Fifth Edition

THE GLOBAL EXPERIENCE

Readings in World History to 1550

Volume I

PHILIP F. RILEY
FRANK A. GEROME
ROBERT L. LEMBRIGHT
HENRY A. MYERS
CHONG-KUN YOON
JAMES MADISON UNIVERSITY

PEARSON
Prentice
Hall

UPPER SADDLE RIVER, NEW JERSEY 07458

Library of Congress Cataloging-in-Publication Data

The global experience / [edited by] Philip F. Riley . . . [et al.].—5th ed.
  p. cm.
   Contents: vol. 1. Readings in world history to 1550.
   ISBN 0-13-117817-2 (v. 1)
   1. World history. I. Riley, Philip F.

D23.G57 2006
909—dc22   2005045929

VP, Editorial Director: Charlyce Jones Owen
Executive Editor: Charles Cavaliere
Editorial Assistant: Maria Guarascio
Executive Marketing Manager: Heather Shelstad
Marketing Assistant: Jennifer Lang
Sr. Managing Editor: Joanne Riker
Production Liaison: Jan H. Schwartz
Buyer: Ben Smith
Cover Designer: Bruce Kenselaar
Cover Art: Wall Hanging, Courtesy of Library of Congress
Director, Image Resource Center: Melinda Reo
Manager, Rights and Permissions: Zina Arabia
Manager, Visual Research: Beth Brenzel
Manager, Cover Visual Research and Permissions: Karen Sanatar
Composition/Full-Service Management: Prepare, Inc./Pietro Paolo Adinolfi
Printer/Binder: R.R. Donnelly, Harrisonburg
Cover Printer: Phoenix Color

Credits and acknowledgments borrowed from other sources and reproduced, with permission, in this textbook appear on appropriate page within text

Pearson Education LTD.
Pearson Education Singapore, Pte. Ltd
Pearson Education, Canada, Ltd
Pearson Education–Japan

Pearson Education Australia PTY, Limited
Pearson Education North Asia Ltd
Pearson Educación de Mexico, S.A. de C.V.
Pearson Education Malaysia, Pte. Ltd

10 9 8 7 6 5 4 3 2

ISBN 0-13-117817-2

FOR
RAYMOND C. DINGLEDINE JR.
1919–1990
TEACHER, SCHOLAR, FRIEND

Contents

Preface   xi

PART I – EARLY CIVILIZATIONS 1

Global Conceptions of the Cosmos and Creation   1

1. The Egyptian Creation Story: The Creation According to Ra 2
2. The Hebrew Creation Story: Genesis 4
3. P'an Ku, China's Creation Story 8
4. A Hindu Creation Story: *Rig Veda* 11
5. A Greek Creation Story: Hesiod's *Theogony* 12
6. A Mayan Creation Story: *Popol Vuh* 14

Culture Heroes in Early Epics   16

7. The Epic of Gilgamesh 16
8. Homer, *The Odyssey* 22
9. Dialli Kieba Koate, *Sunjatta* 28

Law in the Ancient Near East: Babylonian and Hittite   38

10. The Babylonian Code of Hammurabi 39
11. Hittite Laws 42

Origins of Writing in West Asia; the Scribal Profession   45

12. A Sumerian Schoolboy Text 45
13. Papyrus Lansing: A Schoolbook 47

Challenges to Egyptian and Hebrew Tradition   51

14. Hatshepsut: Successful Female Pharaoh 52
15. The Hymn to Aton and Psalm 104 55
16. Isaiah: Prophet of Doom and Hope 60

Military Strategy and Tactics: Assyria and China   62

17. Assyrian War Tactics 63
18. Sun Tzu [Sunzi], *The Art of War* 64

PART II – CLASSICAL CIVILIZATIONS   69

The Hindu Tradition in Classical India   69

19. The Essence of the Universe 71
20. The Laws of Manu 72
21. Bhagavad-Gita 75
22. Duties of a King, Artha Shastra 78
23. Hsuan-tsang [Xuanzang], The Land and People of India 80

The Buddhist Tradition   84

24. Enlightenment of the Buddha 85
25. Pure Land Scripture, *Sukhavativyuha* 87
26. Edict of Ashoka 90

The Golden Age of Chinese Thought   92

27. Confucius, *Analects* 92
28. Taoism [Daoism]: *Lao Tzu [Lao Zi]* 96
29. Legalism: The Writings of Han Fei Tzu [Han Fei Zi] 100
30. Mencius, "Humane Government" 105

Classical Greece   106

31. Sappho, *Lyric Songs* 107
32. Herodotus, *Persian Dialogue* 111
33. Sophocles, *Antigone* 114
34. Thucydides, *Peloponnesian War* 117
35. Xenophon, *The Government of Sparta* 126
36. Aristotle, *Politics* 131

Roman Contributions to Ideologies of Government and Law 134

37. Plutarch, *Numa the Lawgiver* 135
38. Titus Livy, *Heroes of the Early Republic* 145
39. Polybius, "Why Romans and Not Greeks Govern the World" 149
40. Marcus Tullius Cicero, *The Laws* 153

Science in the Greco-Roman and Chinese Worlds 155

41. The Yellow Emperor, *Nei-ching* [*Neijing*] (Canon of Medicine) 156
42. Hippocrates, *On the Sacred Disease* 159
43. Pliny the Elder, *The Nature Story* 162

PART III – CHRISTIANITY TO ISLAM 166

The Rise of Christianity 166

44. The Golden Rule and God's Will 167
45. The Writings of Saint Paul on Women 168

Rome and the Christians 172

46. Pliny the Younger, *Letters to Emperor Trajan* 173
47. St. Augustine of Hippo, *The Just War* 175
48. Paulus Orosius, *History Against the Pagans* 177
49. Monastic Life: *The Rule of St. Benedict* 180

Fusion of Church and State: Byzantine Beginnings 185

50. Eusebius, *Life of Constantine* 186
51. Procopius, *History of the Wars* and *The Secret History* 191

The Rise of Islam 196

52. The Qur'an 197
53. Sayings (*Hadith*) Ascribed to the Prophet: Holy War 205

High Point of Islamic Culture 207

54. Harun al Rashid and the Byzantine Empire 208
55. Kai Kaus, "Scientific Physiognomy and the Purchase of Slaves" 209
56. One Thousand and One Nights: "The Tale of the Fisherman" 214

PART IV – MEDIEVAL EUROPE, AFRICA, AND THE EAST   219

The Germanic Tribes Succeed the Romans in the West   219

57. Gregory of Tours, *History of the Franks* 220
58. Law Code of the Salian Franks 225

Feudalism and Chivalry, West and East   227

59. The Nibelungenlied 228
60. *The Book of Emperors and Kings*, "Charlemagne and Pope Leo III" 234
61. Baha al-Din Ibn Shaddad, "Saladin: The Lion of Islam" 241
62. Tsunetomo Yamamoto, *Hagakure* (The Way of the Samurai) 244
63. The Forty-Seven Ronin 247

East-West Images and Realities   249

64. Liutprand, Bishop of Cremona, *A Mission to Constantinople* 249
65. Memoirs of Usamah Ibn-Munqidh 253
66. Sir John Mandeville, "The Land of Prester John" 257

Islam and Islam's Enemies   260

67. Ibn Battuta in Mali 261
68. Ibn Khaldun, *The Muqaddima* 264
69. Martín Fernández de Figueroa, Confronting the Moors in Somalia 267

Byzantium: The Later Period of Decay   270

70. Micahel Psellus, *Chronographia*, "Empress Zoe" 270
71. Robert of Clari, *The Conquest of Constantinople* 273

Scholasticism, Spirituality, and Mysticism   279

72. Peter Abelard, *The Story of My Misfortunes* 281
73. St. Hildegard of Bingen, *Know the Ways* 284
74. St. Francis of Assisi, *The Rule of Saint Francis* 288

Coping with Deviant Belief: East and West   291

75. Pierre de Vaux-de-Cernay, "What Cathars Believe" 292
76. Thomas Aquinas, *Summa Theologica:* "Whether Heretics are to be Tolerated" 295

77. William Rubruck, *Journey to Cathay* 297

78. The Trial of Joan of Arc 305

Medieval Domestic Life in Western and Eastern Europe   308

79. The Goodman of Paris 308

80. *The Domostroi, Rules for Russian Households in the Time of Ivan the Terrible* 311

Medieval Governments and Societies of China and Japan   314

81. Emperor T'ai-tsung [Taizong]: "On the Art of Government" 315

82. Sung (Song) China: Imperial Examination System 319

83. Chinese Footbinding 320

84. Murasaki Shikibu, *The Tale of Genji* 323

85. John Pian del Carpini, *The Tartars* 328

86. Marco Polo in China 330

The Black Death: Christian and Muslim Views   334

87. The Black Death in Florence 335

88. Ibn Al-Ward*ī,* *An Essay on the Report of the Pestilence* 338

PART V – A WORLD IN CHANGE   343

The Rise of the Ottoman Empire   343

89. Kritovoulos, *History of Mehmed the Conqueror* 344

90. Suleiman the Magnificent and His Courtiers 348

91. Vlad Tsepes, "The Impaler": The Real Dracula or How the Enemy of the Ottomans Became a Legend 351

The Rise of Russia   355

92. The Russian Primary Chronicle 356

93. Heinrich von Staden, *The Land and Government of Muscovy* 359

The Renaissance and Reformation   362

94. Niccolò Machiavelli, *The Prince* and *The Discourses on Titus Livy* 364

95. Erasmus, *Julius II Excluded* 370

96. Martin Luther at the Diet of Worms, 1521 375

97. St. Charles Borromeo: *Instructions to Confessors* 378

Age of Exploration and Expansion   382

98. Cheng Ho [Zheng He]: Ming Maritime Expeditions 384
99. St. Francis Xavier on the Japanese: "The Best People Who Have Yet Been Discovered" 386

Portugal in Asia and Spain in America   390

100. The Travels of Mendes Pinto 390

Spain in America   395

101. Christopher Columbus, *Journal of First Voyage to America* 395
102. An Aztec Account of the Conquest of Mexico: *The Broken Spears* 397
103. Pope Paul III, "Indians are Men"1537 400
104. Bartolomé de las Casas, *Destruction of the Indies* and "The Only Method of Converting the Indians" 402

Preface

This anthology is a brief, balanced collection of primary materials organized chronologically and focused on global themes.

In preparing this collection, we had three concerns in mind. First, any informed understanding of the world at the opening of the third millennium, when the world is rapidly becoming one, must begin with history. We believe the most useful mode of historical study—particularly for college students—is world history. Because men and women make history, the documents we include depict the variety of their experiences over time on a global scale. To help students study and appreciate these experiences, we have included excerpts from both classic texts and less-familiar but equally illustrative material. The resulting selection of readings illustrates patterns of global change and exchange, as well as the distinct achievements of the major civilizations.

Second, to encourage the comparative study of world history and to reinforce the underlying links between civilizations, we have organized the readings into chronological sections. By doing so, we hope to underscore global patterns of development and, at the same time, give our readers access to documents of special interest.

Third, to help with the understanding and retention of our reading selections, particularly those likely to be unfamiliar to students, we have included introductory comments as well as questions to consider. We hope this material will help students gain a better understanding of the text and connect their historical study to contemporary problems and issues.

Our students, particularly in their questions and criticisms, have shaped our work from the outset more than they know. Many of our colleagues at James Madison University have also helped immeasurably. They provided insights and suggestions to make this a better book. Michael J. Galgano, Head, Department of History, has assisted us at every turn; he enthusiastically found for us the means and time to complete this project. Mary Louise Loe not only contributed the selections of Russian and Soviet history but helped us throughout our work. David Owusa-Ansah provided guidance in our introduction to the Sunjatta epic. Nicholas Miller of Boise State University; John A. Murphy of University College, Cork, Republic of Ireland; and John O. Hunwick of Northwestern University kindly advised us on Serbian, Irish, and African selections.

The fifth edition of *The Global Experience*: *Readings in World History* contains new sections, new selections, and new translations, as well as some changes in the selections published in our fourth edition. In Volume I, approximately twenty-five percent of the selections are new. Among the new selections in Volume I are: Pan Ku, China's Creation Story; Hesiod, *Theogony*; The Mayan Creation Story, *Popul Vuh*; Homer, *The Odyssey*; Dialli Kieba Koate, *Sunjatta*; A Sumerian Schoolboy Text; Isaiah, Prophet of Doom and Hope; Edict of Asoka; Mencius, "Humane Government;" Xenephon, *The Spartan Constitution*; Plutarch, *Numa the Lawgiver*; Eusebius of Caesaria, *Life of Constantine*; Harun al Rashid and the Byzantine Empire; *One Thousand and One Nights*, "The Tale of the Fisherman;" Saladin, *Lion of Islam*; Ibn Khaldun, *The Muqaddima* (*The Course of History*); Pierre de Vaux-de-Cernay, "What Cathars Believe;" Saint Thomas Aquinas, *Summa Theologica*: "Whether Heretics Are to be Tolerated?"; William of Rubruck, *Journey to Cathay*; The Trial of Joan of Arc; Giovanni Boccacio, *The Decameron* (description of the Black Plague); Suleiman the Magnificent and His Courtiers; Christopher Columbus, *Journal of First Voyage to America*.

Among the new additions to Volume II are: Akbar on India; Thomas Hobbes, *Leviathan*; Thomas Robert Malthus, *An Essay Concerning the Principle of Population*; Mary Wollstonecraft, *A Vindication of the Rights of Woman*; Harriet Beecher Stowe, *Uncle Tom's Cabin*; Edward Everett Hale, "The Man Without a Country;" Japan's Twenty-One Demands on China; Henry Cabot Lodge, "The Retention of the Philippine Islands;" Francis Russell, "A Journal of the Plague: the 1918 Influenza;" Japan's Imperial Army and War Crimes; George F. Kennan, "The Long Telegram;" Nikolai V. Novikov, U.S. Foreign Policy in the Postwar Period; Jawahrla Nehru on Marxism and Nonalignment; Hasan al-Banna, "Toward the Light;" Ayatollah Ruhollah Khomeini, "Message to the Pilgrims;" Azar Nafisi, "Do I Have Life? Or Am I Just Breathing?;" Roger Wuillaume, "Torture in Algeria;" General Antonio M. Taguba, "Torture in Iraq;" Prime Minister Tony Blair, "Address to Joint Session of U.S. Congress, July 17, 2003."

Acknowledgments

In making these revisions, we were were guided by the advice and criticism of our colleagues, Chris Arndt, Jack Butt, Steven W. Guerrier, Raymond M. Hyser, and Michael Galgano. Sheila Riley helped with the final editing of the first three editions. Allen C. Myers and Marcella A. Smith condensed several of the selections indicated. Gordon Miller and Rebecca Feind, reference librarians, and the James Madison University Inter-Library Loan staff, tirelessly and skillfully assisted us in obtaining materials. JMU History Department Secretaries Jane Crockett and Sonja Lovell guided many student assistants in the work of preparing the selections for publication. Julia Sweeny of the James Madison University Center for Instructional Technology oversaw the technical side of integrating new selections into this fifth edition.

We would also like to thank Raymond Hylton, Virginia Union University and James E. Genova, Indiana State University for their comments and helpful critiques of the manuscript.

Philip F. Riley
Henry A. Myers

Part I

Early Civilizations

Global Conceptions of the Cosmos and Creation

With the dawn of civilization, people sought understanding of the universe and the conditions of their own existence as they described the will or clash of wills that made things the way they were. The resulting creation stories parallel the human experience of birth, with a god or gods arising out of chaos, a primordial ocean, or void, to create the universe. Humanity could be formed from tears, blood, or the earth itself with duties of worship and obedience to the will of the god or gods. Once these myths and the postcreation stories that followed them with a certain logic had been established, they were celebrated at festivals or in rites, often by religious leaders or monarchs whose right to govern was substantiated by these myths.

The most familiar Egyptian creation myth begins with the sun god Ra of Heliopolis, who created the world and other gods. Ra (also called Atum or Khepri) made a place for himself to stand while he created the physical universe, gods and goddesses, and finally humans. The Egyptian kings (pharaohs) of the Old Kingdom (2700–2200 B.C.) traced their right to rule and their funeral practices to Ra and his descendants.

The best-known creation story of the Hebrews, Genesis, developed between 1000 and 400 B.C. from oral and written traditions. Although the Hebrews were influenced by previous accounts of creation, they contributed the idea that there was only one creator god, who stood outside time and space, from whose thought or Word the universe began. In the Hebrew account, God made a conscious decision to create human beings, who were placed in the Garden of Eden. Evil came to this idyllic paradise when a snake persuaded Adam and Eve to disobey God's law and eat out of the Tree of Knowledge. For their "Original Sin," or willful disobedience, humans were forever driven from Paradise.

1

In East Asia, the Chinese creation story features the primordial being, P'an Ku, a giant of formidable proportions, whose body parts became parts of the cosmos. Later, to combat loneliness, the dragon-headed goddess, Nu-kua, formed the first human out of clay.

In India, creation accounts evolved for many centuries before stabilizing in a combination of elements acceptable to most Hindus. These include portrayals of a single, original deity with unlimited creative power ("the One"), similar to the world soul in several other religions and some philosophies, such as Greco-Roman Stoicism, and the story of a cosmic sacrifice establishing a hierarchy of being from the parts of the huge but vulnerable deity, Purusa or Purusha.

Like most other ancient peoples, the Greeks perceived forces of nature as gods. They had no holy scriptures setting forth their deities, but they treated the stories of their earliest known poets as authoritative when they told stories of gods and goddesses, as Homer did around 800 B.C. Some fifty years later, Hesiod, who lived in rural Boetia on the central-eastern Greek mainland, attempted to bring together stories of deities in his *Theogony* (*Origins of the Gods*). In his creation story, the "older gods" came into being as the raw forces of nature. Later, Zeus, son of Kronos, and the other "younger gods," who were more humanlike in motives and activities, would take control of the universe from those senior deities. In contrast with many other creation accounts, the Greek stories of divine origins do not lend themselves to enhancing the power of priests or rulers.

A recurring, parallel story in the Judaeo-Christian tradition begins with God creating angels, many of whom disappoint him with ingratitude and rebellion, leading to their fall. This story sees Adam, Eve, and subsequent humankind as created to furnish replacements for the fallen angels. In a similar vein, although from totally separate origins, the most widespread creation story of the Mesoamericans, the Mayan *Popul Vuh*, presents the first human beings as wooden creatures who showed inadequate respect for their creator and became the ancestors of monkeys. Ultimately, real flesh-and-blood people took their place.

1

The Egyptian Creation Story: "The Creation According to Ra"

The Egyptian religion developed during the Old Kingdom (3100–2200 B.C.). The following selection was created by the priests of Ra, whose central sanctuary was located in Heliopolis, near the city of Memphis. In this account, the great god Ra emerges from the waters of Nun and through an act of will or masturbation creates the Egyptian universe.

QUESTIONS TO CONSIDER

What are the similarities or differences in the Egyptian creation myth compared to those of the Hebrews (see Reading 2), the Chinese (see Reading 3), and the Hindu (see Reading 4)?

1. What is the role or duties of humans in Egypt compared with those in other creation myths? Are there any similarities or differences?
2. Are there any moral or ethical standards in the Egyptian myth compared to the other religions?
3. Some scholars have thought the Benben or primeval mound of Ra might be the prototype of what Egyptian monuments?
4. How did these myths support governmental authority?

The Book of Knowing the Creations of Ra and of Smiting Down Apophis

The words to be spoken:

Thus said the Universal Lord after he had come into being: I am the one who came into being as Khepri.[1] When I came into being, being [itself] came into being. All beings came into being after I came into being. Manifold were the beings from that which came forth from my mouth. Not yet had the heaven come into being; not yet had the earth come into being; not yet had the ground been created or creeping things in this place. I raised some creatures in the Primordial Waters as [still] inert things, when I had not yet found a place upon which I could stand.[2] I found it favorable in my heart, I conceived with my sight. I made all forms, I being all alone. Not yet had I spat out what was Shu, not yet had I emitted what was Tefnut, not yet had there come into being one who could act together with me.

I conceived in my own heart; there came into being a vast number of forms of divine beings, as the forms of children and the forms of their children.[3]

I it was who aroused desire with my fist; I masturbated with my hand, and I spat it from my own mouth. I spat it out as Shu; I spewed it out as Tefnut. By my father Nun, the Primordial Waters, were they brought up, my Eye watching after them since the aeons when they were distant from me.

After I had come into being as the only god, there were three gods aside from me.[4] I came into being in this earth, but Shu and Tefnut rejoiced in Nun, the Primordial Waters, in which they existed. They brought back to me my Eye which had followed after them. After I had united my members, I wept over them, and that was the coming into being of mankind, from the tears which came forth from my Eye.[5] It was wroth against me after it came back and found that I had made another in its place, having replaced it with the Glorious Eye.[6] And so I advanced its place onto my brow,[7] and when it was exercising rule over this entire land, its wrath fell away completely, for I had replaced that which had been taken from it.

---

[1] Throughout this text, as well as in the *Pyramid Texts*, there is a continual play on the verb *kheper*, "come, or bring into being." and *Khepri-Kheprer*, "he who comes into being, or brings into being."

[2] Before he raised the Benben, the Primeval Hill.

[3] Note here the theme of creation by the intellectual conception of the god, which is the central feature of the Memphite theology. Evidently the theme, with its philosophical appeal, was syncretized with the theology of Heliopolis during the intervening millennia.

[4] Nun, Shu, and Tefnut.

[5] The Egyptians loved puns. The word for "mankind" is *remet*, and the word for "tears" is *remyt*.

[6] The sun in its course.

[7] As the uraeus-serpent, which became one of the main emblems of royalty, protecting the king from all enemies. It can be seen on the diadems, crowns, and helmets of all the rulers of Egypt.

From *The Wings of the Falcon: Life and Thought of Ancient Egypt*, edited by Joseph Kaster (New York and Chicago; Holt Rinehart and Winston, 1968), pp. 55–7. Reprinted by permission of Henry Holt and Company, LLC.

I came forth from among the roots,[8] and I created all creeping things, and all that exists among them. Then by Shu and Tefnut were Geb and Nut begotten, and by Geb and Nut were begotten Osiris, Horus, Set, Isis, and Nephthys from the womb, one after the other, and they begot their multitudes in this land.[9]

2

The Hebrew Creation Story: Genesis

In the Hebrew creation story, God creates the world in six days. He gives Adam and Eve the Garden of Eden as their home until they commit the "Original Sin."

QUESTIONS TO CONSIDER

1. Discuss the differences or similarities of Genesis to the other creation stories.
2. Might one say that the Hebrew account is more sophisticated or refined than the others? If so, why? If not, why not?
3. How does the role of human beings in Genesis compare with that found in the Chinese story (see Reading 3)?
4. There are two creation accounts of men and women in Genesis. What are the political and social implications of these differing accounts?

Chapter 1

In the beginning God created the heaven and the earth.

And the earth was without form, and void; and darkness was upon the face of the deep. And the Spirit of God moved upon the face of the waters.

And God said, Let there be light: and there was light.

And God saw the light, that it was good: and God divided the light from the darkness.

And God called the light Day, and the darkness he called Night. And the evening and the morning were the first day.

And God said, Let there be a firmament in the midst of the waters, and let it divide the waters from the waters.

And God made the firmament, and divided the waters which were under the firmament from the waters which were above the firmament: and it was so.

And God called the firmament Heaven. And the evening and the morning were the second day.

And God said, Let the waters under the heaven be gathered together unto one place, and let the dry land appear: and it was so.

And God called the dry land Earth; and the gathering together of the waters he called Seas: and God saw that it was good.

And God said, Let the earth bring forth grass, the herb yielding seed, and the fruit tree yielding fruit after his kind, whose seed is in itself, upon the earth: and it was so.

---

[8]Namely, "which I had created." This refers, no doubt, to the creation of vegetation.

[9]The third and fourth generations of the gods were begotten in normal manner from the womb, differentiating them from Shu and Tefnut, who were begotten from Ra-Atum himself.

From Genesis 1–3 (King James Version), slightly modernized.

And the earth brought forth grass, and herb yielding seed after his kind, and the tree yielding fruit, whose seed was in itself, after his kind: and God saw that it was good.

And the evening and the morning were the third day.

And God said, Let there be lights in the firmament of the heaven to divide the day from the night; and let them be for signs, and for seasons, and for days, and years:

And let them be for lights in the firmament of the heaven to give light upon the earth: and it was so.

And God made two great lights; the greater light to rule the day, and the lesser light to rule the night: he made the stars also.

And God set them in the firmament of the heaven to give light upon the earth,

And to rule over the day and over the night, and to divide the light from the darkness: and God saw that it was good.

And the evening and the morning were the fourth day.

And God said, Let the waters bring forth abundantly the moving creature that hath life, and fowl that may fly above the earth in the open firmament of heaven.

And God created great whales, and every living creature that moveth, which the waters brought forth abundantly, after their kind, and every winged fowl after his kind: and God saw that it was good.

And God blessed them, saying, Be fruitful, and multiply, and fill the waters in the seas, and let fowl multiply in the earth.

And the evening and the morning were the fifth day.

And God said, Let the earth bring forth the living creature after his kind, cattle, and creeping thing, and beast of the earth after his kind: and it was so.

And God made the beast of the earth after his kind, and cattle after their kind, and every thing that creepeth upon the earth after his kind: and God saw that it was good.

And God said, Let us make man in our image, after our likeness: and let him have dominion over the fish of the sea, and over the fowl of the air, and over the cattle, and over all the earth, and over every creeping thing that creepeth upon the earth.

So God created man in his own image, in the image of God created he him; male and female created he them.

And God blessed them, and God said unto them, Be fruitful, and multiply, and replenish the earth, and subdue it: and have dominion over the fish of the sea, and over the fowl of the air, and over every living thing that moveth upon the earth.

And God said, Behold, I have given you every herb-bearing seed, which is upon the face of all the earth, and every tree in which is the fruit of a tree yielding seed; to you it shall be for meat.

And to every beast of the earth, and to every fowl of the air, and to every thing that creepeth upon the earth, wherein there is life, I have given every green herb for meat: and it was so.

And God saw everything that he had made, and, behold, it was very good. And the evening and the morning were the sixth day.

Chapter 2

Thus the heavens and the earth were finished, and all the host of them.

And on the seventh day God ended his work which he had made; and he rested on the seventh day from all his work which he had made.

And God blessed the seventh day and sanctified it: because in it he had rested from all his work which God created and made.

These are the generations of the heavens and of the earth when they were created, in the day that the Lord God made the earth and the heavens.

And every plant of the field before it was in the earth, and every herb of the field before it grew: for the Lord God had not caused it to rain upon the earth, and there was not a man to till the ground.

But there went up a mist from the earth, and watered the whole face of the ground.

And the Lord God formed man of the dust of the ground, and breathed into his nostrils the breath of life; and man became a living soul.

And the Lord God planted a garden eastward in Eden; and there he put the man whom he had formed.

And out of the ground made the Lord God to grow every tree that is pleasant to the sight, and good for food; the tree of life also in the midst of the garden, and the tree of knowledge of good and evil.

And a river went out of Eden to water the garden; and from thence it was parted and became into four heads.

The name of the first is Pishon: that is it which compasseth the whole land of Havilah, where there is gold;

And the gold of that land is good: there is bdellium and the onyx stone.

And the name of the second river is Gihon: the same is it that compasseth the whole land of Ethiopia.

And the name of the third river is Haddekel: that is it which goeth toward the east of Assyria.

And the fourth river is Euphrates.

And the Lord God took the man, and put him into the garden of Eden to dress it and to keep it.

And the Lord God commanded the man, saying, Of every tree of the garden thou mayest freely eat:

But of the tree of knowledge of good and evil, thou shall not eat of it: for in the day that thou eatest thereof thou shalt surely die.

And the Lord God said, It is not good that the man should be alone; I will make him an help mate for him.

And out of the ground the Lord God formed every beast of the field, and every fowl of the air; and brought them unto Adam to see what he would call them: and whatsoever Adam called every living creature, that was the name thereof.

And Adam gave names to all cattle, and to the fowl of the air, and to every beast of the field; but for Adam there was not found an help mate for him.

And the Lord God caused a deep sleep to fall upon Adam, and he slept: and he took one of his ribs, and closed up the flesh instead thereof;

And the rib, which the Lord God had taken from man, made he a woman, and brought her unto the man.

And Adam said, This is now bone of my bones, and flesh of my flesh: she shall be called Woman, because she was taken out of Man.

Therefore shall a man leave his father and his mother, and shall cleave unto his wife: and they shall be one flesh.

And they were both naked, the man and his wife, and were not ashamed.

Chapter 3

Now the serpent was more subtil than any beast of the field which the Lord God had made. And he said unto the woman, Yea, hath God said, Ye shall not eat of every tree of the garden?

And the woman said unto the serpent, We may eat of the fruit of the trees of the garden:

But of the fruit of the tree which is in the midst of the garden, God hath said, Ye shall not eat of it, neither shall ye touch it, lest ye die.

And the serpent said unto the woman, ye shall not surely die:

For God doth know that in the day ye eat thereof, then your eyes shall be opened, and ye shall be as gods, knowing good and evil.

And when the woman saw that the tree was good for food, and that it was pleasant to the eyes, and a tree to be desired to make one wise, she took of the fruit thereof, and did eat, and gave also unto her husband with her; and he did eat.

And the eyes of them both were opened, and they knew that they were naked; and they sewed fig leaves together, and made themselves aprons.

And they heard the voice of the Lord God walking in the garden in the cool of the day: and Adam and his wife hid themselves from the presence of the Lord God amongst the trees of the garden.

And the Lord God called unto Adam, and said unto him, Where art thou?

And he said, I heard thy voice in the garden, and I was afraid, because I was naked; and I hid myself.

And he said, Who told thee that thou wast naked? Hast thou eaten of the tree, whereof I commanded thee that thou shouldest not eat?

And the man said, The woman whom thou gavest to be with me, she gave me of the tree, and I did eat.

And the Lord God said unto the woman, What is this that thou hast done? And the woman said, The serpent beguiled me, and I did eat.

And the Lord God said unto the serpent, Because thou hast done this, thou art cursed above all cattle, and above every beast of the field; upon thy belly shalt thou go, and dust shalt thou eat all the days of thy life:

And I will put enmity between thee and the woman, and between thy seed and her seed; it shall bruise thy head, and thou shalt bruise his heel.

Unto the woman he said, I will greatly multiply thy sorrow and thy conception; in sorrow thou shalt bring forth children; and thy desire shall be to thy husband, and he shall rule over thee.

And unto Adam he said, Because thou has hearkened unto the voice of thy wife, and hast eaten of the tree, of which I commanded thee, saying, Thou shalt not eat of it: cursed is the ground for thy sake; in sorrow shalt thou eat of it all the days of thy life;

Thorns also and thistles shall it bring forth to thee; and thou shalt eat the herb of the field:

In the sweat of thy face shalt thou eat bread, till thou return unto the ground; for out of it wast thou taken: for dust thou art, and unto dust shalt thou return.

And Adam called his wife's name Eve; because she was the mother of all living.

Unto Adam also and to his wife did the Lord God make coats of skins, and clothed them.

And the Lord God said, Behold, the man is become as one of us, to know good and evil: and now, lest he put forth his hand, and take also of the tree of life, and eat, and live for ever:

Therefore the Lord God sent him forth from the garden of Eden, to till the ground from whence he was taken.

So he drove out the man; and he placed at the east of the garden of Eden Cherubims, and a flaming sword which turned every way, to keep the way of the tree of life.

3

P'an Ku, China's Creation Story

Like any other old civilization, China has a number of tales about the origin of the universe. The best known of them all is the tale of P'an Ku, a primordial man who created the world and mankind. This mythology holds that in the beginning the cosmos was a gigantic chaos, dark and swirling, but slowly solidified. Out of the chaos and darkness was born a colossal, formless man named P'an Ku who lived 18,000 years. He grew at a rate of ten feet a day and stood thousands of miles tall. He spent days chopping a huge stone into two parts, one of which turned into heaven and the other earth and he was the great pillar that separated earth and sky. Upon the completion of his work and death, his eyes became the sun and moon, his breath the wind, his beard the stars, the sweat of his brow the rain and dew. His body turned into the mountains, his hands and feet the north and south poles and the extremes of east and west. His blood became the rivers of earth and his veins the roads. His flesh became the soil of the fields, his hair the flowers and trees, his bones and teeth the precious metals beneath the surface of earth. But it remained dull and lonely until the goddess Nu-kua, who had a dragon body with a human head, picked up a piece of clay and fashioned it into the first human being. To proliferate the earth with human beings perpetually, Nu-kua brought man and woman together and taught them the ways of marriage. Then a god named Fu-hsi, Nu-kua's husband, taught human beings how to make fishing nets and entertain themselves with music by the lute. More importantly, Fu-hsi taught men how to make fire for cooking and warmth and taught them how to keep records for their posterity by introducing eight symbols.

Long years of peace and tranquility of the world were broken when a cataclysmic battle between the spirit of Water, Kung-kung, and the spirit of fire, Chu-jung, raged. These battles threatened to end all creation and left many cracks and fissures on the earth. The earth was tilted up in the west and the waters of all the rivers and lakes were spilled over and ran eastward and southeast where the earth was sloped down and formed a vast ocean, presumably today the Yellow Sea and the South China Sea. This cataclysmic event was brought to an end by the goddess Nu-kua who quelled the fire and flood, and peace and order were restored to the world.

QUESTIONS TO CONSIDER

1. Compare and contrast the creation stories of China and India with that of the Hebrews. How are they similar and how are they different?

2. Examine the place of human beings in the Genesis and the Chinese creation story. What cultural significance could be drawn from these stories?

Heaven and Earth and Man

Earth with its mountains, rivers and seas, Sky with its sun, moon and stars: in the beginning all these were one, and the one was Chaos. Nothing had taken shape, all was a dark swirling confusion, over and under, round and round. For countless ages this was the way of the universe, unformed and unillumined, until from the midst of Chaos came P'an Ku. Slowly, slowly, he grew into being, feeding on the elements, eyes closed, sleeping a sleep of eighteen thousand years. At last the moment came when he woke from his sleeping. He opened his eyes: nothing could he see, nothing but darkness, nothing but confusion. In his anger he raised his great arm and struck out blindly in the face of the murk, and with one great crashing blow he scattered the elements of Chaos.

The swirling ceased, and in its place came a new kind of movement. No longer confined, all those things which were light in weight and pure in nature rose upwards; all those things which were heavy and gross sank down. With his one mighty blow P'an Ku had freed sky from earth.

Now P'an Ku stood with his feet on earth, and the sky rested on his head. So long as he stood between the two they could not come together again. And as he stood, the rising and the sinking went on. With each day that passed earth grew thicker by ten feet and the sky rose higher by ten feet, thrust ever farther from the earth by P'an Ku's body which daily grew in height by ten feet also. For eighteen thousand years more P'an Ku continued to grow until his own body was gigantic, and until earth was formed of massive thickness and the sky had risen far above. Thousands of miles tall he stood, a great pillar separating earth from sky so that the two might never again come together to dissolve once more into a single Chaos. Throughout long ages he stood, until the time when he could be sure that earth and sky were fixed and firm in their places.

When this time came P'an Ku, his task achieved, lay down on earth to rest and, resting, died. And now he, who in his life had brought shape to the universe, by his death gave his body to make it rich and beautiful. He gave the breath from his body to form the winds and clouds, his voice to be the rolling thunder, his two eyes to be the sun and moon, the hairs of his head and beard to be the stars, the sweat of his brow to be the rain and dew. To the earth he gave his body for the mountains and his hands and feet for the two poles and the extremes of east and west. His blood flowed as the rivers of earth and his veins ran as the roads which cover the land. His flesh became the soil of the fields and the hairs of his body grew on as the flowers and trees. As for his bones and teeth, these sank deep below the surface of if earth to enrich it as precious metals.

And so P'an Ku brought out of Chaos the heavens in all their glory and the earth with all its splendors. But although the earth could now present its lovely landscapes, although beasts ran in its forests and fish swam in its rivers, still it seemed to lack something, something which would make it less empty and dull for the gods who came down from Heaven to roam over its surface. One day the goddess Nu-kua, whose body was that of a dragon but whose head was of human form, grew weary of the loneliness of earth. After long thought she stooped and took from the ground a lump of clay. From this she fashioned with her dragon claws a tiny creature. The head she shaped after the pattern

From Cyril Birch, *Chinese Myths and Fantasies*, pp. 3–8 (New York: Oxford University Press, 1961).

of her own, but to the body she gave two arms and two legs. She set the little thing back on the ground: and the first human being came to life and danced and made sounds of joy to delight the eyes and ears of the goddess. Quickly she made many more of these charming humans, and felt lonely no longer as they danced together all about her.

Then, as she rested a while from her task and watched the sons and daughters of her own creation go off together across the earth, a new thought came to her. "What would become of the world when all these humans she had made grew old and died?" They were fine beings, well fitted to rule over the beasts of the earth; but they would not live forever. To fill the earth with humans, then when these had gone to make more to take their place, this would mean an endless task for the goddess. And so to solve this problem Nu-kua brought together man and woman and taught them the ways of marriage. Now they could create for themselves their own sons and daughters, and these in turn could continue to people the earth throughout time.

After this gift of marriage from Nu-kua, further blessings came to man from her husband, the great god Fu-hsi. He again had a human head but the body of a dragon. He taught men how to weave ropes to make nets for fishing, and he made the lute from which men first drew music. His also was the priceless gift of fire. Men had seen and feared the fire which was struck from the forest trees by the passing of the Lord of the Thunderstorm. But Fu-hsi, who was the son of this same lord, taught men to drill wood against wood and make fire for their own use, for warmth and for cooking.

Already the creatures of Nu-kua's making could speak their thoughts to one another, but Fu-hsi now drew for them the eight precious symbols with which they could begin to make records for those who were to come after. He drew three strokes to represent Heaven; the three strokes broken represented earth. That symbol whose middle stroke was solid represented water, that whose middle stroke was broken represented fire. A solid stroke above gave the sign for mountains, a solid stroke beneath the sign for storm; a broken line below showed wind, a broken line on top showed marshland. With these eight powerful symbols man could begin to record all he observed of the world about him.

For long years men lived their lives in a world at peace. Then, suddenly, there spread from Heaven to earth a conflict which threatened to put an end to all creation. This was the battle between the Spirit of Water, Kung-kung, and the Spirit of Fire, Chu-jung. Down to earth came the turbulent, wilful Kung-kung to whip up huge waves on river and lake and lead his scaly hordes against his arch-enemy, Fire. Chu-jung fought back with tongues of flame and scorching breath and halted the rebel Water in his path. Kung-kung's armies dispersed and he, their leader, turned and fled. But his flight brought with it a peril greater yet. For, dashing blindly off to the west, Kung-kung struck his head against the mountain Pu-chou-shan, which was none other than the pillar that in the western corner held up the sky.

Kung-kung made good his escape, but he left the world in a disastrous state. Great holes appeared in the sky, whilst the earth tilted up in the west. In that region deep cracks and fissures appeared which are still to be seen to this day. All the rivers and lakes spilled out their waters, which ran off and still run eastwards: off to the south-east, where the earth had slipped down low, ran the waters together to form a vast ocean there. Meanwhile, out of the shaken mountain forests fire still raged forth, and wild beasts of every kind left their lairs to maraud through the world of helpless, terrified men.

It was left to the goddess Nu-kua to bring back order to the world, to quell the fire and flood and tame the wandering beasts. She it was also who selected from the beds of rivers stones of the most perfect coloring. These she heated until they could be molded; then with these stones, block by block, she patched the holes in the sky. Lastly, she killed a giant turtle, and cut off its powerful legs to make pillars between which the sky is firmly held over the earth, never again to fall.

So the peace of the world was restored. But the mountains still rise in the west, and it is to there that the sun, moon and stars still run down the tilted sky; whilst to the east, the waters of the earth still gather into the restless ocean.

4

A Hindu Creation Story: *Rig Veda*

When the Aryans invaded India, they brought with them the diverse pantheon characteristic of the Indo-European peoples, some of them identifiable with prototypes of Greek and Roman deities. The *Rig Veda*, which reflects oral tradition and was written roughly between 1500 and 700 B.C., is the major sourcebook of early Hindu religion, containing descriptions and stories of the early universe and its gods, along with much genealogy and rules for sacrifices. A distinctly Hindu deity, however, was Purusa (Purusha), sacrificed by the other gods to fill creation with worthwhile items ranging from the sacred verses of the *Rig Veda* itself to horses and humankind.

QUESTIONS TO CONSIDER

1. How does the depiction of the universe before human existence compare with the early parts of the previous creation stories?
2. How can the sacrifice of Purusha be seen as justification for the social divisions that developed into the Hindu caste system?

Creation Hymn

Then even nothingness was not, nor existence. There was no air then, nor the heavens beyond it. What covered it? Where was it? In whose keeping? Was there then cosmic water, in depths unfathomed?

Then there were neither death nor immortality, nor was there then the torch of night and day. The One breathed windlessly and self-sustaining. There was that One then, and there was no other.

At first there was only darkness wrapped in darkness. All this was only unilluminated water. That One which came to be, enclosed in nothing, arose at last, born of the power of heat.

In the beginning desire descended on it—that was the primal seed, born of the mind. The sages who have searched their hearts with wisdom know that which is kin to that which is not.

From the *Rig Veda*, Book X, 129, translated by A. L. Basham, *The Wonder That Was India* (New York: Grove Press, 1977), pp. 247–48. Reprinted by permission. "To the Purusha" from the *Rig Veda*, Book X, 90, in Edward J. Thomas, *Wisdom of the East: Vedic Hymns* (London: John Murray, 1923), pp. 120–22. Reprinted by permission.

And they have stretched their cord across the void, and know what was above, and what below. Seminal powers made fertile mighty forces. Below was strength, and over it was impulse.

The Cosmic Sacrifice

Thousand headed was the Purusa, thousand-eyed, thousand-footed. He embraced the earth on all sides, and stood beyond the breadth of ten fingers.

The Purusa is this all, that which was and which shall be. He is Lord of immortality, which he grows beyond through [sacrificial] food.

Such is his greatness, and still greater than that is the Purusa. One fourth of him is all beings. The three fourths of him is the immortal in Heaven.

Three fourths on high rose the Purusa. One fourth of him arose again here [on the earth]. Thence in all directions he spread abroad, as that which eats and that which eats not. . . .

When the Gods spread out the sacrifice with the Purusa as oblation [offering], spring was its ghee [butter offering], summer the fuel, autumn the oblation.

As the sacrifice on the strewn grass they besprinkled the Purusa, born in the beginning. With him the Gods sacrificed, the Sadhyas [demi-gods], and the sages.

From that sacrifice completely offered were born the Verses [*Rig Veda*] and the Saman-melodies [*Sama Veda*]. The metres were born from it. From it was born the Sacrificial formula [*Yajur Veda*].

From it were born horses, and they have two rows of teeth. Cattle were born from it. From it were born goats and sheep.

When they divided the Purusa, into how many parts did they arrange him? What was his mouth? What his two arms? What are his thighs and feet called?

The *brâhman* was his mouth, his two arms were made the *rajanya* [or *kshatriya* warrior], his two thighs the *vaisya* [trader and agriculturist], from his feet the *sûdra* [servile class] was born.

The moon was born from his spirit, from his eye was born the sun, from his mouth Indra and Agni,1 from his breath Vayu [wind] was born.

From his navel arose the middle sky, from his head the heaven originated, from his feet the earth, the quarters from his ear. Thus did they fashion the worlds.

Seven were his sticks that enclose the fire, thrice seven were made the faggots. When the Gods spread out the sacrifice, they bound the Purusa as a victim.

With the sacrifice the Gods sacrificed the sacrifice. These were the first ordinances. These great powers reached to the firmament, where are the ancient Sadhyas, the Gods.

5

A Greek Creation Story: Hesiod's Theogony

This account begins creation with the Greek "old gods." Although they were to be superseded in considerable part by the more anthropomorphic "new gods," none of them were totally erased from the Greek religious system. Tartarus, for example, yielded most of the underworld to Hades (Pluto) but became a place name for its bottom pit (from whence "the Tartars"; see Reading 85), and Erebus became the semi-darkness on the way to the underworld.

Aphrodite (Venus), whose domain was heterosexual love, can be seen either as the first of the new gods to take over the functions of an older one (Eros) or as one of the older deities herself and one of the few to arrive in the classical world with her powers unchallenged. Eros shrank into the cute, winged, cherubic figure we recognize on stereotypical valentines, more familiar by his Roman name, "Cupid." The Furies, whose domain was blood vengeance—a frequent and dreaded threat in early societies—later took on a law-enforcement role as Aeschylus portrayed them in his classic play *Eumenides* (*The Right-Thinking Ones*). In Greek cosmology, aether was the totally pure airspace reserved for gods above the atmosphere that mortals breathed. "Adamant" was the (mythical) hardest of all metals and stones, available only to gods; later it evolved into one of the names for "diamond."

QUESTIONS TO CONSIDER

1. Where might Hesiod's sources have gotten the idea of Heaven and Earth conceiving offspring in a union?
2. What aspects of Hesiod's creation story do you suppose later Greeks who thought of themselves as eminently civilized wanted to suppress or amend?
3. Do you think that perhaps the idea of the Oedipus complex goes all the way back to Greek ideas of the creation?
4. Are there any similarities between the Greek and Chinese creation stories (see Reading 3)?

Chaos was at the beginning, but broad-bosomed Gaia [Earth] soon followed as solid footing for all the immortals who live on the snowy peak of Olympus. Gloomy Tartarus established himself in a deep hole within the broad-pathed Earth. Eros, most handsome of the immortals, also came to be the god who makes other gods and men stumble with their limbs and minds alike.

Black Night and Erebus emerged from Chaos. Then Night bore Aether and Day, whom she had conceived in love with Erebus. Gaia's own first-born was starry Ouranos [Heaven], her own equal, to cover her all around and to provide a secure abode for all the blessed gods forever. Then she brought forth long Hills, the beautiful homes of Nymphs, goddesses who live in their clefts. She also bore—without love— Pontus, the barren sea depths and the raging billows. She then lay with Heaven and bore deepswirling Oceanos. Later she bore cunning, scheming Kronos, who hated his brutal, self-indulgent father.

She went on to bear the arrogant, offensive Cyclopes: Brontes, Stereopes, and spirited Arges; they were to make and give Zeus thunder and the lightning bolt. They resembled other gods except for having only one eye: their name [Cyclopes = the round-eyed] comes from the one round eye set in the middle of the forehead of each one. Their work displayed great strength and craftsmanship. Finally, Heaven and Earth bore three sons, Kottos, Gyes and Briareos, all unspeakably violent, strong and insolent children. From the shoulders of each stretched a hundred arms, flailing about, making it impossible for anyone to come close. Each had fifty heads on his shoulders over all

From Hesiod, "Theogonia," in *Die Hesiodische Theogonie*, ed. F. G. Welcher (Elberfeld: R. L. Friderich, 1865), pp. 30–33; translated by Henry A. Myers.

those arms: nothing could withstand the overwhelming strength of these monstrous creatures. They were the most terrible of the children of Gaia, and their own father hated them from the first. As soon as each was born, Heaven would stuff him away in a secret place far down in Earth and would not let him come up to see the light.

Ouranos gloated over this wickedness of his. Vast Gaia, however, groaning from having her insides strained and stretched, devised a crafty, evil plan. First she created adamant and from it a huge sickle. Then she called on her beloved sons, urging them to join her in vengeance, for her heart was heavy with grief and anger.

"My children, your father is evil and reckless. Do as I say, and we shall avenge his wicked crime against us. He was the first to begin shameful acts."

Those were her words, but fear froze all her sons, and none said a word until finally great but crooked Kronos took heart and answered his dear mother: "I volunteer for this deed, Mother, for I do not love my evil father; he was the first to think up shameful acts."

This is what he said, and vast Gaia was greatly pleased. She hid him in a place of ambush, gave him the serated sickle and revealed the whole plot to him. After a while Ouranos came, bringing Night with him: he spread himself fully over Gaia as he lay with her. From his hiding place, Heaven's son stretched his left hand forward and, with the jagged teeth on the heavy, long sickle in his right hand, quickly severed his father's genitals and threw them behind him. They fell with marvelous results: From all the bloody drops that spurted out and fell Gaia conceived the mighty Furies, also the huge giants in gleaming armor who hold long spears, and those Nymphs everywhere called "Meliae" [Ash-tree Nymphs].

Kronos threw the sickle-severed genitals from land into the stormy sea, where the waves swept them away for a long time. White foam attached itself to the immortal flesh and, in it a girl developed. At first she approached holy Cythera, but afterwards she came to the island of Cyprus. There she came upon land, a beautiful and awesome goddess, and grass grew up around her from under her shapely feet. Gods and men call her "Aphrodite," since she developed in the foam (aphros), also "Cythera," since she first arrived at Cythera, "Cyprogenes," since she first emerged on stormy Cyprus, or "Philommedes" [members-loving] because of the genitalia from which she developed. Eros went along with her, and pretty Desire followed her when she first came on land and when she went to join the assemblage of gods. Among gods and men she has been honored from the first; the fond whisperings of girls pay tribute to her. Her power is in smiles and tricks, sweet delights of love and charm.

But great Ouranos condemned his own sons, calling them "Titans" [those who strain], for he said that they had strained insolently and done a terrible deed which would later be avenged.

And Night bore fearsome Doom and black Fate, as well as Death, Sleep and the whole tribe of Dreams. . . .

6

A Mayan Creation Story: Popol Vuh

Early people of the Americas also had their versions of human origins. The Quiche of Guatemala, a branch of the Mayan civilization, developed one of the most famous accounts in a sacred book, the *Popol Vuh*, which also contained information about Mayan customs, religion, and history. This account was the most important surviving document of the pre-Columbian era and was first published in Spanish in 1857.

QUESTIONS TO CONSIDER

1. What were some of the characteristics of the first men created according to this Mayan legend?
2. Why were the first people who looked and talked like men destroyed by a flood? In what key ways did their successors, the "true humans" differ?
3. Compare and contrast this Mayan version of creation with the others in this section. Are there similarities and/or differences?

And instantly the figures were made of wood. They looked like men, talked like men, and populated the surface of the earth.

They existed and multiplied; they had daughters, they had sons, these wooden figures; but they did not have souls, nor minds; they did not remember their Creator, their Maker; they walked on all fours, aimlessly.

They no longer remembered the Heart of Heaven and therefore they fell out of favor. It was merely a trial, an attempt at man. At first they spoke, but their face was without expression; their feet and hands had no strength; they had no blood, nor substance, nor moisture, nor flesh; their cheeks were dry, their feet and hands were dry, and their flesh was yellow.

Therefore, they no longer thought of their Creator nor their Maker, nor of those who made them and cared for them.

These were the first men who existed in great numbers on the face of the earth. . . .

Immediately the wooden figures were annihilated, destroyed, broken up, and killed.

A flood was brought about by the Heart of Heaven; a great flood was formed which fell on the heads of the wooden creatures.

Of wood the flesh of man was made, but when woman was fashioned by the Creator and the Maker, her flesh was made of rushes. These were the materials the Creator and the Maker wanted to use in making them.

But those that they had made, that they had created, did not think, did not speak with their Creator, their Maker. And for this reason they were killed, they were deluged. A heavy resin fell from the sky. . . .

This was to punish them because they had not thought of their mother, nor their father, the Heart of Heaven, called Hurac'an. And for this reason the face of the earth was darkened and a black rain began to fall, by day and by night.

Then came the small animals and the large animals, and sticks and stones struck their faces. And all began to speak: their earthen jars, their griddles, their plates, their pots, their grinding stones, all rose up and struck their faces.

"You have done us much harm; you ate us, and now we shall kill you," said their dogs and birds of the barnyard.

And the grinding stones said: "We were tormented by you; every day, every day, at night, at dawn, all the time our faces went holi, holi, huqui, huqui, because of you. This was the tribute we paid you. But now that you are no longer men, you shall feel our strength. We shall grind and tear your flesh to pieces," said their grinding stones. And then their dogs spoke and said: "Why did you give us nothing to eat? You scarcely looked at us, but you chased us and threw us out. You always had a stick ready to strike us while you were eating.

"Thus it was that you treated us. You did not speak to us. Perhaps we shall not kill you now; but why did you not look ahead, why did you not think about yourselves? Now we shall destroy you, now you shall feel the teeth of our mouths; we shall devour you," said the dogs, and then they destroyed their faces.

And at the same time, their griddles and pots spoke: "Pain and suffering you have caused us. Our mouths and our faces were blackened with soot; we were always put on the fire and you burned us as though we felt no pain. Now you shall feel it, we shall burn you," said their pots, and they all destroyed their [the wooden men's] faces. The stones of the hearth, which were heaped together, hurled themselves straight from the fire against their heads, causing them pain.

The desperate ones [the men of wood] ran as quickly as they could; they wanted to climb to the tops of the houses, and the houses fell down and threw them to the ground; they wanted to climb to the treetops, and the trees cast them far away; they wanted to enter the caverns, and the caverns repelled them.

So was the ruin of the men who had been created and formed, the men made to be destroyed and annihilated; the mouths and faces of all of them were mangled.

And it is said that their descendents are the monkeys which now live in the forests; these are all that remain of them because their flesh was made only of wood by the Creator and the Maker.

And therefore the monkey looks like man, and is an example of a generation of men which were created and made but were only wooden figures.

Culture Heroes in Early Epics

7

The Epic of Gilgamesh

Gilgamesh, the semilegendary Sumerian king who ruled the city of Uruk around 2700 B.C., is the subject of the world's first great epic poem. Gilgamesh was a roguish king whose lusty appetites were resented by his subjects, who prayed for a deliverer. To punish Gilgamesh for his sins, the gods created the uncivilized Enkidu and sent him to chastise Gilgamesh and spare Uruk further harm. But instead of becoming mortal enemies, Gilgamesh and Enkidu became fast friends and set off together on a series of adventures, detailed in the first half of this epic.

Their first adventure is to secure timber from the distant Cedar Forest, which is guarded by the ogre Humbaba, whom they must kill. Upon their return to Uruk, the fierce Ishtar, goddess of love, tries to entice Gilgamesh into marriage; however, because Gilgamesh and Enkidu spurn Ishtar, she sends down the Bull of Heaven to punish them. Gilgamesh and Enkidu kill this creature, thereby angering the powerful Enlil, king of the gods, who takes his revenge by killing Enkidu. King Gilgamesh is devastated by his friend's death and laments humanity's fate.

The second half of the epic is devoted to Gilgamesh's quest for the secret of life. He descends into the Netherworld in search of Utnapishtim, to whom the gods had granted immortality and from whom he hopes to learn the key to life. When the two meet, Utnapishtim introduces Gilgamesh to the story of the Great Flood, which had killed all life save for Utnapishtim, his family, and the animals he had placed in his great ship. At the end of the Flood tale, Utnapishtim tells Gilgamesh of a certain Plant of Life that can give immortality. Gilgamesh is able to retrieve this plant and bring it back to the living; yet his hopes are dashed when it is eaten by a snake. At the end of the poem, Gilgamesh can only lament the human fate, old age and death.

QUESTIONS TO CONSIDER

1. Why was Enkidu created?
2. Why were Gilgamesh and Enkidu punished?
3. What is the purpose of Gilgamesh's quest?
4. What part of the epic influenced later civilizations?

I will proclaim to the world the deeds of Gilgamesh. This was the man to whom all things were known; this was the king who knew the countries of the world. He was wise, he saw mysteries and knew secret things; he brought us a tale of the days before the flood. He went on a long journey, was weary, wornout with labour, returning he rested, he engraved on a stone the whole story.

When the gods created Gilgamesh they gave him a perfect body. Shamash the glorious sun endowed him with beauty. Adad the god of the storm endowed him with courage; the great gods made his beauty perfect, surpassing all others, terrifying like a great wild bull. Two thirds they made him god and one third man.

In Uruk he built walls, a great rampart, and the temple of blessed Eanna for the god of the firmament Anu, and for Ishtar the goddess of love. . . .

The Coming of Enkidu

Gilgamesh went abroad in the world, but he met with none who could withstand his arms till he came to Uruk. But the men of Uruk muttered in their houses, "Gilgamesh sounds the tocsin for his amusement, his arrogance has no bounds by day or night. No son is left with his father, for Gilgamesh takes them all, even the children; yet the king should be a shepherd to his people. His lust leaves no virgin to her lover, neither the warrior's daughter nor the wife of the noble; yet this is the shepherd of the city, wise, comely, and resolute."

The gods heard their lament, the gods of heaven cried to the Lord of Uruk, to Anu the god of Uruk. . . . When Anu had heard their lamentation the gods cried to

Aruru, the goddess of creation, "You made him, O Aruru, now create his equal; let it be as like him as his own reflection, his second self, stormy heart for stormy heart. Let them contend together and leave Uruk in quiet."

So the goddess conceived an image in her mind, and it was of the stuff of Anu of the firmament. She dipped her hands in water and pinched off clay, she let it fall in the wilderness, and noble Enkidu was created. There was virtue in him of the god of war, of Ninurta himself. His body was rough, he had long hair like a woman's; it waved like the hair of Nisaba, the goddess of corn. His body was covered with matted hair like Samuqan's, the god of cattle. He was innocent of mankind; he knew nothing of the cultivated land.

Enkidu ate grass in the hills with the gazelle and lurked with wild beasts at the water-holes; he had joy of the water with the herds of wild game. But there was a trapper who met him one day face to face at the drinking-hole, for the wild game had entered his territory. On three days he met him face to face, and the trapper was frozen with fear. He went back to his house with the game that he had caught, and he was dumb, benumbed with terror. His face was altered like that of one who has made a long journey. . . .

So the trapper set out on his journey to Uruk and addressed himself to Gilgamesh saying, "A man unlike any other is roaming now in the pastures; he is as strong as a star from heaven and I am afraid to approach him. He helps the wild game to escape; he fills in my pits and pulls up my traps." Gilgamesh said, "Trapper, go back, take with you a harlot, a child of pleasure. At the drinking-hole she will strip, and when he sees her beckoning he will embrace her and the game of the wilderness will surely reject him."

Now the trapper returned, taking the harlot with him. After a three days' journey they came to the drinking-hole, and there they sat down; the harlot and the trapper sat facing one another and waited for the game to come. For the first day and for the second day the two sat waiting, but on the third day the herds came; they came down to drink and Enkidu was with them. The small wild creatures of the plains were glad of the water, and Enkidu with them, who ate grass with the gazelle and was born in the hills; and she saw him, the savage man, come from far-off in the hills. The trapper spoke to her: "There he is. Now, woman, make your breasts bare, have no shame, do not delay but welcome his love. Let him see you naked, let him possess your body. When he comes near uncover yourself and lie with him; teach him, the savage man, your woman's art, for when he murmurs love to you the wild beasts that shared his life in the hills will reject him."

She was not ashamed to take him, she made herself naked and welcomed his eagerness; as he lay on her murmuring love she taught him the woman's art. For six days and seven nights they lay together, for Enkidu had forgotten his home in the hills; but when he was satisfied he went back to the wild beasts. Then, when the gazelle saw him, they bolted away; when the wild creatures saw him they fled. Enkidu would have followed, but his body was bound as though with a cord, his knees gave way when he started to run, his swiftness was gone. And now the wild creatures had all fled away; Enkidu was grown weak, for wisdom was in him, and the thoughts of a man were in his heart. So he returned and sat down at the woman's feet, and listened intently to what she said, "You are wise, Enkidu, and now you have become like a god. Why do you want to run wild with the beasts in the hills? Come with me. I will take you to strong-walled Uruk, to the blessed temple of Ishtar and of Anu, of love and heaven; there Gilgamesh lives, who is very strong, and like a wild bull he lords it over men." . . .

And now she said to Enkidu, "When I look at you you have become like a god. Why do you yearn to run wild again with the beasts in the hills? Get up from the ground, the bed of a shepherd." He listened to her words with care. It was good advice that she gave. She divided her clothing in two and with the one half she clothed him and with the other herself; and holding his hand she led him like a child to the sheepfolds, into the shepherds' tents. There all the shepherds crowded round to see him; they put down bread in front of him, but Enkidu could only suck the milk of wild animals. He fumbled and gaped, at a loss what to do or how he should eat the bread and drink the strong wine. Then the woman said, "Enkidu, eat bread, it is the staff of life; drink the wine, it is the custom of the land." So he ate till he was full and drank strong wine, seven goblets. He became merry, his heart exulted and his face shone. He rubbed down the matted hair of his body and anointed himself with oil. Enkidu had become a man; but when he had put on man's clothing he appeared like a bridegroom.

Now Enkidu strode in front and the woman followed behind. He entered Uruk, that great market, and all the folk thronged round him where he stood in the street in strong-walled Uruk. The people jostled; speaking of him they said, "He is the spit of Gilgamesh." "He is shorter." "He is bigger of bone." "This is the one who was reared on the milk of wild beasts. His is the greatest strength." The men rejoiced: "Now Gilgamesh has met his match. This great one, this hero whose beauty is like a god, he is a match even for Gilgamesh."

In Uruk the bridal bed was made, fit for the goddess of love. The bride waited for the bridegroom, but in the night Gilgamesh got up and came to the house. Then Enkidu stepped out; he stood in the street and blocked the way. Mighty Gilgamesh came on and Enkidu met him at the gate. He put out his foot and prevented Gilgamesh from entering the house, so they grappled, holding each other like bulls. They broke the doorposts and the walls shook. Gilgamesh bent his knee with his foot planted on the ground and with a turn Enkidu was thrown. Then immediately his fury died. When Enkidu was thrown he said to Gilgamesh, "There is not another like you in the world. Ninsun, who is as strong as a wild ox in the byre, she was the mother who bore you, and now you are raised above all men, and Enlil has given you the kingship, for your strength surpasses the strength of men." So Enkidu and Gilgamesh embraced and their friendship was sealed. . . .

[After they had become good friends, Gilgamesh and Enkidu set out for the Cedar Forest (possibly southern Turkey or Phoenicia) in order to secure wood for the city. Before they got to the wood, however, they had to kill a fire-breathing ogre called Humbaba. Succeeding in this mission, they returned to Uruk, where Gilgamesh was offered marriage by the goddess of love, Ishtar (or Inanna).]

Gilgamesh opened his mouth and answered glorious Ishtar, "If I take you in marriage, what gifts can I give in return? What ointments and clothing for your body? I would gladly give you bread and all sorts of food fit for a god. I would give you wine to drink fit for a queen. I would pour out barley to stuff your granary; but as for making you my wife—that I will not. How would it go with me? Your lovers have found you like a brazier which smoulders in the cold, a backdoor which keeps out neither squall of wind nor storm, a castle which crushes the garrison, pitch that blackens the bearer, a water-skin that chafes the carrier, a stone which falls from the parapet, a battering-ram turned back from the enemy, a sandal that trips the wearer. Which of your lovers did you ever love for ever? What shepherd of yours has pleased you for all time?" . . .

[Gravely insulted by the king's words, Ishtar asked her father, Anu, to punish Gilgamesh by sending the Bull of Heaven to ravage the land. Gilgamesh and Enkidu managed to kill the bull, whose hind leg Enkidu tore off and flung at the goddess. Such a serious offense against the gods demanded immediate punishment; thus did Enkidu fall ill and die.]

So Enkidu lay stretched out before Gilgamesh; his tears ran down in streams and he said to Gilgamesh, "O my brother, so dear as you are to me, brother, yet they will take me from you." Again he said, "I must sit down on the threshold of the dead and never again will I see my dear brother with my eyes." . . .

[Gilgamesh was unreconciled to the death of his beloved friend Enkidu. He decided to make a long and difficult journey to the Netherworld in order to search for the secret of immortality. There he encountered the Sumerian Akkadian Noah called Utnapishtim (or Ziusudra). Utnapishtim tells Gilgamesh of a Flood that had been sent by the gods to destroy all life except for Utnapishtim and his family.]

"In those days the world teemed, the people multiplied, the world bellowed like a wild bull, and the great god was aroused by the clamour. Enlil heard the clamour and he said to the gods in council, 'The uproar of mankind is intolerable and sleep is no longer possible by reason of the babel.' So the gods agreed to exterminate mankind. Enlil did this, but Ea because of his oath warned me in a dream. He whispered their words to my house of reeds, 'Reed-house, reed-house! Wall, O wall, hearken reed-house, wall reflect; O man of Shurrupak, son of Ubara-Tutu; tear down your house and build a boat, abandon possessions and look for life, despise worldly goods and save your soul alive. Tear down your house, I say, and build a boat. These are the measurements of the barque as you shall build her: let her beam equal her length, let her deck be roofed like the vault that covers the abyss; then take up into the boat the seed of all living creatures.'

"In the first light of dawn all my household gathered round me, the children brought pitch and the men whatever was necessary. On the fifth day I laid the keel and the ribs, then I made fast the planking. The ground-space was one acre, each side of the deck measured one hundred and twenty cubits, making a square. I built six decks below, seven in all. I divided them into nine sections with bulkheads between. I drove in wedges where needed, I saw to the punt-poles, and laid in supplies. The carriers brought oil in baskets, I poured pitch into the furnace and asphalt and oil; more oil was consumed in caulking, and more again the master of the boat took into his stores. I slaughtered bullocks for the people and every day I killed sheep. I gave the shipwrights wine to drink as though it were river water, raw wine and red wine and oil and white wine. There was feasting then as there is at the time of the New Year's festival; I myself anointed my head. On the seventh day the boat was complete.

"Then was the launching full of difficulty; there was shifting of ballast above and below till two thirds was submerged. I loaded into her all that I had of gold and of living things, my family, my kin, the beast of the field both wild and tame, and all the craftsmen. I sent them on board, for the time that Shamash had ordained was already fulfilled when he said, 'In the evening, when the rider of the storm sends down the destroying rain, enter the boat and batten her down.' The time was fulfilled, the evening came, the rider of the storm sent down the rain. I looked out at the weather and it was terrible, so I too boarded the boat and battened her down. All was now complete, the battening and the caulking; so I handed the tiller to Puzur-Amurri the steersman, with the navigation and the care of the whole boat. . . .

"For six days and six nights the winds blew, torrent and tempest and flood overwhelmed the world, tempest and flood raged together like warring hosts. When the seventh day dawned the storm from the south subsided, the sea grew calm, the flood was stilled; I looked at the face of the world and there was silence, all mankind was turned to clay. The surface of the sea stretched as flat as a roof-top; I opened a hatch and the light fell on my face. Then I bowed low, I sat down and I wept, the tears streamed down my face, for on every side was the waste of water. I looked for land in vain, but fourteen leagues distant there appeared a mountain, and there the boat grounded; on the mountain of Nisir the boat held fast; she held fast and did not budge. One day she held, and a second day on the mountain of Nisir she held fast and did not budge. A third day, and a fourth day she held fast on the mountain and did not budge; a fifth day and a sixth day she held fast on the mountain. When the seventh day dawned I loosed a dove and let her go. She flew away, but finding no resting-place she returned. Then I loosed a swallow, and she flew away but finding no resting-place she returned. I loosed a raven, she saw that the waters had retreated, she ate, she flew around, she cawed, and she did not come back. Then I threw everything open to the four winds, I made a sacrifice and poured out a libation on the mountain top. Seven and again seven cauldrons I set up on their stands, I heaped up wood and cane and cedar and myrtle. When the gods smelled the sweet savour, they gathered like flies over the sacrifice."

[Utnapishtim then revealed to Gilgamesh the secret of immortality. With the aid of his ferryman, Urshanabi, King Gilgamesh secured this mysterious prickly plant, but his hopes for future rejuvenation were not to be.]

"Gilgamesh, I shall reveal a secret thing, it is a mystery of the gods that I am telling you. There is a plant that grows under the water, it has a prickle like a thorn, like a rose; it will wound your hands, but if you succeed in taking it, then your hands will hold that which restores his lost youth to a man."

When Gilgamesh heard this he opened the sluices so that a sweet-water current might carry him out to the deepest channel; he tied heavy stones to his feet and they dragged him down to the water-bed. There he saw the plant growing; although it pricked him he took it in his hands; then he cut the heavy stones from his feet, and the sea carried him and threw him on to the shore. Gilgamesh said to Urshanabi the ferryman, "Come here, and see this marvellous plant. By its virtue a man may win back all his former strength. I will take it to Uruk of the strong walls; there I will give it to the old men to eat. Its name shall be 'The Old Men Are Young Again'; and at last I shall eat it myself and have back all my lost youth." So Gilgamesh returned by the gate through which he had come, Gilgamesh and Urshanabi went together. They travelled their twenty leagues and then they broke their fast; after thirty leagues they stopped for the night.

Gilgamesh saw a well of cool water and he went down and bathed; but deep in the pool there was lying a serpent, and the serpent sensed the sweetness of the flower. It rose out of the water and snatched it away, and immediately it sloughed its skin and returned to the well. Then Gilgamesh sat down and wept, the tears ran down his face, and he took the hand of Urshanabi: "O Urshanabi, was it for this that I toiled with my hands, is it for this I have wrung out my heart's blood? For myself I have gained nothing; not I, but the beast of the earth has joy of it now. Already the stream has carried it twenty leagues back to the channels where I found it. I found a sign and now I have lost it. Let us leave the boat on the bank and go."

After twenty leagues they broke their fast, after thirty leagues they stopped for the night; in three days they had walked as much as a journey of a month and fifteen days. When the journey was accomplished they arrived at Uruk, the strong-walled city. Gilgamesh spoke to him, to Urshanabi the ferryman, "Urshanabi, climb up on to the wall of Uruk, inspect its foundation terrace, and examine well the brickwork; see if it is not of burnt bricks; and did not the seven wise men lay these foundations? One third of the whole is city, one third is garden, and one third is field, with the precinct of the goddess Ishtar. These parts and the precinct are all Uruk."

This too was the work of Gilgamesh, the king, who knew the countries of the world. He was wise, he saw mysteries and knew secret things, he brought us a tale of the days before the flood. He went on a long journey, was weary, worn out with labour, and returning engraved on a stone the whole story.

8

Homer, *The Odyssey*

Greeks differed from peoples of the ancient Near East in many ways, one of which was the reduction of the conceptual distance between gods and people. Greek gods had human failings on a larger-than-life scale as well as superhuman powers. In the earliest surviving Greek literary works of any importance, we find the poet Homer narrating exciting adventures in which the gods side with humans or against them, but mortal beings are always the focal point. Homer's gods are intent on avenging offenses or insults to themselves, their priests, any semidivine offspring, and their "special interests." For example, Artemis, goddess of the chase, avenges wanton destruction of wild animals and Hera, goddess of marriage, gets even with home-wreckers. Somewhat less frequently, Homer's gods reward those who serve them well.

Homer lived and wrote his epics sometime around 800 B.C., during the period of the "Greek Dark Ages," which followed the fall of Mycenaean civilization. Still, he wrote about the earlier Mycenaean-age Greeks, whom he called "Achaeans" or "Danaans," in what for him was the glorious, heroic time of the Trojan War. According to Homer, the war began when a Trojan prince stole away Helen of Troy, the wife of Menelaus, who was King of Sparta. This incident angered the goddess Hera and led King Agamemnon of Mycenae (brother of Menelaus) to gather an all-Achaean expedition for the destruction of Troy.

Two works are attributed to Homer: *The Iliad* (from "Ilium," an ancient name for Troy), which describes the Achaean siege of Troy; and *The Odyssey*, from which the following selection is taken. This latter work deals with the return from Troy of Odysseus, the wily Achaean who designed the "Trojan horse," which brought victory to the Achaeans. In the course of their long and arduous sea voyage, Odysseus and his men come to the land of the Cyclopes, savage one-eyed giants; in the passage excerpted here, Odysseus tells of his encounter with one of these giants, Polyphemus. Afterwards, mounting catastrophes overtake the men, as the curse of Polyphemus is carried out by his father, Poseidon. But the ending is a happy one: Odysseus safely reaches his kingdom of Ithaca, where his faithful wife, Penelope, has waited for many years, resisting the advances of many suitors. Odysseus then kills the suitors in a final glorious battle in the halls of his home.

QUESTIONS TO CONSIDER

1. What does Odysseus find striking about the land of the Cyclopes?
2. How do Odysseus and the men with him become captives in the cave of Polyphemus?
3. When Polyphemus is injured, why do the other Cyclopes show indifference to his fate?

We left (the land of the Lotus-eaters; Odysseus is speaking) and sailed on. . . . And we came to the land of the Cyclopes, a fierce, uncivilized people who never lift a hand to plant or plough but put their trust in Providence. All the crops they require spring up unsown and untilled, wheat and barley and the vines whose generous clusters give them wine when ripened for them by the timely rains. The Cyclopes have no assemblies for the making of laws, nor any settled customs, but live in hollow caverns in the mountain heights, where each man is lawgiver to his children and his wives, and nobody cares a jot for his neighbors.

Not very far from the harbor on their coast, and not so near either, there lies a luxuriant island, covered with woods, which is the home of innumerable goats. The goats are wild, for man has made no pathways that might frighten them off, nor do hunters visit the island with their hounds to rough it in the forests and to range the mountain-tops. Used neither for grazing nor for ploughing, it lies for ever unsown and untilled; and this land where no man goes makes a happy pasture for the bleating goats. I must explain that the Cyclopes have nothing like our ships with their crimson prows; nor have they any shipwrights to build merchantmen that could serve their needs by plying to foreign ports in the course of that overseas traffic which ships have established between the nations. Such craftsmen would have turned the island into a fine colony for the Cyclopes. For it is by no means a poor country, but capable of yielding any crop in due season. Along the shore of the grey sea there are soft water-meadows where the vine would never wither; and there is plenty of land level enough for the plough, where they could count on cutting a deep crop at every harvest-time, for the soil below the surface is exceedingly rich. Also, it has a safe harbor, in which there is no occasion to tie up at all. You need neither cast anchor nor make fast with hawsers: all your crew have to do is to beach their boat and wait till the spirit moves them and the right wind blows. Finally, at the head of the harbor there is a stream of fresh water, running out of a cave in a grove of poplar-trees.

When the fresh Dawn came, we were delighted with what we saw of the island and set out to explore it. Presently, in order that my company might have something to eat, the Nymphs, those Children of Zeus, set the mountain goats on the move. In a short time Providence had sent us, with our curved bows and long spears, a satisfactory bag. So the whole day long till the sun set we sat and enjoyed this rich supply of meat, and as we looked across at the neighboring land of the Cyclopes, we could

From Homer, *The Odyssey*, Book IX, trans. E. V. Rieu (Baltimore: Penguin, 1946), pp. 142–54; condensed by Marcella A. Smith. Copyright by E. V. Rieu. Reproduced by permission of Penguin Books, Ltd.

not only see the smoke from their fires but hear their voices and the bleating of their sheep and goats. The sun went down, night fell, and we slept on the sea-shore.

With the first rosy light of Dawn, I assembled my company. "My good friends," I said, "for the time being I want you to stay here, while I go in my own ship with my own crew to find out what kind of men are over there, and whether they are brutal and lawless savages or hospitable and god-fearing people."

Then I climbed into my ship with my men. It was no great distance to the mainland coast, and as we approached its nearest point, we made out a cave there, close to the sea. Here large flocks of sheep and goats were penned at night: it was the den of a giant, the lonely shepherd of sequestered flocks, who had no truck with others of his kind but lived aloof in his own lawless way. And what a formidable monster he was! No one would have taken him for a man who ate bread like ourselves; he reminded one rather of some wooded peak in the high hills, lifting itself in solitary state.

I picked out the twelve best men in the company and advanced, leaving the rest of the men on guard. I took with me in a goatskin some dark and mellow wine, which had been given to me by Maron son of Euanthes, the priest of Apollo, and a wonderful drink it was. It had been kept secret from all his serving-men and maids, in fact, from everyone in the house but himself, his good wife, and a single stewardess. When they drank this red and honeyed vintage, he used to pour one cupful of wine into twenty of water, and the sweet fumes that came up from the bowl were irresistible.

Well, I filled a big bottle with this wine and took some food in a wallet along with me also; for I had an instant foreboding, though I am no coward, that we were going to find ourselves face to face with some being of colossal strength and ferocity, to whom the law of man and god meant nothing. It took us very little time to reach the cave, but we did not find its owner at home: he was tending his fat sheep in the pastures. So we went inside and had a good look round. There were baskets laden with cheeses, and the folds were thronged with lambs and kids.

Now my men's idea was first to make off with some of the cheeses, then come back, drive the kids and lambs quickly out of the pens down to the good ship, and so set sail across the salt water. They pleaded with me, but though it would have been far better so, I was not to be persuaded. I wished to see the owner of the cave and had hopes of some friendly gifts from my host. As things fell out, my company were to have an unpleasant surprise when he did put in an appearance.

We lit a fire, killed a beast and made offerings, took some cheeses just for ourselves, and when we had eaten, sat down in the cave to await his arrival. At last he came up, shepherding his flocks and carrying a huge bundle of dry wood to burn at supper-time. With a great din he cast this down inside the cavern, giving us such a fright that we hastily retreated to an inner recess. Meanwhile he drove his fat sheep into the wider part of the cave. He then picked up a huge stone, with which he closed the entrance. It was a mighty slab, such as you couldn't have budged from the ground, not with a score of heavy four-wheeled wagons to help you. Next he sat down to milk his ewes and bleating goats: when he had finished all his jobs, he lit up the fire, spied us, and began asking questions.

"Strangers" he said. "And who may you be? Where do you hail from over the highways of the sea? Is yours a trading venture; or are you cruising the main on chance, like roving pirates, who risk their lives to ruin other people?"

Our hearts sank within us. The booming voice and the very sight of the monster filled us with panic. Still, I managed to find words to answer him. "We are Achaeans,"

I said, "on our way back from Troy. We meant to sail straight home; but we lost our bearings, as Zeus, I suppose, intended that we should. We are proud to belong to the forces of Agamemnon, Atreus' son, who by sacking the great city of Ilium and destroying all its armies has made himself the most famous man in the world today. We, less fortunate, are visiting you here as suppliants, in the hope that you may give us friendly entertainment or even go further in your generosity. You know the laws of hospitality: I beseech you, good sir, to remember your duty to the gods. For we throw ourselves on your mercy; and Zeus is there to avenge the suppliant and the guest. He is the travelers' god: he guards their steps and he invests them with their rights."

So said I, and promptly he answered me out of his pitiless heart: "Stranger, you must be a fool, or must have come from very far afield, to preach to me of fear or reverence for the gods. We Cyclopes care not a jot for Zeus with his aegis, nor for the rest of the blessed gods, since we are much stronger than they. It would never occur to me to spare you or your men against my will for fear of trouble from Zeus. But tell me where you moored your good ship when you came. I should like to see her."

He was trying to get the better of me, but I knew enough of the world to see through him and I met him with deceit.

"As for my ship," I answered, "it was wrecked by the Earthshaker Poseidon on the confines of your land. I and my friends here managed to escape with our lives."

To this the cruel brute made no reply. Instead, he jumped up, and reaching out towards my men, seized a couple and dashed their heads against the floor as though they had been puppies. Their brains ran out on the ground and soaked the earth. Limb by limb he tore them to pieces to make his meal, which he devoured like a mountain lion, never pausing till entrails and flesh, marrow and bones, were all consumed, while we could do nothing but weep and lift up our hands to Zeus in horror at the ghastly sight, paralyzed by our sense of utter helplessness. When the Cyclops had filled his great belly with this meal of human flesh, which he washed down with unwatered milk, he stretched himself out for sleep. And now my manhood prompted me to action: I thought I would draw my sharp sword from the scabbard at my side, creep up to him, feel for the right place with my hand and stab him in the breast where the liver is supported by the midriff. But on second thoughts I refrained, realizing that we should have perished there as surely as the Cyclops, for we should have found it impossible with our unaided hands to push aside the huge rock with which he had closed the great mouth of the cave. So for the time being we just sat groaning there and waited for the blessed light of day.

No sooner had the tender Dawn shown her roses in the East, than the Cyclops lit up the fire and milked his splendid ewes, all in their proper order, putting her young to each. This business over and his morning labors done, he once more snatched up a couple of my men and prepared his meal. When he had eaten, he turned his fatted sheep out of the cave, removing the great doorstone without an effort, but he replaced it immediately. Then he drove his rich flocks off towards the high pasture, while I was left, with murder in my heart, beating about for some scheme by which I might pay him back. The best plan I could think of. was this: Lying by the pen, I saw that the Cyclops had a huge staff of green olive-wood, which he had cut to carry in his hand when it was seasoned. To us it looked more like the mast of some black ship of twenty oars. On this piece of timber I set to work and cut off a length and sharpened it to a point. Then I poked it into the blazing fire to make it hard, and finally I laid it carefully by. I then told my company to casts lots among themselves for the dangerous task of helping me to lift the pole and twist it in the Cyclops' eye when he was sound asleep.

Evening came, and with it the Cyclops, shepherding his woolly sheep, every one of which he herded into the broad part of the cave. He raised the great doorstone, set it in its place, and then sat down to milk his ewes and bleating goats. When this business was over and his work finished, he once more seized upon two of us and prepared his supper. Then came my chance. With an ivy-wood bowl of my dark wine in my hands, I went up to him and said:

> "Here, Cyclops, have some wine to wash down that meal of human flesh, and find out for yourself what kind of vintage was stored away in our ship's hold. I brought it for you by way of an offering in the hope that you would be charitable and help me on my homeward way. But your savagery is more than we can bear. Cruel monster, how can you expect ever to have a visitor again from the world of men, after such deeds as you have done?"

The Cyclops took the wine and drank it up. And the delicious draught gave him such exquisite pleasure that he asked me for another bowlful.

"Be good enough," he said, "to let me have some more; and tell me your name, here and now, so that I may make you a gift that you will value. We Cyclopes have wine of our own, but this vintage of yours is nectar and ambrosia distilled."

So said the Cyclops, and I handed him another bowlful of the ruddy wine. Three times I filled up for him; and three times the fool drained the bowl to the dregs. At last, when the wine had fuddled his wits, I addressed him with disarming suavity.

"Cyclops," I said, "you wish to know the name I bear. I'll tell it to you; and in return I should like to have the gift you promised me. My name is 'Nobody.' That is what I am called by my mother and father and by all my friends."

The Cyclops answered me with a cruel jest. "Of all his company I will eat Nobody last, and the rest before him. That shall be your gift."

He had hardly spoken before he toppled over and fell face upwards on the floor, where he lay with his great neck twisted to one side, conquered, as all men are, by sleep. His drunkenness made him vomit, and a stream of wine mixed with morsels of men's flesh poured from his throat. I went at once and thrust our pole deep under the ashes of the fire to make it hot, and meanwhile gave a word of encouragement to all my men, to make sure that no one should play the coward and leave me in the lurch. I withdrew it from the fire and brought it over to the spot where my men were standing ready. Heaven now inspired them with a reckless courage. Seizing the olive pole, they drove its sharpened end into the Cyclops' eye, while I used my weight from above to twist it home. The fiery smoke from the blazing eyeball singed his lids and brow all round, and the very roots of his eye crackled in the heat. He gave a dreadful shriek, which echoed round the rocky walls, and we backed away from him in terror, while he pulled the stake from his eye, streaming with blood. Then he hurled it away from him with frenzied hands and raised a great shout for the other Cyclopes who lived in neighboring caves along the windy heights. These, hearing his screams, came up from every quarter and gathering outside the cave asked him what ailed him:

> "What on earth is wrong with you, Polyphemus? Why must you disturb the peaceful night and spoil our sleep with all this shouting? Is a robber driving off your sheep, or is somebody trying by treachery or violence to kill you?"

Out of the cave came Polyphemus' great voice in reply: "O my friends, it's Nobody's treachery and violence that are doing me to death."

"Well then," they answered, in a way that settled the matter, "if nobody is assaulting you in your solitude, you must be sick. Sickness comes from almighty Zeus and cannot be helped. All you can do is pray to your father, the Lord Poseidon."

And off they went, while I chuckled to myself at the way in which my happy notion of a false name had taken them in. The Cyclops, still moaning in agonies of pain, groped about with his hands and pushed the rock away from the mouth of the cave. But then he sat himself down in the doorway and stretched out both arms in the hope of catching us in the act of slipping out among the sheep. What a fool he must have thought me! Meanwhile I was cudgeling my brains for the best possible course, trying to hit on some way of saving my friends as well as my own skin. Plan after plan, dodge after dodge, passed through my mind. It was a matter of life or death: we were in mortal peril. And this was the scheme I eventually chose. There were in the flock some well-bred, thick-fleeced rams. These I quietly lashed together in threes. The middle one in each case was to carry one of my followers, while its fellows went on either side to protect him. Each of my men thus had three sheep to bear him, but for myself I chose a full-grown ram who was the pick of the whole flock. Seizing him by the back, I curled myself up under his shaggy belly and lay there upside down, with a firm grip on his wonderful fleece and with patience in my heart. Thus in fear and trembling we waited for the blessed Dawn.

As soon as she arrived, the flock began to scramble out and make for the pastures. Their master, though he was worn out by the agonies he had gone through, passed his hand, along the backs of all the animals as they left, but the idiot never noticed that my men were tied up under his own woolly sheep. The last of the flock to come up to the doorway was the big ram, burdened by his own fleece and by me with my teeming brain. As he felt him with his big hands that great Polyphemus broke into speech:

"Sweet ram," he said, "what does this mean? Why are you the last of the flock to pass out of the cave, you who have never lagged behind the sheep, you who always step so proudly out and are the first of them to crop the lush shoots of the grass? Are you grieved for your master's eye, blinded by a wicked man and his accursed friends, when he had robbed me of my wits with wine? Nobody was his name; and I swear that he has not yet saved his skin! Ah, if only you could feel as I do and find a voice to tell me where he's hiding from my fury! Wouldn't I hammer him and splash his brains all over the floor of the cave, till that miserable Nobody had eased my heart of the suffering I owe to him!"

So he passed the ram out; and when we had put a little distance between ourselves and the courtyard of the cave, I first freed myself from under my ram and next untied my men from theirs. Then, quickly, though with many a backward look, we drove our long-legged sheep right down to the ship—and a rich, fat flock they made. My dear companions were overjoyed when they caught sight of us survivors, though their relief soon changed to lamentation for their slaughtered friends. I would have none of this weeping, however, bidding them make haste instead to tumble all the fleecy sheep on board and put to sea.

But before we were out of earshot, I let Polyphemus have a piece of my mind. "Cyclops!" I called. "So he was not such a weakling after all, the man whose friends you meant to overpower and eat in that snug cave of yours! And your crimes came home to roost, you brute, who have not even the decency to refrain from devouring your own guests. Now Zeus and all his fellow-gods have paid you out."

My taunts so exasperated the angry Cyclops that he tore the top off a great pinnacle of rock and hurled it at us. The rock fell just ahead of our blue-painted bows.

As it plunged in, the water rose and the backwash, like a swell from the open sea, swept us landward and nearly drove us on the beach. My crew rowed with a will, but when they had brought us across the water to twice our previous distance I was for giving the Cyclops some more of my talk.

"Cyclops, if anyone ever asks you how you came by your unsightly blindness, tell him your eye was put out by Odysseus, Sacker of Cities, the son of Laertes, who lives in Ithaca."

The Cyclops gave a groan. "Alas!" he cried. "So the old prophecy has come home to me with a vengeance! We had a prophet with us once, a fine upstanding man, who was an excellent seer and grew old among us in the practice of his art. All of that has now happened he foretold, when he warned me that a man called Odysseus would rob me of my sight. But I always expected some big and handsome fellow of tremendous strength to come along. And now, a puny, good for nothing, little runt fuddles me with wine and then puts out my eye! But come here, Odysseus, so that I may make you some friendly gifts and prevail on the great Earthshaker to see you safely home. For I am his son: he is the one who will heal me if he's willing—a thing no other blessed god nor any man on earth could do."

To which I shouted in reply: "I only wish I could make as sure of robbing you of life and breath and sending you to Hell, as I am certain that not even the Earthshaker will ever heal your eye."

At this the Cyclops lifted up his hands to the heavens that hold the stars and prayed to the Lord Poseidon: "Hear me, Poseidon, god of the sable locks, grant that Odysseus, who styles himself Sacker of Cities and son of Laertes, may never reach his home in Ithaca. But if he is destined to reach his native land, to come once more to his own house and see his friends again, let him come late, in evil plight, with all his comrades dead, and when he is landed, let him find trouble in his home."

So Polyphemus prayed; and the god of the sable locks heard his prayer. Then once again the Cyclops picked a boulder up—bigger by far this time—and hurled it with a swing, putting such boundless force into his throw that the rock fell only just astern of our blue-painted ship by inches. The water heaved up as it ploughed into the sea; but the wave that it raised carried us on toward the farther shore. And so we reached our island, where the rest of our good ships were awaiting us in a body, while their crews sat round disconsolate and kept a constant watch for our return. Once there, we beached our ship, jumped out on the shore, and unloaded the Cyclops's sheep and divided our spoil. My comrades-in-arms did me the special honor, when the sheep were distributed, of presenting me with the big ram in addition. Him I sacrificed on the beach, burning slices from his thighs as an offering to Zeus, who is lord of us all. But Zeus took no notice of my sacrifice; his mind must already have been full of plans for the destruction of all my gallant ships and my trusty band.

9

Dialli Kieba Koate, *Sunjatta*

Sunjatta was a quite historical king, whose exploits were decisive in establishing Mali as a great West African kingdom or empire, which he ruled from 1230 to 1255 A.D. Griots, singers who know tribal history, still chant his story among his people, the Malinke, in a great variety of versions, but in all of them Sunjatta stands out for having overcome great hardships as a boy and gone on to display bravery, wisdom, and the ability to work magic.

Mali became the strongest and wealthiest West African kingdom until its decline in the fifteenth century. It included many tribes, but the Malinke or Mandingo, the most prominent Mande-speaking ethnic group, gained ascendancy. Consequently the griot Dialli Kieba Koate's version of Sunjatta, excerpted below, calls what became the Mali kingdom "Mandeland" with some justification. It was essential to the story that Sunjatta's mother should overcome great ugliness as a young woman, and most versions—including the American children's version, Sunjatta the Lion King—make her hunch-backed; this one makes her body covered with boils and running sores.

Islam was gaining ground in Mali in Sunjatta's day, and a century later the great Mansa (King) Musa made Islam a central feature of his kingdom. He is famous for having disbursed so much gold traveling through Egypt on a pilgrimage to Mecca that he brought down the price of Egyptian gold for a decade. Islam figures only marginally in the version excerpted below, which may mark it as one with older roots than most, particularly since it portrays Sunjatta acquitting himself well in a very un-Muslim ordeal of drinking extra-strong beer, while he and his sister spurn the weaker brews.

QUESTIONS TO CONSIDER

1. While the Disney film "The Lion King" features animals rather than humans, would you agree that it reflects some of the themes of Sunjatta?
2. Can you identify common features of the Sunjatta epic in the film "Forrest Gump?"
3. How does Sunjatta compare with Gilgamesh and Odysseus (Readings 7 and 8) in reflecting value-perspectives from different societies?

This is the story of Sunjatta. . . . All people go back to Mamata, the first man: eighty generations lead to Sunjatta, the first king of all the Mande peoples. Sometimes the Sunjatta story is set in the town of Kirrikane, not a particularly big place but noteworthy for having its population stay the same because, whenever someone dies there, someone else is born.

It is also said that Sunjatta came from from Sangara, [which seems more likely]. In Sangara there were once twelve brothers and a sister. All twelve brothers mistreated their sister despite having the same father and mother, so the sister transformed herself into a koba, a kind of horse-antelope, such as is not found anymore, and that koba killed a man in the town every day. She could be recognized by her tail of pure gold.

Two brothers went after the koba with bows and arrows: "One of us will chase the koba and the other will shoot it," they said. [They had no success, and] three hunters, each from a different village, took up the task of finally destroying the koba. When the three went out, they met the koba, but she attacked each one separately, so that each man was driven back into the bush.

From Dialli Kieba Koate, recorded in the *Holy Traditional History of the Malinke*, "as told to him by a snake," ed. Leo Frobenius, *Die Sunjattalegende der Malinke*, in *Atlantis; Volksmaerchen und Volksdichtungen Afrikas* (Munich: Veroeffentlichungen des Instituts fuer Kulturmorphologie, 1925), Vol. V, pp. 330; transl. Henry A. Myers. Phrases in parentheses are in Frobenius' text. Those in square brackets represent condensations of text or clarifications added. The hero's name is often spelled "Sundiata;" "di" is the conventional West African French letter combination to convey the sound of an English "j," so that either spelling of the name (with "di" or "j") should be pronounced "Sunjatta."

"That is no ordinary koba," people said, "just not a bush koba."

The chief, Niamorodiote, announced: "Whoever kills that koba may have the most beautiful girl—or the one who appeals to him most—as his bride."

Sangara had many people, and Chief Niamorodiote had a daughter who, to be sure, was young enough, but whose body was covered with boils and sores.

This woman was named Sugulunkurmang; she was frighteningly ugly. In those days wives were hard to get or very expensive, so that the offer of a free choice among girls was very tempting.

[Two brothers of the Traore clan, Masaulomba and Damba Saulandi, sought advice from a desert oracle, who told them to play up to a foul-tempered old woman who, if they were nice to her, would tell them how to kill the koba; afterwards the boil-covered woman— not the most beautiful girl in twelve villages—was to be chosen. This came to pass: Damba Saulandi killed the koba with an arrow having magic cotton threads attached to it.]

Chief Niamorodiote had all the girls of the land assemble and said the two Traori brothers should choose a bride. All the girls came, although when Sugulunkurmang wanted to present herself, too, her father told her: "You stay away: with your boils and abcesses, you are too ugly."

The two brothers walked along the row of girls and looked them over. "Are all the girls of the land here?" the older Traore brother asked the chief.

Chief Niomorodiote answered: "Yes, except for Sugulunkurmang. She stayed at home because she is so ugly."

The brothers asked: "Just why did she stay home now?"

"Because she has so many boils and abcesses."

"That must be the right one, then," said the brothers.

The people laughed at that. They brought Sugulunkurmang up, and, yes, she was ugly.

[The two brothers took Sugulunkurmang with them as a bride. Each in turn attempted to initiate love-making with her but found her skin magically prickly and burning to the touch. They came to the conclusion that since she was a chief's daughter, she should belong to the Mande King, Farkuma Kakenji. The king was persuaded to give the brothers another woman in exchange for her, and he married Sugulunkurmang himself].

Right away she became pregnant, but the king's first wife became pregnant at the same time. . . .

When Sugulunkurmang became a mother and began recovering her strength, she said to Djalimussu-tumbumannia, [a basically good witch who sang dirges when someone died,] "Go to the king and tell him that I bore him his first son." Djalimussu-tumbumannia went to the king while he was eating. In those days the Mandingoes ate only rice. The king greeted her . . . and then said: " Djalimussu-tumbumannia, come and eat with me." Djalimussa-tumbumannia sat down to eat with the king and in the process completely forgot to deliver her message.

The same day, although a few hours later, the first wife of the king bore a child, summoned Maruni-pempete (a witch practiced in beheading with a knife), and told her: "Go to the king and report to him that I have given him a son." Maruni-pempete made her way to the king. When she reached him, he was [still] eating. When she greeted him, the king greeted her also and said, "Come here and eat with me." "Whoever has swift feet should also have a swift tongue: your first wife has sent me to tell you that she has given you a son," said the witch. "That is truly wonderful," said the king.

Djalimussu-tumbumannia jumped up and said: "I also have a message to report—Oh, in eating I completely forgot to deliver my message—your wife, Sugulun-kurmang sent me to tell you that she gave you your first son. That son is your first-born."

"You are now too late to come and tell me that!" said the king. "The one I heard of first is the older one!" The child of the king's first wife would be called Massa [King] Dangaratuma.

The king said, "Massa Dangaratuma is my older son;" however, this was not true: Sunjatta was the older.

* * *

Years later, Sunjatta's mother asked another mother of a prince: "Give me some of your sirabula (leaves from the monkey-bread tree)."

The other woman answered firmly, "Today I will still give you some, but this is the last time. Your son is older than mine: let him risk his bones and neck climbing around monkey-bread trees. Why is your son, Sunjatta, always sitting and pushing himself across the ground?"

Outside, Sunjatta heard his mother in an argument with somebody and asked, "What are you talking about with that other woman?"

"Oh, it is on account of the sirabula that I asked this lady to give me."

"And are there no smiths in Mandeland? Doesn't my father have any smiths?" asked Sunjatta.

"Yes, your father has smiths," said his mother.

"Then they should make an iron staff for me with which I can raise myself."

The smiths built seven furnaces to smelt iron into a strong staff. They forged the staff and brought it to Sunjatta, who took it and broke it to pieces like a reed, saying: "This is just not good enough. Aren't there any real smiths in Mandeland?"

"Yes, there are real smiths," the people said.

"Then they should make me a decent staff; this one can't bear my weight," said Sunjatta.

The smiths now built seventeen furnaces to smelt the iron for a staff. They forged the staff and brought it to Sunjatta. This staff helped him rise up only a little; then it bent double in his hands into an arch shape. He threw it away and said: "Will you finally bring me something decent? I can't use this kind of stuff."

The smiths then built twenty-seven furnaces to make iron for a single staff.

They forged the staff, and the people carried it: it was thick as a tree trunk.

Sunjatta raised himself on it before the staff began to bend a little. "Mother, come help me!" called Sunjatta, and so he supported himself upon his mother's shoulder on his left and upon the staff on his right.

His mother sang jubilantly: "Today is a wonderful day: the good God has never given me a better one."

* * *

Years later Djalimussu-tumbumannia, the witch who protected Sunjatta, was away on a trip, and the other eight of the nine witches turned Sunjatta into a bull at the instigation of his relatives. Then they led the young bull out and killed him by cutting off his head, after which they cut him up into nine pieces. Each one took her portion, and they saved the ninth part for Djalimussu-tumbumannia. When she returned, Djalimussu-tumbumannia took her portion and asked, "What kind of meat is this?"

The other witches answered, "That is the flesh of Sunjatta, the son of Sugulun-kurmang; we turned him into a bull and then butchered him."

"What has more meat," asked Djalimussu-tumbumannia, "a young bull or nine big bush buffloes?"

"Nine big bush buffaloes have more meat," answered the other eight witches.

"Very well," said Djalimussu-tumbumannia, "so tomorrow bring all the bones and sinews left from your portions, and I will give each of you a big bush buffalo for them."

And so it came to pass: the next morning they brought all the scraps of sinews and bones from the skeleton and assembled them as they had been in the bull; [they each received a big bush buffalo in return.] Then a young bull arose again from the bones and scraps: Djalimussu-tumbumannia struck him on the tail, and he turned back into Sunjatta.

"Run away," said Djalimussu-tumbumannia, "Do not stay here. Leave Mande-land. The young snake must hide himself, if he is not to be killed by people, losing his life at a very young age."

Sunjatta prepared to leave with his mother and let Kengebugurilala, the desert oracle, foretell his fate. The oracle said, "Before you get where you want to go, you will be provoked to anger three times: however, if you do not allow yourself to be carried away by anger, then you will be King of the Malinke. First of all, go away and hide yourself in the land of Mema." Sunjatta began the journey and departed his homeland, taking with him his mother, his little sister, Killikillimadjumasuko and his younger brother, Simbombatanganjati, who was also a big, strong man.

They fled along the way the oracle had set forth and first they came to the land of Dabo. . . . The people of Dabo considered three things sacred [or magical]. First they had doh, a drink like sorghum beer but of different strengths. Some people could stand only the brews that were a month old; others those five months old; others those that were six months old; still others those which were aged for a full ten years. Those last ones, however, had to be very strong people and after they had enjoyed their drink, even they would become tired and drunk.

The second sacred thing centered around a large pot in which much oil boiled. Whoever wanted to swear to something took a bracelet from his arm, threw it into the boiling oil and pulled it out with his bare hand, but the boiling oil burned the flesh down to the bone from the arm of the man who swore falsely. The oil could do no harm to anyone who spoke the truth.

The third sacred thing was their bashi binje, a set of seven doors of double thickness, which they leaned on a tree in the banana-tree family. Someone would swear [to] something before these doors. Whoever swore truthfully could shoot an arrow through two or even three doors, but the arrow of someone who swore falsely could not even begin to penetrate the wood of the first door.

From a distance the people of Dabo saw Sunjatta coming with his companions, and they said: "It is a stranger: let's give him some one-month-old doh."

They handed some of this to Sunjatta, to see how strong he was.

Sunjatta took the cup, [tasted the brew,] and passed it on to Killikillimadjumasuko, saying, "That may be all right for a little girl, but it's nothing for me." [Sunjatta had been given cause for anger at being offered a weak drink, but he kept his composure.]

His sister raised the cup to her lips and then threw cup and drink away on the ground, saying, "Yuck! That's dirty water but not a real drink."

The people of Dabo said, "We shall give you some two-year-old doh."

They held out some to Sunjatta, who raised it to his lips and said: "Where we come from they give stuff like this to children. My little sister might as well try it."

They held out the drink to Killikillimadjumasuko. The girl took a small sip, then threw the drink away with the bowl and said: "That's not good for anything. The women of Dabo just don't understand how to make beer at all."

The Daboans then said: "Let them try the doh that has aged a full ten years."

They extended a small cupfull to Sunjatta, who tried it and said: "That might do for women, but it is really nothing for men. Give that drink to Killikillimadjumasuko. . . ." She raised it to her lips, downed it in a single swallow and said: "I can't say it's good, but when there is nothing better—when the women of Dabo just don't know how to brew anything better—then you could stoop to quench your thirst with it. Go ahead and bring me the big pot."

People brought her the large pot of ten-year-old doh, and she drank it down just to quench her thirst. "These are strong people," said the Daboans. "This man should try the tulu karuli fawa kono (ordeal by boiling oil)."

[Facing this ordeal, Sunjatta swore that he had never been afraid of anything since he was old enough to tell his right hand from his left, tossed a bracelet into the boiling oil, and pulled it out with his bare arm and hand—unharmed except for one slightly singed hair. The Daboans snickered a bit at the singed hair, but Killikillimadjumasuko reminded Sunjatta that the oracle had warned him not to be overcome by anger, even if justified, and he would be king of the Malinke. With more advice from his sister, Sunjatta successfully passed the ordeal by boiling oil; even the one singed hair was restored the second time he tried it.]

The Daboans now set up the binje. They set up the seven doors of double thickness before the old tree like a banana tree and said, "Sunjatta, take your bow and arrow and shoot at the seven doors."

He called his sister and said, "Killikillimadjumasuko, look, I am going to shoot at these seven doors." She came up to him.

The people said to him, "If you are a man of pure, royal blood—if you really are the true son of your father—then you may be confident about shooting at these doors: your arrow will pass through, maybe, two or even three of them. If you are not of true royal blood, your arrow will not be able to go into the wood at all."

Sunjatta put his arrow's notch on the sinew [bowstring] and said: "If I am not of pure, royal blood, may the arrow turn back in the air and kill me." He shot, and the arrow whirred through the air and not only went through all seven doors but penetrated with full force the tree like a banana tree in front of which the doors were standing so hard that the roots tore loose, and the tree fell over. Kissima Dabo, King of Daboland cried out at seeing the old tree fall, and right away the tree rose in the same place it had been before. [This reversal of his deed might have provoked Sunjatta to anger, but instead] Sunjatta cried out, and the tree fell again. Then both cried out at the same time, [the tree split] and half of it rose up again while half lay on the ground, and it remains that way to this day. . . .

The people of Dabo said then: "This is a brave and strong man," and they showed him the way to Mema."

The sand oracle had said to Sunjatta, "Go next and hide yourself in the land of Mema. . . ."

Sunjatta came and entrusted himself to Farambram, King of Mema, saying "I come to you with my dependants because in Mandeland I must fear the witches and my other relatives. . . ." Right after this, he began his stay in Mema.

* * *

Sumanguru attacked Mandeland. This Sumanguru, King of the Susu, had his name from having been borne by two mothers, Sansu and Dabi. When those two became pregnant, one of them was always in that state during the day and the other during the night but during the opposite times each one was not pregnant. They just alternated that way; at night the boy left the one mother's womb and ran around the house [before returning to his other mother], but the women could not give birth to the child.

They turned to the oracle, who told them, "Set up a large wooden mortar of the type you use for grinding grain with a big pestle in the room where both women, Sansu and Dabi, sleep. Then wait and see what happens!"

Just as the oracle advised, a large wooden mortar was set up in the house of the two pregnant women. As always, Sumanguru slipped out of one mother's body and ran around, after which he wanted to go back to the womb of the other mother, but he met up with the wooden mortar and, [overcome by curiosity], climbed into it. Hearing the noise, the two women sat bolt upright in bed, and blood like that which accompanies a delivery flowed from both of them. . . .

Hearing about this, the people said, "Sansu and Dabi have given birth."

They named the boy Susu Sumanguru (Susu with Two Mothers), but the two mothers argued with each other. "He is my son!" said Sansu.

"He is my son!" said Dabi. They fought all over the place, but Sumanguru grew big and strong.

When Sunjatta heard about him, he said, "Nobody will be able to beat Sumanguru."

For his part, however, Sumanguru said, "Nobody can resist Sunjatta."

Susu Sumanguru grew up and started his wars while Sunjatta was staying in Mema and Mansa Dangaratuma ruled in Mandeland. Susu Sumanguru began war against the Mande, attacking their land and conquering one part of it after the other. . . . Mandeland fell, and its people said, "If Sunjatta does not return soon, Mandeland is lost forever."

Others said, "We should call Sunjatta home!"

They thought it over and several of them said, "All Malinke are ready to risk their lives for sirabula [leaves of the monkey-bread tree] to eat, such as grow in no other country. We should send out sirabula to markets everywhere and call out: 'Sirabula! Sirabula!' Sunjatta and his people will come up and want to buy the leaves, and we will recognize them; then we can deliver our message."

That seemed like a good idea, and people were sent out, but Susu Sumanguru heard about what was going on and ordered a load of gold to be gathered together, which he sent to Farambram with the message that he should have Sunjatta killed.

What Farambram loved most was a dice game. He called Sunjatta to play dice with iron cubes; shaking the dice in his hand, he said: "When somebody gives me his father to kill, I kill him; when somebody gives me his mother to kill, I kill her; when somebody gives me their relatives to kill, I kill them." With these words, he threw the dice.

Sunjatta picked up the dice, shook them in his hand, and said, "When somebody gives you an evil task and gold, let the evil task go undone and let the gold go, too." With these words, he threw the dice and won.

* * *

Killikillimadjumasuko told Sunjatta, "A delegation has arrived from Mandeland. Susu Sumanguru has invaded the land, overthrown the king, and now he is destroying everything there. The people of Mandeland ask us to tell you that if you don't come quickly the whole empire will be destroyed. The people have come to call you back."

I can't return now," said Sunjatta, "for my Mother is too old, and she can't stand the long journey anymore."

"You won't want to throw my life away for an uncertain thing," said Sugulunkurmang. "So go to them and swear that you don't want to sacrifice my life for nothing— I mean, you don't want to start something costly without a sure outcome. The fact is that if you become king, I will die; if you don't become king, I will go on living."

Sunjatta went from the town [to the delegation] in the bush and swore: "I promise that I will not go forth if I am not to be King of Mandeland." He returned from the bush to the place in town they were staying, and when he arrived his mother was dead.

Sunjatta went then to Farambram and said, "My mother is dead, and I want to bury her."

"You may bury your mother," said the king, "but you must pay for the place and for the dirt for her burial."

"What will that cost?" asked Sunjatta.

"The space and the dirt that fills it will cost mutukalli (about three and a half ounzes of gold)."

Sunjatta jumped up and said, "I will pay for the space and the earth so that I can bury my Mother." He went off and got the money together, but then he put the feather of a guineafowl, a partridge feather, a broken calabash, a little piece of an old broken pot and an iron musketball—for this was the time when the first guns appeared here[10]—into a calabash which he sent to Farambram with the money. When the gold and the calabash arrived, three wise, old men were sitting with the king, Kemoro-kubelong (he who knows everything), Kemoro-kubakurosi (he who notices and understands everything), and Kemoro-komabefu (he who tells everything, making it clear).

Farambram asked them, "What is that in the calabash?"

Hearing the king's question, Kemoro-kubelong looked at the contents and said only, "Ng."

Kemoro-kubakurosi bent over it and said, "I know what it is."

Kemoro-komabefu, however, raised his head and said, "The piece of a broken calabash means that Sunjatta will once again return to Mema and could be able to destroy the country. The piece of a shattered old pot means that Mema will burst into pieces like a rotten, old jar; the feathers of the guinea-hen and the partridge foretell that wild animals shall forage for food in the ruins of Mema. The musket ball says that your people will fall under gunfire and be scattered."

When Kemoro-homabefu had finished, Farambram shoved the gold and the calabash back and said to Sunjatta, "I don't want your gold. Take your gold and bury your mother. You don't need to take Sugulunkurmang's body back to Mandeland."

Sunjatta then buried his mother and said, "Now, I shall return to my homeland."

---

[10]While much of the narrative appears to be of thirteenth-century origin, the reference to guns and musketballs must be a later addition (Frobenius' note).

Sunjatta began his journey home. Arriving at the border of Mandeland, he sent a messenger to Sumanguru to tell him: "Come with your warriors to Kankinja: there we will wage war." Sumanguru came with his heroes to Kankinja, where the Malinke and the Susu charged each other nine times in battle. At Kankingo the Malinke shed tears [in defeat], while the Susu laughed.

[Sunjatta sent five further challenges to Sumanguru, and each time Sumanguru came with his warriors; in nine encounters at each locale, the Susu were consistently the winners. Finally, Sunjatta challenged him to fight his army at Dagadjalla.]

Sumanguru came, and at the Battle of Dagadjalla the armies charged each other nine times, but at Dagadjalla the Mande laughed in victory, and the Susu were beaten. Sumanguru and the Susu had to leave the country, and Sunjatta became King of Mali.

[Sunjatta sent a message to the King of the Wolofs with gold to buy horses for his warriors, but the Wolof king scornfully gave him five hundred buffalo and five hundred koba hides, saying that the Malinke were all right at hunting and drinking, but they needed leather for their sandals: horses were only for real kings and their warriors, Chiefs serving Sunjatta volunteered to avenge the insult.]

"That is my task, which I must take care of all alone," said Sunjatta.

"Let me avenge this insult," said Tiramaga, the clan leader of the Traore, "and take the field against Djolofemansa [King of the Wolofs]."

"The insult is too great," said Sunjatta. "I must avenge it myself."

"If you don't allow me to go, I will have myself killed and buried," said Tiramaga.

"I shall do it myself," said Sunjatta.

At this, Tiramaga ordered his grave dug, and he wrapped himself in the clothes of death. Once again, he asked Sunjatta: "Permit me to go!"

"I have to do it myself," said Sunjatta.

Then Tiramaga went and laid himself in his grave and sent a messenger to Sunjatta to tell him: "Tiramaga is lying in his grave, and it is about to be closed and filled."

Balla-Fasege-Kuate, the wise griot, was standing by Sunjatta as the messenger arrived, and he told Sunjatta: "Let enough be enough, and let him march against the King of the Wolofs."

"All right, let him have his way," said Sunjatta.

Tiramaga heard the news, stood up from his grave and assembled his men. From there he marched to battle, and in the war, Tiramaga killed Djolofemansa himself and cut off his head. The feet of the Wolofs scraped the ground like the feet of wild buffaloes running away, and so Sunjatta destroyed the Wolof Empire and got the horses he wanted.

Since that day, the song is sung:

"Tiramaga will never be wounded.

No arrow will hit him.

No musketball will hit him,

When the river rises, Tiramaga will stride through it.

When a swamp opens, Tiramaga will walk right through it."

* * *

"Why did you have Djolofemansa killed?" asked Balla-Fasege-Kuate.

"He insulted me—called me a drunkard," said Sunjatta.

"Djolofemansa hasn't been the only one to say that," said Balla-Fasege-Kuate. "Ulimansa said that, too."

Ulimansa was a king who lived close to Djolofemansa's land.

"Well then, I will avenge that insult the same way," said Sunjatta. He sent a military expedition against Ulimansa; he had him killed and the rule of his dynasty ended.

Soon after that it was said that Njanimansa had dared to make the same insult. Sunjatta then sent an expedition against him, had him killed, and had his corpse beheaded. . . .

After all these wars were won, the country became big, and Sunjatta's warriors were equipped with horses, but Kante Numu was a smith to whom Sunjatta had not given a horse, and for that reason he felt very bitter. And so he sent a message to Sumanguru, telling him, "Send me arrows that I may take the field against Sunjatta." Sumanguru received the message and agreed to the request. He sent a large expeditionary force to Kante Numa, who launched a rebellion against Sunjatta by sending troops of warriors against him.

Sunjatta assembled [warriors from many tribes] and marched to war. When the battle began, Kante Numu shot an arrow at Sunjatta, which injured the king. Sunjatta's people wanted to rush at Kante Numau, to kill him.

"Leave him alone: I will take care of him!" said Sunjatta; then he took two arrows and shot them toward Kante Numu. Now these were magical arrows, and Sunjatta had said to them, "Follow Kante Numu, the traitor. Don't kill him at first, but stay just over his head: whether he rides or walks, follow him wherever he goes. Whether he is sleeping, standing, sitting, or resting, you are to stay whirring above his head. Stay with him that way until he comes to Sumanguru, who rules the Susu. When he opens his mouth to start telling about how he struck me with an arrow, then you two kill that traitor." He shot the first arrow. He shot the second arrow.

Kante Numu's troops were scattered, and he was defeated. He fled . . . , attempting to reach Susu Sumanguru. Both of Sunjatta's arrows followed him. At first they didn't kill that rebel, but they followed him everywhere he went and remained constantly above his head. No matter whether he rode or wandered on foot they followed him. If he rested, lay down, sat down or stood up, they circled whirring around his head, and so they stayed with him for his whole journey and never left him. Accompanied by the two arrows, he arrived at [the court of] Sumanguru, the ruler of the defeated Susu. [The arrows followed him through seven gateways and buildings on the way to the royal residence.]

The arrows were still following him, as Kante Numu stepped before the king. He greeted the king and began to tell him: "You sent me warriors, and I marched against Sunjatta with them. . . . We fought all over the place: during the fighting I took an arrow and—"

At that moment the two arrows shot down at Kante Numu and buried themselves in him because Sunjatta had told them they should kill the rebel at the moment when he was about to tell that his arrow had hit the King of Mali. Kante Numu sank dead at the feet of King Sumanguru, who did exercise strong magical powers. [Sumanguru's magic revived Kante Numu three times, but] the fourth time the magic did not succeed because the fellow's body was beginning to disintegrate into dust.

And so, Susu Sumanguru never found out that one of his arrows had injured Sunjatta. That was the end of the war between them: the Susu were defeated. Susu Sumanguru was turned into a mountain, which can be seen to this very day. . . .

Law in the Ancient Near East:
Babylonian and Hittite

L aw is a basic requirement for security in any civilization. Unless imposed on them by foreign conquerors, legal systems reflect the values of the people who create them. Consequently, it is no surprise to find a commercial people punishing commercial fraud much more severely than an agricultural people or feudal lords giving themselves special privileges at the expense of merchants in societies they control.

Throughout the history of civilization, two themes stand out in the construction of law codes: peace and justice. As we will see in the case of the relatively primitive Germanic tribes at the onset of the Western Middle Ages (see Reading 57), peace is the essence of law in this sense: When someone offends another with violence or fraud, a nomadic people who think of themselves as having a valuable population of limited numbers will aim to settle the conflict by letting the guilty party pay his victim or the victim's family enough to settle the matter without a blood feud among families—a dreaded evil for them. On the other hand, people in a settled environment, particularly in an urban one, see justice as the essence of law: This seems to mean punishing the offender severely enough that people believe he has suffered as much or a little more than his victim and enough to deter others in advance from attempting the same act. In sophisticated, urban societies, people who commit acts of violence and fraud are criminals who deserve something drastic to happen to them as punishment. No one worries about losing them or hopelessly alienating them: The danger of blood feuds is a minor one in most urban environments.

One thing we do not find is early historical confirmation of our experience that laws tend to become more humane, assumably as people become more civilized. In Europe, we will see the use of capital punishment go from being rare to common between the sixth and seventeenth centuries A.D. In the ancient Near East, the constant coming and going of civilizations, the sudden appearance of nomadic conquerors, and the relegation of some advanced people to the status of being subjects of a new empire make it difficult to ascertain trends in law before Roman times. Often, laws relating to religious offenses are of different degrees of severity from those instituted to combat secular fraud and violence. The same is true of sex offenses, many of which were seen as violations of religious taboos. Here, primitive peoples were apt to think that the danger of angering a god was a worse threat even than a blood feud, whereas urban peoples were sometimes less worried about divine actions and reactions. The whole question of what sort of religion the people had is another important variable. With the Hebrews in the ancient Near East, for example, religion played a much more important part in their law codes than it did for their neighbors.

10

The Babylonian Code of Hammurabi

Hammurabi (1792–1750 B.C.) was the sixth Amoritic king of Babylon. The people of Babylon were a western Semitic-speaking group who had drifted into Mesopotamia during the third Sumerian dynasty of Ur. As these Amorites invaded the area, the region had deteriorated into several petty city-states, each trying through either diplomacy or attack to maintain its precarious existence.

Inheriting a rather small area (fifty by thirty miles) from his father, King Hammurabi began to enlarge his domain in his twenty-ninth year. He moved against one Sumerian city after another until he had conquered the entire southern region. Then from his thirty-second through his thirty-eighth years, he was able to consolidate his hold upon Assyria and Syria.

In the second year of his reign Hammurabi had the Babylonian code of law carved on an eight-foot block of black basalt. The text consists of a prologue, epilogue, and 282 laws. The cases deal with court procedures, thefts, slaves, crafts, land tenure, farming, domestic life, trade, and consumer protection. The copy we possess comes from late in the reign and was discovered in the Elamite city of Susa, where it had been taken by invaders.

QUESTIONS TO CONSIDER

1. Was there legal equality among the Babylonians?
2. What are the legal rights of women compared to those of men?
3. What consumer protections does the law offer?
4. What similarities are there between Hammurabi's laws and those of the Hittites?

The Laws of Hammurabi

1. If a man accuse a man, and charge him with murder, but cannot convict him, the accuser shall be put to death.

2. If a man charge a man with sorcery, but cannot convict him, he who is charged with sorcery shall go to the sacred river, and he shall throw himself into the river; if the river overcome him, his prosecutor shall take to himself his house. If the river show that man to be innocent and he come forth unharmed, he that charged him with sorcery shall be put to death. He who threw himself into the river shall take to himself the house of his accuser.

3. If a man, in a case (before the court), offer testimony concerning deeds of violence, and do not establish the testimony that he has given—if that case be a case involving life, that man shall be put to death. . . .

14. If a man steal a man's son who is a minor, he shall be put to death. . . .

From D. D. Luckenbill, trans., and Edward Chiera, ed., "The Code of Hammurabi," in J. M. Powis Smith, *The Origin and History of Hebrew Law* (Chicago: University of Chicago Press, 1960), pp. 183, 185–186, 189, 191, 195–196, 199–202, 204–205, 209–210, 212–213, 218. Copyright 1931 by The University of Chicago. Reprinted by permission.

16. If a man harbor in his house a runaway male or female slave of the palace or of a common man and do not bring him forth at the call of the commandant, the owner of the house shall be put to death.

17. If a man catch a runaway male or female slave, in the country, and bring him back to the owner, the owner of the slave shall pay him two shekels of silver. . . .

21. If a man make a breach in a house, they shall put him to death in front of that breach, and they shall bury him there.

22. If a man practice brigandage and be captured, that man shall be put to death.

23. If the brigand be not captured, the man who has been robbed shall establish the amount of his loss before the god, and the city and the governor, in whose land or border the robbery was committed, shall compensate him for whatsoever was lost.

24. If there were loss of life, the city and governor shall pay one mana of silver to his heirs. . . .

42. If a man rent a field for cultivation and do not produce any grain in the field, because he has not performed the necessary work on the field they shall convict him, and he shall give to the owner of the field grain on the basis of the adjacent (fields). . . .

55. If a man open his canal for irrigation and neglect it and he let the water carry away an adjacent field, he shall measure out grain on the basis of the adjacent fields. . . .

98. If a man give silver to a man for a partnership, they shall divide equally before God the profit and the loss, whatever there is (of either). . . .

100. If he (the peddler) made money (*lit.*, saw profit) where he went, he shall write down the interest on all the money he received, and he shall count up his days, and make his return to the merchant.

101. If he made no money where he went, the agent shall double the amount of money obtained and he shall pay it to the merchant. . . .

103. If, when he goes on a journey, an enemy rob him of anything he was carrying, the agent shall take an oath in the name of God and go free. . . .

108. If a barmaid do not take grain in payment of drink, but if she take money by the great stone, or make the measure of drink smaller than the measure of grain, they shall prosecute that barmaid, and they shall throw her into the water.

109. If outlaws hatch a conspiracy in the house of a wine-seller, and she do not arrest these outlaws and bring them to the palace, that wine-seller shall be put to death.

110. If a priestess or a nun who is not resident in a convent open a wineshop or enter a wineshop for a drink, they shall burn that woman. . . .

129. If the wife of a man be taken in lying with another man, they shall bind them and throw them into the water. If the husband of the woman spare the life of his wife, the king shall spare the life of his servant (i.e., subject). . . .

131. If a man accuse his wife and she have not been taken in lying with another man, she shall take an oath in the name of God and she shall return to her house. . . .

137. If a man set his face to put away a concubine who has borne him children or a wife who has presented him with children, they shall return to that woman her dowry and shall give to her part of field, garden, and goods, and she shall bring up her children; from the time that her children are grown up, from whatever is given to her children they shall give to her a portion corresponding to that of a son and the man of her choice may marry her.

138. If a man put away his wife who has not borne him children, he shall give her money to the amount of her marriage settlement and he shall make good to her the dowry which she brought from her father's house and then he may put her away. . . .

142. If a woman hate her husband and say, "Thou shalt not have me," her past shall be inquired into for any deficiency of hers; and if she have been careful and be without past sin and her husband have been going out and greatly belittling her, that woman has no blame. She shall take her dowry and go to her father's house.

143. If she have not been careful, have been going out, ruining her house and belittling her husband, they shall throw that woman into the water. . . .

145. If a man take a wife and she do not present him with children, and he set his face to take a concubine, that man may take a concubine and bring her into his house. That concubine shall not take precedence of his wife. . . .

153. If the wife of a man bring about the death of her husband because of another man, they shall impale that woman. . . .

162. If a man take a wife and she bear him children and that woman die, her father may not lay claim to her dowry. Her dowry belongs to her children. . . .

169. If he have committed a crime against his father sufficiently grave to cut him off from sonship, they shall condone his first (offense). If he commit a grave crime a second time, the father may cut off his son from sonship. . . .

195. If a man strike his father, they shall cut off his hand.

196. If a man destroy the eye of another man, they shall destroy his eye.

197. If he break a man's bone, they shall break his bone.

198. If he destroy the eye of a common man or break a bone of a common man, he shall pay one mana of silver.

199. If he destroy the eye of a man's slave or break a bone of a man's slave, he shall pay one-half his price.

200. If he knock out a tooth of a man of his own rank, they shall knock out his tooth.

201. If he knock out a tooth of a common man, he shall pay one-third mana of silver.

202. If a man smite on the cheek a man who is his superior, he shall receive sixty strokes with an oxtail whip in public. . . .

215. If a physician make a deep incision upon a man (i.e., perform a major operation) with his bronze lancet and save the man's life; or if he operate on the eye socket of a man with his bronze lancet and save that man's eye, he shall receive ten shekels of silver. . . .

218. If a physician make a deep incision upon a man with his bronze lancet and cause the man's death, or operate on the eye socket of a man with his bronze lancet and destroy the man's eye, they shall cut off his hand. . . .

226. If a barber without (the consent of) the owner of the slave cut the hair of the forehead of a slave (making him) unrecognizable, they shall cut off the hand of that barber. . . .

229. If a builder erect a house for a man and do not make its construction firm, and the house which he built collapse and cause the death of the owner of the house, that builder shall be put to death.

230. If it cause the death of a son of the owner of the house, they shall put to death a son of that builder.

231. If it cause the death of a slave of the owner of the house, he shall give to the owner of the house slave for slave. . . .

278. If a man buy a male or female slave, and the slave have not completed his month when epilepsy attacks him, the buyer shall return him to the seller and shall receive the money which he paid.

279. If a man buy a male or female slave of a man in a foreign country, and there be a claim against him, the seller shall be responsible for the claim.

280. If a man buy a male or female slave of a man in a foreign country, and if when he comes back to his own land the (former) owner of the male or female slave recognize his male or female slave, if the male or female slave be natives of the land, their freedom shall be granted without money.

281. If they be natives of another land, the buyer shall declare before God the money which he paid (for them), and the owner of the male or female slave shall give to the merchant the money which he paid out, and shall (thus) redeem his male or female slave.

282. If a male slave say to his master, "Thou art not my master," his master shall prove him to be his slave and shall cut off his ear.

11

Hittite Laws

While the Amorites were creating their Babylonian Empire, a new language group of peoples called the Indo-Europeans, began to invade the ancient world from India to Western Europe after 2000 B.C. They were a nomadic people known for their breeding of horses and their development of the war chariot. In religion, the Indo-Europeans at first worshipped chiefly storm and thunder gods, but as they became settled their civilizations generated families of (often competing, occasionally feuding) deities for each aspect of human existence.

Sometime after 2000 B.C., a branch of the Indo-European peoples, the Hittites, invaded and settled in the center of Anatolia (western Turkey). From their well-fortified capital city of Hattusas (modern Boghazkoy), great warrior kings expanded their realm (in the fourteenth century B.C.) to include most of Anatolia, northern Mesopotamia, and a large part of northern Syria. Yet, by 1200 B.C., the Hittite Empire was destroyed either by native Anatolian peoples or by the notorious "Sea Peoples," who were attacking Egypt at the time.

The Hittite laws in the following selection come from several collections of cuneiform tablets that were found in the archives at Hattusas.

QUESTIONS TO CONSIDER

1. How does the Hittite code differ from that of Hammurabi?
2. What were the capital crimes in the Hittite code?
3. Was there legal equality among the Hittites?

1. If anyone kills a man or a woman in a quarrel, he shall be declared liable for him/her. He shall give four persons, man or woman, and pledge his estate as security.

2. If anyone kills a male or female slave in a quarrel, he shall be declared liable for him/her. He shall give two persons, man or woman, and pledge his estate as security.

From "The Hittite Laws," trans. Albrecht Goetze, in *Ancient Near Eastern Texts Relating to the Old Testament,* 3rd ed., pp. 369–71, with supplement, ed. James B. Pritchard. Copyright © renewed 1969 by Princeton University Press. Reprinted with permission of Princeton University Press.

3. If anyone strikes a free man or woman and he/she dies, (only) his hand doing wrong, he shall be declared liable for him/her. He shall give two persons and pledge his estate as security.

4. If anyone strikes a male or a female slave and he/she dies, (only) his hand doing wrong, he shall be liable for him/her. He shall give one person and pledge his estate as security.

7. If anyone blinds a free man or knocks out his teeth, they would formerly give one mina of silver; now he shall give twenty shekels of silver and pledge his estate as security.

8. If anyone blinds a male or female slave or knocks out his/her teeth, he shall give ten shekels of silver and pledge his estate as security.

9. If anyone batters a man's head, they would formerly give six shekels of silver; he who was battered would receive three shekels of silver, and they would receive three shekels of silver for the palace. Now the king has abolished the (share) of the palace and only he who was battered receives three shekels of silver.

10. If anyone batters a man so that he falls ill, he shall take care of him. He shall give a man in his stead who can look after his house until he recovers. When he recovers, he shall give him six shekels of silver, and he shall also pay the physician's fee. Later version of 10: If anyone injures a free man's head, he shall take care of him. He shall give a man in his stead who can look after his house until he recovers. When he recovers, he shall give him ten shekels of silver, and he shall also pay the physician's fee. If it is a slave, he shall pay two shekels of silver.

11. If anyone breaks a free man's hand or foot, he shall give him twenty shekels of silver and pledge his estate as security.

12. If anyone breaks the hand or foot of a male or a female slave, he shall give ten shekels of silver and pledge his estate as security.
Later version of 11 and 12: If anyone breaks a free man's hand or foot, in case he is permanently crippled, he shall give him twenty shekels of silver. But in case he is not permanently crippled, he shall give him ten shekels of silver. If anyone breaks a slave's hand or foot, in case he is permanently crippled, he shall give him ten shekels of silver. But in case he is not permanently crippled, he shall give him five shekels of silver.

13. If anyone bites off a free man's nose, he shall give thirty shekels of silver and pledge his estate as security.

14. If anyone bites off the nose of a male or female slave, he shall give thirty shekels of silver and pledge his estate as security.

17. If anyone causes a free woman to miscarry—if (it is the ninth or) the tenth month, he shall give ten shekels of silver, if (it is) the fifth month, he shall give five shekels of silver and pledge his estate as security.
Later version of 17: If anyone causes a free woman to miscarry, he shall give twenty shekels of silver.

18. If anyone causes a slave-woman to miscarry, if (it is) the tenth month, he shall give five shekels of silver.

22. If a slave runs away and anyone brings him back—if he seizes him in the vicinity, he shall give him shoes; if on this side of the river, he shall give him two shekels of silver; if on the other side of the river, he shall give him three shekels of silver.

23. If a slave runs away and goes to the country of Luwiya, he shall give to him who brings him back six shekels of silver. If a slave runs away and goes to an enemy country, whoever brings him nevertheless back, shall receive him (the slave) himself.

24. If a male or female slave runs away, the man at whose hearth his master finds him/her, shall give a man's wages for one year, (namely) x shekels of silver, or a woman's wages for one year, namely x shekels of silver.

27. If a man takes a wife and carries her to his house, he takes her dowry with her. If the woman dies, they turn her property into (property) of the man, and the man also receives her dowry. But if she dies in the house of her father, and there are children, the man will not receive her dowry.

29. If a girl is betrothed to a man and he has given the bride-price for her, but the parents subsequently abrogate the contract and withhold her from the man, they shall make double compensation.

32. If a slave takes a free woman, the provision of the law is the same for them.

33. If a slave takes a slave-girl, the provision of the law is the same for them.

57. If anyone steals a bull—if it is a weanling, it is not a bull; if it is a yearling, it is not a bull; if it is a two-year-old, that is a bull—they would formerly give thirty (head of) cattle. Now he shall give fifteen (head of) cattle, (specifically) five two-year-olds, five yearlings (and) five weanlings and he shall pledge his estate as security.

60. If anyone finds a bull and removes the brand, (if) its owner traces it out, he shall give seven (head of) cattle; he shall give (specifically) two two-year-olds, three yearlings, and two weanlings and he shall pledge his estate as security.

61. If anyone finds a stallion and removes the brand, (if) its owner traces it out, he shall give seven horses; he shall give (specifically) two two-year-olds, three yearlings, and two weanlings and he shall pledge his estate as security.

94. If a free man steals a house, he shall give (back) the respective goods; they would formerly give for the theft one mina of silver, but now he shall give twelve shekels of silver. If he has stolen much, they shall impose a heavy fine upon him; if he has stolen little, they shall impose a small fine upon him and pledge his estate as security.

98. If a free man sets a house on fire, he shall rebuild the house. Whatever was lost in the house, whether it is man, cattle or sheep, he shall replace as a matter of course.

99. If a slave sets a house on fire, his master shall make compensation in his stead. They shall cut off the slave's nose (and) ears and shall give him back to his master. But if he does not make compensation, he will lose that (slave).

172. If a man saves a free man's life in a year of famine, he shall give (a person) like himself. If he is a slave, he shall give ten shekels of silver.

173. If anyone rejects the judgment of the king, his house shall be made a shambles. If anyone rejects the judgment of a dignitary, they shall cut off his head. If a slave rises against his master, he shall go into the pit.

188. If a man does evil with a sheep, it is a capital crime and he shall be killed. They bring him to the king's court. Whether the king orders him killed or whether the king spares his life, he must not appeal to the king.

189. If a man violates his own mother, it is a capital crime. If a man violates his daughter, it is a capital crime. If a man violates his son, it is a capital crime.

192. If a man's wife dies (and) he marries his wife's sister, there shall be no punishment.

193. If a man has a wife and then the man dies, his brother shall take his wife, then his father shall take her. If in turn also his father dies, one of the brother's sons shall take the wife whom he had. There shall be no punishment.

197. If a man seizes a woman in the mountains, it is the man's crime and he will be killed. But if he seizes her in (her) house, it is the woman's crime and the woman

shall be killed. If the husband finds them, he may kill them: there shall be no punishment for him.

198. If he brings them to the gate of the palace and declares: "My wife shall not be killed" and thereby spares his wife's life, he shall also spare the life of the adulterer and shall mark his head. If he says, "Let them die, both of them!" . . . the king may order them killed, the king may spare their lives.

199. If anyone does evil with a pig, (or) a dog, he shall die. They will bring him to the gate of the palace and the king may order them killed, the king may spare their lives; but he must not appeal to the king. If an ox leaps at a man, the ox shall die, but the man shall not die. A sheep may be proffered in the man's stead and they shall kill that. If a pig leaps at a man, there shall be no punishment.

Origins of Writing in West Asia; the Scribal Profession

Both the ancient Egyptians and the Chinese devised pictorial writing systems. The artwork of the New Stone Age had often featured stick figures drawn with less realism than were animals in Old Stone Age cave drawings. People who drew these stick figures could well have sacrificed naturalistic detail, we may suppose, in designing them for communication in the way that simple figures on our own signs for "Reserved for Handicapped" or "Deer Crossing" convey a message.

In Egypt, such pictographs evolved into hieroglyphics, which satisfied the Egyptians well enough as a means for recording their language that they were slow to change them. Meanwhile, at the other end of the Eurasian continent the earliest Chinese pictographs developed into ideographs conveying more abstract concepts.

In the Sumerian part of Mesopotamia, the people developed a different style of writing, called cuneiform. Wet clay was shaped into tablets; then a reed was cut into a wedge shape and impressed into the clay to make the hundreds of signs used in writing.

12

A Sumerian Schoolboy Text

Sumer was an area of Mesopotamia composed of 12 major city-states which lay along and between the Tigris and Euphrates rivers. The fertility of the area was increased by careful irrigation, which enabled the Sumerians to produce excess grain, which they traded for wood, stone, and metal ore. Each city was filled with many great temples called "Ziggurats," which served as the homes of the many gods. The cities were controlled from ca. 2700 B.C. by chief executives called lugals or kings, who were advised on the running of government by a council of elders.

Sumerian cuneiform tablets reveal much information about the economic life of the Sumerians as they have left us thousands of lists of sheep, goats, and other material possessions. Our first great epic myth about King Gilgamesh (Reading 7) was created by the Sumerians and became so popular that almost all future Mesopotamian peoples would reproduce versions of this tale. In addition, we have medical texts, proverbs, fragments of legal codes, and the first mention of a schoolhouse or "edubba."

The following selection, composed ca. 2000 B.C., is thought to be by an "ummia" or experienced (teacher) who is asked what he did when he was a boy in school.

QUESTIONS TO CONSIDER

1. Why did the schoolboy have such a hard day?
2. What is different in the Sumerian school from school today?
3. How does this school compare with that of ancient Egypt?
4. How did the schoolboy seek to make a better impression on his teacher?

I recited my tablet, ate my lunch, prepared my [new] tablet, wrote it, finished it; then my model tablets were brought to me; and in the afternoon my exercise tablets were brought to me. When school was dismissed, I went home, entered the house, and found my father sitting there. I explained (?) my exercise-tablets to my father, (?) recited my tablet to him, and he was delighted, [so much so] that I attended him [with joy].

[The author now has the schoolboy turn to the house servants (it was evidently quite a well-to-do home) with these words:]

I am thirsty, give me water to drink; I am hungry, give me bread to eat; wash my feet, set up [my] bed, I want to go to sleep. Wake me early in the morning, I must not be late lest my teacher cane [me].

When I arose early in the morning, I faced my mother and said to her: "Give me my lunch, I want to go to school!" My mother gave me two rolls, and I set out [for] school. In school the fellow in charge of punctuality said: "Why are you late?" Afraid and with pounding heart, I entered before my teacher and made a respectful curtsy.

My headmaster read my tablet and said:
"There is something missing," [and] he caned me.
(There follow two unintelligible lines)
The fellow in charge of neatness(?) said(?)
"You loitered in the street and did not straighten up (?) your clothes (?),"
    [and] caned me.
(There follow five unintelligible lines)
The fellow in charge of silence said:
"Why did you talk without permission?" [and] caned me.
The fellow in charge of the assembly (?) said:
"Why did you 'stand at ease(?)' without permission?" [and] caned me.
The fellow in charge of good behavior said:
"Why did you go out from [the gate] without permission?" [and] caned me.

Samuel Noah Kramer, *The Sumerians* (Chicago: University of Chicago Press, 1963, 1972) pp. 237–40. Used by permission.

The fellow in charge of the whip said:
"Why did you take . . . without permission?" [and] caned me.
The fellow in charge of Sumerian said:
"Why didn't you speak Sumerian?" [and] caned me.
My teacher ("ummia") said:
"Your hand is unsatisfactory," [and] caned me.[and so] I [began to] hate the
   scribal art, and began to neglect the scribal art.

My teacher took no delight in me; [even stopped teaching (?)] me his skill in the
scribal art; in no way prepared me in the matters [essential to the art [of being] a
young scribe, [or the art of being] a "big brother."

He turns to his father for advice and help with his teacher.

Give him a bit extra salary; let him become more kindly(?); let him be free [for a
time] from arithmetic; [when] he shall count up all the school affairs of the students, let
him count me, [too, among them; that is, perhaps, let him not neglect me any longer].

To that which the schoolboy said, his father gave heed. The teacher was brought
from school, and after entering the house, he was seated. . . . The schoolboy attended and served him, and, whatever he learned of the scribal art, he unfolded to his father. Then did the father in the joy of his heart say joyfully to the headmaster of the
school: "My little fellow has opened [wide] his hand, [and] you made wisdom enter
there; you showed him all the fine points of the scribal art; you made him see the so-
lutions of mathematical and arithmetical [problems], you [taught him how] to make
deep (?) the cuneiform script (?).

Pour for him oil; bring it to the table for him. Make fragrant oil flow like water
on his stomach [and] back; I want to dress him in a garment; give him some extra
salary; put a ring on his hand.

The servants do this, and then the teacher says to the boy:

Young fellow, [because] you hated not my words, neglected them not, [may you]
complete the scribal art from beginning to end. Because you gave me everything
without stint, paid me a salary larger than my efforts [deserve], [and] have honored
me, may Nidaba, the queen of guardian angels, be your guardian angel; may your
pointed stylus write well for you; may your exercises contain no faults. Of your brothers, may you be their leader; of your friends may you be their chief; may you rank the
highest among the school graduates, satisfy (?) all who walk (?) to and from in (?)
the palaces. Little fellow, you "know" (your) father, I am second to him; that homage
be paid to you, that you be blessed—may the god of your father bring this about with
firm hand; he will bring prayer and supplication to Nidaba, your queen, as if it were
a matter for your god. Thus, when you put a kindly hand on the . . .

13

Papyrus Lansing: A Schoolbook

The ancient Egyptians had a high regard for education, which meant learning the
complicated hieroglyphic writing. Thousands of papyri, writing tablets, and shards of
pottery have been preserved. These were covered with exercises that young boys had
to reproduce in order to learn the scribal art.

Writing was taught in the "House of Life" by having the students copy ancient texts such as instructions, maxims, prayers, business letters, legal documents, hymns, and religious texts, while their teachers made corrections. As the students copied down these texts, they learned spelling, grammar, and the practical and moral ideas contained within them.

It is thought that the scribal profession was open to any male in Egypt. Once a boy had learned how to read and write, he could enter the House of Life as a teacher. If a student really applied himself, other positions in the civil service—even that of governor or vizir—or service in the temples might provide employment opportunities. Some of the letters suggest that senior officials often wrote instructive letters or literature in order to help a young man advance his career.

The following selection is from a book called the Papyrus Lansing and is dated to the late New Kingdom period (after 1200 B.C.). A royal scribe urges his apprentice to work hard, as the scribal profession is the best when compared to any other. His apprentice responds with appreciation for his mentor's advice.

QUESTIONS TO CONSIDER

1.   Why was the teacher unhappy with his pupil?
2.   How does the scribal profession compare to others in Egypt?
3.   How did the apprentice demonstrate his appreciation to his teacher?

[Beginning of the instruction in letter-writing made by the royal scribe and chief overseer of the cattle of Amen-Re, King of Gods, Nebmare-nakht] for his apprentice, the scribe Wenemdiamun.

Praise of the Scribe's Profession

[The royal scribe] and chief overseer of the cattle of Amen-[Re, King of Gods, Nebmare-nakht speaks to the scribe Wenemdiamun]. [Apply yourself to this] noble profession. . . . You will find it useful. . . . You will be advanced by your superiors. You will be sent on a mission. . . . Love writing, shun dancing; then you become a worthy official. Do not long for the marsh thicket. Turn your back on throw stick and chase. By day write with your fingers; recite by night. Befriend the scroll, the palette. It pleases more than wine. Writing for him who knows it is better than all other professions. It pleases more than bread and beer, more than clothing and ointment. It is worth more than an inheritance in Egypt, than a tomb in the west.

Advice to the Unwilling Pupil

Young fellow, how conceited you are! You do not listen when I speak. Your heart is denser than a great obelisk, a hundred cubits high, ten cubits thick. When it is finished and ready for loading, many work gangs draw it. It hears the words of men; it is loaded on a barge. Departing from Yebu it is conveyed, until it comes to rest on its place in Thebes.

So also a cow is bought this year, and it plows the following year. It learns to listen to the herdsman; it only lacks words. Horses brought from the field, they forget their mothers. Yoked they go up and down on all his majesty's errands. They become like those that bore them, that stand in the stable. They do their utmost for fear of a beating.

But though I beat you with every kind of stick, you do not listen. If I knew another way of doing it, I would do it for you, that you might listen. You are a person fit for writing, though you have not yet known a woman. Your heart discerns, your fingers are skilled, your mouth is apt for reciting.

Writing is more enjoyable than enjoying a basket of . . . and beans; more enjoyable than a mother's giving birth, when her heart knows no distaste. She is constant in nursing her son; her breast is in his mouth every day. Happy is the heart of him who writes; he is young each day.

The Idle Scribe Is Worthless

The royal scribe and chief overseer of the cattle of Amen-Re, King of Gods, Nebmare-nakht, speaks to the scribe Wenemdiamun, as follows. You are busy coming and going, and don't think of writing. You resist listening to me; you neglect my teachings.

You are worse than the goose of the shore, that is busy with mischief. It spends the summer destroying the dates, the winter destroying the seed-grain. It spends the balance of the year in pursuit of the cultivators. It does not let seed be cast to the ground without snatching it ? in its fall. ? One cannot catch it by snaring. One does not offer it in the temple. The evil, sharpeyed bird that does no work!

You are worse than the desert antelope that lives by running. It spends no day in plowing. Never at all does it tread on the threshing-floor. It lives on the oxen's labor, without entering among them. But though I spend the day telling you "Write," it seems like a plague to you. Writing is very pleasant! . . .

All Occupations Are Bad Except That of the Scribe

See for yourself with your own eye. The occupations lie before you.

The washerman's day is going up, going down. All his limbs are weak, from whitening his neighbors' clothes every day, from washing their linen.

The maker of pots is smeared with soil, like one whose relations have died. His hands, his feet are full of clay; he is like one who lives in the bog.

The cobbler mingles with vats. His odor is penetrating. His hands are red with madder, like one who is smeared with blood. He looks behind him for the kite, like one whose flesh is exposed.

The watchman prepares garlands and polishes vase-stands. He spends a night of toil just as one on whom the sun shines.

The merchants travel downstream and upstream. They are as busy as can be, carrying goods from one town to another. They supply him who has wants. But the tax collectors carry off the gold, that most precious of metals.

The ships' crews from every house (of commerce), they receive their loads. They depart from Egypt for Syria, and each man's god is with him. (But) not one of them says: "We shall see Egypt again!"

The carpenter who is in the shipyard carries the timber and stacks it. If he gives today the output of yesterday, woe to his limbs! The shipwright stands behind him to tell him evil things.

His outworker who is in the fields, his is the toughest of all the jobs. He spends the day loaded with his tools, tied to his tool-box. When he returns home at night, he is loaded with the tool-box and the timbers, his drinking mug, and his whetstones.

The scribe, he alone, records the output of all of them. Take note of it!

The Misfortunes of the Peasant

Let me also expound to you the situation of the peasant, that other tough occupation. [Comes] the inundation and soaks him . . . , he attends to his equipment. By day he cuts his farming tools; by night he twists rope. Even his midday hour he spends on farm labor. He equips himself to go to the field as if he were a warrior. The dried field lies before him; he goes out to get his team. When he has been after the herdsman for many days, he gets his team and comes back with it. He makes for it a place in the field. Comes dawn, he goes to make a start and does not find it in its place. He spends three days searching for it; he finds it in the bog. He finds no hides on them; the jackals have chewed them. He comes out, his garment in his hand, to beg for himself a team.

When he reaches his field he finds it ? broken up ? . He spends time cultivating, and the snake is after him. It finishes off the seed as it is cast to the ground. He does not see a green blade. He does three plowings with borrowed grain. His wife has gone down to the merchants and found nothing for ? barter ? . Now the scribe lands on the shore. He surveys the harvest. Attendants are behind him with staffs. Nubians with clubs. One says (to him): "Give grain." "There is none." He is beaten savagely. He is bound, thrown in the well, submerged head down. His wife is bound in his presence. His children are in fetters. His neighbors abandon them and flee. When it's over, there's no grain.

If you have any sense, be a scribe. If you have learned about the peasant, you will not be able to be one. Take note of it! . . .

The Scribe Does Not Suffer Like the Soldier

Furthermore. Look, I instruct you to make you sound; to make you hold the palette freely. To make you become one whom the king trusts; to make you gain entrance to treasury and granary. To make you receive the ship-load at the gate of the granary. To make you issue the offerings on feast days. You are dressed in fine clothes; you own horses. Your boat is on the river; you are supplied with attendants. You stride about inspecting. A mansion is built in your town. You have a powerful office, given you by the king. Male and female slaves are about you. Those who are in the fields grasp your hand, on plots that you have made. Look, I make you into a staff of life! Put the writings in your heart, and you will be protected from all kinds of toil. You will become a worthy official.

Do you not recall the (fate of) the unskilled man? His name is not known. He is ever burdened, like an ass carrying. in front of the scribe who knows what he is about.

Come, let me tell you the woes of the soldier, and how many are his superiors: the general, the troop-commander, the officer who leads, the standard-bearer, the lieutenant, the scribe, the commander of fifty, and the garrison-captain. They go in and out in the halls of the palace, saying: "Get laborers!" He is awakened at any hour. One is after him as (after) a donkey. He toils until the Aten (sun) sets in his darkness of night. He is hungry, his belly hurts; he is dead while yet alive. When he receives the grain-ration, having been released from duty, it is not good for grinding.

He is called up for Syria. He may not rest. There are no clothes, no sandals. The weapons of war are assembled at the fortress of Sile. His march is uphill through mountains. He drinks water every third day; it is smelly and tastes of salt. His body is ravaged by illness. The enemy comes, surrounds him with missiles, and life recedes from him. He is told: "Quick, forward, valiant soldier! Win for yourself a good name!" He does not know what he is about. His body is weak, his legs fail him. When victory is won, the captives are handed over to his majesty, to be taken to Egypt. The foreign woman faints on the march; she hangs herself on the soldier's neck. His knapsack drops, another grabs it while he is burdened with the woman. His wife and children are in their village; he dies and does not reach it. If he comes out alive, he is worn out from marching. Be he at large, be he detained, the soldier suffers. If he leaps and joins the deserters, all his people are imprisoned. He dies on the edge of the desert, and there is none to perpetuate his name. He suffers in death as in life. A big sack is brought for him; he does not know his resting place.

Be a scribe, and be spared from soldiering! You call and one says: "Here I am." You are safe from torments. Every man seeks to raise himself up. Take note of it!

The Pupil Wishes to Build a Mansion for His Teacher

Furthermore. (To) the royal scribe and chief overseer of the cattle of Amen-Re, King of Gods, Nebmare-nakht. The scribe Wenemdiamun greets his lord: In life, prosperity, and health! This letter is to inform my lord. Another message to my lord. I grew into a youth at your side. You beat my back; your teaching entered my ear. I am like a pawing horse. Sleep does not enter my heart by day; nor is it upon me at night. (For I say): I will serve my lord just as a slave serves his master.

I shall build a new mansion for you ,on. the ground of your town, with trees (planted) on all its sides. There are stables within it. Its barns are full of barley and emmer, wheat, ? cumin, ? dates, . . . beans, lentils, coriander, peas, seed-grain, . . . flax, herbs, reeds, rushes, . . . dung for the winter, alfa grass, reeds, . . . grass, produced by the basketful. Your herds abound in draft animals, your cows are pregnant. I will make for you five aruras of cucumber beds to the south.

Challenges to Egyptian and Hebrew Tradition

Ancient Egyptians prided themselves on having a state and society that was not only ancient but totally unchanging. Skeptical as the Greeks often were, Egyptians had them convinced by classical Greek times that Egyptian civilization had flourished as it was for ten thousand years. It can be argued, however, that this image of serene continuity represented more of an ideal than reality: Certainly Egyptian dynasties came and went much more frequently in most centuries than did those of China. Particularly in the New Kingdom, Egyptian traditions were challenged, even two of the most established ones: male rulership and polytheism.

Early Hebrew society was held together in considerable part by the belief in one God (see Reading 2), who had a covenant with his chosen people. The reverse side of being chosen was being specially punished for violating God's laws, and Hebrew defeats by other peoples of the Ancient Near East were to bring forth a series of prophets who berated the Hebrews for immorality, particularly in the form of exploitation of the poor and weak by the rich and powerful. In the teaching of Isaiah, in particular, we can see a challenge to the exclusively ethnocentric orientation of Hebrew religion. The prophet castigates the Hebrews for their sin and iniquity, and then he speaks of a future conversion of other peoples to faith in the one God and the advent of a Messiah, who will gather and guide the faithful of all nations.

14

Hatshepsut: Successful Female Pharaoh

From the earliest organization of the Egyptian state, the kings or pharaohs were considered to be divine and thought of as living images of the god Horus, son of the god Osiris and his sister-wife, Isis. This was true until a woman dared to make herself king, in reality as well as in art.

Hatshepsut (ca. 1504–1482 B.C.) was a daughter of Pharaoh Thutmose I and chief queen to Pharaoh Thutmose II, by whom she had a daughter, Nefrure. When her husband died unexpectedly in 1504 B.C., the next pharaoh was a six-year-old boy, Thutmose III, borne by one of his father's minor wives. For a year, Hatshepsut was content to act as regent, but then her ambition was so great that she overthrew her nephew and had herself declared pharaoh in her own right.

For twenty-two years Pharaoh Hatshepsut reigned alone. She was depicted in art as a male, with men's clothing, and wearing the beard of Osiris. Her main support came from a man named Senmut or Senenmut, who held many titles such as tutor to Hatshepsut's daughter, leader of very famous trade expeditions to the fabled land of Punt, and chief architect of Hatshepsut's tomb at Deir el-Bahri.

Whether Hatshepsut and Senmut died naturally in 1482 B.C. or were violently overthrown is not known. Thutmose III suddenly reappeared and began to erase his aunt's memory through the destruction or obliteration of her inscriptions, statues, and obelisks. She was not counted as one of the true pharaohs in royal annals.

The following selection comes from Hatshepsut's tomb at Deir el-Bahri, where her birth was recorded. In these depictions, Hatshepsut's mother, Queen Aahmes, receives and embraces an unexpected divine lover, the creator god Amen, who tells her that she will have a daughter who would rule as pharaoh.

QUESTIONS TO CONSIDER

1. How is Hatshepsut depicted in art?
2. Why was her reign such a break with Egyptian tradition?
3. Why was it necessary for Hatshepsut to create this fiction of her birth?

Figure 1

The Divine Conception of Queen Hatshepsut

Amen declares the following to these gods [the Great Ennead][11] concerning the heir of the Lord of the Two Lands:

Lo, I have loved the mate whom he [Thothmes] has loved, the Mother of King Ka-Maat-Ra [Hatshepsut], endued with life, the Queen Aahmes. I was the protector of her body when she was exalted. I have endowed her with all lands and foreign countries, that she may lead all the living.

I have joined the Two Lands unto her in contentment. She builds your temples and makes them holy; she keeps fresh your sacrifices and offering tables. Cause the

[11]The Great Ennead is a group of nine gods and goddesses, consisting of Ra-Atum, She, Tefnut, Geb, Nut, Osiris, Isis, and Nephthys.

From *The Wisdom of Ancient Egypt* (pp. 119–21); edited by Joseph Kaster © 1968 by Joseph Kaster. Reprinted by permission of Henry Holt and Company, LLC.

Figure 2

dew in the heavens to come down for her at its proper time, and make a Great Nile[12] for her at its proper time. Extend about her your protection of life and good fortune!

He who shall praise her shall live, but he who shall speak evil of the name of Her Majesty, to him will I give the gift of death forthwith!

The Great Ennead answers:

We have come to extend our protection of life and good fortune about her. She shall build her beautiful monuments in these Two Lands.

[Amen announces his intention to Thoth,[13] who will escort him into the presence of Queen Aahmes. Thoth replies:]

This princess of whom you have spoken, Queen Aahmes is her name. She is more beautiful than all the women in this entire land. She is the wife of the Sovereign, King

---

[12]A good inundation.
[13]The god Thoth was the god of wisdom and learning who functioned as the scribe and keeper of the sacred archives.

Aa-Kheper-Ka-Ra ["great is the becoming of the ka of Ra," that is, Thothmes I], given eternal life. His Majesty is a child of royalty, and thou mayest then go!"

And then he came, this august god Amen, Lord of the Two Lands, and he assumed the form of the Majesty of her husband, King Thothmes. They [the god and the form of the king] found her as she was reclining in the beauty of her palace.

She awakened at the fragrant odor of the god, and laughed in joy before His Majesty. And then he came to her straightway. He was passionate for her. He gave his heart unto her. He let her see him in his divine form after he came to her. She rejoiced when she beheld his beauty; his love went through her limbs. The Palace was flooded with the divine fragrance, and all his odors were those of Punt. The dearest and loveliest one—the Majesty of this god did everything that he desired with her. She let him rejoice over her. She kissed him.

Then spoke the Wife and Mother of the God, Queen Aahmes, to the Majesty of this god, Amen, Lord of the Thrones of the Two Lands:

My Lord, how great is thy splendor! Magnificent it is to see thy presence. Thou hast filled my Majesty with thy glory! Thy sweet savor pervades all my members!

Thus she spoke after the Majesty of this god did everything that he desired with her.

Then spoke Amen, Lord of the Thrones of the Two Lands, unto her:

Hat-Shepsut ["foremost in nobility"] shall be the name of this daughter whom I have implanted in thy body. She shall exercise beneficent kingship in this entire land. My spirit shall be hers. My power shall be hers. My exaltation shall be hers. My crown shall be hers. She shall rule the Two Lands in kingship, and shall lead all the living over all that the heavens embrace and over all which I shine. I have joined unto her the Two Lands in all her names, and upon the throne of Horus of the Living. She shall be under my divine protection every day, together with the god thereof. She is my beloved daughter, out of my own seed.

15

The Hymn to Aton and Psalm 104

The Egyptian pharaoh Amenhotep IV (ca. 1367 B.C.) and his wife Nefertiti attempted to break completely with traditional Egyptian religion. They substituted the worship of the sun disk, Aton, in place of the hundreds of older gods. This radical change caused a revolution in both literary and artistic styles; intimate family scenes now portrayed the pharaoh as a loving father and husband, and hymns and funeral inscriptions prayed to and through him to reach the new cosmic god.

Evidently, priests opposed the pharaoh's new ideas. In his fifth regnal year, Amenhotep and his family left the capital of Thebes for a new city, which the pharaoh called Akhetaton (meaning the gleaming horizon of Aton). Not content with just changing his residence, the pharaoh also changed his name to Akhenaton (meaning one who is serviceable to Aton) as well as all the names and titles of his family. Orders were given to destroy the old gods' names on the temples and tombs, including those of his father, Amenhotep III.

Once the political and religious changes occurred, knowledge about the royal family—especially Nefertiti—became clouded. The queen disappeared from public view and was, perhaps, replaced in the affections of the pharaoh by a man called Smenkhkare, who may have been Akhenaton's son. Although the pharaoh continued his religious reform unabated, the Egyptian Empire began to disintegrate because of attacks from the Hittite Empire or its client states.

The following Hymn to Aton reflects Akhenaton's belief in the universality and, at the same time, the uniqueness of Aton. It often has been compared with Psalm 104. This selection juxtaposes corresponding passages of the Hymn to Aton (left column) and Psalm 104 of the Old Testament (right column).

QUESTIONS TO CONSIDER

1. Why do you suppose Pharaoh Amenhotep IV might have wished to change the Egyptian religion?
2. Why was the worship of Aton a radical reform effort?
3. Who do you suppose might have opposed the Aton religion?
4. When you compare the Aton religion to that of Hebrews, what is missing?

Praise of Re Har-akhti, Rejoicing on the Horizon, in his name as Shu Who Is in the Aton-disc,[14] living forever and ever; the living great Aton who is in jubilee, lord of all that the Aton encircles, lord of heaven, lord of earth, lord of the House of Aton in Akhet-Aton,[15] [and praise of] the King of Upper and Lower Egypt, who lives on truth, the Lord of the Two Lands: Nefer-kheperu-Re Wa-en- Re; the Son of Re, who lives on truth, the Lord of Diadems: Akh-en-Aton, long in his lifetime; [and praise of] the Chief Wife of the King, his beloved, the Lady of the Two Lands: Nefer-neferu-Aton Nefert-iti, living, healthy, and youthful forever and ever; (by) the Fan-bearer on the Right Hand of the King . . . Eye. He says:

Thou appearest beautifully on the horizon of heaven,
Thou living Aton, the beginning of life!
When thou art risen on the eastern horizon,
Thou hast filled every land with thy beauty.

---

[14]The Aton had a dogmatic name written within a royal cartouche and including the three old solar deties, Re, Har-of-the-Horizon, and Shu.

[15]Akhet-Aton was the name of the capital at Tell el-Amarna.

From "The Hymn to the Aton," trans. John A. Wilson, in *Ancient Near Eastern Texts Relating to the Old Testament*, 3rd ed. with supplement, ed. James B. Pritchard (Princeton, NJ: Princeton University Press, 1969), pp. 369–71. Copyright © 1969 by Princeton University Press. Reprinted with permission of Princeton University Press. Psalm 104 is from the King James Version.

Thou art gracious, great, glistening, and
  high over every land;
Thy rays encompass the lands to the limit of
  all that thou hast made:
As thou art Re, thou reachest to the end of
  them;[16]
(Thou) subduest them (for) thy beloved son.[17]
Though thou art far away, thy rays are on
  earth;
Though thou art in *their* faces, *no one knows
  thy* going.
When thou settest in the western
  horizon,
The land is in darkness, in the manner of
  death.
They sleep in a room, with heads wrapped
  up,
Nor sees one eye the other.
All their goods which are under their heads
  might be stolen,
(But) they would not perceive (it).
Every lion is come forth from his den;

All creeping things, they sting.
Darkness *is a shroud,* and the earth is in
  stillness,
For he who made them rests in his horizon.

Thou makest darkness, and it is night:
  Wherein all the beasts of the forest do
  Creep *forth.*
The young lions roar after their prey, and
  Seek their meat from God.

At daybreak, when thou arisest on the horizon,
When thou shinest as the Aton by day,
Thou drivest away the darkness and givest
  thy rays.

The Two Lands are in festivity *every day,*
Awake and standing upon (their) feet,
For thou hast raised them up.
Washing their bodies, taking (their) clothing,
Their arms are (raised) in praise at thy
  appearance.
All the world, they do their work.
All beasts are content with their pasturage;
Trees and plants are flourishing.
The birds which fly from their nests,
Their wings are (stretched out) in praise to
  thy *Ra.*

The sun ariseth, they gather themselves together, and lay them down in their dens.
Man goeth forth unto his work and to his
  labour until the evening.
They give drink to every beast of the field:
  the wild asses quench their thirst.
By them shall the fowls of the heaven have
  their habitation, *which* sing among the
  branches.
He watereth the hills from his chambers:
  the earth is satisfied with the fruit of thy
  works.

[16]Pun: *Ra* "Re," and *er-ra* "to the end."
[17]Akh-en-Aton.

All beasts spring upon (their) feet.
Whatever flies and alights,
They live when thou hast risen (for) them.
The ships are sailing north and south as
  well,
For every way is open at thy appearance.
The fish in the river dart before thy face;
Thy rays are in the midst of the great green sea.

Creator of seed in women,
Thou who makest fluid into man,
Who maintainest the son in the womb of his
  mother,
Who soothest him with that which stills his
  weeping,
Thou nurse (even) in the womb,
Who givest breath to sustain all that he has
  made!
When he descends from the womb to *breathe*
On the day when he is born,
Thou openest his mouth completely,
Thou suppliest his necessities.
When the chick in the egg speaks within the
  shell,
Thou givest him breath within it to maintain
  him.
When thou hast made him his fulfillment
  within the egg, to break it,
He comes forth from the egg to speak at his
  completed (time);
He walks upon his legs when he comes forth
  from it.

How manifold it is, what thou hast made!
They are hidden from the face (of man).
O sole god, like whom there is no other!
Thou didst create the world according to thy
  desire,
Whilst thou wert alone: All men, cattle, and
  wild beasts,

Whatever is on earth, going upon (its) feet,
And what is on high, flying with its wings.
The countries of Syria and Nubia, the *land* of
  Egypt,
Thou settest every man in his place,
Thou suppliest their necessities:

He causeth the grass to grow for the cattle,
  and herb for the service of man: that he
  may bring forth food out of the earth;

So is this great and wide sea, wherein *are*
  things creeping innumerable, both small
  and great beasts.
There go the ships: *there* is that leviathan,
  whom thou hast made to play therein.

O LORD, how manifold are thy works! In wisdom hast thou made them all: the earth is
  full of thy riches.

Everyone has his food, and his time of life is
reckoned.
Their tongues are separate in speech,
And their natures as well;
Their skins are distinguished,
As thou distinguishest the foreign peoples.
Thou makest a Nile in the underworld,
Thou bringest it forth as thou desirest
To maintain the people (of Egypt)[18]

These wait all upon thee; that thou mayest
give *them* their meat in due season.

According as thou madest them for thyself,
The lord of all of them, wearying (himself)
with them,
The lord of every land, rising for them,
The Aton of the day, great of majesty.
All distant foreign countries, thou makest
their life (also),
For thou hast set a Nile in heaven,

That it may descend for them and make
waves upon the mountains,
Like the great green sea,
To water their fields in their
towns.[19]
How effective they are, thy plans, O lord of
eternity!
The Nile in heaven, it is for the foreign
peoples
And for the beasts of every desert that go
upon (their) feet;
(While the true) Nile comes from the underworld for Egypt.

He sendeth the springs into the valleys, *which*
run among the hills.

Thy rays suckle every meadow.
When thou risest, they live, they grow for
thee.
Thou makest the seasons in order to rear all
that thou hast made,
The winter to cool them,
And the heat that *they* may taste
thee.
Thou hast made the distant sky in order to
rise therein,
In order to see all that thou dost make.
Whilst thou wert alone,

---

[18]The Egyptians believed that their Nile came from the waters under the earth, called by them Nun.
[19]The rain of foreign countries is like the Nile of rainless Egypt.

Rising in thy form as the living Aton,
Appearing, shining, *withdrawing or
    approaching,*
Thou madest millions of forms of thyself
    alone.
Cities, towns, fields, road, and river—
Every eye beholds thee over against them,
For thou art the Aton of the day over *the
    earth.* . . .

Thou art in my heart,
And there is no other that knows thee
Save thy son Nefer-kheperu-Re Wa-en-Re,[20]
For thou hast made him well-versed in thy
    plans and in thy strength.[21]
The world came into being by thy hand,
According as thou hast made them.
When thou hast risen they live,
When thou settest they die.
Thou art lifetime thy own self,
For one lives (only) through thee.
Eyes are (fixed) on beauty until thou settest.
All work is laid aside when thou settest in the
    west.
(But) when (thou) risest (again),

[*Everything is*] made to flourish for the
    king, . . .
Since thou didst found the earth
And raise them up for thy son,
Who came forth from thy body: the king of
    Upper and Lower Egypt, . . . Akh-en-Aton,
    . . . and the Chief Wife of the King . . .
    Nefert-iti, living and youthful forever and
    ever.

16

Isaiah: Prophet of Doom and Hope

Isaiah (ca. 740–681 B.C.E.) lived in the kingdom of Judah during the turbulent times when the mighty Assyrian kingdom had spread throughout the Fertile Crescent and was attempting to control the two small Hebrew kingdoms, Israel and Judah. His

---

[20]Even through the hymn was recited by the official Eye, he states that Akh-en-Aton alone knows the Aton.
[21]Pharaoh was the official intermediary between the Egyptians and their gods. The Amarna religion did not change this dogma.

prophecies attacked the moral corruption of his day and demanded a personal responsibility of each person or there would be great destruction, but God would send a Messiah for the entire world.

In addition to his moral prophecies, Isaiah also counseled Judean kings from the time of Ahaz (741–725) until his death at the hands of King Manasseh (696–642). When King Ahaz of Judah was threatened by both Israel and the local Semitic king of Damascus, Syria (732), he turned to Assyria for aid. Isaiah declared this was a mistake and would end in disaster. Yet, when the Assyrian King Sennacherib invaded Judah and surrounded Jerusalem in 701, Isaiah advised King Hezekiah (725–697) not to surrender, as the Assyrians would withdraw, which happened.

The following selections are drawn from Isaiah's thoughts on the moral decay of the Hebrews, the coming of a Messiah, and a new world paradise.

QUESTIONS TO CONSIDER

1. What were some of the things that Isaiah wanted the Hebrews to do?
2. How has the idea of a Messiah or redeemer been used by other religions?
3. How did Isaiah say that God was for all the world?

Isaiah

Hear, O heavens, and give ear, O earth; for the Lord has spoken; I have nourished and brought up children, and they have rebelled against me.

A sinful nation, a people laden with iniquity, a seed of evildoers, children that are corrupters; they have forsaken the Lord, they have provoked the Holy One of Israel unto anger, they are gone away backward.

Wash you, make yourself clean, put away the evil of the doings from before my eyes; cease to do evil:

Learn to do well; see judgment, relieve the oppressed, judge the fatherless, plead for the widow.

If you are willing and obedient, you shall eat of the good of the land:

But if you refuse and rebel, you shall be devoured with the sword: for the mouth of the Lord has spoken it.

Therefore the Lord himself shall give you a sign; Behold a virgin shall conceive, and bear a son, and shall call his name Immanuel.

For unto us a child is born, unto us a son is given; and the government shall be upon his shoulder; and his name shall be called Wonderful, Counselor, The Mighty God, The Everlasting Father, The Prince of Peace.

And there shall come forth a rod out of the stem (family) of Jesse,

And a Branch shall grow out of his roots:

And the spirit of the Lord shall rest upon him, the spirit of wisdom and understanding, the spirit of counsel and might, the spirit of knowledge and of the fear of the Lord;

From *Isaiah* 1: 2, 4, 16–17, 19–20; 7: 14; 9: 6; 11: 1–4, 6, 9–10. King James version, slightly modernized.

And shall make him of quick understanding in the fear of the Lord: and he shall not judge after the sight of his eyes, neither reprove after the hearing of the ears:

But with righteousness shall he judge the poor, and reprove with equity for the meek of the earth; and he shall smite the earth with the rod of his mouth, and with the breath of his lips shall he slay the wicked.

The wolf also shall dwell with the lamb, and the leopard shall lie down with the lamb; and the calf and young lion and the fatling together; and a little child shall lead them.

They shall not hurt nor destroy in all my holy mountain; for the earth shall be full of the knowledge of the Lord, as the waters cover the sea.

And in that day there shall be a root of Jesse, which shall stand for a sign of the people; the Gentiles shall seek him, and his rest shall be glorious.

For thou hast made him well-versed in thy plans and in thy strength.

Military Strategy and Tactics: Assyria and China

Situated in the rolling hills north of Babylonia, Assyria was never a major empire until the late tenth century B.C. The land had been invaded time and again by the Akkadians, Babylonians, Kassites, and, finally, Arameans. In 911 B.C., the Assyrian kings finally confronted the threat posed by the Arameans and expelled them. Thereafter, year by year, the kings went to war and conquered most of the ancient Near East.

The success achieved by Assyria resulted from studying war techniques as a science. The army was divided into light and heavy infantry as well as chariotry, which was supplemented by rolling siege engines. Special schools were set up to teach the techniques of sapping and mining city walls. Conquered areas were welded together through a great system of roads and were controlled by royal governors, supported by garrisons of soldiers. These newly conquered areas saw their populations dispersed or transported throughout Assyria. Booty and tribute kept Assyria constantly expanding. If any city tried to revolt, it could expect swift and severe punishment. The Assyrians were making maximum use of psychological warfare, particularly terror, to encourage quick surrenders of populations marked for annexation and passive acceptance of Assyrian rule once it was in place.

The Chinese took a different approach to warfare. The overall image they projected was one of calm, confident superiority. Their rulers assumed that their own subjects and conquered peoples of any intelligence would recognize the benefits gained from their ties to a wise, paternalistic kingdom. Consequently, terror of the Assyrian type had no place in their scheme of things. Nonetheless, since war was a large part of the real world, Chinese military leaders strove for an understanding of what worked in waging it: speed, restraint, and deception, with actions based on military intelligence in all its forms.

17

Assyrian War Tactics

A typical example of an Assyrian king is Ashurnasirpal (844–859 B.C.). He was at war for most of his reign, attacking northwestern Mesopotamia, Anatolia, Syria, and Phoenicia both for booty and for enlargement of his empire. Nonetheless, he found time to construct a new, six-acre palace at Calah (modern Nimrud) on the Upper Zab, west of the Tigris River—a palace that was well built and beautifully decorated.

The following selection comes from the Assyrian royal archives and describes King Ashurnasirpal's ferocious treatment of rebels.

QUESTIONS TO CONSIDER

1. Why do you suppose that the Assyrian king resorted to such harshness in dealing with rebels?
2. Why would the subjects of Assyria rebel even though they were aware of the consequences?
3. What kingdom and peoples disappeared from history as a result of Assyrian destruction?
4. Are there any parallels in modern times to the policies of the Assyrians?

While I was staying in the land of Kutmuhi, they brought me the word: "The city of Sûru of Bît-Halupê has revolted, they have slain Hamatai, their governor, and Ahi-ababa, the son of a nobody, whom they brought from Bît-Adini, they have set up as king over them." With the help of Adad and the great gods who have made great my kingdom, I mobilized (my) chariots and armies and marched along the bank of the Habur. During my advance I received much tribute from Shulmanu-haman-ilâni of the city of Gardiganni, from Ilu-Adad of the city of Katna,—silver, gold, lead, vessels of copper, and garments of brightly colored wool, and garments of linen. To the city of Sûru of Bît-Halupê I drew near, and the terror of the splendor of Assur, my lord, overwhelmed them. The chief men and the elders of the city, to save their lives, came forth into my presence and embraced my feet, saying: "If it is thy pleasure, slay! If it is thy pleasure, let live! That which thy heart desireth, do!" Ahiababa, the son of no-body, whom they had brought from Bît-Adini, I took captive. In the valor of my heart and with the fury of my weapons I stormed the city. All the rebels they seized and de-livered them up. My officers I caused to enter into his palace and his temples. His sil-ver, his gold, his goods and his possessions, copper, iron, lead, vessels of copper, cups of copper, dishes of copper, a great hoard of copper, alabaster, tables with inlay, the women of his palaces, his daughters, the captive rebels together with their posses-sions, the gods together with their possessions, precious stone from the mountains, his chariot with equipment, his horses, broken to the yoke, trappings of men and trappings of horses, garments of brightly colored wool and garments of linen, goodly oil, cedar, and fine sweet-scented herbs, panels(?) of cedar, purple and crimson wool, his wagons, his cattle, his sheep, his heavy spoil, which like the stars of heaven could not be counted, I carried off. Azi-ilu I set over them as my own governor. I built a pillar over against his city gate, and I flayed all the chief men who had revolted, and I covered the pillar with their skins; some I walled up within the pillar, some I impaled upon the pillar on stakes, and others I bound to stakes round about the pillar; many within the border of my own land I flayed, and I spread their skins upon the walls; and I cut off the limbs of the officers, of the royal officers who had rebelled. Ahiaba-ba I took to Nineveh, I flayed him, I spread his skin upon the wall of Nineveh. My power and might I established over the land of Lakê. While I was staying in the city of Sûru, (I received) tribute from all the kings of the land of Lakê,—silver, gold, lead, copper, vessels of copper, cattle, sheep, garments of brightly colored wool, and garments of linen, and I increased the tribute and taxes and imposed them upon them. At that time, the tribute of Haiâni of the city of Hindani,—silver, gold, lead, copper, *umu*-stone, alabaster, purple wool, and (Bactrian) camels I received from him as tribute. At that time I fashioned a heroic image of my royal self, my power and my glory I inscribed thereon, in the midst of his palace I set it up. I fashioned memorial steles and inscribed thereon my glory and my prowess, and I set them up by his city gate.

18

Sun Tzu [Sunzi], *The Art of War*

This is perhaps the world's oldest known treatise on war and strategy. Although the precise date of composition of this martial classic is not known, most Chinese historians and literary critics place it sometime in the early part of the fourth century B.C. Sun Tzu [Sunzi][22] served as strategist and general under the king of the state of Wu, one of the warring states during the chaotic late Chou [Zhou] period (ca. 1050–256 B.C.).

For well over two millennia, in both war and peace, *The Art of War* has been an important source of wisdom for kings, emperors, feudal lords, generals, and strategists in China, Korea, and Japan. The military thought of Mao Tse-tung [Mao Zedong] was profoundly influenced by Sunzi's work, as evidenced in Mao's writings, such as "On Guerrilla Warfare" and "On Protracted Warfare." *The Art of War* has also received much attention in the West. Since it was first translated into French by a Jesuit named Amiot in 1782, the book has been translated into all major Western languages. Napoleon was supposed to have been an avid reader of it.

QUESTIONS TO CONSIDER

1. How timeless are Sunzi's military strategy and tactics? Discuss.
2. What did Sunzi mean by "All warfare is based on deception"? Explain.

[22]There are at least two ways to transcribe Chinese in the English-speaking world: the Wade-Giles system and the Pinyin system. The Wade-Giles system was first developed by an English Sinologist, Thomas F. Wade, in 1867, and was later modified by Herbert Giles in 1912. It became the standard way of transcribing Chinese. This system is being replaced by the somewhat simpler Pinyin system, the official one of the People's Republic of China, although Wade-Giles continues to be used on Taiwan, where many English-language books are printed. Except where the term is the same in both systems, we will give Pinyin transcriptions in brackets after the Chinese terms when they first occur in the readings.

Laying Plans

Sun Tzu said:

1. The art of war is of vital importance to the State.

2. It is a matter of life and death, a road either to safety or to ruin. Hence it is a subject of inquiry which can on no account be neglected.

3. The art of war, then, is governed by five constant factors, to be taken into account in one's deliberations, when seeking to determine the conditions obtaining in the field.

4. These are: (1) The Moral Law; (2) Heaven; (3) Earth; (4) The Commander; (5) Method and discipline.

5. The Moral Law causes the people to be in complete accord with their ruler;

6. If that is the case, they will follow him regardless of their lives, undismayed by any danger.

7. Heaven signifies night and day, cold and heat, times and seasons.

8. Earth comprises distances, great and small; danger and security; open ground and narrow passes; the chances of life and death.

9. The Commander stands for the virtues of wisdom, sincerily, benevolence, courage and strictness.

10. By method and discipline are to be understood the marshaling of the army in its proper subdivisions, the graduations of rank among the officers, the maintenance of roads by which supplies may reach the army, and the control of military expenditure.

11. These five heads should be familiar to every general: he who knows them will be victorious; he who knows them not will fail.

12. Therefore, in your deliberations, when seeking to determine the military conditions, let them be made the basis of a comparison, in this wise:

13. (1) Which of the two sovereigns is imbued with the Moral law? (2) Which of the two generals has most ability? (3) With whom lie the advantages derived from Heaven and Earth? (4) On which side is discipline most rigorously enforced? (5) Which army is stronger? (6) On which side are officers and men more highly trained? (7) In which army is there the greater constancy both in reward and punishment?

14. By means of these seven considerations I can forecast victory or defeat.

15. The general that hearkens to my counsel and acts upon it, will conquer: let such a one be retained in command! The general that hearkens not to my counsel nor acts upon it, will suffer defeat:—let such a one be dismissed!

16. While heading the profit of my counsel, avail yourself also of any helpful circumstances over and beyond the ordinary rules.

17. According as circumstances are favorable, one should modify one's plans.

18. All warfare is based on deception.

19. Hence, when able to attack, we must seem unable; when using our forces, we must seem inactive; when we are near, we must make the enemy believe we are far away; when far away, we must make him believe we are near.

20. Hold out baits to entice the enemy. Feign disorder, and crush him.

From *Sun Tzu on the Art of War: The Oldest Military Treatise in the World,* trans. Lie Giles (London: Luzac & Co., 1910), pp. 1–3; 4–6; 26–28.

21. If he is secure at all points, be prepared for him. If he is in superior strength, evade him.

22. If your opponent is of choleric temper, seek to irritate him. Pretend to be weak, that he may grow arrogant.

23. If he is taking his ease, give him no rest. If his forces are united, separate them.

24. Attack him where he is unprepared, appear where you are not expected.

25. These military devices, leading to victory, must not be divulged beforehand.

26. Now the general who wins a battle makes many calculations in his temple ere the battle is fought. The general who loses a battle makes but few calculations beforehand. Thus many calculations lead to victory, and few calculations to defeat: how much more no calculation at all! It is by attention to this point that I can foresee who is likely to win or lose.

Attack by Stratagem

Sun Tzu said:

1. In the practical art of war, the best thing of all is to take the enemy's country whole and intact; to shatter and destroy it is not so good. So, too, it is better to recapture an army entire than to destroy it, to capture a regiment, a detachment or a company entire than to destroy them.

2. Hence to fight and conquer in all your battles is not supreme excellence; supreme excellence consists in breaking the enemy's resistance without fighting.

3. Thus the highest form of generalship is to balk the enemy's plans; the next best is to prevent the junction of the enemy's forces; the next in order is to attack the enemy's army in the field; and the worst policy of all is to besiege walled cities.

4. The rule is, not to besiege walled cities if it can possibly be avoided. The preparation of mantlets, movable shelters, and various implements of war, will take up three whole months; and the piling up of mounds over against the walls will take three months more.

5. The general, unable to control his irritation, will launch his men to the assault like swarming ants, with the result that one-third of his men are slain, while the town still remains untaken. Such are the disastrous effects of a siege.

6. Therefore the skillful leader subdues the enemy's troops without any fighting; he captures their cities without laying siege to them; he overthrows their kingdom without lengthy operations in the field.

7. With his forces intact he will dispute the mastery of the Empire, and thus, without losing a man, his triumph will be complete. This is the method of attacking by stratagem.

8. It is the rule in war, if our forces are ten to the enemy's one, to surround him; if five to one, to attack him; if twice as numerous, to divide our army into two.

9. If equally matched, we can offer battle; if slightly inferior in numbers, we can avoid the enemy; if quite unequal in every way, we can flee from him.

10. Hence, though an obstinate fight may be made by a small force, in the end it must be captured by the larger force.

11. Now the general is the bulwark of the State; if the bulwark is complete at all points; the State will be strong; if the bulwark is defective, the State will be weak.

12. There are three ways in which a ruler can bring misfortune upon his army:

13. (1) By commanding the army to advance or to retreat, being ignorant of the fact that it cannot obey. This is called hobbling the army.

14. (2) By attempting to govern an army in the same way as he administers a kingdom, being ignorant of the conditions which obtain in an army. This causes restlessness in the soldier's minds.

15. (3) By employing the officers of his army without discrimination, through ignorance of the military principle of adaptation to circumstances. This shakes the confidence of the soldiers.

16. But when the army is restless and distrustful, trouble is sure to come from the other feudal princes. This is simply bringing anarchy into the army, and flinging victory away.

17. Thus we may know that there are five essentials for victory: (1) He will win who knows when to fight and when not to fight. (2) He will win who knows how to handle both superior and inferior forces. (3) He will win whose army is animated by the same spirit throughout all its ranks. (4) He will win who, prepared himself, waits to take the enemy unprepared. (5) He will win who has military capacity and is not interfered with by the sovereign.

18. Hence the saying: If you know the enemy and know yourself, you need not fear the result of a hundred battles. If you know yourself but not the enemy, for every victory gained you will also suffer a defeat. If you know neither the enemy nor yourself, you will succumb in every battle.

The Use of Spies

Sun Tzu said:

1. Raising a host of a hundred thousand men and marching them great distances entails heavy loss on the people and a drain on the resources of the State. The daily expenditure will amount to a thousand ounces of silver. There will be commotion at home and abroad, and men will drop down exhausted on the highways. As many as seven hundred thousand families will be impeded in their labor.

2. Hostile armies may face each other for years, striving for the victory which is decided in a single day. This being so, to remain in ignorance of the enemy's condition simply because one grudges the outlay of a hundred ounces of silver in honors and emoluments, is the height of inhumanity.

3. One who acts thus is no leader of men, no present help to his sovereign, no master of victory.

4. Thus, what enables the wise sovereign and the good general to strike and conquer, and achieve things beyond the reach of ordinary men, is foreknowledge.

5. Now this foreknowledge cannot be elicited from spirits; it cannot be obtained inductively from experience, nor by any deductive calculation.

6. Knowledge of the enemy's dispositions can only be obtained from other men.

7. Hence the use of spies, of whom there are five classes: (1) Local spies; (2) inward spies; (3) converted spies; (4) doomed spies; (5) surviving spies.

8. When these five kinds of spy are all at work, none can discover the secret system. This is called "divine manipulation of the threads." It is the sovereign's most precious faculty.

9. Having local spies means employing the services of the inhabitants of a district.

10. Having inward spies, making use of officials of the enemy.

11. Having converted spies, getting hold of the enemy's spies and using them for our own purposes.

12. Having doomed spies, doing certain things openly for purposes of deception, and allowing our spies to know of them and report them to the enemy.

13. Surviving spies, finally, are those who bring back news from the enemy's camp.

14. Hence it is that which none in the whole army are more intimate relations to be maintained than with spies. None should be more liberally rewarded. In no other business should greater secrecy be preserved.

15. Spies cannot be usefully employed without a certain intuitive sagacity.

16. They cannot be properly managed without benevolence and straightforwardness.

17. Without subtle ingenuity of mind, one cannot make certain of the truth of their reports.

18. Be subtle! be subtle! and use your spies for every kind of business.

19. If a secret piece of news is divulged by a spy before the time is ripe, he must be put to death together with the man to whom the secret was told.

20. Whether the object be to crush an army, to storm a city, or to assassinate an individual, it is always necessary to begin by finding out the names of the attendants, the aides-de-camp, and door-keepers and sentries of the general in command. Our spies must be commissioned to ascertain these.

21. The enemy's spies who have come to spy on us must be sought out, tempted with bribes, led away and comfortably housed. Thus they will become converted spies and available for our service.

22. It is through the information brought by the converted spy that we are able to acquire and employ local and inward spies.

23. It is owing to his information, again, that we can cause the doomed spy to carry false tidings to the enemy.

24. Lastly, it is by his information that the surviving spy can be used on appointed occasions.

25. The end and aim of spying in all its five varieties is knowledge of the enemy; and this knowledge can only be derived, in the first instance, from the converted spy. Hence it is essential that the converted spy be treated with the utmost liberality.

26. Of old, the rise of the Yin dynasty was due to I Chih who had served under the Hsia. Likewise, the rise of the Chou dynasty was due to Lu Ya who had served under the Yin.

27. Hence it is only the enlightened ruler and the wise general who will use the highest intelligence of the army for purposes of spying and thereby they achieve great results. Spies are a most important element in water, because on them depends an army's ability to move.

Part II
Classical Civilizations

The Hindu Tradition in Classical India

"Hinduism" is the term Westerners have used for the religion of most people living on the Indian subcontinent. Many other religions have originated and flourished in India, however, including Buddhism, Jainism, and Sikhism. Islam has also played a large role in Indian life since around A.D. 1000. Hinduism itself encompasses more than a religion; it includes an entire way of life.

When the Aryan invaders conquered and settled among the native Dravidians in India, the fusion of cultures developed into early Hinduism between approximately 700 B.C. and A.D. 400. In spite of portraying individual divinities in versions much at a variance with one another, Hinduism promoted a comprehensive view of life. It focused on four legitimate goals for which all men and women should strive.

The first and most basic goal was pleasure (*kama*). Wealthy people and the less affluent alike could derive pleasure from elaborate craft traditions in art, music, drama, and many varieties of story-telling. Hindus developed the joys of fine living into highly sophisticated forms.

The second goal was the acquisition of wealth (*artha*), illustrated in the following section on Hindu ideas of the proper use of ruling power. The third goal was abiding by law or duty (*dharma*). Hindu law was believed to be eternal and unchanging, revealed to human seers or prophets at the beginning of time (for example, Manu was the recipient of the Laws of Manu). The essential structure of the law was the fourfold division of social classes—from priests and warriors at the top to the commoners and servile class (the conquered, darker-skinned people) at the bottom. This structure was the basis of the "caste system," whereby one's occupation and social status were completely determined at birth. Hindu law also postulated that after death each person would enter a new life form based on the good or evil done in the previous life. This process is called transmigration or reincarnation (*samsara*).

A final goal of the Hindus was the quest for liberation (*moksha*) from the process of transmigration. This goal involved a quest for transcending the normal human condition of trying to do good and avoid evil, only to be reborn in another life where the struggle would continue indefinitely. Some Hindus sought, and believed that they could attain, a condition of godlike perfection that would be an end to such a cycle.

The Hindu tradition described three valid paths to end transmigration. The first was the path of action (*karma*), which meant properly performing religious rituals as well as doing one's prescribed duty. Most Hindu thinkers, however, believed that following such a path could only partially lead a person to the ultimate goal. Therefore a second, and more favored, path was that of knowledge (*jhana*), first described in the Upanishads, beginning around 700 B.C. This path involved calm contemplation of the universe and the self until one realized that God was present everywhere—including within the self. Only a small percentage of all Hindus would ever reach, or even attempt to reach, this mystical experience of oneness with God and the universe. The journey was a long and difficult one that required sacrificing all usual ways of living and thinking for long hours of private meditation.

The final path to liberation involved devotion (*bhakti*) to God. After the time of the Rig Veda, the Hindus gradually developed the concept that only one God existed. But Hindus did not all agree on the identity of this God; some believed Vishnu was supreme (as did the writer of the Bhagavad Gita), whereas others favored Shiva. They did agree, however, that a person totally devoted to God, in thinking and love, would be saved by God and granted liberation from transmigration. The worship of the supreme deity, the outpouring of love toward God, and the prayerful hope for divine compassion became the major driving forces of Hinduism.

The acquisition and retention of material wealth (*artha*) remained a legitimate goal for Hindus, who frequently linked artha to the subject of power necessary for the secure enjoyment of wealth and to discussions of the proper allocation of resources by those in power. The most famous Hindu text on artha is the Artha Shastra, a work originally intended as a handbook for kings at the outset of the Mauryan Empire, although the surviving version is now believed to have been copied with many alterations over the centuries and to date from the early Gupta Empire.

The last great period of Hindu state and civilization in India before the arrival of Islam came during the Gupta rule (A.D. 320–ca. 540) and the reign of Harsha Vardhana (A.D. 606–647). During this classical age (A.D. 320–ca. 700), Indian art, literature, sculpture, mathematics, medicine, astronomy, and astrology attained new levels of brilliance. Hinduism developed into popular forms while Buddhism gradually withered away in the land of its birth. This happened in spite of the fact that the most detailed and readable description of the workings of the Indian state and society during the late classical period comes from a Chinese Buddhist, who came to visit India as the land where Gautama was born and where he first taught.

The following text selections can give only a small sample of the great variety of writing produced by Hindu India.

19

The Essence of the Universe

This selection, from one of the earliest *Upanishads* (the *Chandogya Upanishad*), takes the form of a dialogue between a father and son. It presents the view that the *Brahman*—the Self of the universe, the abstract, divine power that is present everywhere—is the same as the soul or self (*atman*) dwelling within each individual.

QUESTIONS TO CONSIDER

1. How does the dialogue explain the essential reality underlying the world?
2. How essential is this dialogue in the understanding of Hinduism? Why?

"In the beginning, my dear, this world was just being (*sat*), one only, without a second. Some people, no doubt, say: 'In the beginning, verily, this world was just nonbeing (*asat*), one only, without a second; from that nonbeing, being was produced.' But how, indeed, my dear, could it be so?" said he. "How could being be produced from nonbeing? On the contrary, my dear, in the beginning this world was being alone, one only, without a second. Being thought to itself: 'May I be many; may I procreate.' It produced fire. That fire thought to itself: 'May I be many, may I procreate.' It produced water. Therefore, whenever a person grieves or perspires, then it is from fire [heat] alone that water is produced. That water thought to itself: 'May I be many; may I procreate.' It produced food. Therefore, whenever it rains, then there is abundant food; it is from water alone that food for eating is produced. . . .

"Bring hither a fig from there." "Here it is, sir." "Break it." "It is broken, sir." "What do you see there?" "These extremely fine seeds, sir." "Of these, please break one." "It is broken, sir." "What do you see there?" "Nothing at all, sir." Then he said to Shvetaketu: "Verily, my dear, that subtle essence which you do not perceive—from that very essence, indeed, my dear, does this great fig tree thus arise. Believe me, my dear, that which is the subtle essence—this whole world has that essence for its Self; that is the Real [satya, truth]; that is the Self; that [subtle essence] art thou, Shvetaketu." "Still further may the venerable sir instruct me." "So be it, my dear," said he.

"Having put this salt in the water, come to me in the morning." He did so. Then the father said to him: "That salt which you put in the water last evening—please bring it hither." Even having looked for it, he did not find it, for it was completely dissolved. "Please take a sip of water from this end," said the father. "How is it?" "Salt." "Take a sip from the middle," said he. "How is it?" "Salt." "Take a sip from that end," said he. "How is it?" "Salt." "Throw it away and come to me." Shvetaketu did so thinking to himself: "That salt, though unperceived, still persists in the water." Then Aruni said to him: "Verily, my dear, you do not perceive Being in this world; but it is, indeed, here only: That which is the subtle essence—this whole world has that essence for its Self. That is the Real. That is the Self. That art thou, Shvetaketu."

20

The Laws of Manu

In the Hindu tradition, Manu was the grandson of the Supreme Being, who set down laws for all to follow. The most influential parts of this sacred law book over the ages have been the assignment of duties to the castes, an explanation of cause and effect in the transmigration process, and rules to follow for achieving liberation from reincarnation.

QUESTIONS TO CONSIDER

1. How does the rigidity of castes follow logically from the Cosmic Sacrifice in the Hindu creation story (see Reading 4)?
2. What reasons does Manu give all castes for abiding by his law and doing their prescribed duties?
3. How does the Hindu concept of transmigration compare with the Christian concepts of resurrection, rewards, and punishments?
4. What is final liberation in Hindu-Buddhist thought? Can one achieve this liberation simply by ending one's life in this world?
5. Compare the Hindu goal of liberation with the Judaic, Christian, and Islamic ideas of salvation.

Duties of the Social Classes

31. For the sake of the prosperity of the worlds, Purusha caused the Brâhmana, the Kshatriya, the Vaisya, and the Sûdra to proceed from his mouth, his arms, his thighs, and his feet.

88. To Brâhmanas he assigned teaching and studying (the Veda), sacrificing for their own benefit and for others, giving and accepting (of alms).

89. The Kshatriya he commanded to protect the people, to bestow gifts, to offer sacrifices, to study the Veda, and to abstain from attaching himself to sensual pleasures.

90. The Vaisya to tend cattle, to bestow gifts, to offer sacrifices, to study the Veda, to trade, to lend money, and to cultivate land.

91. One occupation only the lord prescribed to the Sûdra, to serve meekly even these other three castes.

From G. Buhler, trans., *The Laws of Manu* (Oxford: The Clarendon Press, 1886), pp. 13–14, 24–27, 183–85, 196–97, 198–99, 203–6, 214–15, 483–85, 496–97, *passim.*

92. Man is stated to be purer above the navel than below: hence the Self-existent has declared the purest part of him to be his mouth.

93. As the Brâhmana sprang from mouth, as he was the first-born, and as he possesses the Veda, he is by right the lord of this creation.

94. For the Self-existent one, having performed austerities, produced him first from his own mouth, in order that the offerings might be conveyed to the gods and manes[1] and that this universe might be preserved.

95. What created being can surpass him, through whose mouth the gods continually consume the sacrificial meats and the manes the offerings to the dead?

96. Of created beings the most excellent are said to be those which are animated; of the animated, those which subsist by intelligence; of the intelligent, mankind; and of men, Brâhmanas.

97. Of Brâhmanas, those learned in the Veda; of the learned, those who recognize the necessity and the manner of performing those prescribed duties; of those who possess this knowledge, those who perform them; of the performers, those who know the Brahman.

98. The very birth of a Brâhmana is an eternal incarnation of the sacred law; for he is born to fulfill the sacred law, and becomes one with Brahman.

102. In order to clearly settle his duties and those of the other castes according to their order, wise Manu, sprung from the Self-existent, composed these Institutes of the sacred law.

Transmigration

3. Action [karma], which springs from the mind, from speech, and from the body, produces either good or evil results; by action are caused the various conditions of men, the highest, the middling, and the lowest.

4. Know that the mind is the instigator here below, even to that action which is connected with the body, and which is of three kinds, has three locations, and falls under ten heads.

5. Coveting the property of others, thinking in one's heart of what is undesirable, and adherence to false doctrines, are the three kinds of sinful mental action.

6. Abusing others, speaking untruth, detracting from the merits of all men, and talking idly, shall be the four kinds of evil verbal action.

7. Taking what has not been given, injuring creatures without the sanction of the law, and holding criminal intercourse with another man's wife, are declared to be the three kinds of wicked bodily action.

8. A man obtains the result of a good or evil mental act in his mind, that of a verbal act in his speech, that of a bodily act in his body.

9. In consequence of many sinful acts committed with his body, a man becomes in the next birth something inanimate, in consequence of sins committed by speech, a bird or a beast, and in consequence of mental sins he is re-born in a low caste.

10. That man is called a true tridandin in whose mind these three, the control over his speech . . ., the control over his thoughts . . . , and the control over his body . . . , are firmly fixed.

---

[1]Venerated spirits of the dead.

11. That man who keeps this threefold control over himself with respect to all created beings and wholly subdues desire and wrath, thereby assuredly gains complete success. . . .

52. In consequence of attachment to the objects of the senses, and in consequence of the nonperformance of their duties, fools, the lowest of men, reach the vilest births.

53. What wombs this individual soul enters in this world and in consequence of what actions, learn the particulars of that at large and in due order.

54. Those who committed mortal sins . . . , having passed during large numbers of years through dreadful hells, obtain, after the expiration of that term of punishment, the following births:

55. The slayer of a Brâman enters the womb of a dog, a pig, an ass, a camel, a cow, a goat, a sheep, a deer, a bird, a Candala, and a Pukkasa [two low-caste groups].

56. A Brâman who drinks the spirituous liquor called Sura shall enter the bodies of small and large insects, of moths, or birds, feeding on ordure, and of destructive beasts.

57. A Brâman who steals the gold of a Brâhman shall pass a thousand times through the bodies of spiders, snakes and lizards, of aquatic animals and of destructive Pishacas [ghosts].

58. The violater of a Guru's bed enters a hundred times the forms of grasses, shrubs and creepers, likewise of carnivorous animals and of beasts with fangs and of those doing cruel deeds.

59. Men who delight in doing hurt become carnivorous animals; those who eat forbidden food, worms, thieves, creatures consuming their own kind; those who have intercourse with women of the lower castes, Pretas [another kind of ghost].

The Path to Liberation

1. A twice-born householder, who has thus lived according to the law in the order of householders, may, taking a firm resolution and keeping his organs of sense in subjection, dwell in the forest, duly observing the rules given below.

2. When a householder sees his skin wrinkled, and his hair white, and the sons of his sons, then he may resort to the forest.

3. Abandoning all food raised by cultivation, and all his belongings, he may depart into the forest, either committing his wife to his sons, or accompanied by her.

8. Let him be always industrious in privately reciting the Veda; let him be patient of hardships, friendly towards all of collected mind, always liberal. . . .

25. Having reposited the three sacred fires in himself, according to prescribed rule, let him live without a fire, without a house, wholly silent, subsisting on roots and fruit, . . .

33. But having thus passed the third part of a man's natural term of life in the forest, he may live as an ascetic during the fourth part of his existence, after abandoning all attachment to worldly objects.

42. Let him always wander alone, without any companion, in order to attain final liberation, fully understanding that the solitary man, who neither forsakes nor is forsaken, gains his end.

87. The student, the householder, the hermit, and the ascetic, these constitute four separate orders, which all spring from the order of householders.

88. But all or even any of these orders, assumed successively in accordance with the Institutes of the sacred law, lead the Brâman who acts by the preceding rules to the highest state.

89. And in accordance with the precepts of the Veda . . . the householder is declared to be superior to all of them; for he supports the other three.

21

Bhagavad-Gita

The *Bhagavad-Gita*, "The Song of God," is one of the most popular and revered books in Hindu religious literature. For more than two millennia, it has been the principal source of religious inspiration for many millions of South Asian people. It consists of more than seven hundred line verses in the form of a long philosophical dialogue primarily between Krishna, a manifestation of the Supreme Deity in human form, and Arjuna, a warrior-prince, dealing with questions regarding the relationship between man's real self or soul and the body and life and destiny as a whole. In the first of the following two excerpts from the *Bhagavad-Gita*, Krishna explains the deathless life and the indestructibility of the soul and the importance of caste duties, concepts so central to Hindu religious belief, to Arjuna, who is torn by the feelings of worldly and spiritual obligations. In the second excerpt, the importance of devotion to God in achieving salvation in Hindu religion is described.

QUESTIONS TO CONSIDER

1. Explain what Arjuna's worldly and spiritual obligations are and the reason for his dilemma.
2. What spiritual justifications does Krishna offer to Arjuna for killing the enemy in the battlefield?

Deathless Life and Caste Obligation

How can I use my arrows in battle against Bhīshma, my grandsire, and Dro.na, my venerable teacher, who are worthy rather to be worshipped, O Destroyer of all opponents?

Surely would it be better to eat the bread of beggary in this life than to slay these great-souled masters!

If I kill them, all enjoyment of wealth, all gratified desire, is stained by their blood!

Indeed, scarcely can I tell which would be better, that they or we should conquer, for to destroy those sons of Dhritarâstra who oppose us, would be to extinguish forever the savor of life.

Overpowered by my helplessness, and with a mind in confusion, I supplicate Thee! Make clear to me that which is my good; I am Thy disciple. Instruct me, who have sought my refuge in Thee!

From *The Song of God* (pp. 13–21, 86–89), trans. Dhan Gopal Mukerji. Copyright 1931 by Dhan Gopal Mukerji. Used by permission of Dutton, a division of Penguin Putnam Inc.

There is naught to dispel this sorrow which overpowereth my senses. Were I to obtain undisputed and powerful dominion over all the earth, and mastery over the gods, what then would that avail me?

Arjuna, having thus spoken to Krishna, Lord of the Senses, made end, saying:

'I shall not fight!' and with these words fell silent.

But as he remained sorrowing thus in the midst of the two armies, K.rish.na, smiling a little, spoke to him as follows:

Thou hast grieved for those undeserving of grief, Arjuna! Although thou speakest wisely, those who are still wiser mourn neither for the living nor for the dead.

For never hath it been that I was not, nor thou, nor these Kings; nor shall we cease to be, ever.

The self is not interrupted while childhood, youth and old age pass through the flesh; likewise in death the self dieth not, but is released to assume another shape. By this the calm soul is not deluded.

The impressions of the senses, quickened to heat and cold, pain and pleasure, are transitory. Forever on the ebb and flow, they are by their very nature impermanent. Bear them then patiently, O Descendant of Kings!

For the wise man who is serene in pain and pleasure, whom these disturb not, he alone is able to attain Immortality, O Great amongst men!

The unreal can never be; the real can never cease to be. Those who know the truth know that this is so.

The Unnamable Principle which pervadeth all things, none hath power to destroy: know thou certainly that It is indestructible.

By That, immortal, inexhaustible, illimitable, Indweller, is the mortality of this flesh possessed. Fight therefore O Descendant of brave Kings!

He who conceiveth this Indweller, this Self, as slayer, or who conceiveth It as slain, is without knowledge. The Self neither slayeth nor is It slain.

It is never born, nor doth It die, nor having once existed, doth It ever cease to be. Ancient, eternal, changeless, ever Itself, It perisheth not when the body is destroyed.

How can that man who knoweth It to be indestructible, changeless, without birth, and immutable, how can he, Arjuna, either slay or cause the slaying of another?

As a man casteth off an old garment and putteth on another which is new, so the Self casteth off its outworn embodiment and entereth into a new form.

This Self, weapons cut not; This, fire burneth not; This, water wetteth not; and This, the winds dry not up.

This Self cannot be cut, it cannot be burnt, it cannot be wetted, it cannot be dried. Changeless, all-pervading, unmoving, Eternal, it is the Unalterable Self.

This Self is invisible, inconceivable, and changeless. Knowing that It is such, cease, therefore, to grieve!

But whether thou believest this Self of eternal duration or subjected constantly to birth and death, yet Mighty-armèd One, hast thou no cause to grieve.

For, to that which is born, death is certain; to that which dieth, birth is certain, and the unavoidable giveth not occasion for grief.

Nothing may be perceived in its beginning; in its middle state only is it known, and its end again is undisclosed. What herein, Arjuna, is cause for grief?

One man perceiveth the Self as a thing of wonder; another speaketh of It as a wonder; others hear of It as a wonder, but though seeing, speaking, hearing, none comprehendeth It at all.

This, which is the Indweller in all beings, is forever beyond harm. Then, for no creature, Arjuna, hast thou any cause to grieve.

Examine thy duty and falter not, for there is no better thing for a warrior than to wage righteous war.

Fortunate indeed are the soldiers, Arjuna, who, fighting in such a battle, reach this unsought, open gate to heaven.

But to refuse this just fight and forgo thine own duty and honour, is to incur sin.

By so doing the world will also hold thee ever in despite. To the honourable, dishonour is surely worse than death.

The great charioteer warriors will believe that through fear thou hast withdrawn from the battle. Then shalt thou fall from their esteem, who hast hitherto been highly regarded.

Thine enemies moreover, cavilling at thy great prowess, will say of thee that which is not to be uttered. What fate, indeed, could be more unbearable than this?

Dying thou gainest heaven; victorious, thou enjoyest the earth. Therefore, Arjuna, arise, resolved to do battle.

Look upon pain and pleasure, gain and loss, conquest and defeat, as the same, and prepare to fight; thus shalt thou incur no evil.

Now hath been declared unto thee the understanding of the Self. Hearken thou moreover to the Way,[2] following which, O son of Kings, thou shalt break through the fateful bondage of thine act.[3]

On this Way nothing that is begun is lost, nor are there any obstacles, and even a very little progress thereon bringeth security against great fear.

Devotion to God

But those who adore Me, and Me alone, and all beings who are steadfast and supremely dedicated in their worship, I augment in their fullness and fill them up in their emptiness.

Even those who devotedly worship other gods because of their love, worship Me; but the path they follow is not My path.

For I alone am the Deity of all sacrifices, and those who worship other gods than Me reach the end of merit and return to the world, where they must set forth anew upon the way.

One pursueth the gods and attaineth the sphere of the gods suitable to the merit of his works; another worshippeth the Fathers and yet another worshippeth attributes and incarnations, each attaining unto his own place; but he who worshippeth Me cometh unto Me.

Whosoever with devotion offereth Me leaf, flower, fruit, or water, I accept it from him as the devout gift of the pure-minded.

Whatsoever thou doest, Arjuna, whatsoever thou eatest, whatsoever thou givest away, whatsoever thou offerest up as sacrifice, and whatsoever austerity thou shalt practice, do it as an offering unto Me.

---

[2]Yŏga. The exact meaning of Yŏga depends on its context. It signifies any consistent way of spiritual life.

[3]"The bondage of thine act," Karma. "The doctrine of true knowledge and of emancipation by means of it."

Thus shalt thou be released from the fateful bonds of thine acts, and the cage of good and evil. Thine heart shall renounce itself, and being liberated, shall come unto Me.

To Me none is hateful, none dear; but those who worship Me with devotion dwell in Me, and I also in them.

Even a very wicked man who worshippeth Me, eschewing all else in his devotion to Me, shall be regarded as worthy of merit, for great is his faith.

He shall attain righteousness in a short time, Arjuna, and compel everlasting Peace; therefore, proclaim it aloud that no one of My devotees is destroyed.

They also who might be considered of inferior birth, women, tradesmen, as well as day-laborers, even they shall master this world and attain Me, Arjuna, if they seek Me with single mind.

What need, then, to describe priests and kings who have attained holiness? Therefore, Arjuna, in this transient, joyless world, worship thou Me!

Make thy mind My dwelling place; consecrate thyself to Me; sacrifice unto Me, bow down unto Me, make thy heart steadfast in Me thy Supreme Destination, and thou too shalt assuredly come unto Me.

22

Duties of a King, Artha Shastra

The original (lost) version of this manual on kingship is ascribed to Kautilya, Chandragupta's prime minister. What follows is a much later version, still bearing Kautilya's name, possibly adapted for the founders of the Gupta Empire. Its guidelines are not high-minded with any consistency: The writer(s) stress that in the real world "the law of the fishes" prevails—that is, the big fish eat the little ones.

QUESTIONS TO CONSIDER

1. How does this selection compare with Niccolò Machiavelli's *The Prince* and *The Discourses on Titus Livy* (see Reading 94)?
2. Are these guidelines and advice consistent with Hindu-Buddhist religious precepts? How?

Only if a king is himself energetically active, do his officers follow him energetically. If he is sluggish, they too remain sluggish. And, besides, they eat up his works. He is thereby easily overpowered by his enemies. Therefore, he should ever dedicate himself energetically to activity.

He should divide the day as well as the night into eight parts. . . . During the first one-eighth part of the day, he should listen to reports pertaining to the organization of law and order and to income and expenditure. During the second, he should attend to the affairs of the urban and the rural population. During the third, he should take his bath and meal and devote himself to study. During the fourth, he should receive gold and the department heads. During the fifth, he should hold consultations with the council of ministers through correspondence and also keep himself informed of the secret reports brought by spies. During the sixth, he should devote himself freely to amusement or listen to the counsel of the ministers. During the seventh, he should inspect the military formations of elephants, cavalry, chariots, and infantry. During the eighth, he, together with the commander-in-chief of the army, should make plans for the campaigns of conquest. When the day has come to an end he should offer the evening prayers.

During the first one-eighth part of the night, he should meet with the officers of the secret service. During the second, he should take his bath and meals and also devote himself to study. During the third, at the sounding of the trumpets, he should enter the bed chamber and should sleep through the fourth and fifth. Waking up at the sound of the trumpets, he should, during the sixth part, ponder over the teachings of the sciences and his urgent duties for the day. During the seventh, he should hold consultations and send out officers of the secret service for their operations. During the eighth, accompanied by sacrificial priests, preceptors, and the chaplain, he should receive benedictions; he should also have interviews with a physician, the kitchen superintendent, and the astrologer. Thereafter, he should circumambulate by the right a cow with a calf and an ox and then proceed to the reception hall. Or he should divide the day and the night into parts in accordance with his own capacities and thereby attend to his duties.

When he has gone to the reception hall, he should not allow such persons, as have come for business, to remain sticking to the doors of the hall [i.e., waiting in vain]. For, a king, with whom it is difficult for the people to have an audience, is made to confuse between right action and wrong action by his close entourage. Thereby he suffers from the disaffection of his own subjects or falls prey to the enemy. Therefore he should attend to the affairs relating to gods, hermitages, heretics, learned brahmans, cattle, and holy places as also those of minors, the aged, the sick, those in difficulty, the helpless, and women—in the order of their enumeration or in accordance with the importance or the urgency of the affairs.

A king should attend to all urgent business; he should not put it off. For what has been thus put off becomes either difficult or altogether impossible to accomplish. . . .

In the happiness of the subjects lies the happiness of the king; in their welfare, his own welfare. The welfare of the king does not lie in the fulfillment of what is dear to him; whatever is dear to the subjects constitutes his welfare.

[In foreign affairs, observe] the sixfold policy: peace, war, marking time, attack, seeking refuge, and duplicity. . . . "There are only two forms of policy," says Vatavyadhi, "for the sixfold policy is actually accomplished through peace and war." Kautilya says: "The forms of policy are, verily, six in number, for conditions are different in different cases."

Of these six forms: binding through pledges means peace; offensive operation means war; apparent indifference means marking time; strengthening one's position means attack; giving oneself to another [as a subordinate ally or vassal] means seeking refuge; keeping oneself engaged simultaneously in peace and war with the same state means duplicity. These are the six forms of policy.

When one king [the would-be conquerer] is weaker than the other [i.e., his immediate neighbor, the enemy], he should make peace with him. When he is stronger than the other, he should make war with him. When he thinks: "The other is not capable of putting me down nor am I capable of putting him down," he should mark time. When he possesses an excess of the necessary means, he should attack. When he is devoid of strength, he should seek refuge with another. When his end can be achieved only through the help of an ally, he should practice duplicity.

23

Hsuan-tsang [Xuanzang], The Land and People of India

During the reign of Harsha Vardhana, Hsuan-tsang [Xuanzang], the most famous of the Chinese Buddhist scholars and pilgrims renowned for translating Indian Sanskrit Buddhist scriptures into Chinese, visited India. In search of answers to questions on Chinese versions of Buddhist scriptures, Xuanzang set out westward in 629 A.D. from Changan [Zhangan], the capital of T'ang China, along the silk routes via Central Asia. After a difficult journey passing through Turfan, Tashkent, Samarkand, and crossing the Hindu Kush, he entered northwest India. In the following sixteen years, he visited many kingdoms, including Harsha's Kanauji kingdom (area around present-day Luck now); sites sacred to Buddhism; and Nalanda Monastery, the famous Buddhist center of learning. He studied there and returned to China in 645. Upon his return, he translated seventy-three Buddhist works, mainly scriptures, totaling more than one thousand rolls. In addition, Xuanzang left behind voluminous records of his eyewitness accounts of the land, people, government, and society of In-tu (India) known as Records of Western Regions (Si-yu-ki), which provide an invaluable source for reconstructing the history of India's classical age. The following selection is from these records, providing the descriptions of the land, education, military, trial by ordeal, and funeral customs.

QUESTIONS TO CONSIDER

1. How does Xuanzang react to Hindu (as opposed to Buddhist) practices?
2. What does Xuanzang find noteworthy about Buddhism in India? Does he give any indication that Buddhism is in relative decline in India?
3. In what other societies have you heard of trial by ordeal? What is the likely justification for the way it is supposed to work?
4. What aspects of Indian society appear to impress Xuanzang as good or bad?

Adopting a general name that is the most acceptable to the people, we shall call the country "In-tu," which signifies "moon." The moon has many designations, In-tu being one of them. It is said that all living creatures unceasingly transmigrate, revolving through mortal existences in the long darkness of ignorance without having a guiding star. It is like the night after the setting of the bright sun, when, although people get light by candles and have the shining light of the stars, these are not comparable with the brightness of the serene moon. For this reason the spiritual condition of India is allegorically compared with the shining moon. The sages and the

From A. V. Williams Jackson, ed., *History of India*, Vol. IX (London: The Grolier Society, 1906), pp. 122–49, *passim.* Condensed by Chong-kun Yoon.

wise teachers of this country followed the norm (of the Buddha) in succession, guided the people, and exercised rule, as the moon sheds its bright influences—on this account this country is called In-tu.

The towns and villages of India have gates; the surrounding walls are broad and high; the streets and lanes are narrow and crooked. The thoroughfares are dirty and the stalls are arranged on both sides of the road with appropriate signs. Butchers, fishermen, actors, executioners, scavengers, and so on, have their dwellings outside of the city. In coming and going these persons are bound to keep on the left side of the road till they arrive at their homes. As to the construction of houses and the enclosing walls, the land being low and moist, the walls of the towns are mostly built of bricks or tiles, and the enclosures of the houses are matted bamboo or wood. The houses have balconies made of wood, as well as flat roofs with a coating of lime, and are covered with burnt or unburnt tiles. The buildings are very high, and in style of construction they are like those in China. Branches or common grasses or tiles or boards are used for covering them. The walls are covered with lime, the floor is smeared with cow's dung as means of purity, and it is strewn with flowers of the season. In such matters they differ from us.

Many Samgharamas (Buddhist monasteries) are constructed with extraordinary skill. A three-storied tower is erected at each of the four angles. The beams and the projecting heads are carved with strange figures. The doors, the windows, and the walls are painted in many colors; the houses of the ordinary people are luxurious on the inside but plain on the outside. The interior and central rooms vary in height and width. As to the form and construction of the tiers of terraces and the series of salons, there is no fixed rule. The doors open toward the east; the royal throne also faces the east.

When the Hindus sit or rest they all use corded benches; the royal family, great personages, the officials, and the gentry use benches variously ornamented, but in size they are exactly the same. The throne of the reigning sovereign is exceedingly high and broad, and it is set with pearls and precious gems; it is called the "lion-throne." It is covered with extremely fine drapery; the footstool is adorned with gems. The ordinary officials carve their seats in various ways and decorate them beautifully according to their taste.

To educate and encourage the young, they first teach them to study the book of "Twelve Chapters." After arriving at the age of seven years, the young are instructed in the great treatises of the "Five Sciences." The first is called Grammar, the elucidation of sounds. This treatise explains the meaning of words and their derivation.

The second science is called Kiau-ming; it treats of the arts and of mechanics, and it explains the principles of Yin and Yang (Negative and Positive Principles) of the calendar. The third is called the "Medicinal Treatise"; it illustrates the use of charms, medicinal stones, needles and moxa. The fourth science is called "Logic," which determines the right and wrong and discriminates between the true and the false. The fifth science is called the science of "Inward Knowledge"; it relates to the Five Vehicles, and the doctrine of cause and effect (karma).

The Brahmans study the four Veda treatises. The first is called Shau ("longevity," i.e., the Ayur-Veda); it relates to the preservation of life and the regulation of the natural condition. The second is called Sse ("worship," i.e., the Yajur-Veda); it relates to sacrifice and prayer. The third is called Ping ("peace regulation," i.e., the Sama-Veda); it relates to decorum, casting of lots, military tactics, and warfare. The fourth is called Shu ("arts," i.e., the Atharva-Veda); it relates to various branches of science, incantations, medicine.

The doctrines of the Tathagata (Buddha) may be comprehended by men of different qualities; but, as the time is now remote since the Holy One lived, his doctrine is presented in a changed form, and is therefore understood orthodoxly or heterodoxly, according to the intelligence of those who inquire into it. The different schools are constantly at variance, and their contending utterances rise like the angry waves of the sea. The different schools have their separate masters, but they aim to reach one and the same end, though by different ways.

There are eighteen schools, each claiming pre-eminence. The tenets of the Great and the Little Vehicle [Mahayana and Hinayana] differ widely. There are some of the followers who give themselves up to meditation, and devote themselves, whether walking, standing still, or sitting down, to the acquirement of wisdom and insight. Others, on the contrary, differ from these in raising noisy contentions about their faith. According to their fraternity, they are governed by distinctive rules and regulations, which we need not name.

The chief soldiers of the country are selected from the bravest of the people, and as the sons follow the profession of their fathers, they soon acquire a knowledge of the art of war. These dwell in garrison around the palace (during times of peace), but when on an expedition they march in front as an advance guard. There are four divisions of the army, the infantry, the cavalry, the chariots, and the elephants. The elephants are covered with strong armour, and their tusks are provided with sharp spurs. The commander-in-chief rides on an elephant, with two soldiers on the right and left to manage the animal. The ordinary officer rides in a chariot drawn by four horses; he is surrounded by a file of guards, who keep close to his chariot wheels.

The cavalry spread themselves in front to resist an attack, and in case of defeat they carry orders hither and thither. The infantry by their quick movements contribute to the defence. These men are chosen for their courage and strength. They carry a great shield and a long spear; sometimes they hold a sword or sabre, and advance to the front with impetuosity. All their weapons of war are sharp and pointed. Some of them are these—spears, shields, bows, arrows, swords, sabres, battle-axes, lances, halberds, long javelins, and various kinds of slings. All these they have used for ages.

The law of the state is sometimes violated by base persons, and plots are made against the ruler. When the matter has been fully sifted, the offenders are imprisoned for life. There is no infliction of corporal punishment; they are simply left to live or die, and are not counted among men. When the rules of propriety or justice are violated, or when a man fails in loyalty or filial piety, they cut off his nose or his ears, or his hands and feet, or expel him from the country, or drive him out into the desert wilds. For other faults, except these, a small payment of money will commute the punishment. In the investigation of criminal cases there is no use of rod or staff to obtain proofs (of guilt). In questioning an accused person, if he replies with frankness, the punishment is proportioned accordingly; but if the accused obstinately denies his fault, or in spite of it attempts to excuse himself, then in searching out the truth to the bottom, when it is necessary to pass sentence, there are four kinds of ordeal used—ordeal by water, by fire, by weighing, and by poison.

When the ordeal is by water, the accused is placed in a sack connected with a stone vessel and thrown into deep water. They then judge of his innocence or guilt in this way—if the man sinks and the stone floats, he is guilty; but if the man floats and the stone sinks, he is pronounced innocent.

Secondly, by fire. They heat some iron and make the accused kneel on it and then tread on it, and apply it to the palms of his hands; moreover, he is made to pass his tongue over it; if no scars result, he is innocent; if there are scars, his guilt is proved. In the case of timid and weak persons who cannot endure such a horrible ordeal, they take a flower-bud and cast it toward the fire; if it opens, he is innocent; if the flower is burned, he is guilty.

Ordeal by weight is this: A man and a stone are placed in a balance evenly, then they judge according to lightness or weight. If the accused is innocent, then the man weighs down the stone, which rises in the balance; if he is guilty, the man rises and the stone falls.

Ordeal by poison is this: They take a ram, cut off its right hind leg, and put poison upon the portion of flesh that is assigned to the accused to eat; if the man is guilty, the poison takes effect and he dies; if the man is innocent, the poison has no effect and he survives.

Every one who falls sick fasts for seven days. During this interval many recover, but if the sickness lasts they take medicine. The character of these medicines is different, and their names also vary. The doctors differ in their modes of examination and treatment. If a person dies, those who attend the funeral raise lamentable cries and weep together. They rend their garments and tear their hair; they strike their heads, and beat their breasts. There are no regulations as to dress for mourning, nor any fixed period for observing it. There are three methods of paying the last tribute to the dead: first, by cremation—wood being made into a pyre, the body is burnt; second, by water—the body is thrown into a stream to float and fall into dissolution; third, by desertion, in which case the body is cast into some forest-wild to be devoured by beasts.

When the king dies, his successor is first appointed, that he may preside at the funeral rites and fix the different points of precedence. Whilst living they give their rulers titles of merit according to their character; when dead there are no posthumous titles.

In a house where there has been a death there is no eating allowed; but after the funeral they resume their usual habits. There are no anniversaries (of the death) observed. Those who have attended a funeral are regarded as unclean; they all bathe outside the town and then enter their houses.

The old and infirm who are approaching death, or those who are suffering from some incurable disease, who fear to linger to the end of their days, and through disgust at life wish to escape from its troubles, or those who, condemning mortal existence, desire release from the affairs of the world and its concerns—these persons after receiving a farewell meal at the hands of their relatives and friends, they place, amid the sounds of music, on a boat which they propel into the midst of the Ganges, and there these persons drown themselves. They think in this way to secure a birth in Heaven. Hardly one out of ten will not carry out his foolish idea.

The Buddhist brethren are not allowed to lament or weep for the dead; when the father or mother of a monk dies, they recite prayers, recounting their obligations to them and recalling the past, and they carefully attend to them being now dead. They expect by this to increase the happiness of the departed.

The Buddhist Tradition

Buddhism represents one of the few truly unifying threads in the diverse cultures of Asia. From its origins in Northeast India around 500 B.C., this religion spread throughout the subcontinent and beyond, into Sri Lanka and Southeast Asia. The patronage of missionary activity by the Indian king of the Mauryan dynasty, Ashoka (269–232 B.C.), particularly promoted the dissemination of Buddhism. Around the beginning of the Christian Era, this religion was introduced into China, and from there it passed via Korea into Japan by the sixth century A.D.. By the seventh century, Buddhism had become the dominant religion of Tibet.

The Buddha's teaching emphasized that life in the endless cycle of transmigration (*samsara*) is inherently fraught with suffering and frustration. The cause of this suffering is our desire for material things and our ignorance of the fact that there is no "self." Our false notions prompt us to action in search of satisfaction for our "selves"; and all of these actions (which the Buddhists and Hindus call *karma*) produce good or bad consequences, depending on whether they involve good or evil deeds. The results push us into another life in the cycle of transmigration, where we will receive our due rewards. However, the Buddha believed that we are only heaps of *skandhas*, material components, which obey natural laws of causation and which eventually disintegrate like all matter. So, the Buddha reasoned, if people could only abandon the false notion of self and give up all desire, they would be liberated from the effects of actions and, therefore, from the cycle of transmigration. Once liberated, people would achieve a condition of absolute peace and tranquility, which the Buddhists call *nirvana*. To achieve this state, the Buddha provided an Eightfold Path for living a disciplined life of calm detachment.

Only monks and nuns, who constitute the Sangha, completely follow this path to reach nirvana. These rare men—and a few women—totally give up their worldly possessions and ways. Historically, most monks lived in monasteries where they spent their time learning and discussing the Buddha's teaching and meditating in order to achieve a deep, inner calm. The Buddhist laypersons (that is, those who lived normal lives outside the monastery) greatly respected the monks and gained merit by providing them food for their one meal a day. This religious practice still prevails in Sri Lanka and Southeast Asia.

About the time of Christ, two major branches of Buddhism had developed. They are known as *Mahayana* or the Greater Vehicle and *Hinayana* or the Lesser Vehicle (also known as *Theravada* or the Doctrine of Elders). The former claimed to be more tolerant and inclusive than the latter, which spread widely in Sri Lanka and in the Southeast Asian countries of Myanmar (Burma), Thailand, Cambodia, and Laos; rejected all later accretions; and remained closer to original Buddhism, in which the monks were the central element. Over the centuries, Mahayana Buddhism, which had spread to China, Korea, Japan, and Vietnam, developed the concept of salvation by faith in one of many buddhas, including the historical Buddha. It also created a new type of deity, the *Boddhisattvas* ("Buddha-to-be" or "Enlightened Existence"), who were dedicated to selflessly helping as many other creatures as possible and delayed achieving nirvana and becoming a Buddha themselves.

24

Enlightenment of the Buddha

This selection is from the best-known biography of the Buddha, called the *Buddhacarita* and written by the Indian poet Ashvaghosha before A.D. 200. The reading begins with Prince Gautama already having abandoned family and home, intent on conquering the cause of human suffering. This Buddha-to-be decides to sit alone under a tree until an answer to his problem is clear. The episode ends with his achieving enlightenment—insight into the cause of suffering and the way to overcome it. This experience turns him into a Buddha, an Enlightened One.

QUESTIONS TO CONSIDER

1. Compare the achievements of the Buddha with those of Jesus, Muhammad, and Confucius.
2. How important is meditation in achieving enlightenment in Buddhism? Why?

The Bodhisattva [Buddha-to-be], possessed of great skill in Transic meditation, put himself into trance, intent on discerning both the ultimate reality of things and the final goal of existence. After he had gained complete mastery over all the degrees and kinds of trance:

1. In the *first watch* of the night he recollected the successive series of his former births. "There was I so and so; that was my name; deceased from there I came here"—in this way he remembered thousands of births, as though living them over again. When he had recalled his own births and deaths in all these various lives of his, the Sage, full of pity, turned his compassionate mind towards other living beings, and he thought to himself: "Again and again they must leave the people they regard as their own, and must go on elsewhere, and that without ever stopping. Surely this world is unprotected and helpless, and like a wheel it turns round and round." As he continued steadily to recollect the past thus, he came to the definite conviction that this world of Samsara is as unsubstantial as the pith of a plantain tree.

2. Second to none in valour, he then, in the *second watch* of the night, acquired the supreme heavenly eye, for he himself was the best of all those who have sight. Thereupon with the perfectly pure heavenly eye he looked upon the entire world, which appeared to him as though reflected in a spotless mirror. He saw that the decease and rebirth of beings depend on whether they have done superior or inferior deeds. And his compassionateness grew still further. It became clear to him that no

security can be found in this flood of Samsaric existence, and that the threat of death is ever-present. Beset on all sides, creatures can find no resting place. In this way he surveyed the five places of rebirth with his heavenly eye. And he found nothing substantial in the world of becoming, just as no core of heartwood is found in a plantain tree when its layers are peeled off one by one.

3. Then, as the *third watch* of that night drew on, the supreme master of trance turned his meditation to the real and essential nature of this world: "Alas, living beings wear themselves out in vain! Over and over again they are born, they age, die, pass on to a new life, and are reborn! What is more, greed and dark delusion obscure their sight, and they are blind from birth. Greatly apprehensive, they yet do not know how to get out of this great mass of ill." He then surveyed the twelve links of conditioned co-production, and saw that, beginning with ignorance, they lead to old age and death, and, beginning with the cessation of ignorance, they lead to the cessation of birth, old age, death, and all kinds of ill. When the great seer had comprehended that where there is no ignorance whatever, there also the karma-formations are stopped— then he had achieved a correct knowledge of all there is to be known, and he stood out in the world as a Buddha. He passed through the eight stages of Transic insight, and quickly reached their highest point. From the summit of the world downwards he could detect no self anywhere. Like the fire, when its fuel is burnt up, he became tranquil. He had reached perfection, and he thought to himself: "This is the authentic Way on which in the past so many great seers, who also knew all higher and all lower things, have travelled on to ultimate and real truth. And now I have obtained it!"

4. At that moment, in the *fourth watch* of the night, when dawn broke and all the ghosts that move and those that move not went to rest, the great seer took up the position which knows no more alteration, and the leader of all reached the state of all-knowledge. When, through his Buddhahood, he had cognized this fact, the earth swayed like a woman drunken with wine, the sky shone bright with the Siddhas who appeared in crowds in all the directions, and the mighty drums of thunder resounded through the air. Pleasant breezes blew softly, rain fell from a cloudless sky, flowers and fruits dropped from the trees out of season—in an effort, as it were, to show reverence for him. Mandarava flowers and lotus blossoms, and also water lilies made of gold and beryl, fell from the sky onto the ground near the Shakya sage, so that it looked like a place in the world of the gods. At that moment no one anywhere was angry, ill, or sad; no one did evil, none was proud; the world became quite quiet, as though it had reached full perfection. Joy spread through the ranks of those gods who longed for salvation; joy also spread among those who lived in the regions below. Everywhere the virtuous were strengthened, the influence of Dharma increased, and the world rose from the dirt of the passions and the darkness of ignorance. Filled with joy and wonder at the Sage's work, the seers of the solar race who had been protectors of men, who had been royal seers, who had been great seers, stood in their mansions in the heavens and showed him their reverence. The great seers among the hosts of invisible beings could be heard widely proclaiming his fame. All living things rejoiced and sensed that things went well.

The Four Holy Truths

What then is the Holy Truth of Ill? Birth is ill, decay is ill, sickness is ill, death is ill. To be conjoined with what one dislikes means suffering. To be disjoined from what one likes means suffering. Not to get what one wants, also that means suffering. In short, all grasping at any of the five Skandhas involves suffering.

What then is the Holy Truth of the Origination of Ill? It is that craving which leads to rebirth, accompanied by delight and greed, seeking its delight now here, now there, i.e., craving for sensuous experience, craving to perpetuate oneself, craving for extinction.

What then is the Holy Truth of the Stopping of Ill? It is the complete stopping of that craving, the withdrawal from it, the renouncing of it, throwing it back, liberation from it, non-attachment to it.

What then is the Holy Truth of the steps which lead to the stopping of Ill? It is this holy eightfold Path, which consists of right views, right intentions, right speech, right conduct, right livelihood, right effort, right mindfulness, right concentration.

25

Pure Land Scripture, *Sukhavativyuha*

In Mahayana Buddhism, a new concept of Buddhahood emerged. The number of buddhas increased, and multiple paths to salvation or enlightenment evolved. These buddhas reigned over separate Buddha-lands, and each could lead his devotees to rebirth and ultimate enlightenment in his Buddha-land. Among these, one gained prominence in eastern Asia: the "Pure Land" sect, also known as the "Western Paradise of Buddha Amitabha," the land of purity, beauty, and happiness (Sanskrit, "Sukhavati"). According to Pure Land tradition, Dharmakara, an Indian ascetic who was a contemporary of Siddhartha Gautama, took forty-eight vows and eventually gained Buddhahood under the name of Amitabha, meaning "Buddha of Infinite Light." In his eighteenth vow, Amitabha promised that anyone who, at the moment of death, wished salvation need only call upon him by name, and that person would be released from the sufferings of this world, gain rebirth in the Pure Land, and lead a life of peace and happiness until his or her final entry into nirvana. In China, a monk named Hui-yuan (A.D. 334–416) was the first to teach the attainment of salvation through faith in Buddha Amitabha. In time, the Pure Land sect placed less emphasis on the attainment of salvation through one's own efforts than on salvation through the power of another, that is, Amitabha. In the early period of its development, only serious devotees to Amitabha, such as monks and nuns, could attain Pure Land salvation. However, as this sect gained popularity, the Pure Land became accessible to all people, including the poor and downtrodden who sought release from the sufferings of this world but could not afford to practice asceticism, seclusion, and meditation. The practice of invoking Amitabha's name is known as *"nienfo"* in Chinese, *"nembutsu"* in Japanese, and *"yombul"* in Korean. The following excerpt is the Pure Land Sutra (*Sukhavativyuha*), which describes the blissful paradise ruled by Buddha Amitabha.

QUESTIONS TO CONSIDER

1. Compare and contrast Sukhavati with the Garden of Eden.
2. What would Sukhavati offer beyond sensual and material pleasures?
3. What does the follower need to do to gain final entry into nirvana?

This world Sukhavati, Ananda,[4] which is the world system of the Lord Amitabha, is rich and prosperous, comfortable, fertile, delightful and crowded with many Gods and men. And in this world system, Ananda, there are no hells, no animals, no ghosts, no Asuras[5] and none of the inauspicious places of rebirth. And in this our world no jewels make their appearance like those which exist in the world system Sukhavati.

And that world system Sukhavati, Ananda, emits many fragrant odours, it is rich in a great variety of flowers and fruits, adorned with jewel trees, which are frequented by flocks of various birds with sweet voices, which the Tathagata's[6] miraculous power has conjured up. And these jewel trees, Ananda, have various colours, many colours, many hundreds of thousands of colours. They are variously composed of the seven precious things, in varying combinations, i.e. of gold, silver, beryl, crystal, coral, red pearls or emerald. Such jewel trees, and clusters of banana trees and rows of palm trees, all made of precious things, grow everywhere in this Buddha-field. On all sides it is surrounded with golden nets, and all round covered with lotus flowers made of all the precious things. Some of the lotus flowers are half a mile in circumference, others up to ten miles. And from each jewel lotus issue thirty-six hundred thousand kotis of rays. And at the end of each ray there issue thirty-six hundred thousand kotis of Buddhas, with golden-coloured bodies, who bear the thirty-two marks of the superman, and who, in all the ten directions, go into countless world systems, and there demonstrate Dharma.

And further, Ananda, in this Buddha-field there are nowhere any mountains,— black mountains, jewel mountains, Sumerus, kings of mountains, circular mountains and great circular mountains. But the Buddha-field is everywhere even, delightful like the palm of the hand, and in all its parts the ground contains a great variety of jewels and gems. . . .

And many kinds of rivers flow along in this world system Sukhavati. There are great rivers there, one mile broad, and up to fifty miles broad and twelve miles deep. And all these rivers flow along calmly, their water is fragrant with manifold agreeable odours, in them there are bunches of flowers to which various jewels adhere, and they resound with various sweet sounds. And the sound which issues from these great rivers is as pleasant as that of a musical instrument, which consists of hundreds of thousands of kotis of parts, and which, skilfully played, emits a heavenly music. It is deep, commanding, distinct, clear, pleasant to the ear, touching the heart, delightful, sweet, pleasant, and one never tires of hearing it, it always agrees with one and one likes to hear it, like the words "Impermanent, peaceful, calm, and not-self." Such is the sound that reaches the ears of those beings.

And, Ananda, both the banks of those great rivers are lined with variously scented jewel trees, and from them bunches of flowers, leaves and branches of all kinds hang down. And if those beings wish to indulge in sports full of heavenly delights on

[4]Favorite disciple of Buddha.
[5]Evil spirits.
[6]Buddha.

those river-banks, then, after they have stepped into the water, the water in each case rises as high as they wish it to,—up to the ankles, or the knees, or the hips, or their sides, or their ears. And heavenly delights arise. Again, if beings wish the water to be cold, for them it becomes cold; if they wish it to be hot, for them it becomes hot; if they wish it to be hot and cold, for them it becomes hot and cold, to suit their pleasure. And those rivers flow along, full of water scented with the finest odours, and covered with beautiful flowers, resounding with the sounds of many birds, easy to ford, free from mud, and with golden sand at the bottom. And all the wishes those beings may think of, they all will be fulfilled, as long as they are rightful.

And as to the pleasant sound which issues from the water (of these rivers), that reaches all the parts of this Buddha-field. And everyone hears the pleasant sound he wishes to hear, i.e. he hears of the Buddha, the Dharma,[7] the Samgha,[8] . . . the powers, the grounds of self-confidence, of the special dharmas[9] of a Buddha, of the analytical knowledges, of emptiness, the signless, and the wishless, of the uneffected, the unborn, of non-production, non-existence, non-cessation, of calm, quietude and peace, of the great friendliness, the great compassion, the great sympathetic joy, the great evenmindedness, of the patient acceptance of things which fail to be produced, and of the acquisition of the stage where one is consecrated (as a Tathagata). And, hearing this, one gains the exalted zest and joyfulness, which is associated with detachment, dispassion, calm, cessation, Dharma, and brings about the state of mind which leads to the accomplishment of enlightenment. And nowhere in this world-system Sukhavati does one hear of anything unwholesome, nowhere of the hindrances, nowhere of the states of punishment, the states of woe and the bad destinies, nowhere of suffering. Even of feelings which are neither pleasant nor unpleasant one does not hear here, how much less of suffering! And that, Ananda, is the reason why this world-system is called the "Happy Land" (Sukhavati). But all this describes it only in brief, not in detail. One aeon might well reach its end while one proclaims the reasons for happiness in the world-system Sukhavati, and still one could not come to the end of (the enumeration of) the reasons for happiness.

Moreover, Ananda, all the beings who have been reborn in this world-system Sukhavati, who are reborn in it, or who will be reborn in it, they will be exactly like the Paranirmitavasavartin Gods:[10] of the same colour, strength, vigour, height and breadth, dominion, store of merit and keenness of super-knowledges; they enjoy the same dresses, ornaments, parks, palaces and pointed towers, the same kind of forms, sounds, smells, tastes and touchables, just the same kinds of enjoyments. And the beings in the world-system Sukhavati do not eat gross food, like soup or raw sugar; but whatever food they may wish for, that they perceive as eaten, and they become gratified in body and mind, without there being any further need to throw the food into the body. And if, after their bodies are gratified, they wish for certain perfumes, then the whole of that Buddha-field becomes scented with just that kind of heavenly perfumes. But if someone does not wish to smell that perfume, then the perception of it does not reach him. In the same way, whatever they may wish for, comes to them, be it musical instruments, banners, flags, etc.; or cloaks of different colours, or ornaments of various kinds. If they wish for a palace of a certain colour, distinguishing marks, construction, height and

---

[7]Teachings of Buddha.
[8]Community of believers.
[9]Duties.
[10]The gods who live in the sixth of the six heavens of desire.

width, made of various precious things, adorned with hundreds of thousands of pinnacles, while inside it various heavenly woven materials are spread out, and it is full of couches strewn with beautiful cushions,—then just such a palace appears before them. In those delightful palaces, surrounded and honoured by seven times seven thousand Apsaras,[11] they dwell, play, enjoy and disport themselves.

. . . And the beings who are touched by the winds, which are pervaded with various perfumes, are filled with a happiness as great as that of a monk who has achieved the cessation of suffering.

And in this Buddha-field one has no conception at all of fire, sun, moon, planets, constellations, stars or blinding darkness, and no conception even of day and night, except (where they are mentioned) in the sayings of the Tathagata. There is nowhere a notion of monks possessing private parks for retreats.

And all the beings who have been born, who are born, who will be born in this Buddha-field, they all are fixed on the right method of salvation, until they have won Nirvana. And why? Because there is here no place for and no conception of the two other groups, i.e. of those who are not fixed at all, and those who are fixed on wrong ways. For this reason also that world-system is called the "Happy Land." . . .

And further again, Ananda, in the ten directions, in each single direction, in Buddha-fields countless like the sands of the river Ganges, Buddhas and Lords countless like the sands of the river Ganges, glorify the name of the Lord Amitabha, the Tathagata, praise him, proclaim his fame, extol his virtue. And why? Because all beings are irreversible from the supreme enlightenment if they hear the name of the Lord Amitabha, and, on hearing it, with one single thought only raise their hearts to him with a resolve connected with serene faith.

And if any beings, Ananda, again and again reverently attend to this Tathagata, if they will plant a large and immeasurable root of good, having raised their hearts to enlightenment, and if they vow to be reborn in that world system, then, when the hour of their death approaches, that Tathagata Amitabha, the Arhat,[12] the fully Enlightened One, will stand before them, surrounded by hosts of monks. Then, having seen that Lord, and having died with hearts serene, they will be reborn in just that world-system Sukhavati. And if there are sons or daughters of good family, who may desire to see that Tathagata Amitabha in this very life, they should raise their hearts to the supreme enlightenment, they should direct their thought with extreme resoluteness and perseverance unto this Buddha-field and they should dedicate their store of merit to being reborn therein.

26

Edict of Ashoka

This statement was one of several rock inscriptions Ashoka had erected in public so that everyone could be instructed. While the content is not particularly Buddhist, the material was inspired by the Buddhist ideal of compassion. The ideal of rule by *dharma*, a just and humane order, is emphasized.

[11]Female supernatural beings.
[12]One who has achieved Nirvana.

QUESTIONS FOR DISCUSSION

1. Is Buddhism pessimistic about life? Or does this religion seem to offer hope?
2. Which form of Buddhism—the Theravada emphasizing the life of the monk, or the Mahayana, focusing on the Bodhisattva—do you think would inspire and promote more works of art and literature? Why?
3. In what other cases have political leaders been inspired by a religion to promote a humane and just society, as was King Ashoka?
4. Can you identify any of the "realms" in the enumeration of places where Ashoka believes his moral conquest has reached?

The Kalinga country was conquered by King Priyadarsi [Ashoka], Beloved of the Gods, in the eighth year of his reign. One hundred and fifty thousand persons were carried away captive, one hundred thousand were slain, and many times that number died.

Immediately after the Kalingas had been conquered, King Priyadarsi became intensely devoted to the study of Dharma, to the love of Dharma, and to the inculcation of Dharma.

The Beloved of the Gods, conqueror of the Kalingas, is moved to remorse now. For he has felt profound sorrow and regret because the conquest of a people previously unconquered involves slaughter, death, and deportation.

But there is a more important reason for the King's remorse. The Brahmanas and Sramanas [the priestly and ascetic orders] as well as the followers of other religions and the householders—who all practiced obedience to superiors, parents, and teachers, and proper courtesy and firm devotion to friends, acquaintances, companions, relatives, slaves, and servants—all suffer from the injury, slaughter, and deportation inflicted on their loved ones. Even those who escaped calamity themselves are deeply afflicted by the misfortunes suffered by those friends, acquaintances, companions, and relatives for whom they feel an undiminished affection. Thus all men share in the misfortune, and this weighs on King Priyadarsi's mind. . . .

Therefore, even if the number of people who were killed or who died or who were carried away in the Kalinga war had been only one one-hundredth or one one-thousandth of what it actually was, this would still have weighed on the King's mind. King Priyadarsi now thinks that even a person who wrongs him must be forgiven for wrongs that can be forgiven.

King Priyadarsi seeks to induce even the forest peoples who have come under his dominion [that is, primitive peoples in the remote sections of the conquered territory] to adopt this way of life and this ideal. He reminds them, however, that he exercises the power "to punish, despite his repentance, in order to induce them to desist from their crimes and escape execution.

For King Priyadarsi desires security, self-control, impartiality, and cheerfulness for all living creatures.

King Priyadarsi considers moral conquest [that is, conquest by Dharma, Dharmavijaya] the most important conquest. He has achieved this moral conquest repeatedly both here and among the peoples living beyond the borders of his kingdom, even as far away as six hundred yojanas [about three thousand miles], where the Yona [Greek] king Antiyoka rules, and even beyond Antiyoka in the realms of the four

From N. Nikam and R. McKeon, eds. and trans., *The Edicts of Asoka* (Chicago: University of Chicago Press, 1959), pp. 27–30. © 1959 by The University of Chicago. Reprinted by permission.

kings named Turamaya, Antikini, Maka and Alikasudara, and to the south among the Cholas and Pandyas [in the southern tip of the Indian peninsula] as far as Ceylon. . . .

Even in countries which King Priyadasi's envoys have not reached, people have heard about Dharma and about his Majesty's ordinances and instructions in Dharma, and they themselves conform to Dharma and will continue to do so.

Wherever conquest is achieved by Dharma, it produces satisfaction. Satisfaction is firmly established by conquest by Dharma [since it generates no opposition of conquered and conqueror]. Even satisfaction, however, is of little importance. King Priyadarsi attaches value ultimately only to consequences of action in the other world.

This edict on Dharma has been inscribed so that my sons and great grandsons who may come after me should not think new conquests worth achieving. If they do conquer, let them take pleasure in moderation and find mild punishments. Let them consider moral conquest the only true conquest.

This is good, here and hereafter. Let their pleasure be pleasure in morality [Dharma-rati]. For this alone is good, here and hereafter.

The Golden Age of Chinese Thought

The Eastern Chou [Eastern Zhou] dynasty ruled China from 770 to 249 B.C. During the dynasty's last centuries, however, the land was beset by political and social disintegration and bitter civil war. Ironically, despite the chaotic conditions, this time was the most remarkable golden age of Chinese thought. Many of the philosophies developed during this period had a lasting influence on the cultures of East Asia, similar to the influence classical Greece had on European civilization. This great age of intellectual ferment is also known as the age of "The Hundred Schools."

During this period, many philosophical schools such as the Naturalists, Logicians, Mohists, Taoists [Daoists], Confucianists, and Legalists evolved in China. They questioned old values and institutions and sought new meaning and purpose in life and society. The following selections represent the three most important schools of philosophy that emerged during this period.

27

Confucius, *Analects*

Perhaps the one individual who was most responsible for molding Chinese mind and institutions was Confucius (551–479 B.C.). The name "Confucius" is the Latinized version of K'ung Fu-tzu [Kong Fuzi] (or Master Kung). His family name was K'ung [Kong], and his given name was Chiu [Jiu]. As a transmitter of the wisdom of the past and a creator of new ideas, his primary concern was the fundamental issue of creating utopia. He believed in the perfectability of all people and used the word "*chün-tzu*," [junzi] literally meaning "ruler's son," to describe a perfect or morally superior person. This individual possessed among other qualities the five inner virtues of (1) integrity, *chih* [zhi]; (2) righteousness, *i* [yi]; (3) loyalty and conscientiousness toward others, *chung* [chong]; (4) altruism and reciprocity, *shu*; and (5) virtue, love, and human heartedness, *jen* [ren]. The chün-tzu also possessed culture or polish, *wen*, and ritual or proper etiquette, *li*. Confucius' ideal of a well-ordered society was one based on mutual moral obligations in the five basic human relationships. These bonds were between ruler and subject, husband and wife, father and son, elder and younger brother, and friend and friend. All had assigned roles to play in hierarchical society.

The teachings of Confucius were not accepted widely during his lifetime; for the ensuing few centuries, the Confucian school remained only one among many Chinese schools of philosophy. But for more than two thousand years, from around the second century B.C. to the twentieth century, Confucianism was the official creed of the Chinese Empire. The great influence of this philosophy on the civilizations of the East Asian peoples was unmatched by any other body of thinking.

Among the Confucian classics, the most important work is the *Analects* (Lun Yü) [Lunyu], a collection of sayings by Confucius and his disciples. These sayings were selected and compiled, perhaps in the fourth century B.C., long after Confucius' death, by his disciples' followers. The Analects consist of twenty chapters (or "books") with 497 proverbial-style verses.

QUESTIONS TO CONSIDER

1. Compare and contrast the tenets of Confucianism with those of Taoism (Reading 28) and Legalism (Reading 29).
2. How do you compare the ideas of Confucius with that developed during the golden age of Greek philosophy (Reading 36)?
3. What kind of person is "superior" in the Confucian sense?

The Superior Man

1. Tsze-kung [Zigong] asked what constituted the superior man. The Master said, "He acts before he speaks, and afterwards speaks according to his actions."

2. The Master said, "The superior man is catholic and no partizan. The mean man is a partizan and not catholic."

3. (a) The Master said, "Riches and honours are what men desire. If it cannot be obtained in the proper way, they should not be held. Poverty and meanness are what men dislike. If it cannot be obtained in the proper way, they should not be avoided."

(b) "If a superior man abandons virtue, how can he fulfil the requirements of that name?"

(c) "The superior man does not, even for the space of a single meal, act contrary to virtue. In moments of haste, he cleaves to it. In seasons of danger, he cleaves to it."

4. The Master said, "The superior man, in the world, does not set his mind either for anything, or against anything; what is right he will follow."

5. The Master said, "The superior man thinks of virtue; the small man thinks of comfort. The superior man thinks of the sanctions of law; the small man thinks of favours which he may receive."

6. The Master said, "The mind of the superior man is conversant with righteousness; the mind of the mean man is conversant with gain."

7. The Master said, "The superior man wishes to be slow in his speech and earnest in his conduct."

8. The Master said of Tsze-ch'an [Zichan] that he had four of the characteristics of a superior man:—"in his conduct of himself, he was humble; in serving his superiors, he was respectful; in nourishing the people, he was kind; in ordering the people, he was just."

9. The Master said, "The superior man, extensively studying all learning, and keeping himself under the restraint of the rules of propriety, may thus likewise not overstep what is right."

10. The Master said, "The superior man is satisfied and composed; the mean man is always full of distress."

11. (a) Sze-ma Niu [Sima Niu] asked about the superior man. The Master said, "The superior man has neither anxiety nor fear."

(b) "Being without anxiety or fear!" said Niu;—"does this constitute what we call the superior man?"

(c) The Master said, "When internal examination discovers nothing wrong, what is there to be anxious about, what is there to fear?"

12. The Master said, "The superior man is affable, but not adulatory; the mean man is adulatory, but not affable."

13. The Master said, "The superior man has a dignified ease without pride. The mean man has pride without a dignified ease."

14. Tsze-lu [Zilu] asked what constituted the superior man. The Master said, "The cultivation of himself in reverential carefulness." "And is this all?" said Tsze-lu. "He cultivates himself so as to give rest to others," was the reply. "And is this all?" again asked Tsze-lu. The Master said, "He cultivates himself so as to give rest to all the people." He cultivates himself so as to give rest to all the people:—even Yao and Shun were still solicitous about this.

15. Confucius said, "The superior man has nine things which are subjects with him of thoughtful consideration. In regard to the use of his eyes, he is anxious to see clearly. In regard to the use of his ears, he is anxious to hear distinctly. In regard to his countenance, he is anxious that it should be benign. In regard to his demeanour, he is anxious that it should be respectful. In regard to his speech, he is anxious that it should be sincere. In regard to his doing business, he is anxious that it should be reverently careful. In regard to what he doubts about, he is anxious to question others. When he is angry, he thinks of the difficulties (his anger may involve him in). When he sees gain to be got, he thinks of righteousness."

Virtue

16. The Master said, "Fine words and an insinuating appearance are seldom associated with true virtue."

17. The Master said, "Those who are without virtue cannot abide long either in a condition of poverty and hardship, or in a condition of enjoyment. The virtuous rest in virtue; the wise desire virtue."

18. The Master said, "It is only the (truly) virtuous man, who can love, or who can hate, others."

19. The Master said, "Virtue is not left to stand alone. He who practises it will have neighbours."

20. (a) Yen Yuan asked about perfect virtue. The Master said, "To subdue one's self and return to propriety, is perfect virtue. If a man can for one day subdue himself and return to propriety, all under heaven will ascribe perfect virtue to him. Is the practise of perfect virtue from a man himself, or is it from others?"

(b) Yen Yuan said, "I beg to ask the steps of that process." The Master replied, "Look not at what is contrary to propriety; listen not to what is contrary to propriety; speak not what is contrary to propriety; make no movement which is contrary to propriety." Yen Yuan then said, "Though I am deficient in intelligence and vigour, I will make it my business to practise this lesson."

21. Chung-kung [Zonggong] asked about perfect virtue. The Master said, "It is, when you go abroad, to behave to every one as if you were receiving a great guest; to employ the people as if you were assisting at a great sacrifice; not to do to others as you would not wish done to yourself; to have no murmuring against you in the country, and none in the family." Chung-kung said, "Though I am deficient in intelligence and vigour, I will make it my business to practise this lesson."

22. Tsze-chang [Zizhang] asked Confucius about perfect virtue. Confucius said, "To be able to practise five things everywhere under heaven constitutes perfect virtue." He begged to ask what they were, and was told, "Gravity, generosity of soul, sincerity, earnestness, and kindness. If you are grave, you will not be treated with disrespect. If you are generous, you will win all. If you are sincere, people will repose trust in you. If you are earnest, you will accomplish much. If you are kind, this will enable you to employ the services of others."

Virtuous Government

23. The Master said, "He who exercises government by means of his virtue may be compared to the north polar star, which keeps its place and all the stars turn towards it."

24. (a) The Master said, "If the people be led by laws, and uniformity sought to be given them by punishments, they will try to avoid the punishment, but have no sense of shame."

(b) "If they be led by virtue, and uniformity sought to be given them by the rules of propriety, they will have the sense of shame and moreover will become good."

25. The duke Ai asked, saying, "What should be done in order to secure the submission of the people?" Confucius replied, "Advance the upright and set aside the crooked, then the people will submit. Advance the crooked and set aside the upright, then the people will not submit."

26. Chi K'ang [Ji Kang] asked how to cause the people to reverence their ruler, to be faithful to him and to go on to nerve themselves to virtue. The Master said, "Let him preside over them with gravity;—then they will reverence him. Let him be filial and kind to all;—then they will be faithful to him. Let him advance the good and teach the incompetent;—then they will eagerly seek to be virtuous."

27. The Master said, "If a prince able to govern his kingdom with the complaisance proper to the rules of propriety, what difficulty will he have? If he cannot govern it with that complaisance, what has he to do with the rules of propriety?"

28. (a) Tsze-kung [Zigong] asked about government. The Master said, "The requisites of government are that there be sufficiency of food, sufficiency of military equipment, and the confidence of the people in their ruler."

(b) Tsze-kung said, "If it cannot be helped, and one of these must be dispensed with, which of the three should be foregone first?" "The military equipment," said the Master.

(c) Tsze-kung again asked, "If it cannot be helped, and one of the remaining two must be dispensed with, which of them should be foregone?" The Master answered, "Part with the food. From of old, death has been the lot of all men; but if the people have no faith in their rulers, there is no standing for the State."

29. The Master said, "When a prince's personal conduct is correct, his government is effective without the issuing of orders. If his personal conduct is not correct, he may issue orders, but they will not be followed."

30. (a) Tsze-chang [Zizhang] asked Confucius, saying, "In what way should a person in authority act in order that he may conduct government properly?" The Master replied, "Let him honour the five excellent, and banish away the four bad, things;— then may he conduct government properly." Tsze-chang said, "What are meant by the five excellent things?" The Master said, "When the person in authority is beneficent without great expenditure; when he lays tasks on the people without their repining; when he pursues what he desires without being covetous; when he maintains a dignified ease without being proud; when he is majestic without being fierce."

(b) Tsze-chang said, "What is meant by being beneficent without great expenditure?" The Master replied, "When the person in authority makes more beneficial to the people the things from which they naturally derive benefit;—is not this being beneficent without great expenditure? When he chooses the labours which are proper, makes them labour on them, who will repine? When his desires are set on benevolent government, and he secures it, who will accuse him of covetousness? Whether he has to do with many people or few, or with things great or small, he does not dare to indicate any disrespect;—is not this to maintain a dignified ease without any pride? He adjusts his clothes and cap, and throws a dignity into his looks, so that, thus dignified, he is looked at with awe;—is not this to be majestic without being fierce?"

(c) Tsze-chang then asked, "What are meant by the four bad things?" The Master said, "To put the people to death without having instructed them;—this is called cruelty. To require from them, suddenly, the full tale of work, without having given them warning;—this is called oppression. To issue orders as if without urgency, at first, and, when the time comes, to insist on them with severity;—this is called injury. And, generally, in the giving pay or rewards to men, to do it in a stingy way;—this is called acting the part of a mere official."

28

Taoism [Daoism]: *Lao Tzu* [Lao Zi]

Taoism was probably the second most important and influential philosophy after Confucianism in traditional China. It was antithetical to Confucianism. Taoism emphasized individual life, tranquility, nonconformity, and transcendental spirit, whereas Confucianism taught the importance of regulated social order, an active life, conformity, and worldliness. Taoism had two famous founders: Lao Tzu (meaning

"Venerable Master"), a sixth-century B.C. mythical sage whose historicity is questioned, and Chuang-tzu [Zhuang Zi] (369–286 B.C.). The two most important Taoist texts are *Lao Tzu* or *Tao-te-ching* [Dao de Jing] (Classics of the Way and Its Virtue) and *Chuang Tzu*, probably written in the third century B.C.

Taoism attacked moral idealism and political realism, encouraging people to merge with Tao [Dao], meaning "the Way." Tao was conceived as a natural process, the universal force in the natural world. Tao, which could be sensed only intuitively, was the source of everything—all life, both human and natural.

The way to merge with Tao was through nonaction (wu-wei). This concept did not mean complete inaction but rather taking no action contrary to nature. It meant: "Do nothing and nothing will be not done."

According to this theory, human effort to reform morals or to improve nature was a waste of time and destroyed the harmonies of the universe. Taoism taught that the universe was amoral and operated on its own harmonious principles, which ignored human desires or standards of conduct. This philosophy also stressed passivity, simplicity, and a laissez-faire attitude for the individual. Taoism advised the ruler that "the least government is the best government."

The following selections are from Lao Tzu or Tao-te-ching, a small classic of about 5,250 words. No other Chinese book of this size has had so much influence on the Chinese mind, and no other Chinese book has been translated into English more often than this one. This Chinese classic is a combination of poetry, philosophical speculation, and mystical reflection written in vague, subtle, and cryptic language.

QUESTIONS TO CONSIDER

1. What is the Taoist view of the universe? How do Taoists define human happiness?
2. Why is Taoism considered to be antithetical to Confucian philosophy?
3. Does the Taoist way of life have modern-day relevance? How?

Tao (The Way)

Tao can be talked about, but not the Eternal Tao.
Names can be named, but not the Eternal Name.

As the origin of heaven-and-earth, it is nameless:
As "the Mother" of all things, it is nameable.

So, as ever hidden, we should look at its inner essence:
As always manifest, we should look at its outer aspects.

These two flow from the same source, though differently
  named;
And both are called mysteries.

The Mystery of mysteries is the Door of all essence.

John C. H. Wu, tr., *Tao Teh Ching* (Boston: Shambala, 1989), pp. 3, 5, 7, 9, 29, 35, 53, 75.

The Tao is like an empty bowl,
Which in being used can never be filled up.
Fathomless, it seems to be the origin of all things.
It blunts all sharp edges,
It unties all tangles,
It harmonizes all lights,
It unites the world into one whole.
Hidden in the deeps,
Yet it seems to exist forever.
I do not know whose child it is;
It seems to be the common ancestor of all, the father of things.

Look at it but you cannot see it!
Its name is *Formless.*

Listen to it but you cannot hear it!
Its name is *Soundless.*

Grasp it but you cannot get it!
Its name is *Incorporeal.*

These three attributes are unfathomable;
Therefore they fuse into one.

Its upper side is not bright:
Its under side not dim.
Continually the Unnameable moves on,
Until it returns beyond the realm of things.
We call it the formless Form, the imageless Image.
We call it the indefinable and unimaginable.

Confront it and you do not see its face!
Follow it and you do not see its back!
Yet, equipped with this timeless Tao
You can harness present realities.

To know the origins is initiation into the Tao.

Tao never makes any ado,
And yet it does everything.
If a ruler can cling to it,
All things will grow of themselves.
When they have grown and tend to make a stir,
It is time to keep them in their place by the aid of the
   nameless Primal Simplicity,
Which alone can curb the desires of men.
When the desires of men are curbed, there will be peace,
And the world will settle down of its own accord.

Wu-wei (Non Actrion)

When all the world recognizes beauty as beauty,
   this in itself is ugliness.

When all the world recognizes good as good, this in
   itself is evil.
Indeed, the hidden and the manifest give birth
   to each other.
Difficult and easy complement each other.
Long and short exhibit each other.
High and low set measure to each other.
Voice and sound harmonize each other.
Back and front follow each other.
Therefore, the Sage manages his affairs without ado,
And spreads his teaching without talking.
He denies nothing to the teeming things.
He rears them, but lays no claim to them.
He does his work, but sets no store by it.
He accomplishes his task, but does not dwell upon it.
And yet it is just because he does not dwell on it

That nobody can ever take it away from him.

Government

By not exalting the talented you will cause the people
to cease from rivalry and contention.
By not prizing goods hard to get, you will cause the
   people to cease from robbing and stealing.
By not displaying what is desirable, you will cause the
   people's hearts to remain undisturbed.
Therefore, the Sage's way of governing begins by

> Emptying the heart of desires,
> Filling the belly with food,
> Weakening the ambitions,
> Toughening the bones.

In this way he will cause the people to remain without
knowledge and without desire, and prevent the
knowing ones from any ado.
Practice Non-Ado, and everything will be in order.

The highest type of ruler is one of whose existence
the people are barely aware.
Next comes one whom they love and praise.
Next comes one whom they fear.
Next comes on whom they despise and defy.

When you are lacking in faith,
Others will be unfaithful to you.

The Sage is self-effacing and scanty of words
When his task is accomplished and things have been
   completed,

All the people say, "We ourselves have achieved it!"
Heaviness is the root of lightness.

Serenity is the master of restlessness.
Therefore, the Sage, travelling all day,
Does not part with the baggage-wagon;
Though there may be gorgeous sights to see,
He stays at ease in his own home.

Why should a lord of ten thousand chariots
Display his lightness to the world?
To be light is to be separated from one's root;
To be restless is to lose one's self-mastery.

29

Legalism: The Writings of Han Fei Tzu [Han Fei Zi]

During the warring state period (403–221 B.C.) in ancient China, the most radical school of philosophy—and the one with the most influence on political life—was Legalism (*Fa-chia*) [Fajia]. Legalism became the state ideology of the feudal state of Ch'in [Qin] (221–206 B.C.), which overthrew the Chou [Zhou] dynasty and created the first unified Chinese empire (221 B.C.).

Two leading Legalists were Kung-sun Yang [Gongsun Yang] (d. 300 B.C.), also called Wei Yang or Shang Yang (Lord Shang), and Han Fei Tzu [Han Fei Zi] (d. 223 B.C.). Both served in the government of Ch'in and were political strategists rather than philosophers. These Legalists, rejecting the moral and ethical basis of human conduct and society, accepted Hsün-tzu's [Xun Zi] (300–237 B.C.) view that human nature was basically evil but potentially improvable. They advocated rule by force rather than persuasion and favored a strong centralized government under an absolute ruler.

The main concern of this philosophy was how to make the state a powerful instrument in achieving whatever the ruler desired. The Legalists encouraged war, aggression, and regimentation to strengthen the power of the ruler. To make people obedient and loyal, the Legalists advised the ruler to manipulate two presumably basic human drives: greed and fear. Han Fei Tzu proposed the principle of the "Two Handles" by which the ruler could control others: proportional rewards and harsh punishments. According to this theory, proportional rewards would encourage what was beneficial to the state, and harsh punishments would restrain evil. Because Legalists viewed human nature as basically evil and selfish, and officials as self-seeking and untrustworthy, they advised the ruler to draw up an exhaustive set of laws and regulations to define everyone's duties and responsibilities clearly. Any slight infraction was to be dealt with severely. Thus, they strictly regulated the life and thought of the Chinese people. In the following excerpts, Han Fei Tzu provides a summary of Legalist doctrines.

QUESTIONS TO CONSIDER

1. Why did Legalism gain influence among the rulers of China during the last phase of the Chou period, a politically chaotic time?
2. How does the Legalistic philosophy compare with modern-day totalitarian ideologies?

The Way of the Ruler

The Way is the beginning of all beings and the measure of right and wrong. Therefore the enlightened ruler holds fast to the beginning in order to understand the wellspring of all beings, and minds the measure in order to know the source of good and bad. He waits, empty and still, letting names define themselves and affairs reach their own settlement. Being empty, he can comprehend the true aspect of fullness; being still, he can correct the mover. Those whose duty it is to speak will come forward to name themselves; those whose duty it is to act will produce results. When names and results match, the ruler need do nothing more and the true aspect of all things will be revealed.

Hence it is said: The ruler must not reveal his desires; for if he reveals his desires his ministers will put on the mask that pleases him. He must not reveal his will; for if he does so his ministers will show a different face. So it is said: Discard likes and dislikes and the ministers will show their true form; discard wisdom and wile and the ministers will watch their step. Hence, though the ruler is wise, he hatches no schemes from his wisdom, but causes all men to know their place. Though he has worth, he does not display it in his deeds, but observes the motives of his ministers. Though he is brave, he does not flaunt his bravery in shows of indignation, but allows his subordinates to display their valor to the full. Thus, though he discards wisdom, his rule is enlightened; though he discards worth, he achieves merit; and though he discards bravery, his state grows powerful. When the ministers stick to their posts, the hundred officials have their regular duties, and the ruler employs each according to his particular ability, this is known as the state of manifold constancy.

Hence it is said: "So still he seems to dwell nowhere at all; so empty no one can seek him out." The enlightened ruler reposes in nonaction above, and below his ministers tremble with fear.

This is the way of the enlightened ruler: he causes the wise to bring forth all their schemes, and he decides his affairs accordingly; hence his own wisdom is never exhausted. He causes the worthy to display their talents, and he employs them accordingly; hence his own worth never comes to an end. Where there are accomplishments, the ruler takes credit for their worth; where there are errors, the ministers are held responsible for the blame; hence the ruler's name never suffers. Thus, though the ruler is not worthy himself, he is the leader of the worthy; though he is not wise himself, he is the corrector of the wise. The ministers have the labor; the ruler enjoys the success. This is called the maxim of the worthy ruler.

The Way lies in what cannot be seen, its function in what cannot be known. Be empty, still, and idle, and from your place of darkness observe the defects of others.

See but do not appear to see; listen but do not seem to listen; know but do not let it be known that you know. When you perceive the trend of a man's words, do not change them, do not correct them, but examine them and compare them with the results. Assign one man to each office and do not let men talk to each other, and then all will do their utmost. Hide your tracks, conceal your sources, so that your subordinates cannot trace the springs of your action. Discard wisdom, forswear ability, so that your subordinates cannot guess what you are about. Stick to your objectives and examine the results to see how they match; take hold of the handles of government carefully and grip them tightly. Destroy all hope, smash all intention of wresting them from you; allow no man to covet them.

If you do not guard the door, if you do not make fast the gate, then tigers will lurk there. If you are not cautious in your undertakings, if you do not hide their true aspect, then traitors will arise. They murder their sovereign and usurp his place, and all men in fear make common cause with them: hence they are called tigers. They sit by the ruler's side and, in the service of evil ministers, spy into his secrets: hence they are called traitors. Smash their cliques, arrest their backers, shut the gate, deprive them of all hope of support, and the nation will be free of tigers. Be immeasurably great, be unfathomably deep; make certain that names and results tally, examine laws and customs, punish those who act willfully, and the state will be without traitors.

The ruler of men stands in danger of being blocked in five ways. When the ministers shut out their ruler, this is one kind of block. When they get control of the wealth and resources of the state, this is a second kind of block. When they are free to issue orders as they please, this is a third kind. When they are able to do righteous deeds in their own name, this is a fourth kind. When they are able to build up their own cliques, this is a fifth kind. If the ministers shut out the ruler, then he loses the effectiveness of his position. If they control wealth and resources, he loses the means of dispensing bounty to others. If they issue orders as they please, he loses the means of command. If they are able to carry out righteous deeds in their own name, he loses his claim to enlightenment. And if they can build up cliques of their own, he loses his supporters. All these are rights that should be exercised by the ruler alone; they should never pass into the hands of his ministers.

The way of the ruler of men is to treasure stillness and reserve. Without handling affairs himself, he can recognize clumsiness or skill in others; without laying plans of his own, he knows what will bring fortune or misfortune. Hence he need speak no word, but good answers will be given him; he need exact no promises, but good works will increase. When proposals have been brought before him, he takes careful note of their content; when undertakings are well on their way, he takes careful note of the result; and from the degree to which proposals and results tally, rewards and punishments are born. Thus the ruler assigns undertakings to his various ministers on the basis of the words they speak, and assesses their accomplishments according to the way they have carried out the undertaking. When accomplishments match the undertaking, and the undertaking matches what was said about it, then he rewards the man; when these things do not match, he punishes the man. It is the way of the enlightened ruler never to allow his ministers to speak words that cannot be matched by results.

The enlightened ruler in bestowing rewards is as benign as the seasonable rain; the dew of his bounty profits all men. But in doling out punishment he is as terrible as the thunder; even the holy sages cannot assuage him. The enlightened ruler is never overliberal in his rewards, never overlenient in his punishments. If his rewards are too liberal, then ministers who have won merit in the past will grow lax in their duties; and if his punishments are too lenient, then evil ministers will find it easy to do wrong. Thus if a man has truly won merit, no matter how humble and far removed he may be, he must be rewarded; and if he has truly committed error, no matter how close and dear to the ruler he may be, he must be punished. If those who are humble and far removed can be sure of reward, and those close and dear to the ruler can be sure of punishment, then the former will not stint in their efforts and the latter will not grow proud.

The Two Handles

The enlightened ruler controls his ministers by means of two handles alone. The two handles are punishment and favor. What do I mean by punishment and favor? To inflict mutilation and death on men is called punishment; to bestow honor and reward is called favor. Those who act as ministers fear the penalties and hope to profit by the rewards. Hence, if the ruler wields his punishments and favors, the ministers will fear his sternness and flock to receive his benefits. But the evil ministers of the age are different. They cajole the ruler into letting them inflict punishment themselves on men they hate and bestow rewards on men they like. Now if the ruler of men does not insist upon reserving to himself the right to dispense profit in the form of rewards and show his sternness in punishments, but instead hands them out on the advice of his ministers, then the people of the state will all fear the ministers and hold the ruler in contempt, will flock to the ministers and desert the ruler. This is the danger that arises when the ruler loses control of punishments and favors.

The tiger is able to overpower the dog because of his claws and teeth, but if he discards his claws and teeth and lets the dog use them, then on the contrary he will be overpowered by the dog. In the same way the ruler of men uses punishments and favors to control his ministers, but if he discards his punishments and favors and lets his ministers employ them, then on the contrary he will find himself in the control of his ministers.

T'ien Ch'ang [Tian Chang] petitioned the ruler for various titles and stipends, which he then dispensed to the other ministers, and used an extra large measure in doling out grain to the common people. In this way the ruler, Duke Chien [Jian], lost the exclusive right to dispense favors, and it passed into T'ien Ch'ang's hands instead. That was how Duke Chien came to be assassinated.

Tzu-han [Zihan] said to the ruler of Sung [Song], "Since the people all delight in rewards and gifts, you should bestow them yourself; but since they hate punishments and death sentences, I beg to be allowed to dispense these for you." Thereupon the ruler of Sung gave up the exclusive right to hand out penalties and it passed into the hands of Tzu-han. That was how the ruler of Sung came to be intimidated.

T'ien Ch'ang got to bestow favors as he pleased, and Duke Chien was assassinated; Tzu-han got to hand out punishments as he pleased, and the ruler of Sung was intimidated. Hence, if the ministers of the present age are permitted to share in the right to hand out punishments and favors, the rulers of the time will put themselves in greater peril than Duke Chien and the lord of Sung. Invariably when rulers are intimidated, assassinated, obstructed, or forced into the shade, it has always come about because they relinquished the rights to administer punishment and favor to their ministers, and thus brought about their own peril and downfall.

If the ruler of men wishes to put an end to evil-doing, then he must be careful to match up names and results, that is to say, words and deeds. The ministers come forward to present their proposals; the ruler assigns them tasks on the basis of their words, and then concentrates on demanding the accomplishment of the task. If the accomplishment fits the task, and the task fits the words, then he bestows reward; but if they do not match, he doles out punishment. Hence, if one of the ministers comes forward with big words but produces only small accomplishments, the ruler punishes him, not because the accomplishments are small, but because they do not match the name that was given to the undertaking. Likewise, if one of the ministers comes forward with small words but produces great accomplishments, he too is punished, not because the ruler is displeased at great accomplishments, but because he considers the discrepancy in the name given to the undertaking to be a fault too serious to be outweighed by great accomplishments.

Once in the past Marquis Chao [Zhao] of Han got drunk and fell asleep. The keeper of the royal hat, seeing that the marquis was cold, laid a robe over him. When the marquis awoke, he was pleased and asked his attendants, "Who covered me with a robe?" "The keeper of the hat," they replied. The marquis thereupon punished both the keeper of the royal hat and the keeper of the royal robe. He punished the keeper of the robe for failing to do his duty, and the keeper of the hat for overstepping his office. It was not that he did not dislike the cold, but he considered the trespass of one official upon the duties of another to be a greater danger than cold.

Hence an enlightened ruler, in handling his ministers, does not permit them to gain merit by overstepping their offices, or to speak words that do not tally with their actions. Those who overstep their offices are condemned to die; those whose words and actions do not tally are punished. If the ministers are made to stick to their proper duties and speak only what is just, then they will be unable to band together in cliques to work for each other's benefit.

The ruler of men has two worries: if he employs only worthy men, then his ministers will use the appeal to worthiness as a means to intimidate him; on the other hand, if he promotes men in an arbitrary manner, then state affairs will be bungled and will never reach a successful conclusion. Hence, if the ruler shows a fondness for worth, his ministers will all strive to put a pleasing façade on their actions in order to satisfy his desires. In such a case, they will never show their true colors, and if they never show their true colors, then the ruler will have no way to distinguish the able from the worthless. Because the king of Yüeh [Yue] admired valor, many of his subjects defied death; because King Ling of Ch'u [Chu] liked slim waists, his state was full of half-starved people on diets. Because Duke Huan of Ch'i [Chi] was jealous and loved his ladies in waiting, Shu-tiao [Shudiao] castrated himself in order to be put in charge of the harem; because the duke was fond of unusual food, Yi-ya [Yiya] steamed his son's head and offered it to the duke. Because Tzu-k'uai [Zikuai] of Yen admired worthy men, Tzu-chih [Zizhi] insisted that he would not accept the throne even if it were offered to him.

Thus, if the ruler reveals what he dislikes, his ministers will be careful to disguise their motives; if he shows what he likes, his ministers will feign abilities they do not have. In short, if he lets his desires be known, he gives his ministers a clue as to what attitude they had best assume.

Hence Tzu-chih, by playing the part of a worthy, was able to snatch power from his sovereign; Shu-tiao [Shudiao] and Yi-ya, by catering to the ruler's desires, were able to invade his authority. As a result, Tzu-k'uai died in the chaos that ensued, and

Duke Huan was left unburied for so long that maggots came crawling out the door of his death chamber.

What caused this? It is an example of the calamity that comes when the ruler reveals his feelings to his ministers. As far as the feelings of the ministers go, they do not necessarily love their ruler; they serve him only in the hope of substantial gain. Now if the ruler of men does not hide his feelings and conceal his motives, but instead gives his ministers a foothold by which they may invade his rights, then they will have no difficulty in doing what Tzu-chih and T'ien Ch'ang did. Hence it is said: Do away with likes, do away with hates, and the ministers will show their true colors. And when the ministers have shown their true colors, the ruler of men will never be deceived.

30

Mencius, "Humane Government"

Mencius (371–289 B.C.), a contemporary of Socrates, was perhaps the most influential philosopher in Confucian thought after Confucius. Mencius is the Latinized name for Meng Zi (Meng Tzu). He lived some two centuries after his master Confucius. This was during the warring states period (403–221 B.C.) in Chinese history, when China was fragmented into many contentious small states. Like Confucius, he wandered around as an itinerant philosopher in North China. He traveled from one state to another offering advice on the art of government rulers. As a Confucianist, Mencius distinguished himself by expanding the Confucian concepts of innate goodness in human nature, and humane government, which proposed that government was primarily an exercise in ethics. As the following sections show, he advocated that the government should be led by a moral ruler with the consent of the ruled, and recognized the right of the people to dethrone an unworthy evil ruler. He said that people are the most important element in a state and the sovereignty is of the slightest importance. His thoughts are contained in the *Book of Mencius* (*Meng Zi* or Meng Tzu) which is written in a dialogue style similar to the *Analects* of Confucius.

QUESTIONS TO CONSIDER

1. What policies does Mencius advise rulers to adopt, in order to brig about a stable and prosperous society?
2. How does Mencius suggest making people feel they have "ownership" in their ruler's government and possessions?

The King Hsuan of Chi asked, saying, "Was it so that T'ang banished Chieh and that king Wu smote Chau?" Mencius replied, "It is so in the records."

The kings said, "May a minister then put his sovereign to death?"

Mencius said, "He who outrages the benevolence proper to his nature, is called a robber; he who outrages righteousness, is called a ruffian. The robber and ruffian

Source: James Legge, *The Chinese Classics*, Vol. II, 1971 (Oxford, England: Oxford Univ. Press, 1895), Part II, chapter 8, pp. 167–68, 483–84.

we call a mere fellow. I have heard of the cutting off of the fellow Chau, but I have not heard the putting a sovereign to death, in his case."

Mencius, having an interview with the king of Hsuan of Chi, said to him, "If you are going to build a large mansion, you will surely cause the Master of the workmen to look out for large trees, and when he has found such large trees, you will. . ." be glad, thinking that they will answer for the intended object. Should the workmen hew them so as to make them too small, then your Majesty will be angry, thinking that they will not answer for the purpose. Now, a man spends his youth in learning *the principles of right government*, and, being grown up to vigour, he wishes to put them in practice;—if your Majesty says to him, "For the present put aside what you have learned, and follow me," what shall we say?

"Without the rules of propriety and distinctions of right, the high and the low will be thrown into confusion."

"Without the great principles of government and their various business, there will not be wealth sufficient for the expenditure."

Mencius said, "There are instances of individuals without benevolence, who have got possession of a single State. But there has been no instance of the throne's being got by one without benevolence."

Mencius said, "The people are the most important element in a nation; the spirits of the land and grain are the next; the sovereign is the lightest.

"Therefore to gain the peasantry is the way to become sovereign. . ."

Classical Greece

Greeks differed from other peoples of the ancient Near East in many ways. One difference involved their reducing the conceptual distance between gods and people. Greek gods had human failings on a larger-than-life scale as well as superhuman powers. In the earliest surviving Greek literary works of any importance, we find the poet Homer narrating exciting adventures in which the gods side with humans or against them, but mortal beings are always the focal point. Homer's gods are intent on avenging offenses or insults to themselves, their priests, any semidivine offspring, and their "special interests." For example, Artemis, goddess of the chase, avenges wanton destruction of wild animals, and Hera, goddess of marriage, gets even with home-wreckers. Somewhat less frequently, Homer's gods reward those who serve them well.

As their civilization developed, the Greeks recognized three types of poetry: (1) the epic, exemplified by Homer (Reading 8), (2) lyric poetry, and (3) the poetry of drama, exemplified by Sophocles (see Reading 33) and other playwrights of the Classical Age. Lyric poetry antedated the Classical Age: It was originally composed as words to be sung to the accompaniment of a lyre. (Lyres are rare among us now, but notice how we still refer to the "lyrics" of a song.) Lyric poetry fo-

Source: James Legge, *The Chinese Classics*, Vol. II (Oxford, England: Oxford University Press, 1895), pp. 167–68, 483–84.

cused on what the poet believed as an individual, reflecting personal experiences and desires, whereas the epic poets focused much more on descriptions and narratives of their heroes and events than on their own beliefs about them.

The most interesting political and literary developments of classical Greece—roughly those of the fifth century B.C.—were centered in Athens. Athenian democracy reached its fullest development in the half century following the Persian Wars. The success of Pericles (ca. 495–429 B.C.) in centering the Delian League's treasury and judicial system in Athens brought added income and power. The Athenians used the new wealth well: The classical works of architecture, sculpture, and drama set standards for ages to come.

Three great playwrights—Aeschylus (525–456 B.C.), Sophocles (496–406 B.C.), and Euripides (485–406 B.C.)—developed the art of composing tragedies to be performed at Athenian religious festivals. Periclean Athens also produced the first writing of history as we use the term: In his *Histories*, Herodotus (ca. 485–430 B.C.) gave an account of major events in the history of the world accessible to him, events culminating in the great conflict to defend Greek freedom against the Persian threat. The Age of Pericles ended in the great Peloponnesian War, fought between groups of city-states headed by Athens and Sparta from 431 to 404 B.C., although it was interrupted by truces. All modern accounts of that war still rely heavily on the classic work of Thucydides (ca. 455–400 B.C.) as their principal source. His *Peloponnesian War* is far more critical and fact-oriented than is Herodotus' work, and his style conveys the impression of total objectivity in his descriptions. At the same time, his frequent use of speeches and dialogue makes his narrative colorful and readable.

The high point of Greek philosophy came after art, architecture, and drama had reached their peak in the Age of Pericles. Socrates (ca. 469–399 B.C.), his student Plato (427–347 B.C.), and Plato's student Aristotle (384–322 B.C.) are the three greatest philosophers of classical Greece. Philosophy to the Greeks simply meant "love of wisdom," and a philosopher was someone who seriously pursued knowledge relating to human concerns or cosmic matters.

31

Sappho, *Lyric Songs*

One of the earliest and greatest writers of Greek lyric poetry was Sappho of the Island of Lesbos, who had a remarkable gift for conveying a wealth of universal emotions in a few lines. Only a small fraction of her work survives, and most of it is in "fragments" copied by later Greek writers. Although these surviving fragments cover a broad spectrum of topics, the recurring theme in them is love for both women and men. Sappho's poetry made its contribution to the modern meaning of "lesbian," but she appears unaware of anything unusual in her sexual orientation. When she refers to "Lesbian bards" as far excelling those from other parts of Greece, she is including her contemporary male poets on Lesbos. Ancient Greeks of both sexes were expected to be heterosexual enough to have conventional families; beyond that the only frequent caution raised was for moderation, in sex as in all things.

QUESTIONS TO CONSIDER

1. Why does Aphrodite figure so prominently in Sappho's poetry? Elsewhere in Greek poems, Aphrodite is described as "faithless" or "merciless." What characteristics does she have for Sappho?
2. Poems 1 and 3 are given in both prose and verse translations. Which do you prefer? Why? Would your reasons apply to Homer's epics as well? Are there grounds for the modern custom of keeping lyric poetry in verse translation while giving the epics in prose?

1a. Immortal Aphrodite

Immortal Aphrodite of the broidered throne, daughter of Zeus, weaver of wiles, I pray thee break not my spirit with anguish and distress, O Queen. But come hither, if ever before thou didst hear my voice afar, and listen, and leaving thy father's golden house camest with chariot yoked, and fair fleet sparrows drew thee, flapping fast their wings around the dark earth, from heaven through mid sky. Quickly arrived they; and thou, blessed one, smiling with immortal countenance, didst ask, what now is befallen me, and why now I call, and what I in my mad heart most desire to see. "What Beauty now wouldst thou draw to love thee? Who wrongs thee, Sappho? For even if she flies she shall soon follow, and if she rejects gifts shall yet give, and if she loves not shall soon love, however loth." Come, I pray thee, now too, and release me from cruel cares, and all that my heart desires to accomplish, accomplish thou, and be thyself my ally.

1b.

Ah! gold-enthroned immortal Aphrodite,
Daughter of Zeus, through wily cunning mighty,
    Goddess revered, to thee I pray:
    My soul-subduing griefs allay.

And hither come thou, if before this ever
Thou didst my distant voice to hear endeavor,
    Leaving thy father's house of gold,
    If e'er thou camest to me of old.

Upon thy radiant chariot thee ascending
Thy beauteous sparrows, across the earth contending,
    Carried thee down from heaven on high,
    And busily their wings did ply.

From *The Songs of Sappho in English Translation by Many Poets* (Mt. Vernon, NY: Peter Pauper Press, 1942): 1a. trans. Henry T. Wharton (1898), p. 9; 3a. trans. Edwin D. Cox (1913), pp. 18–19; 3b. trans. J. M. Edmonds, pp. 20–21;. Walter Peterson, ed. and trans., *The Lyric Songs of the Greeks* (Boston: The Gorham Press, 1918): 1b. pp. 17–19; 2. pp. 18–19; 4. p. 22; 5–6. pp. 28–29. Percy Osborne, ed. and trans., *The Poems of Sappho* (London: Elkin Matthews, 1909): 7. p. 44. Lord Rennell of Rodd and Edward Arnold, *Love, Worship and Death: Some Renderings from the Greek Anthology*, trans. Rodd (1908). 8–9. p. 5.

Scarce had they passed, O goddess, earth's wide portal,
When thou, with smiling countenance immortal,
    Didst ask concerning my distress,
    What misfortune did me oppress:

"Why call'st thou me, what all-consuming passion
Devoureth thee? The Goddess of Persuasion
    Shall whom constrain to do thy will?
    Who, Sappho, dares to do thee ill?

"Though now she spurns thee, soon she'll friendship proffer;
    Gifts which she now refuses soon she'll offer;
    Though now thy love she from her fling,
Soon 'gainst thy will her love she'll bring."

And now again come to me, cares dispelling,
My soul's tempestuous fiery passion quelling.
    My heart's desire for me fulfill,
    And be my friend and ally still.

2. To a Beloved Maiden

That man who sits before thy face,
    Godlike he seems to me.
He hears thy words' sweet charming grace,
    Conversing joyously.

Thou laugh'st a laugh of pure delight;
    But in my breast my heart
Violently flutters at thy sight:
    No sound from me will start.

My tongue is lamed, a fiery glow
    My limbs completely sears;
My eyes see nothing, rumblings low
    Play havoc in my ears.

Hot perspiration downward drops,
    And trembling seizes me.
I am ghastly pale, my life-blood stops,
    Near death I seem to be.

3a. To Anactoria in Lydia

Some say that the fairest thing upon the dark earth is a host of horsemen, and some say a host of foot soldiers, and others again a fleet of ships, but for me it is my beloved. And it is easy to make anyone understand this. When Helen saw the most beautiful of mortals, she chose for best that one, the destroyer of all the honor of Troy, and thought not much of child or dear parent, but was led astray by Love, to bestow her heart far off, for woman is ever easy to lead astray when she thinks of no account what is near and dear. Even so, Anactoria, you do not remember, it seems, when she is with you, one the gentle sound of whose footfall I would rather hear and the brightness of whose shining face I would rather see than all the chariots and mail-clad footmen of Lydia. I know that in this world man cannot have the best; yet to pray for a part of what was once shared is better than to forget it.

3b.

A host of horse or foot may be
To some the fairest sight to see,
To some a fleet of ships; to me
    The loved one passes all.
And easy 'tis to prove my case;
She that had the fairest face
Man ever looked on, set her joy
Upon the ravisher of Troy,
    And heedless of the call
Of parent dear or sweetest child,
Left her home, by Love beguiled
    To give her heart afar.
For ever easy to mislead
Is woman, when she pays no heed
To what is near to her and dear.
Anactory, though far thou'rt gone,
Let us be remembered by one
Whose sweet footfall I'd rather hear,
Whose beaming smile I'd rather see,
Than all the Lydian chariotry
    And mighty men of war.
Well wot I no mortal wight
May have the best for his delight;
Yet a one-time happy lot
Is better longed-for than forgot.

4. My Daughter, Cleis

For me a pretty child I claim,
    With form like flowers of gold.
Beloved Cleis is her name,
    Admired by young and old.
Were lovely Lydia all my own,
It could not for her loss atone.

5. Truly I Want to Die

Truly I want to die,
Such was her weeping when she said good-bye.
    These words she said to me:
    "What sad calamity!
Sappho, I leave you most unwillingly."
    To her I made reply:
    "Go with good heart, but try

Not to forget our love in days gone by.
    Else let me call to mind,
    If your heart proves unkind,
The soft delightful ways you leave behind.
    Many a coronet
    Of rose and violet,
Crocus and dill upon your brow you set:
    Many a necklace too
    Round your soft throat you threw,
Woven with me from buds of ravishing hue,
    And often balm you spread
    Of myrrh upon my head,
And royal ointment on my hair you shed."

6. The Bridegroom

Lift high the roof to give him room—
Ye workmen, lift again—
Like mighty Ares now doth come
The bridegroom taller than tall men.

His rivals he outstrips with ease,
Like Lesbian bards those of all Greece.

7.A Certain Kind of Woman

Like the sweet apple which reddens, far up on the high tree-top growing,
Up on the loftiest branch, scarce itself to the gatherers showing—
They rathermore could not reach it; although of it easily knowing.

8. Death

Death is an evil; for the gods chose breath;
Had Death been good the gods had chosen Death.

9. To the Goddess of Evening

Thou, Hesper, bringest homeward all
    That radiant dawn sped far and wide:

The sheep to fold, the goat to stall,
    The children to their mother's side.

32

Herodotus, *Persian Dialogue*

Herodotus (ca. 485–ca. 430 B.C.) has at least three major claims to fame. Often called "The Father of History," he is also the first writer of prose and the first Western political scientist whose work survives. Greeks before him all wrote in verse, since lines in poetic meter are easier to memorize than ordinary sentences. Although Herodotus is known to have read his *Histories* aloud to audiences, the scope of his work and his striving for factual accuracy led him to abandon the poetic form for prose. A great cultural geographer along with everything else, he stated his intention of writing about the varied cultural achievements and the great men among the Greeks as well as the "barbarians" (Asians and Africans). In his *Histories*, Herodotus presents all earlier world history as funneling into the great conflict between Europe and Asia in the form of the Persian attempts to conquer Greece; so we usually entitle his sweeping *Histories*, "The Persian Wars." This source focuses on stories of how the freedom-loving Greeks feared the despotic system of the Persians enough to undergo great sacrifices and to defeat many times their own number of invading forces. Writing in the afterglow of the historic Persian Wars, Herodotus felt positive about democracy, which he tended to equate with Greek freedom. While he shared the prejudice of his ethnocentric countrymen that Greeks had higher ideals than the less-than-free Asians (represented by the Persians), he still had abiding respect for foreign things such as the antiquity of Egyptian civilization and the strength with order preserved by Persian society. His basically democratic political philosophy includes the notion that what works best for one people does not necessarily work best for all peoples.

In the following selection, Herodotus records an episode from Persian history, in which, after a break in monarchical rule, three leading Persians—Otanes, Megabyzos, and Darius, who overthrew Magi usurpers—debate rather much like stereotypical Greeks before deciding on the best form of government for Persia. The three forms of government described here–monarchy, aristocracy (oligarchy), and democracy–remained as the basic options in speculative political thought through the eighteenth century.

QUESTIONS TO CONSIDER

1. In your view, which of the three advocates, Otanes, Megabyzos, or Darius, defends "his" system with the strongest arguments? Which with the weakest? Why?
2. Do the twentieth-century terms *dictatorship, elite rule,* and *democracy* mean about the same thing to us that *monarchy, aristocracy,* and *democracy* meant to the ancient Greeks? Why or why not?

Otanes advised putting governmental power in the hands of the Persian people, saying: "I cannot think about one of us becoming a sole monarch with any pleasure or optimism. You can all see how far Cambyses' arrogance of power drove him. You also had to suffer the same thing under the Magi. How can absolute monarchy be compatible with ethical behavior when it allows the king to do whatever he wants with no accountability? Even the very best man picked for this position would abandon the character traits which made us choose him. Envy is something everyone is born with. Limit-breaking pride will overwhelm him from the very fullness of his power and wealth. Envy heightened by pride will implant all other vices in him. Overwhelming pride and envy will lead him into committing foolish crimes. Logically, of course, an ab-

From Herodotus, *Historien*, Book III, ed. H. Stein (Berlin: Weidmann, 1856), pp. 76–82. Trans. Henry A. Myers.

solute monarch should be free of all malice; after all, he owns all the goods in his realm. The truth of the matter, however, is that he will behave in the very opposite way towards citizens. He will envy the very best people for the very fact that they are better than he. He will be attracted to the worst people and eager to listen to slander. The most contradictory thing about him is that he will be annoyed when people admire him in moderation, since they are not showing him enough humility in doing so. But if you express really strong admiration for him, then he will be put off by your flattery. Now I have been saving the worst for last: He will trample traditional laws into the ground. He will have our women seized for his own pleasure and men killed without trials.

"When the people rule, on the other hand, first of all their regime is called 'equality before the law,' and there can be no more pleasant sounding name than that. Secondly, democracy is free of all the vices of absolute monarchy. It assigns offices by lot and keeps office-holders responsible. All decisions are put before the whole people. And so I am of the opinion that we should abolish monarchy and give the people power, for the people and the state really should be thought of as the same thing."

That was the case made by Otanes. Megabyzos, however, advocated oligarchy, saying: "I support Otanes in opposing one-man rule; however, he is wrong in advising us to make the multitude into a ruler. There is really nothing less reasonable or more arrogant than the blind masses: It would be unbearable to flee the deadly whims of a sole ruler only to end up with the conceit of a mob, who recognizes no limits. A king at least knows what he is doing, but a mob does not. Where are common people supposed to get reasoning power from? They are not born with it, nor have they met up with it in their experiences. Instead the multitude hurls itself like a mountain stream into politics and washes everything away before it. We should form a government by giving the very best men power: We will be among them ourselves. The best men will make the best decisions as a matter of course." That opinion was presented by Megabyzos.

Darius was the third to speak, saying: "I concur with what Megabyzos just said about the masses, but not what he says about oligarchy. There are three possible constitutional forms. If we examine them in their purest forms, that is, the purest democracy, the purest oligarchy and the purest monarchy, the last one towers over the other two in my opinion. There is obviously nothing better than sole government by the best man: Nothing will keep him from looking after his people. Decisions against enemies of the people are best kept secret by a single ruler. In an oligarchy on the other hand, violent personal feuds arise when a good number of men compete for distinction. Everybody tries to force himself ahead. That way, real enemies are made. Out of this, factional conflicts arise, leading to assassinations. It will all end up with a return to monarchy again, and so you can see how much better monarchy is than any other form of government. When the people rule, it is impossible to prevent corruption. When conspiracies occur in a democracy, it is not a matter of hostility among the worst elements but the wrong kind of friendships: Those who work against the common good will do so in cooperation with each other, putting their heads together. That will go on until a leader of the people puts an end to their abuses. The people will admire him for that, and the admired man will lead you back again to one-man rule. Again we see monarchy emerge as the best constitution. To sum it all up briefly: How did the Persian Empire become free? Who gave Persia her freedom: the people, an oligarchy, or the monarchy? The answer certainly convinces me, and we must stick with that system. Anyway, we would be very foolish to discard our ancient and traditional laws, when they have served us so well, since any change is bound to be for the worse."

33

Sophocles, *Antigone*

In modern times, Athenian tragedies have enjoyed substantial revivals—remarkable given the fact that they were intended to be performed only once. What keeps them in modern repertoires is their concern with conflicts having universal interest. Some themes appear much more frequently than others, to be sure. For example, the Greek tragic hero is typically hounded by a fate inherited from the misdeeds of his forebears. Very often, too, he brings doom upon himself with *hubris* a mortal's false pride leading to acts that no mortal can get away with.

In Greek drama, the Chorus often recites or chants odes. These relate events on stage to the will of the gods, punishments for those guilty of hubris, the implacability of fate, or similar cosmic concerns. The Chorus leader (or Choragos) enters the dialogue with questions and observations.

Sophocles' *Antigone*, from which the following selection is taken, remains a 21st-century favorite. Along with the themes of implacable fate and punishment for hubris, this excerpt stresses the recurring conflict—truly global in the history of civilization—between the official, promulgated laws of a governing body and the laws believed by an individual to outweigh the claims of the governing body. Athenians saw this problem as a conflict between nature and convention. Later ages would label the conflict as natural law versus positive law (that is, law set down by people) or, returning close to Sophocles' own phrasing, God-made law versus man-made law.

In the play, Creon, King of Thebes, has declared that Polyneices, a member of the royal family, should not be buried. Polyneices—with considerable justification—had led an attack to take Thebes and was killed in single combat by his own brother, Eteocles. In popular Greek belief, the unburied dead found no rest; therefore, Antigone, sister of Polyneices and Eteocles, violates Creon's decree by giving Polyneices burial rites. Ismene, her sister, had shown sympathy for Antigone but lacked the courage to join her in the deed. The guard who appears in this selection is one of a group sent earlier to guard the unburied body; they had failed the first time to stop Antigone as she slipped by them unnoticed.

QUESTIONS TO CONSIDER

1. What is Antigone's attitude toward her "crime" and the death penalty she is facing?
2. How does Creon bring male-female relations into the heated discussion with Antigone?
3. Is Creon guilty of hubris (the crime of overweening pride)? Could Antigone be accused of hubris as well?
4. When have you heard similar arguments in our own time concerning the existence of laws higher than those humans make?

Chorus: But I know her . . .! Antigone, the ill-fated daughter of the ill-fated Oedipus: why is she under arrest?

From Sophocles, *Antigone*, (Gothae: F.A. Perthes, 1883), Lines 382–768, *passim.* Trans Martha B. Caldwell and Henry A. Meyers.

Guard: We have the culprit here! We seized her right when she was burying him. Now where is the king?

Chorus: Coming from the palace right now. (*Creon enters.*)

Creon: What is all this . . .?

Guard: Sire, no man should ever swear he'll never do a thing. After all your threats, I swore you'd never see me return. But being so surprised and so very glad when we captured the one who did it just made a liar out of me. . . . I am bringing you the woman we caught in the very act of burying him. Take her and judge her guilt any way you like. I've done my part and ought to be relieved of any further responsibility.

Creon: Just what was she doing when you arrested her? Tell me.

Guard: Burying him. It's that simple. . . .

Creon: You there, standing with your head bowed, do you admit the truth of what he charges you with or not?

Antigone: I did it. I don't deny it.

Creon (to Guard): Feel free to go. . . . (Guard exits.)

(to Antigone): Did you know that I gave the order that he should not be buried? Just tell me yes or no.

Antigone: I knew your order just as everyone else knew it.

Creon: Then you knowingly broke the law?

Antigone: I knew what I was doing. Zeus would not have approved such an order. Diké [goddess of justice], whose justice rules the world, has other decrees than such laws of men. I did not feel that your royal strength was enough to nullify the unwritten but eternal laws of the gods, laws which were not declared today or yesterday but have kept their living force from origins no mortal can trace or question. . . .

Creon: This girl has outdone herself in insolence: she broke the law, and now she's boasting about breaking it. If she can get away with that, she is the man, not I.

Antigone: Do you want something else besides my execution?

Creon: No, that will be enough for me.

Antigone: Then why wait? Have me killed. Your words are having no effect on me, and you must be getting tired of mine, although you shouldn't be. I deserve all honor for burying my brother. These men right here would all congratulate me for my courage if their fear of you did not keep them quiet. Kings are really fortunate in being able to adjust laws so that whatever they want to do or say is covered by them.

Creon: Not one single Theban thinks that way but you.

Antigone: They think as I do, but you intimidate them.

Creon: Aren't you ashamed to be the only one talking like that?

Antigone: To show respect for a dead kinsman is nothing to be ashamed of. . . . Be what may, Hades requires the rite of burial.

Creon: Not so that good and bad men will be treated equally.

Antigone: Why do you think you know how the gods below will judge this?

Creon: An enemy does not become a friend by dying.

Antigone: Nature inclines me to love, not to hate.

Creon: Go ahead and die then! Love the dead in the world below if you must!

Chorus: Will you really steal your own son's bride from him?

Creon: Hades will take her, not I.

Chorus: Then she really is to die. . . . Now here comes Haemon, your last surviving son. Isn't it grief bringing him here? He's sad and bitter over Antigone's doom. (*Haemon enters.*)

Creon: We'll find out soon enough. . . . Son, have you heard about your bride's death sentence? Have you come here raving mad, or will you accept my decision as an act of love?

Haemon: Father, I belong to you. Your good judgment will steer me, and I will obey. No marriage will mean more to me than your loving guidance.

Creon: That's the right way to act, recognizing your father's authority like a proper son. Men pray for dutiful sons, each one harming his father's enemies and doing good to his father's friends. . . . So you have made the right choice, not to let this woman cloud your mind. You would find her embraces turning cold, Haemon, and then you'd be left with a hateful armful. What is worse than a false love? Let Hades find her a husband! I will not go back on my word to the state, since she alone among my people disobeyed my law. . . . She must surely die. Let her sing her appeal to Zeus who helps guard family ties. If I let my own family rebel, I would be encouraging lawlessness on a grand scale. The man who heads an orderly household is the right one to help with administering the city-state. I will not put up with anyone who wants to bend the law and dictate to his rulers. The ruler entrusted with the power of the state must be obeyed, whether he happens to be right or wrong. . . . There is no greater evil than disrespect for authority, which destroys homes and city-states alike, demoralizing and defeating armies. Discipline makes life orderly and good. With it we will preserve authority and not be led astray by a woman. If I am overthrown, I want it said at least that I was beaten by a man rather than outmaneuvered by a woman.

Chorus: Unless old age is taking its toll, my mind tells me you are speaking sensibly and justly.

Haemon: Father, reason is the greatest gift of the gods to mankind. It's not my place to say you are not using your share of it; however, there are other men around who reason well, and as your son I feel responsible for telling you their thoughts when they pertain to you. The people are afraid of making you angry and will not let you know what they really think, but I have overheard them whispering their complaints and their grief over this girl's fate. You should know how the people are mourning, saying she is doomed to die a shameful death for a glorious deed. They say she refused to leave her brother's body unburied for the vultures and dogs, and they ask: "Doesn't she deserve a prize of gold?" That's what the people are really saying. . . .

Withdraw your anger, and reverse your decree! Young as I am, I do know this: The ideal would be to have absolute wisdom at all times, but since nature doesn't work like that the next best thing is to pay attention to wisdom and reason in good advice.

Chorus: Sire, if what he says makes sense, you would do well to listen. Haemon, you in turn should consider your father's words. Both of you have spoken well.

Creon: You think it's right for a man to take instruction from a boy?

Haemon: Not if I did not have right on my side, but if I do you shouldn't hold my age against me.

Creon: Are you asking me to condone lawlessness?

Haemon: I'm not asking you to protect lawbreakers.

Creon: Isn't that just what this girl is?

Haemon: The people of Thebes don't think so.

Creon: And so the citizens are going to dictate my decrees?

Haemon: It is you now who are talking like a youngster.

Creon: Am I to rule or let others do it?

Haemon: No true city-state obeys one man alone.

Creon: A city-state belongs to its ruler.

Haemon: You might rule well alone in a desert.

Creon: I can tell this boy is under the woman's influence.

Haemon: That's true if you're a woman. I am thinking of your own interests.

Creon: Good for nothing! Getting into a fight of words with your father . . .! All your arguing is for her sake!

Haemon: For yours and mine, too, and for the sake of the gods below.

Creon: You will never marry her while she's alive.

Haemon: She must die then, but another death will follow hers.

Creon: Another? Are you going so far as to make threats?

Haemon: I'm only trying to keep you from carrying out your vain plan.

Creon: You vain fool: you'll regret condescending talk like that.

Haemon: If you weren't my father, I'd say you were crazy. . . .

Creon: That's enough! I swear by Olympus you will not get away with your raving insults! Bring out the hateful creature: She will die this moment before her bridegroom's very eyes, right close to him.

Haemon: Don't deceive yourself. She will not die with me looking on, and you will never see my face again. Keep on raving as long as you think you have a friend to listen. (*Haemon exits.*)

Chorus: He's gone, Sire. A young man made furious can do great harm.

34

Thucydides, *Peloponnesian War*

As Athenian commerce began to dominate the Aegean Sea trade, Athenian naval power kept member states from leaving the Delian League. Trouble came with increasing discontent over this Athenian domination. There was also a perceived (perhaps real, perhaps imagined) Athenian threat to the freedom of the remaining independent Greek city-states. Many of those city-states allied with Sparta in the Peloponnesian League.

Thucydides, whose *Peloponnesian War* is the classic account of the ensuing conflict, was an Athenian general who failed to carry out his mission of relieving the city of Amphipolis from a Peloponnesian siege; in harmony with Athenian democratic principles and practice, he was relieved of his duties by authority of the people. In his history, Thucydides gives detailed information on troop numbers, types of equipment used, and other data in year-by-year accounts of battles until 411 B.C., when his book breaks off unfinished. He makes his work more vivid with speeches by leading figures on both sides. Although Thucydides was not present to hear many of the speeches, which are presented as extended verbatim quotations, he claims to give their approximate content accurately.

In the first excerpt that follows, we find Pericles highlighting the greatness of Athenian democracy in a funeral oration after the first battle casualties. But two years later Pericles was dead, and Athenian democracy became more extreme. As Thucydides saw it, the Athenian people began to suppose that whatever they said was law. In the second excerpt, Thucydides writes about a confrontation with the Melians in the sixteenth year of the war. In this account, the Athenians seem to believe that might makes right and that the Athenian Empire is mighty enough to enforce its policies—even genocidal ones—on all would-be enemies. In the third excerpt, Thucydides describes the Great Plague, which struck Athens from 430 to 426 B.C. and killed about a third of the population. Although he describes the symptoms of the disease, we really do not know what the plague was—some have said it may have been measles, scarlet fever, or yaws—which took the poor and wealthy alike. Even Pericles succumbed to the disease, and Athens would never again know a statesman of his kind.

QUESTIONS TO CONSIDER

1. What does "democracy" appear to mean to Pericles apart from broad participation in government? (the first excerpt)
2. Does Pericles state or imply that the rights of nonconformists or dissenters in Athens are protected under Athenian democracy? (the first excerpt)
3. What does Pericles appear to have in mind when he speaks of Athens as a model for all of Greece? (the first excerpt)
4. These selections contrast Athens as an educational model for Greece (the first excerpt) and as a state demanding compliance through deadly force (the second excerpt). Do you think the contrast is too neat to be true?
5. Does Thucydides—the fired Athenian general—give the impression of writing more as dramatist than as historian when stressing evils in the system that rejected him? Or does he convey the image of a realistic historian regretfully documenting the twisting of democratic ideals? (the second excerpt).
6. How did the plague come to Athens? (the third excerpt)
7. Can you think of other diseases that had a great impact on civilization? (the third excerpt)

Pericles' Funeral Oration

Pericles . . . was chosen to give the funeral oration for the first who had fallen. When the proper time arrived, he advanced from the tomb . . . and spoke as follows:

From Thucydides, *Peloponnesian War*, trans. Richard Crawley (London: J. M. Dent & Co., 1903), Vol. 1, pp. 120–28; 128–33. Vol. 2, pp. 59–67. Language modernized.

"I shall begin with our ancestors. . . . They dwelt in this country without interruption from generation to generation, and handed it down to the present time by their bravery. . . .

"Our constitution does not copy the laws of neighboring states; we are rather a model for others than imitators ourselves. Its administration favors the many instead of the few; this is why it is called a democracy. If we look at the laws, they afford equal justice to all in settling private differences. As for prestige, advancement in public life goes to men with reputations for ability: class considerations are not allowed to interfere with merit, nor again does poverty bar the way. If a man is able to serve the state, he is not hindered by obscure origins or poverty. The freedom we enjoy in our government extends also to our private life. There . . . we do not feel called upon to be angry with our neighbor for doing what he likes, or even to indulge in those injurious looks which cannot fail to be offensive, although they inflict no actual harm. But all this ease in our private relations does not make us lawless as citizens. . . . We obey the magistrates and the laws, particularly those for the protection of the injured, whether they are actually on the statute book, or belong to that code which, although unwritten, yet cannot be broken without acknowledged disgrace.

"Further, we provide plenty of means for the mind to refresh itself from business. We celebrate games and sacrifices all the year round, and the elegance of our private establishments forms a daily source of pleasure and helps to banish our cares. Then, too, the magnitude of our city draws the produce of the world into our harbor, so that to the Athenian the products of other countries are as familiar a luxury as those of his own.

"If we turn to our military policy, there also we differ from our antagonists. We throw open our city to the world, and never pass laws to exclude foreigners from any opportunity of learning or observing, although the eyes of the enemy may occasionally profit from our liberality. We rely less on secrecy than on the native spirit of our citizens. In education, where our rivals from their very cradles seek after manliness through a very painful discipline, at Athens we live as we please, and yet are just as ready to encounter every legitimate danger. . . . And yet if with habits not of labor but of ease, and with courage which is not artificial but real, we are still willing to encounter danger, we have the double advantage of escaping the experience of hardships in anticipation and of facing them in the hour of need as fearlessly as those who are never free from them.

"We cultivate refinement without extravagance and knowledge without effeminacy; wealth we employ more for use than for show, and place the real disgrace of poverty not in admitting the fact of it but in declining the struggle against it. Our public men have, besides politics, their private affairs to tend to, and our ordinary citizens, though occupied with the pursuits of industry, are still fair judges of public matters. Unlike any other nation, we regard a man who takes no part in these duties not as unambitious but as useless. . . . Instead of looking on discussion as a stumbling block in the way of action, we Athenians consider it an indispensable preliminary to any wise action at all.

"In generosity we are equally singular, acquiring our friends by conferring, not receiving, favors. Yet, of course, the doer of the favor is the firmer friend of the two, in order by continued kindness to keep the recipient in his debt; while the debtor feels less keenly from the very consciousness that the return he makes will be a repayment, not a free gift, and it is only the Athenians who, fearless of consequences, confer their benefits not from calculations of expediency, but in the confidence of liberality.

"In short, I say that as a city we are the school of Hellas; while I doubt if the world can produce a man who is equal to so many emergencies where he has only himself to depend upon, and who is graced by so happy a versatility as the Athenian . . . For Athens alone of her contemporaries is found when tested to be greater than her reputation, and alone gives no occasion to her assailants to blush at the antagonist by whom they have been worsted, or to her subjects to question her title by merit to rule. Rather, the admiration of the present and succeeding ages will be ours, since we have not left our power without witness, but have shown it by mighty proofs; and far from needing a Homer for our panegyrist, or another poet whose verses might charm for the moment only for the impression which they gave, to melt at the touch of fact, we have forced every sea and land to be the highway of our daring, and everywhere, whether for evil or for good, have left imperishable monuments behind us. Such is the Athens for which these men, in the assertion of their resolve not to lose her, nobly fought and died; and well may every one of their survivors be ready to suffer in her cause.

"If I have dwelt at some length upon the character of our country, it has been to show that our stake in the struggle is not the same as theirs who have no such blessings to lose, and also that the praise of the men over whom I am now speaking might be confirmed by definite proofs. My speech is now largely complete; for the Athens that I have celebrated is only what the heroism of these and others like them have made her, men whose fame, unlike that of most Hellenes, will be found to be only proportionate to what they deserve. And if a test of worth be wanted, it is to be found in their last scene, and this not only in the cases in which it set the final seal upon their merit, but also in those in which it gave the first intimation of their having any. For there is justice in the claim that steadfastness in his country's battles should be as a cloak to cover a man's other imperfections, since the good more than outweighed his demerits as an individual. . . . And while committing to hope the uncertainty of final success, in the business before them they thought fit to act boldly and trust in themselves. Thus choosing to die resisting, rather than to live submitting.

"So died these men as became Athenians. You, their survivors, must be determined to have as unfaltering a resolution in the field, though you may pray that it may have a happier outcome. . . . You must yourselves realize the power of Athens, and feed your eyes upon her from day to day, till the love of her fills your hearts; and then when all her greatness shall break upon you, you must reflect that it was by courage, sense of duty, and a keen feeling of honor in action that men were enabled to win all this, and that no personal failure in an enterprise could make them consent to deprive their country of their bravery except as a sacrifice of the most serious contribution they could offer. For this offering of their lives made in common by them all, each of them individually receives that renown which never grows old, and for a tomb, not so much that in which their bones have been deposited, but that noblest of shrines wherein their glory is laid up to be eternally remembered upon every occasion on which deed or story shall call for its commemoration. . . . Take these as your model, and recognize that happiness comes from freedom and freedom comes from courage; never decline the dangers of war. For it is not the miserable who have the most reason to risk their lives; they have nothing to hope for: instead, it is they to whom continued life may bring reverses as yet unknown, and to whom a fall, if it came, would be most tremendous in its consequences. Surely, to a man of spirit, the degradation of cowardice must be immeasurably more grievous than the unfelt death which strikes him in the midst of his strength and patriotism.

"Comfort, therefore, not condolence, is what I have to offer to the parents of the dead who may be here. Numberless are the chances to which, as they know, the life of man is subject; but fortunate indeed are they who draw their lot a death so glorious as that which has caused your mourning, and to whom life has been so exactly measured as to terminate in the happiness in which it has been passed. . . . If I must say anything on the subject of female excellence to those of you who will now be in widowhood, it will all be comprised in this brief exhortation: great will be your glory in not falling short of your natural character; and greatest will be hers who is least talked of among the men whether for good or bad. My task is now finished. I have performed it to the best of my ability, and in words at least the requirements of the law are now satisfied. If deeds be in question, those who are here interred have received part of their honors already, and for the rest, their children will be brought up till manhood at the public expense: thus the state offers a valuable prize as the garland of victory in this race of valor, for the reward both of those who have fallen and their survivors. And where the rewards for merit are greatest, there the best citizens are found.

"And now that you have brought to a close your lamentations for your relatives, you may depart."

The Melian Conference

The Melians are a colony of Lacedæmon [Sparta] that would not submit to the Athenians like the other islanders, and at first remained neutral and took no part in the struggle, but afterwards upon the Athenians using violence and plundering their territory, assumed an attitude of open hostility. . . . The generals, encamping in their territory . . . before doing any harm to their land, sent envoys to negotiate. These the Melians did not bring before the people, but bade them state the object of their mission to the magistrates and the few; upon which the Athenian envoys spoke as follows: . . .

Athenians: "For ourselves, we shall not trouble you with specious pretences—either of how we have a right to our empire because we overthrew the Mede, or are now attacking you because of wrong that you have done us—and make a long speech which would not be believed; and in return we hope that you, instead of thinking to influence us by saying that you did not join the Lacedæmonians [Spartans], although their colonists, or that you have done us no wrong, will aim at what is feasible, holding in view the real sentiments of us both; since you know as well as we do that right, as the world goes, is only in question between equals in power, while the strong do what they can and the weak suffer what they must."

Melians: "As we think, at any rate, it is expedient—we speak as we are obliged, since you enjoin us to let right alone and talk only of interest—that you should not destroy what is our common protection, the privilege of being allowed in danger to invoke what is fair and right, and even to profit by arguments not strictly valid if they can be got to pass current. And you are as much interested in this as any, as your fall would be a signal for the heaviest vengeance and an example for the world to meditate upon."

Athenians: "The end of our empire, if end it should, does not frighten us: a rival empire like Lacedæmon, even if Lacedæmon was our real antagonist, is not so terrible to the vanquished as subjects who by themselves attack and overpower their rulers. . . . We will now proceed to show you that we are come here in the interest of our empire, and that we shall say what we are now going to say for the preservation of your country; as we would fain exercise that empire over you without trouble, and see you preserved for the good of us both."

Melians: "And how, pray, could it turn out as good for us to serve as for you to rule?"

Athenians: "Because you would have the advantage of submitting before suffering the worst, and we should gain by not destroying you."

Melians: "So that you would not consent to our being neutral, friends instead of enemies, but allies of neither side."

Athenians: "No; for your hostility cannot so much hurt us as your friendship will be an argument to our subjects of our weakness, and your enmity of our power."

Melians: "Is that your subjects' idea of equity, to put those who have nothing to do with you in the same category with peoples that are most of them your own colonists, and some conquered rebels?"

Athenians: "As far as right goes they think one has as much of it as the other, and that if any maintain their independence it is because they are strong, and that if we do not molest them it is because we are afraid; so that besides extending our empire we should gain in security by your subjection; the fact that you are islanders and weaker than others rendering it all the more important that you should not succeed in baffling the masters of the sea." . . .

Melians: "Well then, if you risk so much to retain your empire, and your subjects to get rid of it, it were surely great baseness and cowardice in us who are still free not to try everything that can be tried, before submitting to your yoke."

Athenians: "Not if you are well advised, the contest not being an equal one, with honour as the prize and shame as the penalty, but a question of self-preservation and of not resisting those who are far stronger than you are."

Melians: "But we know that the fortune of war is sometimes more impartial than the disproportion of numbers might lead one to suppose; to submit is to give ourselves over to despair, while action still preserves for us a hope that we may stand erect."

Athenians: "Hope, danger's comforter, may be indulged in by those who have abundant resources, if not without loss at all events without ruin; but its nature is to be extravagant, and those who go so far as to put their all upon the venture see it in its true colours only when they are ruined. . . ."

Melians: "You may be sure that we are as well aware as you of the difficulty of contending against your power and fortune, unless the terms be equal. But we trust that the gods may grant us fortune as good as yours, since we are just men fighting against unjust, and that what we want in power will be made up by the alliance of the Lacedæmonians. . . ."

Athenians: "When you speak of the favour of the gods, we may as fairly hope for that as yourselves; neither our pretensions nor our conduct being in any way contrary to what men believe of the gods, or practise among themselves. Of the gods we believe, and of men we know, by a necessary law of their nature they rule wherever they can. . . . But when we come to your notion about the Lacedæmonians, which leads you to believe that shame will make them help you, here we bless your simplicity but do not envy your folly. The Lacedæmonians, when their own interests or their country's laws are in question, are the worthiest men alive; of their conduct towards others much might be said, but no clearer idea of it could be given than by shortly saying that of all the men we know they are most conspicuous in considering what is agreeable to be honourable, and what is expedient to be just. Such a way of thinking does not promise much for the safety which you now unreasonably count upon."

Melians: "But it is for this very reason that we now trust to their respect for expediency to prevent them from betraying the Melians, their colonists, and thereby losing the confidence of their friends in Hellas and helping their enemies." . . .

Athenians: "Yes, but what an intending ally trusts to, is not the goodwill of those who ask his aid, but a decided superiority of power for action; and the Lacedæmonians look to this even more than others. At least, such is their distrust of their home resources that it is only with numerous allies that they attack a neighbour; now is it likely that while we are masters of the sea they will cross over to an island? . . . Your strongest arguments depend upon hope and the future, and your actual resources are too scanty, as compared with those arrayed against you, for you to come out victorious. You will therefore show great blindness of judgment, unless, after allowing us to retire, you can find some counsel more prudent than this. You will surely not be caught by that idea of disgrace, which in dangers that are disgraceful, and at the same time too plain to be mistaken, proves so fatal to mankind. . . . You will not think it dishonourable to submit to the greatest city in Hellas, when it makes you the moderate offer of becoming its tributary ally, without ceasing to enjoy the country that belongs to you; nor when you have the choice given you between war and security, will you be so blinded as to choose the worse. And it is certain that those who do not yield to their equals, who keep terms with their superiors, and are moderate towards their inferiors, on the whole succeed best. Think over the matter, therefore, after our withdrawal, and reflect once and again that it is for your country that you are consulting, that you have not more than one, and that upon this one deliberation depends its prosperity or ruin."

The Athenians now withdrew from the conference; and the Melians, left to themselves, came to a decision corresponding with what they had maintained in the discussion, and answered, "Our resolution, Athenians, is the same as it was at first. We will not in a moment deprive of freedom a city that has been inhabited these seven hundred years; but we put our trust in the fortune by which the gods have preserved it until now, and in the help of men, that is, of the Lacedæmonians; and so we will try and save ourselves. Meanwhile we invite you to allow us to be friends to you and foes to neither party, and to retire from our country after making such a treaty as shall seem fit to us both."

Such was the answer of the Melians. The Athenians now departing from the conference said, "Well, you alone, as it seems to us, judging from these resolutions, regard what is future as more certain than what is before your eyes, and what is out of sight, in your eagerness, as already coming to pass; and as you have staked most on, and trusted most in, the Lacedæmonians, your fortune, and your hopes, so will you be most completely deceived."

The Athenian envoys now returned to the army; and the Melians showing no signs of yielding, the generals at once betook themselves to hostilities. . . . Subsequently the Athenians returned with most of their army, leaving behind them a certain number of their own citizens and of the allies to keep guard by land and sea. The force thus left stayed on and besieged the place. . . .

Summer was now over. The next winter the Lacedæmonians intended to invade the Argive territory, but arriving at the frontier found the sacrifices for crossing unfavourable, and went back again. . . . About the same time the Melians again took another part of the Athenian lines which were but feebly garrisoned. Reinforcements afterwards arriving from Athens, . . . the siege was now pressed vigorously; and some treachery taking place inside, the Melians surrendered at discretion to the Athenians, who put to death all the grown men whom they took, and sold the women and children for slaves, and subsequently sent out five hundred colonists and inhabited the place themselves.

Thucydides on the Plague

In the first days of summer the Lacedæmonians and their allies, with two-thirds of their forces as before, invaded Attica, under the command of Archidamus, son of Zeuxidamus, king of Lacedæmon, and sat down and laid waste the country. Not many days after their arrival in Attica the plague first began to show itself among the Athenians. It was said that it had broken out in many places previously in the neighborhood of Lemnos and elsewhere; but a pestilence of such extent and mortality was nowhere remembered. Neither were the physicians at first of any service, ignorant as they were of the proper way to treat it, but they died themselves the most thickly, as they visited the sick most often; nor did any human art succeed any better. Supplications in the temples, divinations, and so forth were found equally futile, till the overwhelming nature of the disaster at least put a stop to them altogether.

It first began, it is said, in the parts of Ethiopia above Egypt, and then descended into Egypt and Libya and into most of the king's country [Persian Empire]. Suddenly falling upon Athens, it first attacked the population in Piraeus [Athenian port],—which was the occasion of their saying that the Peloponnesians had poisoned the reservoir, there being as yet no wells there—and afterwards appeared in the upper city, when the deaths became much more frequent. All speculation as to its origin and its causes, if causes can be found adequate to produce so great a disturbance, I leave to other writers, whether lay or professional; for myself, I shall simply set down its nature, and explain the symptoms by which perhaps it may be recognized by the student, if it should ever break out again. This I can better do, as I had the disease myself, and watched its operation in the case of others.

That year then is admitted to have been otherwise unprecedentedly free from sickness; and such few cases as occurred all determined in this. As a rule, however, there was no ostensible cause; but people in good health were all of a sudden attacked by violent heats (temperatures) in the head, and redness and inflammation in the eyes, the inward parts, such as the throat or tongue, becoming bloody and emitting an unnatural and fetid breath. These symptoms were followed by sneezing and hoarseness, after which the pain soon reached the chest and produced a hard cough. When it fixed in the stomach, it upset it; and discharges of bile of every kind named by the physicians ensued, accompanied by a great distress. In most cases also an ineffectual retching followed, producing violent spasms, which in some cases ceased soon after, in others much later. Externally the body was not very hot to the touch, nor pale in its appearance, but reddish, livid, and breaking out into small pustules and ulcers. But internally it burned so that the patient could not bear to have on him clothing or linen even of the lightest description; or indeed to be otherwise than stark naked. What they would have liked best would have been to throw themselves into cold water; as indeed was done by some of the neglected sick, who plunged into the rain-tanks in their agonies of unquenchable thirst; though it made no difference whether they drank little or much. Besides this, the miserable feeling of not being able to rest or sleep never ceased to torment them. The body meanwhile did not waste away so long as the distemper was at its height, but held out to a marvel against its ravages; so that when they succumbed, as in most cases, on the seventh or eighth day to internal inflammation, they had still some strength in them. But if they passed this stage, and the disease descended further into the bowels, inducing a violent ulceration there accompanied by severe diarrhea, this brought on a weakness which was generally fatal. For the disorder first settled in the head, ran its course from there through the whole of the body, and even where it did not prove mortal, it still left its mark on the extremities; for it settled in the private parts, the fingers and toes, and many escaped with the loss of these, some too with that of their eyes. Others again were seized with an entire loss of memory on their first recovery, and did not know either themselves or their friends.

But while the nature of the distemper was such as to baffle all description, and its attacks almost too grievous for human nature to endure, it was still in the following circumstance that its difference from all ordinary disorders was most clearly shown. All the birds and beasts that prey upon human bodies, either abstained from touching them (though there were many lying unburied), or died after tasting them. In proof of this, it was noticed that birds of this kind actually disappeared; they were not about the bodies, or indeed to be seen at all. But of course the effects which I have mentioned could best be studied in a domestic animal like a dog.

Such then, if we pass over the varieties of particular cases, which were many and peculiar, were the general features of the distemper. Meanwhile the town enjoyed an immunity from all the ordinary disorders; or if any case occurred, it ended in this. Some died in neglect, others in the midst of every attention. No remedy was found that could be used as a specific; for what did good in one case, did harm in another. Strong and weak constitutions proved equally incapable of resistance, all alike being swept away, although [they] dieted with the utmost precaution. By far the most terrible feature in the malady was the dejection which ensued when any one felt himself sickening, for the despair into which they instantly fell took away their power of resistance, and left them a much easier prey to the disorder; besides which, there was the awful spectacle of men dying like sheep, through having caught the infection in nursing each other. This caused the greatest mortality. On the one hand, if they were afraid to visit each other, they perished from neglect; indeed many houses were emptied of their inmates for want of a nurse: on the other, if they ventured to do so, death was the consequence. This was especially the case with such as made any pretensions to goodness: honor made them unsparing of themselves in their attendance in their friends' houses, where even the members of the family were at last worn out by the moans of the dying, and succumbed to the force of the disaster. Yet it was with those who had recovered from the disease that the sick and the dying found most compassion. These knew what it was from experience, and had now no fear for themselves; for the same man was never attacked twice—never at least fatally. And such persons not only received the congratulations of others, but themselves also, in the elation of the moment, half entertained the vain hope that they were for the future safe from any disease whatsoever.

An aggravation of the existing calamity was the influx from the country into the city, and this was especially felt by the new arrivals. As there were no houses to receive them, they had to be lodged at the hot season of the year in stifling cabins, where the mortality raged without restraint. The bodies of dying men lay one upon another, and half-dead creatures reeled about the streets and gathered round all the fountains in their longing for water. The sacred places also in which they had quartered themselves were full of corpses of persons that had died there, just as they were; for as the disaster passed all bounds, men, not knowing what was to become of them, became utterly careless of everything, whether sacred or profane. All the burial rites before in use were entirely upset, and they buried the bodies as best they could. Many from want of proper appliances, through so many of their friends having died already, had recourse to the most shameless sepulchers: sometimes getting the start of those who had raised a pile, they threw their own dead body upon the stranger's pyre and ignited it; sometimes they tossed the corpse which they were carrying on the top of another that was burning, and so went off.

Nor was this the only form of lawless extravagance which owed its origin to the plague. Men now coolly ventured on what they had formerly done in a corner, and not just as they pleased, seeing the rapid transitions produced by persons in prosperity suddenly dying and those who before had nothing succeeding to their property. So they resolved to spend quickly and enjoy themselves regarding their lives and riches as alike things of a day. Perseverance in what men called honor was popular with none, it was so uncertain whether they would be spared to attain the object; but it was settled that present enjoyment, and all that contributed to it, was both honorable and useful. Fear of gods or law of man there was none to restrain them. As for the first, they judged it to be just the same whether they worshipped them or not, as they saw all alike perishing; and for the last, no one expected to live to be brought to trial for his offense, but each felt that a far severer sentence had been already passed upon them all and hung ever over their heads, and before this fell it was only reasonable to enjoy life a little.

Such was the nature of the calamity, and heavily did it weigh on the Athenians; death raging within the city and devastation without.

35

Xenophon, *The Government of Sparta*

Xenophon (ca. 430 B.C.–ca. 354 B.C.), a Greek historian and philosophical essayist, fought for his native Athens in several campaigns in the Peloponnesian War. He came under the influence of Socrates, whom he greatly admired, but he did not stay in Athens after the war ended. In 401 B.C. he was recruited to serve in an expedition of the younger Cyrus in Persia against his brother, Artaxerxes II. When Cyrus was assassinated, most of the Greek officers commanding Greek forces serving him were murdered. Xenophon became a leader of the Greek forces returning to safe territory after a long march under very difficult circumstances, which he records in detail in his *Anabasis* (*Up-Country March*).

Xenophon went on to fight for the Spartans in conflicts following the Peloponnesian War. In the selection below, he gives a description of the basic laws or constitution given to the Spartans by one of their legendary heroes and sages, Lycurgus.

QUESTIONS TO CONSIDER

1. The image of Sparta in our own world focuses rather negatively on Spartan militarism. What do you suppose writers in other ages—such as Nicolo Machiaveli during the Italian Renaissance (Reading 94)—found good enough to be worthy of imitation in the governmental structures and practices attributed to Lycurgus?
2. In what ways are the Spartan ideas associated with Lycurgus different from those of Athens as presented by Pericles (Reading 34)? Are their some similarities in aims? Do you think Xenophon is consciously emphasizing Spartan traits that helped Sparta defeat Athens?
3. Would you agree with Xenophon that women in authoritarian Sparta have a better life than those in democratic Athens or most other Greek states?

Reflecting once how Sparta, one of the least populous of states, had proved the most powerful and celebrated city in Greece, I wondered how this result had been produced. When I proceeded, however, to contemplate the institutions of the Spartans, I wondered no longer.

Lycurgus, who made laws for them, by obedience to which they have flourished, I not only admire, but consider to have been in the fullest sense a wise man; for he rendered his country preeminent in prosperity, not by imitating other states, but by making ordinances contrary to those of most governments.

With regard, for example, to the procreation of children, other people feed their young pregnant women on the most moderate quantity of vegetable food possible, and on the least possible quantity of meat, while they keep them from wine altogether; and as most of the men engaged in trades are sedentary, so the rest of the Greeks think it proper that their young women should sit quiet and spin wool. Lycurgus, on the contrary, thought that female slaves were competent to furnish clothes; and, considering that the production of children was the noblest duty of the free, he enacted that the female should practice bodily exercises no less than the male sex; and he appointed for the women contests with one another, just as for the men, expecting that when both parents were rendered strong, a stronger offspring would be born from them.

Observing, too, that men of other nations associated with their wives, during the early part of their intercourse, without restraint, he made enactments at variance with this practice; for he ordained that a man should think it shame to be seen going in to his wife, or coming out from her. When married people meet in this way, they must feel stronger desire for the company of one another, and whatever offspring is produced must thus be rendered more robust than if the parents were satiated with each other's company.

In addition to these regulations, he also took from the men the liberty of marrying when each of them pleased, and appointed that they should contract marriages only when they were in full bodily vigor, deeming this injunction also conducive to the production of an excellent offspring. Seeing also that if old men chanced to have

From Xenophon, On the Government of Lacedaemon [Sparta] in Xenophon's *Minor Works*, transl. J. S. Watson (London: George Bell & Sons, 1905), pp. 204–239, *passim*; condensed and language slightly modernized by Allen C. Myers.

young wives, they watched their wives with the utmost strictness, he made a law quite opposed to this feeling; for he appointed that an old man should introduce to his wife whatever man in the prime of life he admired for his corporeal and mental qualities, in order that she might have children by him. If, again, a man was unwilling to associate with his wife, and yet was desirous of having proper children, he made a provision that whatever woman he saw likely to have offspring, and of good disposition, he might, on obtaining the permission of her husband, have children by her. Many similar permissions he gave; for women are willing to have two families, and men to receive brothers to their children, who are equal to them in birth and standing, but have no claim to share property.

Let him who wishes, then, consider whether Lycurgus, in thus making enactments different from those of other legislators, in regard to the procreation of children, secured for Sparta a race of men eminent for size and strength.

Having given this account of the procreation of children, I wish also to detail their education. The other Greeks set slaves over their sons to take charge of them, as soon as the children can understand what is said to them, and send them to schoolmasters, to learn letters, music, and exercises. They also render their children's feet delicate by the use of sandals, and weaken their bodies by changes of clothes; and as to food, they regard appetite as the measure of what to take. But Lycurgus, instead of allowing each citizen to set slaves as guardians over his children, appointed a man to have the care of them all, one of those from whom the chief magistrates are chosen; and he is called the Paedonomus. He invested this man with full authority to assemble the boys, and, if he found any one negligent of his duties, to punish him severely. He assigned him also some of the grown-up boys as scourge-bearers, that they might inflict whatever chastisement was necessary; so that great dread of disgrace, and great willingness to obey, prevailed among them.

Instead, also, of making their feet soft with sandals, he enacted that they should harden them by going without sandals; thinking that, if they exercised themselves in this state, they would go up steep places with far greater ease, and descend declivities with greater safety; and that they would also leap, and skip, and run faster unshod, if they had their feet inured to doing so, than shod. Instead of being rendered effeminate, too, by a variety of dresses, he made it a practice they should accustom themselves to one dress throughout the year; thinking that they would thus be better prepared to endure cold and heat.

As to food, he ordained that they should exhort the boys to take only such a quantity as never to be oppressed with repletion, supposing that, they would be the better able, if they should be required, to support toil under a scarcity of supplies, to persevere in exertion, and would be less desirous of sauces, more easily satisfied with any kind of food, and pass their lives in greater health. Yet that the boys might not suffer too much from hunger, Lycurgus, though he did not allow them to take what they wanted without trouble, gave them liberty to steal certain things to relieve the cravings of nature; and he made it honorable to steal as many cheeses as possible; as it is evident that he who designs to steal must be wakeful during the night, and use deceit, and lay plots; and, if he would gain anything of consequence, must employ spies. All these things he taught the children from a desire to render them more dexterous in securing provisions, and better qualified for warfare.

When boys pass from the condition of children to that of young men, the rest of the Greeks withdraw them from the charge of the slaves and the schools, allowing them to live according to their own pleasure. Lycurgus, however, made enactments at variance with this custom; for observing that in youths of such an age there is naturally the greatest spirit and the keenest desire of pleasure prevailing in their minds, he imposed upon them, at that period of life, the most constant toil, and contrived as much occupation for them as possible.

Besides, as he wished to engender in them the deepest feelings of modesty, he enjoined them, when they were in public, to walk along in silence, not to look round in any direction, but to keep their eyes on what was before their feet. Hence you would hear no more sound from them than from stone statues; you would have as much difficulty turning their eyes as if they were made of brass; you would esteem them more bashful than virgins in the bridal chamber.

Lycurgus, having found the Spartans, like the other Greeks, taking meals at home, and knowing that most were guilty of excess at them, made their meals public. He appointed them such a quantity of food that they should neither be overfed nor hungry. Many extraordinary supplies are also furnished from hunting, and for these the rich sometimes contribute bread; so that the table is never without provisions, and yet is never expensive.

In the following particulars, also, he made enactments contrary to most states; for in other communities each individual has the control over his own children, and servants, and property; but Lycurgus, wishing that the citizens might enjoy some advantage from one another, ordained that each should have authority not only over his own children, but those of others. But when a person is conscious that his fellow citizens are fathers of the children over whom he exercises authority, he must exercise it in such a way as he would wish it to be exercised over his own.

He enacted also that a person might use his neighbor's servants, if he had need of them. He also introduced a community of property in hunting dogs; so that those requiring them call on their owner to hunt, who, if he is not at leisure to hunt himself, cheerfully sends them out. They use horses also in like manner; for whoever is sick, or desires to go some place speedily, takes possession of a horse, if he sees one anywhere, and, after making proper use of it, restores it.

In other communities all gain as much by traffic as they can; one cultivates land, another trades by sea, another maintains himself by art. But at Sparta, Lycurgus prohibited free men from having any connection with traffic, and enjoined them to consider as their only occupation whatever secures freedom to states. How, indeed, could wealth be eagerly sought in a community where he had appointed that the citizens should contribute equally to their necessary maintenance, and should take their meals in common? Nor had they to get money for the sake of clothing; for they think themselves adorned, not by expensive raiment, but by a healthy personal appearance. Nor have they to gather money for spending on those who eat with them, since it is more honorable for a person to serve his neighbors by bodily exertion, than by pecuniary expense; making it apparent that the one proceeds from the mind, and the other from fortune.

From acquiring money by unjust means, he prohibited them by such methods as the following. He instituted such a kind of money, that, even if but ten minae came into a house, it could never escape the notice of either masters or servants; for it would require much room, and a carriage to convey it. Also, gold and silver are searched after, and, if they are discovered anywhere, the possessor of them is punished.

It is deserving of admiration, too, in Lycurgus, that he made it a settled principle in the community, that an honorable death is preferable to a dishonorable life; for whoever pays attention to the subject will find that fewer of those who hold this opinion die, than of those who attempt to escape danger by flight. Hence we may say with truth, that safety attends for a much longer period on valor than on cowardice; for valor is not only attended with less anxiety and greater pleasure, but is also more capable of assisting and supporting us.

In other communities, when a man acts as a coward, he merely brings on himself the name of coward, but the coward goes to the same market, and sits or takes exercise, if he pleases, in the same place with the brave man; in Sparta, however, every one would be ashamed to admit a coward into the same tent with him, or to allow him to be his opponent in a wrestling match. Frequently, too, such a person of, when they choose teams to play at ball, is left without any place. On the road he must yield the way to others, and at public meetings he must rise up, even before his juniors. Since such disgrace is inflicted on cowards, I do not wonder that death is preferred at Sparta to a life so dishonorable and infamous.

It is worthy of admiration in him, too, that he attached consideration to the old age of the well-deserving; for by making the old men arbiters in the contest for superiority in mental qualifications, he rendered their old age more honorable than the vigor of those in the meridian of life. This contest is held in the greatest esteem among the people, for gymnastic contests are attended with honor, but they concern only bodily accomplishments; the contest for distinction in old age involves merits of the mind. In proportion as the mind is superior to the body, so much are contests for mental eminence more worthy of regard than those for bodily superiority.

The regulations which I have mentioned are beneficial alike in peace and in war; but if any one wishes to learn what he contrived better than other legislators with reference to military proceedings, he may attend to the following particulars.

For engagements in the field he made the following arrangements. He ordered that each soldier should have a purple robe and a brazen shield; for he thought that such a dress had least resemblance to that of women, and was excellently adapted for the field of battle. He permitted also those above the age of puberty to let their hair grow, as he thought that they thus appeared taller, more manly, and more terrible in the eyes of the enemy.

If any one should ask me, whether the laws of Lycurgus appear to me to continue even at the present time intact, I could certainly no longer reply with any confidence in the affirmative. For I know that the Spartans formerly preferred to associate together at home, though with moderate means, rather than to grow corrupt by governing foreign cities and listening to flatterers. I know that they were formerly afraid to let it be known that they were possessed of gold; but some at present, I am aware are ostentatious of possessing it. I know that for this reason strangers were formerly banished from Sparta, and that citizens were not allowed to reside abroad, lest they should be initiated in licentiousness by foreigners; but now I know, that those who are thought the chief men among them have shown the utmost eagerness to be constantly engaged in governing some foreign city. Hence the Greeks formerly used to resort to Sparta, and request them to be their leaders against those who were convicted of doing wrong; but now many of the Greeks exhort one another to prevent them from ever again taking the lead.

36

Aristotle, *Politics*

Socrates wrote nothing himself but devoted much of his later life to disputations in which he sought to define the eternal "forms" of items of human interest, such as beauty, love, and immortality. Socrates was a master of the "dialectic," defined then as the art of posing and answering questions to separate error and half-truths from reality. Plato wrote many dialogues in which Socrates is the main speaker and practitioner of the dialectic; however, it is impossible to know whether the statements attributed to Socrates were actually his own or Plato's. But because Plato was such a devoted admirer of Socrates, it seems likely that most of his summaries of Socrates' ideas were accurate.

Plato blamed a combination of extreme democracy, ignorantly run and capitalistic, imperialistic expansion for the disastrous Peloponnesian War. Using Socrates as a speaker in his dialogues, he pursued the ideal of an essentially communist society ruled by philosophers unconcerned with acquiring wealth or expanding their territory.

Aristotle studied with Plato for some twenty years, but in his philosophy he reacted against many of the teachings of Socrates/Plato. Aristotle did not believe in a separate, transcendent world of "forms" that could be reached through the dialectic, but rather in gathering knowledge by observing specifics, leading to general conclusions. He shared the very strong interest of Socrates/Plato in examining the ideal state, but his own findings were very different from those in Plato's Republic. In contrast with his teacher, Aristotle did not believe that extensive collective ownership would benefit society, and he looked to the middle class, rather than to philosophers, as the mainstay of the best possible government. "Polity" for Aristotle became the form of government with the best record of providing for stability and human happiness. He uses it, as in the reading that follows, as a synonym for "constitutional government" or "mixed government," containing both aristocratic and democratic elements.

QUESTIONS TO CONSIDER

1. Why does Aristotle consider political science to be the highest field of study? Do you agree with him?
2. What is Aristotle's view of holding property in common as opposed to private property?
3. On the basis of what Aristotle writes about polity or constitutional government, is it possible to see in him an early advocate of the theory of checks and balances?

Ethics as the Search for the Good of Mankind

Every art or systematic inquiry—in reality, every action and goal—seems to aim at some good, so that *the good* is correctly defined as the end at which all things aim. . . .

First section from Aristotelis *Ethica Nicomachea*, ed. Franciscus Susemihl (Leipzig: B. G. Teubner, 1903), I, i, 1904a–b; trans. Henry A. Myers. Remaining sections from *The Politics of Aristotle*, trans. Benjamin Jowett, rev. ed. (New York: Colonial Press, 1899), I, 1., 1252a–1253a; II, v, 1262b–1263b; IV, vii, 1294a–b; IV, xi, 1295b; V, ix, 1309b. Language slightly modernized; condensed by Marcella A. Smith.

Still, ends differ: some are actions, others are results, rather than the actions which bring them about. In the latter case, it is natural for the results to be valued higher than the actions. . . .

If we find something desirable for its own sake and find also that everything else seems desirable for the sake of this one thing . . . , then clearly we have found the good, meaning "the supreme good." Will knowledge of it not be a main determining factor in our lives? Will it not give us, like archers, a proper target to aim at? If there be such a thing, we must try to ascertain what it is and which arts and sciences search for it. It would have to be the object of the most sovereign and comprehensive study.

We find that political study meets the requirements of this master art and science: politics determines what other studies should be pursued in the city-states, what each class of people should learn and how much. We find that politics controls education in the most respected fields of study, such as military strategy, economics and rhetoric. Since it uses the other branches of knowledge and controls what people should and should not do, the goals of political science subsume the goals of the others, making the ends of politics the general ends of mankind. . . .

Origins of the State

Every state is a community of some kind, and every community is established with a view to some good, for mankind always acts in order to obtain what is thought good. But if all communities aim at some good, the state or political community, which is the highest of all, and which embraces the rest, aims at the highest good in greater degree than any other. . . .

Before a state can exist, there must first be a union of those who cannot exist without each other; for example, of male and female, that the race may continue. This is a union which is formed with no deliberate purpose, but because, in common with other animals and even plants, people have a natural desire to leave behind them an image of themselves. Secondly, there must be a union of natural ruler and subject, that both may be preserved. For those who can foresee with their minds are by nature intended to be lords and masters, and those who work with their bodies are subjects and natural slaves; hence master and slave have the same interest. . . .

Of these two relationships, between man and woman, master and slave, the family arises first. . . . The family is the association established by nature for the supply of men's everyday wants. . . . But when several families are united, and the association aims at something more than the supply of daily needs, the village then comes into existence. . . . When several villages are united into a single, complete community, large enough to be nearly or totally self-sufficing, the city-state comes into existence, originating in the bare needs of life and continuing its existence for the sake of a good life. And therefore, if the earlier forms of society are natural, so is the state, for it is the culmination of them. . . . Hence it is evident that the state is a creation of nature and that man is by nature a political animal. He who by nature and not by mere accident is without a state is either above or below humanity. . . . It is a characteristic of man that he alone has any sense of good and evil, of just or unjust, and the like, and the association of living beings who have this sense makes a family and a state. . . .

Private versus Community-Held Property

. . . What should be our arrangements concerning property: should the citizens of the perfect state have their possessions in common or not? . . . When farmers farm their land, questions arising from common ownership will give a world of trouble. If they do not share equally in enjoyments and toils, those who labor much and get little will necessarily complain to those who labor little and receive or consume much. Indeed there is always a difficulty in men living together and having all human relations in common, but especially in their having common property. . . .

In one sense property should be common, but, as a general rule, private. When everyone has a separate interest, men will not complain about one another, and they will make more progress, because each one will be attending to his own business. And yet, by reason of goodness and in matters of use, "Friends," as the proverb says, "have all things in common." Even now there are traces of this principle, showing that it is not impossible, but in well-ordered states, exists already to a certain extent and may be carried further. For although a man has his own property, some things he will place at the disposal of friends, while he will share the use of them with others. The Spartans, for example, use one another's slaves, horses and dogs, as if they were their own; and when they lack provisions on a journey they appropriate what they find in the fields throughout the country. It is clearly better that property should be private, but the use of it common. . . .

The Best Possible State in This Imperfect World

Now let us consider how by the side of oligarchy and democracy, the so-called "polity" or constitutional government springs up and how it should be organized. The nature of it will be at once understood from a comparison of oligarchy and democracy: we must ascertain their different characteristics and, taking a portion from each, put the two together. . . . There are three systems by which fusions of government may be brought about. Using the first, we must combine the laws made by both governments, say concerning the administration of justice. In oligarchies they impose a fine on the rich if they do not serve on juries, and to the poor they give no pay when they do serve, but in democracies they give pay to the poor and do not fine the rich. Now combining these two approaches would achieve a middle ground between them, a characteristic of constitutional government, for it is a union of both. A second way is to take a mean between the enactments of the two: democracies require no property qualification, or only a small one, for serving in the assembly, oligarchies a high one, and here a mean or middle ground can be located between them. There is a third way, in which something is borrowed from the oligarchic and something from the democratic principle. For example, the appointment of magistrates by lot is perceived as democratic and the election of them oligarchic; democratic again when there is no property qualification and oligarchic when there is. In the . . . constitutional state, one element will be taken from each: from oligarchy the principle of electing officials, from democracy the absence of any property qualification to serve. Such are the various modes of combination. There is a true union of oligarchy and democracy when the same state may be termed either a democracy or an oligarchy: those who use both names feel that fusion is complete. . . . Oligarchy or democracy, although a departure from the most perfect form, may yet be a good enough government, but if anyone attempts to push the principle of either to an extreme, he will begin by spoiling the government and end up having none at all. For neither form can begin or continue existence unless both rich and poor are included in it. . . .

We now have to inquire what is the best constitution for most states, and the best life for most men, neither assuming a standard of virtue which is above ordinary persons, nor an education which is exceptionally favored by nature and circumstances . . . , but having regard to the life in which the majority are able to share, and to the form of government which states in general can attain. . . .

Now in all states there are three elements: one class is very rich, another very poor, and a third in a mean. It is well known that moderation and the mean are best, and therefore it will clearly be best to possess the gifts of fortune in moderation; for in that condition of life men are most ready to follow rational principles. But he who greatly excels in good looks, strength, birth or wealth, or on the other hand who is very poor or very weak, or very much disgraced, finds it difficult to follow rational principles. Men of the first sort grow into violent and great criminals, those of the second into rogues and petty rascals. . . . The middle class is least likely to resent rule, or to be over-ambitious for it, both of which are injurious to the state. The evil begins at home: when they are boys, by reason of the luxury in which they are brought up, they never learn the habit of obedience, even at school. On the other hand, the very poor, who are in the opposite extreme, are too degraded. The result is that one class cannot obey, and can only rule despotically; the other does not know how to command and must be ruled like slaves. Thus a city-state arises, not of free men but of masters and slaves, the one despising, the other envying. Nothing can be more fatal to friendship and good fellowship in states than this, for good fellowship springs from friendship, while when men are hostile to one another they would rather not even share the same path. A city-state ought to be composed, as far as possible, of equals and similars, and these are generally the middle classes. Wherefore the city which is composed of middle-class citizens is necessarily best constituted from the elements of which we say the fabric of the state naturally consists. This is the class of citizens which is most secure in a state, for they do not, like the poor, covet their neighbors' goods; nor do others covet theirs, as the poor covet the goods of the rich. As they neither plot against others, nor are themselves plotted against, they pass through life safely. . . . Thus it is obvious that the best political community is formed by citizens of the middle class and that those states are likely to be well-administered, in which the middle class is large, and stronger if possible than both the other classes. . . .

Roman Contributions to Ideologies of Government and Law

Although the Romans were not particularly interested in abstract thought about political matters, they contributed political ideas of lasting significance to succeeding civilizations. They imparted these ideas in large part through stories about heroes and villains who served Rome well or badly and through commentaries on law in many forms.

Ancient Romans saw themselves as descendents of Trojans, and Romulus as the first of seven kings during their period of monarchy (753–509 B.C.). They held the second king, Numa Pompilius, in high regard for his policies on religion and morality, as well as for greatly furthering the respect for a government of law, which Romans thought characterized their culture.

The Roman Republic (ca. 509–31 B.C.) became the model of "mixed government," or a government of checks and balances. Because it lasted a long time and led Rome on its successful rise to world-power status, it presented a viable alternative to monarchy; however, it is characteristic of the Roman indifference to theorizing that the first systematic explanation of why the Roman form of government was so successful came to them from a Greek hostage, Polybius.

Along with the Roman concept of a Republic, Roman law helped to shape the legal systems of future civilizations in Europe and later the New World. The underlying philosophic basis was fairly simple: that laws made by man should be in harmony with Natural Law or, particularly after the triumph of Christianity, with God's Eternal Law. When it came to divisions of man-made law, the Romans refined a lasting distinction between (1) civil law, involving private disputes among citizens, and (2) criminal law, involving the public interest. Later, the Germanic tribes began with a primitive system, in which all disputes were private, but, partly on the basis of the model Roman law codes, they eventually separated "private" from "public" law (see the Law Code of the Salian Franks, Reading 58).

37

Plutarch, *Numa the Lawgiver*

Plutarch or Ploutarchos (ca. A.D. 46–125) was a Greek writer who had the highest regard for the fusion of Greek and Roman cultures, which had shaped his world. His voluminous *Parallel Lives* features paired biographies of famous Greeks and Romans and invites readers to engage in the type of compare-and-contrast thinking that has remained a staple of humanities education to this day.

In the selection which follows, Plutarch presents Numa Pompilius, whom the Romans regarded as successor to Romulus and author of laws governing Roman worship, as a lawgiver of the same basic sort as Lycurgus in Sparta (Reading 35; Plutarch wrote his own life of Lycurgus, based largely on Xenophon's account). For centuries, someone with Lycurgus's or Numa's achievements was called a "legislator" or "lawgiver," not in the sense of being a member of a legislative body but as the author of a new set of laws or constitution in the fashion of the American James Madison or the Japanese Ito Hirobumi.

QUESTIONS TO CONSIDER

1. How would you describe Numa's religious orientation? Why does Plutarch think that Numa's religious laws were improvements?

2. Both Numa and Lycurgus obviously thought that a major task of government was the suppression of vice and the cultivation of virtue, but how did they go about that task differently?
3. How were the aims of Numa and Lycurgus different concerning the role of women in society?

Numa was descended of the Sabines, who declare themselves to be a colony of the Spartans. We will proceed to give the most noticeable events recorded of the life of Numa. It was the thirty-seventh year, counted from the foundation of Rome,[13] when Romulus, then reigning, did, on the fifth day of the month of July, offer a public sacrifice at the Goat's Marsh, in presence of the senate and people of Rome. Suddenly the sky was darkened, a thick cloud of storm and rain settled on the earth; the common people fled in affright; and in this whirlwind Romulus disappeared, his body being never found either living or dead. A foul suspicion was attached to the patricians, as if that they, weary of kingly government, had plotted against his life and made him away, that so they might assume the government into their own hands. This suspicion they sought to turn aside by decreeing divine honours to Romulus, as to one not dead but translated to a higher condition. And Proculus, a man of note, took oath that he saw Romulus caught up into heaven, and heard him, as he ascended, cry out that they should hereafter style him by the name of Quirinus.[14]

This trouble, being appeased, was followed by another, about the election of a new king; for the minds of the original Romans and the new Sabine inhabitants were not as yet grown into that perfect unity of temper, but that there were diversities of factions amongst the commonalty. For those who had been builders of the city with Romulus, and had already yielded a share of their lands and dwellings to the Sabines, were indignant at any pretension on their part to rule over their benefactors. On the other side, the Sabines could plausibly allege, that, at their king Tatius's decease, they had peaceably submitted to the sole command of Romulus; so now it was their turn to have a king chosen out of their own nation; nor did they esteem themselves to have combined with the Romans as inferiors, nor to have contributed less to the increase of Rome, which, without their numbers and association, could scarcely have merited the name of a city.

Lest meanwhile discord, in the absence of all command, should occasion general confusion, it was agreed that the hundred and fifty senators should interchangeably execute the office of supreme magistrate, each in succession; equal distribution of power would preclude all rivalry amongst the senators and envy from the people. Nor yet could they, by this plausible and modest way of rule, escape suspicion of the vulgar, as though they were changing the form of government to an oligarchy without ever choosing a king. Both parties came at length to the conclusion that the one should choose a king out of the body of the other; the Romans make a choice of a Sabine, or the Sabines name a Roman; the prince who should be chosen would have an equal af-

---

[13]The Romans numbered years "from the founding of the city" (753 B.C. in our dating system); the thirty-seventh year would thus be our 716 B.C.

[14]Quirinus was originally a male personification of Rome or god of the Roman state, who was later identified with Romulus.

From *Plutarch's Lives of Illustrious Men*, transl. John Dryden (Chicago/New York: Belford, Clarke & Co., ca. 1904). Vol. I, pp. 74–97, passim. Condensed and language slightly modernized by Allen C. Myers.

fection to the one party as his electors and to the other as his kinsmen. Consultations being accordingly held, the Romans named Numa Pompilius, of the Sabine race.

Numa was endued with a soul disposed to virtue, which he had yet more subdued by discipline and the study of philosophy; means which had not only succeeded in expelling the baser passions, but also the violent temper which barbarians are apt to think highly of; true bravery, in his judgment, was the subjugation of our passions by reason.

He banished all luxury and softness from his own home, and while citizens alike and strangers found in him an incorruptible judge and counselor, in private he devoted himself to the worship of the immortal gods, and rational contemplation of their divine power and nature.

Numa was about forty years of age when ambassadors came to make him offers of the kingdom; the speakers were Proculus and Velesus, one or other of whom it had been thought the people would elect as their new king; the original Romans being for Proculus, and the Sabines for Velesus. Their speech was very short, supposing that, when they came to tender a kingdom, there needed little to persuade to an acceptance; but, contrary to their expectations, they found that they had to use many reasons and entreaties to induce one, that lived in peace and quietness, to accept the government of a city whose foundation and increase had been made, in a manner, in war. In presence of his father and his kinsman Marcius he returned answer that "Every alteration of a man's life is dangerous to him; but madness only could induce one who needs nothing, and is satisfied with everything, to quit a life he is accustomed to; which, whatever else it is deficient in, at any rate has the advantage of certainty over one wholly doubtful and unknown. Though, indeed, the difficulties of this government cannot even be called unknown; Romulus, who first held it, did not escape the suspicion of having plotted against the life of his colleague Tatius; nor the senate the like accusation, of having treasonably murdered Romulus. Yet Romulus had the advantage to be thought divinely born and miraculously preserved and nurtured. My birth was mortal; I was reared and instructed by men that are known to you. The very points of my character that are most commended mark me as unfit to reign, love of retirement and of studies inconsistent with business, a passion for peace, and for the society of men whose meetings are but those of worship and of kindly intercourse, whose lives in general are spent upon their farms and their pastures. I should but be, methinks, a laughingstock, while I should go about to inculcate the worship of the gods and give lessons in the love of justice and the abhorrence of violence and war, to a city whose needs are rather for a captain than for a king."

At length, his father and Marcius, taking him aside, persuaded him to accept a gift so noble in itself, and tendered to him rather from heaven than from men. "Though," said they, "you neither desire riches, being content with what you have, nor court the fame of authority, as having already the more valuable fame of virtue, yet you will consider that government itself is a service of God, who now calls out into action your qualities of justice and wisdom, which were not meant to be left useless and unemployed. Do not turn your back upon an office which is a field for great and honourable actions, for the magnificent worship of the gods, and for the introduction of habits of piety, which authority alone can effect amongst a people. Tatius, though a foreigner, was beloved, and the memory of Romulus has received divine honours; and who knows but that this people, being victorious, may be satiated with war, and be desirous to have a pacific and justice-loving prince to lead them to good order and quiet? Even if their desires are uncontrollably set on war, were it not better to have the reins held by such a moderating hand as is able to divert the fury another way, and that your native city and the whole Sabine nation should possess in you a bond of goodwill and friendship with this young and growing power?"

Numa, yielding to these inducements, having first performed divine sacrifice, proceeded to Rome, being met in his way by the senate and people, who, with an impatient desire, came forth to receive him; so universal was the joy, that they seemed to be receiving, not a new king, but a new kingdom. He descended into the forum, where Spurius Vettius, whose turn it was to be interrex at that hour, put it to the vote; and all declared him king. Then the robes of authority were brought to him; but he refused to be invested with them until he had first been confirmed by the gods; so accompanied by the priests and augurs, he ascended the Capitol. Then the chief of the augurs covered Numa's head, and prayed, turning his eyes every way, in expectation of some auspicious signal from the gods. It was wonderful, meantime, with what silence and devotion the multitude stood assembled in the forum, in similar expectation and suspense, till auspicious birds appeared and passed on the right. Then Numa, apparelling himself in his royal robes, descended from the hill to the people, by whom he was received and congratulated with shouts and acclamations of welcome, as a holy king, and beloved of all the gods.

The first thing he did as king was to dismiss the band of three hundred men which had been Romulus's life-guard, saying that he would not distrust those who put confidence in him; nor rule over a people that distrusted him. The next thing he did was to add to the two priests of Jupiter and Mars a third, in honour of Romulus, whom he called the Flamen Quirinalis.

When Numa had, by such measures, won the favor and affection of the people, he took upon the task of bringing the iron Roman temper to somewhat more of gentleness and equity. Plato's expression of a city in high fever was never more applicable than to Rome at that time; in its origin formed by daring and warlike spirits, it had found in perpetual wars and incursions on its neighbors its sustenance and means of growth, and in conflict with danger the source of new strength. Wherefore Numa, judging it no slight undertaking to mollify and bend to peace the presumptuous and stubborn spirits of this people, began to operate upon them with the sanctions of religion. He sacrificed often and used processions and religious dances; by such combinations of solemnity with refined and humanizing pleasures, seeking to win over and mitigate their fiery and warlike tempers. At times, also, he filled their imaginations with religious terrors, professing that strange apparitions had been seen, and dreadful voices heard; thus subduing and humbling their minds by a sense of supernatural fears.

Numa conceived of the first principle of being as transcending sense and passion, invisible and incorrupt, and only to be apprehended by abstract intelligence. So Numa forbade the Romans to represent God in the form of man or beast, nor was there any painted or graven image of a deity admitted amongst them. Their temples and chapels were kept free and pure from images; to such baser objects they deemed it impious to liken the highest, and all access to God impossible, except by the pure act of the intellect.

The original constitution of the priests, called Pontifices, is ascribed unto Numa, and he himself was, it is said, the first of them; and that they have the name of Pontifices from potens, powerful, because they attend the service of the gods, who have power to command over all.

The office of Pontifex Maximus, or chief priest, was to declare and interpret the divine law, or, rather, to preside over sacred rites; he not only prescribed rules for public ceremony, but regulated the sacrifices of private persons, giving information to every one of what was requisite for purposes of worship or supplication. He was also guardian of the vestal virgins, the institution of whom, and of their perpetual fire, was attributed to Numa, who, perhaps, fancied the charge of pure and uncorrupted flames would be fitly entrusted to chaste and unpolluted persons, or that fire, which consumes, but produces nothing, bears an analogy to the virgin estate. Some think that these vestals had no other business than the preservation of this fire; but others conceive that they were keepers of divine secrets concealed from all but themselves.

The statutes prescribed by Numa for the vestals were these: that they should take a vow of virginity for the space of thirty years, the first ten of which they were to spend in learning their duties, the second ten in performing them, and the remaining ten in teaching and instructing others. For this condition he compensated by great privileges; they had power to make a will in the lifetime of their father; that they had a free administration of their own affairs without guardian or tutor, which was the privilege of women who were mothers of three children; and if in their walks they chance to meet a criminal on his way to execution, it saves his life, upon oath made that the meeting was an accidental one, and not of set purpose. If these vestals commit any minor fault, they are punishable by the high priest only, who scourges the offender, sometimes with her clothes off, in a dark place, with a curtain drawn between; but she who breaks her vow of chastity is buried alive near the gate called Collina.

It is said, also, that Numa built the temple of Vesta, which was intended for a repository of the holy fire, of a circular form, not to represent the figure of the earth, as if that were the same as Vesta, but that of the general universe, in the centre of which the Pythagoreans place the element of fire, and give it the name of Vesta and the unit; and do not hold that the earth is immovable, or that it is situated in the centre of the globe, but that it keeps a circular motion about the seat of fire; in this agreeing with the opinion of Plato, who, they say, conceived that the earth held a lateral position, and that the central space was reserved for some nobler body.

Numa also prescribed rules for regulating the days of mourning, according to certain times and ages. As, for example, a child of three years was not to be mourned for at all; one older, up to ten years, for as many months as it was years old; and the longest time of mourning for any person whatsoever was not to exceed the term of ten months; which was the time appointed for women that lost their husbands to continue in widowhood. If any married again before that time, by the laws of Numa, she was to sacrifice a cow big with calf.

Numa also erected, near the temple of Vesta, the Regia, or king's house, where he spent the most part of his time performing divine service, instructing the priests, or conversing with them on sacred subjects. In all public processions and solemn prayers, criers were sent before to give notice to the people that they should forbear their work, and rest. Numa wished that his citizens should neither see nor hear any religious service in a perfunctory and inattentive manner, but, laying aside all other occupations, should apply their minds to religion as to a most serious business; and that the streets should be free from all noises and cries that accompany manual labor, and clear for the sacred solemnity. By such discipline in religion, the city passed insensibly into such a submissiveness of temper, and stood in such awe and reverence of the virtue of Numa, that they received, with an undoubted assurance, whatever he delivered though never so fabulous, and thought nothing incredible or impossible from him.

Numa's own thoughts are said to have been fixed to such a degree on divine objects, that he once, when a message was brought to him that "Enemies are approaching," answered with a smile, "And I am sacrificing." It was he, also, that built the temples of Faith and Terminus, and taught the Romans that the name of Faith was the most solemn oath that they could swear. They still use it; and to the god Terminus, or Boundary, they offer to this day both public and private sacrifices, upon the borders and stone-marks of their land; living victims now, though anciently those sacrifices were solemnized without blood; for Numa reasoned that the god of boundaries, who watched over peace, and testified to fair dealing, should have no concern with blood. It is very clear that he was the first to prescribe bounds to the territory of Rome; for Romulus would but have openly betrayed how much he had encroached on his neighbours' lands, had he ever set limits to his own; for boundaries are, indeed, a defence to those who choose to observe them, but are only a testimony against the dishonesty of those who break through them. The truth is, the portion of lands which the Romans possessed at the beginning was very narrow, until Romulus enlarged them by war; all those acquisitions Numa now divided amongst the indigent commonalty, wishing to do away with that extreme want which is a compulsion to dishonesty, and, by turning the people to husbandry, to bring them, as well as their lands, into better order. For there is no employment that gives so keen a relish for peace as husbandry and a country life, which leave in men all that kind of courage that makes them ready to fight in defense of their own, while it destroys the license that breaks out into acts of injustice and rapacity. But of all his measures the most commended was his distribution of the people by their trades into companies or guilds; for as the city was divided into two different tribes, the diversity between which prevented all unity and caused perpetual tumult and ill-blood, he resolved to divide the whole population into a number of small divisions, and thus hoped, by introducing other distinctions, to obliterate the original and great distinction, which would be lost among the smaller. So, distinguishing the whole people by the several arts and trades, he formed the companies of musicians, goldsmiths, carpenters, and potters; and all other handicraftsmen he composed and reduced into a single company, appointing every one their proper courts, councils, and religious observances. In this manner all factious distinctions began to pass out of use, no person any longer being either thought of or spoken of under the notion of a Sabine or a Roman; and the new division became a source of general harmony and intermixture.

He is also much to be commended for the repeal of that law which gives power to fathers to sell their children; he exempted such as had been with the liking and consent of both parents; for it seemed a hard thing that a woman who had given herself in marriage to a man whom she judged free should afterwards find herself living with a slave.

He attempted, also, the formation of a calendar, not with absolute exactness, yet not without some scientific knowledge. During the reign of Romulus, they had let their months run on without any certain or equal term; some of them contained twenty days, others thirty-five, others more; they had no sort of knowledge of the inequality in the motions of the sun and moon; they only kept to the one rule that the whole course of the year contained three hundred and sixty days. Numa, calculating the difference between the lunar and the solar year at eleven days, to remedy this incongruity doubled the eleven days, and every other year added an intercalary month, to follow February, consisting of twenty-two days, and called by the Romans the month Mercedinus. That the Romans, at first, comprehended the whole year within ten, and not twelve months, plainly appears by the name of the last, December, meaning the tenth month. He also altered the order of the months; for March, which was reckoned the first he put into the third place; and January, which was the eleventh, he made the first. January was called from Janus, and precedence given to it by Numa before March, which was dedicated to the god Mars; because, as I conceive, he wished to take every opportunity of intimating that the arts and studies of peace are to be preferred before those of war. For this Janus was certainly a great lover of civil and social unity, and one who reclaimed men from brutal and savage living; for which reason they figure him with two faces, to represent the two states and conditions out of the one of which he brought mankind, to lead them into the other. His temple at Rome has two gates, which they call the gates of war, because they stand open in the time of war, and shut in the times of peace; of which latter there was very seldom an example, for, as the Roman empire was enlarged and extended, it was so encompassed with barbarous nations and enemies to be resisted, that it was seldom or never at peace. But, during the reign of Numa, those gates were never seen open a single day, but continued constantly shut for a space of forty-three years together; such an entire and universal cessation of war existed. For not only had the people of Rome itself been softened and charmed into a peaceful temper by the just and mild rule of a pacific prince, but even the neighbouring cities began to experience a change of feeling, and partook in the general longing for the sweets of peace and order. Festival days and sports, and the secure and peaceful interchange of friendly visits and hospitalities prevailed all through the whole of Italy. The love of virtue and justice flowed from Numa's wisdom as from a fountain.

During the whole reign of Numa, there was neither war, nor sedition, nor innovation in the state, nor any envy or ill-will to his person, nor plot or conspiracy from views of ambition. Numa was a living example and verification of that saying which Plato, long afterwards, ventured to pronounce, that the sole and only hope of respite or remedy for human evils was in some happy conjunction of events which should unite in a single person the power of a king and the wisdom of a philosopher, so as to elevate virtue to control and mastery over vice. The mere sight itself of a shining and conspicuous example of virtue in the life of their prince will bring the people spontaneously to virtue, and blessed life of good-will and mutual concord, supported by temperance and justice, which is the highest benefit that human means can confer; and he is the truest ruler who can best introduce it into the hearts and practice of his subjects.

Numa lived something above eighty years, and then, as Piso writes, was not taken out of the world by a sudden or acute disease, but died of old age and by a gradual and gentle decline. It is the fortune of all good men that their virtue rises in glory after their deaths, and that the envy which evil men conceive against them never outlives them long; some have the happiness even to see it die before them; but in Numa's case, also, the fortunes of the succeeding kings served as foils to set off the brightness of his reputation. For after him there were five kings, the last of whom ended his old age in banishment, being deposed from his crown; of the other four, three were assassinated and murdered by treason; the other, who was Tullus Hostilius, that immediately succeeded Numa, derided his virtues, and especially his devotion to religious worship, as a cowardly and mean-spirited occupation, and diverted the minds of the people to war; but was checked in these youthful insolences, and was himself driven by an acute and tormenting disease into superstitions wholly different from Numa's piety, and left others also to participate in these terrors when he died by the stroke of a thunderbolt.

Comparison of Numa with Lycurgus

Having thus finished the lives of Lycurgus and Numa, we shall now put together their points of difference as they lie here before our view. Their points of likeness are obvious; their moderation, their religion, their capacity of government and discipline, their both deriving their laws and constitutions from the gods. Yet in their common glories there are circumstances of diversity; for first Numa accepted and Lycurgus resigned a kingdom; Numa received without desiring it, Lycurgus had it and gave it up; the one from a private person and a stranger was raised by others to be their king; the other from the condition of a prince voluntarily descended to the state of privacy. It was glorious to acquire a throne by justice, yet more glorious to prefer justice before a throne; the same virtue which made the one appear worthy of regal power exalted the other to the disregard of it. Lastly, as the musicians tune their harps, so the one let down the high-flown spirits of the people at Rome to a lower key, as the other screwed them up at Sparta to a higher note, when they were sunken low by dissoluteness and riot. The harder task was that of Lycurgus; for it was not so much his business to persuade his citizens to put off their armor or ungird their swords, as to cast away their gold or silver, and abandon costly furniture and rich tables; nor was it necessary to preach to them, that, laying aside their arms, they should observe the festivals, and sacrifice to the gods, but rather, that, giving up feasting and drinking, they should employ their time in laborious and martial exercises; so that while the one effected all by persuasions and his people's love for him, the other, with danger and hazard of his person, scarcely in the end succeeded. Numa's muse was a gentle and loving inspiration, fitting him well to turn and soothe his people into peace and justice out of their violent and fiery tempers; whereas, if we must admit the treatment of the Helots to be a part of Lycurgus's legislation, a most cruel and iniquitous proceeding, we must own that Numa was by a great deal the more humane and Greek-like legislator, granting even to actual slaves a license to sit at meat with their masters at the feast of Saturn, that they also might have some taste of the sweets of liberty.

In general, it seems that of the virtues, the one set his affection most on fortitude, and the other on justice; unless we attribute their different ways to the different habits and temperaments which they had to work upon by their enactments; for Numa did not out of cowardice affect peace, but because he would not do injustice; nor did Lycurgus promote a spirit of war in his people that they might do injustice to others, but that they might protect themselves from it.

In bringing the habits they formed in their people to a just and happy mean, mitigating them where they exceeded, and strengthening them where they were deficient, both were compelled to make great innovations. The frame of government which Numa formed was democratic and popular to the last extreme, goldsmiths and flute-players and shoemakers constituting his promiscuous, many-coloured commonalty. Lycurgus was rigid and aristocratic, banishing all the base and mechanic arts to the company of servants and strangers, and allowing the true citizens no implements but the spear and shield, the trade of war only, and no other knowledge or study, but that of obedience to their commanding officers, and victory over their enemies. Every sort of money-making was forbid them; and to make them thoroughly so and keep them so through their whole lives, every conceivable concern with money was handed over to slaves and helots. But Numa made none of these distinctions; he only suppressed military rapacity, allowing free scope to every other means of obtaining wealth; nor did he endeavor to obviate, as Lycurgus did, and take measures of precaution against the mischiefs of avarice, mischiefs not of small importance, but the real seed and first beginning of all the great and extensive evils of after-times. The redivision of estates, Lycurgus is not, it seems to me, to be blamed for making, nor Numa for omitting; this equality was the basis and foundation of the one commonwealth; but at Rome, where the lands had been lately divided, there was nothing to urge any redivision or any disturbance of the first arrangement, which was probably still in existence.

With respect to wives and children, and that community which both, with a sound policy, appointed, to prevent all jealousy, their methods, however, were different. For when a Roman thought himself to have a sufficient number of children, in case his neighbor who had none should come and request his wife of him, he had a lawful power to give her up to him who desired her, either for a certain time, or for good. The Spartan husband, on the other hand, might allow the use of his wife to any other that desired to have children by her, and yet still keep her in his house, the original marriage obligation still subsisting as at first. Nay, many husbands, as we have said, would invite men whom they thought likely to procure them fine and good-looking children into their houses. What is the difference, then, between the two customs? Shall we say that the Spartan system is one of an extreme and entire unconcern about their wives, and would cause most people endless disquiet and annoyance with pangs and jealousies? That the Roman course wears an air of a more delicate acquiescence, draws the veil of a new contract over the change, and concedes the general insupportableness of mere community? Numa's directions, too, for the care of young women, are better adapted to the female sex and to propriety; Lycurgus's are altogether unreserved and unfeminine, and have given a great handle to the poets, who call them (Ibycus, for example) Phoenomerides, bare-thighed; and give them the character (as does Euripides) of being wild after husbands

> "These with the young men from the house go out,
> With thighs that show, and robes that fly about."

For in fact the skirts of the frock worn by unmarried girls were not sewn together at the lower part, but used to fly back and show the whole thigh bare as they walked.

And so their women, it is said, were bold and masculine, overbearing to their husbands in the first place, absolute mistresses in their houses, giving their opinions about public matters freely, and speaking openly even on the most important subjects. But the matrons, under the government of Numa, still indeed received from their husbands all that high respect and honor which had been paid them under Romulus as a sort of atonement for the violence done to them; nevertheless, great modesty was enjoined upon them; all busy intermeddling forbidden, sobriety insisted on, and silence made habitual. Wine they were not to touch at all, nor to speak, except in their husband's company, even on the most ordinary subjects. So that as the Greek historians record in their annals the names of those who first unsheathed the sword of civil war, or murdered their brothers, or killed their mothers, so the Roman writers report it as the first example, that Spurius Carvilius divorced his wife, being a case that never before happened, in the space of two hundred and thirty years from the foundation of the city; and that one Thalaea, the wife of Pinarius, had a quarrel (the first instance of the kind) with her mother-in-law, Gegania, in the reign of Tarquinius Superbus; so successful was the legislator in securing order and good conduct in the marriage relation. Their respective regulations for marrying the young women are in accordance with those for their education. Lycurgus made them brides when they were of full age and inclination. Their bodies, also, would be better able to bear the trials of breeding and of bearing children, in his judgment the one end of marriage.

The Romans, on the other hand, gave their daughters in marriage as early as twelve years old, or even under; thus they thought their bodies alike and minds would be delivered to the future husband pure and undefiled. The way of Lycurgus seems the more natural with a view to the birth of children; the other, looking to a life to be spent together, is more moral. However, the rules which Lycurgus drew up for superintendence of children, their collection into companies, their discipline and association, as also his exact regulations for their meals, exercises, and sports, argue Numa no more than an ordinary lawgiver. Numa left the whole matter simply to be decided by the parent's wishes or necessities, uniting to act for the common good only in time of danger upon occasion of their private fears, in general looking simply to their own interest.

We may forbear, indeed, to blame common legislators, who may be deficient in power or knowledge. But when a wise man like Numa had received the sovereignty over a new and docile people, was there anything that would better deserve his attention than the education of children, not to contrariety and discordance of character, but to the unity of the common model of virtue, to which from their cradle they should have been formed and molded? One benefit among many that Lycurgus obtained by his course was the permanence which it secured to his laws. The obligation of oaths to preserve them would have availed but little, if he had not, by discipline and education, infused them into the children's characters, and imbued their whole early life with a love of his government. The result was that the fundamentals of his legislation continued for above five hundred years. But Numa's whole design and aim, the continuance of peace and goodwill, on his death vanished with him; no sooner did he expire his last breath than the gates of Janus's temple flew wide open; and thus that best fabric of things was of no long continuance, because it wanted that cement which should have kept all together, education. What, then, some may say, has not Rome been advanced and bettered by her wars? A question that will need a long answer, if it is to be one to satisfy men who take the better to consist in riches, luxury, and dominion, rather than in security, gentleness, and that independence which is accompanied by justice. However, it makes much for Lycurgus, that, after the Romans had deserted the doctrine and discipline of Numa, their empire grew and their power increased so much; whereas so soon as the Spartans fell from the institutions of Lycurgus, they sank from the highest to the lowest state, and, after forfeiting their supremacy over the rest of Greece, were themselves in danger of absolute extirpation. Thus much, was peculiarly signal and almost divine in the circumstances of Numa, that he accepted a kingdom, the frame of which though he entirely altered, yet he performed it by mere persuasion, and ruled a city that as yet had scarce become one city, without recurring to arms or any violence (such as Lycurgus used, supporting himself by the aid of the nobler citizens against the commonalty), but, by mere force of wisdom and justice, established union and harmony amongst all.

38

Titus Livy, *Heroes of the Early Republic*

Titus Livy (59 B.C.–A.D. 17) gave the Western world a panorama of patriotic heroes with an inspirational force well beyond that given by essays in political philosophy. His *History from the Founding of the City* (Rome since 753 B.C.) is much more comprehensive than that of Polybius, beginning with the arrival of the fabled Trojan Prince Aeneas in Rome. It continues in 142 books, of which thirty-five survive, down to the time of Augustus Caesar, Livy's patron. In the absence of reliable written sources for the early part of his work, Livy was forced to use oral legends that had been recorded much later, but he gave his sketches of people and events in realistic detail.

Livy's subsequent influence was immense. The realistic and cynical Machiavelli was moved by Livy's portrayal of the citizen-soldier-leader Cincinnatus (see Reading 94), and "Horatio at the Bridge" served as a model for patriotic fearlessness into the twentieth century. Almost every educated American of the seventeenth and eighteenth centuries knew Titus Livy stories. Thomas Jefferson thought he had wasted his time laboring through Plato's *Republic*, but he considered Titus Livy's work so valuable that he insisted that his daughter Martha learn to read it with ease enough not to have to ask her tutor for help with it. Livy's story of Tarquin and Lucretia articulated the Roman aversion to kings as potential tyrants and the need to have a government without them. Somewhat as Americans were to consider George III bad enough to make them swear off monarchy forever, many Romans believed that the Tarquins discredited kingship so thoroughly that likely claimants to a crown were public enemies, guilty of high treason and deserving death.

QUESTIONS TO CONSIDER

1. What sort of bet did Collatinus make with the younger Tarquin?
2. How does Lucretia embody a particular type of female virtue?
3. Why does Titus Livy assume that a republic has no place for monarchy in it? Does he differ with Polybius on that subject?
4. How did Horatio Cocles and Caius Mucius Scaevola contribute to the defense of Rome?
5. What made Porsena abandon his attempt to reestablish the Tarquins as kings of Rome?

While . . . the young princes . . . were drinking in the camp quarters of Sextus Tarquin, they began discussing their wives, with each one showering praise upon his

From *Titi Livi ab urbe condita libri*, ed. Wilhelm Weissenborn (Leipzig: B. G. Teubner, 1926), Part One, I, lvii; II, xv, pp. 68–86, *passim.* Trans. Henry A. Myers.

own. When the competitive praise really began to heat up, Collatinus said that there was no reason to settle for verbal displays and that in a few hours they could see how much better than the others his wife Lucretia was: "Why don't we—since we are young and full of energy—get on our horses and see for ourselves what our wives are doing? Let us all agree that the award of 'best wife' will be determined by what she does when her husband comes home unexpected."

"Agreed!" they all shouted, heated with wine, and soon they were urging their horses on towards Rome. It was just beginning to get dark when they arrived there. . . . [Later] they made their way to Collatia, where they discovered Lucretia occupied very differently from the daughters-in-law of the king: they had found them spending their time with their friends at a luxurious banquet. Lucretia, however, even though it was well into the night by then was busy working with her wool; her maids were working by lamplight around her as she sat in the great hall. There was no question then but what Lucretia won the "best wife" competition. The leading contenders were cordially received, and Collatinus, the victor, courteously offered refreshments to the young princes. Then and there wicked lust seized Sextus Tarquin: not only her beauty but her confirmed chastity lit flames of passion within him; however, for the time being they all treated what had happened as youthful sport and rode back to camp.

A few days later, Sextus Tarquin took one servant to Collatia without letting Collatinus know. He was graciously welcomed there, since no one knew what was on his mind. After dinner, he was led to a guest room. Burning with desire, he waited until he was sure that everyone around was asleep, and with sword drawn he entered the room of the sleeping Lucretia. He held her down with his left hand on her breast and told her: "Keep quiet, Lucretia. I am Sextus Tarquin; my sword is in my hand. One sound out of you, and you die!" The woman woke up with a start and saw no help at hand, only the threat of imminent death. Then Tarquin declared his love for her, pleading and threatening together, bringing pressure to bear from every angle on the woman's soul. When he saw she was stubborn and not going to be swayed by fear of death, he added the threat of shame. He said he would kill his slave and drag him naked to lie by her own corpse so that she could be reported killed in adultery with a low-born fellow. With this horrible threat, his lust finally overran her steadfast chastity, and Tarquin left in triumph over his conquest of her woman's honor.

Despairing at her fate, Lucretia sent the same message to her father at Rome and her husband at Ardea, asking each to come with a trustworthy friend and to come quickly for a terrible thing had happened. [With their friends, Valerius and Brutus] the men arrived and found Lucretia sitting sadly in her room. The presence of those dear to her brought tears to her eyes. When her husband asked, "Is everything all right?" she answered:

"Not by far. It can never be 'all right' for a woman whose honor has been stolen. The imprint of a stranger, Collatinus, is on your bed. To be sure, only my body has been violated, not my spirit. Death will be my witness for that. But raise your right hands and swear that the criminal will not escape punishment. It was Sextus Tarquin last night who repaid hospitality with the armed force of hostility to ruin me—and himself if you are men—with his perverted, fatal pleasure-taking."

One after the other each takes a solemn oath. They try to console her, by coaxing the poisonous affliction out of her and onto the perpetrator, telling her that the mind sins but not the body, and where there is no consent there is no guilt. "You will decide what is to happen to him. As for me, I absolve myself of sin but not of the need to suffer the fate which must follow. In time to come, let no defiled woman use Lucretia as an excuse to keep on living." Pulling out a knife she had concealed in her dress, she plunged it into her heart and fell forward upon her wound. . . .

While the others were still overcome by grief, Brutus pulled the knife from Lucretia's wound, and as the blood dripped from it spoke: "I swear by this blood—innocent until polluted by royalty—and you, O gods, I call to witness that I will use sword, fire and every other means of force I can apply to bring down Lucius Tarquin with his evil wife and all his children and that I will not allow any of them, nor anyone else, to rule as king in Rome!" The others swore as he told them to swear. Anger devoured their grief, and they followed Brutus as leader when he called upon them to get rid of the rule of kings. . . .

The reaction to this atrocity was every bit as furious in Rome as at Collatia. People streamed to the Forum from all parts of the city. . . . The city gates were closed to keep out Tarquin [who was at the campsite] and he was banished. . . . Rule by kings had lasted two hundred and forty years at Rome. . . . The new liberty was welcomed by the Romans so enthusiastically because of the wretched tyranny of the last king. . . . [A little later, as first consul] Brutus, for his first act of office, while the people were still jealous of their new freedom, required them to swear never to allow any man to be king in Rome. . . .

By that time the Tarquins had fled to Lars Porsena, King of Clusium, and appealed to him with both pleas and advice. Sometimes they would beg him not to permit them, his fellow Etruscans, who shared blood and family names with him, to languish in exile; sometimes they would warn him not to let this growing practice of expelling kings go unpunished. . . . Porsena, convinced that there was safety in having a king rule Rome, particularly an Etruscan king honoring his people, sent an invading army towards Rome.

Never before had such terror seized the Senators—so great was Clusium's reputation for power and Porsena's own prestige. They worried not only about the invaders but also about their own common people's being seized by such fear as to allow the royal forces into the city and accept servitude as the price of peace. To gain popular support, the Senate passed some measures favoring them: . . . the poor were excused from many obligations and taxes. These burdens were assumed by wealthier people who could afford them, and the Senate justified this with the thought that the poor paid enough by raising children for Rome. And so, with these concessions by the City Fathers, harmony within the city held firm under the suffering which was to come when the city was besieged and hunger reigned—so united were the upper and lower classes in rejecting the name of king in disgust. . . .

When the enemy approached, all the Romans left their farms for the city and surrounded it with armed men. Most of Rome seemed protected by the walls, the rest by the Tiber, but the river bridge almost furnished the enemy a roadway or lane into Rome and would, in fact, have done so had it not been for one man: Horatio Cocles. That day he protected the fortunes of Rome himself. He was on guard at the bridge when a sudden enemy assault overran Janiculum Hill [on the other side of the Tiber from the strongly defended parts of the city]. He saw the invaders coming down the hill from there, with his own people turning into a frightened mob, dropping their weapons behind them as they broke ranks and ran. Confronting them individually, blocking their way and making them listen to him, he told them in the name of gods and men that if they deserted their posts there was no place left to flee to: if they gave up the bridge there would soon be more enemy forces on Palatine Hill and Capitol Hill than on Janiculum. Thus he warned them and ordered them to destroy the bridge with steel, fire or whatever they could find to work with and promised that he would hold back the enemy's charge to the extent that one man's body could block it. Then he walked to the far end of the bridge, his lone figure standing out against the sight of those fleeing from the fight. With his sword and shield ready for single combat, his daring made the invaders pause in amazement. Shame did keep two men from leaving him there alone. . . . With them he withstood the first, most violent onslaught but after a short time he made them retreat to safety, for little support remained under the bridge, and its demolishers were shouting for them to come back. Then, with threatening glances he looked around at the Etruscan elite. Challenging them individually to do combat with him and ridiculing them all as a group, he taunted them for accepting slavery under royal arrogance . . . while coming to take away the liberty of others. The Etruscans looked around at each other, each waiting for his comrade to start fighting with Horatio. Shame finally moved them to attack, and with a loud shout they hurled their spears against their lone enemy. He deflected all these with his shield and, determined as ever, planted his feet in the center of the far end of the bridge. The Etruscans began to advance with a charge to dislodge him, when the crash of falling bridge timbers and the simultaneous roar of joy from the Romans, who saw their work finished in time, stopped them fearfully in their tracks.

"Father Tiber," Horatio began, "I pray reverently that you will receive these arms and this soldier with a kindly current!" Then he jumped, fully armed, into the Tiber and with a shower of spears striking the water around him swam unhurt across the river to his people. . . .

Porsena responded to this defeat in his attempt to conquer Rome by ordering a siege. . . . [After the blockade had been in place for a while], grain supplies were depleted and what remained was selling at very high prices, so that Porsena began to hope that just by sitting still he could take the city. At that point Caius Mucius, a young noble, brooded over the fact that the Roman people had never been blockaded by enemies in the days of their servitude under kings, but now, when they were free, they were being blockaded by the same Etruscans whose armies they had so often defeated, and so he made up his mind to avenge this indignity with some great and daring deed. . . . [Letting the Senate know only that he was leaving], he set out with a dagger concealed in his clothing. Arriving at the Etruscan camp, he wedged himself into a dense crowd near the platform on which the king was sitting. It was payday for his soldiers and a paymaster was sitting by the king, dressed almost the same way as he, and very busy since most of the soldiers transacted their business with him. Mucius was afraid to ask which of the two was the king, lest his ignorance of who the king was give away who he was. Trusting to Fortune, he stabbed the paymaster instead of the king. As he tried to carve a path back through the crowd with his bloody blade, shouts resounded and royal bodyguards surrounded him and led him back to the platform. Yet completely alone and seemingly abandoned by Fortune, his face stayed grim and threatening as befit a man to be feared rather than one afraid: "I am a Roman citizen," he began, "named Caius Mucius. As your enemy, I wanted to kill you, but I am just as ready to die as I was to kill. It is the Roman way to act and to suffer bravely. Nor am I the only one determined to assassinate you. A long line of men behind me will seek the same honor. Get ready if you want for the coming struggle in which you will try to save your life from hour to hour, having one enemy with a dagger after another on your doorstep. This is the kind of war we young men of Rome declare on you. You need fear neither marching ranks nor pitched battles: it will be all between your own self and us, one at a time."

The king, enraged but also very anxious about the danger to himself, ordered the prisoner to be burned alive unless he would give him the details of the plot he had just outlined. "So that you may see how cheap our men who have their eyes fixed on glory consider their bodies—" said Mucius, and with that he shoved his right hand into the altar-fire which had been lit for sacrificing. When he let his hand burn as if his spirit removed any sensation of pain, the king jumped from his seat in astonishment and ordered the young man removed from the altar. "Go free, you who dare injure yourself more than me! I would pray that your bravery be rewarded with success if it were bravery on behalf of my country; at least I am releasing you with no charges of crime and no painful penalties from me."

As if responding to the king's generosity, Mucius answered: "Since you honor bravery, I will give you information in gratitude which you could not have tortured out of me: three hundred young men from Rome's leading families are members of this conspiracy to finish you off by violent means. I drew the first lot. Whoever draws the next and the next after that will seek you out in turn, until Fortune gives one of us an opportunity to get you."

Emissaries from Porsena arrived in Rome following the release of Mucius, who was afterwards known as "Scaevola" (Lefty) because of his missing right hand. . . . The king had been so disturbed . . . that he sent peace proposals to the Romans. . . .

Peace was concluded, but later Porsena sought to open negotiations for the restoration of the Tarquins, and the Romans sent their most distinguished Senators to reply, saying they were in hopes of closing discussion on that issue once and for all and that they wanted to remove any hindrance to mutually beneficial relations—the hindrance being royal requests for something incompatible with Roman liberty, asking them to give up something essential for the sake of being agreeable, requiring the Romans to keep on denying his request to a man to whom they did not wish to deny anything. Rome was not to be a kingdom but was to remain in freedom. The Romans were determined to open their gates to enemies sooner than to kings. The Romans were all united in a single prayer—that the city could come to an end when its liberty ended.

39

Polybius, "Why Romans and Not Greeks Govern the World"

The Romans sent men of prominence or from prominent families from those Greek city-states with a recent history of resistance off to Rome as hostages in order to ensure the good behavior of the Greek leaders now subject to Rome. In this role, Polybius (ca. 205–125 B.C.), who had been a cavalry general and ambassador to Egypt for the Achaean League (of Greek city-states), arrived in Rome around 170 B.C.

Polybius got along splendidly with the Roman leaders he met and seems to have noted a cavernous gap in Roman historiography and political philosophy that he could fill with his Greek erudition. After some twenty years in Rome, the surviving hostages of his group were allowed to return to Greece, but Polybius stayed and wrote his *Universal History* in forty books, which is largely the history of Rome during the hundred years up to his own time and an interpretation of why Rome had become the world power it was. In the following selection, he analyzes the governmental system of the Roman Republic.

QUESTIONS TO CONSIDER

1. Why does Polybius think that checks and balances have given lasting stability to the Roman political system?
2. How does Polybius divide the Roman government into branches? How is his tripartite division both similar to and different from the system outlined in the U.S. Constitution?
3. How does aristocracy fit into the Roman system, according to Polybius? Does the concept of aristocracy play any part in the U.S. Constitution?

With those Greek states which have often risen to greatness and then experienced a complete change of fortune, it is easy to describe their past and to predict their future. For there is no difficulty in reporting the known facts, and it is not hard to foretell the future by inference from the past. But it is no simple matter to explain the present state of the Roman constitution, nor to predict its future owing to our ignorance of the peculiar features of Roman life in the past. Particular attention and study are therefore required if one wishes to survey clearly the distinctive qualities of Rome's constitution.

Most writers distinguish three kinds of constitutions: kingship, aristocracy, and democracy. One might ask them whether these three are the sole varieties or rather the best. In either case they are wrong. It is evident that the best constitution is one combining all three varieties, since we have had proof of this not only theoretically but by actual experience, Lycurgus having organized the Spartan state under a constitution based upon this principle. Nor can we agree that these three are the only kinds of states. We have witnessed monarchical and tyrannical governments, which differ sharply from true kingship, yet bear a certain resemblance to it. Several oligarchical constitutions also seem to resemble aristocratic ones. The same applies to democracies.

We must not apply the title of kingship to every monarchy, but must reserve it for one voluntarily accepted by willing subjects who are ruled by good judgment and not by terror and violence. Nor can we call every oligarchy an aristocracy, but only one where the government is in the hands of a selected body of the justest and wisest men. Similarly the name of democracy cannot be applied to a state in which the masses are free to do whatever they wish, but only to a community where it is traditional and customary to reverence the gods, honor one's parents, respect one's elders, and obey the laws. Such states, provided the will of the greater number prevails, are to be called democracies.

From Polybius, *Historiarum reliquiae* (Paris: Didot, 1839), VI, iii–xvii, pp. 338–48, *passim*. Trans. and condensed by Henry A. Myers.

We should therefore recognize six kinds of governments: the three above mentioned, kingship, aristocracy, and democracy, and the three which are naturally related to them, monarchy, oligarchy, and ochlocracy (mob-rule). The first to arise was monarchy, its growth being natural and unaided; the next is true kingship born from monarchy by planning and reforms. Kingship is transformed into its vicious related form, tyranny; and next, the abolishment of both gives birth to aristocracy. Aristocracy by its very nature degenerates into oligarchy; and when the masses take vengeance on this government for its unjust rule, democracy is born; and in due course the arrogance and lawlessness of this form of government produces mob-rule to complete the cycle. Such is the recurring cycle of constitutions; such is the system devised by nature.

Rome, foreseeing the dangers presented by such a cycle, did not organize her government according to any one type, but rather tried to combine all the good features of the best constitutions. All three kinds of government shared in the control of the Roman state. Such fairness and propriety was shown in the use of these three types in drawing up the constitution, that it was impossible to say with certainty if the whole system was aristocratic, democratic, or monarchical. If one looked at the power of the Consuls, the constitution seemed completely monarchical; if at that of the Senate, it seemed aristocratic; and if at the power of the masses, it seemed clearly to be a democracy.

Roman Consuls exercise authority over all public affairs. All other magistrates except the tribunes are under them and bound to obey them, and they introduce embassies to the Senate. They consult the Senate on matters of urgency, they carry out in detail the provisions of its decrees, they summon assemblies, introduce measures, and preside over the execution of popular decrees. In war their power is almost uncontrolled; for they are empowered to make demands on allies, to appoint military tribunes, and to select soldiers. They also have the right of inflicting punishment on anyone under their command, and spending any sum they decide upon from the public funds. If one looks at this part of the administration alone, one may reasonably pronounce the constitution to be a pure monarchy or kingship.

To pass to the Senate: in the first place it has the control of the treasury, all revenue and expenditure being regulated by it; with the exception of payments made to the consuls, no disbursements are made without a decree of the Senate. Public works, whether constructions or repairs, are under the control of the Senate. Crimes such as treason, conspiracy, poisoning, and assassination, as well as civil disputes, are under the jurisdiction of the Senate. The Senate also sends all embassies to foreign countries to settle differences, impose demands, receive submission, or declare war; and with respect to embassies arriving in Rome it decides what reception and what answer should be given to them. All these matters are in the hands of the Senate, so that in these respects the constitution appears to be entirely aristocratic.

After this we are naturally inclined to ask what part in the constitution is left for the people. The Senate controls all the particular matters I mentioned and manages all finances, and the Consuls have uncontrolled authority as regards armaments and operations in the field. But there is a very important part left for the people. For the people alone have the right to confer honors and inflict punishment, the only bonds by which human society is held together. For where the distinction between rewards and punishment is overlooked, or is observed but badly applied, no affairs can be properly administered. For how can one expect rational administration when good and evil men are held in equal estimation? The people judge cases punishable by a fine, especially when the accused have held high office. In capital cases they are the sole judges. It is the people who bestow office on the deserving, the noblest reward of virtue in a state; the people have the power of approving or rejecting laws, and what is most important of all, they deliberate on questions of war and peace. Further in the case of alliances, terms of peace, and treaties, it is the people who ratify all these. Thus one might plausibly say that the people's share in the government is the greatest, and that the constitution is a democratic one.

Having stated how political power is distributed among the three constitutional forms, I will now explain how each of the three parts is enabled, if they wish, to oppose or cooperate with the other parts. The Consul, when he leaves with his army, appears to have absolute authority in all matters necessary for carrying out his purpose; however, in fact he really requires the support of the people and the Senate. For the legions require constant supplies, and without the consent of the Senate, neither grain, clothing, nor pay can be provided; so that the commander's plans come to nothing, if the Senate chooses to impede them. As for the people it is indispensable for the Consuls to conciliate them, however far away from home they may be; for it is the people who ratify or annul treaties, and what is most important, the Consuls are obliged to account for their actions to the people. So it is not safe for the Consuls to underestimate the importance of the good will of either the Senate or the people.

The Senate, which possesses such great power, is obliged to respect the wishes of the people, and it cannot carry out inquiries into the most grave offenses against the state, unless confirmed by the people. The people alone have the power of passing or rejecting any law meant to deprive the Senate of some of its traditional authority. Therefore the Senate is afraid of the masses and must pay due attention to the popular will.

Similarly, the people are dependent on the Senate and must respect its members both in public and in private. Through the whole of Italy a vast number of contracts, which it would not be easy to enumerate, are given out by the Senate for the construction and repair of public buildings, and besides this there are many things which are farmed out, such as navigable rivers, harbors, gardens, mines, lands, in fact everything that forms part of the Roman domains. Now all these matters are undertaken by the people, and everyone is interested in these contracts and the work they involve. Certain people are the actual purchasers of the contracts, others are the partners of these first, others guarantee them, others pledge their own fortunes to the state for this purpose. In all these matters the Senate is supreme. It can grant extension of time; it can relieve the contractor if any accident occurs; and if the work proves to be absolutely impossible to carry out it can liberate him from his contract. There are many ways in which the Senate can either benefit or injure those who manage public property. What is even more important is that the judges in most civil trials are appointed from the Senate. As a result of the fact that all citizens are at the mercy of the Senate, and look forward with alarm to the uncertainty of litigation, they are very shy of obstructing or resisting its decisions. Similarly anyone is reluctant to oppose the projects of the Consuls as all are generally and individually under their authority when in the field.

Such being the power that each part has of hampering the others or cooperating with them, their union is adequate to all emergencies, so that it is impossible to find a better political system than this. Whenever the menace of some common danger from abroad compels them to act in concord and support each other, the strength of the state becomes great, as all are zealously competing in devising means of meeting the need of the hour. Consequently, this peculiar form of constitution possesses an irresistible power of attaining every object upon which it is resolved. When they are freed from external menace, and reap the harvest of good fortune and affluence which is the result of their success, and in the enjoyment of this prosperity are corrupted by flattery and idleness and become insolent and overbearing, as indeed happens often enough, it is then especially that we see the state providing itself a remedy for the evil from which it suffers. For when one part having grown out of proportion to the others aims at supremacy and tends to become too predominant, it is evident that none of the three is absolute. The purpose of one can be offset and resisted by the others, and none of them will excessively outgrow the others or treat them with contempt. All parts abide by the traditional constitutional practices because any aggressive impulse is sure to be checked and because they fear from the outset the possibility of being interfered with by the others.

40

Marcus Tullius Cicero, *The Laws*

The idea of a higher law than men could make had been a familiar one to the Greeks of the Classical Age. It had been well articulated by Sophocles in *Antigone* (see Reading 33). Consequently, it is a matter of some debate how original the Stoics of the Hellenistic Age were in stressing Natural Law as the body of (obviously unwritten) laws governing both the world of nature and the proper conduct of humankind. Be that as it may, the idea of a law based on nature as the proper model for human law appealed to many Roman commentators on law: Ideally man-made law, called *lex positiva* or "positive law" [15] by the Romans, was to reflect and implement the *lex naturalis* or "law of nature." If it did not, it did not deserve to be called "law." In the following selection, Marcus Tullius Cicero (106–43 B.C.), the Roman orator and political ideologue of the Republic, defends this relationship.

Placing higher value on Greek authority than on a claim to originality, Cicero used Plato's titles *The Republic* and *The Laws* to present his political ideas. In his *Republic*, he gives a short summary of the relationship between natural and positive law:

> "There is in fact a true law—namely, right reason—which is in accordance with nature, applies to all men, and is unchangeable and eternal. By its commands this law summons men to the performance of their duties; by its prohibitions it restrains them from doing wrong. Its commands and prohibitions always influence good men, but are without effect upon the bad. To invalidate this law by human legislation is never morally right, nor is it

---

[15]This was not in the sense of "positive" versus "negative," but rather in the no longer common usage of "set down" or "recorded," as in our common words: "*deposit*" and "*repository*."

permissible ever to restrict its operation, and to annul it wholly is impossible. Neither the Senate nor the people can absolve us from our obligation to obey this law. . . . It will not lay down one rule at Rome and another at Athens, nor will it be one rule today and another tomorrow. But there will be one law, eternal and unchangeable, binding at all times upon all peoples; and there will be, as it were, one common master and ruler of men, namely God, who is the author of this law, its interpreter, and its sponsor. The man who will not obey it will abandon his better self, and, in denying the true nature of a man, will thereby suffer the severest of penalties, though he has escaped all the other consequences which men call punishment."[16]

In his Laws, this connection is defended at much greater length.

QUESTIONS TO CONSIDER

1. Why does Cicero consider Natural Law to have greater power than man-made law? Do you? Why?
2. Why do you suppose that most twentieth-century lawyers prefer not to argue their cases in terms of Natural Law? Can you think of some cases in which Natural Law argumentation has won out?

Those learned men appear to be right who say that law is the highest reason implanted in Nature, which commands what should be done and prohibits what should not be: when this same reason takes root and develops in the human mind it is law. Thus they consider law to be intelligence which has the power to command people to do what is right and to refrain from what is wrong. . . . The way Nature has made us lets us share the concept of justice with each other and pass it on to all men. . . . Those human beings to whom Nature gave reason were also given *right* reason in matters of command and prohibition. . . .

From the time we were children, we have been calling rules that begin: "If a man makes a complaint in court" and similar things by the name "laws." It would be good now if we could establish that with commands to do things or refrain from doing them nations apply the power to steer people towards doing the right things and away from committing crimes; however, this power is not only older than peoples and governments but is of the same age as the God who protects and rules both Heaven and earth. You see, the divine mind cannot exist without reason, and divine reason must have the power to sanction what is right and wrong.

Nothing was ever written to say that one man alone on a bridge should face massed, armed forces of enemies and command the bridge behind him to be destroyed, but that fact should not mislead us into thinking that [Horatio] Cocles was not following to the utmost the law which summons us to deeds of bravery. If there has been no written law in Rome against rape back when Lucius Tarquin ruled as king, that would not mean that Sextus Tarquin was not breaking that eternal law when he took Lucretia by force. . . . The fact is that reason did exist, a gift of Nature,

[16]Marcus Tullius Cicero, *On the Commonwealth*, ed. and trans. George H. Sabine and Stanley B. Smith (Columbus: Ohio State University Press, 1929), III, xxii, pp. 215–16.

From Marcus Tullius Cicero, *De legibus libri*, ed. J. Vahlen (Berlin: F. Vahlenum, 1883), I, vi, 18–19; I, xi, 33; II, iv, 9–v, 13). Trans. Henry A. Myers. Dialogue-personage names omitted.

calling upon man to do right and abstain from wrong. It did not begin to be law when it first came into being, which it did at the same time as the divine mind. . . . The varied ordinances formulated for momentary needs of the peoples bear the name "laws" through being so favored by conventional usage rather than because they are really laws. . . . Men introduced such laws to insure the protection of citizens and states, as well as the peaceful and happy lot of mankind. Those who originated these sanctions persuaded their people that what they were writing down and putting into effect would—if the people lived by them—give them happiness and honor. When these sanctions were formulated and went into effect they were indeed called "laws."

How about all the pernicious and pestilential bits of legislation which nations have been known to enact? These no more deserve the name "laws" than the agreements that gangs of robbers might make among themselves. We know that if ignorant and inexperienced men should recommend poisons instead of medicines with the power to heal these would not be called "physicians' prescriptions." In the same way, nothing causing injury should be called a "law," no matter how it may have been enacted by a state or how the people may accept it. Thus we find that law reflects justice, distinct from injustice, and comes from that most ancient and rightfully dominant of all things: Nature, which all human laws reflect when they punish evildoers while defending and protecting good people.

Science in the Greco-Roman and Chinese Worlds

Greeks and Romans made strides toward a comprehensive philosophy of science with their understanding of cause and effect in the world of nature as a system of regularities functioning without any supernatural causes needed to make things happen. This served them well in medicine as in engineering. They prayed, of course, for divine intervention to ward off and cure diseases and occasionally were not above invoking supernatural aid to curse individuals, families, or projects, but in general they separated their study of the workings of nature from theology.

In astronomy, they inherited considerable data, particularly information related to devising calendars, from Egyptian and Babylonian predecessors and went on to observe with increasing exactness regularities with which planets and stars appeared in the sky, collating the patterns into a basis for more accurately predicting their reoccurrence. With few exceptions, their observations led them to confirm the geocentric theory, according to which the heavenly bodies revolved around the earth, which remained the focal point of the universe in their cosmography.

In general, it was the judgment of the educated Greek, Hellenistic, and Roman worlds that the study of nature should be pursued by observing natural phenomena through sense perception and reflecting upon the data so obtained through reason. This mindset was to surface much later as the formula for scientific—and consequently human—progress sporadically in the Western

European Renaissance and as a powerful force in the Enlightenment of the eighteenth century.

The Chinese, on the other hand, pursued scientific cause and effect to the point of developing valuable treatises, particularly on medicine, but Chinese science was always strongly influenced by cosmology. The concept of *yin* and *yang* as mutually complementary and balancing regulators of the universe remained the constant point of reference in Chinese medicine.

41

The Yellow Emperor, *Nei-ching* [*Neijing*] (Canon of Medicine)

The Yellow Emperor's Classic of Medicine (*Huangdi Neijing Suwen*, abbreviated *Neijing*) is one of the world's oldest medical classics. It remained for more than two thousand years the most basic and influential reference on internal medicine in China, Japan, and Korea in premodern times. Although the authorship of this extraordinary classic is attributed to the Yellow Emperor, one of the most famous legendary rulers of ancient China, who reigned from 2696 to 2598 B.C., the earliest mention of this work is found in the *History of Former Han* (206 B.C.–A.D. 25) by Ban Gu (A.D. 32–92), the great historian of the first century A.D. Various dates for the origin of this classic have been suggested, ranging from 1000 B.C. to the end of the fourth century B.C. It is also difficult to determine who the real author was. Whoever the original author may have been, it is highly likely that the Yellow Emperor's name was used to enhance the authoritativeness of this classic of medicine. This classic is written in the form of dialogue between the Yellow Emperor (Huangdi) and his minister Qi Bo.

The *Neijing* in its currently available form consists of eighty-one chapters. It covers wide-ranging topics such as a cosmological view of humans and health, etiology, diagnoses of various diseases, pulse analysis, methods of treatment, the art of acupuncture, pathology, psychiatry, and admonitions for physicians. The recurring themes that underlie this medical canon are cosmological concepts of *yin* and *yang* and the five elements. This philosophy explains that the universe is basically evolved from *yin* and *yang*, the mutually complementary and balancing cosmic regulators. Yang stands for sun, day, light, male, hot, active, and life; and *yin* for moon, night, dark, female, cold, passive, and death. *Yin* and *yang* are interdependent. *Yang* grows or fades into *yin* and vice versa. The concept of the five elements explains that all nature is made up of varying combinations of the five elements, which are wood, fire, earth, metal, and water. These five elements interact with one another and produce a constant state of internal motion. Such a pattern of motion is similarly extended to the human body. Since humans are very much a part of nature and the universe, traditional Chinese medicine extensively applies the concepts of *yin* and *yang* and the five elements to the understanding of the human body and mind, etiology, physiology, pathology, and treatment.

QUESTIONS TO CONSIDER

1. How similar and how different was traditional Chinese medicine from Hellenic and Hellenistic medicine? Did cosmology play any role in Western medicine in premodern times?
2. What are the reasons behind the growing interest in acupuncture in the West in recent years?
3. How are the concepts of *yin* and *yang* and the five elements reflected in the art of acupuncture?

Manifestation of Yin and Yang

Huang Di said, "The law of yin and yang is the natural order of the universe, the foundation of all things, mother of all changes, the root of life and death. In healing, one must grasp the root of the disharmony, which is always subject to the law of yin and yang.

"In the universe, the pure yang qi energy ascends to converge and form heaven, while the turbid yin qi descends and condenses to form the earth. Yin is passive and quiet, while the nature of yang is active and noisy. Yang is responsible for expanding and yin is responsible for contracting, becoming astringent, and consolidating. Yang is the energy, the vital force, the potential, while yin is the substance, the foundation, the mother that gives rise to all this potential. . . .

"The elements of fire and water are categorized into yang and yin, the fire being yang and the water being yin. The functional aspect of the body is yang and the nutritive or substantive aspect is yin. While food can be used to strengthen and nourish the body, the body's ability to transform it is dependent on qi. The functional part of qi is derived from the jing/essence. Food is refined into jing/essence, which supports the qi, and the qi is required for both transformation and bodily functions. For this reason, when the diet is improper, the body may be injured, or if activities are excessive, the jing/essence can be exhausted.

"The yin and yang in the body should be in balance with one another. If the yang qi dominates, the yin will be deprived, and vice versa. Excess yang will manifest as febrile disease, whereas excess yin will manifest as cold disease. When yang is extreme, however, it can turn into cold disease, and vice versa.

"Cold can injure the physical body, and heat can damage the qi or energetic aspect of the body. When there is injury to the physical body there will be swelling, but if the qi level is damaged, it can cause pain because of the qi blockage. In an injury that has two aspects, such as swelling (yin) and pain (yang), treatment may consist of pungent herbs to disperse swelling and cooling herbs to subdue the pain. If a patient complains of pain first and swelling afterward, this means the qi level was injured first. But if a patient complains of swelling first followed by pain, the trauma occurred at the physical level initially."

* * *

"Overindulgence in the five emotions—happiness, anger, sadness, worry or fear, and fright—can create imbalances. Emotions can injure the qi, while seasonal

From Maoshing Ni, Ph.D., trans., *The Yellow Emperor's Classic of Medicine* (pp. 17–26, 192–94). Copyright © 1995 by Maoshing Ni. Reprinted by arrangement with Shambhala Publications, Inc., Boston, *www.shambhala.com.*

elements can attack the body. Sudden anger damages the yin qi; becoming easily excited or overjoyed will damage the yang qi. This causes the qi to rebel and rise up to the head, squeezing the shen out of the heart and allowing it to float away. Failing to regulate one's emotions can be likened to summer and winter failing to regulate each other, threatening life itself."

* * *

Then Huang Di inquired, "What are the methods to balance yin and yang?"

Qi Bo answered, "If one understands the methods or Tao of maintaining health and the causes of depletion, then one can readily master the balance of yin and yang and stay healthy. Normally, by the age of forty, people have exhausted fifty percent of their yin qi, and their vitality is weakened. At age fifty the body is heavy, the vision and the hearing deteriorated; by age sixty the yin qi is further diminished, the kidneys drained; the sensory organs and the nine orifices, including the excretory organs, have all become functionally impaired. Conditions will manifest such as prostatitis, vision loss, deficiency in the lower jiao (viscera cavity) and excess in the upper jiao, tearing, and nasal drainage problems.

"Thus, the body of one who understands the Tao will remain strong and healthy. The one who does not understand the Tao will age. One who is careless will often feel deficient, while one who knows will have an abundance of energy. Those who are knowledgeable have clear orifices, perceptions, hearing, vision, smell, and taste, and are light and strong. Even though their bodies are old, they can perform most of life's activities."

The Art of Acupuncture

Huang Di said, "Will you please explain to me the nine different needles? And will you also please discuss the methods of tonification and sedation in excess and in deficiency?"

Qi Bo answered, "When acupuncturing deficient conditions one should elicit heat sensation with the needle. Only when the qi is strong will it be able to produce heat. In treating excess conditions one should elicit a cooling sensation. When the pathogenic qi is weakening one will experience a cooling feeling. When there is stagnation in the blood caused by the accumulation of a pathogen, one should promote bloodletting to rid the bad blood. In withdrawing the needle on patients with an excess condition, withdraw the needle quickly. Allow the hole to remain open in order to disperse the pathogen. In deficiency, withdraw the needle slowly and close the hole to prevent loss of qi. . . .

"In order to master the techniques one must be able to use the nine needles with equal ease. Each of the nine has a specific indication. In terms of the timing in tonifying or sedating, one must coordinate the technique with the opening and closing of the hole, and the arrival and departure of the qi. When the qi arrives, we call this opening. At this point, one can sedate. When the qi leaves, we call this closing. Now one can tonify.

"The nine needles are of different size, shape, and use. When acupuncturing excess, one must sedate. Insert the needles and await the arrival of yin qi. When one feels a cooling sensation under the needle, remove the needles. In deficiency, one must tonify. After needle insertion, await the arrival of yang qi. When there is a warming sensation, remove the needles. Once you grasp the qi with the needle, be very attentive and listen so as not to lose the opportunity to manipulate the effects. Treat disease according to where it is located; determine whether to insert deeply or shallowly. When the disease is located deep, insert deeply. When the disease is superficial, needle shallowly. Although there is a difference in depth of penetration, the principle of awaiting the qi is the same.

"When acupuncturing, one should be prepared and careful, as if one is facing a deep abyss. Move carefully so as not to fall. In handling the needle, hold it as if holding the tiger—firmly grasped and in control. One needs a calm mind to observe the patient. Concentrate clearly on the patient and do not become scattered. Upon inserting the needle, be accurate and precise. It should not be crooked or miss the target. When the needle enters the body, the physician should observe the patient closely in order to help guide the patient's attention. This allows the qi in the channels to move more easily, and the results are more effective."

Huang Di said, "I've heard that the nine types of needles have a relationship to yin and yang and the four seasonal energies. Can you please explain this so it may be passed on to later generations as a principle of healing?"

Qi Bo answered, "In Taoist cosmology the number one corresponds to heaven; two to earth; three to man; four to the seasons; five to sounds; six to rhythms; seven to the stars; eight to wind; nine to the continents. People have physical form and connect to nature. The various shapes and forms of the nine needles conform to different types of conditions. The skin of human beings envelops and protects the body, just as heaven envelops and protects the myriad things. Muscles are soft, pliable, and calm, just as earth, which contains the myriad things. . . .

"Therefore, we have the nine needles. The first, called *chan zhen*, superficially punctures the skin. The second needle, called *yuan zhen*, does not penetrate but instead massages the acupoints on the flesh and muscles. The third needle, *ti zhen*, punctures the vessels. The fourth needle, *feng zhen*, punctures and draws blood from capillaries and small veins. The fifth needle, *fei pi zhen*, lances the skin to drain pus. The sixth needle, *yuan li zhen*, punctures the joints for bi conditions. The seventh needle, *hao zhen*, punctures the acupoints on the flesh. The eighth needle, *chang zhen*, punctures deep fleshy locations. The ninth needle, *da zhen*, punctures the abdomen to relieve edema or masses. Choose these needles wisely for the appropriate occasion."

* * *

"The blood and qi within the body circulate throughout the channels and vessels, balancing yin and yang, just as water in rivers and lakes circulates endlessly. The qi of the liver connects with the eyes, and the eyes are part of the nine orifices."

42

Hippocrates, *On the Sacred Disease*

Hippocrates of Cos [460 (?)–375 (?) B.C.] practiced and taught medicine in the days of Socrates and Plato. He forcefully advocated collecting objective data concerning cause and effect in diseases and cautioned against ascribing supernatural causes to any particular category of disease. At the medical school at Cos and then at the much larger one in Greek Alexandria, his writings were copied and new ones ascribed to him long after his death, so that it is impossible to know just which pieces he wrote; however, all the writings that bear his name show the rational, systematic, and secular approach to medicine for which he is known. The famed "Hippocratic Oath" ascribed to him, which physicians in the Western world have taken over the centuries, promising among other things to supply neither a means for abortion nor poison for a physician-assisted suicide, may well reflect some of his concern for ethics in the practice of medicine, but it appears to have been written some four centuries after his death.

The following article deals with epilepsy. Probably because no physician had any clue as to its cause—understandably, since its cause is still unknown—and its convulsions appeared to come out of nowhere and strike the afflicted, it had been called "the sacred disease."

QUESTIONS TO CONSIDER

1. What sort of people, according to Hippocrates, were first inclined to call this disease "the sacred one"?
2. Why does Hippocrates believe that those who stress the "sacred" nature of the disease are less, rather than more, religious than other people?
3. How does Hippocrates go about refuting the claim that this disease is specially sacred?

It is thus with regard to the disease called Sacred: it appears to me to be nowise more divine nor more sacred than other diseases, but has a natural cause from which it originates like other afflictions. Men regard its nature and cause as divine from ignorance and wonder, because it is not at all like to other diseases. And this notion of its divinity is kept up by their inability to comprehend it, and the simplicity of the mode by which it is cured, for men are freed from it by purifications and incantations. But if it is reckoned divine because it is wonderful, instead of one there are many diseases which would be sacred; for, as I will show, there are others no less wonderful and prodigious, which nobody imagines to be sacred. The quotidian, tertian, and quartan fevers seem to me no less sacred and divine in their origin than this disease, although they are not reckoned so wonderful. And I see men become mad and demented from no manifest cause, and at the same time doing many things out of place; and I have known many persons in sleep groaning and crying out, some in a state of suffocation, some jumping up and fleeing out of doors, and deprived of their reason until they awaken, and afterward becoming well and rational as before, although they be pale and weak; and this will happen not once but frequently. And there are many and various things of the like kind, which it would be tedious to state particularly.

They who first referred this malady to the gods appear to me to have been just such persons as the conjurors, purificators, mountebanks, and charlatans now are,

From Hippocrates, *On the Sacred Disease* (pp. 154–55), trans. Francis Adams. Reprinted from *Great Books of the Western World* © 1952, 1990, Encyclopaedia Britannica, Inc.

who give themselves out for being excessively religious, and as knowing more than other people. Such persons, then, using the divinity as a pretext and screen of their own inability to afford any assistance, have given out that the disease is sacred, adding suitable reasons for this opinion, they have instituted a mode of treatment which is safe for themselves, namely, by applying purifications and incantations, and enforcing abstinence from baths and many articles of food which are unwholesome to men in diseases. Of sea substances, the surmullet, the blacktail, the mullet, and the eel; for these are the fishes most to be guarded against. And of fleshes, those of the goat, the stag, the sow, and the dog: for these are the kinds of flesh which are aptest to disorder the bowels. Of fowls, the cock, the turtle, and the bustard, and such others as are reckoned to be particularly strong. And of potherbs, mint, garlic, and onions; for what is acrid does not agree with a weak person. And they forbid to have a black robe, because black is expressive of death; and to sleep on a goat's skin, or to wear it, and to put one foot upon another, or one hand upon another; for all these things are held to be hindrances to the cure. All these they enjoin with reference to its divinity, as if possessed of more knowledge, and announcing beforehand other causes so that if the person should recover, theirs would be the honor and credit; and if he should die, they would have a certain defense, as if the gods, and not they, were to blame, seeing they had administered nothing either to eat or drink as medicines, nor had overheated him with baths, so as to prove the cause of what had happened. But I am of opinion that (if this were true) none of the Libyans, who live in the interior, would be free from this disease, since they all sleep on goats' skins, and live upon goats' flesh; neither have they couch, robe, nor shoe that is not made of goat's skin, for they have no other herds but goats and oxen. But if these things, when administered in food, aggravate the disease, and if it be cured by abstinence from them, godhead is not the cause at all; nor will purifications be of any avail, but it is the food which is beneficial and prejudicial, and the influence of the divinity vanishes.

Thus, they who try to cure these maladies in this way, appear to me neither to reckon them sacred nor divine. For when they are removed by such purifications, and this method of cure, what is to prevent them from being brought upon men and induced by other devices similar to these? So that the cause is no longer divine, but human. For whoever is able, by purifications and conjurations, to drive away such an affection, will be able, by other practices, to excite it; and, according to this view, its divine nature is entirely done away with. By such sayings and doings, they profess to be possessed of superior knowledge, and deceive mankind by enjoining lustrations and purifications upon them, while their discourse turns upon the divinity and the godhead. And yet it would appear to me that their discourse savors not of piety, as they suppose, but rather of impiety, and as if there were no gods, and that what they hold to be holy and divine, were impious and unholy. This I will now explain.

For, if they profess to know how to bring down the moon, darken the sun, induce storms and fine weather, and rains and droughts, and make the sea and land unproductive, and so forth, whether they arrogate this power as being derived from mysteries or any other knowledge or consideration, they appear to me to practice impiety, and either to fancy that there are no gods, or, if there are, that they have no ability to ward off any of the greatest evils. How, then, are they not enemies to the gods? For if a man by magical arts and sacrifices will bring down the moon, and darken the sun, and induce storms, or fine weather, I should not believe that there was anything divine, but human, in these things, provided the power of the divine were overpowered by human knowledge and subjected to it. But perhaps it will be said, these things are not so, but, men being in want of the means of life, invent many and various things, and devise many contrivances for all other things, and for this disease, in every phase of the disease, assigning the cause to a god. Nor do they remember the same things once, but frequently. For, if they imitate a goat, or grind their teeth, or if their right side be convulsed, they say that the mother of the gods is the cause. But if they speak in a sharper and more intense tone, they resemble this state to a horse, and say that Poseidon is the cause. Or if any excrement be passed, which is often the case, owing to the violence of the disease, the appellation of Enodia is adhibited; or, if it be passed in smaller and denser masses, like bird's, it is said to be from Apollo Nomius. But if foam be emitted by the mouth, and the patient kick with his feet, Ares then gets the blame. But terrors which happen during the night, and fevers, and delirium, and jumpings out of bed, and frightful apparitions, and fleeing away—all these they hold to be the plots of Hecate, and the invasions of the Heroes, and use purifications and incantations, and, as appears to me, make the divinity to be most wicked and most impious. For they purify those laboring under this disease, with the same sorts of blood and the other means that are used in the case of those who are stained with crimes, and of malefactors, or who have been enchanted by men, or who have done any wicked act; who ought to do the very reverse, namely, sacrifice and pray, and, bringing gifts to the temples, supplicate the gods. But now they do none of these things, but purify; and some of the purifications they conceal in the earth, and some they throw into the sea, and some they carry to the mountains where no one can touch or tread upon them. But these they ought to take to the temples and present to the god, if a god be the cause of the disease. Neither truly do I count it a worthy opinion to hold that the body of man is polluted by god, the most impure by the most holy; for were it defiled, or did it suffer from any other thing, it would be like to be purified and sanctified rather than polluted by god. For it is the divinity which purifies and sanctifies the greatest of offenses and the most wicked, and which proves our protection from them. And we mark out the boundaries of the temples and the groves of the gods, so that no one may pass them unless he be pure, and when we enter them we are sprinkled with holy water, not as being polluted, but as laying aside any other pollution which we formerly had. And thus it appears to me to hold, with regard to purifications.

But this disease seems to me to be no more divine that others; but it has its nature such as other diseases have, and a cause whence it originates, and its nature and cause are divine only just as much as all others are.

43

Pliny the Elder, *The Nature Story*

Pliny the Elder (A.D. 23–79) ranked high among Romans as a scientist largely on the basis of his *Naturalis Historia*, roughly *The Nature Story* (not *history* in the sense of a chronological narration). Always a busy man, Pliny studied at Rome for an official career, commanded a cavalry squadron in Germany, returned to Rome, and although he kept a low profile during most of Nero's reign, eventually became governor of Spain, a naval commander, and then adviser to Emperor Vespasian, with whom he had served in Germany. He constantly read and took notes on natural phenomena, and two years before his death presented Emperor Titus with *The Nature Story*, containing, as he put it, "twenty thousand things well worth knowing" (none evidently more important than the rest), gathered from research in two thousand volumes by one hundred authors, and enriched by many of his own observations. His was more of a science-hero's death in the line of duty than was the demise of most scientists: When he went to observe what was happening with Mount Vesuvius, it erupted and directed molten lava toward the city of Pompeii. Before Pompeii was wiped out by the volcano, Pliny was overcome by poisonous fumes and died.

Pliny was convinced of the existence of a World Soul, which made and directed the earth, world, and/or universe (he uses the same word, *mundus*, for all three). He saw the World Soul as a living being and consequently as God. The World Soul is central in his scheme of things, and he refers to it in determining what is natural and unnatural. But in the great bulk of his work, he is content to compile a wealth of factual information about places, things, and events on the basis of his observations or those of authors whom he trusts. In this selection, he discusses the world at large and the basic elements. The four elements, as he describes them, were thought to be the elements until modern times, and his description of them may serve to explain why neither ancient Greeks nor Romans nor early Arabs nor Western medieval people got very far with the science of chemistry.

QUESTIONS TO CONSIDER

1. Can you relate Pliny's "World Soul" to "the One" in the Hindu creation story (see Reading 4) or to "the Way" in Taoism (see Reading 28)? What are the similarities and differences?
2. What are the four elements? Why do you suppose Greeks and Romans settled on one of them as "the highest"?
3. What is distinctive about humans, as opposed to other animals, in Pliny's description of the effects of lightning?

The World

The world, and whatever that be which we otherwise call the heavens, by the vault of which all things are enclosed, we must conceive to be a Deity, to be eternal, without bounds, neither created, nor subject, at any time, to destruction. To inquire what is beyond it is no concern of man, nor can the human mind form any conjecture respecting it. It is sacred, eternal, and without bounds, all in all; indeed including everything in itself; finite, yet like what is infinite; the most certain of all things, yet like what is uncertain, externally and internally embracing all things in itself; it is the work of nature, and itself constitutes nature.

From The *Natural History of Pliny*, trans. and ed. John Bostock and H.T. Riley (London: Henry G. Bohn, 1855), Vol. I, pp. 13–20, 84–86, *passim.*

It is madness to harass the mind, as some have done, with attempts to measure the world, and to publish these attempts; or, like others, to argue from what they have made out, that there are innumerable other worlds, and that we must believe there to be so many other natures, or that, if only one nature produced the whole, there will be so many suns and so many moons, and that each of them will have immense trains of other heavenly bodies. As if the same question would not recur at every step of our inquiry, anxious as we must be to arrive at some termination; or, as if this infinity, which we ascribe to nature, the former of all things, cannot be more easily comprehended by one single formation, especially when that is so extensive. It is madness, perfect madness, to go out of this world and to search for what is beyond it, as if one who is ignorant of his own dimensions could ascertain the measure of anything else, or as if the human mind could see what the world itself cannot contain.

That it has the form of a perfect globe we learn from the name which has been uniformly given to it, as well as from numerous natural arguments. For not only does a figure of this kind return everywhere into itself and sustain itself, also including itself, requiring no adjustments, not sensible of either end or beginning in any of its parts, and is best fitted for that motion, with which, as will appear hereafter, it is continually turning round; but still more, because we perceive it, by the evidence of sight, to be, in every part, convex and central, which could not be the case were it of any other figure.

The rising and setting of the sun clearly prove that this globe is carried round in the space of twenty-four hours, in an eternal and never-ceasing circuit, and with incredible swiftness. I am not able to say, whether the sound caused by the whirling about of so great a mass be excessive, and therefore, far beyond what our ears can perceive, nor, indeed, whether the resounding of so many stars, all carried along at the same time and revolving in their orbits, may not produce a kind of delightful harmony of incredible sweetness. To us, who are in the interior, the world appears to glide gently along, both by day and by night.

Various circumstances in nature prove to us, that there are impressed on the heavens innumerable figures of animals and of all kinds of objects, and that its surface is not perfectly polished like the eggs of birds, as some celebrated authors assert. For we find that the seeds of all bodies fall down from it, principally into the ocean, and, being mixed together, that a variety of monstrous forms are in this way frequently produced. And, indeed, this is evident to the eye; for, in one part, we have the figure of a wain, in another of a bear, of a bull, and of a letter; while, in the middle of them, over our heads, there is a white circle.

The Elements and Planets

I do not find that any one has doubted that there are four elements. The highest of these is supposed to be fire, and hence proceed the eyes of so many glittering stars. The next is that spirit, which both the Greeks and ourselves call by the same name, air. It is by the force of this vital principle, pervading all things and mingling with all, that the earth, together with the fourth element, water, is balanced in the middle of space. These are mutually bound together, the lighter being restrained by the heavier, so that they cannot fly off; while, on the contrary, from the lighter tending upwards, the heavier are so suspended, that they cannot fall down. Thus, by an equal tendency in the opposite direction, each of them remains in its appropriate place, bound together by the never-ceasing revolution of the world, which always turning on itself, the earth falls to the lowest part and is in the middle of the whole, while it remains suspended in the center, and, as it were, balancing this center, in which it is suspended. So that it alone remains immoveable, whilst all things revolve round it, being connected with every other part, whilst they all rest upon it.

Between this body and the heavens there are suspended, in this aerial spirit, seven stars, separated by determinate spaces, which, on account of their motion, we call wandering, although, in reality, none are less so. The sun is carried along in the midst of these, a body of great size and power, the ruler, not only of the seasons and of the different climates, but also of the stars themselves and of the heavens. When we consider his operations, we must regard him as the life, or rather the mind of the universe, the chief regulator and the God of nature; he also lends his light to the other stars. He is most illustrious and excellent, beholding all things and hearing all things, which, I perceive, is ascribed to him exclusively by the prince of poets, Homer.

The Laws of Lightning

It is certain that the lightning is seen before the thunder is heard, although they both take place at the same time. Nor is this wonderful, since light has a greater velocity than sound. Nature so regulates it, that the stroke and the sound coincide; the sound is, however, produced by the discharge of the thunder, not by its stroke. But the air is impelled quicker than the lightning, on which account it is that everything is shaken and blown up before it is struck, and that a person is never injured when he has seen the lightning and heard the thunder. Thunder on the left hand is supposed to be lucky, because the east is on the left side of the heavens.

It lightens without thunder more frequently in the night than in the day. Man is the only animal that is not always killed by it, all other animals being killed instantly, nature having granted to him this mark of distinction, while so many other animals excel him in strength. All animals fall down on the opposite side to that which has been struck; man, unless he be thrown down on the parts that are struck, does not expire. Those who are struck directly from above sink down immediately. When a man is struck while he is awake, he is found with his eyes closed; when asleep, with them open. It is not considered proper that a man killed in this way should be burnt on the funeral pile; our religion enjoins us to bury the body in the earth. No animal is consumed by lightning unless after having been previously killed. The parts of the animal that have been wounded by lightning are colder than the rest of the body.

Part III

Christianity to Islam

The Rise of Christianity

In the last century of the Roman Republic, religious and civil conflicts made Palestine vulnerable to Roman intervention in Jewish affairs. Pompey the Great stormed Jerusalem in 63 B.C. and aided an Idumean named Antipater in being named foreign minister to the temple state. Thereafter, Antipater's son, Herod, became friends with Julius Caesar, Mark Antony, and Augustus Caesar. In return for his loyalty and obedience, the Romans permitted Herod to resurrect the monarchy (37–4 B.C.).

Herod's reign was a prosperous one: He was able to rebuild Jerusalem with a great palace, the Second Temple, and to add many forts throughout the kingdom. Nonetheless, many Jews hated Herod because they saw him as proRoman, a murderer of his family, and—above all—not wholly Jewish.

Factions also dominated Judea, where Jesus was born. There were the Sadducees, supported by the upper classes, who controlled the Temple priesthood and were strict supporters of the Torah. Their opponents were the Pharisees, who were seen as more liberal. They supported public education, believed in personal immortality, and sponsored scribal commentaries on the Laws. Other groups, such as the Essenes, had withdrawn from secular life completely and became ascetics in desert communities. One of these latter, the New Covenanters, expected an end to the wicked age and the establishment of a new kingdom of righteousness.

Jesus was born some time near the end of Herod's rule—not, as the later Christians believed, in the year A.D. 1. Although we cannot establish a true date, his parents, Joseph and Mary, had to leave their village of Nazareth and proceed to Bethlehem. They were displaced because Augustus Caesar had ordered a census of the empire, requiring that everyone register in the city of his or her family. In the Gospels, Jesus' lineage is traced back to Bethlehem, the home of David, from whose line the Hebrew prophets had predicted a Messiah would come.

Little information is recorded in the Gospels about the middle years of Jesus' life. Not until he was baptized by his cousin, John the Baptist, would Jesus begin his public ministry. From that time until his crucifixion three years later, Jesus gathered his apostles, preached a new religious message, and worked his miracles.

As Jesus' fame increased in Galilee and Judea, the religious authorities feared disturbances. The Sadducees accused him of religious blasphemy, arrested him, and handed him over to the Roman governor of Judea, Pontius Pilate. Jesus was tried and executed for sedition against Rome.

Within a short period, the apostles announced that Jesus had risen from the grave and would shortly return in the Second Coming, which would inaugurate the Messianic Kingdom. In order to amplify this theology, the Apostle Paul identified Jesus as the son of God, or God-made flesh, whose sacrifice on the Cross made salvation from sin possible for all humanity. The apostles traveled from city to city with these messages, appealing first to the Jews and then to the Gentiles. This was the true foundation of the Christian religion.

44

The Golden Rule and God's Will

In this passage, Jesus explains that the person who hears and does God's will is fulfilling the Law.

QUESTIONS TO CONSIDER

1. What are the Lord's requirements of a true believer?
2. Why are not all prophets acceptable?
3. Compare Jesus' Sermon on the Mount and other teachings with those of Moses and the Hebrews (see Readings 2 and 16), Buddha (see Readings 24 and 25), and Hindu sources (see Readings 21 to 22) touching on the same subjects.

Judge not, that ye be not judged.

For with what judgment ye judge, ye shall be judged: and with what measure ye mete, it shall be measured to you again.

And why beholdest thou the mote that is in thy brother's eye, but considerest not the beam that is in thine own eye?

Or how wilt thou say to thy brother, Let me pull out the mote out of thine eye: and, behold, a beam is in thine own eye?

Thou hypocrite, first cast out the beam out of thine own eye; and then shalt thou see clearly to cast out the mote out of thy brother's eye.

Give not that which is holy unto the dogs, neither cast ye your pearls before swine, lest they trample them under their feet, and turn again and rend you.

Ask, and it shall be given you: seek, and ye shall find: knock, and it shall be opened unto you:

From Matthew 7:1–29 (King James Version); slightly modernized.

For every one that asketh receiveth: and he that seeketh findeth: and to him that knocketh it shall be opened.

> Or what man is there of you, whom if his son ask bread, will he give him a stone?
> Or if he ask a fish, will he give him a serpent?

If ye then, being evil, know how to give good gifts unto your children, how much more shall your Father which is in heaven give good things to them that ask him?

Therefore all things whatsoever ye would that men should do to you, do ye even so to them: for this is the law and the prophets.

Enter ye in at the strait gate: for wide is the gate, and broad is the way, that leadeth to destruction, and many there be which go in there:

Because strait is the gate, and narrow is the way, which leadeth unto life, and few there be that find it.

Beware of false prophets, which come to you in sheep's clothing, but inwardly they are ravening wolves.

> Ye shall know them by their fruits. Do men gather grapes of thorns, or figs of thistles?
> Even so every good tree bringeth forth good fruit; but a corrupt tree bringeth forth evil fruit.
> A good tree cannot bring forth evil fruit, neither can a corrupt tree bring forth good fruit.
> Every tree that bringeth not forth good fruit is hewn down, and cast into the fire.
> Wherefore by their fruits ye shall know them.

Not every one that saith unto me, Lord, Lord, shall enter into the kingdom of heaven; but he that doeth the will of my Father which is in heaven.

Many will say to me in that day, Lord, Lord, have we not prophesied in thy name? and in thy name have cast out devils? and in thy name done many wonderful works?

And then will I profess unto them, I never knew you: depart from me, ye that work iniquity.

Therefore whosoever heareth these sayings of mine, and doeth them, I will liken him unto a wise man, which built his house upon a rock:

And the rain descended, and the floods came, and the winds blew, and beat upon that house; and it fell not: for it was founded upon a rock.

And every one that heareth these sayings of mine, and doeth them not, shall be likened unto a foolish man, which built his house upon the sand:

And the rain descended, and the floods came, and the winds blew, and beat upon that house; and it fell: and great was the fall of it.

And it came to pass, when Jesus had ended these sayings, the people were astonished at his doctrine:

For he taught them as one having authority, and not as the scribes.

45

The Writings of St. Paul on Women

Women in many ancient societies were subordinate to men in legal, political, and religious rights. And at first glance, this might appear to be the case in the Old and New Testaments, where woman (Eve) is depicted as the source of "Original Sin" or compared to Israel, God's unfaithful wife; however, woman is also viewed in the Old Testament as the faithful companion of God and in the Gospels as the way to salvation through the New Eve, Mary.

When all the Gospel accounts are taken as a whole, they seem to reflect a significant change in human relations and an increased importance for women. Jesus' teachings emphasize the idea that men and women have equal duties in marriage; just as divorce is forbidden for both, so adultery is not limited to women. Women such as Mary Magdalene were attracted to Jesus' ministry, and it was to women that Jesus appeared at his tomb. They were also important as helpers (deaconesses) or patrons in the newly established Christian communities.

The ideas of St. Paul reflect both the Old Testament and the Gospel views of women. Born into a Jewish family that had acquired Roman citizenship, Saul of Tarsus (Paul) at first rejected Christianity and joined in the persecution of early Christians. Later, according to his own account, a blinding light appeared to him on the road to Damascus, where God commanded him to stop harming Christians and to begin preaching the Gospel. Under his Roman name of Paul, he became such an effective Christian preacher and teacher that he was listed among the Apostles. His letters became an important part of Christian theology.

St. Paul changed the course of Christianity as he preached to the gentile communities of the Roman world instead of concentrating exclusively on Jews. When doctrinal disputes arose within Christian groups, Paul attempted to settle these problems in his letters through interpretation and application of Jesus' teachings.

St. Paul was frequently in trouble with Jewish leaders, who saw him as a traitor. Roman authorities at first had nothing against Christians but later took a dim view of religious figures, such as Paul, whose speeches provoked an uproar. When some confusion resulted in Paul's being arrested in Palestine, he used his Roman citizenship to appeal his case to the emperor. According to Church tradition, he was sent to the capital and released after several years of captivity. Some seven or eight years later, however, he was one of the Christians executed during Nero's persecution.

The following excerpts from Paul's letters to the Galatians and Corinthians illustrate some of his teachings. These include the equality of men and women in Christ through baptism but their inequality in marriage and sexuality.

QUESTIONS TO CONSIDER

1. What was life like for women in the ancient world? Were there any exceptions?
2. How did the Hebrew religion influence the Christian view of women (see Reading 2)?
3. How does St. Paul argue for equality for all persons?
4. In the area of freedom and responsibilities in marriage, does St. Paul address himself only to men?
5. Many authors say that St. Paul subordinates women to men in I Corinthians 11:2–16. Could his statements express his view of a "natural law" governing men and women?

Baptism and Faith

Wherefore the law was our schoolmaster to bring us unto Christ, that we might be justified by faith.

But after that faith is come, we are no longer under a schoolmaster.

For you are all the children of God by faith in Christ Jesus.

For as many of you as have been baptized into Christ have put on Christ.

There is neither Jew nor Greek, there is neither bond [slave] nor free, there is neither male nor female: for you are all one in Christ Jesus.

Marriage

Now concerning the things whereof you wrote unto me: It is good for a man not to touch a woman.

Nevertheless, to avoid fornication, let every man have his own wife, and let every woman have her own husband.

Let the husband render unto the wife due benevolence: and likewise also the wife unto the husband.

The wife has no power of her own body, but the husband: and likewise also the husband has not power of his own body, but the wife.

Do not refuse one another except by agreement for a time, that you may give yourselves to fasting and prayer; and come together again, lest that Satan tempt you through lack of self-control.

But I speak this by permission, and not of commandment.

For I wish that all men were even as I myself. But every man has his proper gift of God, one after this manner, another after that.

I say therefore to the unmarried and widows, it is good for them if they remain even as I.

But if they cannot contain, let them marry: for it is better to marry than to burn.

And to the married I command, yet not I, but the Lord, Let not the wife depart from her husband:

But and if she depart, let her remain unmarried, or be reconciled to her husband: and let not the husband put away his wife.

But to the rest I speak, not the Lord: If any brother has an unbelieving wife, and she is pleased to live with him, let him not put her away.

And the woman who has an unbelieving husband, and if he is pleased to live with her, let her not leave him.

For the unbelieving husband is sanctified by the wife, and the unbelieving wife is sanctified by the husband: otherwise your children were unclean; but now they are holy.

But if the unbelieving departs, let him depart. A brother or sister is not under bondage in such cases: but God has called us to peace.

For what do you know, Oh wife, whether you shall save your husband? or how do you know, Oh man, whether you shall save your wife?

But as God has distributed to every man, as the Lord has called every one, so let him walk. And so I ordain in all churches. . . .

The first section is from Galatians 3:24–28. The second is from I Corinthians 7:1–17, 25–28, 32–40. The third section is from I Corinthians 11:2–16. (King James Version; slightly modernized.)

Now concerning virgins I have no commandment of the Lord: yet I give my judgment, as one that has obtained mercy of the Lord to be faithful.

I suppose therefore that this is good for the present distress, I say, that it is good for a man so to be.

Art you bound to a wife? seek not to be freed. Art you freed from a wife? seek not a wife.

But if you marry, you have not sinned; and if a virgin marry, she has not sinned. Nevertheless such shall have trouble in the flesh: but I spare you.

But this I say, brothers, the time is short: it remains that both they who have wives be as though they had none; . . .

But I would have you without carefulness. He that is unmarried cares for the things that belong to the Lord, how he may please the Lord:

But he that is married cares for the things that are of the world, how he may please his wife.

There is difference also between a wife and a virgin. The unmarried woman cares for the things of the Lord, that she may be holy both in body and in spirit: but she who is married cares for the things of the world, how she may please her husband.

And this I speak for your own profit; not that I may cast a snare on you, but for that which is proper, and that you may attend upon the Lord without distraction.

But if any man thinks that he behaves improperly toward his virgin, if she is passed the flower of her age, and need requires it, let him do what he will, he does not sin; let them marry.

Nevertheless he that stands steadfast in his heart, having no necessity, but has power over his own will, and has so decreed in his heart that he will keep his virgin, does well.

So then he that gives her in marriage does well; but he that does not give her in marriage does better.

The wife is bound by the law as long as her husband lives; but if her husband is dead, she is at liberty to be married to whomever she will; only in the Lord.

But she is happier if she so abide, after my judgment: and I think also that I have the Spirit of God.

Physical Differences of Sexes

Now I praise you, brothers, that you remember me in all things, and keep the ordinances, as I delivered them to you.

But I would have you know, that the head of every man is Christ; and the head of the woman is the man; and the head of Christ is God.

Every man praying or prophesying, having his head covered, dishonors his head.

But every woman who prays or prophesies with her head uncovered dishonors her head: for that is even all one as if she were shaven.

For if the woman is not covered, let her be shorn: but if it is a shame for a woman to be shorn or shaven, let her be covered.

For a man indeed ought not to cover his head, as he is the image and glory of God: but the woman is the glory of man.

For the man is not of the woman; but the woman of the man.

Neither was the man created for the woman; but the woman for the man.

For this cause ought the woman to have power on her head because of the angels.

Nevertheless neither is the man without the woman, neither the woman without the man, in the Lord.

For as the woman is of the man, even so is the man also by the woman; but all things of God.

Judge in yourselves: is it seemly that a woman pray unto God uncovered?

Does not even nature itself teach you, that, if a man has long hair, it is his shame?

But if a woman has long hair, it is a glory to her: for her hair is given her for a covering.

But if any man seems to be quarrelsome, we have no such custom, neither the churches of God.

Rome and the Christians

For three hundred years, the Roman government showed an unusual tolerance in the area of personal religion. In rare instances, such as during the Great Fire of A.D. 64, the Christians were persecuted; however, the persecution occurred not only for their religious practices: The Emperor Nero needed scapegoats to stop the rumors that he had started the fire. Most persecutions took place in the provinces and were sporadic. They were undertaken by local governors who saw the Christians as unlicensed groups, practicing barbaric rites and refusing to make public sacrifices to the emperors. In the second century, the official government position was established by Emperor Trajan, who decreed that only conspicuous and defiant Christians were to be punished; the rest would be tolerated. As the Roman Empire crumbled in the last half of the third century, Emperor Diocletian viewed the Christians as a danger to the unity of the empire and began the Great Persecution (A.D. 303–311). After Constantine (306–337) conquered the western half of the Roman Empire, however, he issued a declaration of religious toleration in 313 that became the governmental policy until 392, when Emperor Theodosius I made Christianity the sole religion.

The first selection is from Pliny the Younger (A.D. 62–113), whose ten books of *Letters* illustrate travel, court, and daily life, and politics at the turn of the first century. About A.D. 110, Emperor Trajan appointed Pliny proconsul or special imperial representative in the province of Bithynia, which lay along the south coast of the Black Sea.

The next two selections, from St. Augustine's *Twenty-Two Books on the City of God* and Orosius' *Seven Books of History Against the Pagans*, date from the late Western Roman Empire when the Christian Church emerged as the only stable institution amidst the defunct governmental, social, and religious traditions of the past. St. Augustine of Hippo (354–430) was educated by his parents in Africa and Milan to be a teacher of rhetoric. He was not a Christian until after 384, when he listened to the sermons of St. Ambrose, Bishop of Milan. Augustine became a priest and returned to Africa, where he was made the Bishop of Hippo in 390.

Augustine began to write against various Christian heresies and developed explanations of predestination, grace, and free will that became the primary Christian doctrines. His most famous work, *City of God*, was an attempt to create a philosophy of history with the belief that citizens should place their trust in God, or the Heavenly City, and not in the City of Man.

The last selection concerns monasticism as formulated by St. Benedict (480–545). In contrast to the East, where monks often led solitary lives filled with extreme fasts or self-inflicted torments, Benedict's rule prescribed moderation. Each monk took the vows of poverty, chastity, and obedience, but the rule also provided for simple meals, clothing, recreation, and adequate sleep. The most important of a monk's duties was prayer, but manual labor was instituted, as all monasteries were to be self-sufficient.

46

Pliny the Younger, *Letters to Emperor Trajan*

After a senatorial career and consulship, Pliny the Younger was sent by Emperor Trajan as a special representative to the Roman province of Bithynia in Asia Minor. His task was to keep the peace. When he had trouble dealing with the Christians, Pliny wrote to the emperor asking how he should proceed against them. The emperor replied with a surprisingly humanitarian approach.

QUESTIONS TO CONSIDER

1. What caused Pliny to write to Emperor Trajan for advice?
2. What was Emperor Trajan's approach to dealing with Christians?
3. Why did the Christian religion appeal to all classes and sexes?

The Official Treatment of the Christians

It is my custom, Sire, to refer to you all matters in which I am in doubt. For who can better guide my hesitancy or instruct my ignorance? I have never been present at trials of Christians; therefore I do not know what is sought and punished, nor to what extent. I have been puzzled in no small degree as to whether there is any difference in the treatment of ages or if the young, no matter how young, are treated just like more mature defendants; whether pardon is given to those who repent or it avails not at all to have given up the aberration if one has once been a Christian; whether

From Hieronimus, John Paul, trans. "Selected Letters of the Younger Pliny," pp. 366–67 in MacKendrick, Paul and Herbert M. Howe, *Classics in Translation*, Vol. II: *Latin Literature*, © 1952 (Madison: The University of Wisconsin Press). Reprinted by permission of the University of Wisconsin Press.

the name itself, if free from criminal practices, is punished or only the abominations that are associated with the name.

For the present I have followed this procedure in the case of those who were denounced to me as Christians: I asked the defendants in person whether they were Christians. If they admitted it I asked them for a second and third time, threatening punishment: if they persisted, I ordered them to be executed. For I had no doubt that whatever it was they were confessing, their persistence and unbending stubbornness deserved to be punished. There were others of similar folly whom I sent to Rome, since they were Roman citizens. Soon the accusation became common, as usual, from the very fact that cases were being tried, and several variations appeared. An anonymous information was lodged listing a number of names. If defendants who denied that they were now Christians or had been in the past would, following my example, pray to the gods and offer incense and wine to your statue, which I had had placed beside those of the gods for this purpose, and if they would curse Christ, they should, I thought, be dismissed; for it is declared that real Christians cannot be compelled to do any of these acts. Others, named by an informer, said that they were Christians but later denied it; they had indeed been, but had given up the practice, some of them several years ago, one even twenty years ago. All of these also worshipped your image and the statues of the gods, and cursed Christ. However, they asserted that their guilt or mistake had amounted to no more than this, that they had been accustomed on a set day to gather before dawn and to chant in antiphonal form a hymn to Christ as if to a god, and to bind themselves by a pledge, not for the commission of any crime, but rather that they would not commit theft nor robbery nor adultery nor break their promises, nor refuse to return on demand any treasure that had been entrusted to their care; when this ceremony had been completed, they would go away, to reassemble later for a feast, but an ordinary and innocent one. They had abandoned even this custom after my edict in which, following your instruction, I had forbidden the existence of fellowships. So I thought it the more necessary to extract the truth even by torture from two maidservants who were called deaconesses. I found nothing save a vile superstition carried to an immoderate length.

So, postponing further trials, I have resorted to consulting you. For it seemed to me a subject worthy of consultation, especially because of the number of people charged. For many of every age and rank, and of both sexes, are being brought to trial, and will be. The contagion of the superstition has pervaded not only the cities but the villages and country districts as well. Yet it seems that it can be halted and cured. It is well agreed that temples almost desolate have begun to be thronged again, and stated rites that had long been abandoned are revived; and a sale is found for the fodder of sacrificial victims, though hitherto buyers were rare. So it is easy to conjecture what a great number of offenders may be reformed, if a chance to repent is given.

The Emperor's Answer About the Christians

You have followed the proper course, my friend, in examining the cases of those who have been denounced to you as Christians. It is impossible to establish a hard and fast procedure for general use. They are not to be sought out; if they are accused, and the case is proved, they are to be punished, with the restriction, however, that if one denies that he is a Christian and makes it manifest in very deed, that is, by offering sacrifice to our gods, he shall be pardoned because of his repentance, however suspicious his past conduct was. Information lodged anonymously ought not to be regarded in dealing with any charge; it is of an abominable tendency, and not consonant with our enlightened age.

47

St. Augustine of Hippo, *The Just War*

In A.D. 410, the Visigothic armies of Alaric sacked Rome. Not only was this a major military defeat for the Empire in the West, but the victory of Arian Goths also undermined a basic doctrine widely held in Church circles since the time of Constantine: that people of the wrong religion could not prevail against orthodox Christian rulers.

St. Augustine (A.D. 354–430) of Hippo in North Africa began the task of explaining the Roman debacle in the first of what were to become twenty-two books of *The City of God*. At the outset, he attempted to refute pagan claims that Rome had done better under its old gods than under the Christian God by recalling positive experiences for the empire under its Christian rulers and arguing that Christian morality led these emperors, with God's aid and direction, to provide a happier life for Romans than their pagan predecessors had achieved. At the same time, he stressed that true Christians lose nothing of value in worldly calamities; this belief, of course, rendered the havoc of barbarian invasions relatively unimportant.

For St. Augustine, the City of God, or the Heavenly City, includes God, the angels, and mortals predestined for salvation among its citizens. Those citizens of the Heavenly City who are making their way through earthly life pay no attention to material interests. Consequently, if churchgoers show too much concern about loss of property and physical suffering, they are probably citizens of the Earthly City in this life and doomed to hell in the hereafter. Citizens of the Earthly City are identified through their interests, which are limited to those earthly concerns that are insignificant to saved Christians.

St. Augustine was the first father of the church to develop the theory of the just war. His ideas emerged in response to current events, as Christians were required to cope with increasing threats to the security of the empire. Pieced together from numerous topical writings he completed over the years, his theory can be presented in terms of four characteristics that a just war must have: (1) It must be defensive in nature. (2) It must not do more damage than it prevents. (3) Its aim must be the restoration of peace, rather than the expansion of control. (4) It must be waged only by constituted authority.

The first four selections that follow are from the early books of *The City of God*; the next two, from the much later Book XIX; the last selection, from the treatise *Against Faustus*. Faustus was a leading Manichæan. The Manichæans were Dualists who considered the material world altogether evil, a doctrine which led them into a position of total pacifism, since for them all war was waged for material aims.

QUESTIONS TO CONSIDER

1. Why does St. Augustine view the sack of Rome as a cause for heightened, rather than diminished, respect for Christianity?
2. Compare Kautilya's statement from the *Duties of a King* (see Reading 22): "In the happiness of the subjects lies the happiness of the king . . . " with St. Augustine's statement on the happiness of Christian emperors.
3. Why is a temporary peace observable between the City of God and the Earthly City?
4. Why does St. Augustine say that the City of God or the Heavenly City is in a state of pilgrimage on earth?
5. Much of the context of St. Augustine's discussion of just war in the final section is that of wars waged at God's command in the Old Testament. Why do many modern people shy away from approving of wars because they are waged "at God's command" or "in obedience to God"?

It makes sense that if the true God is worshipped and served with true rites and good morals, it is a benefit for good men to have long reigns over great territories. This is actually not of so much use to themselves as it is to their subjects, because as far as they themselves are concerned their own true faith and righteousness, which are great gifts from God, are enough to give them the true happiness that lets them live this life well and attain eternal life afterwards. Thus the reign of good men here on earth does not serve their own good so much as it does human concerns.

All the destruction, killing, looting, burning, and suffering which took place in the recent sack of Rome happened in accordance with the customs of waging war. What was altogether new and previously unheard of, however, was that the barbarian brutality [of the Goths] was so tamed that they picked the largest of the basilicas and allowed them to remain sanctuaries, where no one could be struck down and from which no one could be dragged away. Many people were led there to freedom and safety by soldiers showing sympathy for them. . . . Anyone who does not see fit to credit this to the name of Christ—yes, to Christian times—is blind. Anyone who sees this new turn of events but fails to praise it is most ungrateful.

In the sack of Rome faithful and godly men . . . "lost everything they had." How about their faith? How about their godliness? How about the goods of the inner being which make a person rich before God? Listen to what the Apostle Paul says about the riches of Christianity: " . . . Godliness with contentment is great gain, for we brought nothing into this world and certainly we can carry nothing out. If we have food and clothing, let us be content with them. People who want to be rich fall into temptations and traps. They fall into foolish and harmful desires which drown men in destruction and perdition."[1]

Domestic peace is a harmonious arrangement in matters of command and obedience among those of the same household, and the peace of a [normal] city is a similar one among its citizens. The peace of the Heavenly City is the most perfectly and harmoniously designed communal relationship in the enjoyment of God and in

---

[1] *I Timothy* 6:6–10.

From *De civitate Dei libri xxii*, ed. Emmanuel Hoffman (Vienna: F. Tempsky, 1899–1900), extracts from Books I–V and XIX, *passim*; and *Contra Faustum libri xxxiii*, ed. Josephus Zycha (Vienna: F. Tempsky, 1891), extracts from Book XXII, chs. 74–75. Trans. Henry A. Myers.

the fellowship resulting from union with God. Peace for all beings is tranquility within order. Order is the arrangement of equal and unequal things, with each assigned its proper place.

And so we see that miserable people [lacking faith and godliness] . . . in the very fact that they justly deserve their misery are confined to a condition of misery by the principle of order. This keeps them from being united with saved people. When they live without obvious disturbances they adapt to their bondage, and so there is a bit of tranquil order among them, and so they enjoy a peace of sorts. They still remain miserable, however, since, in spite of not suffering constantly from a total lack of security, they are not within that realm where there is no cause to worry about either suffering or security. . . .

The Earthly City, which does not live by faith, desires an earthly peace, seeking to bring it about through harmony of command and obedience among citizens, even though its scope is limited to uniting people's wills on matters pertaining to this mortal life.

The Heavenly City, however, or, to be more precise, those of its members who are living by faith during their mortal pilgrimages, must make use of this peace, although only until they are through with their transient status on earth, which requires it. For this reason, the Heavenly City sojourning either as a captive or a wandering stranger in the Earthly City does not hesitate to obey earthly authority in matters required by the communal life of mortals. With mortal life common to the people of both Cities, a certain harmony between them may be maintained in relation to its requirements.

While the Heavenly City sojourns on earth, it recruits members from all peoples and forms a pilgrim society of men and women speaking all different languages, which pays no attention to the diversity of customs, laws, and institutions among them, by which earthly peace is established and maintained.

Just what is wrong with war? Is it that some people will die in it—people who will die sometime anyway—so that others may live in peace under authority? That is the objection of cowards, not believers. The real evils in war are: a love of inflicting violence, vengeful cruelty, raging and implacable hatred, ferocity in rebelling, lust for power, and similar things. It is normally to punish under law these very things that, at the command of God or some legitimate authority, good men resort to war against violent offenders. . . . Much depends on the reasons for which and the authority by which men commit themselves to waging war. The natural order among mortal men requires the promotion of peace. It justifies the exercise of military force through the authority and direction of the ruler when he decides it is necessary for soldiers to carry out their duties on behalf of the peace and safety of the community. When men wage war in obedience to God, it is not appropriate to doubt that it is waged justly either to deter, or humble, or subdue the pride of men.

48

Paulus Orosius, *History Against the Pagans*

St. Augustine worked on *The City of God* for thirteen years. Early in the project, he seems to have realized that comprehensive proof of the relative happiness of Christian times should be presented more systematically than he was doing, and so he entrusted that part of his work to Paulus Orosius, a young priest from Spain who had come to serve him and study with him. In writing this dissertation for St. Augustine, Orosius became the first Christian graduate student on record. His work, entitled without the slightest pretense of objectivity, *Seven Books of History Against the Pagans,* became *the* Christian textbook of world history, as opposed to plain Church history, from creation to A.D. 417. In it, Orosius sought to demonstrate once and for all that Christian times were better than pagan times. It was one of the most widely copied and cited books in the Middle Ages and sold so well in the first centuries of printed books that four-hundred-year-old copies of *History Against the Pagans* are not really rare books today. Actually, St. Augustine did not think highly of the finished work of Orosius, but that fact did not become known until the late 1950s, and for some fifteen hundred years Orosius was viewed as having written what the great St. Augustine would have written if he had not given young Paulus this assignment to ease the burdens on his own time.

Orosius selectively rewrites history to make "pagan times," including those periods such as the Age of Pericles and Rome in the Early Republic, which the usual narrative, world-history textbook presents as enjoyable times to have lived in, as characterized by misery and uncertainty of existence. For him, times became happier with the birth of Christ, not only spiritually for those who accepted the Christian faith, but in terms of worldly peace and greater earthly happiness. In stressing this, he has God bestow divine approval on the Empire founded by Augustus Caesar, which, give or take thirty years, came into being when Christ was born. Predictably, times become even better with the reigns of Constantine and Theodosius, who turn the empire into a Christian one. Proving this involves selecting the best aspects of an empire that, in fact, was crumbling all around him. The Roman Empire in the West had only a scant sixty years of life left in it when Orosius wound up his research, but you would never guess from what follows that its weaknesses were severe. Orosius treated the barbarian invasions that rocked his own fifth century as minor inconveniences, ordained by God to facilitate the spread of the Catholic faith to the invaders and to civilize them through their contacts with Roman Christians. Orosius is faithful enough to earlier Christian doctrine to state his love of the City of God, but by an odd quirk of fate and conviction his commitment to it made him a much more avid spokesman for the outgoing Pax Romana than any subsequent pagan writer or orator.

QUESTIONS TO CONSIDER

1. In spite of the great optimism of Orosius, he does give a few hints that the Roman Empire in the West is coming apart at the seams. Can you find one or more of them?
2. Comparing the excerpts from St. Augustine and Orosius, what similarities do you find? Where is the emphasis different?

Let us assume there is no doubt about the fact that it was under Augustus Caesar, following the peace treaty with the Parthians, that for the first time the entire world

From *Historiam adversum paganos libri VII,* ed. Karl Zangemeister (Vienna: C. Gerold, 1882), excerpts from Books III, viii, 5–8, and V, i, 10–13, ii, 1–8. Trans. Allen C. Myers.

laid down its arms and overcame its disagreements under an all-encompassing peace and new tranquility in obedience to Roman laws. Foreign peoples preferred relying on Roman laws to relying on their own arms. All races, all provinces, innumerable city-states, infinite populations—in fact, the whole world—finally united with a single will in freely and honestly serving the cause of peace, ever mindful of the common good. In earlier days, not even one city-state, nor one group of citizens, nor even (more significantly) one household of brothers could get along with another indefinitely. If we confirm that all this came to pass under Augustus as ruler, it is quite clear that in the same empire of Augustus the birth of our Lord Jesus Christ was beginning to light up the world in a most certain manifestation of His approval.

Although it will be against their will, those driven to blasphemy by jealousy will be forced to admit and acknowledge that this worldwide peace and most tranquil serenity was made possible not by the greatness of Augustus Caesar, but by the Son of God, who appeared at the time of Caesar and who came not just to be the ruler of one city-state but rather as the Creator of the universe, to be recognized by everyone, in order to unite the world. In the same way as the rising sun fills the day with light, upon His arrival he mercifully adorned the world with peace.

We need to take a look at ourselves and the lifestyles we have chosen and gotten used to, in order to get our bearings. Our ancestors waged wars until, exhausted by wars, they sought peace by offering to pay tribute. Tribute is the price of peace: we pay tribute to avoid the suffering of war, and we stop and wait in the same harbor (of tribute-paying) where our ancestors sheltered themselves from storms of evils.

It is in this light that we should judge whether our times are happy ones: surely we find them happier than those of old because we continually enjoy the peace they arrived at only late in their game. We are strangers to the violence of wars which exhausted them. In fact, we are able to enjoy that carefree existence from birth to old age, which they could enjoy only in part after the coming of Augustus Caesar's empire and Christ's birth. What we contribute freely for our defense was simply taken from them earlier, as what they owed in their slave-like status. How different modern times are from past ones can be seen when we compare the way Rome extorted money by force of arms from its subject peoples, in order to support Roman luxury, with the way Rome now allocates funds for the general good of all our communities.

For me my native land is everywhere. I can get away to a safe place at the first hint of any sort of disturbance. Right now Africa has taken me in with a hospitality commensurate with my confidence in approaching her. Now Africa receives me into its own community with its carefree enjoyment of peace under laws common to us all. That same Africa, of which it was said in olden days and truly said,

> We dare not ask for refuge on her sand:
> The wars they stir up keep us from this land[2]

now opens wide the doors to her hearths for weary bodies and keeps them warm and welcome. The huge expanse of the East, the abundance produced in the North, the expansive diversity of the South, the great and secure strongholds on our large islands now have my law and name because I come to Christians and Romans as a Christian and Roman. I do not fear any gods of my host. I do not fear that his religion will mean my death. I have none of that fear of strange lands where a native gets away with whatever

---

[2]Vergil, *The Aeneid*, Book I, lines 540–541.

he wants and a traveller cannot tend to his own business in peace or even of lands where the law of foreigners is not mine. One God, loved and feared by all, established this unity of the kingdom at the time He chose to reveal Himself among men: those same laws under one God now rule everywhere. Whenever I arrive unknown, I need not fear sudden violence as if I were alone and deserted. Among Romans, as I was saying, I am a Roman; among Christians, a Christian; among men, a man. I can appeal to the state on the basis of its laws, to the consciences of men on the basis of religion, and to nature on the basis of our common sharing of it. I enjoy time spent in each country, as though it were my own fatherland—keeping in mind that the true fatherland I love most does not have its roots on earth. I have lost nothing where I loved nothing, and I have everything when He whom I do love is with me, particularly since He is the same among all men. He not only gives me an introduction to all men but helps me become a friend of theirs. Nor does He desert me when I am in need, for "The earth is His and the fullness thereof." He instructs that all things from this abundance be made available to all people in common. These are the benefits of our own time, and our ancestors did not enjoy them fully, whether we refer to our present tranquility, or to hope for the future, or to places of refuge for all. Lacking these, they waged wars without end. Since they were not free to move as groups from place to place, they had to cling to their old homes when warfare came and face miserable death or the disgrace of enslavement.

49

Monastic Life: The Rule of St. Benedict

In the midst of a disorderly world, medieval monasteries established communities devoted to achieving salvation. St. Benedict of Nursia (A.D. 480–543), the most influential figure in Western European monastic history, came from a wealthy Italian family; but at age twenty, he renounced all worldly temptations and withdrew to the mountains to live as a hermit. His reputation for holiness led others to seek him out, and in time they became his devoted disciples.

St. Benedict eventually decided that a communal setting was a better environment for most men trying to lead a life pleasing to God. He founded twelve monasteries in Italy before he and his followers built a large one at Monte Cassino around 529, where he applied his "Rule" and lived the rest of his life. Requiring vows of chastity, poverty, and obedience, St. Benedict's Rule became the basis for monastic life in the West.

Unlike the stricter Celtic monasticism of St. Columban, the strength of St. Benedict's Rule lies in its combination of religious commitment, encouragement of good works along with faith, and common-sense moderation in discipline. In contrast, the more extreme Celtic rules required severe punishment for even unintentional lapses. The Benedictine model is the family, with the abbot in the role of a strict, but patient and loving father. Other members of the community overcome unChristian willfulness through continual acts of humility; they complete their tasks in a mutually supportive fashion as brothers. In the year before St. Benedict died, his sister, Scholastica, founded a convent near Monte Cassino. With appropriate modifications, the Benedictine Rule guided nuns as well as monks in the medieval West.

QUESTIONS TO CONSIDER

1. What should the monk do in order to achieve progressively greater degrees of humility?
2. What are St. Benedict's guidelines for correcting the faults of those who commit offenses?
3. What is St. Benedict's basic attitude toward providing food, drink, and other necessities of life for the monks?

What Kind of Man the Abbot Ought to Be

An abbot who is worthy to rule over the monastery ought always to remember what he is called, and correspond to his name of superior by his deeds. For he is believed to hold the place of Christ in the monastery, since he is called by his name, as the apostle says: "You have received the spirit of the adoption of children, in which we cry Abba, Father." And, therefore, the abbot ought not (God forbid) to teach, or ordain, or command anything contrary to the law of the Lord; but let his bidding and his doctrine be infused into the minds of his disciples like the leaven of divine justice.

Let the abbot be ever mindful that at the dreadful judgment of God an account will have to be given both of his own teaching and of the obedience of his disciples. And let him know that to the fault of the shepherd shall be imputed any lack of profit which the father of the household may find in his sheep. Only then shall he be acquitted, if he shall have bestowed all pastoral diligence on his unquiet and disobedient flock, and employed all his care to amend their corrupt manner of life: then shall he be absolved in the judgment of the Lord.

For the abbot in his doctrine ought always to observe the bidding of the apostle, wherein he says: "Reprove, entreat, rebuke"; mingling, as occasions may require, gentleness with severity; showing now the rigor of a master, now the loving affection of a father, so as sternly to rebuke the undisciplined and restless, and to exhort the obedient, mild, and patient to advance in virtue. And such as are negligent and haughty we charge him to reprove and correct. Let him not shut his eyes to the faults of offenders; but as soon as they appear, let him strive with all his might to root them out, remembering the fate of Eli, the priest of Shiloh. Those of good disposition and understanding let him, for the first or second time, correct only with words; but such as are forward and hard of heart, and proud, or disobedient, let him chastise with bodily stripes at the very first offence, knowing that it is written: "The fool is not corrected with words." . . .

Of Obedience

The first degree of humility is obedience without delay. This becomes those who hold nothing dearer to them than Christ, and who on account of the holy servitude which they have taken upon them, either for fear of hell or for the glory of life everlasting, as soon as anything is ordered by the superior, suffer no more delay in

From "The Rule of Saint Benedict," trans. Dom Oswald Hunter Blair, in Emmanuel Heufelder, *The Way to God According to the Rule of St. Benedict* (Kalamazoo, MI: Cistercian Publications, 1983), pp. 224–266, *passim.* Reprinted by permission of Fort Augustus Abbey.

doing it than if it had been commanded by God himself. It is of these that the Lord says: "At the hearing of the ear he has obeyed me." And again, to teachers he says: "He that hears you hears me."

Such as these, therefore, leaving immediately their own occupations and forsaking their own will, with their hands disengaged, and leaving unfinished what they were about, with the speedy step of obedience follow by their deeds the voice of him who commands; and so as it were at the same instant the bidding of the master and the perfect fulfilment of the disciple are joined together in the swiftness of the fear of God by those who are moved with the desire of attaining eternal life.

Of the Practice of Silence

Let us do as says the prophet: "I said, I will take heed to my ways, that I sin not with my tongue, I have placed a watch over my mouth; I became dumb and was silent, and held my peace even from good things." Here the prophet shows that if we ought at times to refrain even from good words for the sake of silence, how much more ought we to abstain from evil words, on account of the punishment due to sin. Therefore, on account of the importance of silence, let leave to speak be seldom granted even to perfect disciples, although their conversation be good and holy and tending to edification; because it is written: "In much speaking you shall not avoid sin." . . . But as for buffoonery or idle words, such as move to laughter, we utterly condemn them in every place, nor do we allow the disciple to open his mouth in such discourse. . . .

Of Humility

The Holy Scripture cries out to us, brothers, saying: "Every one that exalts himself shall be humbled, and he who humbles himself shall be exalted." . . .

The first degree of humility, then, is that a man, always keeping the fear of God before his eyes, avoid all forgetfulness; and that he be ever mindful of all that God has commanded, bethinking himself that those who despise God will be consumed in hell for their sins, and that life everlasting is prepared for them that fear him. . . .

The second degree of humility is, that a man love not his own will, nor delight in fulfilling his own desires; but carry out in his deeds that saying of the Lord: "I came not to do mine own will, but the will of him who sent me." And again Scripture says: "Self-will has punishment, but necessity wins the crown."

The third degree of humility is, that a man for the love of God submit himself to his superior in all obedience; imitating the Lord, of whom the apostle says: "He was made obedient even unto death."

The fourth degree of humility is, that if in this very obedience hard and contrary things, nay even injuries, are done to him, he should embrace them patiently with a quiet conscience, and not grow weary or give in, as the Scripture says: "He that shall persevere to the end shall be saved." And again: "Let your heart be comforted, and wait for the Lord."

The fifth degree of humility is, not to hide from one's abbot any of the evil thoughts that beset one's heart, or the sins committed in secret, but humbly to confess them. Concerning which the Scripture exhorts us, saying: "Make known your way unto the Lord, and hope in him." . . .

The sixth degree of humility is for a monk to be contented with the meanest and worst of everything, and in all that is enjoined him to esteem himself a bad and worthless laborer, saying with the prophet: "I have been brought to nothing, and I knew it not: I am become as a beast before you, yet I am always with you."

The seventh degree of humility is that he should not only call himself with his tongue lower and viler than all, but also believe himself in his inmost heart to be so, humbling himself, and saying with the prophet: "I am a worm and no man, the shame of men and the outcast of the people: I have been exalted, and cast down, and confounded." . . .

The eighth degree of humility is for a monk to do nothing except what is authorized by the common rule of the monastery, or the example of the seniors.

The ninth degree of humility is, that a monk refrain his tongue from speaking, keeping silence until a question be asked him, as the Scripture shows: "In much talking you shall not avoid sin," and, "The talkative man shall not be directed upon the earth."

The tenth degree of humility is, that he be not easily moved and prompt to laughter; because it is written: "The fool lifts up his voice in laughter." . . .

Having, therefore, ascended all these degrees of humility, the monk will presently arrive at that love of God which, being perfect, casts out fear. . . .

Of Those Who, Being Often Corrected, Do Not Amend

If any brother who has been frequently corrected for some fault, or even excommunicated, does not amend, let a more severe chastisement be applied: that is, let the punishment of stripes be administered to him. But if even then he does not correct himself, or perchance (which God forbid), puffed up with pride, even wishes to defend his deeds, then let the abbot act like a wise physician. If he has applied fomentations and the unction of his admonitions, the medicine of the Holy Scriptures, and the last remedy of excommunication or corporal chastisement, and if he see that his labors are of no avail, let him add what is still more powerful, his own prayers and those of all the brothers for him, that God, who is all-powerful, may work the cure of the sick brother. But if he be not healed even by this means, then at length let the abbot use the sword of separation, as the apostle says: "Put away the evil one from you." And again: "If the faithless one depart, let him depart," lest one diseased sheep should taint the whole flock. . . .

What Kind of Man the Cellarer of the Monastery Is to Be

Let there be chosen out of the community, as cellarer of the monastery, a man wise and of mature character, temperate, not a great eater, not haughty, nor headstrong, nor arrogant, not slothful, nor wasteful, but a Godfearing man, who may be like a father to the whole community. Let him have the care of everything, but do nothing without leave of the abbot. Let him take heed to what is commanded him, and not sadden his brothers. If a brother ask him for anything unreasonably, let him not treat him with contempt and so grieve him, but reasonably and with all humility refuse what he asks for amiss. Let him be watchful over his own soul, remembering always that saying of the apostle, that "he that has ministered well, purchases to himself a good degree." Let him have special care of the sick, of the children, of guests and of the poor, knowing without doubt that he will have to render an account of them all on the day of judgment. . . .

Whether Monks Ought to Have Anything of Their Own

The vice of private ownership is above all to be cut off from the monastery by the roots. Let none presume to give or receive anything without leave of the abbot, nor to keep anything as their own, either book or writing-tablet or pen, or anything whatsoever; since they are permitted to have neither body nor will in their own power. But all that is necessary they may hope to receive from the father of the monastery; nor are they allowed to keep anything which the abbot has not given, or at least permitted them to have. Let all things be common to all, as it is written: "Neither did anyone say that anything which he possessed was his own." But if anyone should be found to indulge in this most baneful vice, and after one or two admonitions does not amend, let him be subjected to correction. . . .

Whether All Ought Alike to Receive What Is Needful

As it is written: "Distribution was made to every man, according as he had need." Herein we do not say that there should be respecting of persons—God forbid—but consideration for infirmities. Let him, therefore, that has need of less give thanks to God and not be grieved; and let him who requires more be humbled for his infirmity and not made proud by the kindness shown to him; and so all members of the family shall be at peace. Above all, let not the evil of murmuring show itself by the slightest word or sign on any account whatever. If anyone be found guilty herein, let him be subjected to severe punishment. . . .

Of the Weekly Servers in the Kitchen

Let the brothers wait on one another in turn, so that none be excused from the work of the kitchen, except he be prevented by sickness or by some more necessary employment; for thus is gained a greater reward and an increase of charity. But let assistance be given to the weak, that they may not do their work with sadness; and let all have help according to the number of the community and the situation of the place. If the community be large, let the cellarer be excused from work in the kitchen, and also those, as already mentioned, who are occupied in more urgent business. Let the rest serve each other in turn with all charity. Let him who ends his week in the kitchen make all things clean on Saturday and wash the towels with which the brothers dry their hands and feet. Let both him who goes out and him who is coming in wash the feet of all. Let him hand over to the cellarer the vessels of his office, clean and whole; and let the cellarer deliver the same to him who enters, that he may know what he gives and what he receives.

Let the weekly servers each take a cup of drink and a piece of bread over and above the appointed portion, one hour before the time for reflection, that so they may serve their brothers when the hour comes without murmuring or great labor. . . .

Of Old Men and Children

Although human nature is of itself drawn to feel pity for these two times of life, namely, old age and infancy, yet the authority of the Rule should also provide for them. Let their weakness be always taken into account, and the strictness of the Rule respecting food be by no means kept in their regard; but let a kind consideration be shown for them, and let them eat before the regular hours. . . .

Of the Measure of Food

We think it sufficient for the daily meal, whether at the sixth or the ninth hour, that there be at all seasons of the year two dishes of cooked food, because of the weakness of different people; so that he who perchance cannot eat the one may make his meal of the other. Let two dishes, then, suffice for all the brothers; and if there be any fruit or young vegetables, let a third be added. Let one pound weight of bread suffice for the day, whether there be but one meal or both dinner and supper.

Of the Measure of Drink

Everyone has his proper gift from God, one after this manner, another after that. And, therefore, it is with some misgiving that we appoint the measure of other men's living. Yet, considering the infirmity of the weak, we think that one pint of wine a day is sufficient for each; but let those to whom God gives the endurance of abstinence know that they shall have their proper reward. If, however, the situation of the place, the work, or the heat of summer require more, let it be in the power of the superior to grant it, taking care in every thing that surfeit or drunkenness creep not in. And although we read that wine ought by no means to be the drink of monks, yet since in our times monks cannot be persuaded of this, let us at least agree to drink not to satiety, but sparingly; because "wine makes even the wise to fall away." But where the necessity of the place allows not even the aforesaid measure, but much less, or none at all, let those who dwell there bless God and not murmur. This above all we admonish, that there be no murmuring among them.

Fusion of Church and State: Byzantine Beginnings

After undergoing persecutions of varying intensities by the Roman state, Christians in the early fourth century suddenly found themselves not only tolerated but moving towards dominance. Emperor Constantine (288?–337) attributed his decisive victory at the Battle of the Milvian Bridge to the one God of the Christians and soon embarked on the policy of making the Roman Empire a Christian one.

Following Emperor Diocletian's policy of dividing the empire for administrative purposes, Constantine made Byzantium, a large, commercial, Greek city, just barely in Asia, into "Constantinople" ("Constantine City," "Istanbul" in today's Turkey), the capital of the Roman Empire in the East. After 476, when the Roman Empire in the West became defunct, the eastern Empire survived as the "Byzantine Empire," until it was taken by the Muslim Turks in 1453 (see Reading 89).

The Byzantine Empire featured both splendor and decadence, particularly in contrast with the developing territories of Western Europe in the Middle Ages (see Reading 64). Upon the death of his uncle Justin I, Justinian (A.D. 527–565) became Roman emperor and immediately had his wife, Theodora (a former prostitute), crowned empress. Together they worked hard to meet the challenges of imperial rule. In A.D. 532, Theodora's timely advice helped Justinian successfully suppress the Nika tax riots in Constantinople.

Justinian's central policy was to reunite the Western Roman Empire, which had fallen to various barbarian Germanic peoples, with the East. This goal was temporarily accomplished with the aid of many great generals; for example, Belisarius conquered Vandal-held Africa and led the first invasions of Ostrogothic Italy. Justinian is remembered in considerable part for the great codification of Roman law (*Codex Iuris Civilis*), which took place during his reign. In centuries to come, the Justinian Code would become the foundation of law in continental Europe and, to a lesser extent, the British Isles.

Another imperial objective was peace within the Christian Church, which was disturbed by heretics called Monophysites. These Christians rejected the orthodox view that Christ had two natures, human and divine; they rejected Christ's humanity and stressed only his divine nature. After attempting a series of compromises, Justinian finally resorted to religious persecution that only increased the dissatisfaction of orthodox and heretics alike.

Our major source for Justinian's reign is Procopius. Born about A.D. 500, he went to Constantinople, where he became the private secretary (ca. 527) to General Belisarius. From his pen came three known works: *History of the Wars*, *On the Buildings*, and *The Secret History*. The first book details the events concerning Justinian's wars in Africa, Italy, and Persia. The second work praises the emperor for his architectural contributions such as the rebuilding of Santa Sophia, which had been destroyed in the Nika riots. Yet it is Procopius' third and smallest book—*The Secret History* or *Anecdota*—that has given him the most fame. It records in vitriolic splendor the crimes, vices, and scandals of Justinian, Theodora, General Belisarius, and his wife, Antonina.

50

Eusebius, The Life of Constantine

When Constantine the Great (A.D. 288?–337) was proclaimed emperor by his late father's legions in York (Eboracum), England in 306, this was contrary to the plan which Emperor Diocletian had proposed for choosing new Roman emperors. Almost immediately a rival to Constantine appeared in Rome, Maxentius, son of Maximian, also sought to be recognized as the Western Roman emperor. The two men lived in peace for six years and then in October, 312, Constantine suddenly invaded Italy to confront Maxentius at the Milvian Bridge. After the battle, Constantine became very favorable to the Christians—issuing the Edict of Milan which gave toleration to the Christians in the empire, giving land to the Bishops of Rome (popes), discovering the burial spot of St. Peter, presiding over the First Church Council at Nicaea in 325, founding the city of Constantinople, and receiving baptism on his deathbed in 337. These efforts on behalf of the Christian religion gained for Constantine the title of Great and he was later named a saint in the Church.

The following selection is by Bishop Eusebius of Caesare in Asia Minor, a friend and confidant, the emperor's biographer and tutor to his children. In this piece Eusebius recounts the miraculous events at the Milvian Bridge by which Constantine, with the aid of God, triumphed over Maxentius.

QUESTIONS TO CONSIDER

1. Why was Constantine able to defeat his rival Maxentius?
2. How does Constantine compare to previous emperors such as Nero and Trajan in their relations to the Christians? (See Reading 46.)

How, While He was Praying, God Sent Him a Vision of a Cross of Light in the Heavens at Mid-day, with an Inscription Admonishing Him to Conquer by That

Accordingly, he called on him with earnest prayer and supplications that he would reveal to him who he was, and stretch forth his right hand to help him in his present: difficulties. And while he was thus praying with fervent entreaty, a most marvelous sign appeared to him from heaven, the account of which it might have been hard to believe had it been related by any other person. But since the victorious emperor himself long afterwards declared it to the writer of this history, when he was honored with his acquaintance and society, and confirmed his statement by an oath, who could hesitate to accredit the relation, especially since the testimony of after-time has established its truth? He said that about noon, when the day was already beginning to decline, he saw with his own eyes the trophy of a cross of light in the heavens, above the sun, and bearing the inscription, "Conquer by this!" At this sight he himself was struck with amazement, and his whole army also, which followed him on this expedition, and witnessed the miracle.

How the Christ of God Appeared to Him in His Sleep, and Commanded Him to Use in His Wars a Standard Made in the Form of the Cross

He said, moreover, that he doubted within himself what the import of this apparition could be. And while he continued to ponder and reason on its meaning, night suddenly came on; then in his sleep the Christ of God appeared to him with the same sign which he had seen in the heavens, and commanded him to make a likeness of that sign and to use it as a safeguard in all engagements with his enemies.

The Making of the Standard of the Cross

At dawn of day he arose, and communicated the marvel to his friends and then, calling together the workers in gold and precious stones, he sat in the midst of them, and described to them the figure of the sign he had seen, bidding them represent it in gold and precious stones. And this representation I myself have had an opportunity of seeing.

Eusebius Pamphili, Bishop of Caesarea, *Life of Constantine the Great,* in *Nicene and Post-Nicene Fathers of the Christian Church,* Second Series, ed. Philip Schaff and Henry Wace (New York: Christian Literature Co., 1890), Vol. I, pp. 491–93.

A Description of the Standard of the Cross, which the Romans Now Call the Labarum

Now it was made in the following manner. A long spear overlaid with gold, formed the figure of the cross by means of a transverse bar laid over it. On the top of the whole was fixed a wreath of gold and precious stones and within this, the symbol of the Saviour's name, two letters indictating the name of Christ by means of its initial characters the letter P being intersected by X in its centre; and these letters the emperor was in the habit of wearing on his helmet at a later period. From the cross-bar of the spear was suspended a cloth, a royal piece, covered with a profuse embroidery of most brilliant precious stones; and which, being also richly interlaced with gold, presented an indescribable degree of beauty to the beholder. This banner was of a square form, and the upright staff, whose lower section was of great length, bore a golden half-length portrait of the pious emperor and his children on its upper part, beneath the trophy of the cross, and immediately above the embroidered banner.

The emperor constantly made use of this sign of salvation as a safeguard against every adverse and hostile power, and commanded that others similar to it should be carried at the head of all his armies.

How Constantine Received Instruction, and Read the Sacred Scriptures

These things were done shortly afterwards. But at the time above specified, being struck with amazement at the extraordinary vision, and resolving to worship no other God save Him who had appeared to him, he sent for those who were acquainted with the mysteries of His doctrines, and enquired who that God was, and what was intended by the sign of the vision he had seen. They affirmed that He was God, the only begotten Son of the one and only God; that the sign which had appeared was the symbol of immortality, and the trophy of that victory over death which He had gained in time past when sojourning on earth. They taught him also the causes of His advent, and explained to him the true account of His incarnation. Thus he was instructed in these matters, and was impressed with wonder at the divine manifestation which had been presented to his sight. Comparing, therefore, the heavenly vision with the interpretation given, he found his judgment confirmed; and, in the persuasion that the knowledge of these things had been imparted to him by Divine teaching, he determined thenceforth to devote himself to the reading of the Inspired writings.

Moreover, he made the priests of God his counselors, and deemed it incumbent on him to honor the God who had appeared to him with all devotion. And after this, being fortified by well-grounded hopes in Him, he hastened to quench the threatening fire of tyranny.

How the Wife of a Prefect Slew Herself for Chastity's Sake

Now a certain woman, wife of one of the senators who held the authority of prefect, when she understood that those who ministered to the tyrant in such matters were standing before her house (she was a Christian), and knew that her husband through fear had bidden them take her and lead her away, begged a short space of time for arraying herself in her usual dress, and entered her chamber. There, being left alone, she sheathed a sword in her own breast, and immediately expired, leaving indeed her dead body to the procurers, but declaring to all mankind, both to present and future generations, by an act which spoke louder than any words, that the chastity for which Christians are famed is the only thing which is invincible and indestructible. Such was the conduct displayed by this woman.

Massacre of the Roman People by Maxentius

All men, therefore, both people and magistrates, whether of high or low degree, trembled through fear of him whose daring wickedness was such as I have described, and were oppressed by his grievous tyranny. Nay, though they submitted quietly, and endured this bitter servitude, still there was no escape from the tyrant's sanguinary cruelty. For at one time, on some trifling pretense, he exposed the populace to be slaughtered by his own body-guard; and countless multitudes of the Roman people were slain in'the very midst of the city by the lances and weapons, not of Scythians or barbarians, but of their own fellow-citizens. And besides this, it is impossible to calculate the number of senators whose blood was shed with a view to the seizure of their respective estates, for at different times and on various fictitious charges, multitudes of them suffered death.

Magic Arts of Maxentius Against and Famine at Rome

But the crowning point of the tyrant's wickedness was his having recourse to sorcery: sometimes for magic " purposes . . . ripping up women with child, at other times searching into the bowels of new-born infants. He slew lions also and practiced certain horrid arts for evoking demons, and averting the approaching war, hoping by these means get the victory. In short, it is impossible to describe the manifold acts of oppression by which this tyrant of Rome enslaved his subjects: so that by this time they were reduced to the most extreme penury and want of a necessary food, a scarcity such as our contemporaries do not remember ever before to have existed at Rome.

Defeat of Maxentius's Armies in Italy

Constantine, however, filled with compassion on account of all these miseries, began to arm himself with all warlike preparation against the tyranny. Assuming therefore the Supreme God as his patron and invoking His Christ to be his preserver and aid, and setting the victorious trophy, the salutary symbol, in front of his soldiers and body-guard, he marched with his whole forces, trying to obtain again for the Romans the freedom they had inherited from their ancestors.

And whereas, Maxentius, trusting more in his magic arts than in the affection of his subjects, dared not even advance outside the city gates, but had guarded every place and district and city subject to his tyranny, with large bodies of soldiers the emperor, confiding in the help of God, advanced against the first and second and third divisions of the tyrant's forces, defeated them all with ease at the first assault, and made his way into the very interior of Italy.

Death of Maxentius on the Bridge of the Tiber

And already he was approaching very near Rome itself, when, to save him from the necessity of fighting with all the Romans for the tyrant's sake, God himself drew the tyrant, as it by secret cords, a long way outside the gates. And now those miracles recorded in Holy Writ, which God of old wrought against the ungodly (discredited by most as fables, yet believed by the faithful), did he in every deed confirm to all alike, believers and unbelievers, who were eye-witnesses of the wonders. For as once in the days of Moses and the Hebrew nation, who were worshipers of God, "Pharaoh's chariots and his host hath he cast into the sea, and his chosen chariot-captains are drowned in the Red Sea," so at this time Maxentius, and the soldiers and guards with him, "went down into the depths like a stone," when in his flight before the divinely-aided forces of Constantine, he essayed to cross the river which lay in his way, over which, making a strong bridge of boats, he had framed an engine of destruction, really against himself, but in the hope of ensnaring thereby him who was beloved by God. For his God stood by the one to protect him, while the other, godless, proved to be the miserable contriver of these secret devices to his own ruin. So that one might well say, "He hath made a pit, and digged it, and is fallen into the ditch which he made. His mischief shall return upon his own head, and his violence shall come down upon his own pate." Thus, in the present instance, under divine direction, the machine erected on the bridge, with the ambuscade concealed therein, giving way unexpectedly before the appointed time, the bridge began to sink, and the boats with the men went bodily to the bottom. And first the wretch himself, and then his armed attendants and guards, even as the sacred oracles had before described, "sank as lead in the mighty waters." So that they who thus obtained victory from God might well, if not in the same words, yet in fact in the same spirit as the people of his great servant Moses, sing and speak as they did concerning the impious tyrant of old: Let us sing unto the Lord, for he hath been glorified exceedingly: the horse and his rider. hath he thrown into the sea. He is become my helper and my shield unto salvation. And again, "Who is like unto thee, O Lord, among the gods? Who is like thee, glorious in holiness, marvelous in praises, doing wonders?"

Constantine's Entry into Rome

Having then at this time sung these and such like praises to God, the Ruler of all and the Author of victory, after the example of his great servant Moses, Constantine entered the imperial city in triumph. And here the whole body of the senate, and others of rank and distinction in the city, freed as it were from the restraint of a prison, along with the whole Roman populace, their countenances expressive of the gladness of their hearts, received, him, with acclamations and abounding joy; men, women, and children, with countless multitudes of servants, greeting him as deliverer, preserver, and benefactor, with incessant shouts. But he, being possessed of inward piety toward God, was neither rendered arrogant, by these plaudits, nor uplifted by the praises heard but, being sensible that he had received help from: God, he immediately rendered a thanksgiving to him as the Author of his victory.

Of the Statue of Constantine Holding a Cross, and its Inscription

Moreover, by loud proclamation and monumental inscriptions he made known to all men the salutary symbol, setting up this great trophy of victory over his enemies in the midst of the imperial city, and expressly causing it to be engraven in indelible characters, that the salutary symbol was the safeguard of the Roman government and of the entire empire. Accordingly, he immediately ordered a lofty spear in the figure of a cross to be placed beneath the hand of a statue representing himself, in the most frequented part of Rome, and the following inscription to be engraved on it in the Latin language:

> By virtue of this salutary sign, which is the true test of valor, I have preserved and liberated your city from the yoke of tyranny. I have also set at liberty the roman senate and people, and restored them to their ancient distinction and splendor.

51

Procopius, *History of the Wars* and *The Secret History*

The first selection, from the *History of the Wars*, depicts the causes and results of the A.D. 532 Nika revolt and reveals how Empress Theodora helped to control this uprising. The second selection, from *The Secret History*, records Procopius' true feelings about the moral character of General Belisarius, his wife Antonina, Emperor Justinian, and Theodora.

QUESTIONS TO CONSIDER

1. What caused the Nika revolt, and who did the most to stop it?
2. Who are some of the women in other civilizations we have studied who had great importance?

History of the Wars

At this same time an insurrection broke out unexpectedly in Byzantium among the populace, and, contrary to expectation, it proved to be a very serious affair, and ended in great harm to the people and to the senate, as the following account will show. In every city the population has been divided for a long time past into the Blue and the Green factions; but within comparatively recent times it has come about that, for the sake of these names and the seats which the rival factions occupy in watching the games, they spend their money and abandon their bodies to the most cruel tortures, and even do not think it unworthy to die a most shameful death. And they fight against their opponents knowing not for what end they imperil themselves, but knowing well that, even if they overcome their enemy in the fight, the conclusion of the matter for them will be to be carried off straightway to the prison, and finally, after suffering extreme torture, to be destroyed. So there grows up in them against their fellow men a hostility which has no cause, and at no time does it cease or disappear, for it gives place neither to the ties of marriage nor of relationship nor of friendship, and the case is the same even though those who differ with respect to these colours be brothers or any other kin. They care neither for things divine nor human in comparison with conquering in these struggles; and it matters not whether a sacrilege is committed by anyone at all against God, or whether the

Reprinted by permission of the publishers and the Trustees of the Loeb Classical Library from Procopius, *History of the Wars*, Book I, pp. 2, 19, 221, 223, 231, 233; *The Secret History*, pp. 7, 13, 95, 107, 111, trans. H. B. Dewing (Cambridge, Mass: Harvard University Press, 1914). The Loeb Classical Library is a registered trademark of the President and Fellows of Harvard College.

laws and the constitution are violated by friend or by foe; nay even when they are perhaps ill supplied with the necessities of life, and when their fatherland is in the most pressing need and suffering unjustly, they pay no need if only it is likely to go well with their "faction"; for so they name the bands of partisans. And even women join with them in this unholy strife, and they not only follow the men, but even resist them if opportunity offers, although they neither go to the public exhibitions at all, nor are they impelled by any other cause; so that I, for my part, am unable to call this anything except a disease of the soul. This, then, is pretty well how matters stand among the people of each and every city.

But at this time the officers of the city administration in Byzantium were leading away to death some of the rioters. But the members of the two factions, conspiring together and declaring a truce with each other, seized the prisoners and then straightway entered the prison and released all those who were in confinement there, whether they had been condemned on a charge of stirring up sedition, or for any other unlawful act. And all the attendants in the service of the city government were killed indiscriminately; meanwhile, all of the citizens who were sane-minded were fleeing to the opposite mainland, and fire was applied to the city as if it had fallen under the hand of an enemy. The sanctuary of Sophia and the baths of Zeuxippus, and the portion of the imperial residence from the propylaea as far as the so-called House of Ares were destroyed by fire, and besides these both the great colonnades which extended as far as the market place which bears the name of Constantine, in addition to many houses of wealthy men and a vast amount of treasure. During this time the emperor and his consort with a few members of the senate shut themselves up in the palace and remained quietly there. Now the watchword which the populace passed around to one another was Nika,[3] and the insurrection has been called by this name up to the present time. . . .

Now the emperor and his court were deliberating as to whether it would be better for them if they remained or if they took to flight in the ships. And many opinions were expressed favouring either course. And the Empress Theodora also spoke to the following effect: "As to the belief that a woman ought not to be daring among men or to assert herself boldly among those who are holding back from fear, I consider that the present crisis most certainly does not permit us to discuss whether the matter should be regarded in this or in some other way. For in the case of those whose interests have come into the greatest danger nothing else seems best except to settle the issue immediately before them in the best possible way. My opinion then is that the present time, above all others, is inopportune for flight, even though it brings safety. For while it is impossible for a man who has seen the light not also to die, for one who has been an emperor it is unendurable to be a fugitive. May I never be separated from this purple, and may I not live that day on which those who meet me shall not address me as mistress. If, now, it is your wish to save yourself, O Emperor, there is no difficulty. For we have much money, and there is the sea, here the boats. However consider whether it will not come about after you have been saved that you would gladly exchange that safety for death. For as for myself, I approve a certain ancient saying that royalty is a good burial-shroud." When the queen had spoken thus, all were filled with boldness, and, turning their thoughts towards resistance, they began to consider how they might be able to defend themselves if any hostile force should come against them.

[3]Conquest or victory.

The Secret History

Belisarius was Justinian's most important general. Procopius relates, however, how easily Belisarius was deceived by his unscrupulous wife, Antonina.

QUESTIONS TO CONSIDER

1. Why do you suppose that Procopius would not want this *Secret History* published during his lifetime?
2. Why was Antonina not considered an ideal wife?
3. What is Procopius' view of Emperor Justinian?
4. Why would Theodora's early life not make her a good candidate as a wife for Justinian?

Belisarius had a wife, whom I have had occasion to mention in the previous books; her father and grandfather were charioteers who had given exhibitions of their skill in both Byzantium and Thessalonica, and her mother was one of the prostitutes attached to the theatre. This woman, having in her early years lived a lewd sort of a life and having become dissolute in character, not only having consorted much with the cheap sorcerers who surrounded her parents, but also having thus acquired the knowledge of what she needed to know, later became the wedded wife of Belisarius, after having already been the mother of many children. Straightway, therefore, she decided upon being an adulteress from the very start, but she was very careful to conceal this business, not because she was ashamed of her own practices, nor because she entertained any fear so far as her husband was concerned (for she never experienced the slightest feeling of shame for any action whatsoever and she had gained complete control of her husband by means of many tricks of magic), but because she dreaded the punishment the Empress might inflict. . . .

There was a certain youth from Thrace in the household of Belisarius, Theodosius by name. . . . Now when Belisarius was about to embark on the voyage to Libya, he bathed this youth in the sacred bath, from which he lifted him with his own hands, thus making him the adopted child of himself and his wife, as is customary for Christians to make adoptions, and consequently Antonina loved Theodosius, as she naturally would, as being her son through the sacred word, and with very particular solicitude she kept him near herself. And straightway she fell extraordinarily in love with him in the course of this voyage, and having become insatiate in her passion, she shook off both fear and respect for everything both divine and human and had intercourse with him, at first in secret, but finally even in the presence of servants of both sexes. For being by now possessed by this passion and manifestly smitten with love, she could see no longer any obstacle to the deed. And on one occasion Belisarius caught them in the very act in Carthage, yet he willingly allowed himself to be deceived by his wife. For though he found them both in an underground chamber and was transported with rage, she, without either playing the coward or attempting to conceal the deed, remarked "I came down here in order to hide with the aid of the boy the most valuable of our booty, so that it may not get to the knowledge of the Emperor." Now she said this as a mere pretext, but he, appearing to be satisfied, dropped the matter, though he could see that the belt which supported the drawers of Theodosius, covering his private parts, had been loosened. For under compulsion of love for the woman, he would have it that the testimony of his own eyes was absolutely untrustworthy.

[In another section of *The Secret History*, Procopius describes the nature and moral character of the emperor.]

And I think it not inappropriate to describe the appearance of this man. He was neither tall in stature nor particularly short, but of a medium height, yet not thin but slightly fleshy, and his face was round and not uncomely; for his complexion remained ruddy even after two days of fasting. But that I may describe his appearance as a whole in few words, I would say that he resembled Domitian, son of Vespasian, very closely, an Emperor who so impressed the Romans who suffered under him that even after they had chopped his whole body into pieces they felt that they had not satisfied their rage against him. . . .

Such was Justinian in appearance; but his character I could not accurately describe. For this man was both an evil-doer and easily led into evil, the sort of a person whom they call a moral pervert, never of his own accord speaking the truth to those with whom he conversed, but having a deceitful and crafty intent behind every word and action, and at the same time exposing himself, an easy prey, to those who wished to deceive him. . . .

This Emperor was insincere, crafty, hypocritical, dissembling his anger, double-dealing, clever, a perfect artist in acting out an opinion which he pretended to hold, and even able to produce tears, not from joy or sorrow, but contriving them for the occasion according to the need of the moment, always playing false, yet not carelessly but adding both his signature and the most terrible oaths to bind his agreements, and that too in dealing with his own subjects. But he departed straightway from his agreements and his oaths, just like the vilest slaves, who, through fear of the tortures hanging over them, are induced to make confession of acts which they had denied on oath. He was a fickle friend, a truceless enemy, an ardent devotee of assassination and of robbery, quarrelsome and an inveterate innovator, easily led astray into wrong, but influenced by no counsel to adopt the right, keen to conceive and to execute base designs, but looking upon even the hearing about good things as distasteful. How could any man be competent to describe adequately the character of Justinian? These faults and many others still greater he manifestly possessed to a degree not in accord with human nature. On the contrary, Nature seemed to have removed all baseness from the rest of mankind and to have concentrated it in the soul of this man. And in addition to his other shortcomings, while he was very easy-going as to lending an ear to slanders, yet he was severe as to inflicting punishment. For he never paused for a thorough investigation before reaching a decision, but straightway upon hearing what the slanderer said, he would make his decision and order it published. And he did not hesitate to write orders that called for the capture of towns and the burning of cities and the enslavement of whole peoples, for no reason whatever. Consequently, if one should care to estimate all the misfortunes which have befallen the Romans from the earliest times and then to balance against them those of the present day, it seems to me that he would find a greater slaughter of human beings to have been perpetrated by this man than has come to pass in all the preceding time. And while he had no scruples whatever against the quiet acquisition of other men's money—for he never even made any excuse, putting forward justice as a screen in trespassing upon things which did not belong to him—yet when once these had become his own, he was perfectly ready to shew his contempt for the money, with a prodigality in which there was no trace of calculation, and for no reason at all to fling it away to the barbarians. And, to sum up the whole matter, he neither had any money himself, nor would he allow anyone else in the world to have it, as though he were not a victim of avarice, but simply consumed by envy of those who possessed money. Consequently he lightly banished wealth from the Roman world and became the creator of poverty for all.

[In the following section of *The Secret History*, Procopius describes Theodora's unsavory life before she met and married Justinian.]

The traits, then, of Justinian's character, as far as we are able to state them, were roughly these. And he married a wife concerning whom I shall now relate how she was born and reared and how, after being joined to this man in marriage, she overturned the Roman State to its very foundations. There was in Byzantium a certain Acacius, keeper of the animals used in the circus, an adherent of the Green Faction, a man whom they called Master of the Bears. This man had died a natural death during the reign of Anastasius, leaving three girls, Comito, Theodora and Anastasia, the eldest of whom was not yet seven years of age. And the woman, now reduced to utter distress, entered into marriage with another husband, who, she thought, would later on assist her in both the care of the household and in her first husband's occupation. But the Dancing Master of the Greens, a man named Asterius, was bribed by another man to remove these persons from that office and to make no difficulty about putting in the position the man who had given him the money. For the Dancing Masters had authority to administer such matters as they wished. But when the woman saw the whole populace gathered in the Circus, she put garlands on the heads and in both hands of the three girls and caused them to sit as suppliants. And though the Greens were by no means favourable to receiving the supplication, the Blues conferred this position of honour upon them, since their Master of the Bears also had recently died. And when these children came of age, the mother immediately put them on the stage there— since they were fair to look upon—not all three at the same time, but as each one seemed to her to be ripe for this calling. Now Comito, the first one, had already scored a brilliant success among the harlots of her age; and Theodora, the next in order, clothed in a little sleeved frock suitable to a slave girl, would follow her about, performing various services and in particular always carrying on her shoulders the stool on which her sister was accustomed to sit in the assemblies. Now for a time Theodora, being immature, was quite unable to sleep with a man or to have a woman's kind of intercourse with one, yet she did engage in intercourse of a masculine type of lewdness with the wretches, slaves though they were, who, following their masters to the theatre, incidentally took advantage of the opportunity afforded them to carry on this monstrous business, and she spent much time in the brothel in this unnatural traffic of the body. But as soon as she came of age and was at last mature, she joined the women of the stage and straightway became a courtesan, of the sort whom men of ancient times used to call "infantry." For she was neither a flute-player nor a harpist, nay, she had not even acquired skill in the dance, but she sold her youthful beauty to those who chanced to come along, plying her trade with practically her whole body. Later on she was associated with the actors in all the work of the theatre, and she shared their performances with them, playing up to their buffoonish acts intended to raise a laugh. For she was unusually clever and full of gibes, and she immediately became admired for this sort of thing. For the girl had not a particle of modesty, nor did any man ever see her embarrassed, but she undertook shameless services without the least hesitation, and she was the sort of a person who, for instance, when being flogged or beaten over the head, would crack a joke over it and burst into a loud laugh; and she would undress and exhibit to any who chanced along both her front and her rear naked, parts which rightly should be unseen by men and hidden from them.

And as she wantoned with her lovers, she always kept bantering them, and by toying with new devices in intercourse, she always succeeded in winning the hearts of the licentious to her; for she did not even expect that the approach should be made by the man she was with, but on the contrary she herself, with wanton jests and with clownish posturing with her hips, would tempt all who came along, especially if they were beardless youths. Indeed there was never anyone such a slave to pleasure in all forms; for many a time she would go to a community dinner with ten youths or even more, all of exceptional bodily vigour who had made a business of fornication, and she would lie with all her banquet companions the whole night long, and when they were too exhausted to go on, she would go to their attendants, thirty perhaps in number, and pair off with each one of them; yet even so she could not get enough of this wantonness.

On one occasion she entered the house of one of the notables during the drinking, and they say that in the sight of all the banqueters she mounted to the projecting part of the banqueting couch where their feet lay, and there drew up her clothing in a shameless way, not hesitating to display her licentiousness. And though she made use of three openings, she used to take Nature to task, complaining that it had not pierced her breasts with larger holes so that it might be possible for her to contrive another method of copulation there. And though she was pregnant many times, yet practically always she was able to contrive to bring about an abortion immediately.

And often even in the theatre, before the eyes of the whole people, she stripped off her clothing and moved about naked through their midst, having only a girdle about her private parts and her groins, not, however, that she was ashamed to display these too to the populace, but because no person is permitted to enter there entirely naked, but must have at least a girdle about the groins. Clothed in this manner, she sprawled out and lay on her back on the ground. And some slaves, whose duty this was, sprinkled grains of barley over her private parts, and geese, which happened to have been provided for this very purpose, picked them off with their beaks, one by one, and ate them. And when she got up, she not only did not blush, but even acted as if she took pride in this strange performance. For she was not merely shameless herself, but also a contriver of shameless deeds above all others.

The Rise of Islam

Arabia in the sixth century A.D. was inhabited primarily in the southern area of Yemen, along the western slopes of the Hejaz Mountains, and along scattered desert oases. Large-scale international trade in dates and imported spices from Africa and India was made possible through the use of camel caravans. Religion was well developed; the people worshipped the moon, planets, spirits, stone idols, and rocks.

The major center of religious worship and pilgrimage, however, was the city of Mecca. Within the city there was a sacred precinct containing a well, called the Zamzam, and the holy shrine, referred to as the Kaaba. A great variety of religions were connected with the Kaaba, which housed approximately 300 idols, including statues of Jesus.

Politically, the Byzantines and Persians, each of whom had launched several invasions to gain control of Arabia, were fierce competitors. Yet, despite these struggles, no major power had secured total domination of the independent peoples.

Muhammad (A.D. 570?–632) was born into the Kuraysh clan, which was one of the leading camel-caravan trading groups in Mecca. Unfortunately, before Muhammad's birth his father died. The child was left in the care of his mother until she, too, died when he was six. At this time, he was placed under the protection of his paternal uncle.

There is little information about Muhammad's life until 595, when he became an overseer for a wealthy, older caravan owner, a woman named Khadija. Muhammad did so well at his job that soon Khadija asked him to marry her; this marriage of convenience turned to true affection and lasted until Khadija's death in 619. After her death, Muhammad married many times, in each case to bind new converts to his religion. Despite his numerous marriages, Muhammad never had a son who lived beyond infancy; however, he later adopted a cousin as a foster son.

During the month of Ramadan (Fasting) in the year 610, Muhammad said he was called by God (Allah) to become his prophet. Through the messages of the Archangel Gabriel, which Muhammad received for the rest of his life, he formed the religion called Islam (meaning submission to the Will of God). Muhammad was instructed to preach the message of Allah to the Meccans. At first he was able to convert only members of his family and some young men in the city, while most Meccans resisted his teachings.

Persecution of Muhammad and his small group of followers intensified. When he finally decided to leave Mecca, his Hegira (migration) took him to a small date-palm oasis called Yathrib (Medina), some two hundred and fifty miles north. Once in Yathrib, Muhammad became a political as well as a religious leader for his Muslims; as such, he resorted to the time-honored tradition of raiding caravans that passed near Yathrib. These actions brought swift retaliation from Mecca, but the Meccans were never able to defeat Muhammad, whose prestige continually increased. Finally, the Meccans ended their opposition to Muhammad and allowed him into the city to perform the act of "pilgrimage" (or Hajj). Once inside Mecca, he cleansed the Kaaba of idolatry and rededicated it to the sole worship of Allah.

52

The Qur'an

The Qur'an is the Holy Scripture and basis of the Islamic religion. The work comprises 114 chapters (or suras) arranged according to their length, running from the longest to the shortest. The Qur'an is believed to be the word of God, transmitted by the

Archangel Gabriel to the Prophet Muhammad. The Prophet, in turn, preached these messages, first in Mecca, then in Medina, to his small group of converts (Muslims). Only after Muhammad's death were the messages gathered together and given their final arrangement by the third caliph,[4] Othman.

The basic beliefs of Islam are drawn from contacts with both Jews and Christians and then adapted for the Arab peoples. Essential to the religion is the need for each person to submit to the one and only god, Allah. According to this religion, Allah knows and sees everything. He has determined each person's fate; however, lest one fall into fatalism, each person must account for his or her actions on the Day of Last Judgment.

Drawing upon the scriptures of the "Peoples of the Book" (Jews and Christians), Muhammad preached that Allah had described to his twenty-eight prophets—including Adam, Noah, Moses, John the Baptist, and Jesus—the method in which He was to be worshipped. However, Muhammad thought that the Jews and Christians had deliberately distorted the original messages. Muhammad claimed that the Qur'an was the most perfect guide for worshipping Allah, and that he was the final prophet or "Seal."

In the following Qur'anic selections, note the descriptions of Muhammad's call to God's Word, the Last Judgment, the Islamic view of the "Peoples of the Book," and the duties that each Muslim must follow. Today the Qur'an governs approximately 800 million lives.

QUESTIONS TO CONSIDER

1. What are some of the beliefs and duties of Islam as contained in the following verses?
2. Why does Abraham hold a special position in Islam?
3. Why was there trouble between the Jews, Christians and Muslims?

The Blood Clot

96:1 Recite in the name of your Lord who created,
Created man from clots of blood!
Recite! Your Lord is the Most Bountiful One,
Who taught the use of the pen;
Taught man what he did not know.
Nay, surely, Man is insolent,
Because he sees himself possessed of riches.
Truly, to your Lord is the return of all.

---

[4]*Caliph* means "Successor of the Apostle of God (Muhammad)." A caliph was the head of state, a judge, leader in worship, and commander of the army.

From *The Koran*, trans. By J. M. Rodwell (London: J. M. Dent, New York: E. P. Dutton & Co., 1909), Suras 96:1–8, 5:97, 56:1–27, 41–46, 62:9, 3:42–60, 65–70, 4:34, 24:31–32, 2:174, 177–178, 183–185, 187, 196, 219–220, 17:8–15, 21, 30, 32, 71:199, 16:115. 9:592:178, 184, 186, 196–7, 219, 225, 228, 4:34; 5:96, 22:25, 3:19, 45, 55, 67–70, 84, 115–158, 161, 180, 6:103, 112, 146. Slightly modernized.

The Flood

5:97 God has appointed the Kaaba, the sacred house, to be a maintenance for mankind, and the sacred month, and the offering, and its ornament. Thus, you may know that God loves all that is in the heavens and on the earth, and that God has knowledge of everything. Know that God is severe in punishing, and that God is Forgiving, Merciful.

The Great Event

56:1 When the day that must come shall have come suddenly,
None shall treat that sudden coming as a lie:
Day that shall abase? Day that shall exalt!
When the earth shall be shaken with a shock,
And the mountains shall be crumbed with a crumbling,
And shall become scattered dust,
    And into three bands shall you be divided:
Then the people of the right hand—Oh! How happy shall be the people
of the right hand!
And the people of the left hand—Oh! How wretched shall be the people
of the left hand!
And they who were foremost on earth—the foremost still.
These are they who shall be brought close to God,
In gardens of delight;
A crowd of the former
And a few of the latter generations;
On decorated couches
Reclining on them face to face:
Never changing youths go round about to them
With goblets and ewers and a cup of flowing wine;
They shall not suffer headache from it, nor shall they be exhausted:
And with fruits as shall please them best,
And with flesh of birds, as they shall desire:
And they shall have Virgins, with large dark eyes, like
Pearls hidden in their shells,
In recompense of their past labors.
NO vain discourse shall they hear, nor talk of sin,
But only the cry, Peace! Peace!
And the people of the right hand—Oh! how happy shall the people
Of the right be!

* * *

But the people of the left hand—oh! how wretched shall the people
Of the left hand be!
Amid scorching winds and in scalding water,
And in the shadow of a black smoke,
Not cool, and horrid to behold.
For they truly, formerly, were blessed with worldly good,
But persisted in terrible sin, . . .

Friday

62:9 O you who believe! When you are called to prayer on Friday, hasten to the commemoration of God, and quit your business. This, if you knew it, will be best for you.

The Family of Imram

97:40 Remember when the angel said, " O Mary! Truly God announced to you the Word from Him? His name shall be the Messiah, Jesus son of Mary, illustrious in this world, and in the next, and one of those who have near access to God;

And He shall speak to men alike when in the cradle and when grown up: And he shall be one of the just."

She said, "How, O my Lord! Shall I have a son, when man has not touched me?" He said, "Thus: God will create what He wills; When he decrees a thing, He only says, 'Be' and it is."

And he will teach him the Book (Torah), and the Wisdom, and the Law, and the Gospel: and he shall be an apostle to the children of Israel. "Now have I come," he will say, " to you with a sign from your Lord; Out of clay I will make for you the figure of a bird: and I will breathe into it, and it shall be by God's leave, a bird. And I will heal the blind, and the leper; and by God's leave I will raise the dead; and I will tell you what you may eat, and what you should store up in your houses! Truly this will be a sign for you, if you are believers.

And I have come to uphold the law (Torah) which was before me; and to allow you part of that which had been forbidden to you; and I have come to you with a sign from your Lord: Fear God, then, and obey me; in truth God is my Lord, and your Lord: Therefore worship Him. This is a right way."

And when Jesus saw unbelief on their part, He said, "Who are my helpers with God?" The apostles said, "We will be God's helpers! We believe in God, and bear you witness that we are Muslims.

O our Lord! We believe in what you have sent down, and we follow the apostle; write us up, then, with those who bear witness to him.

And the Jews planned, and God planned: But of those who plan, God is the best.

Remember when God said, "O Jesus! I will cause you to die, and will take you up to myself and deliver you from those who do not believe; and I will place those who follow you above those who do not believe, until the day of resurrection. Then to me you will return, and where you differ I will decide between you.

And as to those who are not believers, I will chastise them with a terrible punishment now and in the next life; and they shall have no one to help them."

But those who believe, and do good things, He will reward them. God does not love the evildoers.

These signs, and this wise warning we remind you.

Truly, Jesus is as Adam was in the sight of God. He created him of dust: He then said to him, "Be"—and he was. . . .

O people of the Book! Why dispute about Abraham, when the Law (Torah) and the Gospel were not sent down until after him? Do you not understand? . . .

Abraham was neither Jew nor Christian; but he was sound in the faith, a Muslim; and not of those who add gods to God . . .

A party among the people of the Book would mislead you: but they only mislead themselves, and do not understand.

O people of the Book! Why disbelieve the signs of God when you have been witnesses?

O people of the Book! Why do you bear false witness? Why knowingly hide the truth?

Women

4:34 Men are superior to women because of the qualities, which God has placed one above the other because of the expenses they make from their property for them. Good women are obedient, careful, during the husband's absence, because God has guarded them. But punish those whom you fear might desert; remove them to other beds and scourge them; But if they are obedient to you, then do not seek a way against them; surely God is High, Great!

The Light

24:31 And say to believing women that they cast down their eyes, and that they do not show their ornaments, except those which are external; and that they throw their veils over their bosoms, and do not display their ornaments, except to their husbands or their fathers, or their brothers, or their brothers' sons, or their sisters' sons, or their women, or their slaves, or male domestics who have no natural force, or to children who do not know women's nakedness. And do not let them strike their feet together, so as to show their hidden ornaments. And all of you turn to God, O you Believers! That it may be well with you.

And marry those among you who are single, and your good servants, and that are maidens. If they are poor, God in His bounty will enrich them. God is all-bounteous, Knowing.

The Cow

2:169 Truly they who hide the Book which God has sent down, and sell it for a small price—these shall swallow into their bellies naught but fire. God will not speak to them, or purify them, on the day of Resurrection: and theirs shall be a grievous torment . . .

There is no piety in turning your faces toward the East or the West, but he is pious who believes in God, and the Last Day, and the Angels, and the Book, and the Prophets; who for the love of God gives his wealth to his kinfolk, and to the orphans, and the needy, and the wayfarer, and those who ask, and for ransoming; who observe prayer, and pay the legal alms and who is faithful to their promises.

When they have promised, and patient under ills and hardships, and in time of troubles: those are they who are just, and these are they who fear the Lord.

O believers! Retaliation for bloodshed is prescribed to you: the free man for the free, and the slave for the slave, and the woman for the woman: but he to whom his brother shall make any admission, is to be dealt with equitably; and to him should he pay a fine with liberality.

This is a relaxation from your Lord and a mercy. For him who after this shall transgress, a harsh punishment! . . .

O believers! A Fast is prescribed to you as it was prescribed to those before you, that you may fear God,

For certain days. But he among you who shall be ill, or on a journey, shall fast that same number of other days: and as for those who are able to keep it and yet break it, the expiation of this shall be the keeping of a poor man. And he who of his own accord performs a good work, shall derive good from it: and good shall it be for you to fast—if you knew it.

As to the month Ramadan in which the Koran was sent down to be man's guide, and an explanation of that guidance, and of that illumination, as soon as any of you observes the moon, let him set about the fast; but he who is sick, or on a journey, shall fast a like number of other days. God wishes you ease, but wishes not your discomfort, and that you fulfill the number of days, and that you glorify God for his guidance, and that you be thankful . . .

You are allowed on the night of the fast to approach your wives: they are your garment and you are theirs. God knows that you delude yourselves, so He turns unto you and forgives you! Now, therefore, go into them full of desire which God has ordained for you; and eat and drink until you can discern a white thread from a black thread at daybreak; then fast strictly till night, and do not go to them, but rather pass the time in the Mosques. These are the bounds set up by God: there come not to them. Thus God makes his signs clear to men that they may fear Him . . .

Accomplish the Pilgrimage and the Visitation of the holy places in honor of God: and if you are stopped by foes, send whatever offering shall be the easiest; and do not shave your heads until the offering reaches the place of sacrifice. But if you are ill, or have an ailment of the head, (you) must satisfy (the requirement) by fasting, alms or an offering; then when you are secure from foes, he who combines the visit to the holy places with the pilgrimage, shall bring whatever offering is the easiest; but he who can not find anything to offer, shall fast three days in the pilgrimage, and seven days when you return: they shall be ten days in all. This is binding on him whose family shall not be present at the Sacred Mosque. And fear God, and know that God is terrible in punishing. . . .

They will ask you about wine and games of chance. Say: In both of them there is great sin, and a means of profit for men; but their sin is greater than their advantage. They will ask you also what they shall give in alms (charity). Say: what you can spare. Thus God shows you his things that you may ponder.

About this present world and the hereafter. They will also ask you concerning orphans. Say: Fair dealing with them is best. But if you mix yourselves up (in their affairs)—they are your brethren: God knows the evil dealer from the fair; and if God pleased, he could indeed afflict you!. Truly, God is Mighty, Wise . . .

Satan, Who Refused

"Adam," We said, "Satan is an enemy to you and to your wife. Let him not turn you out of Paradise and plunge you into affliction. Here you shall not hunger or be naked; you shall not thirst, or feel the scorching heat."

But Satan whispered to him, saying: "Shall I show you the Tree of Immortality and an everlasting kingdom?"

They both ate of its fruit, so that they beheld their nakedness and began to cover themselves with leaves. Thus Adam disobeyed his Lord and went astray.

The Night

17:8-15. This Koran will guide men to that which is most upright. It promises the believers who do good works a rich reward, and threatens those who deny the life to come with a grievous scourge. Yet man prays for evil as fervently as he prays for good. Truly, man is ever impatient . . .

The fate of each man We have bound about his neck. On the Day of Resurrection We shall confront him with a book spread wide open, saying: "Here is your book: read it. Enough for you this day that your own soul should call you to account . . ."

17:21. Serve no other gods besides Allah, lest you incur disgrace and ruin. Your Lord has enjoined you to worship none but Him, and to show kindness to your parents . . .

17:30. Be neither miserly nor prodigal, for then you should either be reproached or be reduced to penury.

17:32. You shall not kill any man whom Allah has forbidden you to kill, except for a just cause . . . Do not interfere with the property of orphans except with the best of motives, until maturity. Keep your promises; you are accountable for all that you promise.

Give full measure, when you measure, and weigh with even scales. That is fair, and better in the end.

The Heights

71:199. Show forgiveness, speak for justice, and avoid the ignorant. If Satan tempts you, seek refuge in Allah; He hears all and knows all.

The Bee

16:115. He has forbidden you carrion, blood, and the flesh of swine; also any flesh consecrated other than in the name of Allah. But whoever is constrained to eat of any of these, not intending to sin or transgress, will find Allah forgiving and merciful.

Repentance

9:59. Alms shall be used only for the advancement of Allah's cause, for the ransom of captives and debtors, and for distribution among the poor, the destitute, the wayfarers, those that are employed in collecting alms, and those that are converted to the faith . . .

The Cow

2:178. Believers, retaliation is decreed for you in bloodshed: a free man for a free man, a slave for a slave, and a female for a female . . .

It is decreed that when death approaches, those of you that leave property shall bequeath shall bequeath it equitable to parents and kindred . . .

2:184. In the month of Ramadan the Koran was revealed, a book of guidance with proofs of guidance distinguishing right from wrong. Therefore whoever of you is present in that month let him fast. But he who is ill or on a journey shall fast a similar number of days later on . . .

2:186. . . . Eat and drink until you can tell a white thread from a black one in the light of coming dawn. Then resume the fast till nightfall and do not approach them, but stay at your prayers in the mosques.

2:196. Make the pilgrimage and visit the Sacred House (the Kaaba) for His sake . . .

2:197. Make the pilgrimage in the appointed months. He that intends to perform it in those months must abstain from sexual intercourse, obscene language, and acrimonious disputes while on pilgrimage . . .

2:219. They ask you about drinking and gambling. Say: "There is great harm in both, although they have some benefit for men; but their harm is far greater than their benefit."

2:225. Those that renounce their wives on oath must wait four months. If they change their mind, Allah is forgiving and merciful; but if they decide to divorce them, know that He hears all and knows all.

2:228. Women shall with justice have rights similar to those exercised against them, although men have a status above women. Allah is mighty and wise.

Women

4:34. Men have authority over women because Allah has made the one superior to the others, and because they spend their wealth to maintain them. Good women are obedient. They guard their unseen parts because Allah has guarded them. As for those from whom you fear disobedience, admonish them and send them to beds apart and beat them. The if they obey you, take no further action against them. Allah is high, supreme.

The Table

5:96. Allah has made the Sacred House of the Kaaba, the sacred month, and the sacrificial offerings with their ornaments, eternal values for mankind; so that you may know that Allah has knowledge of all that the heavens and the earth contain; that He has knowledge of all things.

Pilgrimage

22:25. When We prepared for Abraham the site of the Sacred Mosque We said: "Worship none besides Me. Keep My House clean for those who walk around it and those who stand upright or kneel in worship."

The Imrans

3:19. The only true faith in Allah's sight is Islam. Those to whom the Scriptures were given disagreed among themselves through jealousy only after knowledge had been given them. He that denies Allah's revelations should know that He is swift in reckoning.

3:45. The angels said to Mary: "Allah bids you rejoice in a Word from HIm. His name is the Messiah, Jesus the son of Mary. He shall be noble in this world and in the next, and shall be favored by Allah. He shall preach to men in his cradle and in the prime of manhood, and shall lead a righteous life."

3:55. They plotted, and Allah plotted. Allah is the supreme Plotter. He said: "Jesus, I am about to cause you to die and lift you up to Me. I shall take you away from the unbelievers and exalt your followers above them till the Day of Resurrection; then to Me you shall all return and I shall judge your disputes. The unbelievers shall be sternly punished in this world and in the world to come: there shall be none to help them. As for those that have faith and do good works, they shall be given their reward in full. Allah does not love the evil-doers."

3:67–70. Abraham was neither Jew nor Christian. He was an upright man, one who had surrendered himself to Allah. He was no idolater. Surely the men who are nearest to Abraham are those who follow him, this Prophet, and the true believers. Allah is the guardian of the faithful. Some of the People of the Book wish to mislead you; but they mislead none but themselves, though they may not perceive it.

People of the Book! Why do you deny Allah's revelations when you know that they are true?

3:84. Say: "We believe in Allah and what is revealed to us; in that which was revealed to Abraham and Ishmael, to Isaac and Jacob and the tribes; and in that which Allah gave Moses and Jesus and the prophets. We discriminate against none of them. To Him We have have surrendered ourselves."

3:115. Yet they are not all alike. There are among the People of the Book some upright men who all night long recite the revelations of Allah and worship Him; who believe in Allah and the Last Day; who enjoin justice and forbid evil and vie with each other in good works. These are righteous men: whatever good they do, its reward shall not be denied them. Allah know the righteous.

3:158. If you should die or be slain in the cause of Allah, His forgiveness and His mercy would surely be better than all the riches they amass. If you should die or be slain, before Him you shall all be gathered.

3:161. No prophet would rob his followers; for anyone that steals shall on the Day of Resurrection bring with him that which he has stolen. Then shall every soul be paid what it has earned: none shall be wronged.

3:180. Let no misers who hoard the gifts of Allah think that their avarice is good for them: it is nothing but evil. The riches they have piled up shall become their fetters on the Day of Resurrection. It is Allah who will inherit the heavens and the earth. He is cognizant of all your actions.

Cattle

6:103. No mortal eyes can see Him, though He sees all eyes. He is benignant and all-knowing.

6:112. Thus We have assigned for every prophet an enemy: the devils among men and jinn, who inspire one another with vain and varnished falsehoods . . .

6:146. We forbade the Jews all animals with undivided hoofs and the fat of sheep and oxen, except what is on their backs and intestines and what is mixed with their bones. Such is the penalty with which We rewarded them for their misdeeds.

53

Sayings (*Hadith*) Ascribed to the Prophet: Holy War

Hadith, or sayings, are one source of Islamic law. They are stories or sayings connected with Muhammad's life, which were, and are, used to justify actions in the past and present. Each hadith is connected with the Prophet or one of his Companions through a narrative story that passed from one person to another over the centuries.

The following selection concerns the undertaking of a *Jihād*, or Holy War, in which every *amir* (a political-military leader) should participate. It describes the motivations for the undertaking, the duties and actions of a good warrior, and prohibitions against certain unacceptable actions in warfare.

QUESTIONS TO CONSIDER

1.   What will be the rewards for a warrior of the faith?
2.   How are polytheists, women, and children to be treated and why?
3.   Compare a Jihād with a Christian Crusade. What are the similarities and differences?

Jihād is incumbent upon you with every amir, whether he be godly or wicked and even if he commit major sins. Prayer is incumbent upon you behind every Muslim, be he godly or wicked and even if he commit major sins. Prayer is incumbent upon you for every Muslim who dies, be he godly or wicked and even if he commit major sins.

Paradise is under the shadow of swords.

Where the believer's heart shakes on the path of God, his sins fall away from him as the fruit falls off a date palm.

If anyone shoots an arrow at the enemy on the path of God and his arrow reaches his enemy, whether it hits him or misses, it is accounted equal in merit to liberating a slave.

He who draws his sword in the path of God has sworn allegiance to God.

If anyone ransoms a prisoner from the hands of the enemy, I am that prisoner.

He who fights so that the word of God may prevail is on the path of God.

He who dies fighting on the frontier in the path of God, God protects him from the testing of the tomb.

The unbeliever and the one who kills him will never meet in Hell.

God sent me as a mercy and a portent; He did not send me as a trader or as a cultivator. The worst of the community on the Day of Resurrection are the traders and the cultivators, except for those who are niggardly with their religion.

A day and a night of fighting on the frontier is better than a month of fasting and prayer.

The best thing a Muslim can earn is an arrow in the path of God.

He who equips a warrior in the Holy War for God has the same reward as he, while the warrior's reward is not diminished.

He who when he dies has never campaigned or even intended to campaign dies in a kind of hypocrisy.

Fight against the polytheists with your property, your persons, and your tongues.

Swords are the keys of Paradise.

A sword is sufficient witness.

God wonders at people who are led to Heaven in chains.

A campaign by sea is like ten campaigns by land, and he who loses his bearings at sea is like one who sheds his blood in the path of God.

Every prophet has his monasticism, and the monasticism of this community is the Holy War in the path of God.

If a campaigner by sea is seasick, he has the reward of a martyr; if drowned, of two martyrs.

In Islam there are three dwellings, the lower, the upper, and the uppermost. The lower is the Islam of the generality of Muslims. If you ask any one of them he will answer, "I am a Muslim." In the upper their merits differ, some of the Muslims being better than others. The uppermost is the jihad in the cause of God, which only the best of them attain.

Will you not ask me why I laugh? I have seen people of my community who are dragged to Paradise against their will. They asked, "O Prophet of God, who are they?" He said, "They are non-Arab people whom the warriors in the Holy War have captured and made to enter Islam."

Shoot and ride! Of the two, I would rather have you shoot than ride. Anything in which a man passes his time is vain except for shooting with his bow, training his horse, or dallying with his wife. These three things are right. He who abandons archery after having learned it is ungrateful to the one who taught him.

Accursed be he who carries the Persian bow. Keep to the Arab bow and to the lances by which God gives you power in these lands and gives you victory over your enemy.

Learn to shoot, for what lies between the two marks is one of the gardens of Paradise.

Warfare is deception.

The Muslims are bound by their stipulations.

The Muslims are bound by their stipulations as long as these are lawful.

Of any village that you come to and stay in, you have a share, but of any village that is disobedient to God and His Prophet, one-fifth of it belongs to God and His Prophet and the rest is yours.

Treat an Arab as an Arab and a half-breed as a half-breed. The Arab has two shares and the half-breed one.

Kill the old polytheists, but spare the young ones.

If you find a tithe collector, kill him.

Go in the name of God and in God and in the religion of the Prophet of God! Do not kill the very old, the infant, the child, or the woman. Bring all the booty, holding back no part of it. Maintain order and do good, for God loves those who do good.

Why are some people so bent on killing today that they even kill children? Are not the best of you the sons of idolators? Do not kill children! Do not kill children! Every soul is born with a natural disposition [to the true religion] and remains so until their tongue gives them the powers of expression. Then their parents make Jews or Christians of them.

Expel the Jews and the Christians from the Arabian peninsula.

Accept advice to treat prisoners well.

Looting is no more lawful than carrion.

He who loots is not one of us.

He has forbidden looting and mutilation.

He has forbidden the killing of women and children.

He who flees is not one of us.

The bite of an ant is more painful to the martyr than the thrust of a weapon, which is more desirable to him than sweet, cold water on a hot summer day.

High Point of Islamic Culture

Islam developed during the lifetime of the Prophet Muhammad not only as a religion in the sense of a way of worship and a systematic elaboration of the relationship between man and his creator out through the circumstances of its incubation, but it also evolved as a social and political institution that claimed divine authority for the regulation of relations between man and man, believer and nonbeliever. The Qur'an, the revealed word of God, was the prime and unchanging authority. The early generations of Muslims could also recall decisions made by the Prophet, whose teachings were considered a supplement to and commentary on the divine text. Soon, however, as the community of Islam expanded and embraced former subjects of Byzantium, Sassanid Iran, and others as far west as Spain and as far east as India that belonged to many different nations and cultures, the need arose to formalize the social teachings of Islam and to unify its rituals.

54

Harun al Rashid and the Byzantine Empire

In A.D. 750 the first Islamic dynasty, the Omayyads, was overthrown by the Abbasid family, who moved the center of government from Damascus, Syria, to Iraq and built the fabled capital, Baghdad. The reign of Harun al Rashid (768-809) marked the acme of the Abbasid glory in Baghdad. The wealth of Harun's court became legendary and formed the basis of the "One Thousand and One Nights" tales.

In politics, Harun al Rashid was reported by Westerners to have been in contact with Emperor Charlemagne, sending to the West an organ and a great white elephant to the astonishment of the Europeans. Relations with the Byzantine government were much less cordial as the Abbasids continued the traditional Arab raids into Anatolia. Immediately preceding the overthrow of the infamous Byzantine Empress Irene (796–802) by Emperor Nicephoros I, the empire had been invaded and defeated by Harun's army. As a result, Irene had promised to pay the Abbasids more gold in a large tribute. When Nicephoros seized the throne, he was determined to receive better conditions from the caliph. The following Arab passages reveal the emperor's demand and the swift response from Harun.

QUESTIONS TO CONSIDER

1. Why was the reign of Empress Irene disliked by the Byzantines?
2. How did Nicephoros justify his request for repayment of the monies promised to Harun al Rashid?
3. How did Harun treat this request?

A woman came to rule over the Romans [Byzantines] because at the time she was the only one of their royal house who remained. She wrote to the Caliphs al-Mahdi and al-Hadi and to al-Rashid at the beginning of his Caliphate with respect and deference and showered him with gifts. When her son [Constantine VI] grew up and came to the throne in her place, he brought trouble and disorder and provoked al-Rashid. The empress, who knew al-Rashid and feared his power, was afraid lest the

From *Islam: From the Prophet Muhammad to the Capture of Constantinople, Volume 1: Politics and War*, edited by Bernard Lewis, translated by Bernard Lewis, copyright 1974 by Bernard Lewis. Used by permission of Oxford University Press, pp. 27–30, 210–12.

kingdom of the Romans [the Eastern Roman Empire or Byzantine Empire] pass away and their country be ruined. She therefore overcame her son by cunning and put out his eyes so that the kingdom was taken from him and returned to her. But the people of their kingdom disapproved of this and hated her for it. Therefore Nicephoros, who was her secretary, rose against her, and they helped and supported him so that he seized power and became the ruler of the Romans.

When he was in full control of his kingdom, he wrote to al-Rashid, "From Nicephoros, the king of the Romans, to al-Rashid, the king of the Arabs, as follows: That woman put you and your father and your brother in the place of kings and put herself in the place of a commoner. I put you in a different place, and [I]am preparing to invade your lands and attack your cities, unless you repay me what that woman paid you. Farewell !" When his letter reached al-Rashid, he replied, "In the name of God, the Merciful and the Compassionate, from the servant of God, Harun, Commander of the Faithful, to Nicephoros, the dog of the Romans, as follows: I have understood your letter, and I have your answer. You will see it with your own eye, not hear it." Then he at once sent an army against the land of the Romans of a size the like of which was never heard before and with commanders unrivaled in courage and skill. When news of this reached Nicephoros, the earth became narrow before him and he took counsel. Al-Rashid advanced relentlessly into the land of the Romans, killing, plundering, taking captives, destroying castles, and obliterating traces, until they came to the narrow roads before Constantinople, and when they reached there, they found that Nicephoros had already had trees cut down, thrown across these roads, and set on fire . . . Nicephoros sent gifts to al-Rashid and submitted to him very humbly and paid him the poll tax for himself as well as for his companions . . . Then al-Rashid went back, because of what Nicephoros had given him, and got as far as Raqqa. When the snow fell and Nicephoros felt safe from attack, he took advantage of the respite and broke the agreement between himself and al-Rashid and returned to his previous posture. Yahya ibn Khalid [the vizier], let alone any other, did not dare to inform al-Rashid of the treachery of Nicephoros. Instead, he and his sons offered money to the people to recite poetry and thereby inform al-Rashid of this [treachery] . . . When he recited this, al-Rashid asked, "Has he done that?" and he learned that the viziers had used this device to inform him of it. He then made war against Nicephoros while snow still remained and conquered Heraclea [a city in Anatolia] at that time.

55

Kai Kaus, "Scientific Physiognomy and the Purchase of Slaves"

Slavery was a part of most ancient and many modern societies until the nineteenth century. Slaves inherited their status and were regularly bought and sold on the domestic market, although war captives frequently became slaves and a fair amount of kidnapping by professionals, who could easily sell their human wares to dealers in foreign countries, introduced new slaves to the markets. Slaves were common in Islamic society, where they were used as domestic servants, as guardians of harem women, or as specially trained soldiers. They were sometimes used as field workers, but much less frequently than the victims of the later Atlantic–West African slave trade, who were later, at its height, taken by the hundreds of thousands annually to labor on the plantations and in the mines of the New World.

The following selection is by an eleventh-century ruler of several provinces on the south shore of the Caspian Sea, Kai Kaus, from his guidebook for princes, considered a classic of Persian literature. In it he gives advice on subjects as diverse as love, astrology, and polo. Here he suggests the qualities a buyer should look for in purchasing both black and white and male and female slaves.

QUESTIONS TO CONSIDER

1. What were the qualities a person should look for when buying slaves?
2. How is this article an example of racial or ethnic stereotyping?
3. From the author's description of how to apply it, what does physiognomy involve? Do people occasionally use something like it in our own day in making statements about types of humans?
4. This writer uses the term "science" generally in a way we probably would not. How is our modern notion of "science" different from his?

When you set out to buy slaves, be cautious. The buying of men is a difficult art; because many a slave may appear to be good, who, when regarded with knowledge, turns out to be the opposite. Most people imagine that buying slaves is like any other form of trading, not understanding that the buying of slaves, or the art of doing so, is a branch of philosophy. Anyone who buys goods of which he has no competent understanding can be defrauded over them, and the most difficult form of knowledge is that which deals with human beings. There are so many blemishes and good points in the human kind, and a single blemish may conceal a myriad good points, while a single good point may conceal a myriad faults.

Human beings cannot be known except by the science of physiognomy and by experience, and the science of physiognomy in its entirety is a branch of prophecy that is not acquired to perfection except by the divinely directed apostle. The reason is that by physiognomy the inward goodness or wickedness of man can be ascertained.

Now let me describe to the best of my ability what is essential in the purchasing of slaves, both white and black, and what their good and bad points are, so that they may be known to you. Understand then that there are three essentials in the buying of slaves; first is the recognition of their good and bad qualities, whether external or internal, by means of physiognomy; second is the awareness of diseases, whether latent or apparent, by their symptoms; third is the knowledge of the various classes and the defects and merits of each.

With regard to the first requirement, that of physiognomy, it consists of close observation when buying slaves. Whoever it may be that inspects the slave must first look at the face, which is always open to view, whereas the body can only be seen as occasion offers. Then look at eyes and eyebrows, followed by nose, lips and teeth, and lastly at the hair. The reason for this is that God placed the beauty of human beings in eyebrows, delicacy in the nose, sweetness in the lips and teeth and freshness in the skin. To all these the hair of the head has been made to lend adornment, since [God] created the hair for adornment.

From *Anthology of Islamic Literature from the Rise of Islam to Modern Times, ed. Reuben Levy* (New York: Henry Holt & Co), pp. 160–166.

You must, consequently, inspect everything. When you see beauty in the eyes and eyebrows, delicacy in the nose, sweetness in the lips and teeth and freshness in the skin, then buy the slave possessing them without concerning yourself over the extremities of the body. If all of these qualities are not present, then the slave must possess delicacy; because, in my opinion, one that is delicate without having beauty is preferable to one that is beautiful but not possessed of delicacy.

The learned say that one must know the indications and signs by which to buy the slaves suited for particular duties. The slave that you buy for your private service and conviviality should be of middle proportions, neither tall nor short, fat nor lean, pale nor florid, thickset nor slender, curly-haired nor with hair overstraight. When you see a slave soft-fleshed, fine-skinned, with regular bones and wine-coloured hair, black eyelashes, dark eyes, black eyebrows, open-eyed, long-nosed, slender-waisted, round-chinned, red-lipped, with white regular teeth, and all his members such as I have described, such a slave will be decorative and companionable, loyal, of delicate character, and dignified.

The mark of the slave who is clever and may be expected to improve is this: he must be of erect stature, medium in hair and flesh, broad of hand and with the middle of the fingers lengthy, in complexion dark though ruddy, dark-eyed, open-faced and unsmiling. A slave of this kind would be competent to acquire learning, to act as treasurer or for any other [such] employment.

The slave suited to play musical instruments is marked out by being soft-fleshed (though his flesh must not be over-abundant, especially on the back), with his fingers slender, neither lean nor fat. (A slave whose face is over-fleshy, incidentally, is one incapable of learning.) His hands must be soft, with the middles of the fingers lengthy. He must be bright-visaged, having the skin tight; his hair must not be too long, too short or too black. A slave of this kind will swiftly acquire a delicate art of whatever kind, particularly that of the instrumentalist.

The mark of the slave suited for arms-bearing is that his hair is thick, his body tall and erect, his build powerful, his flesh hard, his bones thick, his skin coarse and his limbs straight, the joints being firm. Shoulders must be broad, the chest deep, the neck thick and the head round; also for preference he should be bald. The belly should be concave, the buttocks drawn in and the legs in walking well extended. And the eyes should be black. Any slave who possesses these qualities will be a champion in single combat, brave and successful.

The mark of a slave suited for employment in the women's apartments is that he should be dark-skinned and sour-visaged and have withered limbs, scanty hair, a shrill voice, little [slender] feet, thick lips, a flat nose, stubby fingers, a bowed figure, and a thin neck. A slave with these qualities will be suitable for service in the women's quarters. He must not have a white skin nor a fair complexion; and beware of a ruddy-complexioned man, particularly if his hair is limp. His eyes, further, should not be languorous or moist; a man having such qualities is either over-fond of women or prone to act as a go-between.

The mark of a slave who is callous [insensitive] and suited to be a herdsman or groom is that he should be open-browed and wide-eyed, and his eyelids should be flecked with red. He should, further, be long in lips and teeth and his mouth should be wide. A slave with these qualities is extremely callous, fearless and uncivilized.

The mark of the slave suited for domestic service and cookery is that he should be clean in face and body, round-faced, with hands and feet slender, his eyes dark inclining to blue, sound in body, silent, the hair of his head wine-colored and falling forward limply. A slave with these qualities is suitable for the occupations mentioned.

Each then, should have the essential characteristics which I have recounted. But I will also mention the defects and virtues which should be known in respect of each separate race. You must understand that Turks are not all of one race, and each has its own nature and essential character. Amongst them the most ill-tempered are the Ghuzz and the Qipchaqs; the best-tempered and most willing are the Khutanese, the Khallukhis, and the Tibetans; the most active are the Tatars and the Yaghma, whereas the laziest of all are the Chigil.

It is a fact well-known to all that beauty or ugliness in the Turks is the opposite of that in the Indians. If you observe the Turk feature by feature [he has] a large head, a broad face, narrow eyes, a flat nose, and unpleasing lips and teeth. Regarded individually the features are not handsome, yet the whole is handsome. The Indian's face is the opposite of this; each individual feature regarded by itself appears handsome, yet looked at as a whole the face does not create the same impression as that of the Turk. To begin with, the Turk has a personal freshness and clearness of complexion not possessed by the Indian; indeed the Turks win for freshness against all other races.

Without any doubt, what is fine in the Turks is present in a superlative degree, but so also is what is ugly in them. Their faults in general are that they are blunt-witted, ignorant, boastful, turbulent, discontented, and without a sense of justice. Without any excuse they will create trouble and utter foul language, and at night they are poor-hearted. Their merit is that they are brave, free from pretense, open in enmity, and zealous in any task allotted to them. For the [domestic] establishment there is no better race.

Slavs, Russians, and Alans are near in their temperament to the Turks, but are more patient. The Alans are more courageous than the Turks at night and more friendly disposed towards their masters. Although in their craftsmanship they are nearer to the Byzantines, being artistic, yet there are faults in them of various kinds; for example, they are prone to theft, disobedience, betrayal of secrets, impatience, stupidity, indolence, hostility to their masters, and escaping. Their virtues are that they are soft-natured, agreeable, and quick of understanding. Further, they are deliberate in action, direct in speech, brave, good road-guides, and possessed of good memory.

The defect of the Byzantines is that they are foul-tongued, evil-hearted, cowardly, indolent, quick-tempered, covetous, and greedy for worldly things. Their merits are that they are cautious, affectionate, happy, economically-minded, successful in their undertakings, and careful to prevent loss.

The defect of the Armenians is that they are mischievous, foul-mouthed, thieving, impudent, prone to fight, disobedient, babblers, liars, friendly to misbelief, and hostile to their masters. From head to foot, indeed, they incline rather towards defects than to merits. Yet they are quick of understanding and learn their tasks well.

The defect of the Hindu is that he is evil-tongued and in the house no slave-girl is safe from him. But the various classes of the Hindus are unlike those that prevail amongst other peoples, because in other peoples the classes mingle with each other, whereas the Hindus, ever since the time of Adam (Upon whom be peace!), have practiced the following custom: namely, no trade will form an alliance with any outside it. Thus, grocers will give their daughters only to grocers, butchers to butchers, bakers to bakers, and soldiers to soldiers.

Each of these groups therefore has its own special character, which I cannot describe one by one because that would entail a book in itself.

However, the best of them, people benevolent, brave or skilled in commerce, are [respectively] the Brahman, the Rawat and the Kirar. The Brahman is clever, the Rawat brave, and the Kirar skilled in commerce, each class being superior to the one after. The Nubian and the Abyssinian are freer of faults, and the Abyssinian is better than the Nubian because many things were said by the Prophet in praise of the former.

These then are the facts concerning each race and the merits and defects of each.

When you buy a slave, you must take and lay him down, press him on both sides and watch closely that he has no pain or swelling. If he has, it will be in the liver or spleen. Having looked for such hidden defects, seek further for the open ones, such as smells from the mouth and nose, hardness of hearing, hesitation in utterance, irregularity of speech, walking off the road, coarseness of the joints, and hardness at the base of the teeth, to prevent any trickery being practiced on you.

When you have seen all that I have mentioned and have made certain, then if you should buy, do so from honest people, and so secure a person who will be of advantage to your household. As long as you can find a non-Arab do not buy an Arabic-speaking slave. You can mould a non-Arab to your ways, but never the one whose tongue is Arabic. Further, do not have a slave-girl brought before you when your appetite is strong upon you; when desire is strong, it makes what is ugly appear good in your eyes. First abate your desires and then engage in the business of purchasing.

Never buy a slave who has been treated with affection in another place. If you do not hold him dear, he will show ingratitude to you, or will flee, or will demand to be sold, or will nourish hatred in his heart for you. Even if you regard him with affection, he will show you no gratitude, in view of what he has experienced elsewhere. Buy your slave from a house in which he has been badly treated, so that he will be grateful for the least kindness on your part and will hold you in affection. From time to time make your slaves a gift of something; do not allow them to be constantly in need of money in such a way that they are compelled to go out seeking it.

Buy slaves of a good price, for each one's value is in accordance with his price. Do not buy a slave who has had numerous masters; a woman who has had many husbands and a slave who has had many masters are held in no esteem. Let those you buy be well-favored. And when a slave truly desires to be sold, do not dispute with him, but sell; when a slave demands to be sold or a wife to be divorced, then sell or divorce, because you will have no pleasure from either.

If a slave is deliberately (and not through inadvertence or mistake) lazy or neglectful in his work, do not teach him under compulsion to improve; have no expectation of that, for he will in no wise become industrious or capable of improvement. Sell him quickly; you may rouse a sleeping man without a shout, but a dead body cannot be roused by the sound of a hundred trumpets and drums.

Provide for your slaves in such fashion that they will not escape, and treat them that you would have well, as benefits your dignity; if you have one person in good condition it is better than having two in ill condition. Do not permit your male slave to take to himself in your household someone whom he calls "brother," nor permit slave-girls to claim sisterhood with each other; it leads to great trouble. On bond and free impose the burdens which they are able to bear, that they may not be disobedient through sheer weakness. Keep yourself ever adorned with justice, that you may be included amongst them that are honored as such.

The slave must recognize your brother, sister, mother or father as his master. Set no store by the slave who always, when called to any work, demands to be sold and never has any fears with regard to being bought and sold; you will gain nothing good from him. Change him quickly for another, seeking out one such as I have described. Thus you will achieve your purpose and suffer no troubles.

56

One Thousand and One Nights: The Tale of the Fisherman

The most famous collection of folk-tales comes to us from many periods, lands, and peoples—the Arabs, Persians, Indians, and Egyptians. They include wondrous tales of magicians, jinn, Aladdin and his Magic Lamp, Sinbad the Sailor, and Ali Baba and the Forty Thieves for popular enjoyment. They were set in a fabulously rich court of King Shahriyar. The king had one new wife each night and executed her the following morning. When the king picked Shahrazad as his next wife, she recited part of one tale each night but left it unfinished so that the king longed to hear the conclusion and would spare her for the next night's conclusion and a new tale. The following selection recounts how a poor fisherman found a bottle containing a jinn and how the fisherman was repaid for freeing the jinn.

QUESTIONS TO CONSIDER

1. Why did the jinn want to kill the fisherman?
2. How did the fisherman trick the jinn?
3. Is there a moral to this story?

The Fisherman and The Jinn

There was a certain fisherman, advanced in age, who had a wife and three children; and though he was in indigent circumstances, it was his custom to cast his net, everyday, no more than four times. One day he went forth at the hour of noon to the shore of the sea, and put down his basket, and cast his net, and waited until it was motionless in the water, when he drew together, its strings; and found it to be heavy: he pulled, but could not draw it up: so he took the end of the cord, and knocked a stake into the shore, and tied the cord to it He then stripped himself; and dived round the net, and continued to pull until he drew it out: whereupon he rejoiced, and put on his clothes, but when he came to examine the net, he found in it the carcass of an ass. At the sight of this he mourned, and exclaimed, There is no strength nor power but in God, the High, the Great!

This is a strange piece of fortune!

He then disencumbered his net of the dead ass and wrung it out; after which he spread it, and descended into the sea, and—exclaiming, "In the name of God!"—cast it again, and waited till it had sunk and was still, when he pulled it, and found it more heavy and more difficult to raise than on the former occasion. He therefore

The Arabian Nights Entertainments or The Thousand and One Nights, trans. Edward William Lane (New York: Tudor Publishing Co., 1927), pp. 21–33.

concluded that it was full of fish: so he tied it, and stripped, and plunged and dived, and pulled until he raised it, and drew it upon the shore; when he found in it only a large jar, full of sand and mud; on seeing which, he was troubled in his heart. . . .

So, saying, he threw aside the jar, and wrung out and cleansed his net; and, begging the forgiveness of God for his impatience, returned to the sea the third time; and he threw the net and waited till it had sunk and was motionless: he then drew it out, and found in it a quantity of broken jars and pots. Upon this, he raised his head towards heaven, and said, "O God, Thou knowest that I cast not my net more than four times; and I have, now cast it three times!" Then—exclaiming, "In the name of God!"—he cast the net again into the sea, and waited till it was still; he attempted to draw it up, but could not, for it clung to the bottom. And he exclaimed, "There is no strength nor power but in God!"—and stripped himself again, and dived round the net, and pulled it until he raised it upon the shore; when he opened it, and found in it a bottle of brass, filled with something, and having its mouth closed with a stopper of lead, bearing the impression of the seal of our Lord Solomon. At the sight of this, the fisherman rejoiced, and said, "This I will sell in the copper-market; for it is worth ten pieces of gold." He then shook it, and found it to be heavy, and said, "I must open it, and see what is in it, and store it in my bag; and then I will sell the bottle in the copper-market."

So he took out a knife, and picked at the lead until he extracted it from the bottle. He then laid the bottle on the ground, and shook it, that its contents might pour out; but there came forth from it nothing but smoke, which ascended towards the sky, and spread over the face of the earth; at which he wondered excessively. And after a little while, the smoke collected together, and was condensed, and then became agitated, and was converted into a jinn whose head was in the clouds, while his feet rested upon the ground. His head was like a dome: his hands were like winnowing forks; and his legs, like masts: his mouth resembled a cavern: his teeth were like stones; his nostrils like trumpets; and his eyes like lamps; and he had disheveled and dust-colored hair.

When the fisherman beheld this jinn, the muscles of his sides quivered, his teeth were locked together, his spittle dried up, and he saw not his way. The jinn, as soon as he perceived him, exclaimed, "There is no deity but God: Solomon is the Prophet of God. O Prophet of God, slay me not; for I will never again oppose thee in word, or rebel against thee in deed!"

"O evil jinn," said the fisherman, "dost thou say, Solomon is the Prophet of God? Solomon hath been dead a thousand and eight hundred years; and we are now at the end of time. What is thy history, and what is thy tale, and what was the cause of thy entering this bottle?" When the evil jinn heard these words of the fisherman, he said, "There is no deity but God! Receive news, O fisherman!" – "Of what," said the fisherman, "dost thou give me news?" He answered, "Of thy being instantly put to a most cruel death."

The fisherman exclaimed, "Thou deservest, for this news, O master of the jinns, the withdrawal of protection from thee. . . . Wherefore wouldst thou kill me? and what requires thy killing me, when I have: liberated thee from the bottle, and rescued thee from the bottom of the sea! and brought thee up upon the dry land?"

The jinn answered, "Choose what kind of death thou wilt die, and in what manner thou shalt be killed."

"What is my offence, said the fisherman, that this should be my recompense from thee?"

The jinn replied, "Hear my story, O fisherman."

"Tell it then," said the fisherman, "and be short in thy words; for my soul hath sunk down to my feet."

"Know then," said he, "that I am one of the heretical jinn: I rebelled against Solomon, the son of David: I and Sakhr the jinn; and he sent to me his vizier, Asaf, the son of Barkhiya, who came upon me forcibly, and took me to him in bonds, and placed me before him: and when Solomon saw me, he offered up a prayer for protection against me, and exhorted me to embrace the faith, and to submit to his authority; but I refused; upon which he called for this bottle, and confined me in it, and closed it upon me with the leaden stopper, which he stamped with the Most Great Name. He then gave orders to the jinn, who carried me away, and threw me into the midst of the sea. There I remained a hundred years; and I said in my heart, 'Whoever shall liberate me, I will enrich him for ever'—but the hundred years passed over me, and no one liberated me.; and I entered upon another hundred years; and I said, 'Whosoever shall liberate me, I will open to him the treasures of the earth;'—but no one did so; and four hundred years more passed over me, and I said, 'Whosoever shall liberate me, I will perform for him three wants;'— but still no one liberated me; I then fell into a violent rage, and said within myself, 'Whosoever shall liberate me now, I will kill him; and only suffer him to choose in what manner he will die.' And lo, now thou has liberated me, and I have given thee thy choice; of the manner in which thou wilt die."

When the fisherman had heard the story of the jinn he exclaimed, "O Allah! that I should not have liberated thee but in such a time as this!" Then be said to the Jinn, "Pardon me, and kill me not, and so may God pardon thee; and destroy me not, lest God give power over thee to one who will destroy thee."

The jinn answered, "I must positively kill thee; therefore choose by what manner of death thou wilt die." The fisherman then felt assured of his death, but he again implored the jinn saying, "Pardon me by way of gratitude for my liberating thee."

"Why?" asked the jinn. "I am not going to kill thee but for that very reason, because thou hast liberated me."

"O Sheykh of the jinns," said the fisherman, "do I not act kindly towards thee, and dost thou not recompense me with baseness?"

The jinn, when he heard these words, answered by saying, "Covet not life, for thy death is unavoidable."

Then said the fisherman within himself, "This is a jinn, and I am a man; and God hath given me sound reason; therefore, I will now plot his destruction with my art and reason, like as he hath plotted with his cunning and perfidy." So he said to the jinn, "Hast thou determined to kill me?"

He answered, "Yes."

Then said he, "By the most Great Name engraved upon the seal of Solomon, I will ask thee one question; and wilt thou answer it to me truly?"

On hearing the mention of the Most Great Name, the jinn was agitated, and trembled, and replied, "Yes; ask, and be brief."

The fisherman then asked, "How wast thou in this bottle? It will not contain thy hand or thy foot; how then can it contain thy whole body?"

"Dost thou not believe that I was in it?" asked the Jinn.

The fisherman answered, "I will never believe thee until I see thee in it."

Upon this, the jinn shook, and became converted again into smoke, which rose to the sky; and then became condensed, and entered the bottle little by little, until it was all enclosed; when the fisherman hastily snatched the sealed leaden stopper, and, having replaced it in the mouth of the bottle, called out to the jinn and said, "Choose in what manner of death thou wilt die. I will assuredly throw thee here, into the sea, and build me a house on this spot; and whosoever shall come here, I will prevent his fishing in this place," and will say to him, "Here is a jinn who to any person that liberates him will propose various kinds of death, and then give him his choice of one of them." On hearing these words of the fisherman the jinn endeavored to escape; but could not, finding himself restrained by the impression of the seal of Solomon, and thus imprisoned by the fisherman as the vilest and filthiest and least of jinns. The fisherman then took the bottle to the brink of the sea.

The Jinn exclaimed, "Nay! nay!—," to which the fisherman answered, "Yea, without fail; yea without fail!"

The evil jinn then addressing him with a soft voice and humble manner, said, "What dost thou intend to do with me, O fisherman?"

He answered, "I will throw thee into the sea; and if thou hast been there a thousand and eight hundred years, I will make thee to remain there until the hour of judgment; Did I not say to thee, 'Spare me and so may God spare thee; and destroy me not, lest God destroy thee?' But thou, didst reject, my petition, and wouldest nothing but treachery; therefore God hath caused thee to fall into my hand; and I have betrayed thee."

"Open to me," said the Jinn, "that I may confer benefits upon thee."

The fisherman replied, "Thou liest, thou accursed! I and thou are like the vizier of King Yoonan and the sage Dooban."

"What," asked the jinn, "was the case of the vizier of King Yoonan and the sage Dooban, and what is their story?" The fisherman then recited a tale of a king, afflicted by leprosy, and a wise man who offered to cure him. The king's wicked vizier advised the king to kill the wise man instead of giving him a reward, but the wise man poisoned the leaves of a book which the king touched and then licked his lips.

"Now, O jinn," continued the fisherman, know that if King Yoonan had spared the sage Dooban, God had spared him; but he refused, and desired his destruction; therefore God destroyed him: and thou, O Jinn if thou hadst spared me, God had spared thee, and I had spared thee; but thou desiredst my death; therefore will I put thee to death imprisoned in this bottle, and will .throw thee here into the sea."

The jinn, upon this, cried out and said, "I conjure thee by Allah, O fisherman, that thou do it not: spare me in generosity and be not angry with me for what I did; but if I have done evil, do thou good, according to the proverb—'O thou benefactor of him who hath done evil, the action that he hath done is sufficient for him.' Do not therefore as Umamer did to Atikeh."

"And what," asked the fisherman, "was their case?"

The Jinn answered, "This is not a time for telling stories, when I am in this prison; but when thou liberatest me, I will relate to thee their case."

The fisherman said, "Thou must be thrown into the sea, and there shall be no way of escape for thee from it! For I endeavored to propitiate thee, and humbled myself before thee; yet thou wouldest have nothing but my destruction, though I had committed no offence to deserve it, and had done no evil to thee, whatever, but only good, delivering thee from thy confinement; and when thou didst thus unto me, I perceived that thou wast radically corrupt: and I would have thee know, that my motive for throwing thee into this sea, is, that I may acquaint with thy story everyone that shall take thee out; and caution him against thee, that he may cast thee in again: thus shalt thou remain in this sea to the end of time, and experience varieties of torment."

The jinn then said, "Liberate me, for this is an opportunity for thee to display humanity; and I vow to thee that I will never do thee harm; but, on the contrary, will do thee a service that shall enrich thee for ever."

Upon this the fisherman accepted his covenant that he would not hurt him, but that he would do him good; and when he had bound him by oaths and vows, and made him swear by the Most Great Name of God, he opened to him; and the smoke ascended until it had all come forth, and then collected together, and became, as before, a jinn of hideous form. The jinn then kicked the bottle into the sea. When the fisherman saw him do this he made sure of destruction, and said, "This is no sign of good:"—but afterwards he fortified his heart, and said, "O jinn, God, whose name be exalted, hath said, 'Perform the covenant, for the covenant shall be inquired into:'—and thou hast covenanted with me, and sworn that thou wilt not act treacherously towards me; therefore, if thou so act, God will recompense thee; for He is jealous; He respiteth, but suffereth not to escape; and remember that I said to thee as said the sage Dooban to King Yoonan, 'Spare me, and so may God spare thee.'"

The jinn laughed, and, walking on before him, said, "O fisherman, follow me." The fisherman did so, not believing in his escape, until they had quitted the neighborhood of the city, and ascended a mountain and descended into a wide desert tract, in. the midst of which was a lake of water. Here the jinn stopped and ordered the fisherman to cast his net and take some fish; and the fisherman, looking into the lake, saw in it fish of different colors, white and red and blue and yellow; at which he was astonished; and he cast his net, and drew it in, and found in it four fish, each fish of a different color from the others, at the sight of which he rejoiced.

The jinn then said to him, "Take them to the Sultan, and present them to him; and he will give thee what will enrich thee; and for the sake of God accept my excuse, for, at present, I know no other way of rewarding thee, having been in the sea a thousand and eight hundred years, and not seen the surface of the earth until now: but take not fish from the lake more than once each day: and now I commend thee to the care of God." Having thus said, he struck the earth with his feet, and it clove asunder, and swallowed him.

The fisherman then went back to the city, wondering at all that had befallen him with the jinn and carried the fish to his house; and he took an earthen bowl, and, having filled it with water, put the fish into it; and they struggled in the water; and when he had done this, he placed the bowl upon his head, and repaired to the King's palace, as the jinn had commanded him, and, going up unto the King, presented to him the fish; and the King was excessively astonished at them, for he had never seen any like them in the course of his life; and he said, "Give these fish to the slave cookmaid." This maid had been sent as a present to him by the King of the Greeks three days before, and he had not yet tried her skill.

The vizier, therefore, ordered her to fry the fish, and said to her, "O maid, the King saith unto thee, 'I have not reserved my tear but for the time of my difficulty:'— today, then, gratify us by a specimen of thy excellent cookery, for a person hath brought these fish as a present to the Sultan. After having thus charged her, the vizier returned, and the King ordered him to give the fisherman four hundred pieces of gold: so the vizier gave them to him; and he took them in his lap, and returned to his home and his wife, joyful and happy, and bought what was needful for his family.

Part IV

Medieval Europe, Africa, and the East

The Germanic Tribes Succeed the Romans in the West

In the declining centuries of the Roman Empire in the West, Roman leaders increasingly relied on Germanic barbarian tribes to do their fighting for them, with the eventual result that more military power was in Germanic hands than in Roman ones. A broad array of Germanic tribes assumed a rather shapeless hegemony in Italy when the last Roman emperor in the West, Romulus Augustulus, was eased out in favor of Odoakar, King of the Scirians, a rather small tribe, in 476. Odoakar called himself *rex* (king) on his coinage but could not decide for the life of him *what* he was king of. He was, in fact, king of the Germanic tribes in Italy, which would have made a poor title. The Romans probably would not have stood for his styling himself "King of Italy" or "King of the Romans," let alone "Roman Emperor," and so he had himself referred to as "Odoakar the King" and let it go at that.

Soon, however, King Theoderic of the Ostrogoths, the most advanced and best organized of the Germanic tribes, invaded Italy, killed Odoakar in 493, and established Ostrogothic rule in Italy. Theoderic ran Italy roughly by keeping military affairs in the hands of his fellow Goths, but entrusting much civilian administration to cooperative Romans. His long reign until 526 was a peaceful and prosperous one, which enabled considerable economic recovery in Italy. Apart from being barbarians in the eyes of the Romans, however, the Goths had a more serious flaw: Like most of the other Germanic tribes, they had accepted Arianism as their version of Christianity. The Arians believed that if the terms "God the Father" and "God the Son" were accurate, there must have been a time when there was a Father and no Son, and consequently the powers of Jesus, the Son, were derivative from God the Father. This meant that they rejected the equality of the persons of the Trinity and were consequently heretics from the Trinitarian or Catholic standpoint, which prevailed in Roman Italy. Consequently, most Roman Italians applauded the forces serving the Eastern Emperor Justinian when they invaded Italy in the early 550s and nearly wiped out the Ostrogoths.

219

Meanwhile the Franks, who had remained pagan until the end of the fifth century, accepted Trinitarian Christianity under Clovis. Their resulting religious identification with Rome meant that they immediately enjoyed the support of the Catholic Church. Partly through Clovis's victories and partly through general Catholic Church support, the Franks became the dominant Germanic tribe and in their own minds, at least, inherited the governance of Western Europe from the Romans. Three centuries after Clovis, the great Frankish king Charlemagne would be acclaimed as Roman emperor and crowned as such by the pope.

Georgius Florentinus Gregorius (538/9–594) came from a Roman family of the senatorial class, which held governing and high Church positions in Gaul and worked with the Frankish conquerors there. As Gregory, Bishop of Tours, he distinguished himself by writing the first substantial work of history in and about that earliest part of the medieval world, often called the "Dark Ages." Although very conscious of his Roman roots, he shows no resentment at all toward the Franks, although he casually refers to them as "barbarians," probably because their native language is not Latin, as is his. His work, which he calls simply *Ten Books of History*, begins as a world history of sorts with the creation and relevant Hebrew history, funneling into Church, Roman, and Gallic history but becoming expansive only with the story of the Franks and how the Church fared under them.

An important aspect of Gregory's work is his portrayal of early medieval kingship. Students frequently assume that because of the superstitious nature of the Dark Ages monarchs could exploit their ignorant, gullible people without hindrance through a claim to rule divinely. Gregory's stories make it clear that this was not the case at all. Kings and queens had about the same totality of power as did chiefs among the Native Americans before the arrival of Europeans, although, taking one with the other, they seem to have been much more ambitious to consolidate their personal power than were the North American chiefs of old. Consequently, they had to bestir themselves, often using deception and violence, when they really wanted to have their way.

People in Gregory's accounts invoke laws, written and unwritten—often to highlight the lawlessness of powerful figures—and there is an underlying consensus that willingness to be law-abiding is a great virtue. The Franks, like other Germanic tribes, had their law codes. At first, Germanic tribal law was not at all severe and resembled that of the Hittites (see Reading 11) considerably more than Roman Law. In time, as the Germanic peoples grew more settled, they began to favor the harsh deterrent laws of the Romans, a trend that accelerated as they became more city-oriented.

57

Gregory of Tours, *History of the Franks*

The first selections that follow present Clovis (ca. 466–511), who made Catholic Christians out of his Franks and greatly extended Frankish rule. He is easily the greatest secular hero of Gregory's work and remains for him an enduring model. Although Clovis is scarcely a Christian model at all by later standards, for Gregory his Christian commitment is shown by the fact that once he was well established, he defended the lands and property of churches and monasteries and never let his Franks take anything from them.

Clovis's domains were divided upon his death: The pieces were combined and redivided throughout the sixth century with Austrasia, Neustria, and Burgundy emerging as the most prominent Frankish kingdoms. The last selections feature Queen Fredegunde of Neustria, who spent much of her life in a feud with Queen Brunhilde of Austrasia. It is difficult to say who got the better of it. Fredegunde died before Brunhilde, but she did succeed in raising her own son to rule as Chlothar II, King of Neustria—no mean achievement in view of the number and strength of her enemies. According to the seventh-century "Chronicle of Fredegar," Chlothar charged Brunhilde, when she was about eighty years old, with the death of ten Frankish kings, including two he had ordered killed himself. Then, after three days of diverse tortures, he consigned her "to be tied by her hair, one leg and one arm to the tail of a very wild horse, so that his hooves and speed tore her limb from limb."

The murderous rivalry between the two queens lived on in medieval legend and was probably one of the inspirations for the lethal conflict between Queens Brunhilde and Kriemhilde in the *Nibelungenlied* (see Reading 59).

QUESTIONS TO CONSIDER

1. How would you rate Clovis on his handling of the valued-vessel incident in Soissons? Did he have any better options, or did he do essentially the right thing?
2. What were Clovis's motives in accepting Christianity? How compatible were his motives with the basic teachings of Christianity in the New Testament (see Readings 44 and 45)?
3. Do you think Fredegunde behaved much differently in dealing with her enemies than a male figure, such as Clovis, would have?
4. Some perhaps turf-conscious medieval historians become defensive when confronted with the term "Dark Ages" for the early medieval centuries. One remarks that the period is "dark" only because we have failed to shed light on it. Do you have the feeling that if you knew more about Clovis and Fredegunde you would not consider their period a particularly "dark" one? Why?

1. The Vessel of Soissons

In the fifth year of his reign, Clovis advanced against Syagrius, a Roman king whose power was centered in the city of Soissons. The two waged a battle against each other, and when Syagrius saw his troops being pushed back he fled.

In those days Clovis's army plundered many churches, for he was still entrapped by the perverse superstition of unbelievers. And so, his Franks took with them a vessel of great size and beauty, along with other treasured pieces used in church services. The Bishop of the church they had robbed then sent a messenger to King Clovis and asked that his church might at least have that pitcher back, even if the

From Gregorius Turonensis, *Historiarum Libri Decem*, ed. Bruno Krusch and Rudolf Buchner (Darmstadt: Wissenchaftliche Buchgesellschaft, 1967), II, 27; IV, 27–28; VIII, 31. Trans. Henry A. Myers.

Franks kept all the other pieces of value. The King listened to the messenger and said: "Follow us to Soissons, for there everything taken as booty must be divided up. If I draw that vessel by lot, I will do as the Bishop desires."

Afterwards they reached Soissons, where all the loot was spread out for display. "Bravest of warriors," the King began, "I am going to ask you to do me a special favor." He pointed to this pitcher: "Let me have that pitcher, not counting it in the lot-drawing."

When the King spoke, the warriors of a healthier mind responded: "Everything we see here is yours, glorious King; we, too, belong under your authority. Do now whatever you like, for no one can withstand your power."

As they said this, however, one impulsive, envious, and thoughtless man struck his battle-ax into the pitcher with a loud shout: "You are not going to get anything except what you get rightfully by lot!"

This upset everyone, but the King took this insult patiently in stride, giving the broken pitcher to the Bishop's messenger, but the shame inflicted on him burned secretly in his heart.

The following year at the annual inspection of arms and gear on March 1, Clovis had all his warriors display their weapons, to show how well they were polished and cared for. As he made his rounds among them, he came to the man who had struck the pitcher and said to him: "No one carries such shabby weapons as you do. Your spear, your sword and your battle-ax are all worthless!" Then he threw the man's battle-ax on the ground, but when its owner leaned over to pick it up, the King raised his own ax with both hands and drove it into the man's head.

"That is what you did with the pitcher at Soissons," said Clovis. When the man was dead, the King told the rest to go home, and his deed seized them with mighty dread. He went on to wage many wars and win many victories.

2. Baptism of Clovis

[Chrodichilde, his Queen] kept imploring Clovis to renounce the false gods and recognize the one true God, but he could not be converted to the faith until he found himself in a war with the Alamanni. Naked need forced him to confess what his heart had previously denied. When the two armies collided, the result was a terrible bloodbath, with Clovis's army coming close to annihilation. When he realized that, he raised his eyes to Heaven, his heart was moved, his eyes filled with tears, and he spoke: "Jesus Christ, Chrodichilde has revealed to me that Thou art the Son of the living God. They say Thou givest help to the hard-pressed and victory to those who have faith in Thee. I humbly plea for Thy mighty assistance. If Thou grantest me victory over these enemies of mine and I experience that might which Thy followers claim to have tested, then I will believe in Thee and have myself baptized in Thy name. For I have called upon my gods, only to find that they are a long ways from helping me. I believe they are powerless, since they don't help those who serve them. Just deliver me from the hands of mine enemies!" When he spoke these words, the Alamanni turned and began to flee. Then when they saw their own king lying there dead they surrendered to Clovis, saying: "Do not let any more people be killed, we plead with you. We belong to you now." Then Clovis stopped the fighting, gave instructions to the people, and they went home in peace. He told the Queen how he had called upon the name of Christ and thus won the victory. . . .

The Queen then had Saint Remigius summoned and asked him to bring the word of salvation to the King's heart. . . .

"Holy Father, I would be glad to obey you, but one thing bothers me: the people who follow me will not stand for my deserting their gods. But I will still go and speak with them, as you ask me to do."

As he met with his people, the whole crowd shouted in unison, even before he could open his mouth: "We renounce the mortal gods, gracious King, and are prepared to follow the immortal God, Whom Remigius preaches."

The King asked Remigius to baptize him first, and so he went, a new Constantine, to the baptismal bath, to wash himself pure of the old leprosy and to cleanse himself of the dirty spots on his past. . . .

And so the King recognized the Almighty God as the Trinitarian One and had himself baptized in the name of the Father, the Son, and the Holy Ghost. Then he was anointed with holy oil under the sign of the cross of Christ. From his army, more than three thousand were baptized.

3. Brunhilde and Fredegunde

When King Sigbert saw that his brothers were marrying wives unworthy of them and were even lowering themselves to the point of marrying servant women, he sent a delegation to Spain with many gifts and asked for [the Visigothic] King Athanagild's daughter, Brunhilde. She was a maiden of noble bearing, beautiful to behold, intelligent and charming to talk with. Her father did not turn down the request but sent her to the King with many treasures. The King assembled his chief nobles, prepared a great banquet for the ceremony and with great rejoicing and merriment all around he married her. She came as an Arian, but the bishop's teaching and the king's own encouragement converted her to believe in the blessed Trinity. . . .

When King Chilperic saw all this, he sent—although he already had several wives—to Spain for Galswintha, Brunhilde's sister. Through his messengers he promised to put away his other wives if he could have her, the daughter of a king and thus his own equal. The father believed these promises and sent off his daughter, as he had the previous one, with a great wealth of riches. . . . When Galswintha arrived at King Chilperic's court she was received with great honors, and she married him. He treated her very lovingly: she had brought really splendid treasures with her, but his scandalous love for Fredegunde, now one of his ex-wives, caused great friction between them. . . . Galswintha complained to the king about the insults she constantly had to endure, insisting that she must not really be important to him. She told him to go ahead and keep the treasures she had brought but to let her return free to her homeland. The king would not agree to this, but cleverly reassured her with soft words. Finally, however, he had a servant strangle her and "found" her dead on her bed.

Upon her death, God worked a great miracle: the cord holding the lamp which hung and burned at her tomb broke, although no one touched it, and the lamp fell upon the cement floor. The hard cement yielded to it, and the lamp sank into it as if it had been a soft mass until it was half covered by it but not damaged in the least. Those who saw this recognized it as an awesome miracle. The king mourned her death but after a few days took Fredegunde back as his wife.

4. Fredegunde and Her Enemies

Fredegunde was staying in Rouen. In a bitter tirade against Bishop Praetestatus she said that the time would return when he would see the exile he had been through before. He replied, "Exiled or not, I remained a bishop, and I will continue to be one. You, however, will not always have your royal power. Through God's grace those such as I may ascend from exile to God's kingdom. You, however, will be cast down to hell from this kingdom. Still, it would be better for you to renounce your stupid and wicked ways and start behaving better: that way you could gain salvation and also succeed in raising the little son you bore to maturity. . . ."

When Sunday dawned, the bishop went to his church early and began, as was his custom, to sing responses to the antiphones of the choir. He knelt during the singing, and a cursed murderer came up, drew a dagger from his belt and stabbed him through his armpit. He shouted to the clergy there to come and help him, but none of those there would come right away. Then he stretched out his bloody hands towards the altar, saying prayers and still giving thanks to God, until finally faithful hands carried him to his room and laid him on his bed. Right away, Queen Fredegunde appeared with Dukes Beppolen and Ansovald and said: "O holy bishop, this really should not have happened to you or your congregation, particularly while you were worshipping! If only we could find out who dared commit such a crime as this, so that he might suffer the punishment he deserves!"

The bishop, however, knew full well how treacherously she was speaking and answered: "And who did this? None other than the one who has murdered kings and who often has spilled innocent blood and unleashed all kinds of evil in this kingdom."

The woman replied: "I have very experienced doctors, who can cure your wound. . . ."

"God is summoning me from this world, but you, who have instigated these wicked acts, are cursed in this world, and God will avenge my blood on your head."

She left then, and the bishop ordered his affairs put in order and breathed his last. Bishop Romachard of Coutances came to his funeral. Grief prevailed among all the people of Rouen, but particularly among the aristocratic Franks of that city. One of these lords came to Fredegunde and spoke: "You have caused a great deal of evil in this world, but you never did anything worse than this—having a priest of God murdered. May God take vengeance upon you for his innocent blood. All of us want to track this evil to its source, so that you will no longer be free to carry out such crimes."

When he had said this, he left the Queen, but she sent someone to him to invite him to join her for a merry meal. When he declined the messenger asked him— since he would not accept the dinner invitation—would he at least drink a cup of wine so that he would not be leaving the royal palace without accepting some hospitality. He did stay and drink a cup of vermouth mixed with honey . . . , but this wine was poisoned. . . . Things turned black before his eyes. He mounted his horse, but when he had ridden about six hundred yards he fell from his horse and died.

Afterwards, Bishop Leudowald sent messengers to all other bishops around Rouen and, after getting their approval, closed all Rouen's churches: the people were not to expect any divine services until those responsible for this crime had been identified; everyone was to join the search. He had several men detained, and when they were tortured they confessed that Fredegunde had ordered these crimes. She denied everything, however, so he could not follow up on what they had said. People were saying that murderers came after him, too, since he was quite determined to resume the investigation, but since he was bravely guarded by his own men they could not do him any harm.

58

Law Code of the Salian Franks

In matters of robbery and homicide, although not in matters of angering gods, relatively primitive law codes have tended to be mild even by modern standards. Their aim is less to do absolute justice than to reestablish "peace," placating the victims or survivors with money, sheep, pigs, or whatever it takes to keep them from unleashing blood feuds. For them, there is little, if any, idea of the "state" that is obliged to punish criminals because fraud and violence are threats to public safety. Each tribal member is considered valuable, and no lives should be taken if offenders can pay compensation enough to aggrieved families in order to pacify them.

At the onset of the Middle Ages, the Franks were less settled than the Goths and retained this sort of tribal thinking in their laws, even when they began recording them in Latin. By way of contrast the Visigoths, who had had more contact with the Roman world than the Franks before the fall of the Empire in the West, reflected something of a Roman outlook in their earliest surviving Latin law code, which allots a substantial independent role to judges and courts as permanent state institutions. What follows from the oldest Frankish code, which was constantly amended or updated through Charlemagne's time, reflects the concept of free people called to meetings on "hills of judgment" to decide the innocence or guilt and appropriate sentences for accused lawbreakers. The stipulated fines appear in denarii or solidi: A denarius began as the equivalent of a Roman worker's daily wage—it is the "penny" of the New Testament—but by the sixth century, denarii were merely copper coins "washed" in silver; solidi were gold coins of fairly constant value since Constantine's time, each worth forty denarii at the time this code was written down.

QUESTIONS TO CONSIDER

1. How does the severity of the Frankish Code compare with that of the Laws of Hammurabi?
2. How are gender and status relations reflected in the code?
3. A frequently accepted distinction between "serf" and "slave" is that serfs could not be sold while slaves could. How does the code show that in some instances the distinction was quite blurred?

II. Hog Stealing

1. Anyone who steals a nursing sow from a sty and is proven guilty of the offense shall pay 120 denarii, which equal 3 solidi.

From *Forschungen über das Recht der Salischen Franken vor und in der Königszeit: Lex Salica und Malbergische Glossen*, ed. Knute Clement and Heinrich Zoepfl (Berlin: Grieben, 1876), pp. 89–90, 149–9, 151–52, and 185–86; trans. Henry A. Myers. The Salic or Salian Franks were those who had settled close to the salt (saline) North Sea, in distinction to the other main branch, the Ripuarian Franks, who had settled along the Rhine River. The texts of the code are in Latin, but in some manuscripts, the earliest being from Malberg, they are supplemented by marginal notes called "glosses" in which some Germanic, Frankish expressions for the Latin terms are written out.

2. Anyone who steals from the field a shoat old enough to live without its mother and is proven guilty of the offense shall pay 40 denarii, which equals 1 solidus.

3. Anyone who strikes a pregnant sow, causing her to miscarry, and is proven guilty of the offense shall pay 280 denarii, which equal 7 solidi and also payment equal to the value of the lost litter and for the time lost [when the sow was fed but produced no litter].

XIV. Killing Children and Women

1. Anyone who kills a [free] boy less than twelve years old and is found guilty of the offense shall pay 24,000 denarii, which equal 600 solidi. . . .

3. He who is found guilty of striking a freeborn, pregnant woman so that she dies shall pay 28,000 denarii, which equals 700 solidi.

4. If instead his act causes the death of an infant in its mother's womb or before it has been given a name, and he is found guilty of the offense, he shall pay 4,000 denarii, which equal 100 solidi.

5. A boy under twelve years old who commits an offense will not be required to pay peace-restitution money.

6. Anyone who kills a free woman after she has begun to bear children and is found guilty of the offense shall pay 24,000 denarii, which equal 600 solidi; however, if he kills her when she is no longer able to bear children, and is found guilty of the offense, he shall pay 8,000 denarii, which equal 200 solidi.

XXV. Fornication with Servant Women

1. If a freeborn man fornicates with a female serf who does not belong to him and is found guilty of the offense, he is to pay the maid's master 600 denarii, which equal 15 solidi. If he does the same with a maid belonging to the King and is found guilty, he is to pay 1,200 denarii or 30 solidi.

2. If a freeborn man publicly marries a female serf belonging to another, he is to fall into serfdom with her.

3. If a male serf fornicates with a female serf belonging to a lord other than his own and she dies as a result of that act,[1] that serf shall either pay 240 denarii, which equal 6 solidi, to the owner of the dead maid or be castrated. The lord to whom that serf belongs shall make full restitution to the owner of the serving maid, according to her value. If the serving maid does not die, the serf shall either receive 300 blows or also pay the maid's lord 120 denarii, which equal 3 solidi.

4. When a male serf abducts a female serf belonging to a lord other than his own against her will, he shall pay 120 denarii or 3 solidi to her lord.

XXXIX. Kidnapping

1. If someone is apprehended in the act of enticing away serfs who do not belong to him and found guilty of the offense, he shall pay 600 denarii or 15 solidi.

2. When a serf belonging to someone else is enticed away in an act of kidnapping, transported across the sea, and there discovered by his rightful lord with the man who treacherously kidnapped him from his homeland; and further, when the

---

[1]The reference is probably to rape-related violence.

rightful lord can name the latter at the public hill of judgment, he is obligated to present three witnesses there. The kidnapped serf, when he has been fetched back from the other side of the sea, shall indicate the guilty party before a second gathering called to pass judgment and likewise present three credible witnesses. The same procedure is to be followed in a third meeting to pass judgment, in which nine witnesses are to swear that they themselves heard the serf speak about the kidnapper in the same way. After that, the man found guilty of abducting the serf through cunning is to pay 1,400 denarii, which equal 35 solidi, in addition to a sum equal to the value of the serf and the cost to his lord due to the serf's absence. This statement of the serf may be used to find up to three kidnappers guilty, but only with the proviso that he can state the names of the people and the places of the offenses.

3. If someone kidnaps and sells a freeborn man but the evidence against him is not compelling, then he is obliged to furnish oath-swearers in his behalf, just as is required in a murder case. If he cannot find the oath-swearers for himself, he is to be considered guilty [of a criminal act] and is to pay 8,000 denarii, which equal 200 solidi.

4. If he abducts a Roman [Gallo-Roman] and is found guilty, he is to pay 2,500 denarii or $62\frac{1}{2}$ solidi.

Feudalism and Chivalry, West and East

The feudal system began to take shape in Western Europe in the early eighth century when Charles Martel, Charlemagne's grandfather, first made the practice of *benefice*—giving land in return for services, previously in the form of grants to monasteries, in return for masses or other Church services—into a secular institution. He entrusted land in a form that would later be called a *fief* to leaders among the Frankish warrior nobility in return for their pledge of military service against the Moors. Owing service for the lands entrusted to them, the Frankish nobles thus functioned as Charles's *vassals*. Under Charlemagne's own, fairly strong central regime, these relationships were not decisive, but with the breakup of the Carolingian Empire and the onset of the second wave of Dark Ages, feudal relations became the dominant way of upholding something like law and order in much of Western Europe.

The term "chivalry" originally meant cavalry, but under feudalism the warrior nobility fighting on horseback developed a value system all its own. Chivalry, as an ideology, stressed courageous loyalty for good reasons: In the centuries when feudalism prevailed, the "state" (in the sense of an independent entity with a legal monopoly on the use of force) did not exist. Dukes, counts, and others in the feudal hierarchy were supposed to keep a semblance of law and order in their territories and assist their liege lords in doing the same, but the responsibilities were a matter of individual contract. For example, a lord promised to uphold his vassal's rights in his fief, and the vassal promised to give "aids" and counsel to his lord. For the system to work properly, it was necessary—in the absence of readily available enforcing power—for both sides to feel a strong sense of honor in carrying out their commitments. Consequently, the utmost value was attached to having sufficient loyalty and courage to stand by the feudal contract despite overwhelming threats.

The ideas of chivalry were conveyed in epics known by their French generic name, *chansons de geste* (songs of deeds), of which the Song of Roland is easily the most famous, but chivalric epics were written in many parts of Europe. The first selection that follows, the *Nibelungenlied* (Song of the Nibelungs), written anonymously in Germany around 1200, mixes elements of the older epic; emphasis is on detailed and bloody battles with elements of the new "courtly" style, in which refinement, good manners, and fine clothing come into their own. In this new courtly style, women play active roles.

The second epic selection, taken from the anonymous *Book of Emperors and Kings*, illustrates among other things the feudal-chivalric theme by having Charlemagne function as vassal of his feudal lord, Saint Peter. It displays the ideology of the Holy Roman Empire in which the Church, secular monarchy, and the feudal nobility were supposed to function in a unity of mutual support.

The medieval Islamic world did not develop feudal institutions of lord and vassal comparable to those in Western Europe or Japan; however, Islamic military figures often held to their own code of chivalrous conduct. Willingness to sacrifice life and fortune in holy wars for Islam (see Reading 53) was certainly comparable to knightly devotion to the Crusader cause in the West. Islamic rulers like Saladin fit into the role of knightly heroes as easily as a western king like Richard the Lion-Hearted.

Feudalism in Japan had very different origins from feudalism in the West. In Japan, leaders of armed groups in the provinces began to challenge the aristocrats who controlled the central government in the ninth century, and by the twelfth century these *bushi* or samurai were effectively in control of Japan. Thus, they replaced one kind of aristocratic rule with another, whereas in Europe from the eighth through the thirteenth century all the nobility who counted were real or imagined descendants of a warrior elite. The samurai culture of Japan developed an ethical system similar to that of European chivalry, which is illustrated by both the Bushido Code or Way of the Samurai and the tale of self-sacrificing heroism for the honor of a feudal lord, The Forty-Seven Ronin.

59

The Nibelungenlied

The following excerpts from this epic sample both the violence-loving older emphasis of the genre and the (by 1200 contemporary but still fairly new) emphasis on what is polite and fashionable. Siegfried, the most heroic among the male figures, is a master of both helmet-splitting combat and the courtly arts. He knows just what to do, just what to say, and just what to wear to cut a fine chivalric picture.

To understand the second and third excerpts, it is necessary to know that Brunhilde, Queen of Iceland, was a beautiful but Amazonian figure who offered her hand in marriage to any aspiring knight who would attempt to defeat her in sports but who would be killed if he lost to her. Gunther, King of Burgundy, was no match for Brunhilde and knew it, but he enlisted the aid of Siegfried by giving him a magic helmet that gave supernatural strength and invisibility to the wearer. In return for his help, Siegfried would have the beautiful Princess Kriemhilde, Gunther's sister, as his wife. Gunther went through the motions of throwing the required spear and a huge stone, but it was the invisible Siegfried who really won the games for him. Later, on their wedding night, Brunhilde refused to yield to Gunther's embraces but rather tied him up and hung him on the wall until dawn. Gunther then enlisted Siegfried's aid again: The next night, the invisible Siegfried physically overcame Brunhilde but then turned her over to Gunther for the consummation of their marriage, after which her Amazonian features left her and she became simply the "home queen" of Burgundy. Siegfried's fatal mistake was in taking a ring and valuable belt from Brunhilde as souvenirs of his adventure and then—an even worse judgment call—giving them to his own bride, Kriemhilde.

Eventually, rivalry between the two women led Kriemhilde to tell Brunhilde that Siegfried was the first man to possess her, and Brunhilde's longing for vengeance led her to persuading Hagen, one of Gunther's vassals who was trusted by Siegfried, to murder Siegfried. Much, much later Kriemhilde got her own revenge by bringing about the bloody deaths of Hagen and other traitors, even though she had to marry Attila the Hun to do so and lost her own life in the process of carrying out the demands of justice as she saw them.

QUESTIONS TO CONSIDER

1. How does the author go about making Siegfried an appealing figure for his audience?
2. Why do you suppose the author starts the conflict with the Danes and the Saxons with a description of single combat and ends it with one combining single combat and mass fray?
3. Where do you suppose the author got the idea of a man risking his life on a wager on his athletic performance for the hand of a desirable woman? Have you met up with a roughly similar story in one or more earlier cultures?
4. The author of this epic announces early on that he intends to tell of disaster brought on "by the conflicts between two noble women." Do you think the story of Brunhilde and Fredegunde (see Reading 57) furnished the inspiration for this story after centuries of retelling? Why or why not?
5. What does the feudal structure have to do with the rivalry between Brunhilde and Kriemhilde?

I

In the Netherlands, a son of the mighty King Siegmund and Queen Sieglinde grew up. There, downstream on the Rhine, the royal castle with the city called Xanten was

From *Das Nibelungenlied*, ed. Friedrich Zarncke (Halle: M. Niemeyer, 1905), verses 20–843. Trans. Henry A. Myers.

known far and wide for its splendor. The bold young prince was named Siegfried. His manly courage was to lead him on tests of his warrior's skill into many kingdoms; his bold strength kept him riding through the lands. . . . He was of an age now to take his own place at the royal court. The people loved to watch him ride by. Many ladies and many girls hoped that his desires might pull him in their direction. Many loved him. . . . Siegmund and Sieglinde kept him very well dressed, and wise men who knew what honor was all about instructed him in winning lands and people to rule. . . .

[Hearing tales of the great beauty and charm of the Burgundian princess, Kriemhilde, Siegfried makes a knightly journey to Worms, the Burgundian capital. While he is there, messengers of the hostile kings of Saxony and Denmark approach her brother, King Gunther:] "If you will permit us, Sire, there is no reason for us to delay in giving you our message: It is that Ludgast and Ludger, the rulers who sent us, declare the feud you have caused by kindling great hatred in them, as we have been told, as reason for marauding your land. They plan an expedition to Worms on the Rhine, and there should be no doubt that many bold knights will follow them here. . . . They will start out in twelve weeks; that is, unless you want to negotiate with them: Then offer what you can. If you choose that course, the vast armies of your mighty enemies will not ride so close to Worms, bringing conflict that will cause you sorrow because so many of your good knights will be killed."

"Give me a little time," the good king said, "until I can think all this over. I will let you know what I decide later. If I indeed have loyal vassals, I will not want to keep this from them. Such a harsh message calls for the advice of my friends."

The best of his men who could be located came to him, and he said: "Ludgast and Ludger intend to invade our lands with strong forces: Just think about the grief that this will bring us."

"Let's defend with swords," said Gernot. "He will die whose lot it is to fall. I will not forget my honor in the fight: Let us welcome our enemies to do battle here."

Then Hagen of Tronya spoke up: "That does not seem like a good idea. Ludgast and Ludger are too full of themselves. We can't get a decent army together in such a short time. Why don't you tell Siegfried about this?"

Gunther directed men to see that the messengers were given lodgings in his city. Even though they were enemies, he had them very well taken care of. His act was generous, and he was doing the right thing until he could find friends who would support him.

But then the boldest of knights [Siegfried] saw how something terrible was depressing the king. He had no way of knowing what had gone on, and so he asked King Gunther to let him know what had happened. . . .

"I don't want to tell everybody about the troubles I have to bear secretly, but there is nothing wrong with opening your heart to your real friends."

At this, Siegfried turned both pale and red and said to the king: "I have never turned you down in anything yet, and I will help you deal with everything that is worrying you. If you need the help of friends, count on me. Trust me to support you through it all with honor until my own end comes."

"May God reward you, Lord Siegfried! I like the way you talk. Even if you don't actually fight in my cause, I'm glad to hear that you are so supportive. If I live through all this, I will see that you are well rewarded. And so, I will let you in on what troubles me so much right now. I just learned from my enemies' messengers that they are going to invade my lands, which no knights have ever done before."

"Don't pay too much attention to that threat," said Siegfried, "and don't let it worry you. Just do what I ask you to. Send for your vassals to come to your aid, but let me win honor and victories for you. If your mighty enemies can enlist thirty thousand knights, I would still beat them even if I had only a thousand. You can count on that."

"If you do, I will see that you receive lasting rewards," said King Gunther. . . .

When the news reached Denmark [that Gunther was going to fight and that the renowned Siegfried was supporting him], the king's men hurried to assemble more and more forces until Ludgast had twenty thousand knights ready to ride under his banner. King Ludger kept recruiting in Saxony until forty thousand and more had pledged to ride against the Burgundians.

[A little later at Gunther's court] "Let your Royal Highness stay at home," said Siegfried, "since your knights are willing to follow me. Look after the ladies and be of good cheer because I will prevent those invaders from attacking you at Worms on the Rhine. They will wish they had stayed at home because we will ride so far back into their own lands that their arrogance will be turned to grief." . . .

From the Rhine, the Burgundian forces rode through Hesse toward Saxony, where the battle was soon to be fought. . . . Never had the Saxons experienced such a devastating attack as this was to be. . . . "I will ride out myself," said Siegfried the hero, "and do some reconnaissance in our enemies' direction until I can establish where their knights are." He rode directly into Saxony . . . , and there he caught sight of a great army encamped in the field. From the forward sentries' position, one noble warrior soon rode out ready for combat. That bold man had seen Siegfried, and Siegfried saw him now.

I'll tell you who that was, riding now from the vanguard and holding a light shield of gold: It was King Ludgast himself, who had come to lead his army in person! Siegfried galloped toward him in all his glory, and Ludgast sought his noble "guest" for single combat as well. . . . Spurred on, their horses bore the two royal warriors, who had lowered their lances to rest on their shields for the charge, toward each other with such lightness that the wind itself appeared to be carrying them.

[The impact did not dislodge either of them, however, and] each grim and determined foe turned his steed around and sought the other with his sword. The field echoed the sounds of clanging metal, as Siegfried struck heavy blows. Under his hero's hand, great red sparks of fire sprayed from Ludgast's helmet. For a while, each of them found the other his equal, for Ludgast struck Siegfried many severe blows, too: Gashes made by the other's sword soon marked both their shields. Thirty of Ludgast's men saw what was going on, but before they reached him, Siegfried won the combat with three deep wounds he dealt the king through his light armor: They were decisive. The cutting edge of his sword drew blood from Ludgast's wounds and destroyed his will to continue. He asked for his life and, letting Siegfried know that he was Ludgast, offered him his lands.

But then his knights, who had seen from the outpost what was happening rode up and attacked Siegfried, all thirty of them, while he was leading Ludgast away. But Siegfried's strong arm let him keep his valuable hostage for himself: That wonderful knight inflicted still more destruction on his foes. Of the thirty, he killed all but one, leaving him to ride back to tell the news of what had happened with the red on his helmet bearing testimony. Denmark's warriors were sad and grim to learn that their ruler had been captured. When his brother, Ludger, heard the news, he went into convulsions of rage and grief.

[After turning Ludgast over to Hagen at the Burgundian camp,] Siegfried told the knights there to tie their flags on their lances: "There is much more to be done on the field of battle," he said. "If I stay alive, the wife of many a fine knight will be grieving in Saxony before sundown. . . . I can lead you to Ludger's forces. There your strong arms will split many helmets before we return." . . .

They led no more than one thousand knights and the twelve brought by Siegfried. Clouds of dust began to rise on the road as they rode over the land, but many an ornamented shield rim still gleamed from their midst.

By then the full army of the Saxons was on the march. With their well-sharpened swords . . . , the Saxons hoped to defend their towns and lands from the stranger. . . . The Danes, too, gave their hands a good try. [When the battle began,] you could hear the clang of blows on many shield rims, while the sharp swords struck many wounds. Eager for combat, the Saxons did plenty of damage, but the Burgundians pressed into the fray, slashing wide wounds everywhere. You could watch the blood flowing over the saddles as those bold and good warriors competed for honor. Yes, you could hear their sharp weapons ring loud and far as they wielded them. Those who had followed Siegfried from the Netherlands pushed forward behind their lord into the thickest combat. You could see a bloody brook flowing through the gleaming helmets split by Siegfried's strong hand until he confronted King Ludger before his comrades at arms. . . .

When brave Ludger caught sight of Siegfried swinging his wonderful sword . . . high and low and slaughtering so many of his men, rage welled up in him. Both kings' followers rushed at each other with loud sword blows, as their leaders tested each other. Hate was seething all around, but then the Saxons began to back off a little. The Saxon king was told that his brother had been captured, and this gave him sad cause to grieve. . . . Siegfried soon took such blows from Ludger's sword that he felt his horse falter under his saddle. . . . In the press of battle, many knights dismounted, as did Siegfried and Ludger, who charged each other on foot. Siegfried's blows sent the rim clasps holding Ludger's shield together flying off, and the hero from the Netherlands felt sure of winning victory. . . . King Ludger recognized the crown painted on Siegfried's shield, and, realizing that the peerless hero must be its owner, began shouting loudly to his followers: "Give up fighting, all you on my side; I now see Siegmund's son before me. Yes, I recognize that strongest of men: The devil himself sent him against us Saxons!"

And so the Saxons lowered their battle flags. Ludger sought peace, and this was granted him with the stipulation that he must go to King Gunther's country as a hostage. Brave Siegfried's strong hand had made him a prisoner.

II

"I want to sail over the North Sea to Brunhilde," said Gunther, the king from the Rhineland. "I don't care what happens to me: I am going to put my life on the line to win her love and die if I fail to win her as my wife."

"I would advise against that," said Siegfried. "That queen has introduced a savage custom at her court: The man who seeks her love will pay dearly for it. You really should find out more what that trip involves."

"If you insist on going," said Hagen, "I would advise you to take Siegfried along to help you with the grave dangers there, since he seems to know so much about the ways of Brunhilde's court."

"Noble Siegfried, will you help me to win my beloved? If you do what I ask and help me win that most desirable of women for my wife, I will risk my own honor and life to repay you."

"If you give me your sister to be my queen, I will do it," answered Siegfried. "I would not want any other reward for my trouble than that exalted princess, the beautiful Kriemhilde."

"I promise!" said Gunther. "Siegfried, let me shake your hand and swear that if the beautiful Brunhilde comes here to my kingdom I will give you my sister as your wife and you shall live happily ever after with your own beautiful bride." And so those bold knights confirmed their promises with oaths.

[A little later, Gunther spoke to Kriemhilde:] "My dearest sister, we cannot make good on what we plan without your help. We are going to undertake real challenges in Brunhilde's country, and for that we will need truly magnificent clothing to wear when we appear before the women there."

The maiden answered him: "My dearest brother, rest assured that I will surely do everything in my power to help you. Kriemhilde would be very sorry indeed if someone else were to let you down. In fact, noble knight that you are, I would rather that you didn't make requests of me as if it worried you to do so. Act confident in letting me know what you would like me to do for you. You will find me not only willing but eager to carry out your wishes. . . ."

"My dear sister, we want to go there wearing the best of clothes. Your own white hands can well see to our needs, but your serving women should help you, too, so that we look splendid for this trip. We wouldn't know where to begin otherwise."

The maiden answered: "I'm glad to let you know that I have just the silk for the task. See that we get a couple of shields full of gems. When we have sewn the gems on the silks, every combination you wear will do you honor before that prized princess. But who is going along to her court with you and will need fine clothes?"

"Four of us," he said. "Siegfried and two of my vassals, Dankwart and Hagen, are going to her court with me. Now pay close attention, sister, to what I am requesting: I would like each of us to have three changes of clothes per day for four days, outfits nice enough that when we leave Brunhilde's kingdom there will be no negative comments."

With cheerful words of parting, the royal lords left her. Princess Kriemhilde then had thirty of her ladies-in-waiting come from their chambers, those who had a keen sense of craftsmanship for the work at hand. They set gems on Arabian silks, white as snow, and the fine silks from Zazamanc, green as clover. Out of these they made fine garments with that wonderful young lady, Kriemhilde, cutting the cloth herself.

They also took some hides from exotic creatures of the deep to serve as bottom layers, sewing the silk on top of them and mounting gold on top of both layers to catch the eyes of their hosts in that foreign land. You can just imagine what comments of amazement those glittering outfits later received! Kriemhilde certainly demonstrated her willing support of the project. She had an abundance of the very best silks that royalty had ever heard of from Morocco and some from Libya, too. Since this was the most exalted of all kinds of expeditions, they would have considered mere ermine furs unworthy. They did use ermine, but they mounted pieces of velvet, black as coals, on it so fine and costly that it would make bold heroes even of our own day stand out at ceremonies. The ladies took great pains with their work, and within seven weeks they had completed the wardrobe, which included garments with gems set in a background of Arabian gold. . . .

III

Kriemhilde and Brunhilde, the two exalted queens, were sitting next to each other [at a palace window, looking on] as outside many knights took part in jousting. They began to speak of two very special heroes who deserved the highest praise. "I have a husband," said the lovely Kriemhilde, "who deserves control over all these domains."

"How could that come about?" Brunhilde responded. "If no other royal kin were still living but you and Siegfried, then the lands could owe allegiance to him, but as long as Gunther is alive they never will."

"Just look at him out there," said Kriemhilde, "riding so nobly and so handsomely in front of the other knights. He displays the moon's radiance dominantly in front of the milder glow of the stars. I have to admit that I derive pleasure from that fact."

"I don't care how well-outfitted your husband is," said Brunhilde, "or how well-mannered or how good-looking, you will still have to concede a higher place to your royal brother, the noble Gunther. You know very well that he must take his place before all other kings."

"My husband is so great," said Kriemhilde, "that I did not exaggerate with my praise of him. He deserves the very highest respect in a good many areas. Take it from me, Brunhilde: He is Gunther's equal and maybe more than that."

[The verbal exchanges escalated in sharpness until] "You are ranking yourself too high," said Brunhilde: "I am just waiting to see if people show you as much respect in public as they do me." Both of the ladies were really getting angry. . . .

[Later the two queens confronted each other upon approaching the door of the cathedral.] The home queen could not suppress her rage and rudely told Kriemhilde to stand where she was, saying: "No vassal's woman has a right to enter before a ruling king's wife."

That infuriated Kriemhilde: "You had better learn to hold your tongue. You brought disgrace on your own lovely body. How do you think another man's mistress can ever hope to be a real queen?"

"Who are you calling 'mistress'?" asked the king's wife.

"That is my name for you," said Kriemhilde, "because it was my dear husband, Siegfried, who first possessed that beautiful body of yours. It just wasn't my brother that you lost your virginity to. What are you so mad about? Or are you just pretending to be hurt? Why did you let him be your lover if he is supposed to be your vassal?"

Brunhilde began to cry. Kriemhilde waited no longer before the home king's wife but strode into the cathedral followed by her retinue.

60

The Book of Emperors and Kings,
"Charlemagne and Pope Leo III"

In the mid-twelfth century, one or more anonymous clerics in the German city of Regensburg made the first attempt since ancient times to present history to a broad—in fact, largely illiterate—audience in its own vernacular language. *The Book of Emperors and Kings*, now referred to with greater frequency and less accuracy as *The Impe-*

rial Chronicle, was composed for reading or chanting aloud. Although it retains the outward form of a rhymed epic, the main author states his intention of telling the true history of the Roman Empire (meaning the Holy Roman Empire as well as the ancient one) from its beginning to the present day. He makes it plain that, unlike other "songs," his will refute lies instead of spreading them.

In the following excerpt, we see this author's idea of truth. He is more concerned throughout with true models of Christian rulership and contrasting examples of falsity than with mere "facticity." For example, he is intent on portraying Charlemagne as a monumental figure of stern faith and courage who collaborated with Pope Leo III in giving new life to the Roman Empire after the Byzantine Greeks, "the preceding house," had let the empire's fortunes slide. To explain the motivation behind their mutual support, the author makes Pope Leo III into Charlemagne's brother.

The episode in which Charlemagne threatens St. Peter may seem extreme by modern standards, but it reminds us that ideas of contract and loyalty thoroughly permeated the religious as well as the secular value system of the feudal world. Charlemagne has kept his part of the feudal contract; when he is convinced that Saint Peter has not kept his, he acts accordingly. Saint Peter responds like a liege lord who has been late in relieving his vassal's distress.

The selection also demonstrates the ambivalence of medieval people in northern Europe toward Rome and the Romans. All of them acknowledged the Bishop of Rome, the pope, as head of the Church, whereas the descent of their empire from Rome was stressed in the German-speaking lands. Still, those loyal to the empire regarded the current inhabitants of Rome as a frequently treacherous group who had to be controlled from time to time by "right-thinking" rulers with armies from the "uncorrupted" countries to the north of Italy.

By the twelfth century, the tradition that electoral princes (ranking members of the nobility and clergy) chose the German king (who officially became Roman Emperor when consecrated by the pope) had become established. In describing Charlemagne's ascension to these positions, the author of *The Book of Emperors and Kings* drifts between historical accounts from learned sources and traditional accounts from his own day.

The Saint Pancras episode reflects the legal view that people of different tribes or nations were entitled to be tried according to their own native laws. At the same time, this account heightens the author's ethnic stereotypes: The brave Germanic peoples settle their disputes through trial by combat, whereas the less courageous Romans settle legal disputes by raising two fingers and swearing oaths. According to legend, Pancras was a youth of fourteen who was martyred during Diocletian's (A.D. 284–305) persecution of Christians. As a reward for his courage in the face of death, God gave him the power to inflict a wasting, terminal illness on any who swore a false oath at his grave.

QUESTIONS TO CONSIDER

1. How does the author establish Charlemagne as a model Christian ruler?
2. What motivates the Romans to attack the pope? Why is Charlemagne ultimately to blame for this conflict?

3.   Why is the pope's requesting mercy for his assailants unacceptable to Charlemagne?
4.   Does *The Book of Emperors and Kings* give any justification for identifying most of the inhabitants of Arles as "heathens"?
5.   How does Charlemagne finally win his struggle in Spain?

The Empire remained without a head. The lords of Rome set the crown on Saint Peter's Altar. Meeting all together, they swore before the people that never again would they choose a king—nor judge, nor anyone else to rule them—from the kin of the preceding house, which had proven unable to maintain faith and honor with them. They wanted kings from other lands. . . .

According to a custom of those days, young princes from all over the Empire were raised and instructed with great care at the court in Rome. The Romans gave them the sword of knighthood when the time came . . . , sending the young heirs back to their homelands. This helped keep all the dominions mindful of serving Rome.

It came to pass that Pippin, a mighty king of Karlingen,[2] had two fine sons. One of them named Leo came to hold Saint Peter's throne after being raised in Rome, while Charles, the other, stayed home.

One night when Charles fell asleep, a voice called out to him three times: "Arise, beloved Charles, and hurry to Rome! Your brother Leo needs you!" And quickly Charles made ready, saying nothing to anyone about what he intended to do until he asked leave of the King to go. . . .

When the young Prince asked for leave, his father granted it to him gladly and bestowed gifts upon his son in a manner worthy of a mighty king. . . .

Charles really undertook his journey more for [the chance to pray at the tombs of] the divine Apostles than for his brother's sake. Early and late in the day his thoughts, which he revealed to no one, were filled with love of God. . . .

When Charles arrived in Rome, he was given a fine reception by old and young. . . . Pope Leo sang a mass then in honor of the Holy Ghost and to strengthen the Prince's spirit. Then he received God's Body. All who were there praised God, finding Charles so worthy and to their liking that the law should make him their ruler.

Charles did not listen to what was being said: He had made his journey for the sake of prayer, and he let no commotion distract him. He entered churches barefoot and, imploring God's mercy, he prayed for his soul. This steadfast devotion brought him every worldly honor, too. . . .

Thus he spent four weeks so wrapped in prayer and meditation that no one could approach him to speak, until once his brother, Pope Leo, and all the people fell at his feet. Charles pointed out to God in Heaven that if he were to prove unworthy he never should have made his journey. Then he received the royal emblems,

[2]"Karlingen," the name given by several medieval German writers to the domain of Charlemagne and his ancestors, is probably a derivation by analogy on the assumption that the name of the great Charles (Karl) was given to his whole family domain. Similarly, his grandson Lothar's name was applied to Lorraine (Lotharingen).

From *The Book of Emperors and Kings (Der keiser und der kunige buoch)*, trans. Henry A. Myers from text published as *Die Kaiserchronik eines Regensburger Geistlichen*, ed. Edward Schröder, in *Monumenta Germaniae Historica, Deutsche Chroniken* (Hannover: Hahn, 1892), Vol. 1, pp. 393–53, *passium.*

and they set a magnificent crown on his head. All those there in Rome rejoiced that day, and all said, "Amen."

Then the King sat in judgment, and the Pope made complaint before him that church properties and the collection of tithes, entrusted to him by his predecessors for his use in the saving of souls, were being granted away from his jurisdiction, and that his benefices had been taken from him. His complaint angered a number of the nobles.

Then Charles spoke these true ruler's words: "Never in this world, I feel sure, did anyone make a gift to honor God in order that another might take it. That would clearly be robbery. . . . Whoever would take anything away from gifts bestowed on God's houses, through which God's work is furthered, would be despised of God and could not remain a good Christian. . . ." Then those nobles departed, full of resentment. Charles also had no desire to remain there any longer.

Charles returned to Ripuaria.[3] The Romans realized very well that he was their rightful judge, but stupid men among them ridiculed the others for ever having proclaimed him ruler. . . . In Saint Peter's Cathedral they caught the Pope and pushed his eyes out of their sockets . . . , and sent him blind to the King in Ripuaria.

Nothing remained for the Pope to do but set out on the journey in his hapless condition. He rode on a donkey and took with him two of his chaplains, desiring no other escort. . . .

The Pope arrived in Ingelheim with his two chaplains and rode into the King's courtyard. When the King saw him coming, he said to one of his men: "Someone has attacked this pilgrim, and we shall do justice in his cause if we can. He seems badly injured. Someone must have robbed him. . . ."

The King strode quickly across the courtyard . . . and said: "Good pilgrim, if you wish to stay here with me, I will gladly take you in. Tell me if your misfortune is such that I can help you with it. Why don't you dismount?"

The noble Pope wanted to draw closer to the King. His head hung at a strange angle, and his eyes stared askew. "That God should have granted me your presence!" he began. . . . "It has not been long since I sang a mass for you at Rome, when I could still see." As he spoke these words, the noble King recognized him and was so shocked that he could neither see nor hear. . . . His body went limp and he could not speak. . . .

When the Emperor had recovered, the Pope told him sorrowfully: "I have come here that you may take pity on me. It was because of you that I lost my eyes: they blinded me to get even with you. Still, Brother, you must pull yourself together, and weep no more. . . ."

The Emperor himself lifted him down and carried him across the courtyard into his private chamber. There they sat together, and Charles told his men to go outside. "Brother," he said, "how did this happen to you? Let me hear your complaint, and then my forces of justice will right the wrong."

Pope Leo answered the King: "Brother, after you left Rome, the Romans very soon betrayed their loyalty to me in a conspiracy. They caught me in the Cathedral and committed this terrible crime upon me. Brother, we must bear this patiently: I seek vengeance only in Heaven, and you must not injure any of them for this."

---

[3]Territorial home of one historic group of the Franks on the Rhine River; for the author, this location is sometimes synonymous with "Karlingen," sometimes one of its provinces.

"It would be doing God a dishonor to spare those murderers!" the noble King replied. "Ah! How sorely that would injure Christendom. I am called 'Judge' and 'Ruler': and this means I have the duty of judging over the peoples. . . . I must defend Christendom with the sword. You will have them sorely regret their crime against you. I will avenge your eyes, or I will renounce my sword."

Then he dispatched messengers to King Pippin to tell him of his great need and let the nobles of Karlingen know that if they ever wanted to render God a loving service they should hurry to him. And there were none in Karlingen but who proclaimed all with one voice: "Woe to the fatal hour that Rome was ever founded!" . . .

The messengers galloped ceaselessly from land to land and from lord to vassal: all men were willing to come to the cause of Charles. Farmers and merchants, too— no one could hold them back. They left all their belongings and set out to join Charles. The mourning and grief over the news traveled through Christendom from people to people, and the streams of warriors converged like clouds over the Great Saint Bernard Pass. . . . The book does not give a number for the total army, but it was the greatest military expedition that ever descended on Rome.

When the army had advanced to within sight of the Aventine Hill in Rome, the worthy King asked three days and nights for himself. This annoyed his great lords, who went to him to say that it ill became his office to pause there, now that they had come so close that they could see the city which had aggrieved them.

"First we must pray to God, for we must gain His leave to carry through," answered the King. "Then we shall fight with ease. . . ."

Early one morning the voice of God spoke to him: "God in Heaven commands you, King, to remain here no longer. Ride on to Rome: God has rendered judgment, and just vengeance shall overtake them."

And so the King's banner was raised, and Charles let word pass through his whole army that when the knights were prepared for battle they should keep their eyes upon the banner and ride in close formation. Hearts swelling with high spirits, Charles's men swarmed over the hill. . . .

Owî, what an army this was that besieged Rome and the Lateran for seven days and seven nights, so menacingly that no one would fight against it! On the eighth day—this is the truth I am telling you—the Romans ordered the city gates opened and offered to let the King enter with this condition: that any man who could prove himself innocent of committing, aiding, or advising the crime would remain in the King's favor, while the King would deal with the guilty ones after deciding on a just sentence. . . .

As the Emperor sat in judgment and the document naming the guilty men was read, the accused all fervently denied their guilt when they were called forward. The King ordered them to submit to trial by combat for their unwillingness to confess. But then the Romans objected that this was not according to their law, and that no Emperor had ever forced such treatment on them before; instead, they should prove their innocence by swearing with their two fingers.

Then King Charles spoke: "I doubt that any crime so great was ever committed before. Don't be overhasty now: I imagine my brother saw at the time who did it." Still, when so very many of the accused offered their oaths in the Cathedral, the King said: I will not deprive you of recourse to your own law any longer; however, I know of a youth here named Pancras. If you are willing to swear an oath at his grave and if he tolerates it, then I will be willing to believe you.

Icy fear seized the Romans at the mention of this test. As they came to the place sacred to Saint Pancras and were supposed to hold up their fingers and to keep asserting their innocence under oath, one man was overcome, and panic gripped all the rest. They retreated in fear and fled back over the bridge although a fair number went back to Saint Peter's Cathedral.

Charles hesitated no longer but rode after them angrily. For three days, he and his men struck them down, and for three days they carried them out. Then they washed down the floor stones. . . . Charles fell on his knees before Saint Peter's tomb and made his plea to Christ: "Lord God in Heaven, how can I be any good to You as King when You let such shame befall me? Sinner that I may be, I do make every attempt to judge the people in a manner worthy of You. The Romans swore allegiance to a Pope, and You granted him a portion of Your power that he might loose the people from their sins and bind them. I [ask] . . . that you give the evil people of Rome something to recognize Your hidden power by: then they will know for certain that You are a true God. Grant me this, Holy Christ!"

A second time Charles, the noble King, fell to the ground and said: "Hail noble Saint Peter! You are really a divine stalwart of God, a watchman of Christendom. Think now, my lord, what I am going through! You are a summoner of the Kingdom of Heaven. Just look at your Pope! I left him sound of body in your care. Blinded was how I found him, and if you do not heal the blind man today I shall destroy your Cathedral and ruin the buildings and grounds donated to you, and then I shall leave him for you blind as he is, and go back again to Ripuaria."

Quickly the noble Pope Leo made himself ready and said his confession. As he spoke the last word, he saw a heavenly light with both his eyes. Great are the hidden powers of God.

The Pope turned around and spoke to the multitude: "My dearest children gathered from afar, be glad of heart, for the Kingdom of God is drawing near to you. God has heard you and because of your holy prayer has turned His face toward you. Here, at this very place, you are called to be public witnesses that a great miracle has happened. . . . I can see with both eyes better than I ever saw in this world." . . .

The Pope consecrated him as Emperor and granted absolution to all his comrades in arms. Owî, what joy there was in Rome then! The whole people rejoiced then and sang: "Gloria in excelsis Deo."

Then Charles laid down the Imperial Law, as an angel recited the true words of God to him. . . . And so the mighty Emperor left us many good laws, which God caused to be spoken before him. . . .

The very first laws the Emperor established dealt with what seemed to him to be the most exalted matters, those concerning bishops and priests, for the Imperial Law of Constantine had been sadly neglected. At the same time, he established laws governing tithes and gifts of property to the Church. . . .

Now I shall tell you about what the peasant is to wear according to the Imperial Law: his clothes may be black or gray, and he is allowed no other. . . . He is to have shoes of cow leather only and seven yards of towcloth for his shirt and breeches. He is to spend six days at the plow and doing plenty of other work; on Sunday he is to go to Church, carrying his animal goad openly in his hand. If a sword is found on a peasant, he is to be led bound to the churchyard fence, where he is to be tied and his skin and hair are to be flayed. If he is threatened by enemies, however, let him defend himself with a pitchfork. This law King Charles established for the peasants. . . .

Emperor Charles besieged a walled city called Arles [France], which actually took him more than seven years. The inhabitants had considered him unworthy of his office. By way of an underground canal, wine was conveyed to them in plentiful supply, but finally Charles's cunning succeeded in cutting off their source. When the inhabitants could not hold out any longer, they threw open the city gates and fought fiercely, offering no terms at all. So many were slain on both sides that there is no man who can tell another how many of either the Christians or the heathens were lying there dead after the battle. No one could tell the dead apart until the Emperor solved the problem with God's help: He found the Christians lying separately in well adorned coffins. Now that is a wonder really worth telling about. . . .

The Emperor and his men turned toward Galicia [in Spain], where the king of the heathens inflicted great losses upon them. The Christian soldiers were all slain, and Charles barely escaped from the battle. Today the stone stays wet on which Charles sat afterwards, weeping passionately as he lamented his sins, saying: "Hail to You, God sublime! Grant me mercy for my poor soul. Take me out of this world, so that my people will no longer be punished because of me. I can never be consoled again."

Then an angel comforted him, saying: "Charles, beloved of God, your joy will come to you quickly. Bid your messengers make haste to summon virgin women—leave the married ones at home—for God will reveal His power through them. If you will fear and love God, the maidens will win your honor back again for you."

The messengers made haste and thoroughly searched through all the lands. They gathered together the maidens and brought them together . . . where the Emperor was waiting for them. Many a young maid came to join the host, fifty-three thousand—I am telling you this as a fact—and sixty-six more. . . .

When all the maidens arrived in a valley since named for Charles, they readied themselves for battle in formations just like men. . . .

Each heathen sentry was struck by wonder as to who this people could be, for it all seemed very strange to them. They hurried back, and one of them said to their king: "Sire, even though we slew the old ones, we must tell you for a fact that the young ones have followed them here. I have the feeling they want to slake their thirst for vengeance. They are big around the chest. Sire, if you fight with them, it will not come to any good end. Their hair is long, and their gait is very graceful: They are fine knights indeed. They are a terrifying lot. . . . No force could ever be assembled on this earth to defeat them. . . ."

At the advice of his experienced counsellors, their king turned over hostages to the Emperor. The king then had himself baptized—how well he suddenly believed in God!—and all his people with him. . . . Thus God made Charles victorious without the thrust of a spear or the blow of a sword, and the maidens well realized that God in Heaven was with them.

Charles and his heroines returned to their own homes back in the Empire. On the way, the worthy maidens came to a green meadow. Tired from the expedition, the heroines stuck their spearshafts into the ground and stretched out their arms in the form of a cross, sleeping on the ground after praising God for the goodness which He had shown them. They stayed there overnight, and a great miracle occurred. Their spearshafts had turned green and had sent forth leaves and blossoms. That is why the place is called "Woods of the Spearshafts"; it can be seen to this day.

Charles, the rich and powerful, built a mighty and beautiful church for the praise of Holy Christ, the honor of Saint Mary and all God's maidens, and the solace of Christendom. Since through chastity and spiritual purity the maids achieved their victory, the church is called Domini Sanctitas.[4]

61

Baha al-Din Ibn Shaddad, "Saladin: The Lion of Islam"

Saladin (A.D. 1137?–1193) proved to be one of the greatest Islamic warriors of all time. His family was of Kurdish descent and had served the Seljuk sultans and local Islamic rulers. Saladin was a young man when he followed his uncle in the capturing of Shi'ite-ruled Egypt in 1169. He was able eventually to rule Egypt and most of Syria, where his rule was seen as benefiting the local populations.

Troubles with Christian crusader raids on Muslim caravans by Reynald de Chatillon finally led Saladin to attack and to defeat the Christians in 1187. He quickly captured the Latin Kingdom of Jerusalem, which caused the formation of the Third Crusade (1189–1192). Although King Richard I (the Lionhearted) of England and King Philip II Augustus of France were able to retake the port of Acre and a strip of land down the seacoast, they were never able to retake Jerusalem.

Just after signing a truce with King Richard, whereby Christian pilgrims were permitted free access to all Christian sites, Saladin died. His lands were divided among his sons and his brother.

The following selection on the Battle of Hattin, where the Christians were defeated, is by Baha al-Din Ibn Shaddad, who was a judge in Saladin's army and his biographer. It depicts Saladin's battle tactics and his subsequent treatment of the defeated crusaders.

QUESTIONS TO CONSIDER

1. How were the Christians defeated by Saladin at the battle?
2. What was the difference in the treatment of King Guy and that of Reynald?
3. Do you know of further attempts by crusaders to recapture Jerusalem?

Account of the Battle of Hattin, a blessing for the Muslims

It took place on Saturday, 24 Rabi II 583, (4 July 1187). The sultan perceived that his gratitude for God's favor towards him, evidenced by his strong grasp on sovereignty, his God-given control over the lands and the people's willing obedience, could only be demonstrated by his endeavoring to exert himself to the utmost and to strive to fulfill the precept of Jihad. He sent to summon all his forces, which gathered on the date given at 'Ashtara. He reviewed them and made his dispositions, then set forth into the God-forsaken enemy's lands at midday on Friday, 17 Rabi II, (26 June). He always sought out Fridays for his battles, especially the times of Friday prayer, to gain the blessing of the preachers' prayers on the pulpits, for they were perhaps more likely to be answered.

---

[4]This church is the Emperor's Chapel, the main and oldest part of the Aachen Cathedral, also called Saint Mary's.

From Baha al-Din Ibn Shaddad, *The Rare and Excellent History of Saladin,* trans. D. S. Richards (Hans, England: Ashgate Publishing Limited, 2001), pp. 72–75. Used by permission.

As he marched out at that time in battle array, he heard that the enemy, when they learnt that he had concentrated his armies, gathered in full on the plain of Safftiriyya in the territory of Acre and intended to come to battle. The same clay, the sultan camped at Lake Tiberias near a village called Sannabra. He then moved and camped west of Tiberias on the top of the mountain, in battle formation and expecting that the Franks, when they heard that, would come against him. However, they did not move from their encampment. He took up this position on Wednesday, 21 Rabi II (1 July), and having seen that they were not moving, he descended upon Tiberias with a light force, leaving the main divisions in position facing the direction in which the enemy were. He attacked Tiberias and took it within one hour after a direct assault. Eager hands then turned to plundering, taking captives, burning and killing. The citadel alone held out.

Learning what had happened to Tiberias, the enemy could not bear not to give into their impulsive zeal, but set out at once and marched to defend Tiberias. The Muslim scouts told the emirs that the Franks were on the move, and they sent people to inform the sultan. He left men in Tiberias to watch the citadel and then he and his force joined the main army. The two armies encountered one another on the slopes of the mountain of Tiberias, to the west of the town, late on Thursday 22, Rabi II (2 July).

Nightfall separated the two sides and both spent the night at battle stations, bristling with weapons, until the morning of Friday, 23rd (3 July). Both armies mounted and clashed together. The vanguard was in operation, then the main divisions moved forward and battle was joined and became very intense. This was around a village called Lubiya. They were closely beset as in a noose, while still marching on as though being driven to a death that they could see before them, convinced of their doom and destruction and themselves aware that the following day they would be visiting their graves.

The conflict continued at close quarters, each horseman clashing with his opponent, until victory [for the Muslims] and for the infidels the onset of disaster was imminent, but night and its darkness intervened. That day there occurred mighty deeds and momentous doings, such as have not been related of past generations. Each party spent the night in arms, expecting his adversary at every moment, though too weak through tiredness to stand up and unable through fatigue to crawl, let alone run.

Eventually, there came the Saturday morning, on which the blessing was vouchsafed. Both sides sought their positions and each realized that whichever was broken would be driven off and eliminated. The Muslims were well aware that behind them was the Jordan and before them enemy territory and that there was nothing to save them but God Almighty.

God had already ordained and prepared the believers' victory, and he duly brought it about according to what he had predestined. The Muslim divisions charged on the wings and in the centre. They let out a shout as one man, at which God cast terror into the hearts of the unbelievers. "It was right for Us to give aid to the believers."[5]

The Count [Raymond] was a clever and shrewd leader of theirs. He saw that the signs of defeat were already upon his co-religionists and no notion of aiding his

---

[5]Koran, xxx, 47.

fellows stopped him thinking of himself, so he fled at the beginning of the engagement before it grew fierce and made his way towards Tyre, pursued by a group of Muslims. He alone was saved, but Islam became safe from his wiles.[6]

The forces of Islam surrounded the forces of unbelief and impiety on all sides, loosed volleys of arrows at them and engaged them hand to hand. One group fled and was pursued by our Muslim heroes. Not one of them survived. Another group took refuge on a hill called the Hill of Hattin, the latter being a village near which is the tomb of Shu'ayb (on him and on the rest of the prophets be blessings and peace). The Muslims pressed hard upon them on that hill and lit fires around them. Their thirst was killing and their situation became very difficult, so that they began to give themselves up as prisoners for fear of being slain. Their commanders were taken captive but the rest were either killed or taken prisoner, and among those who lived were their leader, King Guy, Prince Reynald, the brother of the king, the prince who was lord of Shawbak, the son of Humfrey, the son of the Lady of Tiberias, the Master of the Templars, the lord of Jubayl and the Master of the Hospitallers. The rest of the commanders were killed, and the lowly soldiers were divided up, either to be slain or made captive. Everyone not killed was made prisoner. Some nobles amongst them willingly surrendered in fear for their lives. Someone I trust told me that in the Hawran he met a single person holding a tent-rope with which all by himself he was pulling along thirty odd prisoners because of the desperate defeat that had befallen them.

As for their leaders that survived, we shall recount their fate. The count who fled arrived at Tripoli and was taken ill with pleurisy, and thus God brought about his death. As for the officers of the Hospitallers and the Templars, the sultan chose to put them to death and killed them all without exception. The sultan had vowed to kill Prince Reynald if he got him in his power. This was because a caravan from Egypt had passed through his land at Shawbak during the state of truce. They halted there under safe conduct, but he treacherously killed them. The sultan heard of this and religion and his zeal encouraged him to swear that, if he seized his person, he would kill him. After God had bestowed the great victory on him, the sultan sat in the entrance lobby of his tent, for it had not been fully erected, while people were offering him prisoners and any commanders they had found. The [main] tent was then erected and he sat there in great delight, expressing his gratitude for the favour that God had shown him. Then he summoned King Guy, his brother and Prince Reynald. He handed the king a drink of iced julep, from which he drank, being dreadfully thirsty, and he then passed some of it to Prince Reynald. The sultan said to the interpreter, "Tell the King, 'You are the one giving him a drink. I have not given him any drink.'" According to the fine custom of the Arabs and their noble ways, if a prisoner took food or a drink of water from whoever had captured him, his life was safe. His intention was to follow these noble ways.

He ordered them to proceed to a place assigned for their lodging. They did so and ate something. Then the sultan summoned them again, now having with him none but a few servants. He gave the king a seat in the vestibule and, having summoned Prince Reynald, confronted him as he had said. He said to him, "Here I am, having asked for victory through Muhammad, and God has given me victory over you." He offered him Islam but he refused. The sultan then drew his scimitar and

---

[6]Through his death soon afterwards (see below).

struck him, severing his arm at his shoulder. Those present finished him off and God speedily sent his soul to Hell-fire. His body was taken and thrown down at the door of the tent. The king, when he saw him brought out in this manner, was convinced that he would be next. The sultan called him in and reassured him, saying, "It has not been customary for princes to kill princes, but this man transgressed his limits, so he has suffered what he suffered." That night was spent by our people in the most complete joy and perfect delight, raising their voices in praise of God and gratitude towards him, with cries of "God is great!" and "There is no god but God!" until day-break on Sunday.

62

Tsunetomo Yamamoto, *Hagakure* (The Way of the Samurai)

In the ninth century, as the aristocracy-dominated central government of Japan weakened and lost control of the provinces, the local gentry began to fortify its own armed constabulary forces. The leaders of these armed groups were called "the bushi" or "samurai," and they were largely descendants of the old provincial *uji* (clan) aristocracy. The bushi were mounted; armored; armed with bows, arrows, and curved swords; and accompanied by supporting foot soldiers. By the twelfth century, they had begun to emerge as a dominant social class, providing the key values that permeated life in medieval Japan. They became rulers and guardians of peace as well as fighters.

As clashes among the local armed groups became more frequent, the smaller ones were absorbed into larger and more powerful ones. These groups were eventually consolidated into two powerful rival military clans, one under Minamoto in eastern Japan and the other under Taira in the west. In 1156, a dispute over the imperial succession pitted them against each other in a series of struggles that continued until 1185. At this time, Minamoto Yoritomo (1147–1199) emerged as the unchallenged military master of Japan. In 1192, the court bestowed upon Minamoto Yoritomo the title of *Seii-tai-shogun* ("Barbarian-Subduing Generalissimo"). This title was once given to generals in charge of expeditions against the Ainu (old proto-Caucasoid inhabitants of Japan), but henceforth it was used in the shortened form of "Shogun" to denote supreme military commander. The country was governed from Minamoto's military headquarters at Kamakura. For the next seven hundred years, until the Meiji Restoration in 1868, Japan was ruled by the men of the sword. The samurai culture rooted in *Bushido* (meaning "the way of the warrior") flourished.

Bushido was roughly equivalent to medieval European chivalry or the noblesse oblige of the warrior class. Although it did not evolve into an articulated code of conduct for the ruling samurai class until the late seventeenth century, the incipient stage goes back to about the tenth century. The principles of Bushido were to be observed by the warrior in his daily life as well as in his vocation. An unwritten code consisting of a few maxims, Bushido was primarily transmitted orally or through the pen of some well-known warrior or savant. The principles of Bushido were drawn from Zen Buddhism, Shintoism, and the Confucian moral precepts. They stressed justice, honor, duty, loyalty, courage, self-control, and a transcendent fearlessness in the face of death.

The following excerpt is from *Hagakure* (In the Shadow of Leaves), which is one of the best-known classics on Bushido. This book contains the teachings of Tsunetomo Yamamoto (1659–1719), who was a samurai turned Zen monk. Written and compiled in 1716 by Yamamoto's student Tsuramoto Tashiro, the *Hagakure* emphasizes the samurai philosophy of dying.

QUESTIONS TO CONSIDER

1. Compare and contrast Bushido with the medieval European chivalric code. How were they similar? How were they different? (See Readings 59 and 60.)
2. What aspects of Bushido were drawn from Confucianism and from Buddhism?

The Way of the Samurai is found in death. When it comes to either/or, there is only the quick choice of death. It is not particularly difficult. Be determined and advance. To say that dying without reaching one's aim is to die a dog's death is the frivolous way of sophisticates. When pressed with the choice of life or death, it is not necessary to gain one's aim.

We all want to live. And in large part we make our logic according to what we like. But not having attained our aim and continuing to live is cowardice. This is a thin dangerous line. To die without gaining one's aim is a dog's death and fanaticism. But there is no shame in this. This is the substance of the Way of the Samurai. If by setting one's heart right every morning and evening, one is able to live as though his body were already dead, he gains freedom in the Way. His whole life will be without blame, and he will succeed in his calling. . . .

Being a retainer is nothing other than being a supporter of one's lord, entrusting matters of good and evil to him, and renouncing self-interest. If there are but two or three men of this type, the fief will be secure.

If one looks at the world when affairs are going smoothly, there are many who go about putting in their appearance, being useful by their wisdom, discrimination and artfulness. However, if the lord should retire or go into seclusion, there are many who will quickly turn their backs on him and ingratiate themselves to the man of the day. Such a thing is unpleasant even to think about. Men of high position, low position, deep wisdom and artfulness all feel that they are the ones who are working righteously, but when it comes to the point of throwing away one's life for his lord, all get weak in the knees. This is rather disgraceful. The fact that a useless person often becomes a matchless warrior at such times is because he has already given up his life and has become one with his lord. At the time of Mitsushige's death there was an example of this. His one resolved attendant was I alone. The others followed in my wake. Always the pretentious, self-asserting notables turn their backs on the man just as his eyes are closing in death.

From Tsunetomo Yamamoto, *Hagakurer: The Book of the Samurai*, trans. William Scott Wilson (Tokyo and New York: Kodansha International, Ltd., 1979), pp. 17–18, 20–21, 33–34, 66–67. Reprinted with permission from Kodansha International; © 1979. All rights reserved.

Loyalty is said to be important in the pledge between lord and retainer. Though it may seem unobtainable, it is right before your eyes. If you once set yourself to it, you will become a superb retainer at that very moment. . . .

Every morning, the samurai of fifty or sixty years ago would bathe, shave their foreheads, put lotion in their hair, cut their fingernails and toenails rubbing them with pumice and then with wood sorrel, and without fail pay attention to their personal appearance. It goes without saying that their armor in general was kept free from rust, that it was dusted, shined, and arranged.

Although it seems that taking special care of one's appearance is similar to showiness, it is nothing akin to elegance. Even if you are aware that you may be struck down today and are firmly resolved to an inevitable death, if you are slain with an unseemly appearance, you will show your lack of previous resolve, will be despised by your enemy, and will appear unclean. For this reason it is said that both old and young should take care of their appearance.

Although you say that this is troublesome and time-consuming, a samurai's work is in such things. It is neither busy-work nor time-consuming. In constantly hardening one's resolution to die in battle, deliberately becoming as one already dead, and working at one's job and dealing with military affairs, there should be no shame. But when the time comes, a person will be shamed if he is not conscious of these things even in his dreams, and rather passes his days in self-interest and self-indulgence. And if he thinks that this is not shameful, and feels that nothing else matters as long as he is comfortable, then his dissipate and discourteous actions will be repeatedly regrettable.

The person without previous resolution to inevitable death makes certain that his death will be in bad form. But if one is resolved to death beforehand, in what way can he be despicable? One should be especially diligent in this concern.

Furthermore, during the last thirty years customs have changed; now when young samurai get together, if there is not just talk about money matters, loss and gain, secrets, clothing styles or matters of sex, there is no reason to gather together at all. Customs are going to pieces. One can say that formerly when a man reached the age of twenty or thirty, he did not carry despicable things in his heart, and thus neither did such words appear. If an elder unwittingly said something of that sort, he thought of it as a sort of injury. This new custom probably appears because people attach importance to being beautiful before society and to household finances. What things a person should be able to accomplish if he had no haughtiness concerning his place in society!

It is a wretched thing that the young men of today are so contriving and so proud of their material possessions. Men with contriving hearts are lacking in duty. Lacking in duty, they will have no self-respect. . . .

If one were to say in a word what the condition of being a samurai is, its basis lies first in seriously devoting one's body and soul to his master. And if one is asked what to do beyond this, it would be to fit oneself inwardly with intelligence, humanity and courage. The combining of these three virtues may seem unobtainable to the ordinary person, but it is easy. Intelligence is nothing more than discussing things with others. Limitless wisdom comes from this. Humanity is something done for the sake of others, simply comparing oneself with them and putting them in the fore. Courage is gritting one's teeth; it is simply doing that and pushing ahead, paying no attention to the circumstances. Anything that seems above these three is not necessary to be known.

As for outward aspects, there are personal appearance, one's way of speaking and calligraphy. And as all of these are daily matters, they improve by constant practice. Basically, one should perceive their nature to be one of quiet strength. If one has accomplished all these things, then he should have a knowledge of our area's history and customs. After that he may study the various arts as recreation. If you think it over, being a retainer is simple. And these days, if you observe people who are even a bit useful, you will see that they have accomplished these three outward aspects.

63

The Forty-Seven Ronin

One of the most celebrated episodes in Japanese history is the vendetta of the forty-seven Ronin.[7] This story of the samurai ideals of loyalty and honor has been told innumerable times, on the stage and in literature, and has become an important part of the heritage of the Japanese people. Although its origins can be dated to the early eighteenth century, when the warrior class reigned supreme under the Tokugawa shogunate (1600–1867), the chivalric ideals it expresses were the essence of the samurai culture of feudal Japan. In the spring of 1701, Asano Naganori, lord of the small fief of Ako in western Japan, was charged by the shogunal government with the reception of an imperial envoy from Kyoto. He was put under the guidance of Kira Yoshinaka, the shogun's chief of protocol, to prepare for this event. Lord Asano, who was inexperienced in the fine details of protocol, was ridiculed by Kira, who was reputed to be arrogant and corrupt. Pushed to the limits of his patience, Lord Asano drew his sword and wounded Kira in violation of the law prohibiting the drawing of a sword in the shogun's castle. For this offense, Lord Asano was ordered to commit suicide, and his domain was confiscated. His retainers suddenly found themselves masterless. Believing that Asano was a victim of Kira's arrogance and wrongdoing, forty-seven of Asano's most single-mindedly loyal retainers, led by the senior retainer Oishi Kuranosuke, vowed to avenge their lord's death. After long and careful planning, forty-six conspirators[8] burst into Kira's mansion in Edo[9] and killed Kira Yoshinaka. They carried Kira's head to the Sengakuji temple outside Edo and offered it to their Lord Asano's grave. Their vendetta was thus completed. In February 1703, after much controversy surrounding the case, the Ronin were finally punished by the shogunal government, not for the murder of Kira but for their contempt of authority, and were ordered to commit hara-kiri—ritual disembowelment. The bodies of the samurai, ranging in age from fifteen to seventy-seven, were interred in the Sengakuji temple near their master's grave. The following two letters, the first of which was allegedly found on the person of each of the forty-seven men and the second of which was laid upon the tomb of their master, together with the head of Kira, reflect the fanatical devotion of these samurai to the ideals of the feudal warrior in Japan.

---

[7]Masterless samurai or warriors.

[8]One of the forty-seven did not participate in the final act of the vendetta but remains as an honorary member.

[9]Present-day Tokyo.

QUESTIONS TO CONSIDER

1. If you were the judge assigned to this case, how would you rule? How would you reconcile the conflict between private morality and public law? Should the forty-seven Ronin have been acquitted? Why?
2. How would you compare the issues raised in this reading with the issues suggested in *Antigone* (see Reading 33)?

Last year in the third month, Asano Takumi no Kami (Lord Asano), upon the occasion of the entertainment of the Imperial ambassador, was driven, by the force of the circumstances, to attack and wound my Lord Kotsuke no Suke (Kira Yoshinaka) in the castle, in order to avenge an insult offered to him. Having done this without considering the dignity of the place, and having thus disregarded all rules of propriety, he was condemned to hara kiri, and his property and castle of Ako were forfeited to the State, and were delivered up by his retainers to the officers deputed by the Shogun to receive them. After this his followers were all dispersed. At the time of the quarrel, the high officials prevented [Lord Asano] from carrying out his intention of killing his enemy, my Lord Kotsuke no Suke [Kira]. So Asano Takumi no Kami [Lord Asano] died without having avenged himself, and this was more than his retainers could endure. It is impossible to remain under the same heaven with the enemy of lord or father; for this reason we have dared to declare enmity against a personage of so exalted rank. This day we shall attack Kira Kotsuke no Suke, in order to finish the deed of vengeance which was begun by our dead lord. If any honorable person should find our bodies after death, he is respectfully requested to open and read this document.

15th year of Genroku, 12th month[10]

> Signed, Oishi Kuranosuke, Retainer of Asano
> Takumino no Kami, and forty-six others

The 15th year of Genroku, the 12th month, and the 15th day. We have come this day to do homage here, forty-seven men in all, from Oishi Kuranosuke down to the foot-soldier Terasaka Kichiemon, all cheerfully about to lay down our lives on your behalf. We reverently announce this to the honored spirit of our dead master. On the 14th day of the third month of last year our honored master was pleased to attack Kira Kotsuke no Suke, for what reason we know not. Our honored master put an end to his own life, but Kira Kotsuke no Suke lived. Although we fear that after the decree issued by the Government this plot of ours will be displeasing to our honored master, still we, who have eaten of your food, could not without blushing repeat the verse, "Thou shall not live under the same heaven, nor tread the same earth with the enemy of thy father or lord," nor could we have dared to leave hell and present ourselves before you in paradise, unless we had carried out the vengeance which you began. Every day that we waited seemed as three autumns to us. Verily, we have trodden the snow for one day, nay, for two days, and have tasted food but once. The old and decrepit, the sick and ailing, have come forth gladly to lay down lives. Men might laugh at us, as at grasshoppers trusting in the strength of their arms, and thus shame our honored

[10]1702.

lord; but we could not halt in our deed of vengeance. Having taken counsel together last night, we have escorted my Lord Kotsuke no Suke hither to your tomb. This dirk[11] by which our honored lord set great store last year, and entrusted to our care, we now bring back. If your noble spirit be now present before this tomb, we pray you, as a sign, to take the dirk, and, striking the head of your enemy with it a second time, to dispel your hatred for ever. This is the respectful statement of forty-seven men.

East-West Images and Realities

A t present, most historians agree that they should attempt to write as impartially and factually as possible, even though each is a product of his or her own culture. This was not the case, however, with the historians of the distant past.

The first two selections that follow substantiate the xenophobic stance common in early historical accounts. They reflect an aversion to alien things, supported by a view that the writer's own culture is somehow morally or culturally superior to that of the strange and barbaric or decadent peoples with whom he or she has had some contact. Liutprand's *A Mission to Constantinople* describes nothing that is good about the Byzantines (e.g., their food, clothing, or entertainments) compared with people at the German court. Christian Crusaders were seen by most Muslim authors as ruthless, unbelieving barbarians who carved out their feudal states in the Near East at the expense of the native population.

The fourth selection, from *The Travels of Sir John Mandeville*, illustrates the opposite extreme of stereotyping: the portrayal of faraway places as utopian, abounding in riches and harmonious relationships among their peoples. Generally in the medieval West, the not-too-distant East populated by Byzantines and Arabs was viewed with suspicion, whereas what their writers called "the Far East" tended to be viewed much more favorably.

64

Liutprand, Bishop of Cremona, *A Mission to Constantinople*

In theory, all medieval Christians recognized the leadership within a single church until 1054, when the leaders of what we know as the Roman Catholic Church in the West and the Greek Orthodox Church in the East broke with each other and remain separate to this day. In reality, differences in style and theology had come to alienate the Greek-oriented Easterners from their counterparts in the West well before 1054. The self-image of the Easterners was one of pride in continuing Roman civilization with sophistication and refinement; Westerners appeared rough and

---

[11]A dirk is a dagger. The dirk with which Lord Asano disemboweled himself, and with which Oishi Kuranosuke cut off Kira's head.

savage by contrast. The self-image of Westerners was one of being honest and straightforward, as well as fearless in facing enemies; Easterners appeared devious and decadent by contrast.

In 968, the Western or Holy Roman Emperor Otto I sent Bishop Liutprand of Cremona, Italy, to the court of the Eastern Emperor Nicephorus Phocas to negotiate a marriage between his son, Otto II, whom he had made his coruler, and Princess Theophano, the daughter of Romanus II, Byzantine emperor between 959 and 963. His hope was that the marriage would help overcome strife between Greeks and Saxons over territories in Italy claimed by both empires. Liutprand's account of his stay in Constantinople, a much-condensed version of which follows, conveys the conflict of cultural images vividly. In reporting to the Ottos, he is determined not to let Easterners get away with their boasts of living on a higher plane of civilization. (Some of his complaints were also reported by Western crusaders in the following centuries.) His complaints range from an emphatic rejection of the most common Greek wine to indignation over Greek attempts to overcharge him for everything. (Even today, Western travelers in Greece are likely to remark that retsina, the resinated wine that Greeks favor above all others, "tastes a little like turpentine" or, more kindly, "is going to take a little getting used to.") Like many Westerners then and later, Liutprand found the eunuchs at the Eastern capital to be proof of the degraded and effeminate nature of Byzantine society. Wearing apparel was another source of conflict. The fur-trimmed leather garments, in which Germanic Europeans took much pride, seem to have been harshly criticized by their southern and eastern counterparts since the days of the great migrations. In the selection that follows, Liutprand is very defensive on this score. In a section not included in the reading, he refers to the long-sleeved, silky garments of the East as of a type "that only streetwalkers and sorcerers wear" in the West.

Still, both East and West were moved by the feeling that they should pull toward unity, particularly in the face of the Muslim threat. Liutprand's mission foundered at the time on the shoals of mutual dislike, but the following year Nicephorus was assassinated by his nephew, John Zimisces, who became emperor; and in 972, under this new Eastern regime, Otto II did, in fact, marry the Princess Theophano, whom Liutprand had attempted to secure for him as a bride. From the perspective of centuries, however, Theophano's genteel influence scarcely put a dent in East-West ethnic prejudices. The mutual excommunications of 1054 and the sacking of Constantinople by western crusaders a hundred and fifty years after that attest to the fragile nature of East-West medieval Christian harmony.

QUESTIONS TO CONSIDER

1. How does Liutprand mentally cope with the wealth and scope of the Byzantine Empire?
2. What main elements in the Westerners' self-image emerge in Liutprand's account?
3. Nearly a thousand years after Liutprand's mission, we find *Webster's Biographical Dictionary*, which we generally recognize as a fairly dispassionate source of in-

formation, noting that when Princess Theophano married Otto and came to the West, she "had great influence at his court, introducing much of the refinement of Constantinople."[12] Liutprand died in 972 or thereabouts, but if he had lived another ten or fifteen years, how do you suppose he would have judged the efforts of a Byzantine-born empress to upgrade the culture of the Saxon court?

When we arrived in Constantinople on June 4, we were received very shabbily as a sign of disrespect to you, and afterwards treated the same way. They shut us up in a palace of sorts, which was big enough, all right, but had no roof to keep out heat or cold. Armed soldiers stood guard outside, to keep any of my companions from going out or anyone else from coming in. We were located so far away from the palace of Nicephorus that we were always out of breath from the long walk up to it whenever we went. We found the Greek wine, which is mixed with tar, resin, and plaster unfit to drink, but we could not even *buy* water to quench our thirst. No earthly being, but only one from hell, could be compared to the warden assigned to look after our daily needs. Like a drenching cloudburst, his inventiveness soaked us with misfortunes, extortions, torture, and grief for a hundred and twenty days.

On June 7, I was led before Nicephorus, a human freak with a very wide head and eyes as small as a mole's. He is thoroughly repulsive to look at with a thick neck less than an inch in length, long and bristly hair, Ethiopian skin color, drooping paunch and short stature. He is of a type you would hope not to meet up with after dark. And his clothes! They are very costly but ancient, faded, and bad-smelling. I always thought of my own august lords and emperors as handsome, but this horrible sight made me appreciate your handsome qualities all the more. In the same way, I was always aware of your great magnificence, power, kindness, and virtue: How much more did being with Nicephorus make me appreciate these even more!

Both these rulers . . . , the King of the Greeks and the King of the Franks[13] are men . . . , but they are as different from each other—I would exaggerate only a little if I said: as species of animals differ from each other—as people of a sound mind differ from the insane. The King of the Greeks wears long hair and a tunic with long sleeves and a hood. He is lying, scheming, without mercy, fox-like, proud, insincerely humble, stingy, and greedy. He eats garlic, onions, and leeks, and he drinks bathwater. By way of contrast, the King of the Franks wears his hair tastefully trimmed, his clothing is altogether different from a woman's, and he wears a hat. He is truthful, straightforward, merciful when this is appropriate but severe when it is not. He is always sincerely humble and never stingy. He does not live on garlic, onions, and leeks, nor does he pile up money by saving animals to sell rather than having them to eat. . . .

[Liutprand was defending the Western imperial position on governing areas in Italy claimed by the Byzantines, when Nicephorus interrupted him:][14] "It is time for

---

[12]*Webster's Biographical Dictionary* (Springfield, MA: G. & C. Merriam, 1960), p. 1131.

[13]By Liutprand's time, the term "Frank" no longer applied simply to the original ethnic group of that name, but to any people associated with running the Germanic or Holy Roman Empire. By the time of the Crusades, it had become a rather generic term for Westerners as opposed to inhabitants of the East, and Asians from Arabia to China called all Western peoples "Franks."

[14]Material in brackets is the editor's condensed summary of Liutprand's writing.

From "*Legatio*," in *Liudprandi episcopi Ceremonensis opera omina* (Hannover: Hahn, 1877), chs. i.–xl, *passim*. Trans. and condensed by Henry A. Myers: calendar usage modernized.

the solemn procession to the church. Let us attend to the needs of the hour, and when I have some time I will take up your requests again."

And what a procession it was indeed, with craftsmen and base-born people lining both sides of the road in masses thick as walls from the palace to Saint Sophia's. They were made even uglier than they already were by the thin little shields and flimsy spears which many of them carried. The fact that they came barefooted, which I think was to honor Nicephorus, made them more disgusting than ever to look at. The nobles who passed through that multitude of low-lifes were wearing tunics that were really old. Their grandfathers must have worn those self-same garments, which were very, very old even when their grandfathers wore them. None of them was wearing any gold, not even jewels, except Nicephorus himself; however, the symbols of imperial majesty which had been made for his imperial predecessors simply made him all the more loathsome to look at. I swear by your very salvation, which I value more than my own, that one precious garment of any of your nobles is worth more than a hundred of the things his were wearing. I had to take part in this procession and ended up on a platform next to the singers.

When Nicephorus, like a slithering reptile, reached the cathedral's interior, the singers chanted loudly: "Behold the Morning Star as he approaches. His glances do reflect the sun's own rays: Nicephorus, our ruler, who brings swift death to Muslims." They kept on like that: "A long life to our ruler, Nicephorus! Worship him, O people, adore him; bow your heads to him alone." It would have been much more appropriate if they had sung: "Come to us, burnt-out wood-ember that you are, fool who looks like an evil spirit of the forest and walks like an old woman; you double-jointed rebel, scaly-headed, bristly of hide, totally rural, barbarian, rude serf-by-nature, most at home in filthy places!" And so, blown up by the lying chants of dunces, he entered Saint Sophia's.

That day he asked me to dinner, but, acting as if I were unworthy to be placed above any of his nobles, he assigned me a seat fifteen places away from him without even a tablecloth in front of me. The meal was completely disgusting; everything smelt bad. All the food was soaked in oil, and they washed it all down with a perfectly awful kind of spicy fish juice. During that meal he asked me many questions about you, the lands you rule, and the forces which serve you. Then when I had given him true and straightforward answers, he accused me of lying.

Eight days later, he invited me back again, thinking no doubt that I would appreciate the food and drink he served. Many bishops were there, including the Patriarch of Constantinople. He asked me many Bible questions, which I answered eloquently enough, but then he tried to make fun of us by comparing the great church councils which have been held in the East with the lack of them in the West. [The Patriarch implied that the dearth of councils held in Western cities showed that the Christian faith there was not mature; for Liutprand, however, councils had the function of coping with heresies, so that a lack of them meant a lack of heresy in the region.] I answered: "It is the member of the body which is afflicted that must be cauterized with a hot iron. All heresies have come from your territory. We of the Western nations have strangled them and put an end to them. The Saxon people have produced no heresies from the time they first received baptism and the knowledge of God. With no errors of doctrine among them, they had no need of holding church councils. I am willing to agree with you that faith among the Saxons is young: Faith in Christ is always young, not old, in people who actually live according to it. Where people do not live according to the faith, where people scorn it and throw it away like worn-out clothes—that is where faith is old. But let me add that I do know for sure of one council held by Saxons: It determined that it is better to fight with swords than with pens and to submit to death than run from the enemy. Your own army has learned the truth confirmed by that council." And to myself I said: "May the Saxons soon have a chance to show what they can do in war!"

I just hope you believe me—and, of course, I know that you will believe me—when I tell you that [if war reoccurs in Italy] four hundred of your fighting men can slay the whole army dispatched by Nicephorus, unless they survive by hiding behind ditches and walls. It seems to me that it is as if to show his scorn of you that he has given the command of this army to a kind of man—I say "kind of" because he has ceased to be a male and has not yet been able to become a female.

[By mid-September, the outcome of Liutprand's mission seemed very much in doubt. When Nicephorus appeared reluctant to let him leave, Liutprand indicated to a group of Byzantine nobles that Emperor Otto might consider taking vengeance on the Greeks for having detained his messenger so long.] "If he tries it," they said, "neither Italy, nor the poor region of Saxony, land of his birth, where the natives go around in wild animal skins, will be able to protect him. Our money gives us power, and with it we will rally all manner of peoples against him. We will break him like a clay pot, which, once shattered, cannot be put back together again." [These nobles also seized some purple garments from Liutprand and his companions in a forced purchase, saying that they were too good for people from the West.] How totally inappropriate it is that these soft, effeminate, lying, neutered, idle creatures with their long sleeves, hoods, and veils should go around in purple, while heroes representing you, strong warriors that they are, experienced in the military arts, possessing love and the true faith—men who hold God in real reverence and are full of virtues—may not. What is this, if not horrendous vanity!

Those who seek God upon false paths shall never find Him!

65

Memoirs of Usamah Ibn-Munqidh

By the mid-tenth century, the once mighty Abbasid caliphs [the head of state] of Baghdad were puppets of their own bodyguards. About a century later, Turkish nomads, the Seljuks, who had come from Central Asia into Iran and had converted to Islam, rescued the caliphs. These Seljuk sultans slowly extended their political power from Iran-Iraq through Syria and Palestine. In 1071, the Byzantine emperor, Romanus IV Diogenes, tried to stop Seljuk raids into Anatolia (modern Turkey), but he was defeated at Manzikert. The Seljuks soon took over most of Anatolia from the Byzantine government.

Soon, however, the Seljuk sultanate broke up into quarreling petty states. This situation, plus appeals from the Byzantines and the Seljuk restrictions on the number of Christian pilgrims to the Holy Land, led Pope Urban II in 1095 to call for the First Crusade (1096–1099). The Crusaders, or Franks, as Muslim authors refer to them, were able to create a series of Western states along the Mediterranean coast from Anatolia to Egypt. These states did not last. The Turkish lord of Mosul, Zangi, and the Kurdish warrior Saladin became the anti-crusading champions as they recaptured northern Syria and then Jerusalem by 1187.

One Arab-Syrian who lived through this period was Usamah Ibn-Munqidh. He was born in 1095 to one of the most important families of the area who controlled the Castle of Shayzar on the Orontes River, which guarded routes into northern Syria or south into Lebanon. Usamah was given such a well-rounded education by his father that he not only gained military fame in fighting the Franks but was also considered a world traveler, poet, and scholar. His fame was so great that Saladin appointed him a lecturer on Islamic law and tutor in rhetoric in one of the academies in Damascus.

The following selections from Usamah's memoirs relate a personal view of the Franks. Although the Crusaders are referred to as "devils" or "infidels" whose morals were both shocking or amusing to a conservative Muslim, Usamah developed a friendship with and respect for some of the Christians.

QUESTIONS TO CONSIDER

1. Compare the culture and society of Western Europe to that of the Near East. Why did the Franks seem barbaric to the Muslims?
2. Why would the sexual customs of the Franks shock Usamah?
3. How did Western Europe and Islamic society treat women?
4. Is there any indication that relations between the Franks and Muslims were not solely as enemies?
5. Compare the present selection with the Portuguese and Spanish relations with Africa and the New World (see Readings 101 to 104). What are some similar or different attitudes?

Their curious medication

A case illustrating their curious medicine is the following:

The lord of al-Munaytirah[15] wrote to my uncle asking him to dispatch a physician to treat certain sick persons among his people. My uncle sent him a Christian physician named Thābit. Thābit was absent but ten days when he returned. So we said to him, "How quickly hast thou healed thy patients!" He said:

They brought before me a knight in whose leg an abscess had grown; and a woman afflicted with imbecility.[16] To the knight I applied a small poultice until the abscess opened and became well; and the woman I put on diet and made her humor wet. Then a Frankish physician came to them and said, "This man knows nothing about treating them." He then said to the knight, "Which wouldst thou prefer, living with one leg or dying with two?" The latter replied, "Living with one leg." The physician said, "Bring me a strong knight and a sharp ax." A knight came with the ax. And I was standing by. Then the physician laid the leg of the patient on a block of wood and bade the knight

---

[15]In Lebanon near Afqah, the source of Nahr-Ibrāhīm, i.e., ancient Adonis.

[16]Ar. *nashāf,* "dryness," is not used as a name of a disease. I take the word therefore to be Persian *nishāf*—"imbecility."

strike his leg with the ax and chop it off at one blow. Accordingly he struck it—while I was looking on—one blow, but the leg was not severed. He dealt another blow, upon which the marrow of the leg flowed out and the patient died on the spot. He then examined the woman and said, "This is a woman in whose head there is a devil which has possessed her. Shave off her hair." Accordingly they shaved it off and the woman began once more to eat their ordinary diet—garlic and mustard. Her imbecility took a turn for the worse. The physician then said, "The devil has penetrated through her head." He therefore took a razor, made a deep cruciform [cross-shaped] incision on it, peeled off the skin at the middle of the incision until the bone of the skull was exposed and rubbed it with salt. The woman also expired instantly. Thereupon I asked them whether my services were needed any longer, and when they replied in the negative I returned home, having learned of their medicine what I knew not before.

Newly arrived Franks are especially rough: One insists that Usāmah should pray eastward

Everyone who is a fresh emigrant from the Frankish lands is ruder in character than those who have become acclimatized and have held long association with the Moslems. Here is an illustration of their rude character.

Whenever I visited Jerusalem I always entered the Aqsa Mosque, beside which stood a small mosque which the Franks had converted into a church. When I used to enter the Aqsa Mosque, which was occupied by the Templars,[17] who were my friends, the Templars would evacuate the little adjoining mosque so that I might pray in it. One day[18] I entered this mosque, repeated the first formula, "Allah is great," and stood up in the act of praying, upon which one of the Franks rushed on me, got hold of me and turned my face eastward saying, "This is the way thou shouldst pray!" A group of Templars hastened to him, seized him and repelled him from me. I resumed my prayer. The same man, while the others were otherwise busy, rushed once more on me and turned my face eastward, saying, "This is the way thou shouldst pray!" The Templars again came in to him and expelled him. They apologized to me, saying, "This is a stranger who has only recently arrived from the land of the Franks and he has never before seen anyone praying except eastward." Thereupon I said to myself, "I have had enough prayer." So I went out and have ever been surprised at the conduct of this devil of a man, at the change in the color of his face, his trembling and his sentiment at the sight of one praying towards the qiblah.[19]

Another wants to show to a Moslem God as a child

I saw one of the Franks come to al-Amīr [chieftain] Mu'īn-al-Dīn (may Allah's mercy rest upon his soul!) when he was in the Dome of the Rock[20] and say to him, "Dost thou want to see God as a child?" Mu'īn-al-Din said, "Yes." The Frank walked ahead of us until he showed us the picture of Mary with Christ (may peace be upon him!) as an infant in her lap. He then said, "This is God as a child." But Allah is exalted far above what the infidels say about him!

---

[17]Knights Templars were members of a military religious order called the Knights of the Temple of Solomon, named from their house in Jerusalem.
[18]About 1140.
[19]The direction of the Ka'bah in the holy city, Mecca.
[20]The mosque standing near al-Aqṣa in Jerusalem.

Franks lack jealousy in sex affairs

The Franks are void of all zeal and jealousy. One of them may be walking along with his wife. He meets another man who takes the wife by the hand and steps aside to converse with her while the husband is standing on one side waiting for his wife to conclude the conversation. If she lingers too long for him, he leaves her alone with the conversant and goes away. . . .

We had with us a bath-keeper named Sālim, originally an inhabitant of al-Ma'arrah,[21] who had charge of the bath of my father (may Allah's mercy rest upon his soul!). This man related the following story:

I once opened a bath in al-Ma'arrah in order to earn my living. To this bath there came a Frankish knight. The Franks disapprove of girding a cover around one's waist while in the bath. So this Frank stretched out his arm and pulled off my cover from my waist and threw it away. He looked and saw that I had recently shaved off my pubes. So he shouted, "Sālim!" As I drew near him he stretched his hand over my pubes and said, "Sālim, good! By the truth of my religion, do the same for me." Saying this, he lay on his back and I found that in that place the hair was like his beard. So I shaved it off. Then he passed his hand over the place and, finding it smooth, he said, "Sālim, by the truth of my religion, do the same to madame" (al-dāma in their language means the lady), referring to his wife. He then said to a servant of his, "Tell madame to come here." Accordingly the servant went and brought her and made her enter the bath. She also lay on her back. The knight repeated, "Do what thou has done to me." So I shaved all that hair while her husband was sitting looking at me. At last he thanked me and handed me the pay for my service.

Consider now this great contradiction! They have neither jealousy nor zeal but they have great courage, although courage is nothing but the product of zeal and of ambition to be above ill repute.

Their judicial trials: a duel

I attended one day a duel in Nāblus between two Franks. The reason for this was that certain Moslem thieves took by surprise one of the villages of Nāblus. One of the peasants of that village was charged with having acted as guide for the thieves when they fell upon the village. So he fled away. The king[22] sent and arrested his children. The peasant thereupon came back to the king and said, "Let justice be done in my case. I challenge to a duel the man who claimed that I guided the thieves to the village." The king then said to the tenant who held the village in fief, "Bring forth someone to fight the duel with him." The tenant went to his village, where a blacksmith lived, took hold of him and ordered him to fight the duel. The tenant became thus sure of the safety of his own peasants, none of whom would be killed and his estate ruined.

I saw this blacksmith. He was a physically strong young man, but his heart failed him. He would walk a few steps and then sit down and ask for a drink. The one who had made the challenge was an old man, but he was strong in spirit and he would rub the nail of his thumb against that of the forefinger in defiance, as if he was not worrying over the duel. Then came the viscount, i.e., the seignior of the town, and

---

[21]Ma'arrah-al-Nu'mān, between Ḥamāh and Aleppo.

[22]Fulk of Anjou, King of Jerusalem (1131–1142).

gave each one of the two contestants a cudgel and a shield and arranged the people in a circle around them.

The two met. The old man would press the blacksmith backward until he would get him as far as the circle, then he would come back to the middle of the arena. They went on exchanging blows until they looked like pillars smeared with blood. The contest was prolonged and the viscount began to urge them to hurry, saying, "Hurry on." The fact that the smith was given to the use of the hammer proved now of great advantage to him. The old man was worn out and the smith gave him a blow which made him fall. His cudgel fell under his back. The smith knelt down over him and tried to stick his fingers into the eyes of his adversary, but could not do it because of the great quantity of blood flowing out. Then he rose up and hit his head with the cudgel until he killed him. They then fastened a rope around the neck of the dead person, dragged him away and hanged him. The lord who brought the smith now came, gave the smith his own mantle, made him mount the horse behind him and rode off with him. This case illustrates the kind of jurisprudence and legal decisions the Franks have—may Allah's curse be upon them!

Ordeal by water

I once went in the company of al-Amīr Mu'īn-al-Dīn (may Allah's mercy rest upon his soul!) to Jerusalem. We stopped at Nāblus. There a blind man, a Moslem, who was still young and was well dressed, presented himself before al-amīr carrying fruits for him and asked permission to be admitted into his service in Damascus. The amīr consented. I inquired about this man and was informed that his mother had been married to a Frank whom she had killed. Her son used to practice ruses against the Frankish pilgrims and coöperate with his mother in assassinating them. They finally brought charges against him and tried his case according to the Frankish way of procedure.

They installed a huge cask and filled it with water. Across it they set a board of wood. They then bound the arms of the man charged with the act, tied a rope around his shoulders and dropped him into the cask, their idea being that in case he was innocent, he would sink in the water and they would then lift him up with the rope so that he might not die in the water; and in case he was guilty, he would not sink in the water. This man did his best to sink when they dropped him into the water, but he could not do it. So he had to submit to their sentence against him— may Allah's curse be upon them! They pierced his eyeballs with red-hot awls [drills].

66

Sir John Mandeville, "The Land of Prester John"

One of the most widely read accounts of travel to the East in the centuries preceding those of the Age of Exploration was *The Travels of Sir John Mandeville*. Nothing of significance is known of the author: It is now generally doubted that he was a knight, and what scanty evidence there is points to an Englishman who fled to France after committing a crime in his homeland and took this name as a pseudonym. Whoever he was, his stories of the fabulous East fascinated audiences in England, France, Spain, and Portugal and helped to strengthen the image of the East as a land of untold riches.

Medieval people had been captivated since the twelfth century by the story of the (fictional) Prester John, who ruled a great Christian kingdom to the East. "Prester" is an English contraction of the Latin *presbyter* (priest), and the man was supposed to combine kingship with priesthood, ruling over vast domains as a benign leader of peoples living in perfect Christian harmony. The earliest accounts of Prester John put him somewhere east of India. Mandeville's geography is problematic when he writes of Prester John. On the one hand, he describes his main capital as Susa, which was in the Persian Empire, but elsewhere his lands appear to be not only east of India but farther away than "Cathay" (China). In the minds of Europeans interested in geography, the locale of Prester John's kingdom shifted from (very roughly) Mongolia to India, and from there to Africa, where the Portuguese were still looking for Prester John in the fifteenth century. Mandeville claimed to have set out on his journey at dates given in the various surviving manuscripts from 1322 to 1332. There is some factuality in his accounts of Arab and Ottoman-controlled territory, including Egypt, which he may well have visited, but it seems doubtful that he actually traveled farther east than that.

QUESTIONS TO CONSIDER

1. What does Mandeville find most striking about Prester John and his kingdom?
2. Some modern commentators believe that Mandeville's attitude toward religion in Prester John's land hints that he may be a heretic, perhaps sympathetic to pre-Reformation criticism of the Roman Catholic Church. Do you get this impression? Why or why not?
3. What impression do Mandeville's pointed assurances that his experiences in Asia are to be trusted make on you?

This emperor Prester John has many diverse countries under his empire, in which are many noble cities and fair towns and many islands great and large. For this land of India is separated into islands because of the great floods that come out of Paradise and run through and divide it. And also in the sea he has many great islands. . . .

This very royal king Prester John and the great Caan of Tartary are evermore allied together through marriage; for each of them weds the daughter or sister of the other one. In the land of Prester John are a great plenty of precious stones of diverse kinds, some of them so great and so large that they make vessels out of them: dishes, bowls, cups and so many other kinds it would take a long time to list them all.

Now I will speak of some of the principal islands of Prester John's land, and of the royalty of his state and what law and belief his people hold. This emperor Prester John is a Christian man, and the most part of his land is also, even if it be so that they do not have all of the articles of our belief so clearly as we have. Not for nought do they trust in God, Father and Son and Holy Ghost, and full devout men they are and true, one to the other, and there is no fraud or guile among them. The emperor has

From *The Voyage and Travaile of Sir John Ma(u)ndeville, Knight, Which Treateth of the Way to Hierusalem [Jerusalem], and of Marvayles of Inde [India] with Other Islands and Countries,* ed. J. O. Halliwell (London: F.S. Ellis, 1866), 121–22, 187–93, *passim;* language modernized.

under his subjection seventy-two provinces, and in each one of them is a king. And these kings have other kings under them, and all are tributaries to the emperor Prester John. In the land of Prester John are many marvels. Among them is a great sea all of gravel and sand and no drop of water therein. And it ebbs and flows as the great sea does in other countries with great waves and nevermore stands still without moving. That sea no man may pass, neither by ship nor otherwise; and therefore it is unknown to any man what kind of land or country is on the other side of that sea. And although there be no water in that sea, nevertheless there is a great plenty of good fishes taken at its seabanks. They are right savory in the mouth, but they are of a different shape from the fishes of other waters. I, John Mandeville, ate of them: therefore, trust me, for surely it is so.

Three days' journey from that sea are great hills, out of which flows a great river that comes from Paradise; and it is full of precious stones but not a drop of water. It runs with great waves into the Gravelly Sea, and then the waves are seen no more. Three days out of every week this river runs so fast that no man dare step into it, but on all the other days men may go into it whenever they will and gather precious stones.

Beyond that river towards the wilderness is a great plain among hills, all sandy and gravelly. On this plain are trees, as it seems, which begin to grow at the rising of the sun and fruit begins to spring out of them. They grow so until it be mid-day, and then they begin to dwindle and turn again into the earth, so that by sunset there is nothing to be seen of them, and they keep doing this every day. . . .

In the aforesaid wilderness are many wild men with horns upon their heads. They dwell in the woods as beasts and do not speak but grunt as swine do. Also in some woods of that land are wild hounds that never will come to men, anymore than foxes will do in this country. And there are fowls who speak in their own way, and they will hail men who come through the deserts, speaking as openly as if they were men. These fowls have large tongues and five nails on each foot. There are others that have only three nails on each foot, and they speak neither so well nor so openly.

When this very great king and emperor Prester John marches into battle against his enemies, he has no banner borne before him, but instead of a banner three crosses of fine gold are borne before him. These are great and high and are well studded with precious stones. Then a thousand knights and more than a hundred thousand men on foot are assigned to guard each cross, in the same way that men guard a banner or a standard in other places. This number of men is always assigned to guard the aforesaid crosses when the emperor sets off for battle: it does not include his principal army, or those of his nobles with their own men—those who are actually to fight the battle—nor does it include wings of troops that are assigned to foraging for provisions.

When he rides forth in peacetime with his personal company of men, a cross of wood is borne before him, with no gold or painting or precious stones on it, in remembrance of Christ's suffering on a cross of wood. Also he has borne before him a plate of gold full of earth, as a token of the fact that he came from the earth and to the earth he shall return. And there is borne before him another vessel full of gold and of such precious stones as rubies, diamonds, sapphires, emeralds, topazes, olivines and many others as a token of his great nobility, lordship and might.

Now I will tell you of the adornment of Prester John's palace, where he commonly resides, at the city of Susa. That palace is so rich, so delightful and so noble, that it is a wonder to tell. For above the principal tower are two large balls of gold, and in each of these are two glowing rubies, great and fair, which shine right clear upon the night.

The principal gates of the palace are of those precious stones that men call "sardonyxes"[23] and their bars are of ivory. The windows of the hall and the chambers are of crystal. All the tables on which they eat are of emeralds, amethysts and some of gold set full of precious stones; and the pillars that bear the tables are of the same manner of precious stones. The steps on which the emperor goes up to his throne where he sets at the meal are: one of onyx, another of crystal, another of jasper, another of amethyst, another of sardony, and another of coral; the highest step, on which he sets his feet at the meal, is of olivine. All these steps are bordered with fine gold, set full of precious stones. The pillars in his chamber are of fine gold, set full of precious stones, of which many are glowing rubies, which give great light at night. Nevertheless, in his chamber he also has twelve crystal vessels full of balm, burning to give off a good and sweet smell and to drive away wicked air. The frame of his bed is all of sapphires, well bound with gold, for to make him sleep well and for to destroy lechery; for he will not lie with wives except four times a year and then only to beget children. . . .

Ye shall understand that every day at his court Prester John has more than thirty thousand people eating, not counting comers and goers. . . . This emperor has seven kings in his court to serve him, and when they have served him a month they return home and another seven kings come and serve another month. And with these kings seventy-two dukes and three hundred and sixty earls are always serving, along with many other lords and knights. Every day twelve archbishops and twenty bishops eat at his court. All archbishops, bishops and abbots there are kings and are great lords over fiefs. And the Patriarch of Saint Thomas is there, as it were, pope. . . .

At the foot of a mountain [in a nearby land] is a well, noble and fair, and the water thereof has a sweet savor and pungent, as it were, of a diverse manner of spicery. And every hour of the day the water changes diversely its savor and smell. And whosoever, fasting, drinks thrice of that well, he shall be whole of whatever manner of malady he has. And thus those who live nearby drink the other therefrom, and therefore they nevermore have sickness, but evermore they seem young. I, John Mandeville, saw this well and drank thereof thrice, and all my fellows, and evermore since that time I feel me the better and the wholer. . . .

It is four months' journey across the width of his land, and its length is beyond measuring. Trust me in all this, for surely I saw it with my own eyes and much more than I have told you. For my fellows and I were dwelling with him in his court a long time and saw all that I have told you and much more than I have leisure for to tell.

Islam and Islam's Enemies

From a world-historical perspective the success of Islamic culture as an enriching and stabilizing force stands out particularly in the centuries between the rise of the Abbasids (see Reading 54) and the beginning of lasting Western, global expansion at the end of the Middle Ages.

In black Africa, the Kingdom of Mali (see Reading 9) embodied the strength and stability of an Islamic society having room to accommodate traditional African values. Such compromises worried Islamic observers with more ortho-

---

[23]Onyxes with parallel layers of sard, a deep-orange variety of chalcedony.

dox backgrounds, such as Ibn Battuta, but they turned out to be quite helpful, providing flexibility for the expansion of Islam throughout most of West Africa.

What corresponds roughly to the medieval period in the West was also the time of greatest academic achievement in the Arab-Islamic world, where universities began thriving in places like Mali's Timbuktu centuries before they took root in the Christian West. Towards the end of the epoch, Ibn Khaldun, probably one of the greater historians and philosophers of history in any culture, set forth his conclusions about the simultaneously inevitable but destructive influences of flight from the countryside and urbanization, basing his work on a huge base of what would later be called "case studies."

Islamic culture in Africa and Spain tended to be relatively tolerant of non-Muslims—making them often pay extra taxes and denying them office-holding privileges but seldom threatening them with violence. The Christian conquest of Jerusalem during the First Crusade had been full of slaughter with Western observers later calmly testifying how the blood of unbelievers flowed in streams through the streets, but the relatively short-lived crusader states of necessity developed patterns of Christian-Muslim coexistence (see Reading 65). In Iberia, after their final victories over the Moors, Spanish rulers saw no reason to tolerate Muslims or Jews in a meaningful way at all, while the Portuguese, as they set up fortified trading stations around the coast of Africa, considered Muslims in Africa fair game—they were all "Moors" to the Portuguese, even in East Africa—although some of them expressed reservations about Christians inflicting violence and death on them for material gain.

67

Ibn Battuta in Mali

Born in Algiers, Ibn Battuta (1304–1368) was the premier world traveler of the Middle Ages. Although Marco Polo's adventures are better known in the West, never did Polo travel as far or see as many different countries as this indefatigable Berber did. In 1325, Ibn Battuta made the first of four visits to the Holy City of Mecca, thereby beginning an itinerary of 75,000 miles. Later in life, this devout Muslim would dictate to a Moroccan scribe an account of his journeys.

For nearly thirty years, Ibn Battuta traveled continuously throughout Africa, the Middle East, Persia, Russia, India, China, and Spain. He made it a rule, if possible, never to travel the same road twice, and he frequently paid the price for taking the less-traveled road. He often was stranded or overcome by disease. His African editors note: "He seems to have experienced most travellers' diseases from Lahore sore to Delhi belly. Only the fact that the New World had not been discovered saved him from Montezuma's revenge."[24]

[24]Said Hamdun and Noel King, eds. and trans., *Ibn Battuta in Black Africa* (London: Rex Collings, 1975), p. 4.

The following selection illustrates the range of Ibn Battuta's travels and also suggests that, by the fourteenth century, Islamic civilization, spanning four continents, was truly the "world" civilization. In 1344, Ibn Battuta left the Malabar coast of India and sailed south to the Maldive Islands, where for eighteen months he served as a judge of Islamic sacred law.

Later, after journeys to Ceylon, China, and Syria, he returned to Algiers. In 1352, on his last journey, he set off on foot across the Sahara to visit the African kingdoms of the Niger basin. His account of this experience is one of the primary records of the social customs in the Kingdom of Mali, particularly the city of Iwalatan (Walata).

In reporting on Black Africa, Ibn Battuta's accounts are basically favorable, but his enthusiasm over the devout acceptance of Islam is offset by reservations about non-Islamic elements in living customs.

QUESTIONS TO CONSIDER

1. Why was Ibn Battuta so troubled by his African hosts' methods of tracing genealogy? Are there political implications of this genealogical system?

The condition of these people [of Iwalatan] is strange and their manners are bizarre. As for their men, there is no sexual jealousy about them. None of them is named after his father, but each traces his genealogy from his maternal uncle. A man's inheritance is not passed to his own sons but to the sons of his sister. I have never seen such a thing in any other part of the world except among the infidels who live on the Malabar coast of India. These people are Muslims who follow exactly the prescribed laws for prayer, study the laws of Islam, and know the Koran by heart. Their women are not modest in the presence of men; despite reciting their prayers punctually, they do not veil their faces. Any male who wishes to marry one of them can do so very easily, but the women do not travel with their husbands for her family would not allow it. In this country, the women are permitted to have male friends and companions among men who are not members of her family. So too for men; they are permitted to have female companions among women who are not members of his family. It happens quite often that a man would enter his own house and find his wife with one of her own friends and would not rebuke her.

Anecdote

One day I entered the home of Aboû Mohammed Yandecán, a man of the Mesoûfah tribe. He was sitting on a rug while in the middle of his house was a bed covered with a canopy. On it was his wife in conversation with another man sitting at her side. I said to Aboû Mohammed "Who is this woman?" "She is my wife," he responded "And who is the man with her?" I asked. "He is her friend," replied the judge. I asked how

From Ibn Battuta, *Voyages D'Ibn Batoutah*, trans. from the Arabic by C. Defrémery and B. R. Sanguinétti (Paris: Imprimerie Impériale, 1858), IV, 387–90, 421–24. Trans. Philip F. Riley.

he, who knew the divine law on such matters, could permit such a thing. He replied that "The companionship of women with men in this country is proper and honorable: It does not inspire suspicion. Our women are not like the women of your country." I was shocked at his stupid answer and immediately left his home and never returned. . . .

Good and Bad Qualities

Among their good qualities we can cite the following:

1. There is a small amount of crime, for these people obey the law. Their sultan does not pardon criminals.

2. Travelers and natives alike are safe from brigands, robbers, and thieves.

3. The natives do not confiscate the property of white men who die in this country, even if they are very wealthy; instead they entrust it to another, respected white man to dispose of it properly.

4. The prayers are offered punctually and with fervor. Children who neglect their prayers are beaten. If you do not come to the mosque early on a Friday you cannot find a place to pray because the crowds are so large. Quite often they send their slaves to the mosque with a prayer rug to find and hold a place for their masters. These prayer rugs are made from the leaves of trees similar to palm trees, but one that bears no fruit.

5. White garments are worn on Fridays. If by chance one does not have a proper white garment, regular clothing is washed and cleaned to wear for public prayer.

6. They are committed to learn by heart the sublime Koran. Children who fail to learn the Koran by heart have their feet shackled and these shackles are not removed until they memorize the Koran. On a feast day I visited a judge who had his children in chains. I said to him, "Why don't you release them?" He said, "I will not do so until they know the Koran by heart." Another day I passed a handsome young black man dressed superbly, but shackled by a heavy chain on his feet. I asked my companion, "What has this young man done? Is he a murderer?" The handsome young black man laughed and my companion told me, "He has been chained so that he will learn the Koran by heart."

Among their bad qualities we can cite the following:

1. Their female servants, slave women and small daughters appear before men completely naked, exposing their private parts. Even during the month of Ramadan [a period of fast], military commanders broke their fast in the palace of the Sultan. Twenty or more naked servant girls served them food.

2. Nude women without veils on their faces enter the palace of the Sultan. On the twenty-seventh night of Ramadan, I saw about a hundred naked female slaves coming out of the palace of the Sultan with food. Two of the Sultan's daughters, who have large breasts, were with them and they were naked.

3. These natives put dust and ashes on their head to show their education and as a sign of respect.

4. They laugh when poets recite their verse before the Sultan.

5. Finally, they eat impure meat such as dogs and donkeys.

68

Ibn Khaldun, *The Muqaddimah*

Ibn Khaldun (1332–1496) was an Arab diplomat, who achieved good relations for his various sultans in Muslim Spain and North Africa with such difficult individuals as King Pedro the Cruel of Portugal and the great warlord Tamerlane. At other times he studied, taught, and wrote about history, philosophy and what our world calls "political science" and "sociology." He wrote a comprehensive history of the Arabs, Persians, and Berbers; like the Roman Titus Livy (see Reading 38) and the Italian Nicolo Machiavelli (see Reading 94), he treated historical narratives as case studies to illustrate general principles of politics and society. The first part of this work, *The Muqaddimah* ("Introduction"), sets forth the outline of what is for him the way history works.

QUESTIONS TO CONSIDER

1. Why does Ibn Khaldun think that Bedouins are better people among the Arabs than the inhabitants of cities?
2. How does Ibn Khaldun assess the basis for developing wide power in the political sphere?
3. Ibn Khaldun obviously thinks of mosque and state as working together. How do his views here compare with those of Christian sources (see Reading 50) who deal with church-state relations?

Bedouins are closer to being good than sedentary people

The reason for it is that the soul in its first natural state of creation is ready to accept whatever good or evil may arrive and leave an imprint upon it. Mohammed said:

"Every infant is born in the natural state. It is his parents who make him a Jew or a Christian or a Magian." To the degree the soul is first affected by one of the two qualities, it moves away from the other and finds it difficult to acquire. When customs proper to goodness have been first to enter the soul of a good person, and he has thus acquired the habit of goodness, that person moves away from evil and finds it difficult to do anything evil. The same applies to the evil person when customs proper to evil have been first to affect them. Sedentary people are much concerned with all kinds of pleasures. They are accustomed to luxury and success in worldly occupations and to indulge in worldly desires. Therefore, their souls are colored with all kinds of blameworthy and evil qualities. The more of them they possess, the more remote do the ways and means of goodness become to them. Eventually they lose all sense of restraint. Bedouins may be as concerned with earthly affairs as sedentary people are.

However, such concern would touch only the necessities of life and not luxuries, nor anything calling for desires or pleasures. The customs they follow in their mutu-

From Ibn Khaldun, *The Muqaddimah: An Introduction to History*, transl. Franz Rosenthal (Princeton: Princeton University Press, 1958), pp. 252–55, 264–65, 284–85, 319–20, 322–24, 380–81, 385–87; condensed by Allen C. Myers.

al dealings are, therefore, appropriate. They are closer to the first natural state and more remote from the evil habits that have been impressed upon the souls of sedentary people. It will become clear that sedentary life constitutes the last stage of civilization and the point where it begins to decay. It also constitutes the last stage of evil. It has thus become clear that Bedouins are closer to being good than sedentary people. "God loves those who fear God."

Group feeling results only from blood relationship or something corresponding to it. In military affairs, and also every other human activity that requires a mass undertaking, nothing can be achieved without fighting for it. And for fighting, one cannot do without group feeling, such as emerges from ties of kinship. This should be taken as the guiding principle of this exposition. God gives success. Respect for blood ties is something natural among men, with the rarest exceptions. It leads to affection for one's relations, the feeling that no harm ought to befall them. One feels shame when one's relatives are treated unjustly or attacked, and one wishes to intervene between them and whatever peril threatens them. If the direct relationship between persons who help each other is very close, so that it leads to close contact and unity, the ties are obvious. If, however, the relationship is distant, it is often forgotten in part. However, some knowledge of it remains and this causes a person to help his relations to avoid the shame of injustice to a blood relative. Clients and allies belong in the same category. The reason for it is that a client relationship leads to close contact in approximately the same way as does common descent. When common descent is no longer clear and has become a matter of scientific knowledge, it can no longer move the imagination and is denied the affection caused by group feeling. The goal toward which group feeling leads is royal authority.

This is because group feeling gives protection and makes possible mutual defense, the pressing of claims, and every other kind of social activity. According to their nature, human beings need a restraining influence and mediator in every social organization, in order to keep the members from fighting with each other. That person must, by necessity, have superiority over the others in the matter of group feeling. If not, his power to act as a restraining influence could not materialize. Such superiority is royal authority. It is more than leadership. Leadership means being a chieftain, and the leader is obeyed, but he has no power to force others to accept his rulings. Royal authority means superiority and the power to rule by force. When a person sharing in the group feeling has reached the rank of chieftain and commands obedience, and when he then finds the way open toward superiority and force, he follows that way, because it is something desirable. He cannot completely achieve his goal except with the help of the group feeling, which causes obedience to him. Thus, royal superiority is a goal to which group feeling leads. Even if an individual tribe has different "houses" and many diverse group feelings, still there must exist a group feeling stronger than all the other group feelings combined, that is superior to them all and makes them subservient, and in which all the diverse group feelings coalesce to become one greater group feeling.

Dynasties of wide power have their origin in religion

This is because royal authority results from superiority. Superiority results from group feeling. Only by God's help in establishing His religion do individual desires come together in agreement, and hearts become united. The secret of this is that when hearts succumb to false desires and are inclined toward the world, mutual jealousy and widespread differences arise. But when they are turned toward the truth and reject the world and whatever is false, and advance toward God, they become one in their outlook. Jealousy disappears. There are few differences. Mutual cooperation and support flourish. As a result, the extent of the state widens, and the dynasty grows.

Religious propaganda cannot materialize without group feeling

This is because, as we have mentioned before, every mass undertaking requires group feeling. This is indicated in the tradition: "God sent no prophet who did not enjoy the protection of his people." If this was the case with the prophets, who among human beings are those most likely to perform wonders, one would expect it to apply all the more so to others. One cannot expect them to work the wonder of achieving superiority without group feeling. To this chapter belong cases of revolutionaries from among the common people and of jurists who undertake to reform evil.

The true character and different kinds of royal authority

Royal authority is an institution that is natural to mankind. Human beings cannot live and exist except through social organization and cooperation for the purpose of obtaining food and other necessities of life. When they have organized, necessity requires that they deal with each other and satisfy their needs. Each one will reach out for whatever he needs and take it, since injustice and aggressiveness are in the animalistic side of human nature. The others, in turn, will try to prevent him from taking it. This causes dissension. Dissension leads to hostilities, and hostilities lead to bloodshed, which leads to the destruction of mankind. Now the human species is one of the things the Creator has especially told us to preserve.

People, thus, cannot persist in a state of anarchy and without a ruler who keeps them apart. Therefore, they need a person to restrain them. He is their ruler. As is required by human nature, he must be a forceful ruler, one who exercises authority. In this connection, group feeling is absolutely necessary, for aggressive and defensive enterprises can succeed only with the help of group feeling. As one can see, royal authority of this kind is a noble institution, toward which all claims are directed, and one that must be defended.

The meaning of Caliphate and Imamate

The real meaning of royal authority is that it is a form of organization necessary to mankind. It requires superiority and force, which express the wrathfulness and animality of human nature. The decisions of the ruler will therefore, as a rule, deviate from what is right. They will be ruinous to the worldly affairs of the people under his control, since he forces them to execute his trouble and bloodshed. Therefore, it is necessary to have reference to ordained political norms, which are accepted by the mass. If these norms are ordained by the intelligent and leading personalities and minds of the dynasty, the result will be political authority on an intellectual basis.

If they are ordained by God through a lawgiver who establishes them, the result will be political authority on a religious basis, which will be useful for life in both this and the other world.

This is because the purpose of human beings is not only their worldly welfare. This entire world is trifling and futile. It ends in death and annihilation. The purpose of human beings is their religion, which leads them to happiness in the other world. Therefore, religious laws gave as their purpose to cause men to follow the path of God in all their dealings with Him and their fellow men. This also applies to royal authority. Anything that is dictated merely by considerations of policy or political decisions without this supervision is reprehensible, because it is vision lacking the divine light. "He for whom God makes no light has no light whatsoever." The Lawgiver knows better than the mass itself what is good for them so far as the affairs of the other world, which are concealed from the mass itself, are concerned. Political laws consider only worldly interests. The Lawgiver's intentions, however, concern the welfare of mankind in the other world. Therefore, it is necessary to cause the mass to act in accordance with the religious laws in all their affairs touching both this world and the other world.

The authority to do so was possessed by the representatives of the religious law, the prophets. Later on it was possessed by those who took their place, the caliphs. This makes it clear what caliphate means. To exercise natural royal authority means to cause the masses to act as required by intellectual insight into the means of furthering their worldly interests and avoiding anything harmful in that respect. The caliphate means to cause the masses to act as required by religious insight into their interests in the other world as well as in this world. Thus, the Caliphate in reality substitutes for the Lawgiver in as much as it serves, like him, to protect the religion and to exercise leadership of the world. God is wise and knowing.

69

Martín Fernández de Figueroa, Confronting the Moors in Somalia

Martín Fernández de Figueroa was from Castile in Spain, but in 1505 he went to Lisbon, where he joined a Portuguese fleet bound for "the Indies," a rather expansive concept at the time, including in its Eastern sweep alone territories from Ethiopia through what today is Indonesia. Figueroa spent six years traveling with the Portuguese in Africa and Asia and participated in the initial Portuguese seizure of Goa in India in 1510. A year later, he returned home and published an account of his travels. Figueroa's narrative was one of the earliest attempts to bring to the attention of Spain the world of the East that the Portuguese were discovering and conquering.

QUESTIONS TO CONSIDER

1. Why does Figueroa seem to think it is normal enough for the Portuguese to attack the inhabitants of Brava and Mogadishu in Somalia? For what acts does he reproach them as exceeding acceptable limits in the behavior of victors?
2. Why do the Portuguese and Spanish seem to get along so well with most of the people of Socotra, the large island about equally far east of Somalia and south of the Arabian peninsula?

3. What sort of limited community of interests and harmony of action among the Portuguese and Spanish does Figueroa's account bear testimony to? What do you suppose the Africans and Arabians they encountered thought of the Iberians coming to their shores?

Afonso de Albuquerque had set out for the Strait of Mecca as captain major of six ships. He then informed them of his arrival at a city on the mainland called Brava. The Portuguese entered it by force of arms, killed many Moors, and carried off great riches which their owners had not thought to save, thinking they could defend the city. Nor could they save their women, very rich and handsome with seven and eight bracelets on each arm, and just as many, thick and valuable, on their legs. This occasioned severe cruelty, for the men, blinded by avarice rather than enlightened by mercy, so as not to lose a moment's time, cut off the arms, the legs, and the ears which bore the jewelry, without a trace of pity. Good men would never do such a thing, if only because women are "vessels of generation" and of tender, delicate flesh and gentle condition. What man would not have been moved to pity contemplating their beauty! What man would not have cast down his sword before bloodying it on a woman! Worthy of reprimand are such cruel victors and their cruel deeds, but you may be sure that the ones who did such foul things were not the ordinary nor the best of men. The women all ran crying through the streets, covered with blood. Some went fleeing with children in their arms but could find no haven. Quite a few of them were defended and sheltered by the virtuous men who were there.

The city was finally ordered burned, which was done, whereupon they set out for another city, Mogadishu, which was nearby. There, although the army was sore afraid, the ferocity of contrary winds kept the Christians from waiting and attacking, and thus hostile weather frustrated their good and worthy goal. They left that place and went to Socotra,[25] whose inhabitants consider themselves Christians. They fast during Lent and Advent, eating neither meat nor fish. They have churches and altars with crosses on them. They observe most of the principal feast days, as well as those of the Apostles, whose names they take. They give alms. Every day they hear Matins, Vespers, and Compline. They hold the Cross in such veneration that he who wears it goes about without fear of harm from the enemies or the authorities. So states at length the King Manuel letter written in Portuguese that I had in hand. . . . This land is completely surrounded by water. They anchored opposite the castle, and as soon as it was realized that they were Portuguese, mortars were hauled out and a stout defense made ready. They did not want peace or even to let the Portuguese take on Socotran water. There the Christians killed a Socotran captain. The battle was very rough, and a captain named Leonel Coutinho proved himself unflinchingly courageous. With the fierce blows he dealt them, he sorely pressed the castle defenders. As he drove the Moors back from the walls, he put up scaling ladders. Thus, the first Christians who succeeded in entering opened the castle gates, and the Christians entered and captured the fort. No Moor survived, because, rather than surrender and live without their patrimony, they chose to die. Then the conquerers consolidated the land. Although these people were

[25] An island in the Indian Ocean off Cape Guardafui, at the horn of Africa.

Reprinted by permission of the publishers and the Loeb Classical Library from James B. McKenna, *A Spaniard in the Portuguese Indies: The Narrative of Martín Fernández de Figueroa*, pp. 73–85. Cambridge, MA: Harvard University Press, © 1967.

defeated, they died courageously. When winter passed, the men of Hispania attacked the city of Hormuz under the orders of Captain Afonso de Albuquerque. They conquered and took possession of it. The Moors rose up against the Christians, so they went to Socotra again and from there to Cape Guardafui to lie in wait for infidel ships.

During their voyage, the captains came upon Mogadishu, of which we have already spoken. They sighted a Moorish ship and drove it ashore. When they reached it, they saw that everyone was gone, so they set it afire along with its entire rich cargo. Without stopping, they journeyed to Afonso de Albuquerque, by whom they were honorably welcomed. Cape Guardafui is called a cape because there the seacoast comes to an end. There is another cape there, called Fartak, and between these two enters the sea they call the Strait of Mecca. Arabia is a wretched land; the airs are torrid. Its inhabitants are Arabs, cattle-raisers. Fresh water is far away and is brought there in leather gourds to be sold. From there they went to Socotra to spend the winter.

The captains, and Martín Fernández de Figueroa with them, spent the entire winter (which out there runs from the month of April through the middle of August) on the island of Socotra. On this island one finds good-natured men. Their churches do not have statues of men or women saints, only crosses. They sound for Mass with wooden tablets. The men enter church by one door and the women by another, and this practice never varies. On solemn occasions they anoint the cross with lard. The women dearly love the Christians of Hispania. Some of these people know Arabic, but they have their own language. The men go about naked except for their shameful parts. The women wear Moorish tunics; they wear their hair long and comb it down their backs. Women are held in common, which is an abominable custom. Thus the husband will invite you to sleep with his wife, and fathers and mothers with their daughters. They are a libidinous people. In that land it rarely rains except for the dew. No wheat grows there, nor rice, millet, nor barley. There are lots of cattle and palm groves. A pitcher of wine there costs sixteen hundred maravedis, a needle twenty maravedis, and similar prices must be paid for many other necessary things.

A knight from Captain Major Afonso de Albuquerque's company scrupulously related to the captains of the other coast the conquest of Hormuz. He told how, after they had seized the fort from the Fartaks, who fight like Swiss mercenaries, they left it strongly garrisoned and set out in search of provisions. Sailing along the Arabian coast, they came to Kalhat, a rich port city, and the Captain Major was delighted to have come upon a land of good supplies. They entered the harbor, although with difficulty, for it was occupied by many handsome ships and ringed by elegant buildings along the shore. They gave a thunderous artillery display to frighten the inhabitants. They took the supplies the Moors had provided, and the Captain did not harm them, because he had given them a guarantee and one of his rings as token thereof. Kalhat, later destroyed when Hormuz revolted, was more populated outside the city than within. Afonso de Albuquerque departed the next day, and they went to a port named Quryat, which also belongs to the King of Hormuz. It is a very wealthy town located at the water's edge, well stocked with mortars. The Captain Major requested provisions, but the Moors paid no attention. So the next day Afonso de Albuquerque organized his men and the captains of the rear guard and commenced the attack. He destroyed the enemy, and, with Moors fleeing and Christians killing, the ships were well stocked with the riches and supplies they found ashore, namely an abundance of wheat, flour, rice, dates, fish, lard, and honey. They rested there for three days. In all this said encounter or battle no Christian was killed, only one of the Captain Major's Negroes who had strayed off. After this victory, they boarded their ships. They had burned and razed the mosque, the land, and the ships; nothing remained. They sailed forth to Masqat, which belongs to the King of Hormuz. Larger than Kalhat, it had a good port and stout defenses. However, the Moors met with the Captain Major (who truly awed and terrified them) under a flag of truce, whereupon they did as he directed and became vassals of the King of Portugal. There the Christians secured very fresh and rich provisions, but first they had to fight a fierce and cruel battle, for the Moors broke their promise of peace. The city was sacked, the ruler killed, and one Christian captain wounded. The city, its ships and riches were burned and reduced to ashes. With this victory they returned to the ships; the battle had taken place on a Sunday morning and lasted three hours. From there Afonso de Albuquerque and his men moved along the coast to a town called Suhar, where there was a fort garrisoned by a captain and men of the King of Hormuz. As soon as they saw the Christian ships, the captain and his men were terrified, so Suhar and its Moors became vassals of King Manuel of Portugal. Great celebrations were held, and the Portuguese banner was raised over the fort, with Moors and Christians shouting: "Portugal and Spain!"

Byzantium: The Later Period of Decay

After the glorious reign of Emperor Basil II (976–1025), during which the Byzantine Empire subdued the Russians, Bulgars, Muslims, and powerful Byzantine nobles, the empire began to decline. Among the reasons for this disintegration were the disinterested leadership of later emperors; a reemergence of the powerful nobility; the politically inexperienced empresses; the coming of Seljuk Turks; and a competition for the imperial throne, which ultimately led to the disastrous effects of the Fourth Crusade on the empire.

Two selections illustrate the tragedies of this period. The first concerns the intrigues and loves of Empress Zoe, daughter of Emperor Constantine VIII, whose life and lovers are chronicled by the most illustrious writer of the period, Michael Psellus. The second selection marks the permanent decay of the empire. It is a report by Robert of Clari of the Fourth Crusade, which details the attack by Western crusaders on Constantinople that left the empire a mere shadow of its former glory.

70

Michael Psellus, *Chronographia*, "Empress Zoe"

Michael Psellus (1018–1078) achieved much during his lifetime: He was a professor of rhetoric, government minister, monk, and polished historian. His firsthand observations and keen eye for detail makes his *Chronographia* an extremely important source for the period from Emperor Basil II (976–1025) through the reign of Psellus's own pupil and emperor, Michael VII (1071–1078).

In the following selection, Psellus describes the three marriages and one adoption by Empress Zoe, daughter of Constantine VIII. On his deathbed, Constantine VIII tried to keep the succession within the family by making a governmental official, Romanus III Argyus, ascend the throne as husband to his daughter Zoe. When Romanus III's ardor cooled, Zoe found solace with a young man named Michael. Once on the throne as Michael IVth, he kept Zoe confined to the women's quarters of the palace until his early death in 1042. Zoe was then induced to adopt a nephew of her second husband, a young man named Michael V ("The Caulker"). When this last husband tried to force Zoe out of the palace and into a convent, the crowds made short work of him. They then demanded that Zoe and her sister Theodora share the throne. This joint rule of empresses lasted only a short time when Zoe married Constantine IX (1042–1055), with whom she lived peaceably until her death in 1055.

QUESTIONS TO CONSIDER

1. How do these pieces show Empress Zoe's determination to remain in power?
2. How do the Byzantines compare with people of other civilizations in their treatment of rulers?

Romanus III and Zoe

Having been judged worthy of the crown, . . . Romanus deceived himself in the belief that he would reign for many years, and leave to succeed him a family destined to inherit the throne for many generations. Apparently it did not occur to him that Constantine's daughter, with whom he lived after his acclamation, was too old to conceive and already barren (she was in her fiftieth (actually her forty-eighth) year when she married him). Even in the face of natural incapacity, he clung ever more firmly to his ambitions, . . . Nevertheless, he did have recourse to the specialists who deal with sexual disorders and claim the ability to induce or cure sterility. He submitted himself to treatment with ointments and massage, and he enjoined his wife to do likewise. In fact, she went further: she was introduced to most of the magical practices, fastening little pebbles to her body, hanging charms about her, wearing chains, decking herself out with the rest of the nonsense. As their hope were never realized, the emperor at last gave up in despair and paid less attention to Zoe.

A Plot Is Conceived Against the Life of Romanus III

[When Emperor Romanus III and Zoe failed to produce an heir, John the Orpanotrophus, who was in charge of public orphanages, brought his younger brother, Michael, to Zoe. She fell instantly in love and they began to form a plot versus the emperor.]

Whether the loving couple themselves, and their accomplices, committed a very horrible crime against him, I would not say with any certainty, because it is no easy thing for me to bring accusations in matters that I still do not understand. However, it was universally accepted among the rest that they first bewitched him with drugs,

From Michael Psellus, *Fourteen Byzantine Rulers: The Chronographia of Michael Psellus*, trans. E. R. A. Senter (Middlesex, England: Penguin Books Ltd., 1966; reprint 1987), pp. 65, 75–76, 81–82, 95, 134, 144–45, 149–51. Copyright 1966 by E. R. A. Sewter. Reprinted by permission of Penguin Books Ltd.

and later had recourse to a mixture of hellebore as well. I am not disputing that for the moment—it may or may not be true—but I do maintain that Zoe and Michael were the cause of his death. His state of health being what it was, the emperor made his preparations for the Resurrection that awaits all of us alike. At the same time, he was making himself ready for public services on the morrow (Good Friday). Before dawn he set out to bathe in one of the baths situated near the imperial quarters. There was no one to assist him, and he was certainly not at death's door then. He got up in a perfectly normal way to anoint and bathe himself and take his aperitive. So he entered the bath. First he washed his head, then drenched his body as well, and as he was breathing strongly, he proceeded to the swimming pool, which had been deepened in the middle. To begin with, he enjoyed himself swimming on the surface and floating lightly, blowing out and refreshing himself with the greatest of pleasure. Later on some of his retinue came in to support him and give him a rest, according to his own orders. Whether they made an attempt on the emperor's life after they entered the bath I cannot say with any conviction. At any rate, those who see some connection between these events and the rest of their version say that when Romanus plunged his head under the water—his usual custom—they all pressed his neck and held him down for some considerable time, after which they let him go and went away. The air inside him, however, caused his body to rise and it brought him to the surface, almost breathless. There he floated about in a haphazard way, like a cork. When he had recovered a little and saw in what evil plight he was, he stretched out his hand and begged someone to take hold of it and help him to his feet. In pity for him, and because of his sad condition, one man did indeed go to his aid. Putting his arms round him, he drew him out of the water and carried him to a couch, where he laid him, just as he was, in a pitiable state. At this an uproar ensued. Several persons came into the room, among them the empress, without any bodyguard and apparently stricken with grief. After one look at him, however, she went off, having satisfied herself with her own eyes that he was a dying man.

Michael IV and Zoe

. . . For some time he treated Zoe with marked consideration, but that phase soon passed. He suspected her motives—there were reasons for suspicion in that house— and he proceeded to deny her any liberty whatever. Permission to leave the palace in her usual way was refused, and she was shut up in the women's quarters. No one was allowed to approach her, unless the captain of the guard had first given authority after careful scrutiny of the visitor's identity, origin, and purpose—so close was the watch kept over her. She was, quite naturally, embittered by this sort of treatment. Surely it was hardly to be wondered at, when the benefits she had conferred upon the emperor were being repaid with such hatred. Nevertheless, she restrained herself, reflecting that to rebel against Michael's decisions would be improper, and in any case she had no opportunity, even if she wished, to take any action or oppose his will, for she was deprived of all protection from the Imperial Guard and bereft of all power.

Empress Zoe and Michael V

[Michael IV suffered from epilepsy and eventually resigned as emperor. His uncle, John the Orphanotrophus, persuaded Zoe to adopt another nephew, Michael, as the next emperor. Once in power, however, Michael V turned first on his uncle John, whom he exiled, and promoted another uncle, Constantine, as his chief adviser. They then exiled Zoe from the palace, which led to the following dire consequences.]

Certain charges were fabricated against his adopted mother, who was innocent of any plot aimed at himself, and the wretched boy condemned her as a poisoner. She, still knowing nothing of his machinations, was driven from her bedchamber— she who had been born there, driven out by a parvenu! She, the daughter of a most noble family, was dispossessed by a man sprung from the gutter. Witnesses were suborned to give false evidence and he proceeded to question her on matters of which she knew nothing. She was compelled to account for her actions and was then convicted of the most abominable crimes. At once she was put on board a ship, together with certain persons who were given full liberty to insult her. Exiled from the palace, she was landed on one of the islands lying off Byzantium, called Prinkipo.

[A riot ensued when the citizens learned what had happened to Zoe. Michael V and his uncle Constantine tried to flee but were captured. Their fate is detailed by Psellus.]

. . . The emperor, overwhelmed by the situation and his dreadful misfortunes, showed the same weakness of character throughout the whole time of his tribulation. He moaned and wailed loud, and whenever anyone approached him, he begged for help. He humbly called on God, raised hands in supplication to Heaven, to the Church, to anything he could think of. His uncle (Constantine), on the other hand, although at first he followed his companion's example, once he was convinced that safety really was out of the question, braced himself for the trial and, having armed himself, as it were, against the shock of the catastrophe, faced suffering bravely. The fact is, he was a man of more dignified and steadfast character than his nephew, a man who would not willing surrender to adversity. Seeing the executioners all ready for their work, he at once offered himself as the first victim and calmly approached the mob. They waited with hands athirst for his blood. As there was no clear space between himself and the mob—for everyone there present wished to be the first witness of their punishment—the Nobilissimus (Constantine) [a Byzantine title of high office] quietly looked round for the man to whom the miserable job had been entrusted. "You there," he said, "please make the people stand back. Then you will see how bravely I bear my calamity!"

When the executioner tried to tie him down, to prevent movement at the time of blinding, he said, "Look here. If you see me budge, nail me down!" With these words he lay flat on his back on the ground. There was no change of color in his face, no crying out, no groaning. It was hard to believe that the man was still alive. His eyes were then gouged, one after the other. Meanwhile the emperor, seeing in the other's torment the fate that was about to overtake him, too, lived through Constantine's anguish in himself, beating his hands together, smiting his face, and bellowing in agony.

71

Robert of Clari, *The Conquest of Constantinople*

The purpose of the Fourth Crusade (1202–1204), as envisioned by Pope Innocent III, was to continue the Western attack on the Muslim-held holy places in the Near East. The French Norman crusaders were diverted from their original task, however, because of the Venetian desire to control the trade routes to the Near East coupled with a plea for aid from Alexius Angelus. Angelus was the son of the imprisoned, blinded, and dethroned Byzantine emperor, Isaac.

Although the crusaders were able to restore Isaac and his son to their rightful positions, the Byzantine emperors were not able to fulfill their bargain to pay the Normans for the restoration. As a result, tensions between the natives and the crusaders eventually led to the usurpation of the Byzantine throne as well as to the deaths of Isaac and his son. In 1204, the crusaders decided to attack Constantinople, which fell amid scenes of violence and rapacity on the part of the Normans. In the period from 1204 to 1261, a Latin kingdom, ruled by Franks, arose in the East. The Crusade also forcibly instituted Roman Catholicism in place of the Eastern Orthodox Church. These actions left a lasting religious bitterness and an Eastern empire that never recovered from the devastation.

Robert of Clari, a participant in the Fourth Crusade, left an eyewitness account from the perspective of a simple soldier. After returning home in 1205, Robert dictated his memoirs, adding one last piece concerning the death of the second Latin emperor, Henry I, in 1216.

This chronicle is the best single Western source describing the motivations and actions of the crusaders. Robert, with great accuracy, describes the Great Palace, Santa Sophia, and the Golden Gate; he also offers diversions concerning miracle cures and sacred relics such as the True Cross, the head of John the Baptist, and perhaps the Shroud of Turin, thought by many to be the burial cloth of Jesus.

QUESTIONS TO CONSIDER

1. Why was the Fourth Crusade a perversion of the crusading spirit?
2. What was the cause of the religious problems between Rome and Constantinople?
3. What caused the Crusaders to sack the city?
4. What miraculous objects or places impressed the Crusaders?
5. What comparison can you make between Robert of Clari's description and the Spanish conquest of Mexico (see Reading 102)?

In the meantime, while the crusaders and the Venetians were staying there [on the Dalmatian coast] that winter, the crusaders bethought them that they had spent a great deal. And they talked with one another and said that they could not go to Babylon or to Alexandria or to Syria, because they had neither provisions nor money for going there. For they had spent nearly everything, on the long delay they had made as well as on the great price they had given for the hire of the fleet. . . .

The doge of Venice saw right well that the pilgrims were in sore straits, and he spoke to them and said: "Lords, in Greece there is a land that is very rich and plenteous in all good things. If we could have a reasonable excuse for going there and taking provisions and other things in the land until we were well restored, it would seem to me a good plan. Then we should be well able to go oversea." . . .

Now you have heard how Isaac arose and how he became emperor and how his son went to Germany—he for whom the crusaders and the Venetians were going to send, on the advice of the marquis of Montferrat, their leader, . . . so that they might have an excuse for going to the country of Constantinople. And now we shall tell you about this youth and the crusaders, how the crusaders sent for him and how they went to Constantinople and how they conquered it. . . .

When they of Constantinople saw this fleet which was so finely arrayed, they gazed at it in wonder, and they were mounted on the walls and on the houses to look upon this marvel. And they of the fleet also regarded the great size of the city, which was so long and so wide, and they marveled at it exceedingly.

When the emperor of Constantinople learned of it, he sent good envoys to ask them what they sought there and why they were come there, and he sent word to them that if they wanted any of his gold or his silver, he would right gladly send it to them. When the high men heard this, they answered the envoys that they did not want any of his gold or his silver, but rather they wanted the emperor to surrender the empire, for he held it neither rightfully nor loyally, and they sent word to him that they had the rightful heir with them, Alexius, the son of Isaac the emperor. Thereupon the envoys answered and said that the emperor would do nothing of the sort, and with that they went away. . . .

While the French and the Venetians were talking together, there arose a great clamor in the city, for they of the city told the emperor that he ought to deliver them from the French who were besieging them, and that if he did not fight with them they would seek out the youth whom the French had brought and make him emperor and lord over them.

When the emperor heard this, he gave them his word that he would fight them on the morrow. But when it came near midnight, the emperor fled from the city with as many people as he could take with him.

When the morning was come on the morrow and they of the city knew that the emperor was fled, what do they do but go to the gates and open them and issue forth and come to the camp of the French and ask and inquire for Alexius, the son of Isaac. And they were told that they would find him at the tent of the marquis. When they came there, they found him, and his friends did him great honor and made great rejoicing over him. And they thanked the barons right heartily and said that they who had done this thing had done right well and had done a great deed of baronage. And they said that the emperor had fled, and that they [the crusaders] should come into the city and into the palace as if it all belonged to them. Then all the high barons of the host assembled, and they took Alexius, the son of Isaac, and they led him to the palace with great joy and much rejoicing. And when they were come to the palace, they had Isaac, his father, brought out of prison, and his wife also. This was the one who had been imprisoned by his brother, the recent emperor. When Isaac was out of prison, he made great rejoicing over his son and embraced and kissed him, and he gave great thanks to the barons who were there and said that it was by the help of God first and next by theirs that he was out of prison. Then they brought two golden chairs and seated Isaac on one and Alexius his son on the other beside him, and to Isaac was given the imperial seat. . . .

Afterwards the emperor sought out the barons and said to them that he had nothing save Constantinople and that this was worth little to him by itself, for his uncle held all the cities and castles that ought to be his. So he asked the barons to help him conquer some of the land around, and he would right gladly give them still more of his wealth. Then they answered that they would be very glad to do it, and that anyone who wanted to profit by this could go. Then a good half of the host went with Alexius and the other half stayed in Constantinople to receive the payment, and Isaac stayed behind to make the payment to the barons. So Alexius went with all his host and conquered full twenty cities and full forty castles or more of the land, and Alexius, the other emperor, his uncle, fled always before him. . . .

When this respite was past and the French saw that the emperor was not going to pay them anything, all the counts and the high men of the host came together, and they went to the palace of the emperor and asked again for their payment. Then the emperor answered them that he could not pay them anything, and the barons answered that if he did not pay them they would seize enough of his possessions to pay themselves. . . .

While these things were going on, those of the Greeks who were traitors toward the emperor and this Murzuphlus whom the emperor had freed from prison came together and plotted a great treason. For they wanted to make someone else emperor, someone who would deliver them from the French, because Alexius did not seem good to them any longer. And finally Murzuphlus said: "If you will leave it to me," said he, "and will make me emperor, I will deliver you from the French and from this emperor, so that you will never have any more trouble from them." And they said that if he would deliver them they would make him emperor, and Murzuphlus vowed to free them within a week, and they agreed to make him emperor.

Then Murzuphlus went and lost no time. He took sergeants with him and entered by night into the chamber where his lord the emperor, who had freed him from prison, was sleeping, and he had them tie a cord around his neck and strangle him and his father Isaac also. . . . It was not long afterwards that Murzuphlus sent word to the count of Flanders, to Count Louis, to the marquis, and to all the other high barons, telling them to go away and vacate his land, and letting them know that he was emperor and that if he came on them there a week from then he would slay them all. When the barons heard the message that Murzuphlus had sent, they replied: "What?" said they, "He who has treacherously murdered his lord by night has sent this word to us?" And they sent back word to him that they defied him and let him now beware of them, for they would not abandon the siege until they had avenged him whom he had murdered and had taken Constantinople again and had secured in full the payment which Alexius had promised them. . . .

Then it came about on a Friday, about ten days before Palm Sunday, that the pilgrims and the Venetians got their ships and their engines ready and prepared for the assault. So they ranged their ships side by side, and the French had their engines loaded on barges and galleys, and they set out to go toward the city, and the navy extended fully a good league along its front. . . .

When the navy was about to make land, they took strong cables and drew their ships as close as they could to the walls, and the French had their engines set up, their "cats" and "carts" and "sows," to mine the walls. And the Venetians mounted on the bridges of their ships and hardily assailed the walls and the French likewise assailed them with their engines. When the Greeks saw the French attacking them thus, they set to hurling huge blocks of stone, more than enough, onto the engines of the French, and they began to crush and break to pieces and destroy all these engines, so that no one dared to remain inside or under them. And the Venetians on their part were not able to reach the walls or the towers, they were so high. Nor ever that day were the Venetians or the French able to accomplish anything at the walls or at the city. When they saw that they could not do anything, they were greatly disheartened and drew off. When the Greeks saw them withdrawing, they began to hoot and to call out more lustily than a great deal, and they mounted on the walls and let down their clouts and showed them their backsides. . . .

Then when the bishops had preached and had shown the pilgrims that the battle was a righteous one, they all confessed themselves right well and were given communion. When it came to Monday morning, the pilgrims all made themselves ready and armed themselves right well, and the Venetians also. Then they repaired the bridges on their ships and got ready their transports and their galleys and ranged them side by side for the assault, and the navy had fully a good league of front. When they reached the shore and had drawn up as close as they could to the walls, they cast anchor. And when they were at anchor, they began to attack vigorously and to shoot and hurl stones and throw Greek fire on the towers, but the fire could not take hold on them because of the hides with which they were covered. And those within the city defended themselves right hardily, and they had fully sixty petraries [medieval military engines for discharging stones] hurling missiles, and at each cast they hit the ships, but the ships were so well covered with planks and with grapevines that they did not do them any harm, and the stones were so large that a man could not lift one of them from the ground. . . . When my lord Pierre of Amiens saw that those who were in the towers were not advancing and saw the condition of the Greeks, what does he do but descend to the land on foot, he and his people with him, on a little piece of ground that was between the sea and the wall. When they were on land, they looked ahead and saw a false postern, the door of which had been removed and it had been walled up again. . . .

When they were come to this postern, they began to attack it hardily with their picks, and the quarrels of the crossbows were flying so thick and they were hurling so many stones down on them from the walls, that it seemed as if they would be buried under them, so many were thrown. And those below had shields and targes with which they covered those who were picking at the postern. And the others hurled down on them pots full of boiling pitch and Greek fire and immense stones, so that it was a miracle of God they were not all crushed. And my lord Pierre of Amiens and his people endured there labors and difficulties more than a great deal. So they picked away at this postern with axes and with good swords, with pieces of wood, with bars and with picks, until they made a great hole in it. . . .

When those who were defending the towers and the walls saw that the French were entered into the city and their emperor had fled away, they did not dare remain there but fled away each one as best he could. Thus was the city taken. When the city was taken in this way and the French were inside, they stayed right where they were. Then the high barons assembled and took counsel among them as to what they should do. And finally it was cried through the host that no one should dare to go on into the city, for it was a great peril to go there, lest they should cast stones on them from the palaces, which were very large and high, or lest they should slay them in the streets, which were so narrow that they would not be able to defend themselves, or lest the city should be set on fire behind them and they be burned. Because of these dangers and perils, they did not dare seek quarters or disperse, but remained there right where they were. . . .

When the city was captured and the pilgrims were quartered, . . . and the palaces were taken over, then they found in the palaces riches more than a great deal. And the palace of Boukoleon was very rich and was made in such a way as I shall tell you. Within this palace, . . . there were fully five hundred halls, all connected with one another and all made with gold mosaic.[26] And in it there were fully thirty chapels, great and small, and there was one of them which was called the Holy Chapel. . . .[27] Within this chapel were found many rich relics. One found there two pieces of the True Cross as large as the leg of a man and as long as half a toise, and one found there also the iron of the lance with which Our Lord had His side pierced and two of the nails which were driven through His hands and feet, and one found there in a crystal phial quite a little of His blood, and one found there the tunic which He wore and which was taken from Him when they led Him to the Mount of Calvary, and one found there the blessed crown with which He was crowned, which was made of reeds with thorns as sharp as the points of daggers. And one found there a part of the robe of Our Lady and the head of my lord St. John the Baptist and so many other rich relics that I could not recount them to you or tell you all the truth. . . .

Now I will tell you about the church of Saint Sophia, how it was made. Saint Sophia in Greek means Sainte Trinité ["Holy Trinity"] in French [sic]. The church of Saint Sophia was entirely round, and within the church there were domes, round all about, which were borne by great and very rich columns, and there was no column which was not of jasper or porphyry or some other precious stone, nor was there one of these columns that did not work cures. There was one that cured sickness of the veins when it was rubbed against, and another that cured sickness of the side, and others that cured other ills. . . . On the ring of the great door of the church, which was all of silver, there hung a tube, of what material no one knew; it was the size of a pipe such as shepherds play on. This tube had such virtue as I shall tell you. When an infirm man who had some sickness in his body like the bloat, so that he was bloated in his belly, put it in his mouth, however little he put it in, when this tube took hold it sucked out all the sickness and it made the poison run out of his mouth and it held him so fast that it made his eyes roll and turn in his head, and he could not get away until the tube had sucked all of this sickness out of him. And the sicker a man was the longer it held him, and if a man who was not sick put it in his mouth, it would not hold him at all, much or little. . . .

And among the rest, there was another of the churches which they called My Lady Saint Mary of Blachernae, where was kept the sydoine in which Our Lord had been wrapped, which stood up straight every Friday so that the features of Our Lord could be plainly seen there.[28] And no one, either Greek or French, ever knew what became of this sydoine after the city was taken. . . .

Afterwards it came about that all the counts and all the high men came together one day at the palace of Boukoleon, which belonged to the marquis, and they said to one another that they ought to decide on an emperor and ought to choose their ten

[26]In these terms Robert attempts to describe the great complex of building lying between the Hippodrome and the sea walls, which was known as the Great Palace. . . .

[27]This is the celebrated church of the Blessed Virgin of the Pharos (lighthouse). . . .

[28]Robert seems to have confused the *sudarium* (the sweat cloth or napkin, the True Image of St. Veronica) with the *sindon* (the grave cloth in which the body of Jesus was wrapped for entombment). Both relics were in the church of the Blessed Virgin in the Great Palace, and not in the church in the palace of Blachernae, as Robert says.

electors, and they told the doge of Venice to choose his ten. When the marquis heard this, he wanted to put in his own men and those who he thought would choose him as emperor, and he wanted to be emperor forthwith. . . . This discord lasted a good fortnight without their ever being able to agree. And there was no day on which they did not assemble for this affair, until at length they agreed that the clergy of the host, the bishops and abbots who were there, should be the electors. . . .

When the mass was chanted, the electors assembled and took counsel together, and they talked of one and of another, until the Venetians and the bishops and abbots, all twenty electors, agreed all together that it should be the count of Flanders, nor was there one of them who was against it.

Scholasticism, Spirituality, and Mysticism

A great deal of reading and copying went on in medieval monasteries and nunneries, as did occasional writing of letters and longer original works. Monks and nuns not only read godly works themselves but at mealtimes a reader would often read to them, usually from Scripture, commentary, or saints' lives. Improving literacy among the clergy and encouraging the copying of religious books had been a main aim of the Carolingian Renaissance, but in the later ninth century a second wave of Dark Ages swept over Europe with the invasions of Norsemen and Magyars, among others, causing the erosion of what modest central government Charlemagne and his family had established on the continent. Sometime after 1050, however, new stirrings of revived learning led to the Renaissance of the Twelfth Century.

In the twelfth century, some clerics pursued their studies beyond the Scriptures and works of the Church Fathers into writings from pagan antiquity in search of better sources of philosophy. Philosophy included all subjects not medical, legal, nor strictly theological, but its devotees often focused particularly on questions of being and reality. Two schools of medieval philosophy picked up this part of philosophy where the ancients had left off: The Realists, following Socrates and Plato, taught that reality existed only in the eternal essences or ideal forms of things, but not in actual, observable things in this world, whereas the Nominalists, following the Sophists and some ambiguous statements of Aristotle, taught that general ideas reflect only the names of things that are agreed upon by human convention, with basic reality residing in the things named. In the early twelfth century, Pierre (Peter) Abelard rose to youthful distinction by reconciling the two positions to his own satisfaction and that of his students. In modern times, to be sure, Abelard is less known for his philosophical achievements than for his calamitous personal history, which, apart from its enduring romantic content, highlights some of the mindsets of the twelfth century concerning fame, academics, and the clergy.

Most nonacademic clergymen of the twelfth century harbored at least a mild dislike for Realism, Nominalism, or Abelard's new Conceptualism, preferring good old divine revelation and traditional teaching as the source of knowledge. Mysticism, in the sense of a person's longing for nearness to God through pious living, prayer, and revelations flourished right along with the study of critical philosophies revived from the Greek and Roman worlds. In the twelfth century, the mystics' search for God included more of an attempt to understand the total unity of creation than was later typical of Western European mysticism, with all parts of creation fitted together through explanations of visions and the words of heavenly voices. In writing vivid, easily communicated visions, in which all parts of the universe fall into their sanctioned places, St. Hildegard of Bingen knows no equal. A younger contemporary of Abelard, she actually shared his underlying (Dualistic) conviction that the spirit is good and the flesh is evil, but she was content to relate to the struggle between the two forces as a recorder and interpreter of revelations—rather than participate in the struggle as he had—and certainly came away from it much better off than he did.

The Church's acquisition of early wealth and power produced a variety of reactions among faithful medieval Christians. Some groups voiced open criticism of Church worldliness and demanded that churchmen return to the simple lifestyle of the Apostles, but overt condemnation of Church practices was likely to lead to charges of heresy and an untimely end for the critics. In the early thirteenth century, the Franciscan Order offered a living model of Apostolic poverty without attacking Church leaders for their non-Apostolic riches and political influence. St. Francis of Assisi personified personal sacrifices and total commitment to spiritual endeavors; however, he did not advocate rejection of the world by seclusion from it, as was the practice of the more austere religious orders. Instead, he and his followers went boldly and joyfully into the world with the Gospel message. The Franciscans flourished in Europe and soon sent many of the more successful missionaries abroad.

Although the Renaissance of the twelfth century furthered a great revival of interest in the ancient Greek and Roman classics, Church leaders in the West occasionally expressed reservations about this enthusiastic propagation of secular learning. They were all the more concerned because many Greek philosophical and scientific works had reached Europe through the new universities in Arab works on alchemy, astronomy, mathematics, and medicine. The most comprehensive commentary on Aristotle before 1200 was that of the Spanish Muslim, Averroes.

The reservations of Church authorities concerning pagan or Muslim learning influenced Scholasticism toward attempts to harmonize useful pagan learning with Christian teachings. During the earlier Carolingian Renaissance, teachers of the liberal arts had been called "scholastics," or "school-men"; as a loose and general term, the earlier Scholasticism had signified the teaching of theology and philosophy, particularly at points where the two overlapped. During the thirteenth century, however, Scholasticism became the systematic defense of approved dogma with a combination of secular philosophy and scriptural authority.

The censoring aspect of Scholasticism had stifled some of the open in-quisitiveness of the Renaissance of the twelfth century. Soon, however, the great Italian Renaissance would develop a still more independent attitude toward science and philosophy. Meanwhile, St. Hildegard's type of mysti-cism, with its concern for explaining the totality of existence, was giving way to more nearly exclusive searches on the part of mystics for unions of their souls with God. They placed less stress on identifying analogies to re-late the workings of nature to the human condition, leaving that sort of study to "natural philosophers." The later mystics conveyed their revela-tions as more personal, less easily describable experiences than was true of their predecessors.

72

Peter Abelard, *The Story of My Misfortunes*

Peter Abelard (1079–1142), son of a Breton nobleman, felt drawn to philosophy early in life and came to the cathedral school at Paris, where his energy and insights gained him a following among its students. He soon aroused suspicion with a book, *Sic et Non (Yes and No)*, featuring statements of the Church Fathers contradicting each other and leaving them unreconciled, remarking in his preface that this was to stimu-late students into a search for truth on their own. His own "Conceptualism" opposed the notion of the Realists that only eternal essences, ideas, and ideals have reality but rejected the Nominalist conviction that names of things were mere conventions. He sought to prove that those general concepts we arrive at by extracting the common features from particular phenomena have an existence of their own once they are for-mulated. Such concepts are necessary for human discourse, and what is necessary has a good claim to being real.

Abelard's life was full of controversy. His questioning of doctrine brought him into conflict with St. Bernard of Clairvaux, a great mystic, ascetic, and Church re-former. St. Bernard succeeded in having a Church council condemn some of Abelard's writings, and Abelard set off for Rome to appeal his condemnation but died on the way. The following excerpt from his autobiography has the form of a long let-ter written to an anonymous friend.

QUESTIONS TO CONSIDER

1. One modern reaction to Abelard's story is: Why in the world did that man be-come a clergyman, since he obviously did not have the personality for it? What do you think? Would he have been better adjusted in a different medieval occu-pation, or did he probably sense no other option?
2. Why did Abelard think—or at least say that he thought—that he deserved his severe punishment?

Now there dwelt in that same city of Paris a certain young girl named Heloise, the niece of a canon who was called Fulbert. Her uncle's love for her was equalled only by his desire that she should have the best education which he could possibly procure for her. Of no mean beauty, she stood out above by reason of her abundant knowledge of letters. Now this virtue is rare among women, and for that very reason it doubly graced the maiden, and made her the most worthy of renown in the entire kingdom. It was this young girl whom I, after carefully considering all those qualities which are wont to attract lovers, determined to unite with myself in the bonds of love, and indeed the thing seemed to me very easy to be done. So distinguished was my name, and I possessed such advantages of youth and comeliness, that no matter what woman I might favor with my love, I dreaded rejection of none.

Thus, utterly aflame with passion for this maiden, I sought to discover means whereby I might have daily and familiar speech with her, thereby the more easily to win her consent. For this purpose I persuaded the girl's uncle to take me into his household in return for the payment of a small sum. My pretext for this was that the care of my own household was a serious handicap to my studies, and likewise burdened me with an expense far greater than I could afford. Now, he was a man keen in avarice, and likewise he was most desirous for his niece that her study of letters should ever go forward, so, for these reasons, I easily won his consent to the fulfillment of my wish, for he was fairly agape for my money, and at the same time believed that his niece would vastly benefit by my teaching. He entrusted her wholly to my guidance, begging me to give her instruction whensoever I might be free from the duties of my school, and to punish her sternly if ever I should find her negligent of her tasks. In all this the man's simplicity was nothing short of astounding to me; I should not have been more smitten with wonder if he had entrusted a tender lamb to the care of a ravenous wolf. What had he done save to give free scope to my desires, and to offer me every opportunity to bend her to my will?

Why should I say more? Under the pretext of study we spent our hours in the happiness of love, and learning held out to us the secret opportunities that our passion craved. Our speech was more of love than of books which lay open before us; our kisses far outnumbered our reasoned words. Our hands sought less the book than each other's bosoms; love drew our eyes together far more than the lesson drew them to the pages of our text.

In measure as this passionate rapture absorbed me more and more, I devoted ever less time to philosophy and to the work of school. My lecturing became utterly careless and lukewarm; I did nothing because of inspiration, but everything merely as a matter of habit. I had become nothing more than a reciter of my former discoveries, and though I still wrote poems, they dealt with love, not with the secrets of philosophy. Of these songs you yourself well know how some have become widely known and have been sung in many lands.

A thing so manifest could deceive only a few, no one, methinks, save him whose shame it chiefly bespoke, the girl's uncle, Fulbert. The truth was often enough hinted to him, and by many persons, but he could not believe it. But no matter how slow a matter may be in disclosing itself, it is sure to come forth at last, nor is it easy to hide from one what is known to all. So, after the lapse of several months, did it happen to us. Oh, how great was the uncle's grief when he learned the truth, and how bitter was the sorrow of the lovers when we were forced to part! Each grieved most, not for himself, but for the other. Each sought to allay, not his own sufferings, but those of the one he loved. Once the first wildness of shame had passed, it left us more shameless than before, and as shame died within us the cause of it seemed to us ever more desirable. And so it chanced with us as, in the stories that the poets tell, it once happened with Mars and Venus when they were caught together.

It was not long after this that Heloise found that she was pregnant, and of this she wrote to me in the utmost exultation, at the same time asking me to consider what had best be done. Accordingly, I stole her secretly away from her uncle's house, sending her without delay to my own country. She remained there with my sister until she gave birth to a son, whom she named Astrolabe. Meanwhile her uncle, after his return, was almost mad with grief, only one who had seen him could rightly guess the burning agony of his sorrow and the bitterness of his shame. What steps to take against me, or what snares to set for me, he did not know. If he should kill me or do me some bodily hurt, he feared greatly lest his dear-loved niece should be made to suffer for it among my kinsfolk.

At length, however, in pity for his boundless grief, and bitterly blaming myself for the suffering which my love had brought upon him through the baseness of the deception I had practiced, I went to him to entreat his forgiveness, promising to make any amends that he himself might decree. I pointed out that what had happened could not seem incredible to any one who had ever felt the power of love, or who remembered how, from the very beginning of the human race, women had cast down even the noblest men to utter ruin. And in order to make amends even beyond his extremest hope, I offered to marry her whom I had seduced, provided only the thing could be kept secret, so that I might suffer no loss of reputation thereby. To this he gladly assented, pledging his own faith and that of his kindred.

Forthwith I repaired to my own country, and brought back thence my mistress, that I might make her my wife. She, however, most violently disapproved of this, and for two chief reasons: the danger thereof, and the disgrace which it would bring upon me. She swore that her uncle would never be appeased by such satisfaction as this, as, indeed, afterwards proved only too true. She asked how she could ever glory in me if she should make me thus inglorious, and should shame herself along with me. What penalties, she said, would the world rightly demand of her if she should rob it of so shining a light! What curses would follow such a loss to the Church, what tears among the philosophers would result from such a marriage! How unfitting, how lamentable it would be for me, whom nature had made for the whole world, to devote myself to such humiliation!

Her final argument was that it would be dangerous for me to take her back to Paris, and that it would be far sweeter for her to be called my mistress than to be known as my wife; nay, too, that this would be more honorable for me as well. In such case, she said, love alone would hold me to her, and the strength of the marriage chain would not constrain us. Even if we should by chance be parted from time to time, the joy of our meetings would be all the sweeter by reason of its rarity. But when she found that she could not convince me or dissuade me from my folly by these and like arguments, and because she could not bear to offend me, with grievous sighs and tears she made an end of her resistance, saying: "Then there is no more left but this, that in our doom the sorrow yet to come shall be no less than the love we two have already known." Nor in this, as now the whole world knows, did she lack the spirit of prophecy.

So, after our little son was born, we left him in my sister's care, and secretly returned to Paris. A few days later, in the early morning, having kept our nocturnal vigil of prayer unknown to all in a certain church, we were united there in the benediction of wedlock, her uncle and a few friends of his and mine being present. We departed forthwith stealthily and by separate ways, nor thereafter did we see each other save rarely and in private, thus striving our utmost to conceal what we had done. But her uncle and those of his household, seeking solace for their disgrace, began to divulge the story of our marriage, and thereby to violate the pledge they had given me on this point. Heloise, on the contrary, denounced her own kin and swore that they were speaking the most absolute lies. Her uncle, aroused to fury thereby, visited her repeatedly with punishments. No sooner had I learned this than I sent her to a convent of nuns at Argenteuil, not far from Paris, where she herself had been brought up and educated as a young girl. I had them make ready for her all garments of a nun, suitable for the life of a convent, excepting only the veil, and these I bade her put on.

When her uncle and his kinsmen heard of this, they were convinced that now I had completely played them false and had rid myself forever of Heloise by forcing her to become a nun. Violently incensed, they laid a plot against me, and one night, while I, all unsuspecting, was asleep in a secret room in my lodgings, they broke in with the help of one of my servants, whom they had bribed. There they had vengeance on me with a most cruel and most shameful punishment, such as astounded the whole world, for they cut off those parts of my body with which I had done that which was the cause of their sorrow. This done, straightaway they fled, but two of them were captured, and suffered the loss of their eyes and their genital organs. One of these two was the aforesaid servant, who, even while he was still in my service, had been led by his avarice to betray me.

73

St. Hildegard of Bingen, *Know the Ways*

As was true of their male contemporaries, women served in the formative years of the Christian Church as deaconesses or later helped to convert relatives or barbarian peoples. A few, such as St. Teresa of Avila and St. Catherine of Siena, became famous for their teaching roles and were sometimes even called "Doctors," but for the most part female mystics remained relatively unknown, although their writings would be gathered and recopied over the centuries. It was only in the twentieth century that their important contributions are being recognized.

A notable exception to the general rule that female mystics received little attention was St. Hildegard (1098–1179), mother superior of a community of Benedictine nuns at Rupertsburg near Bingen on the Rhine. Over a period of many years, she spoke and wrote of experiencing large-scale, highly detailed visions with figures or voices explaining the significance of their related parts. She also wrote on medical subjects and the world of nature; occasionally she brought her natural-scientific observations to bear on the interpretation of her visions. In 1150, she finished recording her visions of the preceding nine years in a book, *Scivias* ("Sci Vias" means "Know the Ways"), which enhanced her contemporary recognition. As long as she lived after that, people from all walks of life sought her out for advice and help with prophecy, which she freely gave.

QUESTIONS TO CONSIDER

1. How does St. Hildegard relate body and soul to each other?
2. What are the main attributes of Holy Mother Church, as she appears in a vision?
3. Why does Hildegard refer to secular authority, even in its royal ruling form, as "inferior"?

Body and Soul

The body is a tent and the resting place of all spiritual powers, for the soul, who lives outside the body, works with it—and it with her—for both good and evil. . . . The soul is the lady in charge, the flesh truly is her serving-maid. In what way? The soul rules the body in giving life to it; the body submits to the soul's governance for living, since the body dissolves when the soul no longer sustains life in it. When a person does an evil deed with the soul conscious of it, it is as bitter for the soul as if the body knowingly took some poison, but then the soul rejoices at a good deed in the way that the body finds delight in a tasty dish.

The soul flows through the body as sap through a tree. What is that? The sap enables the tree to send forth green leaves, to blossom and to bear fruit. But what makes the fruit of the tree ripen? The weather gives it sunny days with their warmth and rainy ones with water, and so it ripens under the influence of the weather. What does that mean? That, like the sun, the merciful grace of God gives light to man, the breath of the Holy Spirit, like the rain, gives him the water of encouragement and, like the weather elements in turn, they bring good fruit in him to full development.

The soul is thus for the body what the sap is for the tree, applying its powers to the tree as it grows into its ordained form. How so? Gathering knowledge is like unto the greening of the tree's twigs and leaves, directing the will is like unto its blossoming, while feelings resemble the fruit in its early stages and reason the fully developed fruit. Finally, the development of understanding is like unto the spreading growth of the tree to its full dimensions.

And so in this way the soul strengthens and sustains the body. Therefore, o man, recognize what you are in your soul, you who reject the good of knowledge as if wanting to put yourself on the same level as cattle!

From *Scivias* in *S. Hildegardis Abbatissae Opera Omnia, Patrologia,* Vol. CXCVII (Paris: J.P. Migne, 1853), columns 427–28, 453–57, 625–33, *passim.* Trans. Henry A. Myers.

Holy Mother Church

After this I saw a female image, so huge that it was like looking at a large city. She wore a wonderfully decorated crown on her head. Bright rays of light, beaming from Heaven to earth, fell from her arms like flowing sleeves. Her lower abdomen resembled a net, full of open spaces through which a great throng of humanity entered. . . . And this image spread her radiance out like a garment and spoke: "I must conceive and bear!"

Then I saw black children swimming through the air, close to the ground, like fish in water. Through the openings they entered the womb of the great figure. She then took a deep breath, drawing them up to her head, from whence they came out of her mouth. She herself was not hurt by all this.

And behold: there appeared a bright light and within it a human figure, surrounded by a fiery red glow. This apparition pulled the black skin off every child and threw it aside, clothed every single one of them with a garment of blinding white and caused a bright light to beam upon them all. "Take off," she said to each of them, "your old clothing of unrighteousness and put on the new garment of holiness, for the gates to your inheritance have been opened. . . ."

And again, I heard the voice from Heaven, saying to me: "The edifice of living souls is built in Heaven to its perfection. It receives the virtues of its sons, which become its building stones of priceless gems, like a huge city absorbs throngs of people and a wide net pulls up great numbers of fish together. . . . The woman you see, so tall that she resembles a large city when you look at her, is my Son's bride, who keeps on giving him new children, those born again from the spirit and the water. The most stout-hearted warrior of all has chosen her to gather in the great throng of His chosen ones . . . and make them perfect. No attacking enemy can storm her towers, for she hurls unbelief into flight, and through the faith of believers she continues to grow. . . .

Her head is crowned with wonderful adornments. When the Church first came into being, awakened in the blood of the Lamb, the apostles and martyrs fittingly crowned her the true bride wed to my Son with their deeds. From the blood of His wounds she went through faith into the world, where she builds her own structure with hallowed souls. For this reason, bright rays of light descend from her arms like flowing sleeves. This signifies the working of divine power in the priests, who present the holiest of sacrifices at the consecrated altar in the mystery of the flesh and blood of their Redeemer. . . .

Like a net, the lower abdomen of the woman is open in many places through which a great crowd of people enter: this is her maternal love, opening for a catch of believing souls. . . . You see black children swimming through the air close to the ground, like fish in water. Through the openings they enter the figure's womb. . . . Their blackness signifies the foolishness of people who are not yet washed in the bath of redemption. Although they love earthly things, run about in the world and set up their dwellings in it, they have finally succeeded in reaching the mother of holiness. . . .

It is for this reason that the figure takes a deep breath, drawing them up inside her head, where they come out through her mouth. The process does not hurt her in the least. As often as a baptism is carried out . . . the Holy Mother [Church] takes a deep breath—her breath is the Holy Spirit—so that the human being is drawn up to the highest bestower of blessedness, the Head of all, and becomes a member of

Christ[29] when he is born again, this time to salvation, calling upon the Holy Trinity through the mouth of the Holy Mother. . . .

The human figure shimmering in the fiery red glow . . . pulls the black skin off each individual child and casts it aside, then clothes all of them in garments of blinding white and reveals a brightly shining light to them with words of salvation bringing admonition. The divine power, which looks into the hearts of men, mercifully takes away all sinful unbelief with the bath of baptism, for in Christ there is no death but rather life through the righteous acknowledgment of Him and the washing away of sins.

The Walls of Authority

And then I was looking from inside the great building between the north and west corners out at the surrounding walls. The inner wall was one of arches filled with lattice work, but filled in solidly and not with any empty space in the usual fashion of lattice work. . . . Out from this inner wall, I saw two lesser walls running parallel to it from the north corner to the west corner. . . . On both ends they turned towards the inner wall, joining at the top in the way that plates on a turtle's shell come together. Both of these walls were a yard and a half high. Half a yard's distance separated the middle wall from the inner one with only the width of a child's palm between it and the outer one. . . .

While I was attentively observing, He who was sitting on the throne spoke to me again: "Let no believer who wants to serve God humbly withhold in doubt his submission to earthly authority. For the Holy Spirit has established government over the people, to further the people's wellbeing. . . .

"These two outer walls, each a yard and a half high, signify that, following the division into two estates on earth—those situated high and those low[30]—three groups make up the second estate: those leaders with exalted ruling powers, those who are free and not bound in [manorial] service, and those who are obedient to lords to whom they owe [manorial] services. And so the reason that there is a distance of half a yard from the middle wall to the inner one of arches is that this signifies the distance in dignity between those who rank higher because of their spiritual office and those who are assigned lesser titles because their occupations are earthly ones. They enjoy one faith together, but the differentiation still exists according to God's will until the final gathering together of His subjects. But between the outer and middle wall the space is only the width of a child's palm, because between the power of secular rulership, with its inferior ranking, and those who are bound to serve their higher-ups the distance—justly considered—is very limited, so that with the single-minded, simple devotion of innocent children they can touch each other and carry out the chores hand in hand.

---

[29]Her meaning here is not exactly "church member" as we would understand it. She is using the organic analogy of Christian tradition in which the Church is a living body with believing Christians functioning as its members in the sense of arms, legs, and the like, and with Christ functioning as the body's head.
[30]For Hildegard, the difference in authority that really counts is between the spiritual authority of clergymen, making up the first order or estate, and the rest of mankind, making up the second order of laymen. In stressing this, the plays down the importance of divisions among laymen, paying no attention to the distinction between serfs and free townspeople nor to the distinction between townspeople and the nobility; the categories of free townspeople and serfs thus appears as subdivisions of the second state.

74

St. Francis of Assisi, "The Rule of St. Francis"

Francis of Assisi (1182–1226), founder of the Franciscan Order, is one of the most celebrated saints of medieval Europe. As the son of a prosperous merchant, young Francis enjoyed a carefree life of pleasure and paid little attention to religion. But in 1206, he underwent a conversion experience and committed the rest of his life to ministering to the poorest of the poor living in the burgeoning cities of his native Italy. In imitation of the first apostles, Francis accepted a life of absolute poverty. He gave away all of his property and made his way by begging. Francis was an open, joyful man who loved animals and loved to laugh. Despite the hardships of his ministry, he naturally drew people to him. Francis was loath to establish detailed regulations for his followers, but by 1210, so many people had joined in his work that he was compelled to organize a rule for his followers. To underscore the virtue of humility, Francis called his followers the Order of Friars Minor. Unlike monks, who retreated from the world to live in monasteries, his "little brothers" or friars were to live among the people.

The Franciscan Friars, and the women's order of the Poor Clare nuns that he inspired, were to own nothing. Like Francis, they were to earn their way by manual labor or by begging. The focus of their ministry was the poor of the inner cities. Soon the Franciscans had established hospitals for lepers, orphanages for abandoned children, and shelters for the homeless. By 1217, Franciscan missionaries had been sent to France, Germany, Hungary, Spain, and North Africa and would soon be in China and Japan (see Reading 99). By the end of the thirteenth century, fourteen hundred Franciscan convents and friaries had been established. Because of the tremendous growth of the Franciscan movement, Francis was forced to revise his rule of 1210, and in 1223, three years before his death, he produced a more detailed rule to guide his Franciscans.

QUESTIONS TO CONSIDER

1. Why would the Rule of St. Francis be so attractive to thousands of men and women throughout medieval Europe?
2. Why did Francis exempt his followers from certain periods of fasting and permit them to "eat whatever food is set before them"?
3. What does the success of the Franciscan order suggest about social conditions in thirteenth-century Europe?
4. How would you compare the life of a Franciscan with that of a Benedictine (see Reading 49)?
5. Why would the Franciscans excel as foreign missionaries (see Readings 77 and 85)?

1. This is the rule and life of the Minor Brothers, namely, to observe the holy gospel of our Lord Jesus Christ by living in obedience, in poverty, and in chastity. Brother Francis promises obedience and reverence to Pope Honorius and to his suc-

From Oliver J. Thatcher and Edgar J. McNeal, eds., *A Source Book for Medieval History: Selected Documents* (New York: Charles Scribner's Sons, 1905), pp. 499–504.

cessors who shall be canonically elected, and to the Roman Church. The other brothers are bound to obey brother Francis, and his successors.

2. If any, wishing to adopt this life, come to our brothers [to ask admission], they shall be sent to the provincial ministers, who alone have the right to receive others into the order. The provincial ministers shall carefully examine them in the catholic faith and the sacraments of the church. And if they believe all these and faithfully confess them and promise to observe them to the end of life, and if they have no wives, or if they have wives, and the wives have either already entered a monastery, or have received permission to do so, and they have already taken the vow of chastity with the permission of the bishop of the diocese [in which they live], and their wives are of such an age that no suspicion can rise against them, let the provincial ministers repeat to them the word of the holy gospel, to go and sell all their goods and give to the poor [Matt. 19:21]. But if they are not able to do so, their good will is sufficient for them. And the brothers and provincial ministers shall not be solicitous about the temporal possessions of those who wish to enter the order; but let them do with their possessions whatever the Lord may put into their minds to do. Nevertheless, if they ask the advice of the brothers, the provincial ministers may send them to God-fearing men, at whose advice they may give their possessions to the poor. Then the ministers shall give them the dress of a novice, namely: two robes without a hood, a girdle, trousers, a hood with a cape reaching to the girdle. But the ministers may add to these if they think it necessary. After the year of probation is ended they shall be received into obedience [that is, into the order], by promising to observe this rule and life forever. And according to the command of the pope they shall never be permitted to leave the order and give up this life and form of religion. For according to the holy gospel no one who puts his hand to the plough and looks back is fit for the kingdom of God [Luke 9:62]. And after they have promised obedience, those who wish may have one robe with a hood and one without a hood. Those who must may wear shoes, and all the brothers shall wear common clothes, and they shall have God's blessing if they patch them with coarse cloth and pieces of other kinds of cloth. But I warn and exhort them not to despise nor judge other men who wear fine and gay clothing, and have delicious foods and drinks. But rather let each one judge and despise himself.

3. The clerical brothers shall perform the divine office according to the rite of the holy Roman church, except the psalter, from which they may have breviaries. The lay brothers shall say 24 Paternosters at matins, 5 at lauds, 7 each at primes, terces, sexts, and nones, 12 at vespers, 7 at completorium, and prayers for the dead. And they shall fast for All Saints' day [November 1] to Christmas. They may observe or not, as they choose, the holy Lent which begins at epiphany [January 6] and lasts for 40 days, and which our Lord consecrated by his holy fasts. Those who keep it shall be blessed of the Lord, but those who do not wish to keep it are not bound to do so. But they shall all observe the other Lent [that is, from Ash-Wednesday to Easter]. The rest of the time the brothers are bound to fast only on Fridays. But in times of manifest necessity they shall not fast. But I counsel, warn, and exhort my brothers in the Lord Jesus Christ that when they go out into the world they shall not be quarrelsome or contentious, nor judge others. But they shall be gentle, peaceable, and kind, mild and humble, and virtuous in speech, as is becoming to all. They shall not ride on horseback unless compelled by manifest necessity or infirmity to do so. When they enter a house they shall say, "Peace be to this house." According to the holy gospel, they may eat of whatever food is set before them.

4. I strictly forbid all the brothers to accept money or property either in person or through another. Nevertheless, for the needs of the sick, and for clothing the other brothers, the ministers and guardians may, as they see that necessity requires, provide through spiritual friends, according to the locality, season, and the degree of cold which may be expected in the region where they live. But, as has been said, they shall never receive money or property.

5. Those brothers to whom the Lord has given the ability to work shall work faithfully and devotedly, so that idleness, which is the enemy of the soul, may be excluded and not extinguish the spirit of prayer and devotion to which all temporal things should be subservient. As the price of their labors they may receive things that are necessary for themselves and the brothers, but not money or property. And they shall humbly receive what is given them, as is becoming to the servants of God and to those who practise the most holy poverty.

6. The brothers shall have nothing of their own, neither house, nor land, nor anything, but as pilgrims and strangers in this world, serving the Lord in poverty and humility, let them confidently go asking alms. Nor let them be ashamed of this, for the Lord made himself poor for us in this world. This is that highest pitch of poverty which has made you, my dearest brothers, heirs and kings of the kingdom of heaven, which has made you poor in goods, and exalted you in virtues. Let this be your portion, which leads into the land of the living. Cling wholly to this, my most beloved brothers, and you shall wish to have in this world nothing else than the name of the Lord Jesus Christ. And wherever they are, if they find brothers, let them show themselves to be of the same household, and each one may securely make known to the other his need. For if a mother loves and nourishes her child, how much more diligently should one nourish and love one's spiritual brother? And if any of them fall ill, the other brothers should serve them as they would wish to be served.

7. If any brother is tempted by the devil and commits a mortal sin, he should go as quickly as possible to the provincial minister, as the brothers have determined that recourse shall be had to the provincial ministers for such sins. If the provincial minister is a priest, he shall mercifully prescribe the penance for him. If he is not a priest, he shall, as may seem best to him, have some priest of the order prescribe the penance. And they shall guard against being angry or irritated about it, because anger and irritation hinder love in themselves and in others.

8. All the brothers must have one of their number as their general minister and servant of the whole brotherhood, and they must obey him. At his death the provincial ministers and guardians shall elect his successor at the chapter held at Pentecost, at which time all the provincial ministers must always come together at whatever place the general minister may order. And this chapter must be held once every three years, or more or less frequently, as the general minister may think best. And if at any time it shall be clear to the provincial ministers and guardians that the general minister is not able to perform the duties of his office and does not serve the best interests of the brothers, the aforesaid brothers, to whom the right of election is given, must, in the name of the Lord, elect another as general minister. After the chapter at Pentecost, the provincial ministers and guardians may, each in his own province, if it seems best to them, once in the same year, convoke the brothers to a provincial chapter.

9. If a bishop forbids the brothers to preach in his diocese, they shall obey him. And no brother shall preach to the people unless the general minister of the brotherhood has examined and approved him and given him the right to preach. I also

warn the brothers that in their sermons their words shall be chaste and well chosen for the profit and edification of the people. They shall speak to them of vices and virtues, punishment and glory, with brevity of speech, because the Lord made the word shortened over the earth [Rom. 9:28].

10. The ministers and servants shall visit and admonish their brothers and humbly and lovingly correct them. They shall not put any command upon them that would be against their soul and this rule. And the brothers who are subject must remember that for God's sake they have given up their own wills. Wherefore I command them to obey their ministers in all the things which they have promised the Lord to observe and which shall not be contrary to their souls and this rule. And whenever brothers know and recognize that they cannot observe this rule, let them go to their ministers, and the ministers shall lovingly and kindly receive them and treat them in such a way that the brothers may speak to them freely and treat them as lords speak to, and treat, their servants. For the ministers ought to be the servants of all the brothers. I warn and exhort the brothers in the Lord Jesus Christ to guard against all arrogance, pride, envy, avarice, care, and solicitude for this world, detraction, and murmuring. And those who cannot read need not be anxious to learn. But above all things let them desire to have the spirit of the Lord and his holy works, to pray always to God with a pure heart, and to have humility, and patience in persecution and in infirmity, and to love those who persecute us and reproach us and blame us. For the Lord says, "Love your enemies, and pray for those who persecute and speak evil of you" [cf. Matt. 5:44]. "Blessed are they who suffer persecution for righteousness' sake, for theirs is the kingdom of heaven" [Matt. 5:10]. He that endureth to the end shall be saved [Matt. 10:22].

11. I strictly forbid all the brothers to have any association or conversation with women that may cause suspicion. And let them not enter nunneries, except those which the pope has given them special permission to enter. Let them not be intimate friends of men or women, lest on this account scandal arise among the brothers or about brothers.

12. If any of the brothers shall be divinely inspired to go among Saracens and other infidels they must get the permission to go from their provincial minister, who shall give his consent only to those who he sees are suitable to be sent. In addition, I command the ministers to ask the pope to assign them a cardinal of the holy Roman church, who shall be the guide, protector, and corrector of the brotherhood, in order that, being always in subjection and at the feet of the holy church, and steadfast in the catholic faith, they may observe poverty, humility, and the holy gospel of our Lord Jesus Christ, as we have firmly promised to do. Let no man dare act contrary to this confirmation.

Coping with Deviant Beliefs: East and West

In the medieval West, drastic action against deviants in the faith emerged from the combined beliefs that (1.) salvation was the most important thing in human existence; (2.) salvation rested squarely on accepting Christian beliefs as taught by the Catholic Church; (3.) those who taught false beliefs were depriving their hearers of salvation; and (4.) that such *heretics*—"those who would split off" (from the true Church)—merited death, to get them out of this world, where they were actively spoiling their hearers' chances of salvation.

People cited by the Church as heretics, of course, did not accept the idea that they were mistaken. Generally, they saw themselves as reformers, trying to set better examples than an impure church could provide. This was particularly true of the Cathars ("purifying ones"), who held their own faith and lifestyle to be much closer to the true Christian model than that of their persecutors.

Toleration of heretics made no more sense to medieval people than the toleration of drug dealers or counterfeiters would in our own society. In the Age of Scholasticism, St. Thomas Aquinas struck what he seems to have thought was the proper balance between Christian compassion and the need to eliminate the activities of soul-destroying heretics.

By way of contrast, competing belief systems had occasionally brought on retribution in East Asia, such as the persecution of Confucians under the "Legalist" Qin Dynasty (see Reading 29), but the norm there was to be much less concerned about what people believed than how they acted. The thirteenth century produced not only Scholasticism but also much new knowledge of East Asia, as Franciscan monks and Venetian merchants, enjoying the openness of Mongol rulers with their religiously diverse subjects and welcoming policy towards many foreigners, brought back news of "The Far East." Friar William of Rubruck's *Journal* reports on toleration of different Asian religions and even heretical ("Nestorian") Christianity as a matter of considerable interest, although certainly not as something to be imitated by Westerners back home.

The famous Trial of Joan of Arc illustrates the lasting strength of antiheretical feeling, as the Middle Ages neared its end. Joan is treated as the same sort of criminal destroyer of souls through bad teachings and modeling that St. Thomas Aquinas had discussed some century and a half earlier.

75

Pierre de Vaux-de-Cernay, "What Cathars Believe"

The Cathar heresy, which proved most threatening to orthodox Catholic belief in France during the thirteenth century and fourteenth centuries, was in many ways the reemergence of the old third-century Manichean heresy, a belief that viewed life as a battle for supremacy between the forces of light and the forces of darkness. This dualist belief had never been eradicated in Christian Europe and by the thirteenth century had resurfaced in the rugged mountainous terrain of the Balkan Peninsula, the Alpine region of northern Italy, and in the foothills of the Pyrenees Mountains in southern France, and especially in the French city of Albi. Cathar comes from the Greek word, *katharos* meaning "pure." Cathars believed Satan created their fleshy bodies and God created their incorruptible souls. For Cathars life was a continual struggle to purify or free the soul from its imprisonment in the sinful body. The Cathar ideal was to become a "perfect," the believer who through fasting and celibacy would overcome Satan and conquer his body. Yet, Cathars readily admitted that becoming a "perfect," was very difficult and quite unlikely for most believers. As a consequence, Cathars were quite tolerant of sin and failure. All sins were considered equal; fornication and adultery were no more reprehensible than lying or eating meat. Sexual promiscuity was therefore not uncommon. Indeed, Cathar communities in southern France were frequently charged with this sin. In 1209 King Philip II of France launched the first of a series of crusades to root out the heresy in Languedoc, Provence, Toulouse, and in cities such as Albi, from which we have the term "Albigensians" describing this anti-Cathar crusade. Convinced the Cathar heresy was an especially lethal threat to Christendom, crusading armies frequently massacred entire towns shouting, "Kill them all—God will judge the innocent." Because the Cathars were secretive and few in number (perhaps a few thousand members) virtually none of their beliefs were written down. Much of what we know of their beliefs comes from the records of the inquisitional courts, established by the Church to extirpate the heresy and extend the full power and authority of the kings of France throughout the territories of Lanquedoc, Provence and Toulouse.

On February 28, 1320, Jacques Fournier, Bishop of Pamiers and future Pope Benedict XII, presided over the inquisition of Arnauld Gélis, a man accused of being a Cathar. Under questioning, Arnauld admitted that Cathars believe the following: 1) Souls of the dead never do penance; they wander from church to church depending on their sins. 2) Souls of children who die without baptism go to limbo and will enter paradise on judgment day. 3) God will have mercy on all who profess to be Christians; no one will ever be sent to hell. 4) God will have mercy on all the souls of heretics, Jews, and nonbelievers. None of them will be sent to hell. 5) Hell is a place only for demons. 6) Souls both before and after death, have their own fleshy form. They have hands, eyes and feet.

Bishop Fournier condemned Arnauld Gélis for these beliefs, insisting that all orthodox Catholics were required to believe the following: 1) Souls of the dead go to purgatory and after being purged of their sins go to paradise. 2) Souls of children who die without baptism will never go to paradise. 3) Christians who did not keep the commandments will be sent to hell. 4) Heretics, Jews, and pagans are dammed and will receive eternal punishment in hell. 5) Wicked people along with demons reside in hell. 6) Souls are completely spiritual. They do not eat or drink nor do they have any bodily form.[31]

A century earlier, in 1212 Pierre de Vaux-de-Cernay, a Cistercian priest joined the first crusade against the Cathars. He gives us another first-hand account of what Cathars believe.

---

[31]Jean Duvernoy, *Le register d'inquisition de Jacques Fournier (Évêque de Pamiers)*, 1318–1325. *3 vols. (Paris: Mouton, 1978), 1: 165–68.*

QUESTIONS TO CONSIDER

1. Although their numbers were few, the Cathar heresy attracted a considerable number of women. Why would this be the case? What is it about these beliefs women would find so appealing?
2. Based upon your understanding of the Cathar heresy why do you think a crusade, the only one launched in the Christian West, was necessary to deal with this heresy?
3. Many of the crusaders who attacked the Cathar communities were convinced that Cathars were irredeemable sinful heretics, quite undeserving of conversion, who deserved to die. Why would this be the case?

First it is to be known that the heretics held that there are two creators: viz. one of invisible things, whom they called the benevolent god, and another of visible things, whom they named the malevolent god. The New Testament they attributed to the benevolent god, but the Old Testament to the malevolent god, and rejected it altogether, except certain authorities which are inserted in the New Testament from the Old, which, out of reverence to the New Testament, they esteemed worthy of reception. They charged the author of the Old Testament with falsehood, because the Creator said, "In the day that ye eat of the tree of the knowledge of good and evil ye shall die"; nor (as they say) after eating did they die, when, in fact, after the eating the forbidden fruit they were subjected to the misery of death. They also call him a homicide, as well, because he burned up Sodom and Gomorrah and destroyed the world by the waters of the deluge, as because he overwhelmed pharaoh and the Egyptians in the sea. They affirmed also that all the fathers of the Old Testament were damned, that John the Baptist was one of the greater demons. They said also, in their secret doctrine, (*in secreto su*) that the Christ who was born in the visible and terrestrial Bethlehem and crucified in Jerusalem was a bad man, and that Mary Magdalene was his concubine; and that she was the woman taken in adultery, of whom we read in the gospel. For the good Christ, as they said, never ate, nor drank, nor took upon him true flesh, nor ever was in this world, except spiritually in the body of Paul. I say in the terrestrial and visible Bethlehem, because the heretics feigned that there was another new and invisible country, and in that country, according to some, the good Christ was born and crucified, Also the heretics said that the good god had two wives, Collant and Colibant, and from them begat sons and daughters. There were other heretics who said that there is one Creator but that he had for sons Christ and the devil. These, also, said that all creatures were good, but that by the daughters of whom we read in the Apocalypse [*marg.* Genesis], all things had been corrupted.

They said that almost all the Church of Rome was a den of thieves, and that it was the harlot of which we read in the Apocalypse. They so far annulled the sacraments of the Church, as publicly to teach that the water of holy baptism was just the same as river water, and that the Host of the most holy body of Christ did not differ from common bread, instilling into the ears of the simple this blasphemy, that the body of Christ, even though it had been as great as the Alps, would have been long ago consumed and annihilated by those who had eaten of it. Confirmation and con-

From Pierre de Vaux-de-Cernay, *Historia Albegensis* in Samuel Roffery Maitland, *Facts and Documents Illustrative of the History, Doctrine and Rites of the Ancient Albigenses and Waldenses* (London: C.J.G and F. Rivington, 1832), pp. 392–96.

fession they considered as altogether vain and frivolous. They preached that holy matrimony was meretricious, and that none could be saved in, it if they should beget children. Denying also the resurrection of the flesh, they invented some unheard of notions, saying that our souls are those of angelic spirits who, being cast down from heaven by the apostasy of pride, left their glorified bodies in the air; and that these souls themselves, after successively inhabiting seven terrene bodies of one sort or another, having at length fulfilled their penance, return to those deserted bodies.

It is also to be known that some among the heretics were called "perfect" or "good men"; others "believers of the heretics." Those who were called perfect wore a black dress, falsely pretended to chastity, abhorred the eating of flesh, eggs and cheese, wished to appear not liars when they were continually telling lies, chiefly respecting God. They also said that they ought not on any account to swear.

Those were called "believers" of the heretics, who, lived after the manner of the world, and who, though they did not attain so far as to imitate the life of the perfect, nevertheless hoped to be saved in their faith; and though they differed as to their mode of life, they were one with them in belief and unbelief. Those who were called believers of the heretics were given to usury, rapine, homicide, lust, perjury, and every vice; and they, in fact, sinned with more security and less restraint, because they believed that without restitution, without confession and penance, they should be saved, if only, when on the point of death, they could say a Pater Noster, and receive imposition of hands from the teachers.

As to the "perfect" heretics, however, they had a magistracy whom they called deacons and bishops, without the imposition of whose hands, at the time of his death, none of the believers thought he could be saved; but if they laid their hands upon any dying man, however wicked, if he could only say a Pater Noster, they considered him to be so saved that without any satisfaction and without any other aid, he immediately took wing to heaven.

76

Thomas Aquinas, *Summa Theologica*: "Whether Heretics Are to Be Tolerated"

St. Thomas Aquinas (ca. 1225–1274), a Dominican monk, was easily the greatest of the Scholastic writers. His *Summa Theologica* uses human reason and ancient philosophy, particularly that of Aristotle, to confirm revealed religious propositions, especially those found in the letters of St. Paul. In Thomas's work, like that of many other Scholastics, Aristotle is simply called the "Philosopher" and St. Paul the "Apostle":

In the following selection from the Treatise on God, part of the *Summa Theologica*, St. Thomas employs the dialectic, the ancient Greek form of argumentation effectively used by Plato in his dialogues. By the thirteenth century, the dialectic no longer had separate speakers designated in it. It had come to mean presenting a bit of theory as a question; examining all the arguments for it, if it was a false proposition, or against it, if it was a true one; and finally, answering these wrong arguments with reason and evidence.

QUESTIONS TO CONSIDER

1. What shows this to be a medieval document? Why could it definitely not be an ancient Greek or a modern one?
2. Why does St. Thomas leave the whole issue of human rights outside his discussion? Why does freedom of speech seem totally irrelevant to him as he discusses how to handle heretics?
3. Why is Thomas convinced that his method of dealing with heretics does them, as well as the community, a great favor?

Proposition 1. It appears that heretics are to be tolerated. The Apostle [Paul] writes:

> "The servant of the Lord must reject strife, but be gentle unto all men, patient and ready to teach, in meekness instructing those who have offered opposition, if God may bring them to repentance so that they may acknowledge the truth. [II Timothy, ii 24]" But if heretics are put to death rather than being tolerated there is no possibility of repentance, which appears contrary to the teaching of the Apostle.

Beyond that, whatever is necessary in the Church must be tolerated, since Saint Paul tells us: "For there must also be heresies among you, in order that they who are approved may be manifest" (I Corinthians. xi. 19). Therefore it would seem that heretics are to be tolerated.

Further, the Lord commanded his servants to let the weeds grow until the harvest, that is, the end of the world as the same text explains.[32] Therefore it would seem that Heretics are to be tolerated. Now, according to holy interpreters, "weeds" signify "heretics:" consequently heretics are to be tolerated.

But against this conclusion the words of the Apostle tell us: "Reject a man who is a heretic after being admonished the first and second times, as his own words are proof against him" (Titus. Hi. 10–11).

Consequently this is the reply: two things are to be considered concerning heretics, one with regard to themselves, the other with regard to the Church. As for the heretics themselves, their sin is such that they deserve not only exclusion from the Church by excommunication but also from the world by death. To falsify the faith by which the soul lives is far more serious than to falsify earthly coin, which is among the necessities of secular life. Since counterfeiters and similar criminals are quickly condemned to a just death by the civil authorities, how much greater justice is there in putting to death—not merely excommunicating—heretics, as soon as they have been convicted of heresy.

With regard to the Church there is mercy, which aims at the conversion of the erring. This is the reason she does not condemn immediately, but, as the Apostle pre-

---

[32] "Lest while you gather up the weeds, you also uproot the wheat with the weeds, let both grow together until the harvest, and at the time of harvest I will say to the reapers, 'First gather together the weeds, and bind them in bundles to burn them, but gather the wheat unto my barn'" (Matthew, xiii. 29–30).

Not only does the Church readmit those through penance who return from heresy, but she also protects their lives. When, however, heretics lapse into [their old] error after once having been forgiven, this points to their being habitually unfaithful; therefore, when they are brought to renounce their error again, they are given the rites which follow penance, but they are not spared the punishment of death.

From St. Thomas Aquinas, *Summa Theologica*, Second Part of the Second Part, Treatise on Faith; *Questio 11., de haeresi; Art. 3, Utrum haeretici sint tolerandi;* last paragraph from Art. 4. Series: *Patrologia Latina* (Paris: J. P. Migne, 1844–1864), Vol. CXCI, pp. 156–59. Trans. Henry A. Myers.

scribes, only after the first and second admonition. Afterwards, however, if the heretic persists in his error, the Church can no longer be confident of his re-conversion [back to the true faith], and so she promotes the salvation of others by removing him from the Church by excommunication and then delivers him to secular authorities for obliterating him from the world by death. Saint Jerome says, and [Gratian's] Decretal repeats: "The putrefying flesh is to be cut off, and the sheep with rotting sores expelled from the fold, so that the whole house, the whole body and the whole flock, do not bum, . . . become infected, putrefy or die. In Alexandria, Arius was only a single spark, but as that spark was not put out right away, the ensuing flames wrought destruction on the entire world.[33]

77

William of Rubruck, *Journey to Cathay*

In the thirteenth century, encouraged by stories of Mongol leaders having converted to Christianity—or, at least being favorably disposed towards Christians—and ever hopeful of bringing about some sort of alliance between East Asian forces and Europeans against the Muslims, several expeditions were sent out by European rulers, which collectively go by the name, "The Mongol Mission."

In 1253, King Louis IX (St. Louis) of France dispatched the Franciscan Friar William of Rubruck (1215–1270) to make contact with Sartach, the reportedly Christian son of Batu, commander of Mongol forces in Russia. From Sartach's court, William went on to that of Batu; eventually he reached the court of Mangu (or Moengke) Khan, the overall ruler or Great Khan of the Mongols or Tartars before returning home after a trip of some five thousand miles. Like John Pian del Carpini (see Reading 85), who preceded him on the Mongol Mission, William was impressed by the strange material culture and practices of his hosts and ended up bringing back much information about peoples of the East. His "Journey to Cathay" (addressed to Louis IX) reports numerous examples of religious co-existence among people of differing religious persuasions. These people had no fear of anything like heresy.

QUESTIONS TO CONSIDER

1. Why might Mongol rulers have considered it a positive advantage to have so many religions flourishing among their peoples?
2. What was Mangu Khan's evaluation of Christianity? What was it based on?
3. Why was it totally out of the question for William of Rubruck to consider the Mongol religious policy of toleration as anything other than a curiosity?

[33]Reference is to the Arian heresy, promoted by Arius, a priest in Alexandria, Egypt, in the time of Emperor Constantine I. It stressed Jesus as Son of God in a sense which made his powers derivative from God the Father and denied the equally co-eternal existence of the two. It became popular, particularly among Christian communities in the East and later among the Germanic tribes who were about to overrun the Roman Empire in central and western Europe.

The Journal of Friar William's Journey to Cathay

Batu had caused a great tent to be erected, because his house, or ordinary tent, could not contain so many men and women as were assembled. Our guide cautioned us not to speak, till Batu had given us order to do so, whether your Majesty had sent ambassadors to the Tartars or not; I answered, that you had sent messengers to Kuyuk Khan; and that you would not have sent messengers to him, or letters to Sartach, had you not believed that they had become Christians. Then he led us into the pavilion, and brought us into the center of the tent. We stood before him, all men silent.

Batu himself sat upon a seat long and broad like a bed, gilt all over, with three stairs to ascend to it, and one of his ladies sat beside him. At the entrance of the tent, stood a bench furnished with with stately great cups of silver and gold, set with precious stones. Batu beheld us earnestly, and commanded us to speak.

Then our guide asked that we should bow our knees and speak. I bowed one knee, as to a man, but he signaled that I should kneel upon both knees. Thinking I was praying to God, as I knelt on both knees, I began: "Sir, we beseech the Lord, that it would please him hereafter to make you partaker of his heavenly blessings: because the former without these are but vain and unprofitable." And I added further, "Be it known that you shall not obtain the joys of heaven, unless you become a Christian: for God saith, Whosoever believes and is baptized shall be saved; but he that believes not shall be condemned." At this he smiled modestly; but the other Moals (Mongols) began to clap their hands, and to laugh at us. After silence was reestablished, I said to him: "I came to your son, because we heard he was a Christian; and I brought him letters on behalf of my sovereign lord, the King of France, and your son sent me here to you."

Then he gave us of his milk to drink, which they regard to be a great favor. I sat looking down upon the ground and he commanded me to lift up my face, wishing to get a better view of us, or else because of superstition. They hold it a sign of ill luck, or evil, when any man sits in their presence, holding down his head, as if he were sad.

Then we departed, and immediately after us came our guide, and conducting us unto our lodging, said to me: "The Lord King requests that you remain in this land, but Batu cannot grant this without the knowledge and consent of Mangu Khan. Wherefore you must go to Mangu Khan."

Chapter 26: How the Nestorians, Saracens and Idolaters Are Joined Together

Among the Jugures (idolaters) I found a man having a cross painted with ink upon his hand, and I supposed him to be a Christian; for he answered like a Christian to all questions which I asked of him. I asked him why, therefore, he had not the cross with the image of Jesus Christ? And he answered: "We have no such custom." At this I concluded that they were Christians, but that for lack of instruction they omitted the above ceremony. I noticed behind a certain chest, which was to them an altar, where they set candles and oblations, an image having wings like the image of St.

From, William of Rubruck, "Journey to Cathay" in Manuel Komroff, ed., *Contemporaries of Marco Polo* (New York: Boni and Liveright, 1929), pp. 159–98, *passim*; condensed by Allen C. Myers.

Michael; and other images also, holding their fingers as if they were blessing. That evening I could find out nothing more, for the Saracens shun these idolaters so much that they will not allow them to speak of their religion. And when I inquired of the Saracens concerning these ceremonies, they were offended.

On the following day, which was the first of the month, I took up my lodging near another idol temple. Entering the temple, I found the priests of the idols there. At the first of the month they open their temples, and the priests put on vestments and offer the oblation of bread and fruits. They all worship towards the north, clapping their hands together and prostrating themselves on their knees. The Nestorians here do not join their hands together in prayer, but hold their hands before their breasts.

Their temples are build east and west; and upon the north side is a chamber, in manner of a vestry. Within this chamber they place a chest long and broad like a table, and behind this, facing south, stands their principal idol. A certain Nestorian priest, who had been in Cathay, said that in that country there is an idol so huge that it may be seen two days' journey away. They place other idols round about the principal one, all of them finely gilt over with pure gold; and upon the chest, which is in manner of a table, they set candles and offerings. The doors of their temples always open towards the south, which is contrary to the customs of the Saracens. They have also great bells like we have. And that is the reason, I believe, why the Christians in the East will not use great bells.

Chapter 28: Of Various Nations, and of Certain People Who Eat their Parents

Those Jugures, who live among the Christians and the Saracens, have been brought to believe that there is but one God only. The city of Caracarum itself is in a manner within their territory; and the whole country of the king, Prester John, and of his brother Unc, is near their dominions.

So it happened that the Moals adopted their letters from them. And they are the best scribes and nearly all the Nestorians know their writing. Beyond them is the nation of Tangut, who are a most valiant people, and once took Genghis in battle. But after peace was made he was freed by them, and afterwards he subdued them.

Beyond these are the people of Tibet, men known to eat the carcasses of their deceased parents. However, they have recently left off this custom, as they became abominable and odious to all other nations on account of it. But they still to this day make cups of the skulls of their parents, so that when they drink out of them, they may call their dead parents to remembrance. This was told to me by one who saw it.

Chapter 33: Of the Audience with Mangu Khan, Our Message and His Reply

. . . We were conducted to the court, and Nestorian preachers, whom I would not know whether they were Christians or not, approached and asked us in what direction we turn to pray. I answered, "To the east." They asked us this because we had our beards shaved, at the advice of our guide, so as to appear before the Khan according to the custom of our country. It was this that made them take us for Tuins, that is, idolaters. They asked us what ceremony we would observe before the Khan—theirs or ours? I answered them, "We are priests consecrated to the service of God. In our country, our noblemen do not allow priests to kneel before them, if it be not to honor God. We come from afar; so, first, if it please you, we will sing praises to God who has conducted us in safety so far, then we will do all that which shall please your master, except that which would be contrary to the worship and glory of God."

They entered the house and repeated my words to the Khan, who was pleased. Having stopped before the door, we sang a hymn; then they felt our legs, chests, and arms to see if we had knives upon us. Then we entered and were seated on a bench. The house was covered with gold cloth, and in the center was burning a fire of briars and wormwood roots, abundant in these regions, and of cattle dung.

The Khan was seated on a couch, dressed in very glossy fur skin, like that of a seal. He is of medium height, aged 45 years; at his side was his young wife and a grown girl called "Cherina" was seated with some other little children on a couch behind that of their parents. This house had belonged to a Christian lady, whom the Khan had loved very much and of whom he had this girl. He married his young wife, but the young girl is the lady of all the court that had once been her mother's. . . .

Chapter 45: Of the Theological Discussion, and the Provisions from the Khan

At this time a difficulty arose between the Armenian monk and a certain priest, called "Jonas," a well-educated man, whose father had been an archdeacon, and whom the other priests looked upon as their teacher. The monk said that man had been created before paradise, and that it was so written in the Gospel. I was then called to decide the question. I said that paradise had been created on the third day, with the trees of the earth, and that man was created on the sixth day. So the monk said: "Has not the devil brought, on the first day, earth from the four parts of the world, and did he not of this mud, form the human body, in which God had breathed the soul?" Hearing this Manichean heresy, publicly upheld with such impudence, I upbraided him sharply and told him to be quiet, since he did not know the Holy Scriptures. But he scoffed at me because I knew not the language. So I left, returning to my lodgings.

Then the priests and he went in procession to the court, without inviting me, because the monk, since the reprimand, did not speak with me and did not want to take me along. When they came in the presence of Mangu, the Khan asked them where I was and why I was not with them. The priests were afraid and excused themselves. When they returned they told me the words of Mangu and complained of the monk. After that the monk and I were reconciled, and I asked him to aid me in understanding the language of the country, promising to aid him in the study of the Holy Scriptures; for the brother who is aided by a brother is like a strong city. . . .

The Nestorians and the Armenians never ate fish during Lent. So they gave us a leather bottle of wine. We ate but once a day and in great misery; for when they learned that Mangu Khan had given us wine, they rushed upon us impudently and like dogs, these Nestorian priests who every day became drunk at court, and these Moals and these attendants of the monk. The monk, when any one visited him and he wanted to offer a drink, sent to us for wine. That wine was to us more an affliction than a consolation, for we could not refuse it to him without offending him. If we gave it to him, we were short, and we dared not ask for more at the court.

Chapter 51: How the Khan Ordered the Different Priests to Defend Their Own Religions, and Our Last Audience with Mangu Khan

On the Sunday before Pentecost I was conducted to the court. The secretaries of the state served drinks to the Khan, and the others, Saracens, asked me why I had come to their country. So I repeated what I had said already, how I came to Sartach and from Sartach to Batu, and how Batu had sent me here. I said to them: "I have nothing to say on the part of any man, for it ought to be known what Batu has written; I have only to preach the words of God, if they wish to hear them."

At these words, they asked me what words of God I wished to pronounce, for they thought I was going to foretell some good news, like so many of the others do. I answered them: "Of him to whom much has been given, much will be required."

After these words, I said to Mangu Khan, that God has given him a great power, and that his riches were not from the Tuin idols but from Almighty God who made the heavens and the earth, in whose hand are all kingdoms. If he loves God, all will be assured him; if not, he must know that he will have to account for his last farthing.

Then said one of the Saracens: "Is there a man who loves not God?" I answered: "It is God who knows: he who loves me obeys my commandments; he who does not observe the commandments of God does not love God." At this the Saracen said: "Have you been to heaven that you know the commandments of God?" "No," said I, "but he has sent them from heaven to holy men, and himself descended from heaven to teach all men, and it is in the Bible and we see it, by the works of men, when they observe them or do not." But he replied: "Do you mean to say that Mangu Khan does not follow God's precepts?" And I answered, "If Mangu Khan authorizes me, I will tell which are the commandments of God, and he shall judge himself if he obeys them or not." They left me and reported to the Khan that I had said he was an idolater, or Tuin, and that he did not observe the commandments of God.

The following day the Khan sent his secretaries to me, and they said: "You here are Christians, Saracens and Tuins. Each of you says that his law is the best and that his Scriptures are the truest. That is why he wishes that you all assemble in the same place, and that each write down his laws, so that the truth may be known." So I said: "Blessed be God who has inspired the Khan with such a thought. But our Scriptures teach that the servant of God must not dispute, only be kind to all. I am thus ready to explain, without hatred, the faith of the Christians to whoever wishes to question me." They wrote down my response and took it to the Khan. The Nestorians, Saracens and Tuins were also ordered to write down all they wished to say.

The eve of Pentecost arrived. The Nestorians read the chronicle since the creation of the world to the Passion of Christ, they said a few things about the Ascension and the resurrection of the dead and of the last judgment. There was much to reprove there, and I pointed it out to them. We wrote the symbol of the mass: "I believe in one God." Then I asked them how they wished to proceed. They answered that they first wished to discuss with the Saracens. I made them see that it was not well, for the Saracens agreed with us that there is but one God: "You will thus from them have aid against the Tuins." They agreed with me. Then I asked them if they knew how idolatry came into the world. They did not know. I explained it to them and they said: "Tell them that and speak in our place, for it is difficult to talk through an interpreter." I answered: "Look how you will act regarding them. I will uphold the cause of the Tuins, and you will defend that of the Christians. Let us suppose of that sect who claims there is no God; prove that God exists." For there is a sect who believe that all soul, all virtue there is in no matter what thing, is the God of that thing, and there is no other God. And the Nestorians could not prove anything, only repeat what is written in the Bible. I said to them: "They do not believe in the Bible; you allege one thing and they another." Then I advised them to let me discuss with them, for if I were vanquished, they would still find a way to talk.

Therefore on the eve of Pentecost, we assembled in our oratory and Mangu Khan sent three secretaries as arbitrators—one a Christian, another a Saracen, and the third a Tuin; and these proclaimed: "This is the order of Mangu and no one dare say that the commandment of God differs from it. He orders that no one use disagreeable or injurious terms toward his adversary under penalty of death." So all kept their silence. And there were a great number of people there, for each side had called the most learned of his race, and many others were present.

The Christians placed me in the center and told the Tuins to discuss with me. They then placed me opposite some one who came from Cathay. The Tuin asked me about what I wished to discuss first, the origin of the world or the destiny of the soul after death. I answered: "That should not be the beginning of our conference. All things pass from God, and he is the principal source of all things; we must begin to speak of God, of whom you have not the same idea as we, and Mangu wants to know the best opinion." The arbitrators judged that this was right.

He wished to begin with these questions for they had studied them better; for they are all of the Manichean heresy, and believe that one-half of things is evil, the other half good, and they all believe that the soul passes from one body into another.

To confirm this error, so master William told me, there had been brought a child from Cathay who, from their judgment, was not more than three years old. He was, however, capable of all reasoning and it was said that he had been incarnated three times, and that he knew how to read and write. So I said to the Tuin: "We believe firmly and with all our heart, and we confirm with our mouth that there is a God and one God only, and of a perfect unity. What do you believe in?" And he answered: "Only fools say there is but one God, but the wise uphold that there are several. Are there not, in our country, several great lords, and a greater one here, who is Mangu Khan? Even so there are different Gods, for they are different in each country." I answered: "Your example is a poor one; there cannot be similarity between men and God; for in that case a powerful man in his country would be called God."

He then asked: "What is then your God, that you say is the only one?" I answered: "Our God is all powerful, and there is no other than he, and he needs the help of no one; but we all need his protection. It is not so with man. No one can do all by himself; that is why it is necessary that there be several leaders on earth, for one alone cannot govern by himself. Our god also knows everything, and needs no advice. All science comes from him. He is infinitely good. We live and we move and we are in him. Such is our God, and he must not be thought of otherwise."

"No," said he, "he is not like that. It is true that there is a supreme God in heaven, but under him there are ten other Gods, and under us an inferior God. They are innumerable in the countries of the world." I asked him if he believed that the supreme God was all powerful, and I questioned him about some other God.

Evading my question, he in turn asked me: "If your God is what you say, why did he create half the things evil?" "It is not true," I said to him; "the one who created evil is not God. And all that is, is good." The Tuins were astonished at this reply.

I was then asked: "From where does evil come?" "You put your question wrong," I replied. "You should first ask what is evil, before searching whence it comes. But let us go back to the first question: Do you believe that an all-powerful God exists? And I will answer you then all that you ask me." He sat for a long time refusing to reply. At last he said that there did not exist a God all-powerful.

I said: "Then none of your Gods can ever save you, for it can happen that he have no power. Besides, no one can serve two masters; how then, can you serve so many Gods in heaven and on earth?" Those present told him to reply, but he did not. I then yielded, and as the Nestorians were preparing to discuss with the Saracens, the others replied: "We agree that yours is the true law and that all that is in the Gospel is true; so on no account do we wish to argue with you." And they confessed that in all their prayers they asked God to accord them grace to die as the Christians die.

There was an old priest there, of the sect Jugures, who say there is one God yet make idols. They talked a long time with him, telling him all that came to pass till the coming of the Antichrist into the world. Every one listened without objection. Yet no one said: "I believe; I want to become a Christian." Then the Nestorians and the Saracens sang together; the Tuins said not a word and everybody drank deeply.

On Pentecost day, Mangu Khan called me and the Tuin with whom I had discussed. Then the Khan professed his faith to me. "We Moals," said he, "we believe that there is but one God, by whom we live and by whom we die, and we have for him an upright heart." Then I said to him, "May God grant you grace, for without it you can do nothing." And he replied: "Even as God has given several fingers to the hand, so has he given man several ways. God has made us know the Holy Scriptures, and you Christians do not observe them. You do not see in them that one should blame another, do you?" "No, my lord," I said, "but I told you from the start that I did not want to have any differences with anyone." "God has given you a Testament and you do not follow it," he said. "To us, he has given soothsayers, and we do what they tell us and we live peacefully."

While I was waiting for him to confess still another phase of his faith, he began to talk of my return, saying: "You have been here a long while; I wish that you leave. You have said that you do not want to take my ambassadors with you; will you forward my letters or deliver my words?" So I replied I would write down his words, and I willingly undertook to convey them as best I could.

When he had finished, I asked for permission to speak. Permission granted, I began: "My lord, we are not men of war. We want that the authority of the world belong to him who governs with most justice, by the will of God. Our work is to instruct men to live by the will of God. This is why we have come to your land, and we would remain gladly had you wished it. But if you wish we leave, so it will be."

Chapter 52: Of the Soothsayers, Their Customs, and How They Evoke the Devil

Their soothsayers were their priests, and all they command to be done is executed immediately. People from all over the world consult these soothsayers. Some among them are versed in astronomy, predicting the eclipses of the sun and moon. When that happens, the whole population provides itself with food, so that they need not leave their houses. And when the eclipse is taking place, they ring the bells and sound the trumpets, hurling loud cries; and there is much ado. The eclipse past, they give themselves to unbounded joy and excessive drinking and eating.

The soothsayers arrange to pass over fire all that is sent to the court, and for this they get a large part of it. When anyone dies, they take away all that belonged to him, and noone in the court is allowed to touch any object that is not purified. If anything falls to the ground during purification by fire, it becomes property of the soothsayer. The soothsayers are also called in at the birth of a child, to foretell his fate, and then if someone falls ill, to judge if the malady is natural or the result of witchcraft.

The wife of Metz told me something extraordinary about this. Once, a present of valuable furs was given to the court of her mistress, a Christian. The soothsayers had it passed over the fire, and retained more of this than was their due. A woman under whose care was the treasure of this lady, accused them of it before her, and the latter reprimanded them. Then it happened that this lady fell ill and suffered sudden pains over all of her body. The soothsayers were called. They ordered a young girl to place her hand upon the painful spot, and to take off whatever she found. So the young girl arose, did what she was told and found under her hand a piece of felt or something like it. They told her to put it on the ground, and instantly that thing began to crawl like a living animal. They put it in water and it was like a leech, and the soothsayers said: "Madam, some sorcery has been cast on you and has hurt you." And they accused the woman who had accused them of stealing the furs. outside the camp, she was beaten for seven days and otherwise tortured to make her confess. . . .

Some of these soothsayers evoke demons. They assemble, at night, in their house those who wish to have answers from the devil; they put cooked meat in the center of the dwelling, and the cham who invokes begins by saying mysterious words, and holding a drum in his hand, he strikes it hard on the ground. Then he passes into a fury and they bind him. Then the devil appears in the midst of the darkness; the cham gives him this meat to eat and commands his answers.

Once, as was told to me by my interpreter, a Hungarian hid in the house of the soothsayers, and the devil, who was on the roof, complained that he could not enter for there was a Christian there. At this noise he fled, for they began to look for him. They had done that and many other things, too long to relate.

Chapter 54: Of the Letters of Mangu Khan to St. Louis

Finally, the letters to you being finished, they called me and told them to me:

"The eternal commandment of God is this: in heaven there is but one eternal God; on earth, there is no other master than Genghis Khan, the Son of God Demugin, or Genghis the sound of Iron. This is the message sent you. By the eternal virtue of God, through the great world of the Moals, the order of Mangu Khan is sent to the lord of the French, King Louis, to understand our words. The two monks who came from you to Sartach, Sartach sent to Batu and Batu sent to us, for Mangu Khan is the greatest lord in the world of the Moals. And now to the end, that your people all live in peace and rejoice in the welfare and that the commandment of God is obeyed among you, we wanted to send you, with your priests, Moal ambassadors, but they answered us, that between us and you there are countries at war and many wicked men, and that the roads are bad. He feared that they would not be able to take our ambassadors in safety as far as your country; but he proposed to bring our letters and transmit them to King Louis himself. We, therefore, are sending you written order of the eternal God, by your above-named priests, the order of the eternal God that we are making you understand. And when you shall have received and believed it, if you want to obey us, you will send us your ambassadors to let us know if you wish to be at peace or at war with us. When, by the power of the eternal God, the whole world shall be united in joy and in peace, thus shall it be known what we are to be. . . .

78

The Trial of Joan of Arc

During the Hundred Years War between the French and the English, the English won three major battles—Crecy in 1346, Poitiers in 1356, and Agincourt in 1415—and forced the French king, Charles VI, to sign the Treaty of Troyes in 1420. The treaty forced the French king to declare his own son, Charles, a bastard and agree to a marriage between his daughter Catherine and King Henry V of England, who was to become the heir apparent.

When in 1422 both the French and English kings died within a month of each other, the English claimed France in the name of Henry V's infant son, Henry VI, while the "Bastard" Charles retired to his castle of Chinon in southern France; thus the kingdom was divided between the two claimants. Then in 1428 an illiterate French peasant girl named Joan of Arc appeared at Charles's castle, claiming to be sent by God to rescue France from the English. At first there were many disbelievers in her but after she was tested, she was given men's clothing, a suit of armor, and put in charge of Charles's army. She successfully saved the city of Orleans from the English in 1429, earning her title "the Maid of Orleans." Joan then took Charles to Reims and had him crowned King Charles VII in order to gain more French support. She then continued her fights against the English until 1430 when she was captured outside the city of Compiegne and sold to the English, who put Joan on trial as a witch before the Inquisition.

The following is an account of Joan's trial and the charges, which eventually resulted in her death at the stake as a religious heretic.

QUESTIONS TO CONSIDER

1. Why would the English wish Joan to be found guilty by the Inquisition?
2. What were the most serious charges against Joan?
3. What effect would Joan's death have on the French?

May 23, 1431

I

Firstly, Jeanne, you have said that from the age of thirteen years you have had revelations and apparitions of angels, St. Catherine and St. Margaret, whom you have frequently seen with your eyes; and they have often spoken with you and told you many things . . .

The Trial of Jeanne D'Arc, trans by W. P. Barrett, (New York: Gotham House, Inc. 1932), pp. 331–36, 361–62. Slightly modernized.

On this point the clergy of the University of Paris and others have considered the manner and end of these revelations, . . . they declare that is all false, seductive, pernicious, that such revelations and apparitions are superstitions and proceed from evil and diabolical spirits.

II

You have said that your king (Charles VII) received a sign by which he knew that you were sent by God, that it was St. Michael, in the company of a host of angels, . . . coming to you in the town and castle of Chinon. They all mounted the stairs of the castle in your company up to the chamber of your king, before whom the angel who bore the crown bowed . . .

Regarding this article, the clergy say it is not probable, but rather a presumptuous, misleading and pernicious lie, an undertaking contrary and derogatory to the dignity of angels.

V

You have said that you wore and still wear man's dress at God's command and to His good pleasure, for you had instruction from God to wear this dress, and so you have put on a short tunic, jerkin, and hose with many points. You even wear your hair cut short above the ears, without keeping about you anything to denote your sex, . . . And although you have many times been admonished to put it off, you would not, saying that you would rather die than put off this dress, unless it were God's command; . . .

Regarding such matters, the clergy declare that you blaspheme against God, despising Him and His sacraments, that you transgress divine law, Holy Scripture and the canons of the Church, that you think evil and err from the faith, that you are full of vain boasting, that you are given to idolatry and worship yourself and your clothes, according to the customs of the heathen.

VII

You have said that according to revelations given you at the age of seventeen, you left your parents' house against their will . . . You went to Robert de Baduricourt, who, at your request, gave you a man's dress and a sword, also men at arms to take you to your king. And when you came to the king, you told him that his enemies should be driven away, you promised to bring him into a great kingdom, to make him victorious over his foes, and that for this God had sent you. . . .

Regarding such things, the clergy declare that you have been irreverent to your father and mother, . . . disobeying God's commandment, that you have given occasion for scandal, that you have blasphemed; that you have erred from the faith; and that you have made a rash and presumptuous promise.

IX

You have said that St. Catherine and St. Margaret promised to lead you to Paradise provided you preserved the virginity which you vowed and promised them, and that you are well assured of it as if you had already entered into the glory of the Blessed . . .

Such an assertion the clergy declare to be a pernicious lie, presumptuous and rash, that it contains a contradiction of what you had previously said, and that finally your beliefs err from the true Christian faith.

X

You have declared that you know well that God loves certain living persons better than you, and that you learned this by revelation from St. Catherine and St. Margaret; also that those saints speak French, not English, as they are not on the side of the English . . .

Such matters the clergy pronounce to be a rash and presumptuous assertion, a superstitious divination, a blasphemy uttered against St. Catherine and St. Margaret, and a transgression of the commandment to love our neighbors.

XII

And you have said that if the Church wished you to disobey the orders you say God gave you, nothing would induce you to do so; that you know that all the deeds of which you have been accused in your trial were wrought according to the command of God and it was impossible for you to do otherwise. Touching these deeds, you refuse to submit to the judgment of the Church on earth or of any living man, and will submit therein to God alone . . .

Wherefore the clergy declare you to be schismatic, an unbeliever in the unity and authority of the Church, apostate and obstinately erring from the faith.

> On May 24th, 1431, Joan was convinced to abjure her actions and put on women's dress. Her excommunication from the faith was revoked and she was sentenced to perpetual imprisonment. Yet, within four days time Joan once more put on men's dress, saying that she had made the confession from fear of being burned. Joan was said to have fallen once more into heresy.

Wednesday, May 30, 1431 The Final Sentence

"In the name of the Lord, amen. As often as the poisonous virus of heresy obstinately attaches itself to a member of the Church and transforms him into a limb of Satan, most diligent care must be taken to prevent the foul contagion of this pernicious leprosy from spreading to other parts of the mystic body of Christ. The decrees of the holy Fathers have laid down that hardened heretics must be separated from the midst of the just, rather than permit such pernicious vipers to lodge in the bosom of Our Holy Mother Church, to the great peril of the rest . . . have declared by a just judgment that you, Jeanne, commonly called **The Maid**, have fallen into divers errors and crimes of schism, idolatry, invocation of demons and many other misdeeds. Nevertheless, since the Church never closes her bosom to the wanderer who returns, esteeming that with a pure spirit and unfeigned faith you had cut yourself off from these errors and crimes because on a certain day you renounced them, swore in public, vowed and promised never to return to the said errors or heresy under any influence or in any manner whatsoever; but rather to remain indissolubly in the unity of the Catholic Church and the communion of the Roman pontiff. . . . Since subsequently, after this abjuration of your errors the author of schism and heresy has arisen in your heart which he has seduced and since you are fallen again—O, sorrow!—into these errors and crimes as the dog returns to his vomit, as it is sufficiently and manifestly clear from your willing confessions and statements, we have concluded in most celebrated decisions that the denial of your previous inventions and errors was merely verbal.

Therefore we declare that you are fallen again into your former errors and under the sentence of excommunication, which you originally incurred; we decree that you are a relapsed heretic; and by this sentence which we deliver in writing and pronounce from this tribunal, we denounce you as a rotten member, which, so that you shall not infect the other members of Christ, must be cast out of the unity of the church, cut off from her body, and given over to the secular power: we cast you off, separate and abandon you, praying this same secular power on this side of death and the mutilation of your limbs, to moderate its judgment towards you, and if true sign of repentance appear in you to permit the sacrament of penance to be administered to you."

Medieval Domestic Life in Western and Eastern Europe

Domestic life in early modern France and Russia centered on relations between husbands and wives, the preparation of food, cleaning of the living quarters, the disciplining of children and servants, and the smooth running of the household. Although separated by two hundred years, the following two accounts provide useful insights into domestic life in fourteenth-century Paris and sixteenth-century Moscow. Both were capital cities with burgeoning populations, replete with muddy, insect-infested streets and foul drinking water that ensured frequent outbreaks of disease, especially cholera and dysentery. Although public-health measures were virtually unknown at the time, both readings emphasize that cleanliness was of high priority. But a smooth-running household involved much more than clean rooms, a well-swept foyer, and a clean-burning, smokeless chimney fire. Domestic harmony could be achieved only if husbands and especially wives understood their place within the household and discharged their responsibilities properly. In different but revealing ways, each reading tells us much about gender relations and the importance of love, obedience, piety, affection, and discipline in ensuring domestic harmony in early modern France and Russia.

79

The Goodman of Paris

Written late in the fourteenth century by an elderly, anonymous author ("The Goodman of Paris") to his much younger new wife, these instructions center on the importance of a tidy house and good relations between husband and wife. In this communication to her, the Goodman of Paris indicates that he loves his young wife so much that he not only wants her to manage his house efficiently but, after his death, if she should marry again, he wants her to please her new husband by performing properly all of her domestic responsibilities.

QUESTIONS TO CONSIDER

1. What does this reading tell you about the character and quality of domestic life in fourteenth-century Parisian homes?
2. According to the Goodman of Paris, how should a wife keep the love of her husband and of her children? What does the author mean when he urges wives to "bewitch and bewitch again your husband"? Do you agree with his advice?
3. How would the Goodman of Paris react to the *Domostroi*'s advice about the proper method of disciplining wives (see Reading 80)?

Indeed fair sister, certain services make a man love and want to return home to see his good wife, and keep away from others. Therefore I advise you to comfort your husband all the while, persevere and be at peace with him. Remember the rustic proverb that says there are three things that drive a goodman from home: a leaking roof, a smoking chimney, and a scolding woman.

Dear sister I beg you, if you want to keep the love and good will of your husband, be gentle, loving, and sweet. Do for him what the good, simple women of our country say other people have done to their own sons, when these sons give their love elsewhere, and their own mothers cannot win them back. For it is certain that when fathers and mothers are dead and stepfathers and stepmothers scold their stepsons, rebuke them, or pay no attention to where they sleep, what they eat or drink, to their stockings, to their shirts, or other needs, these children will find a good home and counsel with some other woman, one who gives them warm shelter, soup, a bed, keeps them clean, mends their stockings, breeches, shirts, and other clothes. These children follow her, they want to be with her and to sleep and be cradled between her breasts. Soon they will be completely estranged from their step parents who neglected them, but now want them back.

But it is too late, for now these children prefer the company of strangers who care for them, rather than their own relatives who cared so little for them. These step parents lament and cry and say that these women have bewitched their children and have used spells to turn their children against them. But, no matter what they say, this is not witchcraft. For it is done for the sake of the love, the care, the intimacies, the joys and pleasures that these women have shown them in all things and, on my soul, there is no witchcraft. For whoever gives pleasure to a bear, a wolf, or a lion, that same bear, wolf, or lion will follow them. And so the other beasts might say, if they could speak, that those tamed animals must be bewitched. And, by my soul, I believe that this is not witchcraft; it is simply doing good. One does not bewitch a man by doing what pleases him.

From Jérôme Pichon, ed., *Le Ménagier de Paris: Traité de Morale et d'Économie domestique composé vers 1393 par un Bourgeois Parisien.* 2 vols. (Paris: Imprimerie Crapelet, 1847), 1:169–76; trans. Philip F. Riley.

Therefore dear sister, I ask that you bewitch and bewitch again your husband. Protect him from a poorly roofed house, a smoky chimney, and do not scold him, but be sweet, gentle, amiable and peaceable. See to it that in winter he has a good, smokeless fire. Be certain that he rests well between your breasts, and bewitch him there!

And in summer ensure that there be no fleas in your room nor in your bed. I have heard you may do this in six ways. Some suggest that if the room be strewn with alder leaves, the fleas will be caught on them. Also I have heard that at night if you set out in your room one or two slices of bread spread with glue or turpentine, along with a lighted candle, the fleas will come stick to the bread. Another way I have tried that works, is to take a rough cloth: spread it about your room and over your bed; then all the fleas that land on it will be caught, and you can whisk them away with the cloth. Also sheepskins or white wool set on the straw or on the bed works well, for when the black fleas land on this white background they can be seen and killed. But the best way is to be mindful that there are fleas in the coverlets, the furs, and the clothing you wear. One way I have tried to get rid of fleas is to take the infested coverlets, furs, or dresses, fold them and shut them tightly up in a chest, that is cinched tightly with straps. Another way is to put all the clothing in an air-tight bag so that the fleas will not have any light or air and will eventually die. Occasionally I have seen rooms full of mosquitoes, which were attracted by the sleeper's breath, so that they sat on their face, stung them so hard, that they were forced to awake, light a fire of hay to make a smoke to drive the mosquitoes away. Certainly this can be done in daytime as well. Also, if you have a mosquito net use it.

If you have a chamber or a passage where there are many flies, take little cuttings of fern and tie them together and hang them up in the evening so that the flies will land on them; then take down the cuttings and throw them out. In the evening close off all your room save a little opening in the wall towards the east. At first light, all the flies will go through this opening; afterwards close the opening.

Take a bowl of milk and a hare's gall;[34] mix them together and then set out two or three bowls in places where the flies light so that all the flies that drink this mixture will die.

Tie a piece of linen to the bottom of a pot with an opening in its neck, and set that pot in the place where the flies gather and smear it within with honey, apples, or pears; when it is full of flies, cover it and shake it.

Take raw red onions, dice them and pour the juice into a bowl and set it where the flies are so that when they drink it they will die. Have fly swatters to kill them by hand. Have little twigs covered with glue in a bowl of water. Shut your windows tightly with oil cloth, parchment or something else, so that no fly can enter, and those that do can be killed with a fly swatter. Soak a string in honey, and after the flies land on it, gather them up each evening in a bag. Remember that flies will not stop in a room where there are no standing tables, dressers or other things they can light on and rest. For if they have nothing but broad, flat surfaces to settle and cling to, they will not settle. Nor will they light in a place that is watered and shut up. Therefore, it seems to me that if the room is well watered, closed and sealed, and if nothing is left on the floor, no fly will settle there.

---

[34]Hare's gall refers to a rabbit's gallbladder.

Protect your husband from all discomforts, give him all the comforts you can think of, serve him and have him well served in your house. You can expect him to take care of matters outside the home, for if he is good, he will do even more than you could wish. Do what I have said and he will treasure you and give his heart to you. He will avoid all other houses, all other women, and all other services and households. None of these will interest him, but follow the example of horsemen who as soon as they return from a journey give their horses fresh bedding up to their bellies. These horses are unharnessed and made comfortable. They are given hay and oats, and they are well cared for in their own stables. If the horses are treated this way, the same should be done for persons, especially the masters when they return home. Upon returning from the woods and from hunting, the master gives his dogs fresh litter and a place before the fire. Their feet are greased with soft cream, they are given treats and are made as comfortable as possible.

Wives should do at least as much for their husbands as men do for their horses, dogs, asses, mules, and other beasts. If this is the case, all other houses, where their husbands have been served, will seem like dark prisons and strange places, when compared to their own home, which will be a restful haven for them. And so, when traveling, husbands will think only of their wives. No burden will be too heavy, for they will think only of their wives, whom they want to see again, just as the poor hermits and penitents wish to see the face of Jesus Christ. If cared for in this way, these husbands will never be content to live elsewhere. For all other places will seem to them to be a bed of stones compared to their home. Never stop loving: do it honestly and with a good heart.

80

The Domostroi, Rules for Russian Households in the Time of Ivan the Terrible

Although *The Domostroi* (which means "house order") has no clearly identified author, it is most often attributed to a Russian Orthodox priest, Sil'vester, who lived in Moscow in the late sixteenth century. Like *The Goodman of Paris, The Domostroi* is a complete set of domestic instructions on piety, entertaining, needlework, food preparation, the rearing of children, dress for formal occasions, the disciplining of servants, and the proper conduct between husbands and wives.

QUESTIONS TO CONSIDER

1. What does this reading tell you about the character and tone of family life in the households of sixteenth-century Moscow?
2. How does the author of *The Domostroi* suggest a Russian husband love, instruct, and discipline his wife and servants? Is it possible for a husband to bring "understanding with the lash"? Why must a Russian housewife, but not her husband, grieve over their servants' punishments? Would the Goodman of Paris (see Reading 79) agree?

Husbands should instruct their wives lovingly and with due consideration. A wife should ask her husband every day about matters of piety, so she will know how to save her soul, please her husband, and structure her house well. She must obey her husband in everything. Whatever her husband orders, she must accept with love; she must fulfill his every command. Above all, she must fear God and keep her chastity as decreed above.

When she rises from her bed, she should first wash herself, then complete her prayers. Then she should order the daily work for women and maids: telling each which embroidery to work, which food to cook that day, which breads to bake of finely sifted wheat flour. . . .

Wash the table, dishes, jars, spoons, ladles, and goblets. Rinse them off and dry them. Do the same after dinner and in the evening. Wash the pails, trays, kneading troughs, sieves, colanders, clay pots, pitchers, and metal saucepans as well. Rinse them, dry them, and put them in a clean suitable place. Every dish and every utensil should always be clean and accounted for.

Dishes should not be carried about the shop, the courtyard, or the house. Dishes, goblets, ladles, and spoons should not be scattered about the shop. They should be arranged somewhere in a clean place. They should be turned upside down. Any dish that contains food or drink should be covered, even inside the house. Tie the cover down to protect the contents from cockroaches and other unclean things.

Jars, dishes, spoons, goblets, ladles, and all the best dishes—silver, pewter, and wood—should be kept under lock and key in a safe place. When you have guests or a celebration with respectable people, bring them out to the table. After the feast, look them over, have them washed and counted. Then lock them up again. Treat the everyday dishes as described above.

Inside the house, wash the walls, benches, floors, windows, doors, storerooms, and porches. Rinse them, sweep them, and scrape off the dirt. A house should always be clean; so should the staircases and the entranceway. Everything should be washed, raked out, rinsed, and swept.

Put straw in front of the entranceway for wiping muddy feet, so the staircase will not be muddied. Before the doors of the warehouses and granaries, put a bast mat, an old piece of felt, or a towel for wiping muddy feet so they will not dirty the pavement. In muddy weather change the hay or straw in the entranceway and change the bast mat or the piece of felt at the doors. Either put down a clean mat or rinse the dirty mat and dry it; then it will be ready to put down under people's feet again.

By doing these things, an orderly woman will always have a clean and well-arranged house.

Your servants should always sweep in the courtyard, and in the street before your gates, and should rake when it is muddy. They should shovel snow in the winter as well. They should pile up the kindling, the wood, and the lumber. Then everything will be neat and clean.

From *The Domostroi: Rules for Russian Households in the Time of Ivan the Terrible*, ed. and trans. Carolyn Johnston Pouncy (Ithaca and London: Cornell University Press, 1994), pp. 124–25, 141–44. Copyright © 1994 by Cornell University. Reprinted by permission of the publisher, Cornell University Press.

In the stables, the bakery and all the workrooms, all should be in order, everything put away in some appropriate place, clean and swept. To enter such order is like entering Paradise.

The wife should supervise all this and should teach her servants and children in goodly and valiant fashion. If someone fails to heed her scoldings, she must strike him. If the husband sees something amiss for which his wife or her servants are responsible, or notices that all is not in accord with what is written in this document, he should reason with his wife and correct her. If she heeds him and does everything according to this book, he should love her and reward her.

But if your wife does not live according to this teaching and instruction, does not do all that is recommended here, if she does not teach her servants, then the husband should punish his wife. Beat her when you are alone together; then forgive her and remonstrate with her. But when you beat her, do not do it in hatred, do not lose control. A husband must never get angry with his wife; a wife must live with her husband in love and purity of heart.

You should discipline servants and children the same way. Punish them according to the extent of their guilt and the severity of their deed. Lay stripes upon them but, when you have punished them, forgive them.

The housewife must grieve over her servants' punishment, insofar as that is reasonable, for that gives the servants hope.

Only if his wife or son or daughter will not pay attention to scoldings, if they show no respect and refuse to do what they were told to do, should a husband or father bring understanding with the lash. But do not beat the culprit before others; punish him alone, then talk to him and grant him forgiveness.

A wife should not get angry at her husband about anything, nor a husband at his wife.

Do not box anyone's ears for any fault. Do not hit them about the eyes or with your fist below the heart. Do not strike anyone with a stick or staff or beat anyone with anything made of iron or wood. From such a beating, administered in passion or anguish, many misfortunes can result: blindness or deafness, dislocation of an arm, leg or finger, head injury, or injury to a tooth. With pregnant women or children, damage to the stomach could result, so beat them only with the lash, in a careful and controlled way, albeit painfully and fearsomely. Do not endanger anyone's health; beat someone only for a grave fault.

When you must whip someone, take off the culprit's shirt. Beat him in a controlled way with the lash, holding him by the hands while you think of his fault. When you have punished him, you must talk with him; there should be no anger between you. Your people should know nothing of it.

There should be no fights among your people that stem from past quarrels or rumors unsupported by direct investigation. Whenever you discover signs of bad feeling or unkind words, question the offender alone, kindly. If he sincerely repents, punish him lightly and forgive him. If the person is innocent, do not connive with the slanderer. To prevent enmity henceforth, punish appropriately and only after personal investigation. If an offender does not repent, punish him severely. Otherwise the guilty remain guilty and only the righteous learn righteousness.

Medieval Governments and Societies of China and Japan

After nearly four centuries of disruption and disunity following the end of the first great imperial period under the Ch'in [Qin] (221–206 B.C.) and Han (206 B.C.–A.D. 220) dynasties, China, reunified by the short-lived Sui dynasty (589–618), rejuvenated itself and entered into the second great imperial period under the T'ang (618–907) and Sung (960–1279) dynasties. The Han and the T'ang periods are often viewed as the two golden ages of the Chinese Empire, but the T'ang exceeded the Han in material splendor, cultural refinement, and international influence. Its empire was vast; its military was powerful and feared; its bureaucracy was elaborate and dependable; its laws were codified; its art and literature, especially its poetry, achieved new heights of sophistication. Changan, its capital, was large and cosmopolitan; it attracted scholars, diplomats, missionaries, and merchants from surrounding lands and as far away as Persia and Arabia. The religious life of this period was rich in diversity. Although Confucianism strengthened its hold on China, Buddhism and Taoism [Daoism] grew to maturity, and several foreign cults such as Zoroastrianism, Manichaeism, Judaism, Islam, and Nestorian Christianity entered China. Also, the Chinese invention of printing greatly stimulated intellectual life. The world's oldest extant printed book, a whole Buddhist *sutra*, printed in 868, can be traced to this period. Thus T'ang China furnished the models of advanced institutions and a way of life for neighboring countries to emulate. The foundation of this brilliant civilization was initially laid by the second ruler and cofounder of this dynasty, Emperor T'ai-tsung [Taizong]. A heroic warrior and an ardent Confucianist, he was firm but willing to be guided by the counsel of his ministers on matters of state (see Reading 81).

The Sung dynasty came into existence in 960 after more than a half century of disruptions and fragmentation of the empire and remained in power until the Mongols overran the whole empire in 1279. By 1127, the Sung had lost the northern half of its empire to the Tungusic tribal people of Manchuria. Although it was militarily feeble, Sung China fostered great social and cultural development and economic prosperity. The advanced state of its material civilization was unmatched by any other civilization. Trade and industry flourished; urbanization spread, and the inventive genius of the Sung craftsmen was unexcelled in the technical perfection of their silk, lacquer, and porcelain. Gunpowder, an earlier Chinese invention, was now employed for the first time in warfare. Socially, the institution of concubinage grew, and the practice of foot-binding among the upper-class women can be dated to the Sung period (see Reading 83). To run their large imperial bureaucracy efficiently, the Sung government relied heavily upon the imperial examination system, which had been reinaugurated by the Sui and reinvigo-rated by the T'ang (see Reading 82). The widespread use of the imperial ex-amination system contributed to a revival of interest in Confucianism (see Reading 27) and the development of a neo-Confucian movement during the Sung period.

By the time the T'ang dynasty arose in China, farther to the east the Yam-ato clan was busy consolidating its power in central Japan. Nara became the first permanent Japanese capital in A.D. 710. A heavy infusion of cultural in-fluences from Korea and China, particularly T'ang China (618–907), provided models of advanced government, society, and culture for Japan. Although Japan borrowed extensively from China, ranging from art to Zen Buddhism from the fifth to around the mid-ninth centuries, Japan did not become mere-ly a smaller replica of China. During the ensuing Heian period (794–1185),[35] Japan made major adjustments to what it had derived from the Chinese. These included reasserting some of its own native traditions, including the institu-tion of aristocracy, by rejecting the Chinese imperial examination system. Heian was the center of a refined aristocratic culture. The life and romance of the aristocracy were dominant themes in Heian literature, which vividly re-flected Heian aesthetic sensibility and was mostly authored by court ladies. The greatest of the classics of Japanese literature is *The Tale of Genji* by Lady Murasaki Shikibu.

81

Emperor T'ai-tsung [Taizong]: "On the Art of Government"

China under the T'ang [Tang] dynasty (618–907), which was contemporaneous with Charlemagne's empire in Western Europe, marked one of the most brilliant eras of Chinese history. At the height of its power, the empire stretched from Korea in the east to Central Asia in the west, and from Siberia in the north to Annam (Vietnam) in the south. Its culture was sophisticated and cosmopolitan. Although Confucianism was the state cult, other religions were tolerated, and its art, architecture, and literature reached new levels of excellence. Changan, the capital of the empire, was one of the finest in the world, with two million people, including hundreds of foreign students who were eagerly seeking a model of civilized life.

The foundation of this great T'ang empire was largely laid by Emperor T'ai-tsung (also known as Li Shimin, 626–649), who had helped his father Kao-tsu [Gao Zu] (also known as Li Yuan) found the T'ang dynasty by overthrowing the Sui dynasty. Ambitious, energetic, and versatile, Emperor T'ai-tsung created an elaborate

---

[35]The capital was moved to Heian, the city now called Kyoto, where the emperor's court remained for more than a thousand years until 1867. Its first three and a half centuries are usually called the Heian period.

system of imperial bureaucracy, rebuilt palaces, constructed more canals, tolerated foreign religions, established publicly supported state colleges in provincial capitals and a university in Changan, and compiled extensive law codes. Externally, he pursued an aggressive foreign policy and expanded the empire. His extraordinary reign was thus the first high point of the three-century-long T'ang period. The following article by Emperor T'ai-tsung reflects his thoughts on the good ruler and good government.

QUESTIONS TO CONSIDER

1. How do you compare Emperor T'ai-tsung with Charlemagne? How similar and how different are these two rulers (see Reading 60)?
2. What aspects of Emperor T'ai-tsung's essay reflect his being a great ruler? Why?

As a young man, I loved archery and prided myself as an expert in the evaluation of bows and arrows. Recently I came into possession of a dozen bows, the quality of which was the best I had ever observed. I showed them to the bow makers and was surprised to hear that they were not as good as they looked. "Why?" I asked.

"The center of the wood is not located at the center of the bow; consequently all the wood grain moves in a bizarre fashion," replied the bow makers. "Though the bow is strong and durable, an arrow released from it cannot travel straight for a long distance."

I used a countless number of bows and arrows in unifying the country; yet I still do not know enough about them. Now that I have the country for only a short time, how can I say that I know enough about it to govern it successfully, taking into consideration the fact that my knowledge of it is certainly inferior to my knowledge of bows which I have used throughout my life? . . .

Lately the draft decrees that originate from the First Secretariat are often contradictory and in some cases correct one another. To clarify this point, let me say that the purpose of having both the First and the Second Secretariats is for them to check and balance each other, so that the error of one will be corrected by the other and that an error, whoever commits it, will not remain undetected for a long time and thus cause irreparable damage.

Different people are bound to have different opinions; the important thing is that differences in opinion should not degenerate into personal antagonism. Sometimes to avoid the possibility of creating personal grievances or causing embarrassment to a colleague, an official might decide to go ahead with the implementation of a policy even though he knows that the policy is wrong. Let us remember that the preservation of a colleague's prestige, or the avoidance of embarrassment to him, cannot be compared with the welfare of the nation in importance, and to place personal consideration above the well-being of the multitude will lead to defeat for the government as a whole. I want all of you to understand this point and act accordingly.

During the Sui dynasty all officials, in the central as well as the local governments, adopted an attitude of conformity to the general trend in order to be amiable and agreeable with one another. The result was disaster as all of you well know. Most of them did not understand the importance of dissent and comforted themselves by saying that as long as they did not disagree, they could forestall harm to themselves that might otherwise cross their path. When the government, as well as their families, finally collapsed in a massive upheaval, they were severely but justifiably criticized by their contemporaries for their complacency and inertia, even if they themselves may have been fortunate enough to escape death through a combination of circumstances. This is the reason that I want all of you to place public welfare above private interest and hold steadfastly the principle of righteousness, so that all problems, whatever they are, will be resolved in such a way as to bring about a most beneficial result. Under no circumstances are you allowed to agree with one another for the sake of agreement. . . .

As for Sui Wen-ti [Wendi], I would say that he was politically inquisitive but mentally closed. Being close-minded, he could not see truth even if it were spotlighted for him; being overinquisitive, he was suspicious even when there was no valid reason for his suspicion. He rose to power by trampling on the rights of orphans and widows[36] and was consequently not so sure that he had the unanimous support of his own ministers. Being suspicious of his own ministers, he naturally did not trust them and had to make a decision on every matter himself. He became a hard worker out of necessity and, having overworked, could not make the right decision every time. Knowing the kind of man he was, all his ministers, including the prime minister, did not speak as candidly as they should have and unanimously uttered "Yes, sir" when they should have registered strong dissent.

I want all of you to know that I am different. The empire is large and its population enormous. There are thousands of matters to be taken care of, each of which has to be closely coordinated with the others in order to bring about maximum benefit. Each matter must be thoroughly investigated and thought out before a recommendation is submitted to the prime minister, who, having consulted all the men knowledgeable in this matter, will then present the recommendation, modified if necessary, to the emperor for approval and implementation. It is impossible for one person, however intelligent and capable, to be able to make wise decisions by himself. Acting alone, he may be able, if he is fortunate, to make five right decisions out of ten each day. While we congratulate him for the five right decisions he has made that bring benefit to the country, we tend to forget the enormous harm that results from the implementation of the other five decisions that prove to be wrong. How many wrong decisions will he accumulate in a period of days, months, and years if he makes five such decisions every day? How, in that case, can he not lose his country or throne? Instead he should delegate authority to the most able and virtuous men he can find and supervise their work from above most diligently. When he makes clear to them that he will not tolerate any violation of the law, it is doubtful that they will abuse the authority with which they have been entrusted.

---

[36]In 581 Sui Wen-ti forced Chou Ching-ti [Zhou Jingdi], aged seven, to abdicate the throne on his behalf. The boy's father had died only one year earlier; his mother was a young widow at the time of the abdication. Four months after his abdication, the boy died under suspicious circumstances.

I want all of you to know that whenever an imperial decree is handed down you should carefully study its content and decide for yourselves whether all or part of it is or is not wise or feasible. If you have any reservations, postpone the enforcement and petition me immediately. You can do no less as my loyal ministers. . . .

Governing a country is like taking care of a patient. The better the patient feels, the more he should be looked after, lest in a moment of complacency and neglect one irrevocably reverse the recovery process and send him to death. Likewise, when a country has only recently recovered from chaos and war, those responsible for running the country should be extremely diligent in their work, for false pride and self-indulgence will inevitably return the country to where it used to be and perhaps make it worse.

I realize that the safety of this nation relies to a great extent on what I can or may do and consequently I have not relaxed for a moment in doing the best I can. But I cannot do it alone. You gentlemen are my eyes and ears, legs and arms, and should do your best to assist me. If anything goes wrong anywhere in the empire, you should let me know immediately. If there is less than total trust between you and me and consequently you and I cannot do the best we can, the nation will suffer enormous damage. . . .

As the ancients say, a friend in need is a friend indeed. If mutual assistance governs the relations between two friends, how can it not do so between a king and his ministers? Whenever I read of Chieh's [Jie] execution of Kuan Lung-feng [Guan Lung feng] and Han Chingti's [Han Jingdi] execution of Ch'ao Ts'o [Chao Cuo],[37] I cannot but feel deeply about the mistakes these monarchs made. Contrary to these monarchs, I am asking you gentlemen to speak candidly on matters that you believe are most important to the well-being of the nation, even though the opinion you express may not coincide with my own. Needless to say, there will be no penalty of any kind, let alone execution, for opinions honestly held.

Recently I have made several decisions that are clear violations of the law, even though such violations were not apparent to me at the time when the decisions were made. You gentlemen obviously thought that these violations were inconsequential and therefore abstained from speaking about them. The truth is that the most consequential acts are usually an accumulation of acts of less consequence and in order to prevent the greatest harm, one has to make sure that even the smallest harm does not occur. It will be too late to reverse the course after small disasters have coalesced to become a great one. Keep in mind that a government does not fall because of the occurrence of a major catastrophe; rather, its demise usually results from an accumulation of small misfortunes.

It enlightens one to note that not a single person expressed regret when Sui Yang-ti [Sui Yangdi], a brutal and merciless tyrant, met his death at the hands of a group of assassins. If you gentlemen keep in mind the reason why I have been able to overthrow the Sui regime, I, on my part, will constantly remind myself of the injustice suffered by Kuan Lung-feng and Ch'ao Ts'o. Only in this way can you and I be permanently secure.

---

[37]Kuan Lung-feng was a loyal but outspoken minister under King Chieh (r. 1818–1765 B.C.), last ruler of the Hsia [Xia] dynasty. He was executed because of his criticism of the king's policies and personal behavior. Han Ching-ti (ca. 156–141 B.C.) ordered the execution of Ch'ao Ts'o (d. 154 B.C.) to appease some of the feudal lords who were then in rebellion. Previously Ch'ao Ts'o had recommended breaking up large feudal domains into smaller ones, a recommendation that angered the lords.

82

Sung (Song) China: Imperial Examination System

One of the unique features of the imperial government of China was the imperial examination system. Through it, the Chinese government recruited the members of its bureaucracy from the general populace, rather than leaving the imperial administration to the hereditary nobles. This system evolved gradually, starting in the second century B.C. during the former Han dynasty (206 B.C.–A.D. 8), becoming more elaborate and institutionalized during the early part of the Sung [Song] dynasty (960–1279), and continuing with only slight modifications down to the early years of this century. The last imperial examinations were held in 1905.

Millions of young men in China during the imperial period invested their time, energy, money, and passion in an effort to pass the examination, since this was the road to power and wealth. Aspirants for imperial bureaucratic posts usually spent ten or more years preparing for the examination, primarily by reading, analyzing, and memorizing the voluminous Confucian classics. During the Sung period, prospective candidates for imperial administrative posts were expected to pass three levels of highly competitive examinations—prefectural, metropolitan, and palace—and attain the Presented Scholar (Chin-shih [Jinshi]) degree, which was the most coveted degree, roughly comparable to a Ph.D. in the West. The candidates in the palace examination were ranked in order of their achievements in the examination. The higher the rank the candidates achieved, the better the chances were that they would receive more powerful and prestigious imperial appointments. The candidate for the Chin-shih degree was required to produce, among other things, poems in various styles, a rhyme prose piece, a policy essay, answers to five policy questions, and answers to ten "written elucidation" questions on Confucian classics such as the *Spring and Autumn Annals* and the *Book of Rites*. The following selection is an example of an essay question on policy matters.

QUESTIONS TO CONSIDER

1. What do you think are the merits and demerits of the Chinese imperial examination system?
2. How does this system compare with the way the Ottoman Empire recruited Janissaries (see Reading 89)?

It is stated in the Book of Kuan-tzu [Guan Zi][38] "the method by which a sage rules the world is this: he does not let the four classes of people live together. Therefore,

---

[38]Kuan-tzu or Master Kuan [Guan], who lived in the middle of the seventh century B.C., is regarded in Chinese history as one of the most innovative government reformers in ancient China. He was a great supporter of a centralized form of government.

there are no complaints, and things run smoothly. As a result, scholars know how to spend their leisure, laborers abide with the orders of officials, merchants go to the marketplaces and farmers go to the fields. Everyone goes to his appropriate place and lives there satisfactorily. Young children are sent to study; their wills are satisfied and they do not change their minds when they see strange things." The *Kuan-tzu Book* further states: "Children of scholars and farmers must always be scholars and farmers and children of merchants and laborers must also always be merchants and laborers, so that a scholar can give instructions and take care of his proper status, and a farmer can work attentively in cultivating his crops to feed the people. Everyone is satisfied with his occupation and does not seek to change. This is truly good! Otherwise, hundreds of laborers might all go to the marketplaces and ten thousand merchants might all try to work in the same [most profitable] business; they would all become cunning, deceitful, eager to play tricks, and they would also become capricious, greedy and seek only profits."

Now, to fit people in their occupations is not to improve morals. To see something better and change—what harm is there in this? Take the example of Tuan-mu [Duanmu] who became a merchant [after being a disciple of Confucius], Chiao Li [Jiao Li] who became a fisherman [after being an important official] and Wang Meng who went to sell dust-baskets [after being a prime minister]; these men responded to their times and changed in myriad ways, why should they have been restricted to their fixed occupations? Similarly, Huang Hsien [Huang Xian] was originally a lowly veterinarian, Sang Hung-yang [Sang Hongyang] a merchant, Sun Shu-ao a wood-cutter, and yet they all were able to preserve their intelligence and help strengthen their states. How can we accuse them of responding to their times and of going to take up responsibilities other than their own occupations! We now have a regulation keeping the descendants of those in despised occupations from taking the civil service examinations. Although this rule has been in force for some time, I consider that it still is a good time to examine this regulation. You candidates have excelled yourselves in knowledge of the past, and in debating various problems; I would like you to spend time considering the issue I have just outlined above.

83

Chinese Footbinding

One of the most bizarre and painful customs of old China was the binding of women's feet. It is difficult to determine precisely when and how this custom came to be, but historical records seem to indicate that it began with the dancers of the imperial harem of the Southern T'ang [Tang] dynasty (937–975), sometime in the tenth century. In the beginning, the custom was practiced only by fashionable women of the upper class, but footbinding gradually spread down to the rest of the female population and persisted well into the twentieth century. The custom persisted even after the end of the last imperial dynasty (1644–1912), despite a series of official efforts to end it, beginning with an antifootbinding edict issued by Empress Dowager Tz'u-hsi [Ci Xi] in 1902. In the following selection, a middle-aged maidservant named Chang, probably born around the turn of the century, recalls her painful footbinding experience for her master. The story is told sometime in the early 1930s.

QUESTIONS TO CONSIDER

1. Compare the footbinding custom of old China with a comparable custom from another society.
2. Why did such a painful custom continue for so long in China?

I was born in a certain district in western Honan Province, at the end of the Manchu dynasty. In accordance with custom, at the age of seven I began binding. I had witnessed the pain of my cousins, and in the year it was to begin was very much frightened. That autumn, distress befell me. One day prior my mother told me: "You are now seven, just at the right age for binding. If we wait, your foot will harden, increasing the pain. You should have started in the spring, but because you were weak we waited till now. Girls in other families have already completed the process. We start tomorrow. I will do this for you lightly and so that it won't hurt; what daughter doesn't go through this difficulty?" She then gave me fruit to eat, showed me a new pair of phoenix-tip shoes, and beguiled me with these words: "Only with bound feet can you wear such beautiful shoes. Otherwise, you'll become a large-footed barbarian and everyone will laugh at and feel ashamed of you." I felt moved by a desire to be beautiful and became steadfast in determination, staying awake all night.

I got up early the next morning. Everything had already been prepared. Mother had me sit on a stool by the bed. She threaded a needle and placed it in my hair, cut off a piece of alum and put it alongside the binding cloth and the flowered shoes. She then turned and closed the bedroom door. She first soaked my feet in a pan of hot water, then wiped them, and cut the toenails with a small scissors. She then took my right foot in her hands and repeatedly massaged it in the direction of the plantar.[39] She also sprinkled alum between my toes. She gave me a pen point to hold in my hands because of the belief that my feet might then become as pointed as it was. Later she took a cloth three feet long and two inches wide, grasped my right foot, and pressed down the four smaller toes in the direction of the plantar. She joined them together, bound them once, and passed the binding from the heel to the foot surface and then to the plantar. She did this five times and then sewed the binding together with thread. To prevent it from getting loosened, she tied a slender cotton thread from the tip of the foot to its center.

She did the same thing with the left foot and forced my feet into flowered shoes which were slightly smaller than the feet were. The tips of the shoes were adorned with threads in the shape of grain. There was a ribbon affixed to the mouth of the shoe and fastened on the heel. She ordered me to get down from the bed and walk, saying that if I didn't the crooked-shaped foot would be seriously injured. When I first touched the ground, I felt complete loss of movement; after a few trials, only the toes hurt greatly. Both feet became feverish at night and hurt from the swelling. Except for walking, I sat

---

[39]Relating to the sole of the foot.

From Howard S. Levy, *Chinese Footbinding: The History of a Curious Erotic Custom* (New York: Walton Rawls Publisher, 1966), pp. 224–27. Reprinted by permission.

by the k'ang [Kang].[40] Mother rebound my feet weekly, each time more tightly than the last. I became more and more afraid. I tried to avoid the binding by hiding in a neighbor's house. If I loosened the bandage, mother would scold me for not wanting to look nice. After half a year, the tightly bound toes began to uniformly face the plantar. The foot became more pointed daily; after a year, the toes began to putrefy. Corns began to appear and thicken, and for a long time no improvement was visible. Mother would remove the bindings and lance the corns with a needle to get rid of the hard core. I feared this, but mother grasped my legs so that I couldn't move. Father betrothed me at the age of nine to a neighbor named Chao, and I went to their house to serve as a daughter-in-law in the home of my future husband. My mother-in-law bound my feet much more tightly than mother ever had, saying that I still hadn't achieved the standard. She beat me severely if I cried; if I unloosened the binding, I was beaten until my body was covered with bruises. Also, because my feet were somewhat fleshy, my mother-in-law insisted that the foot must become inflamed to get the proper results. Day and night, my feet were washed in a medicinal water; within a few washings I felt special pain. Looking down, I saw that every toe but the big one was inflamed and deteriorated. Mother-in-law said that this was all to the good. I had to be beaten with fists before I could bear to remove the bindings, which were congealed with pus and blood. To get them loose, such force had to be used that the skin often peeled off, causing further bleeding. The stench was hard to bear, while I felt the pain in my very insides. My body trembled with agitation. Mother-in-law was not only unmoved but she placed tiles inside the binding in order to hasten the inflammation process. She was deaf to my childish cries. Every other day, the binding was made tighter and sewn up, and each time slightly smaller shoes had to be worn. The sides of the shoes were hard, and I could only get into them by using force. I was compelled to walk on them in the courtyard; they were called distance-walking shoes. I strove to cling to life, suffering indescribable pain. Being in an average family, I had to go to the well and pound the mortar unaided. Faulty blood circulation caused my feet to become insensible in winter. At night, I tried to warm them by the k'ang, but this caused extreme pain. The alternation between frost and thawing caused me to lose one toe on my right foot. Deterioration of the flesh was such that within a year my feet had become as pointed as new bamboo shoots, pointing upwards like a red chestnut. The foot surface was slightly convex, while the four bean-sized toes were deeply imbedded in the plantar like a string of cowry shells.[41] They were only a slight distance from the heel of the foot. The plantar was so deep that several coins could be placed in it without difficulty. The large toes faced upwards, while the place on the right foot where the little toe had deteriorated away pained at irregular intervals. It left an ineffacable scar.

My feet were only three inches long, at the most. Relatives and friends praised them, little realizing the cisterns of tears and blood which they had caused. My husband was delighted with them, but two years ago he departed this world. The family wealth was dissipated, and I had to wander about, looking for work. That was how I came down to my present circumstances. I envy the modern woman. If I too had been born just a decade or so later, all of this pain could have been avoided. The lot of the natural-footed woman and mine is like that of heaven and hell.

[40]A brick-bed warmed by a fire.

[41]A type of shell somewhat resembling the female sex organ; it was used as a sort of primitive money in prehistoric times in China.

84

Murasaki Shikibu, *The Tale of Genji*

The Tale of Genji was written during the last years of the tenth and first of the eleventh centuries by Murasaki Shikibu (978–ca. 1016), a lady-in-waiting to the empress in the Heian court. The Heian period (794–1185) in Japanese history produced some of Japan's greatest prose and poetry that reflect details of the daily life of the upper classes and their values and tastes. *The Tale of Genji* not only is Japan's most famous prose literature but is also considered to be the world's first novel, written long before the novel was developed in the West. In this lengthy work of one thousand pages in translation or some three-quarters of a million words, Lady Murasaki, drawing upon her own personal experiences at the imperial court, recounts the life, romance, and tragedy of the royal family and aristocracy, centering on the amorous adventures of handsome Prince Genji, a son of an emperor, a great lover, and a man of impeccable taste. The following selection is a conversation between four young men in the court—Prince Genji; his best friend and brother-in-law, Tō-no-Chūjō; a guards officer; and an official in the Ministry of Rites—on the question of what makes the perfect woman. This excerpt mirrors the male view of an ideal woman in medieval Japan.

QUESTIONS TO CONSIDER

1. How do you compare the male view of an ideal woman in medieval Japan with that in medieval Europe?
2. How did the men characterize women from three different classes? In their view, was an ideal woman necessarily one from the aristocracy?
3. How have Japanese views on women changed from the premodern ideals illustrated here?

It had been raining all day. There were fewer courtiers than usual in the royal presence. Back in his own palace quarters, also unusually quiet, Genji pulled a lamp near and sought to while away the time with his books. He had Tō-no-Chūjō with him. Numerous pieces of colored paper, obviously letters, lay on a shelf. Tō-no-Chūjō made no attempt to hide his curiosity.

"Well," said Genji, "there are some I might let you see. But there are some I think it better not to."

"You miss the point. The ones I want to see are precisely the ones you want to hide. The ordinary ones—I'm not much of a hand at the game, you know, but even I am up to the ordinary give and take. But the ones from ladies who think you are not doing right by them, who sit alone through an evening and wait for you to come—those are the ones I want to see."

It was not likely that really delicate letters would be left scattered on a shelf, and it may be assumed that the papers treated so carelessly were the less important ones.

"You do have a variety of them," said Tō-no-Chūjō, reading the correspondence through piece by piece. This will be from her, and this will be from her, he would say. Sometimes he guessed correctly and sometimes he was far afield, to Genji's great amusement. Genji was brief with his replies and let out no secrets.

"It is I who should be asking to see your collection. No doubt it is huge. When I have seen it I shall be happy to throw my files open to you."

"I fear there is nothing that would interest you." Tō-no-Chūjō was in a contemplative mood. "It is with women as it is with everything else: the flawless ones are very few indeed. This is a sad fact which I have learned over the years. All manner of women seem presentable enough at first. Little notes, replies to this and that, they all suggest sensibility and cultivation. But when you begin sorting out the really superior ones you find that there are not many who have to be on your list. Each has her little tricks and she makes the most of them, getting in her slights at rivals, so broad sometimes that you almost have to blush. Hidden away by loving parents who build brilliant futures for them, they let word get out of this little talent and that little accomplishment and you are all in a stir. They are young and pretty and amiable and carefree, and in their boredom they begin to pick up a little from their elders, and in the natural course of things they begin to concentrate on one particular hobby and make something of it. A woman tells you all about it and hides the weak points and brings out the strong ones as if they were everything, and you can't very well call her a liar. So you begin keeping company, and it is always the same. The fact is not up to the advance notices."

Tō-no-Chūjō sighed, a sigh clearly based on experience. Some of what he had said, though not all, accorded with Genji's own experience. "And have you come upon any," said Genji, smiling, "who would seem to have nothing at all to recommend them?"

"Who would be fool enough to notice such a woman? And in any case, I should imagine that women with no merits are as rare as women with no faults. If a woman is of good family and well taken care of, then the things she is less than proud of are hidden and she gets by well enough. When you come to the middle ranks, each woman has her own little inclinations and there are thousands of ways to separate one from another. And when you come to the lowest—well, who really pays much attention?"

He appeared to know everything. Genji was by now deeply interested.

"You speak of three ranks," he said, "but is it so easy to make the division? There are well-born ladies who fall in the world and there are people of no background who rise to the higher ranks and build themselves fine houses as if intended for them all along. How would you fit such people into your system?"

At this point two young courtiers, a guards officer and a functionary in the ministry of rites, appeared on the scene, to attend the emperor in his retreat. Both were devotees of the way of love and both were good talkers. Tō-no-Chūjō, as if he had been waiting for them, invited their views on the question that had just been asked. The discussion progressed, and included a number of rather unconvincing points.

"Those who have just arrived at high position," said one of the newcomers, "do not attract the same sort of notice as those who were born to it. And those who were born to the highest rank but somehow do not have the right backing—in spirit they may be as proud and noble as ever, but they cannot hide their deficiencies. And so I think that they should both be put in your middle rank.

"There are those whose families are not quite of the highest rank but who go off and work hard in the provinces. They have their place in the world, though there are all sorts of little differences among them. Some of them would belong on anyone's list. So it is these days. Myself, I would take a woman from a middling family over one who has rank and nothing else. Let us say someone whose father is almost but not quite a councillor. Someone who has a decent enough reputation and comes from a decent enough family and can live in some luxury. Such people can be very pleasant. There is nothing wrong with the household arrangements, and indeed a daughter can sometimes be set out in a way that dazzles you. I can think of several such women it would be hard to find fault with. When they go into court service, they are the ones the unexpected favors have a way of falling on. I have seen cases enough of it, I can tell you."

Genji smiled. "And so a person should limit himself to girls with money?"

"That does not sound like you," said Tō-no-Chūjō.

"When a woman has the highest rank and a spotless reputation," continued the other, "but something has gone wrong with her upbringing, something is wrong in the way she puts herself forward, you wonder how it can possibly have been allowed to happen. But when all the conditions are right and the girl herself is pretty enough, she is taken for granted. There is no cause for the least surprise. Such ladies are beyond the likes of me, and so I leave them where they are, the highest of the high. There are surprisingly pretty ladies wasting away behind tangles of weeds, and hardly anyone even knows of their existence. The first surprise is hard to forget. There she is, a girl with a fat, sloppy old father and boorish brothers and a house that seems common at best. Off in the women's rooms is a proud lady who has acquired bits and snatches of this and that. You get wind of them, however small the accomplishments may be, and they take hold of your imagination. She is not the equal of the one who has everything, of course, but she has her charm. She is not easy to pass by."

He looked at his companion, the young man from the ministry of rites. The latter was silent, wondering if the reference might be to his sisters, just then coming into their own as subjects for conversation. Genji, it would seem, was thinking that on the highest levels there were sadly few ladies to bestow much thought upon. He was wearing several soft white singlets with an informal court robe thrown loosely over them. As he sat in the lamplight leaning against an armrest, his companions almost wished that he were a woman. Even the "highest of the high" might seem an inadequate match for him.

They talked on, of the varieties of women.

"A man sees women, all manner of them, who seem beyond reproach," said the guards officer, "but when it comes to picking the wife who must be everything, matters are not simple. The emperor has trouble, after all, finding the minister who has all the qualifications. A man may be very wise, but no man can govern by himself. Superior is helped by subordinate, subordinate defers to superior, and so affairs proceed by agreement and concession. But when it comes to choosing the woman who is to be in charge of your house, the qualifications are altogether too many. A merit is balanced by a defect, there is this good point and that bad point, and even women who though not perfect can be made to do are not easy to find. I would not like to have you think me a profligate who has to try them all. But it is a question of the woman who must be everything, and it seems best, other things being equal, to find someone who does not require shaping and training, someone who has most of the qualifications from the start. The man who begins his search with all this in mind must be reconciled to searching for a very long time.

"He comes upon a woman not completely and in every way to his liking but he makes certain promises and finds her hard to give up. The world praises him for his honest heart and begins to note good points in the woman too; and why not? But I have seen them all, and I doubt that there are any genuinely superior specimens among them. What about you gentlemen so far above us? How is it with you when you set out to choose your ladies?

"There are those who are young enough and pretty enough and who take care of themselves as if no particle of dust were allowed to fall upon them. When they write letters they choose the most inoffensive words, and the ink is so faint a man can scarcely read them. He goes to visit, hoping for a real answer. She keeps him waiting and finally lets him have a word or two in an almost inaudible whisper. They are clever, I can tell you, at hiding their defects.

"The soft, feminine ones are likely to assume a great deal. The man seeks to please, and the result is that the woman is presently looking elsewhere. That is the first difficulty in a woman.

"In the most important matter, the matter of running his household, a man can find that his wife has too much sensibility, an elegant word and device for every occasion. But what of the too domestic sort, the wife who bustles around the house the whole day long, her hair tucked up behind her ears, no attention to her appearance, making sure that everything is in order? There are things on his mind, things he has seen and heard in his comings and goings, the private and public demeanor of his colleagues, happy things and sad things. Is he to talk of them to an outsider? Of course not. He would much prefer someone near at hand, someone who will immediately understand. A smile passes over his face, tears well up. Or some event at court has angered him, things are too much for him. What good is it to talk to such a woman? He turns his back on her, and smiles, and sighs, and murmurs something to himself. 'I beg your pardon?' she says, finally noticing. Her blank expression is hardly what he is looking for.

"When a man picks a gentle, childlike wife, he of course must see to training her and making up for her inadequacies. Even if at times she seems a bit unsteady, he may feel that his efforts have not been wasted. When she is there beside him her gentle charm makes him forget her defects. But when he is away and sends asking her to perform various services, it becomes clear, however small the service, that she has no thoughts of her own in the matter. Her uselessness can be trying.

"I wonder if a woman who is a bit chilly and unfeeling cannot at times seem preferable."

His manner said that he had known them all; and he sighed at his inability to hand down a firm decision.

"No, let us not worry too much about rank and beauty. Let us be satisfied if a woman is not too demanding and eccentric. It is best to settle on a quiet, steady girl. If she proves to have unusual talent and discrimination—well, count them an unexpected premium. Do not, on the other hand, worry too much about remedying her defects. If she seems steady and not given to tantrums, then the charms will emerge of their own accord.

"There are those who display a womanly reticence to the world, as if they had never heard of complaining. They seem utterly calm. And then when their thoughts are too much for them they leave behind the most horrendous notes, the most flamboyant poems, the sort of keepsakes certain to call up dreadful memories, and off they go into the mountains or to some remote seashore. When I was a child I would hear the women reading romantic stories, and I would join them in their sniffling and think it all very sad, all very profound and moving. Now I am afraid that it suggests certain pretenses.

"It is very stupid, really, to run off and leave a perfectly kind and sympathetic man. He may have been guilty of some minor dereliction, but to run off with no understanding at all of his true feelings, with no purpose other than to attract attention and hope to upset him—it is an unpleasant sort of memory to have to live with. She gets drunk with admiration for herself and there she is, a nun. When she enters her convent she is sure that she has found enlightenment and has no regrets for the vulgar world.

"Her women come to see her. 'How very touching,' they say. 'How brave of you.'

"But she no longer feels quite as pleased with herself. The man, who has not lost his affection for her, hears of what has happened and weeps, and certain of her old attendants pass this intelligence on to her. 'He is a man of great feeling, you see. What a pity that it should have come to this.' The woman can only brush aside her newly cropped hair to reveal a face on the edge of tears. She tries to hold them back and cannot, such are her regrets for the life she has left behind; and the Buddha is not likely to think her one who has cleansed her heart of passion. Probably she is in more danger of brimstone now in this fragile vocation than if she had stayed with us in our sullied world.

"The bond between husband and wife is a strong one. Suppose the man had hunted her out and brought her back. The memory of her acts would still be there, and inevitably, sooner or later, it would be cause for rancor. When there are crises, incidents, a woman should try to overlook them, for better or for worse, and make the bond into something durable. The wounds will remain, with the woman and with the man, when there are crises such as I have described. It is very foolish for a woman to let a little dalliance upset her so much that she shows her resentment openly. He has his adventures—but if he has fond memories of their early days together, his and hers, she may be sure that she matters. A commotion means the end of everything. She should be quiet and generous, and when something comes up that quite properly arouses her resentment she should make it known by delicate hints. The man will feel guilty and with tactful guidance he will mend his ways. Too much lenience can make a woman seem charmingly docile and trusting, but it can also make her seem somewhat wanting in substance. We have had instances enough of boats abandoned to the winds and waves. Do you not agree?"

Tō-no-Chūjō nodded. "It may be difficult when someone you are especially fond of, someone beautiful and charming, has been guilty of an indiscretion, but magnanimity produces wonders. They may not always work, but generosity and reasonableness and patience do on the whole seem best."

His own sister was a case in point, he was thinking, and he was somewhat annoyed to note that Genji was silent because he had fallen asleep. Meanwhile the young guards officer talked on, a dedicated student of his subject. Tō-no-Chūjō was determined to hear him out. . . .

"So it is with trivialities like painting and calligraphy. How much more so with matters of the heart! I put no trust in the showy sort of affection that is quick to come forth when a suitable occasion presents itself. Let me tell you of something that happened to me a long time ago. You may find the story a touch wanton, but hear me through all the same."

He drew close to Genji, who awoke from his slumber. Tō-no-Chūjō, chin in hand, sat opposite, listening with the greatest admiration and attention. There was in the young man's manner something slightly comical, as if he were a sage expostulating upon the deepest truths of the universe, but at such times a young man is not inclined to conceal his most intimate secrets.

85

John Pian del Carpini, *The Tartars*

John (Giovanni) del Carpini (1182?–1252) had been a companion and disciple of St. Francis of Assisi (see Reading 74). He led the Franciscan expedition sent by Pope Innocent IV to Kuyuk Khan and wrote extensively of his travels and experiences at the Mongol court. It is not known how he entitled his work, which is often called the *History of the Mongols*, even though there is relatively little *history* in it. One of the surviving manuscripts has the simple title *A Book About the Tartars*, which seems more accurate. The following excerpts from it are fairly typical in showing his admiration for the hardiness and capacity for cooperation the Mongols exhibited among themselves, coupled with his revulsion at their ferocity and lack of scruples in dealing with foreign peoples. John was less hopeful of converting the Mongols to Christianity than were most of the explorer-missionaries who followed him; both his travel book and the letter he brought to the pope from Kuyuk Khan indicate why. His Franciscan successors who visited China under Mongol conquest had better experiences, however; they and Venetian traders, particularly the very observant Marco Polo, who became a Mongol administrator in China, were beginning to acquaint Europe with some of the real East Asia.

QUESTIONS TO CONSIDER

1. Why does John consider the Mongol threat a real one?
2. What does John think Westerners could learn from the Mongols?

The Tartars have a very different appearance from other peoples. There is more space between their eyes and between their cheekbones than is true of other men. . . . They have flat noses and rather small eyes. . . . Almost all of them are of medium height. Their men have only sparse growths of beard, some letting their wispy mustaches droop long. . . .

From *Historia Mongalorum*, in *Studi Italiani di Filologia Indo-Iranica*, Vol. IX (Firenze: Carnesecchi e Figli, 1913), pp. 54–101, *passim.* Trans. Henry A. Myers.

I will tell something of their good characteristics and then of their bad ones. . . . They show greater respect to their superiors than any other people in the world. . . . They deceive their own masters rarely or never with words and never at all with deeds. . . . They do not fight among themselves: Internal warfare, brawls and assaults do not occur. . . . If a large animal strays, whoever finds it either lets it go or leads it to men of authority from whom the owner can get it back with no difficulty at all simply by asking for it. They respect each other quite well enough and . . . throw frequent banquets in spite of the scarcity of good things to eat among them. At the same time, they are so hardy that they can go a day or even two without eating and still sing and joke around as if they had had plenty to eat. . . . Tartar women are chaste: There are not even rumors of immodest female behavior among them, although the women do sometimes use filthy language. . . . Even though the Tartars get quite drunk often, this does not lead to hostile words or actions among them.

Having said this much about their good side, let me go on to their bad one. Their pride is terrible when they confront non-Tartars—nobles and commoners alike—whom they are apt to despise. . . . They show their angry and totally condescending natures to foreigners, to whom they habitually lie. When Tartars speak to non-Tartars the truth is seldom in them. When they start off, their conversation is nice enough, but they sting like scorpions before they are through talking. They are cunning, crafty, and very elusive with their falsehoods. When they have hostile plans toward foreigners, they are experts in concealing them so that the foreigners will not know to be on guard. . . . They are very greedy and shameless with their outrageous demands, while they hold fast to what is theirs and are unbelievably stingy givers. Killing off foreign peoples simply does not bother them.

Chinghiz Khan arranged their order of battle by putting ten men under the command of a squad leader, ten squad leaders under one centurion, ten centurions under a battalion commander, thus giving him a thousand men, ten battalion commanders under a colonel and the whole army under two or three generals, but with one of them clearly the theater commander. If in battle, one, two, or three—any number—of men flee from a squad, the whole squad is executed; if the whole squad flees, then the hundred soldiers with the centurion over them are all executed; and, to summarize this point briefly, units with men in them who flee are wiped out. . . . If members of a squad are captured and not rescued by the rest, the rest are executed. The minimum arms they are required to carry are: two bows . . . , three quivers full of arrows, one ax, and ropes to pull along machines of war. To be sure, their nobles carry . . . slightly curved swords with sharp points, and their horses wear armor of multiple thickness of leather shaped to fit their bodies. . . .

Some of them have a hook attached to the necks of their lances with which they will pull a rider off his saddle if they can. Their arrows are about two feet, eight inches long . . . and each man carries a file in his quiver to sharpen their heads. . . .

When they come to a river, they cross it with the higher-ups using large, lightweight leather bags with loops and drawstrings to seal up their clothes and necessary equipment for the crossing. The resulting pack floats. Tied to the tails of their horses, who swim over, the pack serves as a sort of boat. . . . Even the common soldiers have nearly waterproof leather bags, into which they stuff their things . . . and then hang them securely on the bases of their horses' tails before crossing.

You should know that the Tartar emperor told me in person that he wanted to send his armies into Livonia [on the Baltic Sea] and Prussia and that he intended to destroy the whole countryside or reduce it to servitude. They enslave people in a way which we find intolerable. . . . Their tactics include using captives from lands just conquered to fight against a province still holding out against them. They put these captives in the front ranks: If they fight poorly, they kill them; if they fight well, they encourage them with cheering words and promise to make them great lords so that they will not escape. However, once the dangers of battle are passed, they keep these people in line by making hapless serfs out of them, while taking the women they want for serving maids and concubines. Their use of men from one defeated country after another against the next country makes it impossible for any single country to resist them, unless God chooses to fight for them. . . .

Thus, if Christians wish to defend themselves, their countries, and Christianity, it will be necessary for kings, princes, barons, and other chiefs of the lands to cooperate as one and to send men under a consolidated command into battle against them before they have so drained the earth of men that there will be nowhere to draw aid from. . . . This army should be ordered as they do it, from officers commanding a thousand through officers commanding a hundred and overall commanders of the army. These generals should never enter the fighting themselves, just as Tartar commanders do not enter it, but they should be able to observe the army's action and direct it. Our people should make it a regulation that the soldiers advance into battle together or elsewhere in the order established.

86

Marco Polo in China

The creation of a huge Eurasian empire by the Mongols in the thirteenth century again opened the overland routes—the roads once used by the ancient silk traders and Buddhist pilgrims—that had been blocked since the eleventh century by the expansion of Islam. Caravans of traders and pilgrims were again able to move to and from the East. Many European missionaries and merchants made overland journeys to the court of the Mongol Khans. Perhaps the best-known European traveler to the court of Kublai Khan in Cambaluc (Peking) was Marco Polo (1254–1324), the son of a Venetian merchant.

In about 1264, young Marco's adventurous father Nicolo and uncle Maffeo reached the Grand Khan's court after a long and difficult journey through southern Russia, Bukhara, and Chinese Turkestan. They aroused much curiosity in Kublai's mind about Europe and the papacy. In 1266, they were sent back to Europe as Kublai's ambassadors to ask the pope to send one hundred well-schooled missionaries and scholars to China. The Holy See failed to take Kublai's request seriously and sent two priests who made it only as far east as Armenia. Had the pope sent one hundred dedicated and well-trained missionaries, the course of history might have been altered.

In 1271, Marco Polo joined his father and uncle in their second journey to the court of the Kublai Khan. After three and a half years of difficult, overland journey, they reached Shang-Tu (Xandu), the summer residence of Kublai Khan. The Grand Khan was delighted to see them and grew particularly fond of Marco, whom he appointed as his personal, roving administrator for important missions in several distant provinces. In 1292, after seventeen years of service at Kublai Khan's court, the three Polos set out for Europe. This time they went by ship and took with them a young princess whom Kublai was sending as a bride to the Mongol Khan of Persia. In 1295, the Polos returned to Venice, where the Venetians lionized Marco with the nickname "Il milione" (the million).

Shortly after Marco Polo's return, a war broke out between Venice and Genoa. While serving as a Venetian naval commander in this war, Marco was captured and sent to a Genoese prison for three years. During this time, Marco Polo dictated the account of his adventures and travels in China to a fellow prisoner. His book, later printed in Italian, Latin, French, and other languages, introduced Asia to Renaissance Europe and also inspired the great explorers, such as Christopher Columbus, to begin the Age of Discovery in the fifteenth century.

The following excerpts are Marco Polo's eyewitness accounts of the Grand Khan and the capital city of Cambaluc.

QUESTIONS TO CONSIDER

1. Compare and contrast the Kublai Khan's power and palace with those of one of the powerful medieval kings of Europe (see Reading 60).
2. From a historical perspective, what do you think are the most important contributions made by Marco Polo?
3. How would you compare Marco Polo's views on China with Ibn Battuta's views on Africa (see Reading 67)?

Concerning the Person of the Great Kaan

The personal appearance of the Great Kaan [Khan], Lord of Lords, whose name is Cublay, is such as I shall now tell you. He is of good stature, neither tall nor short, but of a middle height. He has a becoming amount of flesh, and is very shapely in all his limbs. His complexion is white and red, the eyes black and fine; the nose well formed and well set on. He has four wives, whom he retains permanently as his legitimate consorts; and the eldest of his sons by those four wives ought by rights to be emperor;—I mean when his father dies. Those four ladies are called empresses, but each is distinguished also by her proper name. And each of them has a special court of her own, very grand and ample; no one of them having fewer than 300 fair and charming damsels. They have also many pages and eunuchs, and a number of other attendants of both sexes; so that each of these ladies has not less than 10,000 persons attached to her court.

When the Emperor desires the society of one of these four consorts, he will sometimes send for the lady to his apartment and sometimes visit her at her own. He has also a great number of concubines, and I will tell you how he obtains them.

You must know that there is a tribe of Tartars called Ungrat, who are noted for their beauty. Now every year a hundred of the most beautiful maidens of this tribe are sent to the Great Kaan, who commits them to the charge of certain elderly ladies

From Henry Yule, trans. and ed., *The Book of Ser Marco Polo*, Vols. 1 and 2 (London: John Murray, 1903), pp. 356–58, 362–64, 374–75.

dwelling in his palace. And these old ladies make the girls sleep with them, in order to ascertain if they have sweet breath [and do not snore], and are sound in all their limbs. Then such of them as are of approved beauty, and are good and sound in all respects, are appointed to attend on the Emperor by turns. Thus six of these damsels take their turn for three days and nights, and wait on him when he is in his chamber and when he is in his bed, to serve him in any way, and to be entirely at his orders. At the end of the three days and nights they are relieved by another six. And so throughout the year, there are reliefs of maidens by six and six, changing every three days and nights.

Concerning the Palace of the Great Kaan

You must know that for three months of the year, to wit December, January, and February, the Great Kaan resides in the capital city of Cathay, which is called Cambaluc [Beijing]. . . . In that city stands his great Palace, and now I will tell you what it is like.

It is enclosed all round by a great wall forming a square, each side of which is a mile in length; that is to say, the whole compass thereof is four miles. This you may depend on; it is also very thick, and a good ten paces in height, whitewashed and loop-holed all around. At each angle of the wall there is a very fine and rich palace in which the war-harness of the Emperor is kept, such as bows and quivers, saddles and bridles, and bowstrings, and everything needful for an army. Also midway between every two of these Corner Palaces there is another of the like; so that taking the whole compass of the enclosure you find eight vast Palaces stored with the Great Lord's harness of war. And you must understand that each Palace is assigned to only one kind of article; thus one is stored with bows, a second with saddles, a third with bridles, and so on in succession right round.

The great wall has five gates on its southern face, the middle one being the great gate which is never opened on any occasion except when the Great Kaan himself goes forth or enters. Close on either side of this great gate is a smaller one by which all other people pass; and then towards each angle is another great gate; also open to people in general; so that on that side there are five gates in all.

Inside of this wall there is a second, enclosing a space that is somewhat greater in length than in breadth. This enclosure also has eight palaces corresponding to those of the outer wall, and stored like them with the Lord's harness of war. This wall also hath five gates on the southern face, corresponding to those in the outer wall, and hath one gate on each of the other faces, as the outer wall hath also. In the middle of the second enclosure is the Lord's Great Palace, and I will tell you what it is like.

You must know that it is the greatest Palace that ever was. [Towards the north it is in contact with the outer wall, whilst towards the south there is a vacant space which the Barons and the soldiers are constantly traversing. The Palace itself] hath no upper story, but is all on the ground floor, only the basement is raised some ten palms above the surrounding soil [and this elevation is retained by a wall of marble raised to the level of the pavement, two paces in width and projecting beyond the base of the Palace so as to form a kind of terrace-walk, by which people can pass round the building, and which is exposed to view, whilst on the outer edge of the wall there is a very fine pillared balustrade; and up to this the people are allowed to come]. The roof is very lofty, and the walls of the Palace are all covered with gold and silver. They are also adorned with representations of dragons [sculptured and gilt], beasts and birds, knights and idols, and sundry other subjects. And on the ceiling too you see nothing but gold and silver and painting. [On each of the four sides there is a great marble staircase leading to the top of the marble wall, and forming the approach to the Palace.]

The Hall of the Palace is so large that it could easily dine 6000 people; and it is quite a marvel to see how many rooms there are besides. The building is altogether so vast, so rich, and so beautiful, that no man on earth could design anything superior to it. The outside of the roof also is all coloured with vermilion and yellow and green and blue and other hues, which are fixed with a varnish so fine and exquisite that they shine like crystal, and lend a resplendent lustre to the Palace as seen for a great way round. This roof is made too with such strength and solidity that it is fit to last for ever.

[On the interior side of the Palace are large buildings with halls and chambers, where the Emperor's private property is placed, such as his treasures of gold, silver, gems, pearls, and gold plate, and in which reside the ladies and concubines. There he occupies himself at his own convenience, and no one else has access.] . . .

Concerning the City of Cambaluc

Now there was on that spot in old times a great and noble city called Cambaluc, which is as much as to say in our tongue "The city of the Emperor." But the Great Kaan was informed by his Astrologers that this city would prove rebellious, and raise great disorders against his imperial authority. So he caused the present city to be built close beside the old one, with only a river between them. And he caused the people of the old city to be removed to the new town that he had founded; and this is called Taidu. . . .

As regards the size of this (new) city you must know that it has a compass of 24 miles, for each side of it hath a length of 6 miles, and it is four-square. And it is all walled round with walls of earth which have a thickness of full ten paces at bottom, and a height of more than 10 paces; but they are not so thick at top, for they diminish in thickness as they rise, so that at top they are only about 3 paces thick. And they are provided throughout with loop-holed battlements, which are all whitewashed.

There are 12 gates, and over each gate there is a great and handsome palace, so that there are on each side of the square three gates and five palaces; for (I ought to mention) there is at each angle also a great and handsome palace. In those palaces are vast halls in which are kept the arms of the city garrison.

The streets are so straight and wide that you can see right along them from end to end and from one gate to the other. And up and down the city there are beautiful palaces, and many great and fine hostelries, and fine houses in great numbers. [All the plots of ground on which the houses of the city are built are four-square, and laid out with straight lines; all the plots being occupied by great and spacious palaces, with courts and gardens of proportionate size. All these plots were assigned to different heads of families. Each square plot is encompassed by handsome streets for traffic; and thus the whole city is arranged in squares just like a chess-board, and disposed in a manner so perfect and masterly that it is impossible to give a description that should do it justice.]

Moreover, in the middle of the city there is a great clock—that is to say, a bell—which is struck at night. And after it has struck three times no one must go out in the city, unless it be for the needs of a woman in labour, or of the sick. And those who go about on such errands are bound to carry lanterns with them. Moreover, the established guard at each gate of the city is 1000 armed men; not that you are to imagine this guard is kept up for fear of any attack, but only as a guard of honour for the Sovereign, who resides there, and to prevent thieves from doing mischief in the town.

The Black Death: Christian and Muslim Views

The outbreak of the Black Death in the fourteenth century is an example of how cross-cultural disease contacts can dramatically change the course of history for millions of people. The Black Death was a combination of three disease strains: a bubonic strain (so called because of buboes, or swelling of the victim's glands) that attacked the lymphatic system, a pneumonic strain that invaded the lungs, and a septicemic strain that was lethal upon entering the bloodstream. In all likelihood, Mongol horsemen carried these disease bacilli westward out of Asia so that by the 1340s, the disease had spread from the Gobi Desert to the Black Sea. In 1347, Genoese traders, returning from the Crimea, brought the disease to Italy. Because of a vigorous and hearty flea and rat population, it spread quickly throughout most of Europe and parts of the Middle East, killing at least twenty million people by 1350. Once a victim was infected, death was certain, usually coming within four days. Certain groups of people, such as bakers, suffered particularly heavy losses because their warm ovens were the choice nests for infected rats. Monasteries, too, seemed to have suffered high mortality rates, as did virtually all the large urban areas.

What is certain is that after the first outbreak of plague, the Black Death recurred at regular intervals. Over time, the huge population losses were restored, not because Europe or the Middle East ever fully conquered the plague, but because the population slowly developed a greater tolerance for the disease. By the eighteenth century, the Black Death had lost much of its lethal effect.

Although these facts are clear, there is no way to determine the degree to which the disease contributed to political, religious, and social change after 1350. Postplague European art, for example, showed a fascination with themes of death, decay, and suffering. Popular culture soon developed new rituals celebrating death, such as the dance of death (the word "macabre" describing this dance appeared first in 1376) and the processional liturgy of flagellants seeking deliverance while scourging themselves. High society's rituals changed as well. Postplague nobility now often hired musicians to play at elaborate funerals. In Paris, polite society now sought the cemetery of the Holy Innocents for its Sunday promenades and amorous rendezvous.

87

The Black Death in Florence

The following account is from Giovanni Boccaccio (1313–1375) whose *The Decameron*, is a collection of tales told by a group of young men and women who had fled Florence during the plague and passed their time telling each other stories. Boccaccio's literary account encapsulates elements of the Christian view of the plague and captures much of the horrors of the Black Death, though, unlike many other accounts, he omits the all too frequent explanation that Jews were responsible for the plague. Jean de Venette, a French Carmelite monk, a contemporary of Boccaccio's, for example, was an observer who reported that many people in France and Germany were convinced that Jews had secretly infected the air and the water supply, thereby causing the Black Death. Not surprisingly the arrival of the Black Death in Europe was followed by widespread incidents of anti-Semitism and the slaughter of thousands of Jews throughout Europe.

QUESTIONS TO CONSIDER

1. How does Boccaccio's account explain the origins of the Black Death?
2. What does the account reveal about the character and assumptions of fourteenth century medicine? According to Boccaccio, what precautions should one take to avoid the plague?
3. How did the plague affect family life, burial customs and prevailing notions of privacy and modesty?
4. What were some of the plague's aftereffects in Italy?

I say, then, that the years of the era of the fruitful Incarnation of the Son of God had attained to the number of one thousand three hundred and forty-eight, when into the notable city of Florence, fair over every other of Italy, there came the death-dealing pestilence, which, through the operation of the heavenly bodies or of our own iniquitous dealings, being sent down upon mankind for our correction by the just wrath of God, had some years before appeared in the parts of the East, and after having bereft these latter of an innumerable number of inhabitants, extending without cease from one place to another, had now unhappily spread towards the West.

To the cure of these maladies neither counsel of physician nor virtue of any medicine appeared to avail or profit aught; on the contrary—whether it was that the nature of the infection suffered it not or that the ignorance of the physicians availed not to know whence it arose and consequently took not due measures thereagainst—not only did few recover thereof, but well nigh all died within the third day from the appearance of the aforesaid signs, this one sooner and that later, and for the most part without fever or other accident, And this pestilence was the more virulent because by communication with those who were sick thereof, it got hold upon

From *The Decameron of Giovanni Boccaccio.* Translated by John Payne (London: Villion Society, 1886), pp. 1–7.

the sound, as fire upon things dry or greasy, when they are brought very near thereunto, Nay, the harm was yet greater; for that not only did conversation and consorting with the sick give infection to the sound or cause of common death, but the mere touching of the clothes or of whatsoever other thing had been touched or used by the sick appeared of itself to communicate the malady to the toucher. A marvelous thing to hear is that which I have to tell and one which, had it not been seen of many men's eyes and of mine own, I had scarce dared credit, much less set down in writing, though I had heard it from one worthy of belief. I say, then, that of such efficience was the nature of the pestilence in question in communicating itself from one to another, that, not only did it pass from man to man, but this, which is much more, it many times visibly did; to wit, a thing which had pertained to a man sick or dead of the aforesaid sickness, being touched by an animal foreign to the human species, not only infected this latter with the plague; but in a very brief space of time killed it. Of this mine own eyes . . . had one day, among others, experience, to wit, that the rags of a poor man, who had died of the plague, being cast out into the public way, two hogs came up to them and having first, after their wont, rooted amain among them with their snouts, took them in their mouths and tossed them about their jaws; then, in a little while, after turning round and round, they both, as if they had taken poison, fell down dead upon the rags with which they had in an ill hour intermeddled.

In this sore affliction and misery of our city, the reverend authority of the laws, both human and divine, was all in a manner dissolved and fallen into decay, for lack of the ministers and executors thereof, who, like other men, were all either dead or sick or else left so destitute of followers that they were unable to exercise any office, wherefore every one had license to do whatsoever pleased him. Many others held a middle course between the two aforesaid, not straitening themselves so exactly in the matter of diet as the first, neither allowing themselves such license in drinking and other debauchery as the second, but using things in sufficiency, according to their appetites; nor did they seclude themselves, but went about, carrying in their hands, some flowers, some odoriferous herbs and other some divers kinds of spices, which they set often to their noses, accounting it an excellent thing to fortify the brain with such odors, more by token that the air seemed all heavy and attainted with the stench of the dead bodies and that of the sick and of the remedies used. Some were of a more barbarous thought, perhaps, a surer way of thinking, avouching that there was no remedy against pestilence better than—no, nor any so good as—to flee before them; wherefore, moved by this reasoning and reeking of nought but themselves, very many, both men and women, abandoned their own city, their own houses and homes, their kinsfolk and possessions, and sought the country seats of others or, at the least, their own, as if the wrath of God, being moved to punish the iniquity of mankind, would not proceed to do so wheresoever they might be, but would content itself with afflicting those only who were found within the walls of their city, or as if they were persuaded that no person was to remain therein and that its last hour was come. And albeit these, who opined thus variously, died not all, yet neither did they all escape; nay, many of each way of thinking and in every place sickened of the plague and languished on all sides, well nigh abandoned, having themselves, what while they were whole, set the example to those who abode in health.

Indeed, leaving be that townsman avoided townsman and that well nigh no neighbor took thought unto other and that kinsfolk seldom or never visited one another and held no converse together save from afar, this tribulation had stricken such terror to the hearts of all, men and women alike, that brother forsook brother, uncle nephew and sister brother and oftentimes wife husband; nay (what is yet more extraordinary and well nigh incredible) fathers and mothers refused to visit or tend their very children, as though they had not been theirs. By reason whereof there remained unto those (and the number of them, both males and females, was incalculable) who fell sick, none other succor than that which they owed either to the charity of friends (and of these there were few) or the greed of servants, who tended them, allured by high and extravagant wage; albeit, for all this, these latter were not grown many, and those men and women of mean understanding and for the most part unused to such offices, who served for well nigh nought but to reach things called for by the sick or to note when they died; and in the doing of these services many of them perished with their gain.

Few, again, were they whose bodies were accompanied to the church by more than half a score or a dozen of their neighbors, and of these no worshipful and illustrious citizens, but a sort of bloodsuckers, sprung from the dregs of the people, who styled themselves pickmen and did such offices for hire, shouldered the bier and bore it with hurried steps, not to that church which the dead man had chosen before his death, but most times to the nearest, behind five or six priests, with little light and sometimes none at all, which latter, with the aid of the said pickmen, thrust him into whatever grave they first found unoccupied, without troubling themselves with too long or too formal a service.

The condition of the common people (and belike, in great part, of the middle class also) was yet more pitiable to behold, for these, for the most part retained by hope or poverty in their houses and abiding in their own quarters, sickened by the thousand daily and being altogether untended and unsuccored died well nigh all without recourse. Many breathed their last in the open street, whilst other many, for all they died in their houses, made it known to the neighbors that they were dead rather by the stench of their rotting bodies than otherwise; and the whole city was full of these and others who died all about. For the most part one same usance was observed by the neighbors, moved more by fear lest the corruption of the dead bodies should imperil themselves than by any charity they had for the departed; to wit, that either with their own hands or with the aid of certain bearers, when they might have any, they brought the bodies of those who had died forth of their houses and laid them before their doors, where especially in the morning, those who went about might see corpses without number; then they fetched biers and some, in default thereof, they laid upon some board or other: Nor was it only one bier that carried two or three corpses, nor did this happen but once; nay, many might have been counted which contained husband and wife, two or three brothers, father and son or the like. And an infinite number of times it befell that, two priests going with one cross for some one, three or four biers, borne by bearers, ranged themselves behind the latter, and whereas the priests thought to have but one dead man to bury, they had six or eight, and sometimes more. Nor therefore were the dead honored with any tears or candles or funeral train; nay, the thing was come to such a pass that folk reeked no more of men that died than nowadays they would of goats; whereby it very manifestly appeared than that which the natural course of things had not availed, by dint of small and infrequent harms, to teach the wise to endure with patience, the very greatness of their ills had brought even the simple to expect and make no account of. The consecrated ground sufficing not to the burial of the vast multitude of corpses aforesaid, which daily and well nigh hourly came carried in crowds to every church especially if it were sought to give each his own place, according to ancient usance—there were made throughout the churchyards, after every other part was full, vast trenches, wherein those who came after were laid by the hundred and being heaped up therein by layers, as goods are stored aboard ship, were covered with a little earth, till such time as they reached the top of the trench. Moreover—not to go longer searching out and recalling every particular of our past miseries, as they befell throughout the city—I say that, whilst so sinister a time prevailed in the latter, on no way therefore was the surrounding country spared, wherein (letting be the castles, which in their littleness were like unto the city) throughout the scattered villages and in the fields, the poor and miserable husbandmen and their families, without succor of physician or aid of servitor, died, not like men, but well nigh like beasts, by the ways or in their tillages or about the houses, indifferently by day and night. By reason whereof, growing lax like the townsfolk in their manners and customs, they reeked not of any thing or business of theirs; nay, all, as if they looked for death that very day, studied with all their wit, not to help to maturity the future produce of their cattle and their fields and the fruits of their own past toils, but to consume those which were ready to hand. Thus it came to pass that the oxen, the asses, the sheep, the goats, the swine, the fowls, nay, the very dogs, so faithful to mankind, being driven forth of their own houses, went straying at their pleasure about the field where the very grain was abandoned, without being cut, much less gathered in; and many, well nigh like reasonable creatures, after grazing all day, returned at night, glutted, to their houses, without the constraint of any herdsman.

To leave the country and return to the city, what more can be said save heaven (and in part, perhaps, that of men) that, between March and the following July, what with the virulence of that pestiferous sickness and the number of sick ill-tended or forsaken in their need, through the fearfulness of those who were well, it is believed for certain that upward of an hundred thousand human beings perished within the walls of the city of Florence, which, peradventure, before the advent of that death-dealing calamity, had not been believed to hold so many? Alas, how many great palaces, how many goodly houses, how many noble mansions once full of families of lords and of ladies, abode empty even to the meanest servant! How many memorable families, how many ample heritages, how many famous fortunes were seen to remain without lawful heir! How many valiant men, how many fair ladies, how many sprightly youths, whom, not others only, but Galen, Hippocrates or Aesculapius themselves, would have judged most hale, breakfasted in the morning with their kinsfolk, comrades and friends and that same night supped with their ancestors in the other world!

88

Ibn Al-Wardī, *An Essay on the Report of the Pestilence*

Ibn al-Wardī,s account of the Black Death, written at the same time as Giovanni Boccaccio's describes the infestation of the plague in Aleppo, a city in northwestern Syria near the Turkish border, where this author died of the plague in 1349. His account parallels Boccaccio's by attributing the plague's origins and deadly consequences to God's wrath but, as a Muslim scholar, he incorporates the teachings of Islam to explain the Black Death.

QUESTIONS TO CONSIDER

1. Why would Ibn al-Wardī advise his readers that the Black Death for Muslims could be a "martyrdom and a reward," but for the infidel it is strictly a punishment? Would Boccaccio agree with this advice?
2. According to this author the Black Death was not caused by infection, but came directly from God; therefore a Muslim should not enter nor flee from a plague-stricken land. Would Boccaccio agree with his diagnosis and advice?
3. What are the major differences between the explanations of Giovanni Boccaccio and Ibn al-Wardî? Are there areas of agreement between these two observers of the plague?
4. How would you compare the literary styles of Ibn al-Wardī and Boccaccio? Which of the two styles presents a more powerful description of the plague? Why?
5. Are there any parallels between these two explanations of the Black Death and modern epidemics?

God is my security in every adversity. My sufficiency is in God alone. Is not God sufficient protection for His servant? Oh God, pray for our master, Muhammad, and give him peace. Save us for his sake from the attacks of the plague and give us shelter.

The plague frightened and killed. It began in the land of darkness. Oh, what a visitor! It has been current for fifteen years. China was not preserved from it nor could the strongest fortress hinder it. The plague afflicted the Indians in India. It weighed upon the Sind. It seized with its hand and ensnared even the lands of the Uzbeks. How many backs did it break in what is Transoxiana![42] The plague increased and spread further. It attacked the Persians, extended its steps toward the land of the Khitai, and gnawed away at the Crimea. It pelted Rūm with live coals and led the outrage to Cyprus and the islands. The plague destroyed mankind in Cairo. Its eye was cast upon Egypt, and behold, the people were wide-awake. It stilled all movement in Alexandria. The plague did its work like a silkworm. . . .

Then, the plague turned to Upper Egypt. It, also, sent forth its storm to Barqah. The plague attacked Gaza, and it shook 'Asqalān severely. The plague oppressed Acre. The scourge came to Jerusalem and paid the zakāt[43] [with the souls of men]. It overtook those people who fled to the al-'Aqsā Mosque, which stands beside the Dome of the Rock. If the door of mercy had not been opened, the end

---

[42]Sind is a province in northwestern India. The Uzbeks were the Mongol tribes east and southeast of the Ural River. Transoxiana is in central Asia, south and east of the Aral Sea.

[43]*Zakāt* is an annual charitable tax each Muslim was expected to pay.

From Michael Dols, *"IBN Al-WARDĪ's RISĀLHA AL-NABA"* An Al-Waba, "A Translation of Major Source for the History of the Black Death in the Middle East," in Dickran K. Kouymjian, ed., *Near Eastern Numismatics, Iconography, Epigraphy and History: Studies in Honor of George C. Miles* (Beirut: American University of Beirut, 1974), pp. 443–55, *passim.* Reprinted by permission.

of the world would have occurred in a moment. It then hastened its pace and attacked the entire maritime plain. The plague trapped Sidon and descended unexpectedly upon Beirut, cunningly. Next, it directed the shooting of its arrows to Damascus. There the plague sat like a king on a throne and swayed the power, killing daily one thousand or more and decimating the population. It destroyed mankind with its pustules.[44] May God the Most High spare Damascus to pursue its own path and extinguish the plague's fires so that they do not come close to her fragrant orchards. . . .

The plague and its poison spread to Sarmīn. It reviled the Sunnī and the Shī'ī.[45] It sharpened its spearheads for the Sunnī and advanced like an army. The plague was spread in the land of the Shī'ī with a ruinous effect. To Antioch the plague gave its share. Then, it left there quickly with a shyness like a man who has forgotten the memory of his beloved. Next, it said to Shayzar and to al-Hārim: "Do not fear me. Before I come and after I go, you can easily disregard me because of your wretchedness. And the ruined places will recover from the time of the plague." Afterward, the plague humbled 'Azāz and took from the people of al-Bāb its men of learning. It ravished Tel Bāshar. The plague subjected Dhulūl and went straight through the lowlands and mountains. It uprooted many people from their homes.

Then, the plague sought Aleppo, but it did not succeed. By God's mercy the plague was the lightest oppression. I would not say that plants must grow from their seeds. . . .

How amazingly does it pursue the people of each house! One of them spits blood, and everyone in the household is certain of death.[46] It brings the entire family to their graves after two or three nights.

Oh God, it is acting by Your command. Lift this from us. It happens where You wish; keep the plague from us. Who will defend us against this horror other than You the Almighty?

How many places has the plague entered? It swore not to leave the houses without its inhabitants. It searched them out with a lamp. The pestilence caused the people of Aleppo the same disturbance. It sent out its snake and crept along. It was named the "Plague of the Ansāb." It was the sixth plague to strike in Islam.[47] To me it is the death of which our Prophet warned, on him be the best prayers and peace.

Oh, if you could see the nobles of Aleppo studying their inscrutable books of medicine. They multiply its remedies by eating dried and sour foods. The buboes which disturb men's healthy lives are smeared with Armenian clay.[48] Each man treated his humours and made life more comfortable.[49] They perfumed their homes with

---

[44]Pustules are swelling of the skin similar to a blister and were an early sign of the plague.

[45]Sunnī and Shī'ī are two major religious divisions within Islam.

[46]Spitting of blood probably refers to the pneumonic form of plague, which is infectious and quite fatal.

[47]Ibn al-Wardī is referring to the fact that Islamic chroniclers recorded five great plagues before the Black Death's arrival in the fourteenth century.

[48]Buboes are an inflamed swelling of the lymphatic glands, especially in the area of the armpit or groin. The ancient Greek medical authority, Galen, recommended the use of Armenian clay as an astringent for wounds and, because of its abundant iron oxide, he also recommended it for the prevention and treatment of the plague.

[49]Humours refers to the fourteenth-century's physiology of the four body fluids (humours) of blood, phlegm, choler, and black bile. Medieval medical authorities believed that illness resulted when the humours were not in proper equilibrium.

ambergris and camphor, cyperus and sandal.[50] They wore ruby rings and put onions, vinegar, and sardines together with the daily meal. They ate less broth and fruit but ate the citron and similar things.

If you see many biers and their carriers and hear in every quarter of Aleppo the announcements of death and cries, you run from them and refuse to stay with them. In Aleppo the profits of the undertakers have greatly increased. Oh God, do not profit them. Those who sweat from carrying the coffins enjoy this plague-time. Oh God, do not let them sweat and enjoy this. They are happy and play. When they are called by a customer, they do not even go immediately.

The Grey [i.e., Aleppo] became blackened in my eyes because of the anxiety and deceit. The sons of the coffins [i.e., the undertakers] are themselves about to follow death.

We ask God's forgiveness for our souls' bad inclination; the plague is surely part of His punishment. We take refuge from His wrath in His pleasure and from His chastisement in His restoring.

They said: the air's corruption kills. I said: the love of corruption kills. How many sins and how many offenses does the crier call our attention to!

Among the things which exasperated the Muslims and brought suffering is that our enemy, the damned people of Sis, are pleased by our trial.[51] They act as if they are safe from the plague—that there is a treaty so that it will not approach them or that they have triumphed over it. Our Lord does not create us as an enticement for those who disbelieve.

The dwellers of Sis are happy with what afflicts us, and this is what you can expect from the enemies of the true religion. God will spread it to them soon so that He will put plague upon plague.

This plague is for the Muslims a martyrdom and a reward, and for the disbelievers a punishment and a rebuke. When the Muslim endures misfortune, then patience is his worship. It has been established by our Prophet: God bless him and give him peace, that the plague-stricken are martyrs. This noble tradition is true and assures martyrdom. And this secret should be pleasing to the true believer. If someone says it causes infection and destruction, say: God creates and recreates. If the liar disputes the matter of infection and tries to find an explanation, I say that the Prophet, on him be peace, said: who infected the first? If we acknowledge the plague's devastation of the people, it is the will of the Chosen Doer. So it happened again and again.

I take refuge in God from the yoke of the plague. Its high explosion has burst into all countries and was an examiner of astonishing things. Its sudden attacks perplex the people. The plague chases the screaming without pity and does not accept a treasure for ransom. Its engine is far-reaching. The plague enters into the house and swears it will not leave except with all of its inhabitants. "I have an order from the qadi [a judge] to arrest all those in the house." Among the benefits of this order is the removal of one's hopes and the improvement of his earthly works. It awakens men from their indifference for the provisioning of their final journey.

---

[50]Ambergris is a waxlike substance often found floating on tropical seas; camphor is a white, crystalline solid with a pungent odor and taste; cyperus is an aromatic marsh plant; and sandal probably refers to a medicinal ointment derived from sandalwood.

[51]Sis was the ancient capital of the Cilician Armenian kingdom and is reported to have suffered from the Black Death after Aleppo.

Nothing prevented us from running away from the plague except our devotion to the noble tradition. Come then, seek the aid of God Almighty for raising the plague, for He is the best helper. Oh God, we call You better than anyone did before. We call You to raise from us the pestilence and plague. We do not take refuge in its removal other than with You. We do not depend on our good health against the plague but on You. We seek Your protection, Oh Lord of creation, from the blows of this stick. We ask for Your mercy which is wider than our sins even as they are the number of the sands and pebbles. We plead with You, by the most honored of the advocates, Muhammad, the Prophet of mercy, that You take away from us this distress. Protect us from the evil and the torture and preserve us. For You are our sole support; what a perfect trustee!

Part V

A World in Change

The Rise of the Ottoman Empire

Osman, after whom the Ottomans were named, was the son of Ertogrul, who had led a small group of Turks out of Asia in advance of the Mongols during the second half of the thirteenth century. Ertogrul eventually received a small fief in northeastern Anatolia and became a frontier warrior against the Byzantines.

By the time Osman succeeded his father, the Ottomans had converted to Islam, which only served to reinforce their military ambitions. The territory expanded slowly until 1354, when a descendant of Osman crossed into Europe (Thrace) and began to attack Byzantine lands as well as other Balkan states.

In 1366, Sultan Murad I decided to move the Ottoman capital from Anatolia to Europe. The emphasis of Ottoman policy for the next century was to be on Christian Europe with the ultimate goal of Constantinople. This was achieved by Mehmed II in 1453, when he captured the former Byzantine capital and made it the center of Ottoman government.

Having eliminated the Byzantine Empire, which had been the chief opposing force to Ottoman expansion toward the West, the Turks moved up the Balkan peninsula and reduced many of the peoples of (the then "future," now "former") Yugoslavia to subjection. Within seventy-five years, under Suleiman the Magnificent, the westward expansion of Ottoman power went beyond the Balkans, to include control of Hungary and threats to Vienna.

In the Balkans proper, only the Bosnians were willing to accept Islam in any numbers. Most Balkan peoples accepted Turkish occupation passively, but on the northern edge of the Balkans the Wallachians, under their colorful but probably psychopathic leader Dracula, continued to make life difficult for Sultan Mehmed.

89

Kritovoulos, *History of Mehmed the Conqueror*

Mehmed II assumed the throne of the Ottoman Empire on the death of his father, Murad II. The new sultan began at once to plan his greatest achievement—the seizure of Constantinople from the last Byzantine emperor, Constantine XI. This successful capture would earn Mehmed II the title of "The Conqueror."

In 1452, Mehmed gathered thousands of cavalry, Janissaries,[1] irregular troops, naval personnel, and military engineers for the undertaking. For fifty-four days during the months of April and May 1453, the sultan's forces pounded on the 1,100-year-old impenetrable land walls. Finally, on May 29 of that same year, his men, spying an inadvertently unlocked sally port, poured into the capital with a frenzy. That fateful day extinguished Greek independence for almost four centuries.

After taking the city, Sultan Mehmed's troops were not allowed to rest. For almost the next thirty years, they raided and captured land and inhabitants in the Balkans, Wallachia-Moldavia (Romania), and even in the hinterland of Venice.

The History of Mehmed the Conqueror is by a contemporary Greek historian named Kritovoulos. Little is known of this writer except that he was not at the fall of Constantinople but arrived soon after at that city to record Mehmed's life. Kritovoulos eventually entered the sultan's service and became a governor on the island of Imbros.

QUESTIONS TO CONSIDER

1. Why was Mehmed II successful in his naval attack on the city?
2. Can you find an example that illustrates the superstitious nature of the Byzantines?
3. How would you compare the actions of the Ottoman warriors with those of the sultan when the city had been taken?
4. How did the fall of the Byzantine Empire affect the growth of the Russian monarchy (see Reading 92)?

He also resolved to carry into execution immediately the plan which he had long since studied out and elaborated in his mind and toward which he had bent every purpose from the start, and to wait no longer nor delay. This plan was to make war against the Romans [Byzantines or Greeks] and their Emperor Constantine and to besiege the city.

Sultan Mehmed considered it necessary in preparation for his next move to get possession of the harbor and open the Horn for his own ships to sail in. So, since every effort and device of his had failed to force the entrance, he made a wise decision, and one worthy of his intellect and power. It succeeded in accomplishing his purpose and in putting an end to all uncertainties.

---

[1]Janissaries were young boys taken by the Ottoman sultans as tribute from the Balkan areas. They were converted to Islam and trained as an elite fighting force.

From Kritovoulos, *History of Mehmed the Conqueror*, trans. Charles T. Riggs (Princeton NJ: Princeton University Press, 1954), pp. 22–23, 55–59, 66–67, 70–72, 76–77, 82–83. Copyright 1954 © renewed 1984 by Princeton University Press. Reprinted with permission of Princeton University Press.

He ordered the commanders of the vessels to construct as quickly as possible glide-ways leading from the outer sea to the inner sea, that is, from the harbor to the Horn, near the place called Diplokion, and to cover them with beams. This road, measured from sea to sea, is just about eight stadia. It is very steep for more than half the way, until you reach the summit of the hill, and from there again it descends to the inner sea of the Horn. And as the glideways were completed sooner than expected, because of the large number of workers, he brought up the ships and placed large cradles under them, with stays against each of their sides to hold them up. And having undergirded them well with ropes, he fastened long cables to the corners and gave them to the soldiers to drag, some of them by hand, and others by certain machines and capstans. . . .

Thus, then, there was assembled in the bay called Cold Waters, a little beyond Galata, a respectable fleet of some sixty-seven vessels. They were moored there.

The Romans, when they saw such an unheard-of-thing actually happen, and war-ships lying at anchor in the Horn—which they never would have suspected—were as-tounded at the impossibility of the spectacle, and were overcome by the greatest consternation and perplexity. They did not know what to do now, but were in de-spair. In fact they had left unguarded the walls along the Horn for a distance of about thirty stadia, and even so they did not have enough men for the rest of the walls, either for defense or for attack, whether citizens or men from elsewhere. In-stead, two or even three battlements had but a single defender.

And now, when this sea-wall also became open to attack and had to be guarded, they were compelled to strip the other battlements and bring men there. This con-stituted a manifest danger, since the defenders were taken away from the rest of the wall while those remaining were not enough to guard it, being so few. . . .

During those same days there occurred the following divine signs and portents of the terrors that were very soon to come to the city. Three or four days before the battle, when all the people in the City were holding a religious procession, men and women together, and marching around with the Ikon of the Mother of God, this latter slipped suddenly from the hands of its bearers without any cause or power being apparent, and fell flat on the ground. And when everybody shouted immediately, and rushed to raise up the ikon, it sank down as if weighted with lead, and as if fastened to the ground, and became well-nigh impossible to raise. And so it continued for a consider-able time, until, by a great effort and much shouting and prayers by all, the priests and its bearers barely managed to raise it up and place it on the shoulders of the men.

This strange occurrence filled everyone with much terror and very great agony and fear, for they thought this fall was no good omen—as was quite true. Later, when they had gone on but a short distance, immediately after that, at high noon, there was much thunder and lightning with clouds, and a violent rain with severe hail followed, so that they could neither stand against it nor make any progress. The priests and the bearers of the ikon and the crowds that followed were depressed and hindered by the force of the waters that flowed down and by the might of the hail. Many of the children following were in danger of being carried away and drowned by the violent and pow-erful rush of water, had not some men quickly seized them and with some difficulty dragged them out of the flood. Such was the unheard-of and unprecedented violence of that storm and hail which certainly foreshadowed the imminent loss of all, and that, like a torrent of fiercest waters, it would carry away and annihilate everything. . . .

The hour was already advanced, the day [May 28, 1453] was declining and near evening, and the sun was at the Ottomans' backs but shining in the faces of their enemies. This was just as the Sultan had wished; accordingly he gave the order first for the trumpets to sound the battle-signal, and the other instruments, the pipes and flutes and cymbals too, as loud as they could. All the trumpets of the other divisions, with the other instruments in turn, sounded all together, a great and fearsome sound. Everything shook and quivered at the noise. After that, the standards were displayed.

To begin, the archers and slingers and those in charge of the cannon and the muskets, in accord with the commands given them, advanced against the wall slowly and gradually. When they got within bowshot, they halted to fight. And first they exchanged fire with the heavier weapons, with arrows from the archers, stones from the slingers, and iron and leaden balls from the cannon and muskets. Then, as they closed with battleaxes and javelins and spears, hurling them at each other and being hurled at pitilessly in rage and fierce anger. On both sides there was loud shouting and blasphemy and cursing. Many on each side were wounded, and not a few died. This kept up till sunset, a space of about two or three hours.

Sultan Mehmed, who happened to be fighting quite near by, saw that the palisade and the other part of the wall that had been destroyed were now empty of men and deserted by the defenders. He noted that men were slipping away secretly and that those who remained were fighting feebly because they were so few. Realizing from this that the defenders had fled and that the wall was deserted, he shouted out: "Friends, we have the City! We have it! They are already fleeing from us! They can't stand it any longer! The wall is bare of defenders! It needs just a little more effort and the City is taken! Don't weaken, but on with the work with all your might, and be men and I am with you!"

Capture of the City

So saying, he led them himself. And they, with a shout on the run and with a fearsome yell, went on ahead of the Sultan, pressing on up to the palisade. After a long and bitter struggle they hurled back the Romans from there and climbed by force up the palisade. They dashed some of their foe down into the ditch between the great wall and the palisade, which was deep and hard to get out of, and they killed them there. The rest they drove back to the gate.

Death of Emperor Constantine

He had opened this gate in the great wall, so as to go easily over to the palisade. Now there was a great struggle there and great slaughter among those stationed there, for they were attacked by the heavy infantry and not a few others in irregular formation, who had been attracted from many points by the shouting. There the Emperor Constantine, with all who were with him, fell in gallant combat. . . .

Then a great slaughter occurred of those who happened to be there: some of them were on the streets, for they had already left the houses and were running toward the tumult when they fell unexpectedly on the swords of the soldiers; others were in their own homes and fell victims to the violence of the Janissaries and other soldiers, without any rhyme or reason; others were resisting, relying on their own courage; still others were fleeing to the churches and making supplication—men, women, and children, everyone, for there was no quarter given.

The soldiers fell on them with anger and great wrath. For one thing, they were actuated by the hardships of the siege. For another, some foolish people had hurled taunts and curses at them from the battlements all through the siege. Now, in general they killed so as to frighten all the City, and to terrorize and enslave all by the slaughter. . . .

Other women, sleeping in their beds, had to endure nightmares. Men with swords, their hands bloodstained with murder, breathing out rage, speaking out murder indiscriminate, flushed with all the worst things—this crowd, made up of men from every race and nation, brought together by chance, like wild and ferocious beasts, leaped into the houses, driving them out mercilessly, dragging, rending, forcing, hauling them disgracefully into the public highways, insulting them and doing every evil thing.

They say that many of the maidens, even at the mere unaccustomed sight and sound of these men, were terror-stricken and came near losing their very lives. And there were also honorable old men who were dragged by their white hair, and some of them beaten unmercifully. And well-born and beautiful young boys were carried off. . . .

After this the Sultan entered the City and looked about to see its great size, its situation, its grandeur and beauty, its teeming population, its loveliness, and the costliness of its churches and public buildings and of the private houses and community houses and of those of the officials. He also saw the setting of the harbor and of the arsenals, and how skillfully and ingeniously they had everything arranged in the City—in a word, all the construction and adornment of it. When he saw what a large number had been killed, and the ruin of the buildings, and the wholesale ruin and destruction of the City, he was filled with compassion and repented not a little at the destruction and plundering. Tears fell from his eyes as he groaned deeply and passionately: "What a city we have given over to plunder and destruction!" . . .

The Sultan Mehmed, when he had carefully viewed the City and all its contents, went back to the camp and divided the spoils. First he took the customary toll of the spoils for himself. Then also, as prizes from all the rest, he chose out beautiful virgins and those of the best families, and the handsomest boys, some of whom he even bought from the soldiers. He also chose some of the distinguished men who, he was informed, were above the rest in family and intelligence and valor. . . .

Then, with the notable men, and his courtiers, he went through the City. First he planned how to repopulate it, not merely as it formerly was but more completely, if possible, so that it should be a worthy capital for him, situated, as it was, most favorably by land and by sea. Then he donated to all the grandees, and to those of his household, the magnificent homes of the rich, with gardens and fields and vineyards inside of the City. And to some of them he even gave beautiful churches as their private residences.

For himself, he chose the most beautiful location in the center of the City for the erection of a royal palace. After this, he settled all the captives whom he had taken as his portion, together with their wives and children, along the shores of the city harbor, since they were sea-faring men whom they previously had called Stenites. He gave them houses and freed them from taxes for a specified time.

He also made a proclamation to all those who had paid their own ransom, or who promised to pay it to their masters within a limited time, that they might live in the City, and he granted them, also, freedom from taxes, and gave them houses, either their own or those of others.

90

Suleiman the Magnificent and his Courtiers

The pinnacle of Ottoman power was reached during the reign of Sultan Suleiman the Magnificent (r. 1520–1565). Suleiman successfully attacked Belgrade in 1521 and Hungary (1526), which were added to his empire. He then began many wars with the Holy Roman Emperor Charles V and, in 1529, unsuccessfully besieged Vienna, but did eliminate the Hapsburgs from most of Hungary by 1565.

Suleiman also fought the Safavid Persians three times and was able to add Mesopotamia. His army and navy were able to win control of the Red Sea and extend his rule along the Barbary coast to Morocco. Suleiman also attacked and captured the island of Rhodes (1522) from the Knights of the Temple, freeing the area from these Christian pirates.

One would assume that Suleiman's successes might have marked the complete downfall of his enemies and complete triumph of the Ottomans; yet, several of his practices—abandoning the strict merit system of the Palace School and the growing influence of his favorite wife—were to sow the seeds of Ottoman decline in the following centuries.

The following piece by Richard Knolles, a contemporary English historian, describes the role of Roxolana, Suleiman's most famous concubine and wife, and her dominating influence over the sultan and his government.

QUESTIONS TO CONSIDER

1. What caused Suleiman to kill his first- born son, Mustapha?
2. Why would the influence of the women of the harem not be beneficial for the Ottoman government in the future?

Roxolana

Suleiman after the manner of the Othoman [Ottoman] kings, who to avoid the participation of the sovereignty, was not oftentimes to marry (but otherwise to satisfy their pleasure with such beautiful concubines as it pleaseth them to make choice of, out of the fairest captives of all nations, most daintily brought up for that purpose in the court) had by a Circadian bondwoman, a son called Mustapha who for his wonderful towardliness and rare perfection was among the Turks had in such expectation and admiration, as that they in nothing accounted themselves more happy, than in the hope laid up in him: whose noble carriage was such, as that thereby he so possessed the minds of all men in general, but especially of the men of war, that he was reputed the glory of the court, the flower of chivalry, the hope of the soldiers, and the joy of the people.

Richard Knolles, The Generall Historie of the Turkes, from the first beginning of that Nation to the rising of the Othoman Familie: with all the notable expeditions of the Christian Pricnes against them. Together with the Lives and Conquests of the Othoman Kings and Emperours (London: A. Islip, 1603), pp. 757–63.

While he thus grew increasing both in years and favor: it fortuned with Suleiman as it doth with men delighting in change, that he became amoured of Roxolana, of some called Rosa (but more truly Hazathya) by condition a captive, but so graced with beauty and courtly behavior, that in short time she became mistress of his thoughts, and commandress of him that all commanded: And that which more established her in possession of his love, she had in time made him father of four fair sons, Mehmed, Selim, Baiazet, and Jehangir, and one daughter called Chameria married to Rustam or Tustemes the great Pasha. In this height of worldly bliss nothing troubled her more than the exceeding credit of Mustapha, Suleiman's eldest son by the Circadian woman; who honored of the greatest, and beloved of the rest, stood only in her light, embarring her and hers {as she thought) of the hope of the empire, which she now above all things sought to bring to one of her own sons: which the better to compass, she under the color of great good will and love procured that Mustapha the young prince and his mother should as it were for their greater honor and state with a princely allowance be sent into Caramania to govern that great country, far from the court . . . Roxolana having at once thus cunningly rid the court of the great competitors both of her love and of the empire . . . rested not so, but began straightway to plot in her malicious head the utter destruction of him, to whom all others wished all happiness.

This she saw was not to be brought to pass without some complies: . . . at last she made choice of Rustam Pasha, her son-in-law, upon whom she would set up her rest. This Rustam was a man basely born in Epirus, altogether composed of dissimulation and flattery, ever serving his own turn, were it never so much to the hurt or grievance of others; by which means he, although none of the best soldiers, was yet by many degrees grown up to be the great man in the court and Suleiman's son in law; him she probably thought to wish the succession of the empire to one of her own sons. . . .

[Roxolana achieved what no other woman had done for many years; she persuaded Suleiman to free her and marry her. This made her the most important woman of the Sultan's harem.]

This woman of late a slave, but now become the greatest empress of the East, flowing in all worldly felicity, attended upon with all the pleasures her heart could desire, wanted nothing she could wish, but how to find means that the Turkish empire right after the death of Suleiman, be brought to some one of her own sons. This was it that had . . . long troubled her aspiring mind; and in the midst of all her bliss, suffered her yet to take no rest . . . Which to bring to pass, the wicked woman labored cunningly by little and little to breed in Suleiman's head no small suspicion of Mustapha, that he being a young man of a haughty spirit, delirious of sovereignty, generally beloved, and swelling with the immoderate favor of the men of war, which were all at his devotion, left nothing else to be expected of him, but when he should . . . lay hand upon the empire, and work his aged father's destruction.

[Rustan secretly wrote to the governors of Syria to report any suspicious activities of Mustapha]

And she (Roxolana) still as occasion best served her purpose, ceased not with pleasing allurements and flattery . . . to infect Suleiman's mind, that whensoever he should chance to have any speech of Mustapha, she might take the fitter occasion to bring forth those letters. Neither was she in her drift deceived, but having found a fit opportunity, with tears trickling down her cheeks(which to serve their turns subtle women seldom want) she told the emperor in what danger he stood, recounting amongst other things, how Selim his father had by such means deprived Bayazid his grandfather, both of his life and empire together: and therefore most instantly besought him, as if it had altogether proceeded of a careful love; . . . so that she little prevailed thereby . . . she still grew more and more in favor and obtained that her sons might by turns be still present in the court: of purpose, that by their daily presence and continual flattery, they should more and more procure their father's love; and if by chance Mustapha should come thither, she might have the better means to dispatch him. . . . But Mustapha never coming . . . she easily devised another practice: that her sons should wait upon their father, not in the city only, but in the provinces also. . . . Certain years thus spent, and she still hammering her mischievous devises; at length fortune favoring her wicked desire, got from the pasha which had the government of Mustapha and the province of Amasia . . . certain suspicious letters; wherein was contained, that there was speech of a marriage to be made between Mustapha and the Persian king's daughter. . . . These letters being brought to Rustam, he thought he had now as good as half brought to end the long desired ruin of Mustapha: so making no stay, he opened the matter to Roxolana, and afterwards both together went to the court, and declared all the matter to the emperor.. .saying, That he as a proud and ambitious young man, ravished with the desire of so glorious an empire, sought against the laws both of God and nature, to take his father out of the way, so that he might with more speed satisfy his aspiring mind. And to give the more credit to this their most false suggestion, they warned him of the alliance by him purposed with the Persian king, the ancient enemy of the Othman emperors; wishing him to beware, least Mustapha supported by the strength of Persia, . . .

In the year 1552 he (Suleiman) caused proclamation to be made almost in all provinces of his empire, That for as much as the Persians without resistance with a great army invaded Syria, burning and destroying the country before them, he to repress their outrageous insolence, was enforced to send thither Rustam Pasha with an army: . . . Now when all things were in readiness, as if it had been for such a war as was pretended, he commanded Rustam, which as much secrecy and as little tumult as was possible, to lay hands upon Mustapha, and to bring him bound to Constantinople: which if he could not conveniently effect, then, by any other means to take him out of the way. With this wicked and cruel charge Rustam with a strong army marched towards Syria. Mustapha understanding of his coming, without delay with 7,000 of the best horsemen in all Turkey made towards Syria also: whereof Rustam hearing, and perceiving that he cold not . . . conveniently execute the cruel command of the unnatural father, forthwith turned his back, and treading the same steps he came, returned with the army to Constantinople with such speed, . . . giving it out,That he certainly understood, that the province was in quiet . . . and that he thereupon returned. But unto Suleiman he told another tale in secret, which he maliciously had devised, That he by most apparent signs and manifest presumptions had perceived the whole army so inclined towards Mustapha, that if he should have attempted anything against him by plain force, he should have been utterly forsaken, and therefore in so dangerous a case left the matter as it was to his further direction. This tale suspiciously told, raised in the wicked and unnatural father . . . new and great suspicions, whereof to disburden his disquieted mind, he conceived with himself a most horrible device. Where the year following, . . . (1553), he raised a great army, giving it out, That the Persians had with greater power than before invaded Syria, and that therefore he for the love of his country and defence of his empire was determined to go thither with his army, and in person himself to repel the attempts of his enemies. Wherefore the army being assembled, . . . he commanded to set forward, and in a few days after followed himself: who coming at length in to Syria, presently by trusted messengers commanded Mustapha to come to him at Aleppo, for there he lay encamped. . . . Neither could Mustapha himself but marvel, that his aged father without any apparent reason should come so far with so great an army: yet trusting to his own innocence, . . . he resolved (although it were with the extreme danger of his life) to obey and yield this father's command: for he thought it more commendable and honorable to incur the danger of death, than living, to fall into the sole suspicion of disloyalty, . . . foreseeing as it were the approach of his own end; . . . set forward towards his father, and making great haste, came at length to his father's camp, and not far off pitched his tents in the open field.

But this his so hasty coming the more increased the suspicion in the mind of his wicked father: neither spared Rustam in the mean time with his crafty and subtle devices to augment the same: for by a sign given he caused the Janissaires and chief men in the army to go as it had been for honors sake to meet Mustapha. . . . In the mean time, he (Rustam) the most crafty varlet with troubled countenance . . . as a man half dismayed came in haste to Suleiman's pavilion, and falsely told him, that the Janissaires and almost all the best soldiers of the army were of themselves without leave gone to meet Mustapha, and that he feared what would ensue thereof. Which news so troubled the old tyrant, that he became pale for fear, and going out of his tent, and finding them gone, easily believed all to be true that the false Pasha had told him, . . . he came to his father's camp, and pitching his tents . . . suited himself all in white, in token of his innocence, and writing certain letters . . . and putting them in his bosom, attended upon with a few of his most trusted followers, came with great reverence towards the tent of his father, fully resolving to have kissed his hand, as their usual manner is. . . . So when he came into the more inward rooms of the tent, he was with such honor as belonged to his state cheerfully received by his father's eunuchs. But seeing nothing else provided but one seat whereon to sit himself alone, he perplexed in mind stood still a while musing, at length asked where the emperor was? Whereunto they answered, that he should by and by see him: and with that casting his eye aside, he saw seven Mutes (these are strong men, bereft of their speech, whom the Turkish tyrants, have always in readiness, the more secretly to execute their bloody butchery) coming from the other side of the tent towards him, at whose sight stricken with a sudden terror, he said no more, but "Lo my death!" and with that, arising, was about to have fled: but in vain, for he was caught hold on by the eunuch and the Mutes, and by force drawn to the place appointed for his death: where without further stay the Mutes cast a bow string about his neck, he poor wretch still striving, and requesting that he might speak but two words to his father before he died.

91

Vlad Tsepes, "The Impaler": The Real Dracula or How the Enemy of the Ottomans Became a Legend

Vlad Tsepes (1431–1476) was born to Vlad Dracul (Order of the Dragon), who was the *voivode* (governor) of Wallachia (modern Romania). Hemmed between his sovereign, the Christian king of Hungary, and the Ottoman Empire south of the Danube,

Vlad Dracul tried to placate both sides in order to keep his power. He was to lose on all counts. In 1444, Sultan Murad II forced Dracul to give his sons Vlad Tsepes and a younger brother, Radu the Handsome, as hostages, and three years later King Mathias of Hungary ordered Dracul's assassination for disloyalty.

Vlad Tsepes managed to escape Ottoman captivity in 1448. He set about regaining control of Wallachia through intrigue and invasions. He finally achieved his goal in 1456 and ruled the area until 1462. It was during these years that Dracula engaged in a frenzy of killing; none were immune to his savage nature—the poor, nobles, or Ottoman Turks were killed by impaling, skinning, boiling, or decapitation. Finally, in 1462, Sultan Mehmed II invaded Wallachia, chased Vlad out, and placed Vlad's brother Radu in power.

Vlad fled to Hungary, where he was kept in prison and house arrest under suspicion of disloyalty until 1474. He was able to rehabilitate himself in the eyes of Mathias, with whose aid he tried once more, in 1476, to regain Wallachia from his brother. He was successful for two months. When the Hungarian forces who had helped him left the lands, a native uprising cost Vlad his throne and his head.

The following two selections contrast Dracula's personality and actions. The first selection details Dracula's strategy against an invasion of Wallachia by Sultan Mehmed II. The second comes from manuscripts and folktales that were created about Dracula and have passed into legend in Russia, Germany, and Romania. Most of these stories relate Dracula's vicious nature, but some, we might say, contain a sense of "black humor."

QUESTIONS TO CONSIDER

1. How do Dracula's methods compare with those of King Ashurnasirpal of Assyria (Reading 17)?
2. Can you cite similar examples of inhumanity in the present time?
3. Why could Dracula be called a national savior for Wallachia?
4. What constitutes Dracula's "black humor"?

Dracula Defends Wallachia against Sultan Mehmed II

In the year 6970 [1462] Mehmed dispatched an ambassador to the voivode of Vlachia[2] commanding him to come quickly to make obeisance and to bring with him five hundred boys as well as the annual tribute of ten thousand gold coins. He replied that whereas the gold coins were ready for payment, he was unable to deliver the boys, and moreover, for him to come and make obeisance was completely out of the question. When the tyrant[3] heard this he became wild with rage. He dispatched one of his nobles and one of his secretaries, and told them, "Bring me the tribute, and I myself will give some thought to the rest." When, on their arrival, they disclosed the tyrant's message to the Vlach, he impaled them on stakes, condemning

[2]Vlad Tsepes (Dracula).
[3]"The tyrant" is Mehmed II, not Dracula ("The Vlach").

From Michael Doukas, *Decline and Fall of Byzantium to the Ottoman Turks,* trans. Harry J. Magoulias (Detroit: Wayne State University Press, 1975), pp. 259–61. Copyright © 1975 by Wayne State University Press. Reprinted with permission.

them to an inhuman, excruciating, and ignominious death. The Vlach afterward crossed the Danube with his troops and overran the environs of Dristra. He took captive many of the rabble and transported them to Vlachia, after which he took their lives by meting out the same death by impalement.

One of the tyrant's commanders who was stationed along these borders, desiring to display his prowess, crossed into Vlachia with ten thousand Turkish troops. The Vlach engaged them in battle and all those Turks who were not killed but taken alive, he condemned to bitter death by impalement, together with their commander Hamza.

The tyrant, apprised of these events, was distraught. Mustering from all quarters a force of more than one hundred and fifty thousand men, he marched out of Adrianople in the spring and came to the Danube. There he pitched his tents and waited until the entire army was assembled. The Vlach, deploying all his troops along mountain defiles and wooded areas, left the plains deserted. Flocks of all kinds of animals were driven into the interior toward the borders of the Alans and Huns [Poland and Hungary], while he passed the days with his troops in the dense woodlands and forest areas. The tyrant crossed the Danube and, during a march of over seven days, found nothing whatsoever, neither man nor animal nor food nor drink of any kind. He came upon a meadow where he saw countless stakes planted in the ground, laden not with fruit but with corpses, and on a stake in the middle was transfixed Hamza, still wearing his purple and red garments. When the tyrant beheld this terrible portent, he was panic-stricken. Terrified of the night, he raised trench embankments in the area where he had pitched his tents and lay down between the trenches. The Vlach, rising in the half-light of dawn and drawing up his troops in battle array, descended while it was still dark. He came by chance upon the right side of the camp, and made a sudden charge inside; by morning he had already cut down countless numbers. Until dawn broke, the Turks were killing one another. With the coming of daylight, the Vlachs returned to their bivouacs and bedded down. The tyrant, in disgrace, crossed the Danube and returned to Adrianople.

Folktales about Dracula

There lived in the Wallachian lands a Christian prince of the Greek faith who was called Dracula in the Wallachian language, which means devil in our language, for he was as cruelly clever as was his name and so was his life.

Once some ambassadors from the Turkish sultan came to him. When they entered his palace and bowed to him, as was their custom, they did not take their caps from their heads and Dracula asked them: "Why have you acted so? You ambassadors have come to a great prince and you have shamed me." The ambassadors answered, "Such is the custom which our land has, Lord." And Dracula told them, "Well, I want to strengthen you in your law. Behave bravely." And he ordered that their caps be nailed to their heads with small iron nails. And then he allowed them to go. He said, "Go tell your lord, for he is a cultured man: let him accept this shame from us. For

From Raymond T. McNally and Radu Florescu, *In search of Dracula: a true history of Dracula and vampire legends* (New York: Galahad Books, 1972), pp. 193–94, 196, 198, 207–08. The German stories come from Ms. 806 at the Monastery Library of St. Gall, Switzerland, the Russian stories are from Ms. 11/1088 in the Kirillov-Bolozersky Monastery Collection in the Saltykov-Schredin Public Library in St. Petersburg and the Romanian stories are word of mouth. They were all translated by the authors. Copyright 1972 by Raymond T. McNally and Radu Florescu.

you seem to think that we are not cultured. Let him not impose his customs on other rulers who will not accept them, but let him keep his customs in his own land."

Once Dracula ordered throughout the land that whoever was old or sick or poor should come to him. And there gathered at the palace a huge multitude of poor and old people, who expected a great act of mercy. And he ordered that all these miserable people be gathered together, in a large palace which was prepared with this idea in mind. And he ordered that they be given food and drink in accordance with their wishes. So they began to eat, and they became happy. Later on Dracula personally came to see them and spoke to them in the following way: "What else do you need?" And they answered him in unison, "Our good lord, God knows how to give, and your highness surely understands the wishes of God." He then said to them, "Do you want me to make you without any further cares, so that you have no other wants in this world?" And they all expected some great gift and they answered, "We wish it so, my lord." Then he ordered that the palace be locked and he set it on fire, and all of them perished within it. Later he told his nobles, "Know that I have done this so that these unfortunate people will have no further burdens, and so that there should be no more poor in my land but only rich people, and in the second place I freed these people so that they no longer suffer in this world either because of poverty, or because of sickness."

If a woman made love with a man who was not her husband Dracula ordered that her vagina be cut and he skinned her alive and tied her skin to a pole. And the skin was usually hanging on the pole in the middle of the city right there in the market place. He did the same thing with young girls who had not preserved their virginity and also widows. In some cases he cut the nipples off their breasts. In other cases he took the skins from their vagina and he placed an iron poker, reddened by fire, up their vaginas so far upwards that the iron bar emerged from their mouths. They remained naked, tied to a pole until the flesh and bones detached themselves or served as food for the birds.

Dracula had a mistress. Her house was located in a dark and isolated suburb of Targoviste. When Dracula went to see her he was oblivious of everything, for this woman unfortunately happened to be to his taste. For her, he had mere physical attraction, nothing else.

The unfortunate woman tried in every way to be pleasing to Dracula. And he reciprocated all the outward manifestations of love which she showed him. One might also say that Dracula expressed a certain gaiety when he was by her side.

One day when she saw his expression somewhat gloomier, she wished in some way to cheer him up and she dared tell him a lie. "Your highness, you will be glad to hear my tidings." "What news can you give me?" answered Dracula. "The little mouse," she answered allegorically, "has entered the milk churn." "What does this mean?" questioned Dracula, grinning. "It means, Your Highness, that I am with child." "Don't you dare prattle such tales." The woman knew Dracula's method of punishing lies and wished to justify her statement. "It is, Your Highness, as I have said." "This will not be," said Dracula, frowning with his eyebrows. "But if it were possible I reckon that Your Highness would be glad," dared she continue. "I told you this will not be," retorted Dracula, rudely stamping his foot, "and I will show you it will not happen." Unsheathing his sword, he opened her entrails in order to see for himself whether she had spoken the truth or had lied.

As the woman lay dying, Dracula told her: "You see that it cannot be." He left while she agonized in great pain. She was punished because, hoping to cheer up her lover, she had told a lie.

The sultan sent an ambassador once to Dracula, in order that he be given the yearly tribute. Dracula greatly honored this ambassador and showed him the whole treasury which he had. And said, "I not only wish to give the sultan the yearly tax, but I also wish to go in his service with my whole army and with my whole treasury. I shall do as he commands and you shall announce this to your emperor, so that when I shall place myself at his disposal, he will give orders in his whole land that no harm should come to me or to my men. And I shall come to my sultan, my liege, quickly after you get back. And I shall bring him the yearly tribute, and I shall personally place myself at his disposal."

When the sultan heard from his ambassador that Dracula wished to come into his service, he honored the ambassador and gave him gifts, and was happy because at that time the Turkish sultan was at war with many of the eastern countries. Immediately the sultan sent to all his fortresses and towns and throughout his land the message that when Dracula comes, no one should do him any harm. On the contrary, they should honor him. Dracula set out with his whole army. With him were his various yeomen. And he was greeted and greatly honored by the emperor. And he traveled throughout the Turkish empire for about five days. But then suddenly instead of helping the sultan, he began to rob and attack the towns and the villages. And he captured many prisoners whose heads he cut off. Some he impaled, others he cut in two, and others he burned. The whole country which he penetrated was laid to waste. He allowed no one to remain alive, not even the babes in the arms of their mothers. But others, that is, those who were Christian, he spared and set them up in his own lands. After taking much booty, he returned to Wallachia. And he set a few prisoners free and said, "Go and tell your sultan what you have seen. As much as I could, I have served him. If my service was pleasing to him, I shall serve him again with as much power as I can." And the sultan could do nothing against him and fled in shame. [This episode from 1462 is confirmed by historical documents.] Dracula so hated evil in his land that if someone stole, lied or committed some injustice, he was not likely to stay alive. Whether he was a nobleman, or a priest or a monk or a common man, and even if he had great wealth, he could not escape death if he were dishonest. And he was so feared that the peasants say that in a certain place, near the source of the river, there was a fountain; at this fountain at the source of this river, there came many travelers from many lands and all these people came to drink at the fountain, because the water was cool and sweet. Dracula had purposely put this fountain in a deserted place, and had set a cup wonderfully wrought in gold and whoever wished to drink the water, had to drink it from this gold cup and had to put it back in its place. And so long as this cup was there no one dared to steal it. [Romanian folklore stresses Dracula's maintenance of law and order.]

The Rise of Russia

The Byzantine Greeks converted the pagan Russians to Orthodox Christianity in the tenth century. With their conversion, the Russians obtained an alphabet, so they might copy religious texts; they also adopted many aspects of Byzantine culture, which merged with their pagan Slavic and Viking culture. In the thirteenth century, the close ties between Constantinople and

Russia—still only a loose confederation of city-states—were broken by the Mongol conquest, which lasted more than two hundred years. It was not until the fifteenth century that the Moscovite Grand Princes succeeded in casting off the Mongol yoke and unifying Russia into a nation-state. Russian ties with Orthodox Christendom were then renewed; but, by coincidence, Constantinople and the Eastern Roman Empire fell in 1453 to the Ottoman Turks. In the face of the Turkish threat, even before Constantinople fell, many Byzantine-Greek artists and literary people made their way to Western Europe, where they were generally welcomed as contributors to the cultural work of what would be called "the Renaissance" (see Reading 94). The Greek Orthodox clergy, however, were not welcome in Catholic Western Europe; many of them headed for Russia.

In the early sixteenth century with the encouragement of Greek clergy, Vasily III, Grand Prince of Moscow, became "Tsar" (the Russian version of "Caesar"). He was hailed as the heir to the Roman emperorship and entrusted with guidance of the Church. According to this line of thinking, Moscow became the Third Rome, since both the original Rome and Constantinople, the Second Rome, had fallen. (Notice how in Reading 89 the people of Constantinople are called "Romans" by the Ottoman Turks). This enhancement of the Russian ruling title was, of course, useful in strengthening the claims of Russian tsars to absolute power.

92

The Russian Primary Chronicle

The Russian Primary Chronicle is the first written document for Russian history. It is a collection of different texts, written by monks in the twelfth century, about the period 852–1120. Modeled on Greek sources, the *Chronicle* offers a religious interpretation of past events, incorporating legendary and mythical stories about the early Russian princes and nobles (*boyars*).

QUESTIONS TO CONSIDER

1. Why did the Russians choose Greek Orthodoxy over other religions?
2. How did this choice affect Russia's relations with Western Europe?

Vladimir summoned together his boyars and the city-elders, and said to them, "Behold, the Bulgars came before me urging me to accept their religion. Then came the Germans and praised their own faith; and after them came the Jews. Finally the Greeks appeared, criticizing all other faiths but commending their own, and they spoke at length, telling the history of the whole world from its beginning. Their words were artful, and it was wondrous to listen and pleasant to hear them. They preach the existence of another world. 'Whoever adopts our religion and then dies shall arise and

From *The Russian Primary Chronicle: Laurentian Text*, trans. and ed. Samuel Hazzard Cross and Olgerd P. Sherbowitz-Wetzor (Cambridge, MA: The Medieval Academy of America, 1953), pp. 110–13. Reprinted by permission of The Medieval Academy of America. Footnotes omitted.

live forever. But whosoever embraces another faith, shall be consumed with fire in the next world.' What is your opinion on this subject, and what do you answer?" The boyars and the elders replied, "You know, oh Prince, that no man condemns his own possessions, but praises them instead. If you desire to make certain, you have servants at your disposal. Send them to inquire about the ritual of each and how he worships God." Their counsel pleased the prince and all the people, so that they chose good and wise men to the number of ten, and directed them to go first among the Bulgars and inspect their faith. The emissaries went their way, and when they arrived at their destination they beheld the disgraceful actions of the Bulgars and their worship in the mosque; then they returned to their country. Vladimir than instructed them to go likewise among the Germans, and examine their faith, and finally to visit the Greeks. They thus went into Germany, and after viewing the German ceremonial, they proceeded to Tsar' grad, where they appeared before the Emperor. He inquired on what mission they had come, and they reported to him all that had occurred. When the Emperor heard their words, he rejoiced, and did them great honor on that very day.

On the morrow, the Emperor sent a message to the Patriarch to inform him that a Russian delegation had arrived to examine the Greek faith, and directed him to prepare the church and the clergy, and to array himself in his sacerdotal robes, so that the Russes might behold the glory of the God of the Greeks. When the Patriarch received these commands, he bade the clergy assemble, and they performed the customary rites. They burned incense, and the choirs sang hymns. The Emperor accompanied the Russes to the church, and placed them in a wide space, calling their attention to the beauty of the edifice, the chanting, and the pontifical services and the ministry of the deacons, while he explained to them the worship of his God. The Russes were astonished, and in their wonder praised the Greek ceremonial. Then the Emperors Basil and Constantine invited the envoys to their presence, and said, "Go hence to your native country," and dismissed them with valuable presents and great honor.

Thus they returned to their own country, and the Prince called together his boyars and the elders. Vladimir then announced the return of the envoys who had been sent out, and suggested that their report be heard. He thus commanded them to speak out before his retinue. The envoys reported, "When we journeyed among the Bulgars, we beheld how they worship in their temple, called a mosque, while they stand ungirt. The Bulgar bows, sits down, looks hither and thither like one possessed, and there is no happiness among them, but instead only sorrow and a dreadful stench. Their religion is not good. Then we went among the Germans, and saw them performing many ceremonies in their temples; but we beheld no glory there. Then we went to Greece, and the Greeks led us to the edifices where they worship their God, and we knew not whether we were in heaven or on earth. For on earth there is no such splendor or such beauty, and we are at a loss how to describe it. We only know that God dwells there among men, and their service is fairer than the ceremonies of other nations. For we cannot forget that beauty. Every man, after tasting something sweet, is afterward unwilling to accept that which is bitter, and therefore we cannot dwell longer here." Then the boyars spoke and said, "If the Greek faith were evil, it would not have been adopted by your grandmother Olga who was wiser than all other men." Vladimir then inquired where they should all accept baptism, and they replied that the decision rested with him.

After a year had passed, in 6496 (988), Vladimir proceeded with an armed force against Kherson, a Greek city, and the people of Kherson barricaded themselves therein. Vladimir halted at the farther side of the city beside the harbor, a bowshot from the town, and the inhabitants resisted energetically while Vladimir besieged the town. Eventually, however, they became exhausted, and Vladimir warned them that if they did not surrender, he would remain on the spot for three years. When they failed to heed this threat, Vladimir marshalled his troops and ordered the construction of an earthwork in the direction of the city. While this work was under construction, the inhabitants dug a tunnel under the city-wall, stole the heaped-up earth, and carried it into the city, where they piled it up in the center of the town. But the soldiers kept on building, and Vladimir persisted. Then a man of Kherson, Anastasius by name, shot into the Russ camp an arrow on which he had written, "There are springs behind you to the east, from which water flows in pipes. Dig down and cut them off." When Vladimir received this information, he raised his eyes to heaven and vowed that if this hope was realized, he would be baptized. He gave orders straightway to dig down above the pipes, and the water-supply was thus cut off. The inhabitants were accordingly overcome by thirst, and surrendered.

Vladimir and his retinue entered the city, and he sent messages to the Emperors Basil and Constantine, saying, "Behold, I have captured your glorious city. I have also heard that you have an unwedded sister. Unless you give her to me to wife, I shall deal with your own city as I have with Kherson." When the Emperors heard this message they were troubled, and replied, "It is not meet for Christians to give in marriage to pagans. If you are baptized, you shall have her to wife, inherit the kingdom of God, and be our companion in the faith. Unless you do so, however, we cannot give you our sister in marriage." When Vladimir learned their response, he directed the envoys of the Emperors to report to the latter that he was willing to accept baptism, having already given some study to their religion, and that the Greek faith and ritual, as described by the emissaries sent to examine it, had pleased him well. When the Emperors heard this report, they rejoiced, and persuaded their sister Anna to consent to the match. They then requested Vladimir to submit to baptism before they should send their sister to him, but Vladimir desired that the Princess should herself bring priests to baptize him. The Emperors complied with his request, and sent forth their sister, accompanied by some dignitaries and priests. Anna, however, departed with reluctance. "It is as if I were setting out into captivity," she lamented; "better were it for me to die at home." But her brothers protested, "Through your agency God turns the land of Rus' to repentance, and you will relieve Greece from the danger of grievous war. Do you not see how much harm the Russes have already brought upon the Greeks? If you do not set out, they may bring on us the same misfortunes." It was thus that they overcame her hesitation only with great difficulty. The Princess embarked upon a ship, and after tearfully embracing her kinfolk, she set forth across the sea and arrived at Kherson. The natives came forth to greet her, and conducted her into the city, where they settled her in the palace.

By divine agency, Vladimir was suffering at that moment from a disease of the eyes, and could see nothing, being in great distress. The Princess declared to him that if he desired to be relieved of this disease, he should be baptized with all speed, otherwise it could not be cured. When Vladimir heard her message, he said, "If this proves true, then of a surety is the God of the Christians great," and gave order that he should be baptized. The Bishop of Kherson, together with the Princess's priests, after announcing the tidings, baptized Vladimir, and as the Bishop laid his hand upon him, he straightway received his sight. Upon experiencing this miraculous cure, Vladimir glorified God, saying, "I have now perceived the one true God." When his followers beheld this miracle, many of them were also baptized.

Vladimir was baptized in the Church of St. Basil, which stands at Kherson upon a square in the center of the city, where the Khersonians trade. The palace of Vladimir stands beside this church to this day, and the palace of the Princess is behind the altar. After his baptism, Vladimir took the Princess in marriage.

93

Heinrich von Staden, *The Land and Government of Muscovy*

In 1565, a troubled and perhaps demented Tsar Ivan IV ("Ivan the Terrible," 1533–1584) created a special administrative apparatus, the *oprichnina* (from the Russian word *oprich*, meaning apart or beside) to govern over one third of the Russian state, leaving the remaining part of his realm, the *zemshchina*, under the control of his traditional imperial officials. Between 1565 and 1572 the *oprichniki*, the servants who administered the *oprichnina*, launched a reign of terror by relentlessly attacking all who opposed the tsar. Dressed in black and bearing special symbols of their authority, the *oprichniki* cruelly inflicted devastation on large parts of Russia. One of these *oprichniki* was Heinrich von Staden, a German who had come to Russia and joined the imperial state service. His account gives us insight into this bleak chapter of Russian history.

QUESTIONS TO CONSIDER

1. Are there any connections between *The Domostroi*'s description of domestic life in the time of Ivan the Terrible (see Reading 80) and this account?
2. What does this reading tell us about Ivan IV's approach to governance? Which other periods of Russian history does this description of the *Oprichnina* suggest?

Ivan Vasilievich [Ivan IV], Grand Prince of all Russia, . . . chose from his own and foreign nations a hand-picked order, thus creating the *oprichnina* and the *zemshchina*.

The oprichnina was [composed of] his people; the zemshchina, of the ordinary people. The Grand Prince thus began to inspect one city and region after another. And those who, according to the military muster rolls, had not served [the Grand Prince's] forefathers by fighting the enemy with their [estates] were deprived of their estates, which were given to those in the oprichnina.

The princes and boyars who were taken into the oprichnina were ranked not according to riches but according to birth. They then took an oath not to have anything to do with the zemskie people or form any friendships with them. Those in the oprichnina also had to wear black clothes and hats; and in their quivers, where they put their arrows, they carried some kind of brushes or brooms tied on the ends of sticks. The oprichniki were recognized in this way.

Because of insurrection [in Moscow in December 1564], the Grand Prince left Moscow for Aleksandrova Sloboda, a two-day trip. He placed guards in this sloboda,[4] and had any nobles that he wanted called to him from Moscow and other cities.

The Grand Prince sent an order to the zemskie people saying that they must judge justly: " . . . Judge justly, ours [the oprichniki] shall not be in the wrong." Because of this order, the zemskie people became despondent. A person from the oprichnina could accuse someone from the zemshchina of owing him a sum of money. And even if the oprichnik had never known nor seen the accused from the zemshchina, the latter had to pay him immediately or he was publicly beaten in the marketplace with knouts or cudgels every day until he paid. No one was spared in this, neither clerics nor laymen. The oprichniki did a number of indescribable things to the zemskie people to get all their money and property. . . .

The Grand Prince arrived in Moscow from Aleksandrova Sloboda and murdered one of the chief men of the zemshchina, Ivan Petrovich Cheliadnin. In the Grand Prince's absence from Moscow, this man was the chief boyar and judge. He willingly helped the poor people find justice quickly, and for a number of years he was governor and commander in Livonia—at Dorpat and at Polotsk. . . .

Prince Andrei Kurbskii was governor and commander after him. When [Kurbskii] became aware of the oprichnina business, he rode off to King Sigismund August in Poland, leaving behind his wife and children. In his place came the boyar Mikhail Morozov. . . .

Afterward [Cheliadnin] was summoned to Moscow. In Moscow he was killed and thrown into a filthy pit near the Neglinna river. The Grand Prince then went with his oprichniki and burned all the [estates] in the country belonging to this Ivan Petrovich. The villages were burned with their churches and everything that was in them, icons and church ornaments. Women and girls were stripped naked and forced in that state to catch chickens in the fields. The oprichniki caused great misery in the country, and many people were secretly murdered.

This was too much for the zemskie people. They began to confer, and they decided to elect as grand prince Vladimir Andreevich [Staritskii]. . . .

Prince Vladimir Andreevich [Staritskii] revealed the compact to the Grand Prince, and revealed everything that the zemskie people had planned and prepared. The Grand Prince . . . returned by post road to Aleksandrova Sloboda, and had someone write down [the names of] those zemskie leaders whom he wanted slaughtered, killed, and executed first. . . .

The Grand Prince continued to have one [zemskii] leader after another seized and killed as it came into his head, one this way, another that way.

Metropolitan Philip could remain silent about this business no longer, and spoke affably to the Grand Prince saying that he ought to live and rule as his forefathers had. The good metropolitan fell into disgrace with these words, and he had to live in very large iron chains until he died. The Grand Prince then chose a metropolitan according to his wishes.

After that the Grand Prince set out from Aleksandrova Sloboda with all his oprichniki. Every city, road, monastery from the sloboda to Livonia was occupied by oprichnina guards, as though it were done because of plague, so that one city or monastery could learn of nothing from another.

[4]Sloboda: a large village inhabited by free peasants.

The oprichniki came to the iam—or post station—at Chernaia and began to plunder. The places where the Grand Prince spent the night were set afire and were burned down the next morning.

All those who came from Moscow to the guard post and wanted to go to the camp of [Ivan's] own hand-picked people, whether they were princes or boyars or their servants, were seized by the guards, bound, and immediately killed. Some were stripped naked in front of the Grand Prince and rolled around in the snow until they died. The same thing happened to those who wanted to leave the camp for Moscow and were caught by the guards.

The Grand Prince then arrived at the city of Tver and had everything plundered, even churches and monasteries. And he had all the prisoners killed, likewise his own people who had befriended or married foreigners. All the bodies had their legs cut off, because of the ice, and were then stuck under the ice of the Volga River. The same occurred in the city of Torzhok. Neither church nor monastery was spared here.

The Grand Prince arrived again outside the city of Great Novgorod. He settled down three furlongs from the city and sent in an army commander with his retinue. He was to spy and reconnoiter. The rumor was that the Grand Prince wanted to march to Livonia. Then the Grand Prince moved into Great Novgorod, into the bishop's palace, and took everything belonging to the bishop. He took the largest bells and whatever he wanted from the churches. The Grand Prince thus left the city alone. He ordered the merchants to buy and sell and to ask a just price from his soldiers, the oprichniki. Every day he arose and moved to another monastery. He indulged his wantonness and had monks tortured, and many of them were killed. There are three hundred monasteries inside and outside the city and not one of these was spared. Then the pillage of the city began. . . .

This distress and misery continued in the city for six weeks without interruption [in January and February 1570]. Every shop and room where money or property were thought to be was sealed. Every day the Grand Prince could also be found in the torture chamber in person. Nothing might remain in the monasteries and the city. Everything that the soldiers could not carry off was thrown into the water or burned. If one of the zemskie people retrieved anything from the water, he was hanged. . . .

The oprichniki ransacked the entire countryside and all the cities and villages of the zemshchina, although the Grand Prince had not given them permission to do that. They drew up instructions themselves, as though the Grand Prince had ordered them to kill this or that merchant or noble—if he was thought to have money— along with his wife and children, and to take his money and property to the Grand Prince's Treasury. In the zemshchina, they thus committed many murders and assassinations, which are beyond description. . . .

When the oprichniki had tortured Russia—the entire zemshchina—according to their will and pleasure so that even the Grand Prince realized it was enough, the oprichniki still had not sated themselves with the money and property of the zemskie people. If one of the zemskie people brought a suit for a thousand rubles, he would accept a hundred rubles or less, but give a receipt [to the oprichniki] for the full amount. All the petitions were set aside together with the records and receipts. [The oprichniki] had sworn to maintain no friendships with the zemskie people and to have nothing to do with them; but then the Grand Prince turned the tables and had all petitions accepted. And when the oprichniki were indebted for a thousand and had a receipt, but had not fully paid, these oprichniki had to pay the zemskie people again. The oprichniki did not at all like this situation. . . .

Then the Grand Prince began to wipe out all the chief people of the oprichnina. Prince Afanasii Viazemskii died in chains in the town of Gorodets. Aleksei [Basmanov] and his son [Fedor], with whom the Grand Prince indulged in lewdness, were killed. Maliuta Skuratov was shot near Weissenstein [Paide] in Livonia. He was the pick of the bunch, and according to the Grand Prince's order, he was remembered in church. Prince Mikhail, the son of the Grand Prince's brother-in-law from the Circassian land, was chopped to death by the harquebusiers [musketeers] with axes or halberds [weapons combining the virtues of the spear and the battle axe]. Prince Vasilii Temkin was drowned. Ivan Saburov was murdered. Peter Seisse was hanged from his own court gate opposite the bedroom. Prince Andrei Ovtsyn was hanged in the Arbatskaia street of the oprichnina. A living sheep was hung next to him [an ovtsa is a sheep, thus the murderers played a prank on his name]. The marshal Bulat wanted to marry his sister to the Grand Prince. He was killed and his sister was raped by five hundred harquebusiers. The captain of the harquebusiers, Kuraka Unkovskii, was killed and stuck under the ice. In the previous year [name unclear] was eaten by dogs at the Karinskii guard post of Aleksandrova Sloboda. Grigorii Griaznoi was killed and his son Nikita was burned alive. His brother Vasilii was captured by the Crimean Tatars. The scribe and clerk Posnik Suvorov was killed at the Land Chancellery. Osip Il'in was shamefully executed in the Court Chancellery.

All the chief men of the oprichnina and zemshchina and all those who were to be killed were first publicly whipped in the marketplace until they signed over all their money and property, if they had any, to the Treasury of the Grand Prince. Those who had no money and property were killed in front of churches, in the street, or in their homes, whether asleep or awake, and were thrown into the street. The cause of the death, and whether it was legal or not, was written on a note, which was then pinned to the clothes of the corpse. The body had to lie in the street day and night as a warning to the people.

The Renaissance and Reformation

By 1500, a sharp contrast had developed between Italy and northern Europe. Most northern European states, except the Holy Roman Empire, were evolving toward centralized political authority, whereas in Italy fragmentation became the norm. Italian rulers had none of the feudal loyalties with which they might have ruled their subjects. If rulers wished to succeed, they had to rely solely on what was termed *virtu*; they had only their own political, diplomatic, or military abilities to maintain their position. Constant maneuvering for supremacy among the states led to instability.

Economic prosperity of Italian cities was based on manufacturing and international trade. Individual cities and families were known for wool and silk weaving and for banking and the importation of luxury goods from the Near and Far East. The accumulated wealth was used to patronize artists and writers whose works enhanced the reputations of cities and patrons alike.

Italian scholars returned to a study of antiquity and sought to revive classical education in their own period. These studies or "liberal arts" included grammar, rhetoric, poetry, history, and moral philosophy and produced an educated elite called Renaissance humanists.

Perhaps the most famous Italian civic humanist and politician was Niccolò Machiavelli (1469–1527), who served as a secretary and diplomat to the Florentine Republic (1498–1512). Machiavelli's most famous works include *Discourses on the First Ten Books of Livy* (1518), *Mandragola* (1512–1520?), *The History of Florence* (1525), and *The Prince* (1513).

In northern Europe, feudal traditions and gothic art were the norm. Social change developed slowly, but with the growth of capitalism, scholars and princes came to admire the Italian humanist movement. Kings, princes, emperors, and high Church officials became patrons of humanists. Yet, there was a difference— northern scholars emphasized the need to purify the Christian Church.

The greatest northern humanist was Desiderius Erasmus of Rotterdam (1469–1536). He was born and educated for the priesthood in Holland, studied in France, and traveled and taught in England and on the Continent. His Christian humanism was based not on a search for religious relics, buying indulgences, or doing good works but, rather, on a desire to restore Christianity through true piety and a love of Christ. In this last respect, Erasmus hoped for an internal religious reform and refused to break with the Catholic Church as Martin Luther did.

Among Erasmus's works were classical Latin quotations or the *Adages* (1500), *The Handbook of a Christian Knight* (1508), and a new translation of the New Testament (1516). Erasmus's most noted work was his satire on European morals, entitled *The Praise of Folly* (1511), whose Latin title was a pun on the name of his English fellow humanist, Sir Thomas More.

Although Christian humanists flourished in every country, those in the Germanies led the general revolt against the Catholic Church. Among the causes of the Reformation were reactions against the gross abuses in the Church, lack of moral leadership of the popes, textual criticisms of the humanists, and the political disunity within the Holy Roman Empire.

Martin Luther (1483–1546) was to combine the demands for purification of the Church with a new theology. The son of a prosperous mine owner, Luther was educated for the law at Erfurt University until a crisis of conscience made him enter an Augustinian monastery and become a priest. Luther continued his studies and received a doctorate while teaching theology at Wittenberg University in Saxony. It was while lecturing on St. Paul's Letters to the Romans that Luther came to believe that God's salvation comes to each person through faith, not by personal actions or good works.

Luther might have remained a little-noted priest had he not chosen to attack indulgence selling by posting his Ninety-five Theses on the Castle Church door in Wittenberg in 1517. Almost immediately, he became the center of a controversy that eventually led to his condemnation as a heretic. Luther took up the challenge and in a stream of pamphlets and treatises further elaborated his theology into what has become the Lutheran Church.

Although initially slow to respond to Luther's criticism, the Roman Catholic Church eventually called the Council of Trent (1545–1563). Trent acknowledged that there were abuses within the Church but insisted that the Church had been addressing these issues long before Luther posted his Ninety-five Theses. Furthermore, Trent insisted that Luther was not calling for traditional authentic reform but was leading a theological revolution. Insisting that the true and proper theological meaning of the verb "reform" was to "re-form," that is, to put back together again, Trent launched a Catholic Reformation aimed at "re-forming" Christendom. Never did Trent try to answer Luther's challenge directly. Instead, it set about reforming Catholicism by insisting upon strict obedience to Church teachings, aggressively sponsoring the baroque style in art and architecture, promoting the new Jesuit order's elitist approach to education and active political engagement, and launching a vigorous attack on the dissent, sin, and lack of discipline in Catholic Europe.

94

Niccolò Machiavelli, *The Prince* and *The Discourses on Titus Livy*

Niccolò Machiavelli (1469–1527) remains one of the most articulate spokesmen for the Italian Renaissance, marking a shift toward secular or humanistic values, away from the church-oriented values of the Middle Ages. Like most men of the later Renaissance, Machiavelli looked back to the pagan Roman Republic for inspiration in addressing problems of his own times.

In defending a set of political, social, economic, and religious norms, Machiavelli writes as a philosopher in the sense of one who attempts to integrate knowledge from different fields into a coherent world outlook. He would probably not qualify as a philosopher under the more narrow contemporary meaning of that term. Machiavelli's Renaissance philosophy typically sets itself apart from that of the Middle Ages by its understanding of *virtu* as human excellence. Based on the Latin word *vir* (man), *virtu* in practice meant making the absolute most of human talents for human ends—as today a virtuoso violinist is one who gets the most out of a violin. In the first section of the reading, Pope Alexander VI (Rodrigo Borgia) and his son, Duke Valentine (Cesare Borgia)—who were too much tainted by intrigue and violent crime to qualify as "virtuous" by current standards—are both treated as virtuoso statesmen. Their grand designs may have been thwarted by fortune, but they made the most of their talents nonetheless.

The first two excerpts are from Machiavelli's most notorious work, *The Prince*, in which he appears to justify nearly any measures to gain and keep rulership. For example, he advises princes to break faith and treaties to keep themselves in power. One can interpret Machiavellianism as a cynical combination of the ideas that "Might makes right" and "The end justifies the means." Yet even in *The Prince*, as the second excerpt illustrates, there are limits. The best form of government for Machiavelli, as for most people of the later Renaissance, was a republic rather than the monarchy (or "princely rule," as Machiavelli calls it) advocated by Dante. Consequently, someone who subverts a successful republic to establish selfish, personal rule is guilty of nothing less than "villainy."

Machiavelli wrote *The Prince* in a short period of time as he attempted to find employment in the service of the Medicis, one of the leading "princely families" of Italy. The Medicis had ruled Florence in the late fifteenth century and had recently come to power again after the overthrow of the republican government of Florence, which Machiavelli had served as an administrator and diplomat.

Machiavelli gives a better presentation of his world outlook in the much longer *Discourses on the First Ten Books of Titus Livy*, from which the second two excerpts are taken. Here, he describes the means for founding and preserving republics, using the early Roman method described by Livy as his primary model. Notice that in the section entitled "The Religion of the Romans," Machiavelli takes a totally humanistic view of religion. The truth or falsity of pagan Roman religion is irrelevant; he is merely interested in illustrating the type of religion that supports a healthy social and political order. In the final excerpts, Machiavelli praises moderate poverty as a positive good, since he believes that small farmers are more likely than rich men to use their political talents for the public benefit.

QUESTIONS TO CONSIDER

1. Why were the activities of Pope Alexander VI contrary to his official position?
2. In modern textbooks, Pope Alexander VI generally gets bad reviews. Why does Machiavelli like him so much?
3. Why was Cesare Borgia an example of *virtu*, and not the villainous Agathocles the Sicilian?
4. Why was L. Quintius Cincinnatus an ideal Roman citizen according to Machiavelli?

Territories Acquired by Virtue or by Fortune

They who from private condition become princes, and, merely by the indulgence of fortune, arrive without much trouble at that dignity, though it costs them dear to maintain it, meet but little difficulty in their passage, being hurried as it were with wings, yet when they come to settle and establish then begins their misery.

. . . About the arrival at this authority, either by virtue or by good fortune, I shall instance two examples that are in our memory; one is Francesco Sforza, the other Caesar Borgia. Sforza, by just means and extraordinary virtue, made himself Duke of Milan, and enjoyed it in great peace, though it was gained with much trouble. Borgia, on the other hand, (called commonly Duke of Valentine), got several fair territories by the fortune of his father, Pope Alexander, and lost them all after his death, though he used all his industry, and employed all the arts that a wise and brave prince ought to use to fix himself in the sphere where the arms and fortune of other people had placed him. . . .

First two excerpts from Niccolò Machiavelli, *The Prince*, trans. S. G. W. Benjamin (n.p.: The National Alumni, 1907), pp. 25–39, *passim*. Latter two excerpts from Niccolò Machiavelli, *The Discourses*, in *The Prince and The Discourses*, trans. Luigi Ricci, E. R. P. Vincent, and Christian E. Detmold (New York: Modern Library, 1950), pp. 145–48, 486–88, *passim*.

Pope Alexander VI had a desire to make his son Duke Valentine great, but he saw many impediments in the way, both for the present and for the future. First, he could not see any way to advance him to any territory that depended not upon the Church; and to those in his gift he was sure the Duke of Milan and the Venetians would never consent; for Faenza and Riminum had already put themselves under Venetian protection. He was likewise sensible that the forces of Italy, especially those that were capable of assisting him, were in the hands of those that ought to apprehend the greatness of the Pope . . . and therefore could not repose any great confidence in them; besides, the laws and alliances of all the states in Italy must of necessity be disturbed before he could make himself master of any part, which was no hard matter to do, finding the Venetians, upon some private interest of their own, inviting the French to another expedition into Italy, which his Holiness was so far from opposing that he promoted it by dissolution of King Louis's former marriage. Louis therefore passed the Alps by the assistance of the Venetians and Alexander's consent, and was no sooner in Milan than he sent forces to assist the Pope in his enterprise against Romagna, which was immediately surrendered upon the King's reputation. Romagna being in this manner reduced by the Duke, and the Colonnesi defeated, he was ambitious both to keep what he had got, and to advance in his conquests. . . .

When the Duke had possessed himself of Romagna, finding it had been governed by poor and inferior lords, who had rather robbed than corrected their subjects, and given them more occasion of discord than of unity, insomuch as that province was full of robberies, riots, and all manner of disturbances, to reduce them to unanimity and subjection to monarchy, he thought it necessary to provide them a good governor, and thereupon he conferred that office upon Remiro d'Orco, with absolute power, though he was a cruel and passionate man. Orco soon settled it in peace, with no small reputation to himself. Afterward the Duke, apprehending that so large a power might become odious to the people, erected a court of judicature in the center of the province, in which every city had its advocate, and an excellent person was appointed to preside. And as he discovered that his past severity had made him many enemies, to remove that ill opinion, and recover the affections of the people, he had a mind to show that, if any cruelty had been exercised, it proceeded not from him but from the arrogance of his minister; and for their further confirmation he caused the said governor to be apprehended, and his head chopped off one morning in the market-place at Cesena, with a wooden dagger on one side of him and a bloody knife on the other; the ferocity of which spectacle not only appeased but amazed the people for a while.

The Duke, finding himself powerful enough, and secure against present danger, being as strong as he desired, and his neighbors in a manner reduced to an incapacity of hurting him, was willing to go on with his conquests. Nothing remained but jealousy of France, which was without cause, for he knew that King Louis had found his error at last, and would be sure to obstruct him. Hereupon he began to look abroad for new allies, and to hesitate and stagger toward France, as appeared when the French army advanced into the kingdom of Naples against the Spaniards, who had besieged Cajeta. His main design was to secure himself against the French, and he would doubtless have done it if Alexander had lived.

These were his provisions against the dangers that were imminent; but those that were remote were more doubtful and uncertain. The first thing he feared was, lest the next Pope should be his enemy and reassume all that Alexander had given him, to prevent which he considered four ways. The first was by destroying the whole line of those lords whom he had dispossessed, that his Holiness might have no occasion to restore them. The second was to cajole the nobility in Rome, and draw them over to his party, that thereby he might put an awe and restraint upon the Pope. The third was, if possible, to make the College of Cardinals his friends. The fourth was to make himself so strong before the death of his father as to be able to stand upon his own legs and repel the first violence that should be practised against him. Three of these four expedients he had tried before Alexander died, and he was in a fair way for the fourth. . . .

On serious examination, therefore, of the whole conduct of Duke Valentine, I see nothing to be reprehended; it seems rather proper to me to present him, as I have done, as an example for the imitation of all such as by the favor of fortune, or the supplies of other princes, have got into power; for, his mind being so large, and his intentions so high, he could not do otherwise, and nothing could have opposed the greatness and wisdom of his designs but his own infirmity and the death of his father. He, therefore, who thinks it necessary in the minority of his dominion to secure himself against his enemies, to gain himself friends; to overcome, whether by force or by fraud; to make himself beloved or feared by his people; to be followed and reverenced by his soldiers; to destroy and exterminate such as would do him injury; to repeal and suppress old laws, and introduce new; to be severe, grateful, magnanimous, liberal, cashier and disband such of his army as were unfaithful, and put new in their places; manage himself so in his alliances with kings and princes that all should be either obliged to requite him or afraid to offend him—he, I say, cannot find a fresher or better model than the actions of this prince.

Of Such Who Have Arrived at Dominion by Wicked Means

Agathocles, the Sicilian, not only from a private but from a vile and abject condition was made King of Syracuse; and being but the son of a potter, he continued the dissoluteness of his life through all the degrees of his fortune. Nevertheless, his vices were accompanied with such courage and activity that he applied himself to the wars, by which, and his great industry, he came at length to be the Pretor of Syracuse. Being settled in that dignity, and having determined to make himself prince, and hold by violence, without obligation to anybody, that which was conferred upon him by consent, he came to an understanding with Hamilcar the Carthaginian, who was then at the head of an army in Sicily; and, calling the people and the Senate of Syracuse together one morning, as if he intended to consult them on some matter of importance to the state, on a signal appointed he caused his soldiers to kill all the senators and the most wealthy of the people; after whose death he usurped the dominion of that city without any obstruction.

Nevertheless it cannot be called virtue in him to kill his fellow-citizens, betray his friends, and be without faith, pity, or religion; these are ways that may get a man empire, but no glory or reputation. Yet, if the wisdom of Agathocles be considered, his dexterity in encountering and overcoming of dangers, his courage in supporting and surmounting his misfortunes, I do not see why he should be held inferior to the best captains of his time. But his unbounded cruelty and barbarous inhumanity, added to numerous other vices, will not permit him to be numbered among the most excellent men. So, then, that which he performed cannot justly be attributed either to fortune or to virtue. . . .

It may seem wonderful to some that it should come to pass that Agathocles, and such as he, after so many treacheries and acts of inhumanity, should live quietly in their own country so long, defend themselves so well against foreign enemies, and none of their subjects conspire against them at home; since several others, by reason of their cruelty, have not been able, even in time of peace, to maintain their government. I conceive it fell out according as their cruelty was well or ill applied. I say well applied (if that word may be applied to an ill action), and it may be called so when committed but once, and that of necessity for one's own preservation, but never repeated, and even then converted as much as possible to the benefit of the subjects. Ill applied are such cruelties as are but few in the beginning, but in time do rather multiply than decrease. . . .

Whence it is to be observed that he who usurps the government of any State is to execute and put in practice all the cruelties that he thinks material at once, that he may have no occasion to renew them often, but that by his discontinuance he may mollify the people, and by benefits bring them over to his side. He who does otherwise, whether from fear or from ill counsel, is obliged to be always ready with his knife in his hand; for he never can repose any confidence in his subjects, while they, by reason of his fresh and continued inhumanities, cannot be secure against him.

So then injuries are to be committed all at once, that the last being the less, the distaste may be likewise the less; but benefits should be distilled by drops, that the relish may be the greater.

The Religion of the Romans

Although the founder of Rome was Romulus, yet the gods did not judge the laws of this prince sufficient for so great an empire, and therefore inspired the Roman Senate to elect Numa Pompilius as his successor, so that he might regulate all those things that had been omitted by Romulus. Numa, finding a very savage people, and wishing to reduce them to civil obedience by the arts of peace, had recourse to religion as the most necessary and assured support of any civil society; and he established it upon such foundations that for many centuries there was nowhere more fear of the gods than in that republic, which greatly facilitated all the enterprises which the Senate or its great men attempted. Whoever will examine the actions of the people of Rome as a body, or of many individual Romans, will see that these citizens feared much more to break an oath than the laws, like men who esteem the power of the gods more than that of men . . . , which can be ascribed to nothing else than the religious principles which Numa had instilled into the Romans. And whoever reads Roman history attentively will see in how great a degree religion served in the command of the armies, in uniting the people and keeping them well conducted, and in covering the wicked with shame. . . . In truth, there never was any remarkable lawgiver amongst any people who did not resort to divine authority, as otherwise his laws would not have been accepted by the people; for there are many good laws, the importance of which is known to the sagacious lawgiver, but the reasons for which are not sufficiently evident to enable him to persuade others to submit to them; and therefore do wise men, for the purpose of removing this difficulty, resort to divine authority. Thus did Lycurgus and Solon, and many others who aimed at the same thing.

The Roman people, then, admiring the wisdom and goodness of Numa, yielded in all things to his advice. It is true that those were very religious times, and the people with whom Numa had to deal were very untutored and superstitious, which made it easy for him to carry out his designs, being able to impress upon them any new form. And doubtless, if any one wanted to establish a republic at the present time, he would find it much easier with the simple mountaineers, who are almost without any civilization, than with such as are accustomed to live in cities, where civilization is already corrupt; as a sculptor finds it easier to make a fine statue out of a crude block of marble than out of a statue badly begun by another. Considering then, all these things, I conclude that the religion introduced by Numa into Rome was one of the chief causes of the prosperity of that city; for this religion gave rise to good laws, and good laws bring good fortune, and from good fortune results happy success in all enterprises. And as the observance of divine institutions is the cause of the greatness of republics, so the disregard of them produces their ruin; for where the fear of God is wanting, there the country will come to ruin.

Cincinnatus: Illustration of Poverty as Good for Republics

It is of the greatest advantage in a republic to have laws that keep her citizens poor. Although there does not appear to have been any special law to this effect in Rome . . . , yet experience shows that even so late as four hundred years after its foundation there was still great poverty in Rome. We cannot ascribe this fact to any other cause than that poverty never was allowed to stand in the way of the achievement of any rank or honor, and that virtue and merit were sought for under whatever roof they dwelt; it was this system that made riches naturally less desirable. We have a manifest proof of this on the occasion when the Consul Minutius and his army were surrounded by the Equeans, and all Rome was full of apprehensions lest the army should be lost, so that they resorted to the creation of a Dictator, their last remedy in times of difficulty. They appointed L. Quintius Cincinnatus, who at the time was on his little farm, which he cultivated with his own hands. This circumstance is celebrated by Titus Livius in the following golden words: "After this let men not listen to those who prefer riches to everything else in this world, and who think that there is neither honor nor virtue where wealth does not flow." Cincinnatus was engaged in ploughing his fields, which did not exceed four acres, when the messengers of the Senate arrived from Rome to announce his election to the dictatorship, and to point out to him the imminent danger of the Roman republic. He immediately put on his toga, gathered an army, and went to the relief of Minutius; and having crushed and despoiled the enemy, and freed the Consul and his army, he would not permit them to share the spoils, saying, "I will not allow you to participate in the spoils of those to whom you came so near falling a prey." He deprived Minutius of the consulate, and reduced him to the rank of lieutenant, saying to him, "You will remain in this grade until you have learned to be Consul."

Cincinnatus had chosen for his master of cavalry L. Tarquinius whose poverty had obliged him to fight on foot. Let us note here how Rome honored poverty, (as has been said), and how four acres of land sufficed for the support of so good and great a citizen as Cincinnatus. We find also that poverty was still honored in the times of Marcus Regulus, who when commanding an army in Africa asked permission of the Roman Senate to return to look after his farm, which was being spoiled by the laborers in whose charge it had been left by him. These instances suggest two reflections: the one, that these eminent citizens were content to remain in such poverty, and that they were satisfied merely to win honor by their military achievements, and to leave all the profits of them to the public treasury; for if they had thought of enriching themselves by their wars, they would have cared little whether their fields were being spoiled or not; and the other, as to the magnanimity of these citizens, who, when placed at the head of an army, rose above all princes solely by the grandeur of their souls. . . .

I might demonstrate here at length that poverty produces better fruit than riches,—that the first has conferred honor upon cities, countries, and religions, whilst the latter have only served to ruin them,—were it not that this subject has been so often illustrated by other writers.

95

Erasmus, *Julius II Excluded*

Popes generally supported the artistic and literary creativity of the Renaissance. At the same time, humanistic scholars north of Italy felt increasingly inclined to turn their learning and persuasive skills against the worldliness of the papacy as well as the backwardness of monastic orders.

Erasmus of Rotterdam (1469–1536) was a literary genius who thought that he had been unfairly coerced as a youth into taking monastic vows. Believing himself to be a defender of true Christianity while attacking monastic narrowness, he advocated both the study of Scripture and the study of classical, pre-Christian literature. In his words, the proper "weapons" for the struggle of life were "prayer and knowledge."

His major contribution to the Renaissance in northern Europe was his edition of the Greek New Testament with a Latin translation and commentaries. Printed by a market-oriented publisher in Switzerland, it was a runaway best-seller: One hundred thousand copies were sold in France alone. Erasmus's popular Latin translation and commentaries greatly heightened the debate on the nature of the Church and its function in society.

The following excerpts from a play by Erasmus illustrate sentiments of the coming Reformation. The play was first staged in 1514 for a sympathetic audience, largely composed of students and faculty members, in Paris. Julius II, the pope from 1503 to 1514, had earned Machiavelli's admiration for his military and diplomatic skills. His excellent artistic taste led him to employ both Michelangelo and Raphael as he sought to adorn the Vatican. Yet for Christian humanists, Julius left something to be desired as the spiritual leader of Christendom. In an early version of an enduring story, the play presents St. Peter dealing with someone with doubtful credentials for entering Heaven. Its serious theme—contrasting the headstrong success of Church leaders in accumulating worldly power with the totally different goals of the early fathers of the Church, or Christ himself—has resurfaced periodically in literary satire; the best-known modern example is perhaps the "Grand Inquisitor" episode in Dostoyevsky's *Brothers Karamazov*.

When he wrote the play, Erasmus was looking to France as the country where leaders were most likely to further Church reform. The play's Julius II calls the French "barbarians," as did Machiavelli and other Italians of the time. But Erasmus sees a connection between the uncorrupted, natural, "barbarian" characteristics of the French and the hope of changing the Church for the better. Within a decade, Martin

Luther would make a similar link in relating German national character to his program of reform.

Erasmus, who hated being caught up in the middle of controversies, despite a lifetime of helping to instigate them, disowned the authorship of the play. But the overwhelming similarities in sentiments, observations, and style between *Julius II Excluded* and other works he published make him the only likely candidate for consideration as its author.

QUESTIONS TO CONSIDER

1. Why was Pope Julius II not considered a reforming pope such as Gregory VII and Innocent III?
2. Why would Machiavelli never have written this satire (see Reading 94)?
3. Whom did Erasmus favor, the "barbarians" or the papacy?
4. Why would the Protestant reformers have welcomed this satire?

Scene—Gate of Heaven

Julius: What the devil is this? The gate's not opened! Something is wrong with the lock. . . .

Peter: Well that the gates are adamant, or this fellow would have broken in. He must be some giant, or conqueror. Heaven, what a stench! Who are you? What do you want here? . . .

Julius: Enough of this. I am Julius . . ., P.M., as you can see by the letters if you can read.

Peter: P.M.! What is that? Pestis Maxima?

Julius: Pontifex Maximus, you rascal. . . .

Peter: . . . Let me look at you a little closer. Hum! Signs of impiety in plenty . . . not precisely like an apostle. Priest's cassock and bloody armour below it, eyes savage, mouth insolent, forehead brazen, body scarred with sins all over, breath loaded with wine, health broken with debauchery. Ay, threaten as you will, I will tell you what you are for all your bold looks. You are Julius the Emperor come back from hell. . . .

Julius: Make an end, I say, or I will fling a thunderbolt at you. I will excommunicate you. I have done as much to kings before this. . . .

Peter: You must show your merits first; no admission without merits. . . .

Julius: The invincible Julius ought not to answer a beggarly fisherman. However, you shall know who and what I am. First, I am a Ligurian, and not a Jew like you. My mother was the sister of the great Pope Sextus IV. The Pope made me a rich man out of Church property. I became a cardinal. I had my misfortunes. I had the French pox. I was banished, hunted out of my country; but I knew all along that I should come to be Pope myself in the end. . . . I succeeded. I rose to the top, and I have done more for the Church and Christ than any Pope before me.

Peter: What did you do?

From Erasmus, *Julius II Exclusus: A Dialogue.* Translated and included by J. A. Froude in his *Life and Letters of Erasmus* (New York: Charles Scribner's Sons, 1894), pp. 149–68, *passim.*

Julius: I raised the revenue. I invented new offices and sold them. . . . Then I annexed Bologna to the Holy See. I have torn up treaties, kept great armies in the field. I have covered Rome with palaces, and I have left five millions in the Treasury behind me. . . .

Peter: Invincible warrior! All this is quite new to me. Pardon my simplicity, who are these fair curly-haired boys that you have with you?

Julius: Boys I took into training to improve their minds.

Peter: And those dark ones with the scars?

Julius: Those are my soldiers and generals who were killed fighting for me. They all deserve heaven. I promised it to them under hand and seal if they lost their lives in my service, no matter how wicked they might be. . . .

Peter: My orders are not to admit men who come with Bulls, but to admit those who have clothed the naked, fed the hungry, given the thirsty drink, visited the sick and those in prison. Men have cast out devils and worked miracles in Christ's name and yet have been shut out. . . .

Julius: If I had but known.

Peter: What would you have done? Declared war?

Julius: I would have excommunicated you.

Peter: . . . When I was Pope the difficulty was to find men who would be priests or deacons.

Julius: Naturally, when bishops and priests had nothing for their reward but fasts, and vigils, and doctrines, and now and then death. Bishops nowadays are kings and lords, and such positions are worth struggling for. . . .

Peter: Why did you take Bologna . . .?

Julius: Because I wanted the revenue for my own treasury, and because Bologna was otherwise convenient for me. So I used my thunderbolts, the French helped me, and now Bologna is mine, and every farthing of the taxes goes to Rome for the Church's use. If you had only seen my triumphal entry. . . .

Peter: He who represents Christ ought to try to be like Christ. But, tell me, is there no way of removing a wicked Pope?

Julius: Absurd! Who can remove the highest authority of all?

Peter: That the Pope is the highest is a reason why he should be removed if he causes scandal. Bad princes can be removed. The Church is in a bad way if it must put up with a head who is ruining it.

Julius: A Pope can only be corrected by a general council, but no general council can be held without the Pope's consent; otherwise it is a synod, and not a council. Let the council sit, it can determine nothing unless the Pope agrees; and, again, a single Pope having absolute power is superior to the council. Thus he cannot be deposed for any crime whatsoever. . . .

Peter: A novel privilege for my successors—to be the wickedest of men, yet be safe from punishment. So much the unhappier the Church which cannot shake such a monster off its shoulders.

Julius: Some say there is one cause for which a Pope can be deposed.

Peter: When he has done a good action, I suppose, since he is not to be punished for his bad actions.

Julius: If he can be convicted publicly of heresy. But this is impossible, too. For he can cancel any canon which he does not like. . . .

Peter: In the name of the papal majesty, who made these fine laws?

Julius: Who? Why, the source of all law, the Pope himself, and the power that makes a law can repeal it.

Peter: What else can you do?

Julius: What else? How do kings levy revenues? They persuade the people that they owe their fortunes to them, and then they ask, and the people give. So we make the people believe that they owe to us their knowledge of God, though we sleep all our lives. Besides, we sell them indulgences in small matters at a cheap rate, dispensations for not much more, and for blessings we charge nothing. . . .

Peter: This is all Greek to me. But why do you hate the barbarians, and move heaven and earth to get rid of them?

Julius: Because barbarians are superstitious, and the French worst of all.

Peter: Do the French worship other gods besides Christ?

Julius: No; but they have precise notions of what is due to Christ. They use hard words about certain things which we have left off.

Peter: Magical words, I presume?

Julius: No, not magical. They talk of simony and blasphemy, sodomy, poisoning, witchcraft, in language expressing abomination of such actions.

Peter: I do not wish to be personal, but can it be that such crimes are to be found among yourselves, professing Christians?

Julius: The barbarians have vices of their own. They censure ours and forget theirs. We tolerate ours and abominate theirs. Poverty, for instance, we look on as so wicked that anything is justifiable to escape from it, while the barbarians scarcely approve of wealth if innocently come by. . . . Barbarians forbid usury; we regard it as a necessary institution. They think looseness with women polluting and disgusting; we—well, we do not think so at all. They are shocked at simony; we never mention it. They stick to old laws and customs; we go for novelty and progress. While our views of life are so different, we don't like to have the barbarians too close to us. They have sharp eyes. They write letters about us to our friends. . . . Thus the Church suffers: we sell fewer dispensations, and get a worse price for them, and we receive less money for bishoprics and abbeys and colleges; worst of all, people are no longer frightened at our thunderbolts. Once let them think that a wicked Pope cannot hurt them, we shall be starved out. So we mean to keep the barbarian at a distance.

Peter: The Church is a community of Christians with Christ's Spirit in them. You have been a subverter of the Church.

Julius: The Church consists of cathedrals, and priests, and the Court of Rome, and myself at the head of it.

Peter: Christ is our Head, and we are His ministers. Are there two Heads? How have you increased the Church?

Julius: I found it poor: I have made it splendid.

Peter: Splendid with what? With faith? . . .

Julius: I have filled Rome with palaces, trains of mules and horses, troops of servants, armies and officers.

Spirit: With scarlet women and the like.

Julius: With purple and gold, with revenues so vast that kings are poor beside the Roman Pontiff. Glory, luxury, hoards of treasure, these are splendours, and these all I have created.

Peter: Pray, inform me. The Church had nothing of all this when it was founded by Christ. Whence came all this splendour, as you call it? . . .

Julius: You are thinking of the old affair, when you starved as Pope, with a handful of poor hunted bishops about you. Time has changed all that, and much for the better. You had only the name of Pope. Look now at our gorgeous churches, our priests by thousands; bishops like kings, with retinues and palaces; cardinals in their purple gloriously attended, horses and mules decked with gold and jewels, and shod with gold and silver. Beyond all, myself, Supreme Pontiff, borne on soldiers' shoulders in a golden chair, and waving my hand majestically to adoring crowds. Hearken to the roar of the cannon, the bugle notes, the boom of the drums. Observe the military engines, the shouting populace, torches blazing in street and square, and the kings of the earth scarce admitted to kiss my Holiness's foot. Behold the Roman Bishop placing the crown on the head of the Emperor, who seems to be made king of kings, yet is but the shadow of a name. Look at all this, and tell me it is not magnificent!

Peter: I look at a very worldly tyrant, an enemy of Christ and a disgrace to the Church.

Julius: Mere envy! You perceive what a poor wretch of a bishop you were compared to me.

Peter: Insolent wretch! Dare you compare your glory with mine?—and mine was Christ's, and not my own. Christ gave to me the keys of the Kingdom of Heaven, trusted His sheep to my feeding and sealed my faith with His approval. Fraud, usury, and cunning made you Pope, if Pope you are to be called. I gained thousands of souls to Christ: you have destroyed as many thousands. I brought heathen Rome to acknowledge Christ: you have made it heathen again. I healed the sick, cast out devils, restored the dead to life, and brought a blessing with me where I went. What blessings have you and your triumphs brought? I used my power for the good of all: you have used yours to crush and vex mankind. . . .

Julius: Do you mean to say I am to give up money, dominion, revenues, pleasures, life? Will you leave me to misery?

Peter: Yes, if you count Christ as miserable. He who was Lord of all became the scorn of all, endured poverty, endured labour, fasting, and hunger, and ended with a death of shame.

Julius: Very admirable, no doubt. But He will not find many imitators in these times of ours.

Peter: To admire is to imitate. Christ takes nothing good from any man. He takes what is falsely called good, to give him instead eternal truth, as soon as he is purged from the taint of the world. Being Himself heavenly, He will have His Church like Him, estranged from the world's corruption, and those who are sunk in pollution cannot resemble One who is sitting in heaven. Once for all, fling away your imagined wealth, and receive instead what is far better.

Julius: What, I beseech you?

Peter: The gift of prophecy, the gift of knowledge, the gift of miracles, Christ Himself. The more a man is afflicted in the world the greater his joy in Christ, the poorer in the world the richer in Christ, the more cast down in the world the more exalted in Christ. Christ will have His followers pure, and most of all His ministers, the bishops. The higher in rank they are the more like Christ they are bound to be, and the less entangled in earthly pleasures. Yet you, the bishop next to Christ, who make yourself equal with Christ, think only of money, and arms, and treaties, to say nothing of vicious pleasures, and you abuse His name to support your own vanities. You claim the honour due to Christ, while you are Christ's enemy. You bless others, you are yourself accursed. You pretend to have the keys of heaven, and you are yourself shut out from it. . . .

Julius: Then you won't open the gates?

Peter: Sooner to anyone than to such as you. We are not of your communion in this place. You have an army of sturdy rogues behind you, you have money, and you are a famous architect. Go build a paradise of your own, and fortify it, lest the devils break in on you.

96

Martin Luther at the Diet of Worms, 1521[5]

Although the Holy Roman Emperor Charles V (1500–1558) saw rebellion against the Church as leading to rebellion against the state, he could neither ignore the aroused German nationalism nor Luther's powerful princely support. It is for these reasons that the emperor did not immediately publish the papal bull[6] *"Exsurge domine"* against Luther but, rather, granted Luther a safe conduct so that he could appear before the Diet of Princes at Worms in order to defend his religious views.

The following excerpt is from Luther's reply to the Diet at Worms on April 18, 1521.

QUESTIONS TO CONSIDER

1. What were Luther's criticisms of the Church?
2. What would have convinced Luther to change his opinions?
3. Why would the Catholic Church not favor Luther's individual interpretation of the Scriptures?
4. From your general reading, how did the Protestant Reformation affect the political situation during the sixteenth century?

---

[5]The imperial Diet had been created in the fifteenth century; it included three houses: (1) the seven electors who chose the emperors, (2) the House of Princes, and (3) the House of Free Cities. The Diets always tried to stop the emperors from exercising any real authority over them. The emperors had to depend for any moneys or troops on voluntary contributions from the Diet. The imperial free city of Worms, located in Hesse on the Rhine, had been designated as the meeting place of the Emperor Charles V and the Diet in 1520. The emperor had promised the princes that no German should be branded an outlaw before a hearing in the empire; he, therefore, had to follow constitutional practices and give Martin Luther a safe-conduct pass to the meeting of the Diet.

[6]A papal bull [*Bulla*] is the most solemn official pronouncement of a pope. It was sealed with lead or a *Bulla.*

Most serene emperor, most illustrious princes, concerning those questions proposed to me yesterday on behalf of your serene majesty, whether I acknowledged as mine the books enumerated and published in my name and whether I wished to persevere in their defense or to retract them, I have given to the first question my full and complete answer, in which I still persist and shall persist forever. These books are mine and they have been published in my name by me, unless in the meantime, either through the craft or the mistaken wisdom of my emulators, something in them has been changed or wrongly cut out. For plainly I cannot acknowledge anything except what is mine alone and what has been written by me alone, to the exclusion of all interpretations of anyone at all.

In replying to the second question, I ask that your most serene majesty and your lordships may deign to note that my books are not all of the same kind.

For there are some in which I have discussed religious faith and morals simply and evangelically, so that even my enemies themselves are compelled to admit that these are useful, harmless, and clearly worthy to be read by Christians. Even the bull, although harsh and cruel, admits that some of my books are inoffensive, and yet allows these also to be condemned with a judgment which is utterly monstrous. Thus, if I should begin to disavow them, I ask you, what would I be doing? Would not I, alone of all men, be condemning the very truth upon which friends and enemies equally agree, striving alone against the harmonious confession of all?

Another group of my books attacks the papacy and the affairs of the papists as those who both by their doctrines and very wicked examples have laid waste the Christian world with evil that affects the spirit and the body. For no one can deny or conceal this fact, when the experience of all and the complaints of everyone witness that through the decrees of the pope and the doctrines of men the consciences of the faithful have been most miserably entangled, tortured, and torn to pieces. Also, property and possessions, especially in this illustrious nation of Germany, have been devoured by an unbelievable tyranny and are being devoured to this time without letup and by unworthy means. . . . If, therefore, I should have retracted these writings, I should have done nothing other than to have added strength to this [papal] tyranny and I should have opened not only windows but doors to such great godlessness. It would rage farther and more freely than ever it has dared up to this time. Yes, from the proof of such a revocation on my part, their wholly lawless and unrestrained kingdom of wickedness would become still more intolerable for the already wretched people; and their rule would be further strengthened and established, especially if it should be reported that this evil deed had been done by me by virtue of the authority of your most serene majesty and of the whole Roman Empire. Good God! What a cover for wickedness and tyranny I should have then become.

I have written a third sort of book against some private and (as they say) distinguished individuals—those, namely, who strive to preserve the Roman tyranny and to destroy the godliness taught by me. Against these I confess I have been more violent than my religion or profession demands. But then, I do not set myself up as a saint; neither am I disputing about my life, but about the teaching of Christ. It is not proper for me to retract these works, because by this retraction it would again hap-

Reprinted from *Luther's Works*, Volume 32, pp. xxxii, 109–13, edited by George W. Forell, copyright © 1958 Muhlenburg Press. Used by permission of Augsburg Fortress.

pen that tyranny and godlessness would, with my patronage, rule and rage among the people of God more violently than ever before.

However, because I am a man and not God, I am not able to shield my books with any other protection than that which my Lord Jesus Christ himself offered for his teaching. When questioned before Annas about his teaching and struck by a servant, he said: 'If I have spoken wrongly, bear witness to the wrong.' . . . If the Lord himself, who knew that he could not err, did not refuse to hear testimony against his teaching, even from the lowliest servant, how much more ought I, who am the lowest scum and able to do nothing except err, desire and expect that somebody should want to offer testimony against my teaching! Therefore, I ask by the mercy of God, may your most serene majesty, most illustrious lordships, or anyone at all who is able, either high or low, bear witness, expose my errors, overthrowing them by the writings of the prophets and the evangelists. Once I have been taught I shall be quite ready to renounce every error, and I shall be the first to cast my books into the fire.

From these remarks I think it is clear that I have sufficiently considered and weighed the hazards and dangers, as well as the excitement and dissensions aroused in the world as a result of my teachings, things about which I was gravely and forcefully warned yesterday. To see excitement and dissension arise because of the Word of God is to me clearly the most joyful aspect of all in these matters. For this is the way, the opportunity, and the result of the Word of God, just as He [Christ] said, 'I have not come to bring peace, but a sword. For I have come to set a man against his father, etc.' . . . Therefore, we ought to think how marvelous and terrible is our God in his counsels, lest by chance what is attempted for settling strife grows rather into an intolerable deluge of evils, if we begin by condemning the Word of God. And concern must be shown lest the reign of this most noble youth, Prince Charles (in whom after God is our great hope), become unhappy and inauspicious. I could illustrate this with abundant examples from Scripture—like Pharaoh, the king of Babylon, and the kings of Israel who, when they endeavored to pacify and strengthen their kingdoms by the wisest counsels, most surely destroyed themselves. For it is He who takes the wise in their own craftiness . . . and overturns mountains before they know it. . . . Therefore we must fear God. I do not say these things because there is a need of either my teachings or my warnings for such leaders as you, but because I must not withhold the allegiance which I owe my Germany. With these words I commend myself to your most serene majesty and to your lordships, humbly asking that I not be allowed through the agitation of my enemies, without cause, to be made hateful to you. I have finished."

When I had finished, the speaker for the emperor said, as if in reproach, that I had not answered the question, that I ought not call into question those things which had been condemned and defined in councils; therefore what was sought from me was not a horned response, but a simple one, whether or not I wished to retract.

Here I answered:

Since then your serene majesty and your lordships seek a simple answer, I will give it in this manner, neither horned nor toothed: Unless I am convinced by the testimony of the Scriptures or by clear reason (for I do not trust either in the pope or in councils alone, since it is well known that they have often erred and contradicted themselves), I am bound by the Scriptures I have quoted and my conscience is captive to the Word of God. I cannot and I will not retract anything, since it is neither safe nor right to go against conscience.

"I cannot do otherwise, here I stand, may God Help me, Amen."

97

St. Charles Borromeo: *Instructions to Confessors*

One of the most effective instruments for teaching Catholic Reformation theology and for infusing discipline amongst the faithful was the sacrament of confession. To refute Luther's claim that Confession was an abuse of priestly power, the Council of Trent insisted that it was a sacrament inspired directly by God and for this reason the faithful must confess their sins at least once a year. When administering this sacrament, the priestly confessor combined the three functions of teacher, spiritual physician, and judge. To assist confessors and to bring a greater degree of uniformity to the sacrament, St. Charles Borromeo (1538–1554), archbishop of Milan, published *Instructions to Confessors* (1572), listing recommended "penances" for all sins, including sins violating the Ten Commandments. Very quickly Borromeo's *Instructions* became the most influential confessional manual for the Catholic Reformation.

When confessing, the penitent entered a semi-enclosed boxed cubicle. The confessor was seated in the center cubicle and could receive two kneeling penitents who spoke indirectly to the confessor through a screen. In some respects confessional architecture, adopted by Charles Borromeo, was not unlike the space of a monastic cell or even a prison. But unlike a prison, the confessional was truly a sacred place, for it was here that the priest ministered to his penitent and, in the words of St. Charles Borromeo, would "exorcise the serpent of sin with all the dexterity of a midwife." Although Borromeo's Instructions did suggest specific penances for some sins, in most cases he expected the confessor, after hearing a penitent's full confession, to determine the proper penance, and therefore he does not always specify the full details of the penance. Following are the Ten Commandments along with Charles Borromeo's suggested penances for violating them.

QUESTIONS TO CONSIDER

1. In what ways might the *Instructions to Confessors* be regarded as the "moral arithmetic" of the Catholic Reformation?
2. Which sins does Borromeo consider the most grievous? Why?
3. What do the sins against the *First Commandment* suggest about the place of magic and divination in early modern Europe?
4. In discussing sins against the *Second Commandment*, does Borromeo consider perjury or blasphemy the more serious sin? Why?
5. Drawing upon Borromeo's discussion of the sins against the *Fourth, Fifth, Sixth,* and *Ninth Commandments*, can we gain any understanding of the Roman Catholic Church's views on parental and clerical authority, birth control, and sex in early modern Europe?
6. Do you believe this approach to the sacrament of penance and reconciliation would be acceptable today? Why? Why not?

First Commandment: I am the Lord, your God; you shall not have false gods before me.

1. Penitents who have renounced their faith and now seek readmittance to the Church should make penance for two years.

2. Penitents who have taken part in any pagan superstitions should do penance for two years.

3. Penitents who have consulted fortunetellers and diviners or who have made satanic sacrileges should receive a penance of seven years.

4. Penitents who have consulted magicians are obliged to endure a penance of five years.

5. Penitents who have collected medicinal herbs for charms should receive a penance of twenty days.

6. Penitents who have used malicious spells intended to induce impotence or sterility in their enemies, or who have employed charms or magic, should receive a penance of two years.

Second Commandment: You shall not take the Lord's name in vain.

7. Penitents who have knowingly perjured themselves should receive a penance of forty days of bread and water. Furthermore, they should be required to do penance of seven years and must not be given Holy Communion without full repentance nor should they ever be asked to give testimony.

8. Penitents who have perjured themselves in Church should be given a penance of ten years.

9. Penitents who have sworn against their neighbor and have not made peace with him should be put on bread and water for forty days, and denied Holy Communion for one year. They must be urged to reconcile as soon as possible with their neighbor.

10. If anyone has blasphemed against God or his Blessed Mother or any other saint, he must appear at the door of his parish church seven Sundays in a row without cloak or shoes, wearing a leather strap or cord around his neck. For these seven weeks he should eat bread and water for six days a week (Sunday excluded) and must not enter a Church. On Sundays he must feed the poor (at least one beggar), but if unable to do so he should be given an appropriate substituted penance. If he refuses this penance he is forbidden to enter a church and upon his death should be denied a Christian burial.

11. If the penitent who confesses perjury appears wealthy he should be referred to a magistrate who should fine him 40 sous or at the very least 20 sous.

Third Commandment: You shall keep holy the Sabbath day.

12. Penitents who have not kept the spirit of the Sabbath or Holy Days and have performed unnecessary servile work should be given a penance of three days of bread and water.

13. Penitents who have traveled on Sunday should be given a penance of seven days.

From Louis Habert, *Pratique du sacrement de pénitence; ou méthode pour l'administrer utilement: imprimée par l'order de Mgr. Lévêque de Verdun. Nouvelle édition qui contient un extrait des canons pénitentiaux tirés de Instructions de S. Charles aux confesseurs* (Paris: Chez Jean-Thomas Herissant, 1755), pp. 503–9. Trans. Philip F. Riley. Arabic numerals in this selection have been added by the translator.

14. Penitents who have deliberately danced in front of a Church on a Sunday or a Holy Day should be given a penance of three years but only after having promised never to commit this sin again.

15. Penitents who confess to eating a full meal before attending Mass should be given three days of bread and water.

16. Penitents who converse and talk with others in Church during the sacred liturgy should be given a penance of ten days of bread and water.

17. Penitents who violate the fast days of the Holy Church should be given a penance of bread and water for twenty days; if they confess to violating the Lenten fast days, they should receive a penance for seven days for each fast day they have violated.

18. Penitents who eat meat during Lent, without good cause, should not be permitted to receive Holy Communion at Easter.

Fourth Commandment: Honor your parents.

19. Children who curse their parents should be given a penance of bread and water for forty days.

20. Children who wish their parents harm or injury should receive a penance of three years.

21. Any child who strikes their parents should receive a penance for seven years.

22. Children who preach rebellion against their bishop, their pastor, or their fathers should be sentenced to a monastery for the rest of their days.

23. A child who is contemptuous of or who ridicules the orders of his bishop or his priest should be given a penance of bread and water for forty days.

Fifth Commandment: Do not murder.

24. A penitent who accidentally kills a priest must abstain from meat and wine (except on Sundays and Holy Days) for the rest of his life. Never should he be permitted to ride a horse or to ever carry a weapon. Only after five years of public penance each Sunday at the Church portal may he be permitted to reenter a church. He should not be permitted to receive Holy Communion for ten years.

25. Anyone, who kills his father, mother, sister or brother, may not receive Holy Communion until his deathbed. He must abstain from meat and wine and fast the second, fourth and sixth days of the week.

26. A female penitent who deliberately aborts her pregnancy must do penance for three years; if she has a spontaneous abortion she must do penance for three Lents.

27. A penitent who involuntarily suffocates an infant must immediately fast for forty days on bread and water, herbs and legumes; if married this sinner must refrain from all conjugal relations during this period. In addition, they should perform this exact penance for the next three successive Lenten seasons.

28. Parents whose child, because of their negligence, dies without receiving either the sacrament of Baptism or Confirmation must do penance for three years, the first year of which must be a diet of bread and water.

29. If a woman kills her husband because of fornication she should leave her home and make her penitence in a monastery.

30. If anyone kills a person they must venture no further than the portal of a church and may receive Holy Communion only on their deathbed.

31. Penitents who counsel others to commit homicide should receive a penance of forty days of bread and water, which should be followed by a penance of seven years.

32. Penitents who accidentally commit homicide should make penance for two weeks, be denied Holy Communion for five years and, at the discretion of their confessor, be required to abstain from eating meat for the rest of their life.

33. A penitent who wounds or mutilates another person should be required to fast, eat bread and water on all Sundays and Holy Days for one year.

34. Anyone who strikes another without provocation must be given a penance of three days of bread and water.

35. If anyone confesses hatred for his neighbor and makes no effort to reconcile with his neighbor, he should be required to eat bread and water until he reconciles with his neighbor.

Sixth Commandment: Do not commit adultery.

36. Depending upon the circumstances, adultery is a sin requiring penance for five, seven, or even ten years.

37. If an unmarried sinner confesses fornication with a woman he is neither engaged to nor married to, he must do penance for three years.

38. Penitents who confess to using conjugal relations in a shameful manner should receive a penance of forty days.

39. Anyone who confesses to fornicating with two sisters or with a nun must receive a perpetual penance.

40. Anyone who confesses the sin incest (of even the slightest degree) should receive a penance of twelve years.

41. If a married woman confesses that she wears rouge and paints her face so as to please men other than her husband, she should be given a penance of three years.

42. A penitent, who by negligence confesses to self-pollution because of indecent conversation or indecent glances, should be given a penance of twenty days.

Seventh Commandment: Do not steal.

43. Penitents who confess to stealing any kind of Church property should perform penance for three Lents and the seven following years.

44. Sinners who steal money from the Church or any kind of Church offering should spend seven years in penance.

45. Sinners who refuse (or neglect) to pay their Church tithe should for their penance pay four times the amount of their tithe and receive a penance of twenty days of bread and water.

46. Sinners who confess embezzling funds from their employers must make full restitution of their theft and perform penance for three years.

47. Anyone who confesses that he has oppressed a poor person should receive a penance of bread and water for thirty days.

48. Penitents who confess to having charged usurious rates of interest should be given a penance of three years, the first year of which they should eat only bread and water.

Eighth Commandment: Do not lie.

49. Penitents who would affirm something to be true knowing that it is false should receive the same penance as an adulterer.

50. Penitents who consent to give false testimony should be given a penance of five years.

51. Penitents who slander their neighbors should receive a penance of bread and water for seven days.

Ninth Commandment: Do not have adulterous desires.

52. Bishops who confess their desire to commit fornication should receive a penance of seven years.

53. A priest who confesses the desire to fornicate should receive a penance of five years; a deacon or monk who confesses this sin should be given a penance of three years.

54. A layman who confesses the desire to fornicate should receive a penance of two years.

55. Penitents who admit to self-pollution while sleeping due to impure desires should receive a penance of thirty days.

Tenth Commandment: Do not covet your neighbors' goods.

56. Penitents who wickedly desire the goods of another should receive a penance of three years.

57. Penitents who desire the goods lost by their neighbor so that they might find them and claim them as their own should receive the same penance as a thief.

Age of Exploration and Expansion

Almost a century before Portuguese captain Vasco da Gama successfully rounded the Cape of Good Hope and reached the Malabar coast of India in 1498, Emperor Yung-lo (1403–1424) of the Ming dynasty (1308–1644) had launched the first of a series of grand-scale maritime expeditions in 1405. Over the next twenty-eight years, the Chinese court dispatched six more large-scale naval expeditions to Southeast Asia, India, Persia, and the east coast of Africa. These gigantic expeditions involved more than 70,000 men and hundreds of vessels and covered thousands of nautical miles. In contrast with the goals of the European adventurers who came to Asia several decades later, the main purpose of these grand undertakings was neither conquest nor trade. The Ming government was mainly interested in spreading and enhancing its dynastic prestige and power as well as winning for China the nominal control of those distant regions. By 1415, nineteen kingdoms had sent tributes to the Ming court; however, after nearly three decades of naval expeditions, not a single permanent overseas Ming colony was established.

Then, in 1433, the great Ming naval expeditions suddenly ceased, never to resume. Although scholars do not know the precise reasons why China refused to embark on her own Age of Exploration, possible explanations might include the high cost of the naval expeditions; China's long-held tradition of anticommercialism; and the ruling Confucian scholars' and officials' prejudice toward the seafaring people, who neglected to observe two important Confucian virtues—namely, filial piety and ancestor worship. Had those Chinese seafarers sustained support from a leader such as Portugal's Prince Henry, the course of world history might have been quite different; certainly China would have "discovered" such distant lands as Spain, England, and France. A little more than six decades after the last Ming naval expedition of 1433, Vasco da Gama opened an era of European domination of the Asian waters. The compass and gunpowder, two important gifts of China to the West, permitted the Europeans to develop empires in Asia.

As the demand for Oriental products increased in Western Europe in the fifteenth century, merchants and monarchs, hoping to break the Italian monopoly of that trade, began their search for an all-water route to the East. Another powerful impetus was a strong sense of Christian duty to convert pagans and infidels. For centuries, Portuguese and Spaniards had struggled to expel the Muslims who occupied their land. That effort generated a religious fervor and missionary zeal and also helped establish a sense of national identity. By the early fifteenth century, Portugal had become a unified state, separate from the expanding Spanish kingdoms of Leon and Castile. The Iberians, with their strategic location facing the Atlantic and with new knowledge of navigation and shipbuilding gained from Italian seafarers on the Mediterranean, initiated the age of European exploration and expansion.

Prince Henry, the third son of King John I of Portugal (1385–1433), focused the small nation's attention on various maritime projects. Under his leadership, Portugal became a center of knowledge for shipbuilding, navigation, and the study of geography. Portugal also was the first European nation to embark on colonial expansion. Prince Henry took the initiative in settling Portuguese adventurers in the Azores, and in 1415 he crossed the Strait of Gibraltar to capture the North African port of Ceuta, the terminal of the caravan routes into Africa. In succeeding years, lured by the potential profits in trading gold, ivory, and slaves, Prince Henry directed Portuguese explorations down the West African coast and established trading centers there. He had also obtained from the papacy a monopoly of missionary activities in the area. When he died in 1460, Prince Henry's economic and religious rights in West Africa passed to the Portuguese monarchs, who continued sending explorers to probe the African coast. They rounded the Cape of Good Hope by 1488 and a decade later arrived in the Indian Ocean, where Muslim states had a monopoly of the trade with India and the Far East. In the New World, Pedro Cabral landed on the east coast of South America in 1500, strengthening Portugal's claim to Brazil.

As a youth, Christopher Columbus (1451–1506) had served as a seaman on various ships in the Mediterranean. He eventually settled in Portugal, where he developed his idea of sailing west to Asia. He was unable to gain financial support from the Portuguese monarchs, who favored opening the sea route to India by way of Africa, but he continued his search for a sponsor in Spain. After the fall of the Muslim stronghold of Granada on January 2, 1492, Queen Isabella finally agreed to his terms. His four voyages established Spanish influence in the Caribbean.

It did not take long, however, for Spain and other European countries to begin conquering the New World that Columbus had stumbled upon. The final reading in this section describes the conquest of Mexico.

98

Cheng Ho [Zheng He]: Ming Maritime Expeditions

Most of the large naval expeditions of the Ming dynasty were led by a Muslim court eunuch named Cheng Ho (1371–1433). The following selection describes China's Columbus and the maritime explorations he led.

QUESTIONS TO CONSIDER

1. What does the size, organization, and nature of the Ming maritime fleet indicate about China's capabilities in the early fifteenth century?
2. What do the Ming emperor's bans on imperial naval explorations suggest about Chinese views of the world?
3. Compare and contrast the Ming maritime expeditions with the Age of Discovery in Western history. What motives inspired Cheng Ho, Columbus, and Magellan?
4. How might the course of world history have been altered had the Chinese seafarers received sustained support from a leader such as Prince Henry of Portugal?

Cheng Ho (1371–1433), eunuch and commander-in-chief of the Ming expeditionary fleets in the early years of the fifteenth century, was born into a family named Ma at K'un-yang [Kunyang] in central Yunnan. His great-grandfather was named Bayan, and his grandfather and father were both named Hājjī, which suggests that the two probably visited Mecca and that the family had a long tradition of Islamic faith and may have been of Mongol-Arab origin. At the beginning of the Ming dynasty, a number of generals who fought on the frontier were in charge of recruiting eunuchs for the court. In 1381, when Yunnan was pacified by an army under Fu Yu-de, Cheng Ho, at that time about ten years old, was one of the children selected to be castrated. As a trainee for eunuch service, he was assigned to the retinue of Chu Ti [Zhu Di] [Emperor Yung-lo]. In his early twenties, he accompanied Chu Ti on a series of military campaigns and in the course of them took up a career in the army. As his family records relate, "when he entered adulthood, he reportedly became seven feet tall and had a waist about five feet in circumference. His cheeks and forehead were high but his nose was small. He had glaring eyes and a voice as loud as a huge bell. He knew a great deal about warfare and was well accustomed to battle." . . .

From Carrington Goodrich, ed., *Dictionary of Ming Biography, 1368–1644*, pp. 194–98, *passim.* Copyright © 1936 Columbia University Press. Reprinted with permission of the publisher.

Cheng Ho first achieved official prominence early in 1404 when he was promoted to the position of director of eunuch affairs and granted the surname of Cheng [Zheng]. Shortly afterward he received the appointment of commander-in-chief of the first expedition. Meanwhile local officials of the eastern coastal regions were ordered to build ocean-going vessels. By July, 1405, some 1,180 ships of various sizes and types had been constructed. The large or treasure ships were, according to measures of that time, as much as 440 feet long and 186.2 wide, and those of medium size, or horse ships, 370 feet long and 150 wide. There were supply ships which measured 280 feet in length and 120 in breadth, and billet ships measuring 240 feet by 94. The battleships equipped with cannon were much smaller, measuring only 180 feet by 68. Most of the treasure ships were the product of the Lung-chiang [Long Jiang] shipyard near Nanking [Nanjing]. None of these has survived, but near the site of the shipyard was recently discovered (1957) a large wooden rudder (length 11 meters) thought to have been fashioned for one of the bigger vessels. It is now preserved in the Kiangsu [Jiangsu] provincial museum.

The first voyage began in the summer of 1405 with a 27,800 man crew and 62 (or 63) large and 255 smaller vessels. . . . [In the second voyage, which was launched in late autumn of 1407, the expedition sailed into the Indian Ocean.]

In the summer of 1409 Cheng Ho returned to Nanking to report on his mission to the emperor. Here he built a temple in honor of T'ien-fei [Tianfei], the goddess of the sea, to whose virtue and power he attributed the safe voyages of his fleets. The inscription on the stele erected later (May 3, 1416) has been partly translated into French by Claudine Lombard-Salmon; the complete Chinese text may be found in the book by Louis Gaillard.

After a brief stay in the capital, Cheng Ho was again sent overseas, accompanied by Wang Ching-hung [Wang Jinghong] and Hou Hsien [Hou Xian]. His third voyage was comparable to the first and second in the number of men but with only 48 vessels; it lasted from September, 1409, to June, 1411. This expedition reached the same destination on the Malabar coast of India, but along the way several excursions were made, including brief visits to Siam, Malacca, Sumatra, and Ceylon. It also undertook lumbering operations and gathered fragrant herbs in the Sembilan Islands. . . .

It was the fourth voyage, which began in 1413 and ended in August, 1415, that took the expedition far beyond its earlier destinations. Under the same command but with a crew of 27,670 men and some 63 large vessels, the expedition touched at a number of new places, including the Maldives, Hormuz, the Hadramaut coast, and Aden. In Sumatra the expedition became involved in a local power struggle at Ch'iao-shan [Qiaoshan] (Samudra-Pasai). A usurper by the name of Su-wa-la, after murdering the king, directed his forces against the expedition, but was subsequently defeated and pursued as far as Lambri, where he and his family were captured. The prisoners were taken to Nanking on the return of the fleet. As a result of this voyage, nineteen countries sent envoys and tribute to the Ming court. Chu Ti was so pleased with the results that he rewarded all participants in the expedition according to their ranks.

In December, 1416, Cheng Ho was commissioned to escort home the envoys of the nineteen states, and embarked, possibly in the autumn of 1417, on his fifth voyage, which lasted up to August, 1419. The returning envoys, who had witnessed the delight of the Ming emperor at his first sight of a giraffe, spread the news to other countries. Hence an impressive collection of strange animals, among them lions, leopards, single-humped camels, ostriches, zebras, rhinoceroses, antelopes, and giraffes offered by rulers of several states highlighted this journey.

The spring of 1421 saw the launching of the sixth voyage, but Cheng may not have joined the fleet until later. It returned on September 3, 1422, accompanied by a large number of envoys from such states as Hormuz, Aden, Djofar, La-sa (Al-shsā?), Brawa, Mogadishu, Calicut, Cochin, Cail, Ceylon, the Maldive Islands, Lambri, Sumatra, Aru, Malacca, Kan-pa-li (Coyampadi?), Sulu, Bengal, Borneo, Ku-ma-la (-lang, Cabarruyan Islands?), and Ts'eng-pa (Zanzibar). The number of countries visited on this trip has not been listed, but the expedition reached at least as far as Aden, near the mouth of the Red Sea, and Mogadishu and Brawa on the coast of east Africa. . . .

In the meanwhile Chu Ti had died (August 12, 1424), and almost at once the idea of another maritime expedition came under attack. The emperor designate, Chu Kao-chih [Zhu Gaozhi], promptly (August 28) released from prison Hsia Yüan-chi [Xia Yuanji], perhaps the most outspoken critic of the treasure fleets, and on September 7, the very day of Chu's accession to the throne as the fourth Ming emperor, other voices joined Hsia's in recommending their abolition. This protest seems to have settled the matter, for in the following February Cheng Ho received an appointment as garrison commander of the Nanking district, and was told to maintain order in his own expeditionary forces, and consult with Wang Ching-hung and two other eunuchs. . . .

Only a few months later the fourth emperor died and for several years the plan to launch another expedition lay dormant. Finally in June, 1430, his successor, the fifth emperor, Chu Chan-chi [Zhu Zhanji], issued an order for the seventh (and what proved to be the last) voyage, but it was not to leave the Fukien [Fujian] coast until a year and a half later. It returned in July, 1433. The mission was intended to regenerate the tributary relationships once maintained under Chu Ti, which had significantly weakened since his death. A score of states were revisited, including those along the coasts of the Arabian peninsula and eastern Africa. In this instance too ambassadors returned with the fleet, bringing such gifts as giraffes, elephants, and horses. Cheng Ho, who was already in his sixties, did not perhaps visit all of them in person, and some of the side missions were conducted by his aides. . . .

What happened to Cheng Ho from this point is not clear. It has customarily been said that he died in 1435 or 1436 at the age of sixty-five, no specific date or site of burial being indicated in contemporary sources. A later source, the T'ung-chih Shang Chiang liang-hsien chih [Tongzhi Shang Jiang liangxian Zhi] (preface of 1874), 3/39a, however, maintains that Cheng Ho died at Calicut and was buried at Niushoushan outside Nanking. If this be true, he must have passed away early in 1433.

99

St. Francis Xavier on the Japanese: "The Best People Who Have Yet Been Discovered"

In 1549, St. Francis Xavier (1506–1552), an ethnic Basque from Spain and one of the founding members of the Society of Jesus, introduced Christianity to Japan, the land of Buddhism and Shintoism. As an apostolic nuncio (highest-ranking papal legate permanently accredited to a civil government) for Asia, he left Europe in 1541 for Goa, an important Portuguese outpost located on the west coast of India. He traveled far and wide along the coastal towns of India, Ceylon, and Malaya to proselytize indigenous Asian people. Glowing accounts of Japan by a Japanese fugitive named Anjiro (Yajiro), whom he met in Malacca in 1547, persuaded Xavier to carry his evangelical endeavor to Japan. On August 15, 1549, Xavier, accompanied by two Jesuit priests and Anjiro as an interpreter, reached Kagoshima, Anjiro's native town, located on the southern tip of Japan's Kyushu island. There, Xavier preached Christianity and won approximately one hundred converts. Apparently, many believed that Christianity was just another version of Buddhism. Encouraged by the good reception to his message in Kagoshima, he traveled to Kyoto, then the Imperial capital, in February 1551. There, he explored the possibility of obtaining official approval for expanding evangelical work throughout the country. Xavier probably did not realize that the country he was visiting was in the throes of bloody civil wars among contending feudal *daimyo* (feudal territorial warlords). Furthermore, he was probably unaware that the Ashikaga shogunate (1336–1573) was in the last phase of its demise. Disappointed by not being able to have an audience with the emperor, Xavier returned to Kyushu. After two years and three months of his proselytizing work in Japan, he left the country for India at the end of 1551.

The following is a letter written by Xavier to fellow Jesuits in Goa, a few months after his arrival in Kagoshima. In this letter he describes the Japanese people as "the best who have yet been discovered."

QUESTIONS TO CONSIDER

1. What aspects of Japanese life and character impressed Xavier to give such high praise?
2. What were the reasons for the more receptive attitudes of the provincial lords and people in western Japan toward Christianity than those in the rest of the country?

By the experience which we have of this land of Japan, I can inform you thereof as follows. Firstly, the people whom we have met so far, are the best who have yet been discovered, and it seems to me that we shall never find among heathens another race to equal the Japanese. It is a people of very good manners, good in general, and not malicious; they are men of honor to a marvel, and prize honor above all else in the world. They are a poor people in general; but their poverty, whether among the gentry or those who are not so, is not considered as a shame. They have one quality which I cannot recall in any people of Christendom; this is that their gentry howsoever poor they may be, and the commoners howsoever rich they may be, render as much honor to a poor gentleman as if he were passing rich. On no account would a poverty-stricken gentleman marry with someone outside the gentry, even if he were given great sums to do so; and this they do because they consider that they would lose their honor by marrying into a lower class. Whence it can clearly be seen that they esteem honor more than riches. They are very courteous in their dealings one with another; they highly regard arms and trust much in them; always carrying sword and dagger, both high and low alike, from the age of fourteen onwards. They are a people who will not submit to any insults or contemptuous words. Those who are not

From C. R. Boxer, *The Christian Century in Japan, 1549–1650* (Berkeley: University of California Press, 1967), pp. 401–5. Reproduced by permission of Carcent Press Limited.

of gentle birth give much honor to the gentry, who in their turn pride themselves on faithfully serving their feudal lord, to whom they are very obedient. It seems to me that they act thus rather because they think that they would lose their honor if they acted contrarily, than for fear of the punishment they would receive if disobedient.

They are small eaters albeit somewhat heavy drinkers, and they drink rice wine since there are no ordinary wines in these parts. They are men who never gamble, because they consider it a great dishonor, since those who gamble desire what is not theirs and hence tend to become thieves. They swear but little, and when they do it is by the Sun. There are many persons who can read and write, which is a great help to their learning quickly prayers and religious matters. It is a land where there are but few thieves in some kingdoms, and this by the strict justice which is executed against those that are, for their lives are never spared. They abhor beyond measure this vice of theft. They are a people of very good will, very sociable and very desirous of knowledge; they are very fond of hearing about things of God, chiefly when they understand them. Of all the lands which I have seen in my life, whether those of Christians or of heathens, never yet did I see a people so honest in not thieving. Most of them believe in the men of old, who were (so far as I understand) persons who lived like philosophers; many of them adore the Sun and others the Moon. They like to hear things propounded according to reason; and granted that there are sins and vices among them, when one reasons with them pointing out that what they do is evil, they are convinced by this reasoning. I discerned fewer sins in the laity and found them more obedient to reason, than those whom they regard as fathers and priests, whom they call Bonzes.

Two things have astonished me greatly about this country. The first, to see how lightly they regard great sins; and the reason is because their forebears were accustomed to live in them, from whom those of the present generation take their example; see how continuation in vices which are against nature corrupts the people, in the same manner as continual disregard of imperfections undermines and destroys perfection. The second point is to see that the laity live better in their state than the Bonzes in theirs; and withal this is so manifest, it is astonishing in what esteem the former hold the latter. There are many other errors and evils among these Bonzes, and the more learned are the worst sinners. I spoke many times with some of the wiser, chiefly with one who is highly regarded by all in these parts, both for his letters, life, and dignity, as for his great age, he being eighty years old, and called Ningit [Ninjitsu], which is to say in Japanese "truthful heart"; he is as a bishop amongst them, and if the term could be applied to him, might well be called "blessed." In many talks which I had with him, I found him doubtful, and unable to decide whether our soul is immortal, or whether it dies with the body; sometimes he told me yes, at others no, and I fear that the other learned are alike. This Ningit is so great a friend of mine, that it is a marvel to see. All, both laity and Bonzes like us very much, and are greatly astonished to see how we have come from such distant lands as from Portugal to Japan, which is more than six thousand leagues, only to speak of the things of God, and how people can save their souls by belief in Jesus Christ; saying that our coming to these lands is the work of God. One thing I tell you, for which you may give many thanks to God Our Lord, that this land of Japan is very fit for our holy faith greatly to increase therein; and if we knew how to speak the language, I have no doubt whatsoever that we would make many Christians. May it please Our Lord that we may learn it soon, for already we begin to appreciate it, and we learned to repeat the ten commandments in the space of forty days which we applied ourselves thereto. . . .

God granted us a signal favor in bringing us to these lands which lack such abundancies, so that even if we wished to minister to our bodies with these superfluities, the country does not allow of it. They neither kill nor eat anything which they rear. Sometimes they eat fish; there is rice and corn, albeit little; there are numerous herbs, on which they live, and some fruit but not much. This people live wonderfully healthy lives and there are many aged. The Japanese are a convincing proof of how our nature can subsist on little, even if it is not a pleasing sustenance. We live in this land very healthy in body, God grant that we may be likewise in our souls. A great part of the Japanese are Bonzes, and these are strictly obeyed in the places where they are, even if their sins are manifest to all; and it seems to me that the reason why they are held in such esteem is because of their rigorous abstinence, for they never eat meat, nor fish, but only herbs, fruit, and rice, and this once a day and very strictly, and they are never given wine. There are many Bonzes and their temples are of but little revenue. By reason of their continual abstinence and because they have no intercourse with women (especially those who go dressed in black like clergy) on pain of death, and because they know how to relate some histories or rather fables of the things in which they believe, it seems to me they are held in great veneration. And it may well happen that since they and we feel so differently about God and the method of salvation, that we may be persecuted by them with something stronger than words. What we in these parts endeavor to do, is to bring people to the knowledge of their Creator and Saviour, Jesus Christ Our Lord. We live with great hope and trust in him to give us strength, grace, help, and favor to prosecute this work. It does not seem to me that the laity will oppose or persecute us of their own volition, but only if they are importuned by the Bonzes. We do not seek to quarrel with them, neither for fear of them will we cease to speak of the glory of God, and of the salvation of souls.

It is well that we should give you an account of our stay in Cangoxima [Kagoshima]. We arrived here at a season when the winds were contrary for going to Miaco [Kyoto], which is the chief city of Japan, where the King and the greatest lords of the Kingdom reside. And there is no wind that will serve us to go thither, save only five months from now, and then we will go with the help of Our Lord. It is three hundred leagues from here to Miaco, according to what they tell us, and we are likewise told great things of that city, which is said to contain more than ninety thousand houses; there is also a great university frequented by students therein, which has six principal colleges and more than two hundred houses of Bonzes, and of others like friars who are called Ieguixu [Zen-shu], and of nuns who are called Hamacata [Amakata]. Besides this university of Miaco, there are five other chief universities whose names are these, Coya [Koya], Nenguru [Negoro], Feizan [Hieizan], Taninomine [Tamu no mine]. These are in the neighborhood of Miaco, and it is said that there are more than 3,500 students in each one of them. There is another university, a great way off, which is called Bandou [Bando, the Ashikaga Gakko] which is the best and biggest in Japan, and more frequented by students than any other. Bandou is a great lordship where there are six dukes, and a chief one among them, whom the others obey. This chief owes allegiance to the King of Japan who is the great King of Miaco. They tell us such things of the greatness of these lands and universities, that we would prefer to see them before affirming and writing them; and if things be as they tell us, then we will write of our experiences in detail. In addition to these principal universities, they say that there are many other smaller ones throughout the kingdom. During the year 1551, we hope to write you at length concerning the disposition that there is in Miaco and its universities for the knowledge of Jesus Christ Our Lord to be spread therein. This year two Bonzes are going to India who have studied in the universities of Bandou and Miaco, and with them many other Japanese to learn the things of our law. . . .

From Cangoxima, fifth of November of the year 1549.
Your most loving brother wholly in Christ,
Francisco

Portugal in Asia and Spain in America

Portugal played a key role in initiating the Age of Discovery and Exploration. Prince Henry "the Navigator" (1394–1460) devoted much of his life to directing explorations along the west coast of Africa and advancing Portuguese commercial interests.

We recall that the Portuguese continued the medieval search for Prester John until they finally "found" him in the Christian emperor of Ethiopia (see Reading 66) and that they carried the Iberian struggle against the Moors around the coast of Africa to the Persian Gulf (see Reading 69). Under Afonso Albuquerque (1453–1515), occasionally called "the Portuguese Mars," the Portuguese went on to take Goa, a city-state in India, which became a Portuguese colony and functioned as one of the capitals in their expanding maritime empire. By the 1530s, the Portuguese had established bases at many points in East Asia, including Ning-po on the Chinese mainland near Canton, where, as Fernão Mendes Pinto tells us, they confidently built an enclave town of expensive houses, oblivious to the fact that the Chinese Empire was not so weak yet as to allow them to settle in permanently.

100

The Travels of Mendes Pinto

Fernão Mendes Pinto (1510?–1583) was born in Portugal and was in his late twenties when he sailed for India in 1537. He became wealthy as a merchant adventurer and spent many years in China and Japan. His account of his travels became important in Portuguese literature. The following selections describe his adventures on the China coast, where the Portuguese had established Ning-po as an enclave near Canton.

QUESTIONS TO CONSIDER

1. What was the Portuguese motive in attacking Nouday?
2. What were the practices of warfare on both sides that could be seen as making Chinese-Portuguese relations difficult, in spite of the fact that China and Portugal were officially at peace with each other?
3. How does religion enter into Pinto's narrative?

The Sack of Nouday

The following morning, shortly before daybreak, Antonio de Faria sailed up the river with the three junks, the *lorcha*[7] and the four fishing barges he had seized, and dropped anchor in six and a half fathoms of water right up against the walls of the city. Dispensing with the noisy salvo of artillery, he lowered the sails and hoisted the flag of commerce in keeping with the Chinese custom, intent upon observing all the outward signs of peace and leaving nothing undone by way of complying with the formalities, though he knew full well, from the way matters stood with the mandarin, that it would do him no good.

From here he sent him another letter which was extremely polite and friendly in tone, offering to raise the ransom for the captives; but it made that dog of a mandarin so angry, that he had the poor Chinese messenger crucified on an X-shaped cross and exhibited from the top of the wall in full view of the fleet. The sight was enough to make Antonio de Faria abandon the last shred of hope to which some of the men still made him cling, and at the same time, it made the soldiers so furious that they told him that, as long as he had decided to go ashore, there was no point in his waiting any longer because he would just be giving the enemies time to increase their strength.

Since this seemed like good advice to him, he embarked immediately with all the men who were determined to go ashore, leaving orders behind for the junks to direct a steady barrage of fire against the enemies and the city, wherever major gatherings were to be seen, provided he was not engaged in a battle with them. And after disembarking at a spot about a culverin[8]-shot's distance below the roadstead, without encountering the slightest opposition, he marched along the shore in the direction of the city where, by this time, many people were stationed on top of the walls, waving an enormous number of silk banners, trying to put on a brave show by shouting and playing their martial music and generally carrying on like people who put more stock in words and outward appearances than in actual deeds.

As our men came within a musket-shot's distance of the moat surrounding the wall, about 1,000 to 1,200 soldiers—a guess hazarded by some—sallied forth from two gates; and of this number, about 100 to 120 were mounted on horseback, or to put it in a better way, they were mounted on some rather sorry looking nags. They began by putting on a fine show of skirmishing, running back and forth just as free and easy as you please, getting in each other's way most of the time, and often colliding and falling down in heaps of three and four, from which it was obvious that they were country bumpkins who were there not so much out of a desire to fight, but because they had been forced to come.

Antonio de Faria gently spurred his men on, and after signalling to the junks, he waited for the enemy out in the field, for he thought that they would want to engage him there, judging by the brave show they were putting on. But instead, they went right on with their skirmishing, running around in circles for a while, as though they

---

[7]A junk a Chinese sailing vessel distinguished by a high poop, overhanging stem, little or no keel, high pole masts, and a deep rudder. A lorcha is a three-masted sailing vessel combining features of Chinese and European ship building.

[8]A long cannon.

From Fernão Mendes Pinto, *The Travels of Mendes Pinto*, ed. and trans. Rebecca D. Catz (Chicago: University of Chicago Press, 1989), pp. 123–27. Reprinted with permission of The University of Chicago Press.

were threshing wheat, thinking that this alone would be enough to scare us off. However, when they saw that we would not turn tail and run as they thought or probably hoped we would, they got together in a huddle and remained that way for a while, in a single body, in great disorder, without coming any closer.

Seeing them in that way, our captain ordered all the muskets, which had been silent until then, to fire at once; and, as God willed, they hit the mark so well that more than half of the cavalrymen, who were in the vanguard, were knocked to the ground. Off to a good start, we rushed them all together, calling on the name of Jesus as we went; and he, in his mercy, caused the enemy to abandon the field to us and sent them fleeing so wildly that they were falling on top of each other; and when they reached the bridge spanning the moat, they got themselves jammed in there so tightly that they were unable to move either backward or forward.

At this juncture, the main body of our men caught up to them and handled them so efficiently that, before long, more than three hundred of them were lying on top of each other—a pitiful sight indeed—for not a single one of them ever drew a sword.

Exhilarated by this victory, we made a dash for the gate, and there in the entrance we found the mandarin, surrounded by nearly six hundred men, mounted astride a fine horse, wearing an old-fashioned gilt-studded breastplate of purple velvet, which we found out later had belonged to a certain Tome Pires, whom King Manuel, of glorious memory, had sent as an ambassador to China. . . . The mandarin and his men tried to stop us at the entrance, where a cruel battle ensued, during which, little by little, in the time it would take to recite four or five Credos, they began to drive us back with a lot less fear than the ones on the bridge had shown, and they would have given us a little difficult time had it not been for one of our slave boys who knocked the mandarin off his horse with a musket ball that struck him right in the chest. At that, the Chinese became so frightened that they all spun around and immediately began retreating through the gates in complete disorder, and we along with them, knocking them down with our lances, while not a single one of them had enough presence of mind to shut the gates. And off we went, chasing them before us like cattle, down a very long road, until at last they swept through another gate that led to the forest where every last one of them disappeared from sight.

Next, to prevent disorder, Antonio de Faria gathered his soldiers together and, in a single corps, marched with them straight to the prison where they were holding our men, who at the sight of us let out such a loud and terrifying cry of "Lord God, have mercy on us!" that it was enough to send the shivers down one's spine. He immediately had the prison doors and bars broken with axes, a task that our men threw themselves into with such great enthusiasm that it took but a moment to smash everything to bits and remove the prisoners' shackles, so that in a very short time all our companions were unfettered and free.

The order was given to our soldiers and the others in our company that each man was to lay hold of as much as he could for himself, because there would be no sharing of the spoils, and everyone was to keep whatever he could carry; but he asked them to be quick about it, for he would allow them no more than the brief space of half an hour in which to do it. And they all answered that they would be perfectly satisfied with that.

And then they all disappeared into the houses, while Antonio de Faria headed straight for the mandarin's, which he had staked out for himself, and there he found eight thousand taels in silver alone, as well as five huge jars of musk, all of which he had gathered up. The rest, which he left for the slaves accompanying him, consisted of large quantities of silk, yarn, satin, damask, and fine-quality porcelain packed in straw, which they carried until they were ready to collapse.

As a result, the four barges and three sampans that had been used as landing craft had to make four trips to transfer the loot to the junks, and there was not a slave or sailor among them who did not speak of his booty in terms of whole cases and bales of piece goods, to say nothing of the secrets each one kept locked in his heart.

When he saw that more than an hour and a half had gone by, Antonio de Faria quickly ordered the men to return to the ships, but there was absolutely no way of getting them to stop their looting, and this was especially true of the men of most account. But with night coming on, he was afraid some disaster might befall them, and he had the torch put to the city in ten or twelve different places, and since most of the buildings were constructed of pine and other woods, the fire spread so fiercely that in less than a quarter of an hour it looked like a blazing inferno.

Withdrawing to the beach with all the men, he embarked, with not a murmur of protest from any of them, for they were all leaving very rich and happy; and they had many pretty girls in tow, which was really pathetic to see, for they were tied up with musket wicks by fours and fives, and they were all crying while our men were laughing and singing.

Pirates at the Gates of Ning-po

Since it was already late when Antonio de Faria and all his men got back to the ship, there was no time left for anything but to attend to the wounded, who numbered fifty—eight of them Portuguese and the rest slaves and sailors—and to bury the dead, who numbered nine, counting one Portuguese. And after spending the night with a careful lookout on account of the junks up the river, at daybreak he departed for a small town located at water's edge on the opposite bank, and discovered that it was completely deserted, all the inhabitants having fled. But he found the houses filled to overflowing with their goods and enormous quantities of food which Antonio de Faria had loaded on board the junks out of fear that in the ports along the way people would refuse to sell him anything because of what he had done.

After that was decided, since everyone thought it best and advised him to do so, that the three winter months he still had to wait before he could set out on his voyage should be spent on a deserted island called Pulo Hinhor, located out to sea fifteen leagues from Ning-po, where there was fresh water and good anchorage, because he thought that his presence in Ning-po would be detrimental to the commerce of the Portuguese merchants who spent their winters there peacefully carrying on their trade. And everyone praised him highly for this decision and his good intentions.

We departed from the port of Nouday, and after five days of sailing between the mainland and the islands of Comolem, at midday on a Saturday we were attacked by a robber named Premata Gundel, a bitter enemy of the Portuguese people, who had already done them a great deal of harm several times before, not only in Patani but in Sunda and Siam and other places as well, wherever he chanced to meet them in a way that suited his purposes. Mistaking us for Chinese, he attacked us with two huge junks carrying two hundred fighting men, not counting the crew that worked the sails. One of them, after sinking its grappling hooks into Mem Taborda's junk, nearly finished him off. However, when Quiay Panjao, who was a little way out to sea, saw what was happening, he turned back and rammed the enemy junk, going after it under full sail and smashing into its starboard quarter with such force that both of them promptly sank to the bottom, leaving Mem Taborda free of the danger threatening him. Then three of our lorchas, which Antonio de Faria had brought from the port of Nouday, came running to the rescue at top speed and—thanks be to God—they saved most of our people while those on the enemy side all drowned.

About this time, Premata Gundel had reached the big junk that Antonio de Faria was on and tackled it with a pair of grappling hooks attached to very long iron chains, immobilizing him fore and aft, and engaging him in a battle that was truly remarkable to see. For more than half an hour the enemy fought so bravely that most of Antonio de Faria's men were wounded, leaving him, on two occasions, in danger of being taken. However, at that point the three lorchas and a small junk commanded by Pero da Silva came to his aid, and—as God willed—with their help our men soon regained the ground they had lost. They pressed the enemy so hard that in no time at all the whole business was over, ending with the death of the eighty-six Moors who had boarded Antonio de Faria's junk and given him such a bad time that the only part of the ship still held by our men was the poop deck. And from here, they boarded the pirate's junk and put everyone they found on it to the sword, sparing none, though the crew had already dived into the sea.

However, the price of this victory was not cheap by any means, for it cost us the lives of seventeen men, five of them Portuguese—the best and bravest soldiers in the whole company—and left forty-three badly wounded, one of them Antonio de Faria, who came out of it with a spear injury and two sword cuts.

The battle over, an inventory was taken of what was found on the enemy junk and the booty was appraised at eighty thousand taels, the bulk of it in Japanese silver that the pirate had stolen from three merchant junks. That meant that, on this ship alone, the pirate was carrying 120,000 cruzados; and they said that he had been carrying almost as much on the junk that went down, which aggrieved many of our men.

With this prize, Antonio de Faria withdrew to a little island called Buncalou, located three or four leagues to the west where there was fresh water and good anchorage. He went ashore and remained there for eighteen days, sleeping in huts that were improvised for the large numbers of wounded men where—as it pleased the Lord—all of them regained their health.

And from there, we proceeded on our determined course with Antonio de Faria on his big junk, Mem Taborda and Antonio Henriques on theirs, Pero da Silva on the small one that had been captured in Nouday, and Quiay Panjao and all his people on the one just taken from the robber, which was given to him to compensate him for the one he had lost, in addition to twenty thousand taels from the common funds, with which he felt completely satisfied and well paid for his trouble; and all our men were also pleased with this arrangement because Antonio de Faria had been most adamant about it and had promised to make up for it handsomely in the future.

We went sailing along in this manner, and within six days we reached the Gates of Ning-po, which are actually two islands located three leagues from where the Portuguese traded in those days. It was a town they had built ashore with over a thousand houses that was governed by a city council, a high court magistrate, constables, six or seven judges, and administrative officers of state, where the notaries would sign the legal documents they drew up in the following manner: "I, So-and-So, Notary Public of the Archives and Judiciary of the city of Ning-po, in the name of His Majesty, the King . . . ," as though it were situated between Santarem and Lisbon.

And they felt so sure of themselves and were so complacent about it that they had gone so far as to build homes costing between three and four thousand cruzados, all of which, from large to small, were later destroyed and completely leveled by the Chinese—for our sins—with not a trace of them left to show for it, as I will explain more fully at the proper time when I come to it. And then it will be plain to see how uncertain things are in China, about which there is such great interest in Portugal and for which some people mistakenly have such high regard, for at every hour of the day they are exposed to all kinds of disasters and misfortunes.

Spain in America

The Spanish conquest and colonization of the indigenous people of the New World was a significant event in world history. After his initial voyage, Christopher Columbus led three additional expeditions that established Spain's base for expansion in the Indies and the Western Hemisphere. In 1519 the governor of Cuba sent an expedition of some six hundred men led by Hernán Cortés to the mainland of Mexico, where the conquistadors met strong Indian resistance. The first two readings that follow are accounts of this historic encounter of the Spaniards and the "Indians," as Columbus called them. Early in the sixteenth century, Spaniards began debating many issues relating to the nature of the Indians and colonial policies. Did the Indians have souls? Were they capable of reason? How should they be treated? Was it the responsibility of Spaniards not only to convert them to Christianity but to educate them? The Roman Catholic pope addressed some of these questions, as did some members of the Church's religious orders, which played a key role in extending Spanish influence in the New World. One of the most influential of those who spoke and wrote in defense of the rights of the Indians was Bartolomé de Las Casas.

101

Christopher Columbus, Journal of *First Voyage to America*

Columbus and his crew of ninety sailed from Spain on August 3, 1492, arriving at San Salvador in the Bahamas in October. After three additional voyages exploring the Yucatan peninsula and Central America, he died in poverty and neglect, still believing he had discovered the coast of Asia.

QUESTIONS TO CONSIDER

1. What did Columbus tell his crew in order to pacify and encourage them when they complained and became impatient with the length of the voyage?
2. What was the nature of this initial encounter between Spaniards and the natives? What were the reactions of each?

From Christopher Columbus, *Journal of First Voyage to America* (New York: A. & C. Boni, 1924), pp. 20–26, *passim*.

3. In what ways do these journal notes reveal some of Spain's motives for exploration, conquest, and colonization?

4. Consider how the Age of Exploration and Expansion changed the course of world history.

Monday, Oct. 8th. Steered W.S.W. and sailed day and night eleven or twelve leagues; at times during the night, fifteen miles an hour, if the account can be depended upon. Found the sea like the river at Seville, *"thanks to God,"* says the, Admiral. The air soft as that of Seville in April, and so fragrant that it was delicious to breathe it. The weeds appeared very fresh. Many land birds, one of which they took, flying towards the S. W.; also *grajaos*, ducks, and a pelican were seen.

Tuesday, Oct. 9th. Sailed S. W. five leagues, when the wind changed, and they stood W. by N. four leagues. Sailed in the whole day and night twenty leagues and a half; reckoned to the crew seventeen. All night heard birds passing.

Wednesday, Oct. 10th. Steered W.S.W. and sailed at time ten miles an hour, at others twelve, and at others, seven; day and night made fifty-nine leagues' progress; reckoned to the crew but forty-four. Here the men lost all patience, and complained of the length of the voyage, but the Admiral encouraged them in the best manner he could, representing the profits they were about to acquire, and adding that it was to no purpose to complain, having come so far, they had nothing to do but continue on to the Indies, till with the help of our Lord, they should arrive there.

Thursday, Oct. 11th. Steered W.S.W.; and encountered a heavier sea than they had met with before in the whole voyage. Saw pardelas and a green rush near the vessel. The crew of the Pinta saw a cane and a log; they also picked up a stick which appeared to have been carved with an iron tool, a piece of cane, a plant which grows on land, and a board. The crew of the Nina saw other signs of land, and a stalk loaded with roseberries. These signs encouraged them, and they all grew cheerful. Sailed this day till sunset, twenty-seven leagues.

After sunset steered their original course W. and sailed twelve miles an hour till two hours after midnight, going ninety miles, which are twenty-two leagues and a half; and as the Pinta was the swiftest sailer, and kept ahead of the Admiral, she discovered land and made the signals which had been ordered. . . . At two o'clock in the morning the land was discovered, at two leagues' distance; they took in sail and remained under the squaresail lying to till day, which was Friday, when they found themselves near a small island, one of the Lucayos, called in the Indian language Guanahani. Presently they descried people, naked, and the Admiral landed in the boat, which was armed, along with Martin Alonzo Pinzon, and Vincent Yanez his brother, captain of the Nina. The Admiral bore the royal standard, and the two captains each a banner of the Green Cross, which all the ships had carried; this contained the initials of the names of the King and Queen each side of the cross, and a crown over each letter. Arrived on shore, they saw trees very green, many streams of water, and divers sorts of fruits. The Admiral called upon the two Captains, and the rest of the crew who landed, as also to Rodrigo de Escovedo, notary of the fleet, and Rodrigo Sanchez, of Segovia, to bear witness that he before all others took possession (as in fact he did) of that island for the King and Queen his sovereigns, making the requisite declarations, which are more at large set down here in writing. Numbers of the people of the island straightway collected together. Here follow the precise words of the Admiral: "As I saw that they were very friendly to us, and perceived that they could be much more easily converted to our holy faith by gentle means than by force, I presented them with some red caps, and strings of beads to wear upon the neck, and many other trifles of small value, wherewith they were much delighted, and became wonderfully attached to us. Afterwards they came swimming to the boats, bringing parrots, balls of cotton thread, javelins and many other things which they exchanged for articles we gave them, such as glass beads, and hawk's bells; which trade was carried on with the utmost good will. But they seemed on the whole to me, to be a very poor people. They all go completely naked, even the women, though I saw but one girl. All whom I saw were young, not above thirty years of age, well made, with fine shapes and faces; their hair short, and coarse like that of a horse's tail, combed toward the forehead, except a small portion which they suffer to hang down behind, and never cut. . . . It appears to me, that the people are ingenious, and would be good servants; and I am of opinion that they would very readily become Christians, as they appear to have no religion.

They very quickly learn such words as are spoken to them. If it please our Lord, I intend at my return to carry home six of them to your Highnesses, that they may learn our language. I saw no beasts in the island, nor any sort of animals except parrots." These are the words of the Admiral.

102

An Aztec Account of the Conquest of Mexico: *The Broken Spears*

Spaniards wrote a number of accounts of the conquest of Mexico in 1521. The following reading, however, is an account translated from the Aztec Nahuatl language by Spanish missionaries after the conquest.

QUESTIONS TO CONSIDER

1. What was the "great plague" that spread throughout the Aztec capital of Tenochtitlán? How important a factor was disease in the Spanish victory over the Aztecs? Can you think of other instances in which disease played a decisive role in determining the outcome of such an encounter? Explain.
2. Consider how this account of the conquest reveals other factors that indicate how relatively few Spaniards were able to conquer so many.

The Plague Ravages the City

While the Spaniards were in Tlaxcala, a great plague broke out here in Tenochtitlán. It began to spread during the thirteenth month and lasted for seventy days, striking everywhere in the city and killing a vast number of our people. Sores erupted on our faces, our breasts, our bellies; we were covered with agonizing sores from head to foot.

The illness was so dreadful that no one could walk or move. The sick were so utterly helpless that they could only lie on their beds like corpses, unable to move their

From Miguel Leon-Portilla, *The Broken Spears*, pp. 92–93, 96–101. © 1962, 1990 by Miguel Leon-Portilla. Expanded and Updated Edition © 1992 by Miguel Leon-Portilla. Reprinted permission of Beacon Press, Boston.

limbs or even their heads. They could not lie face down or roll from one side to the other. If they did move their bodies, they screamed with pain.

A great many died from this plague, and many others died of hunger. They could not get up to search for food, and everyone else was too sick to care for them, so they starved to death in their beds.

Some people came down with a milder form of the disease; they suffered less than the others and made a good recovery. But they could not escape entirely. Their looks were ravaged, for wherever a sore broke out, it gouged an ugly pockmark in the skin. And a few of the survivors were left completely blind.

The first cases were reported in Cuatlán. By the time the danger was recognized, the plague was so well established that nothing could halt it, and eventually it spread all the way to Chalco. Then its virulence diminished considerably, though there were isolated cases for many months after. The first victims were stricken during the fiesta of Teotleco, and the faces of our warriors were not clean and free of sores until the fiesta of Panquetzaliztli.

Defensive Tactics of the Aztecs

When the Aztecs discovered that the shots from the arquebuses and cannons always flew in a straight line, they no longer ran away in the line of fire. They ran to the right or left or in zigzags, not in front of the guns. If they saw that a cannon was about to be fired and they could not escape by running, they threw themselves to the ground and lay flat until the shot passed over them. The warriors also took cover among the houses, through a desert.

Then the Spaniards arrived in Huitzillán, where they found another wall blocking the road. A great crowd of our warriors was hiding behind it to escape gunfire.

The Spaniards Debark

The brigantines came up and anchored nearby. They had been pursuing our war canoes in the open lake, but when they had almost run them down, they suddenly turned and sailed toward the causeway. Now they anchored a short distance from the houses. As soon as the cannons in their bows were loaded again, the soldiers aimed and fired them at the new wall.

The first shot cracked it in a dozen places, but it remained standing. They fired again: this time it cracked from one end to the other and crumpled to the ground. A moment later the road was completely empty. The warriors had all fled when they saw the wall collapsing; they ran blindly, this way and that, howling with fear.

Then the Spaniards debarked and filled in the canal. Working hurriedly, they threw in the stones from the shattered wall, the roof beams and adobe bricks from the nearest houses, anything they could find, until the surface of the fill was level with the causeway. Then a squad of about ten horsemen crossed over it. They galloped to and fro, scouting both sides of the road; they raced and wheeled and clattered back and forth. Soon they were joined by another squad that rode up to support them.

A number of Tlatelolcas had rushed into the place where Motecuhzoma lived before he was slain. When they came out again, they unexpectedly met the Spanish Cavalry. The lead horseman stabbed one of the Tlatelolcas, but the wounded man was able to clutch the lance and cling to it. His friends ran to his aid and twisted it from the Spaniard's hands. They knocked the horseman from his saddle, beat and kicked him as he lay on his back on the ground, and then cut off his head.

The Spaniards now joined all their forces into one unit and marched together as far as the Eagle Gate, where they set up the cannons they had brought with them. It was called the Eagle Gate because it was decorated with an enormous eagle carved of stone. The eagle was flanked on one side by a stone jaguar; on the other side there was a large honey bear, also of carved stone.

Two rows of tall columns led into the city from this gate. Some of the Aztecs hid behind the columns when they saw the Spaniards and their guns; others climbed onto the roofs of the communal houses. None of the warriors dared to show his face openly.

The Spaniards wasted no time as they loaded and fired the cannons. The smoke belched out in black clouds that darkened the sky, as if night were falling. The warriors hidden behind the columns broke from cover and fled; those on the rooftops climbed down and ran after them. When the smoke cleared away, the Spaniards could not see a single Aztec.

The Spaniards Advance to the Heart of the City

Then the Spaniards brought forward the largest cannon and set it up on the sacrificial stone. The priests of Huitzilopochtili immediately began to beat their great ritual drums from the top of the pyramid. The deep throbbing of the drums resounded over the city, calling the warriors to defend the stairway to the temple platform, cut the priests down with their great swords and pitch them headlong over the brink.

The great captains and warriors who had been fighting from their canoes now returned and landed. The canoes were paddled by the younger warriors and the recruits. As soon as the warriors landed, they ran throughout the streets, hunting the enemy and shouting: "Mexicanos, come find them!"

The Spaniards, seeing that an attack was imminent, tightened their ranks and clenched the hilts of their swords. The next moment, all was noise and confusion. The Aztecs charged into the plaza from every direction, and the air was black with arrows and gunsmoke.

The battle was so furious that both sides had to pull back. The Aztecs withdrew to Xoloco to catch their breath and dress their wounds, while the Spaniards retreated to their camp in Acachinanco, abandoning the cannon they had set up on the sacrificial stone. Later the warriors dragged this cannon to the edge of the canal and toppled it in. It sank at a place called the Stone Toad.

The Aztecs Take Refuge

During this time the Aztecs took refuge in the Tlatelolco quarter. They deserted the Tenochtitlán quarters all in one day, weeping and lamenting like women. Husbands searched for their wives, and fathers carried their small children on their shoulders. Tears of grief and despair streamed down their cheeks.

The Tlatelolcas, however, refused to give up. They raced into Tenochtitlán to continue the fight and the Spaniards soon learned how brave they were. Pedro de Alvarado launched an attack against the Point of the Alders, in the direction of Nonhualco, but his troops were shattered as if he had sent them against a stone cliff. The battle was fought both on dry land and on the water, where the Indians had to draw back to Tlacopán.

On the following day, two brigantines came up loaded with troops, and the Spaniards united all their forces on the outskirts of Nonhualco. The soldiers in the brigantines came ashore and the whole army marched into the very heart of Tenochtitlán. Wherever they went, they found the streets empty, with no Indians anywhere in sight.

The Last Stand

Then the great captain Tzilcatzin arrived, bringing with him three large, round stones of the kind used for building walls. He carried one of them in his hand; the other two hung from his shield. When he hurled these stones at the Spaniards, they turned and fled the city.

Tzilcatzin's military rank was that of Otomi, and he clipped his hair in the style of the Otomies. He scorned his enemies, Spaniards as well as Indians; they all shook with terror at the mere sight of him.

When the Spaniards found out how dangerous he was, they tried desperately to kill him. They attacked him with their swords and spears, fired at him with their crossbows and arquebuses, and tried every other means they could think of to kill or cripple him. Therefore he wore various disguises to prevent them from recognizing him.

Sometimes he wore his lip plug, his gold earrings and all the rest of his full regalia, but left his head uncovered to show that he was an Otomi. At still other times, he wore only his cotton armor, with a thin kerchief wrapped around his head. At still other times, he put on the finery of the priests who cast the victims into the fire: a plumed headdress with the eagle symbol on its crest, and gleaming gold bracelets on both arms, and circular bands of gleaming gold on both ankles.

The Spaniards came back again the next day. They brought their ships to a point just off Nonhualco, close to the place called the House of Mist. Their other troops arrived on foot, along with the Tlaxcaltecas. As soon as they had formed ranks, they charged the Aztec warriors.

The heaviest fighting began when they entered Nonhualco. None of our enemies and none of our warriors escaped harm. Everyone was wounded, and the toll of the dead was grievous on both sides. The struggle continued all day and all night.

Only three captains never retreated. They were contemptuous of their enemies and gave no thought whatever to their own safety. The first of these heroes was Tzoyectzin; the second, Temoctzin; and the third, the great Tzilcatzin.

At last the Spaniards were too exhausted to keep on fighting. After one final attempt to break the Aztec ranks, they withdrew to their camp to rest and recover, with their allies trailing behind.

103

Pope Paul III, "Indians Are Men," 1537

The belief that Indians were less than human provided justification for the behavior of many Spaniards in the New World in the early sixteenth century. If the Indians were not human and did not have souls to save, then the activities of the various missionary programs were questionable. In an effort to settle this provocative question, Pope Paul III addressed this issue in his papal bull of 1537.

QUESTIONS TO CONSIDER

1. Summarize and analyze the key elements of the pope's decree. Do you agree with them? Explain why or why not.
2. How might the Spanish conquistadors who had settled in the colonies have re-acted to this official position? Why?
3. Describe how the pope's statement reflected the Church-state tensions of sixteenth-century Spain.

Paul III Pope

To all faithful Christians to whom this writing may come, health in Christ our Lord and the apostolic benediction.

The sublime God so loved the human race that He created man in such wise that he might participate, not only in the good that other creatures enjoy, but endowed him with capacity to attain to the inaccessible and invisible Supreme Good and behold it face to face; and since man, according to the testimony of the sacred scriptures, has been created to enjoy eternal life and happiness, which none may obtain save through faith in our Lord Jesus Christ, it is necessary that he should possess the nature and faculties enabling him to receive that faith; and that whoever is thus endowed should be capable of receiving that same faith. Nor is it credible that any one should possess so little understanding as to desire the faith and yet be destitute for the most necessary faculty to enable him to receive it. Hence Christ, who is the Truth itself, that has never failed and can never fail, said to the preachers of the faith whom He chose for the office "Go ye and teach all nations." He said all, without ex-ception, for all are capable of receiving the doctrines of the faith.

The enemy of the human race, who opposes all good deeds in order to bring men to destruction, beholding and envying this, invented a means never before heard of, by which he might hinder the preaching of God's word of Salvation to the people: he inspired his satellites who, to please him, have not hesitated to publish abroad that the Indians of the West and the South, and other people of whom We have recent knowledge should be treated as dumb brutes created for our service, pretending that they are incapable of receiving the catholic faith.

We, who, though unworthy, exercise on earth the power of our Lord and seek with all our might to bring those sheep of His flock who are outside, into the fold committed to our charge, consider, however, that the Indians are truly men and that they are not only capable of understanding the catholic faith but, according to our information, they desire exceedingly to receive it. Desiring to provide ample remedy for these evils, we define and declare by these our letters, or by any translation there-of signed by any notary public and sealed with the seal of any ecclesiastical dignitary, to which the same credit shall be given as to the originals, that, notwithstanding whatever may have been or may be said to the contrary, the said Indians and all other people who may later be discovered by Christians, are by no means to be deprived of their liberty or the possession of their property, even though they be outside the faith of Jesus Christ; and that they may and should, freely and legitimately, enjoy

From the translation by F. A. MacNutt, *Bartholomew de Las Casas: His Life, His Apostolate, and His Writings* (New York and London, 1909), pp. 426–31, *passim.*

their liberty and the possession of their property; nor should they be in any way enslaved; should the contrary happen, it shall be null and of no effect.

By virtue of our apostolic authority We define and declare by these present letters, or by any translation thereof signed by any notary public and sealed with the seal of any ecclesiastical dignitary, which shall thus command the same obedience as the originals, that the said Indians and other peoples should be converted to the faith of Jesus Christ by preaching the word of God and by the example of good and holy living.

Given in Rome in the year of our Lord 1537.
The fourth of June and of our Pontificate, the third year.

104

Bartolomé de Las Casas, *Destruction of the Indies* and "The Only Method of Converting the Indians"

Bartolomé de Las Casas was born in Seville in 1474, educated in law at Salamanca, and came to Hispaniola as a soldier of fortune in 1502. He acquired land and Indians and in 1510 was ordained to the priesthood but maintained his position as an *encomendero*.[9] He was present when Montesinos delivered his sermon to the colonists and strongly resented it, as did others who heard it. In 1514, however, Las Casas gave up his lands and Indians and for the rest of his life worked to abolish Indian slavery and the forced labor of the encomienda. To a considerable degree, his efforts led the Spanish Crown to issue the New Laws of 1542, which intended to abolish the *encomienda* system in the New World. Las Casas is best known for his strong indictment of Spanish cruelty to the Indians in his famous work *The Brief Account of the Destruction of the Indies* (1552). In the following excerpt from this work, Las Casas describes the Spanish conquest of Cuba. The final selection is taken from another of his writings, *The Only Method of Attracting All People to the True Faith*, arguing that conversion should be accomplished by peaceful means.

QUESTIONS TO CONSIDER

1. What advice does the Indian ruler Hatuey suggest to his followers in an effort to survive the arrival of Spaniards?
2. Might Las Casas have exaggerated his account of the decimation of the native inhabitants?
3. Did the realities of colonial existence in the New World overrule the voice of morality and religion? What other examples could you cite where this occurred?
4. Why were many of Spain's competitors and enemies in Europe eager to seize on Las Casas's descriptions of the Spanish character? In what ways did this reflect national rivalries and stereotypes of the era?

[9]The person in charge of an *encomienda*, an assignment of Indians who were to serve the Spanish grantee with tribute and labor.

In the year 1511 the Spaniards passed over to the island of Cuba, which as I said, is as long as from Valladolid to Rome, and where there were great and populous provinces. They began and ended in the above manner, only with incomparably greater cruelty. Here many notable things occurred. A very high prince and lord, named Hatuey, who had fled with many of his people from Hispaniola to Cuba, to escape the calamity and inhuman operations of the Christians, having received news from some Indians that the Christians were crossing over, assembled many or all of his people, and addressed them thus.

"You already know that it is said the Christians are coming here; and you have experience of how they have treated the lords so and so and those people of Hayti (which is Hispaniola); they come to do the same here. Do you know perhaps why they do it?" The people answered no; except that they were by nature cruel and wicked. "They do it," said he, "not alone for this, but because they have a God whom they greatly adore and love; and to make us adore Him they strive to subjugate us and take our lives." He had near him a basket full of gold and jewels and he said: "Behold here is the God of the Christians, let us perform Areytos before Him, if you will (these are dances in concert and singly); and perhaps we shall please Him, and He will command that they do us no harm."

All exclaimed: it is well! it is well! They danced before it, till they were all tired, after which the lord Hatuey said: "Note well that in any event if we preserve the gold, they will finally have to kill us to take it from us: let us throw it into this river." They all agreed to this proposal, and they threw the gold into a great river in that place.

This prince and lord continued retreating before the Christians when they arrived at the island of Cuba, because he knew them, but when he encountered them he defended himself; and at last they took him. And merely because he fled from such iniquitous and cruel people, and defended himself against those who wished to kill and oppress him, with all his people and offspring until death, they burnt him alive.

When he was tied to the stake, a Franciscan monk, a holy man, who was there, spoke as much as he could to him, in the little time that the executioner granted them, about God and some of the teachings of our faith, of which he had never before heard; he told him that if he would believe what was told him, he would go to heaven where there was glory and eternal rest; and if not, that he would go to hell, to suffer perpetual torments and punishment. After thinking a little, Hatuey asked the monk whether the Christians went to heaven; the monk answered that those who were good went there. The prince at once said, without any more thought, that he did not wish to go there, but rather to hell so as not to be where Spaniards were, nor to see such cruel people. This is the renown and honour, that God and our faith have acquired by means of the Christians who have gone to the Indies.

On one occasion they came out ten leagues from a great settlement to meet us, bringing provisions and gifts, and when we met them, they gave us a great quantity of fish and bread and other victuals, with everything they could supply. All of a sudden the devil entered into the bodies of the Christians, and in my presence they put to the sword, without any motive or cause whatsoever, more than three thousand persons, men, women, and children, who were seated before us. Here I beheld such great cruelty as living man has never seen nor thought to see.

Once I sent messengers to all the lords of the province of Havana, assuring them that if they would not absent themselves but come to receive us, no harm should be done them; all the country was terrorized because of the past slaughter, and I did this by the captain's advice. When we arrived in the province, twenty-one princes and lords came to receive us; and at once the captain violated the safe conduct I had given them and took them prisoners. The following day he wished to burn them alive, saying it was better so because those lords would some time or other do us harm. I had the greatest difficulty to deliver them from the flames but finally I saved them.

After all the Indians of this island were reduced to servitude and misfortune like those of Hispaniola, and when they saw they were perishing inevitably, some began to flee to the mountains; others to hang themselves, together with their children, and through the cruelty of one very tyrannical Spaniard whom I knew, more than two hundred Indians hanged themselves. In this way numberless people perished.

There was an officer of the King in this island, to whose share three hundred Indians fell, and by the end of the three months he had, through labour in the mines, caused the death of two hundred and seventy; so that he had only thirty left, which was the tenth part. The authorities afterwards gave him as many again, and again he killed them: and they continued to give, and he to kill, until he came to die, and the devil carried away his soul.

In three or four months, I being present, more than seven thousand children died of hunger, their fathers and mothers having been taken to the mines. Other dreadful things did I see.

Afterwards the Spaniards resolved to go and hunt the Indians who were in the mountains, where they perpetrated marvellous massacres. Thus they ruined and depopulated all this island which we beheld not long ago; and it excites pity, and great anguish to see it deserted, and reduced to a solitude.

The Only Method of Converting the Indians

The one and only method of teaching men the true religion was established by Divine Providence for the whole world, and for all times: that is, by persuading the understanding through reasons, and by gently attracting or exhorting the will. This method should be common to all men throughout the world, without any distinction made for sects, errors, or corrupt customs.

This conclusion will be proved in many ways: by arguments drawn from reason; by examples of the ancient Fathers; by the rule and manner of preaching which Christ instituted for all times; by the practices of the Apostles; by quotations from holy teachers; by the most ancient tradition of the Church and by her numerous ecclesiastical decrees.

And first, this conclusion will be proved by arguments drawn from reason, among which let this be the first. There is only one method peculiar to Divine Wisdom by which it disposes and moves created beings gently to actions and to their natural ends. But among created beings, rational creatures are higher and more excellent than all others which were not made in the image of God. . . . Therefore, Divine Wisdom moves rational creatures, that is, men, to their actions or operations gently. . . . Therefore, the method of teaching men the true religion ought to be gentle, enticing, and pleasant. This method is by persuading the understanding and by attracting the will.